9.21

NEVER A "CRAFT" MOMENT

A Memoir-cum-Abattoir

ROBIN ANDERSON

Definition of "CRAFT"

"CAN'T REMEMBER A FUCKING THING!"

AUTHOR'S NOTE: Three proverbs can apply to my memoir-cum-abattoir. "You sow what you reap." "The proof of the pudding is in the eating" and "Revenge is a dish best served cold." All incidents mentioned - pleasant or otherwise - are based on fact and opinions along with comments of others.

To Stephen (August)

enjoy - if you Dare!

Cover and photographic layouts: Michael Marsden

DEDICATION

To ABEL MABEL MORTIS, ME, MYSELF and therefore US

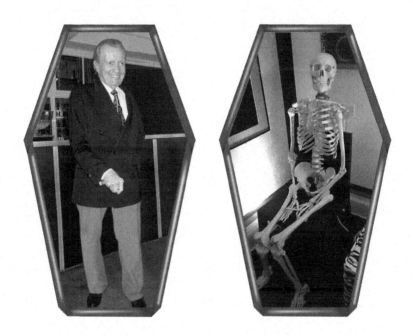

With undying love

FOUR EXCEPTIONAL PEOPLE WITH WHOM I'D ADORE SPENDING
A FEW MORE FABULOUS, UNBEATABLE MOMENTS

DAVID LLOYD-LOWLES

PEGGY POWELL

BEN COLMAN

DONALD CAMERON

NEVER FORGOTTEN

NEVER A "CRAFT" MOMENT

(A MEMOIR-CUM-ABATTOIR)

SECTIONS AS OPPOSED TO CHAPTERS

THE AFFLATUS

REMINISCENCES - IN THE BEGINNING - SOUTHERN RHODESIA

RHODES! RHODES! GLORIOUS RHODES!
THE "OXFORD OF SOUTH AFRICA" WITHOUT THE DREAMING SPIRES

ROBERT BECOMES ROBIN

"FROM NOW ON IT'S JS"

IN THE INTERIM ONE

RAD

IN THE INTERIM TWO

BELLA ITALIA

THE FRENCH ERECTION

CARIBBEAN CAPERS

TREADING WATER - RAD BECOMES RADC

TREADING WATER TO TURBULENT TREADMILL

SAMBA, CARMEN MIRANDA & MACHU POPPINS

MAGIC CARPET RIDES

HALCYON DAZE

NEVER A "CRAFT" MOMENT

A Memoir-cum-Abattoir

Robin Anderson

THE AFFLATUS

It began as a normal Thursday morning; a moment's contemplation whilst lying in bed as to the day ahead - namely the latest shenanigans planned for Miss Miranda Maracona and her "tranny in charms" the uber-glamorous Miss Kookie Kombuis - followed by an unexpected loss of balance as I attempted to hoist myself from supine to sitting. Finding myself falling heavily on to the floor I somehow managed to pull the telephone from the bedside table down next to me and dial 111.

Several hours later I was in hospital where - thanks to my total loss of balance, use of my right arm and a problem with my speech - I was informed by a charming, devastatingly handsome turbaned doctor I had suffered a "serious stroke".

Let me assure you there is nothing quite so startling, so unforeseen, so unexpected or terrifying as a stroke. However, I consider myself extremely lucky and all thanks to a team of dedicated physiotherapists I was soon back to further moments of further "contemplation"; moments mainly made up of what *I* consider to have been and (hopefully) will continue to be a fun, mischievous roller coaster ride of a life well-lived.

Fortunately my mind remains as sharp as ever if not even more lethally honed. Whereas many a fastidious soul may keep a "Dear Diary" I have had to rely on a memory bank; hence the title of my journey into the past. A title inspired by a charming dinner companion, a Miss Marple lookalike and the widow of some former bigwig in the Foreign Office who, having read several of my *La Di Da Di Bloody Da!* series had spent most of the meal avidly discussing these particular books plus a few other titles along with my endless travels.

Changing tack I turned the conversation from *me* back from to *her* along with the tongue-in-cheek suggestion that as the former wife of some former official of some standing surely she too had enough anecdotes to inspire a book.

"Oh no, my dear," she chirruped in reply, "that's something I could never, *ever* do."

"And why not?" I continued in my most charming if somewhat patronising manner.

"Because, unlike *you*, dear, I'm a bona fide member of those who suffer from what is known as 'craft syndrome'."

I stared back at her sweetly smiling face.

"Sorry to appear a tad naïve er . . . Madam, but could you please explain er . . . 'craft syndrome'?"

"Of course dear; 'craft' - spelt c-r-a-f-t. Meaning 'I can't remember a fucking thing'!"

As I am most definitely *not a* sufferer of this dreaded ailment - hence my use of the prefix "never" in the title of my tome - a tome which I should also explain contains multiple observations and inspirational rattles from the erudite "I'm always right" Abel Mabel Mortis: my constant companion and confidant.

A major part of this "at least *I'll* read the bloody thing myself even if nobody else does!" takes on the form of imaginary verbal reminiscing between the elegant Abel Mabel and myself resulting in you, dear reader - dependant of course on your existence plus perception of matters sincere and insincere - being suitably shocked, scandalised and deliciously traumatised by what you are about to perceive.

Whether accepted as *Never A "Craft" Moment* or the equally pedantic *Can Remember* All *Fucking Things*, let the spillage begin.

REMINISCENSES

IN THE BEGINNING - SOUTHERN RHODESIA

For some bizarre reasoning known to his oh so not-at-all bizarre, dull, ordinary self my father - a mining engineer named Robert Anderson, a Scotsman and an émigré to the then Southern Rhodesia (now Zimbabwe) in the nineteen thirties - insisted on my mother travelling to the "Land of the Haggis" for "the great event".

The female parent, an inveterate snob and descendant of the Afrikaner *Voortrekker* Louis Trichardt (she had been named Martha Jacoba Trichardt but had soon changed her given names an early stage to the more socially acceptable and encompassing Jean) could never resist her exalted claim "yew mey hev the brrrains bet I hev the brieding" delivered in a clipped South African accent and a daily mantra in the berating of her "whipping boy" husband along with those whom she considered a rung or two down her rickety social ladder.

Perhaps the term "in-breeding" amongst her unwanted group of ancestors was responsible for these "delusions" of which there were many. (The *Voortrekkers* being a group of Dutch settlers in the Cape area of South Africa who - quite rightly - believed themselves unwanted and unloved by the British; therefore *trekking* north to establish their own settlements.) Relentless uncalled-for beatings with a *sjambok* (a whip made out of animal) hide to "insure my childrin grrow up little gentlemen en not hooligans" plus the bizarre decision to send me, aged six, to Vumba Heights School, a type of "boot camp" for difficult children set amidst the rolling Vumba Hills in the eastern part of Southern Rhodesia being part of her off-key way of thinking.

How a solemn, silent, withdrawn child could be branded "difficult" by this confused, alcoholic nightmare beggars belief: the first "sundowner" or

19

evening drink poured at five p.m. without fail giving yet another example of the woman's Pontius Pilate attitude to matters in general. She simply washed her hands of the problem. As someone so accurately put it, "Childhood never lasts long and what's worse; you never get over it". Doubtless a psychiatrist would rub his hands with glee on hearing such memories but all I can say is the memories are well justified.

Another unsavoury aspect of "Mummy Dearest" was her fiendish delight in tweaking what she gleefully referred to as my "mousie". Obviously realising my whimpers were more whimpers of terror as opposed to whimpers of delight she returned to the heady delights of whipping my elder brother ("Wun yeer en sevin months differince!") ensuring once again her offspring grew up "little gentlemen en not hooligans". Despite the brief number of months between us, elder brother Ian and self were destined never to be friends; never mind close.

"Jean" Martha Jacoba Trichardt deserves every damnatory word said - or written - against her. A repellent, repugnant woman and if by chance you find my introductory words a tad lethal: "Just you wait 'Enry 'Iggins. Just you wait"!

Not to be outdone the male parent's apparent reason for his spouse's visit (perhaps a *trek*) to the Land of his Forefathers was simple and announced in an exaggerated Scottish brogue no doubt: "I want a son of mine born on Scottish soil!" Poor misguided man: little did he know.

My "well-bred" mother, having duly "hatched" the desired Scottish-born son sardonically named Robert Beattie (the same as His) returned in triumph to take up regal residence in the small goldmining town of Gatooma (Population Whites: 2,000. Population Blacks: Not recorded). *What* an achievement! What an accolade! I cannot elaborate on my early days in glittering Gatooma as these definitely *are* a "craft" moment. However all was soon to change; the major happening taking place with "Brains" being promoted to Chief Government Mining Engineer of Gwelo (Population Whites: 8,000. Blacks: Not recorded). What a step-up on both professional and social ladders. Although not exactly Louis Trichardt in the northern Transvaal - great, great grandfather Louis having "hed a town nemmed after him" - it could be seen as a rickety rung in the right direction.

To give Him his due in a one and only early effort to bond with his Scottish-born offspring he duly took me on a visit to a local gold mine outside Gatooma where I - a curious five year old - was cheerfully introduced to my one and only corpse in all its blood splattered technicolour glory. The "star" of the show being an unfortunate mine boy (mine worker) who had lost his footing on a genuine rung while climbing down the mine shaft. The man's broken body was finally brought to the surface on a sheet of rusty corrugated iron serving as a makeshift stretcher and casually laid down in full view of all and sundry including five year old me.

I remember being acutely puzzled as to how the man could be staring wide-eyed at the dazzling blue African sky, his mouth twisted in a grotesque rictus grin despite him lying on his stomach. Before going to sleep that night I must have spent several minutes lying on *my* stomach while trying to look up at the top of the mosquito net covering my bed but simply could not get my head to do what the staring mine boy had been able to do with his. On being asked about this intriguing phenomena at the time Him chose to ignore the question and began talking loudly to Chris Dreyer the owner of the mine instead. This left me no alternative but to go and have a further, closer look at the curiously positioned man with the weird grin. Again, any psychiatrist worth his salt - read "extortionate fee" - would say this clearly explains my fascination for skulls and my fabulous skull collection all of who charmingly sport what I call "a genuine mine boy's grin". Little did I realise at the time I would meet someone else many years later who not only shared the same fascination for skulls but was also connected to a former royal who bore a strong resemblance to a skull! I too would become connected to a similar skull of regal bearing but more about the elegant Miss Abel Mabel Mortis later.

It was in Gwelo this chrysalis of a child prodigy began to emerge into what would become a brilliant, self-confident butterfly and all thanks to a marvellous woman named Peggy Powell; the woman I still hold most dear and the woman I saw as my surrogate mother. The woman to whom my biological mother could never hold a burnt-out match to; never mind a blown-out candle. Peggy Powell - think Wonder Woman with the breathtaking looks of Margaret, Duchess of Argyll (a "hint of things to come") and a touch of the comedienne akin to Joyce Grenfell - and you still couldn't or wouldn't do this amazing woman justice. Today the comparisons would probably be a case of Kirstin Scott Thomas meets Joanna Lumley.

Peggy was married to a pompous dullard - I'll be a tad polite here and call him a "resting" metallurgist - named Roger: a tall, gangling, humourless

Telly Savalas lookalike who, to this day, I still cannot see how or why he ever managed to "hook" Peggy. (It should be remembered in those halcyon days I was totally unaware of "matters below the belt" and who knows, perhaps the "Powell projectile" was the irresistible attraction?) They had two children, a daughter named Frances burdened with the unflattering nickname "Gugs" and a younger son similarly burdened with the unfortunate nickname "Liggy" or "Ligs". A further burden for Gugs was the fact she grew to be a female version of her father whilst Liggy (or Ligs) grew into the spitting image of Peggy. Gugs became a tremendous childhood friend but sadly a friendship that was not to last. All I know is she married, divorced and remained incognito for a while before making a brief reappearance several decades later. Liggy meanwhile wafted into the priesthood. I use the term "wafted" as this is literally what he did. While some people of his generation were finding their "inner selves on the beaches of Goa" Liggy (or Ligs) was apparently doing something similar back in London where he became closely affiliated with God.

Peggy had been previously married and divorced. I eventually met her two daughters from her first marriage and here the contrast between Peggy and her daughters would have put the phrase "as different as chalk and cheese" to shame. The girls were named Caroline and Margaret with Caroline eventually ending up a bossy spinster and Margaret, a vague, Pre-Raphaelite beauty who ended up marrying her male equivalent, a lecturer named Tony, and living in Rome.

As a young boy Liggy (Ligs) possessed an uncanny aptitude for bursting into tears at the slightest provocation; the tears accompanied by siren-like wailing. I'd be telling an untruth if Gugs and I didn't take a secret delight in setting off this siren sound-alike.

Peggy epitomised the term of a Colonial "English woman abroad" and despite the stultifying confines of Gwelo brought a tsunami of technicolour into the lives pf anyone who had the privilege of meeting her. She also indirectly introduced me to the wonderful term "eccentric" with such fads as wearing a rakish Robin Hood-style hat, complete with feather when "going shopping" in what glamorous Gwelo claimed to be a host of "unbeatable" shops with the number five being an exaggeration. Having "afternoon tea" served "on the dot of four" every day was another much-loved "Peggy-ism"; this very English ritual invariably partaken on the veranda - or *stoep* - and promising a fare of de rigueur cucumber sandwiches or sandwiches filled with Heinz's "international" sandwich spread. This much-looked-forward to happening was duly served by Cookie, the Powell's white-jacketed, sneakers or *takkies*-wearing cook.

In true English fashion Peggy was also an avid gardener and included in Peggy's "exotic" persona was the daily cry of "Aargh Bungo aargh!" directed at Bungo the family Ridgeback dog with a penchant for taking a sprawled nap on one of Peggy's endless seedling beds. Poor Bungo, no wonder he always looked so put-out and inclined to greet everybody with a growl. As expected, Gugs and I took great delight in adding our versions of "Aargh Bungo! Aargh!" but without the effectiveness of Peggy's demands!

The indefatigable Peggy also organised endless picnics and exciting paper chases which took place in the adventurous square miles of surrounding *bundu* or bushland surrounding Randolph House, the name of the neighbouring Powell homestead; plus fun charades and endless exhausting games of Bumble-Puppy. Bumble-Puppy being a where two nimble, quick-footed players hit a ball - attached by string to a tall post - in order to see who can be first to wind the ball tightly around the post. With Peggy everything was always "Fun" with a capital "F".

We played Bumble-Puppy using a tennis ball and tennis racquets and it's again thanks to Peggy and her introduction to this zany game which saw me developing my enthusiasm for tennis; an enthusiasm which still exists today. Peggy's introduction to paper chases included brother Ian, a few of his "gang" and several of Gugs' other friends. How we loved racing through the *bundu* in pursuit of the "hare", a role usually played with relish by the agile Ian. Here again Peggy showed great foresight by insisting the only pieces of paper dropped by the "hare" were torn up rolls of toilet paper which would eventually disintegrate following several showers of rain. Herewith the marvellous Peggy Powell already doing her bit for "saving the planet" and she wasn't even an ecologist! This insistence of Peggy's we should do all we could to prevent any contamination of our surroundings with inexcusable litter was a lesson well taught and something I still fervently believe in.

Peggy also introduced us to a contraption known as a spring and hopping stick, an earlier version of what would become known as a pogo stick. According to Peggy I showed a natural talent for bouncing up and down on a sturdy, upright pole.

In earlier years when it came to Guy Fawkes Night and prior to the advent of Peggy Powell (to me an advent on a par with the bomb dropped on Hiroshima!) Ian and I were given a few sparklers to wave about while Cur, armed with a large G and T, would querulously instruct Him on how to set off one or two rockets from their launch pad of a milk bottle. With Peggy, Guy Fawkes Night became a night to remember! On one of Noakie's now harvested maize fields Peggy duly supervised the building of a gigantic bonfire with a suitably wicked-looking Guy perched on top. Whirring Catherine wheels, exploding Roman candles and a spray of rockets decorated the starry night as a crackling Guy Fawkes was made to pay for his wicked misdemeanours.

However, before proceeding with any further rapturous comments regarding Peggy, I must explain that on our arrival in "glamorous step-up the social ladder Gwelo" my ambitious parents (from now onwards simply referred to as "Him" and "Cur") rented a small house several miles out of Gwelo and by some incredible stroke of luck, twist of fate or "see it as ordained", our next door neighbours (read half a mile away) turned out to be the Powell family who lived - like us - in a typical, sprawling bungalow with a corrugated iron roof, large veranda (or *stoep*) set amidst acres of farmland and bushveld. While our modest homestead was known as "Noakie's House" (named after the owner but due to Cur's rung grasping this venue was soon to change) the Powell's resided in the more grandly christened Randolf House. Both surrounding farmland and bush was owned by the mysterious Mr Noakes aka "Noakie" who farmed acres of maize and owned an impressive beef producing herd of cattle.

"Getting lost" in the endless of towering seven to eight foot high maize plants prior to harvesting proved to be a great game as was sliding down the corrugated iron roofs of "Noakie's" derelict pig sties. Even more exhilarating was Ian's construction of splendid *foefie* (filthy) slide; a daredevil slide comprising of a long wire strung between two trees; one end attached to the top on one tree and the other attached much lower down to the second tree forming a sharp gradient between the two. *Pièce de résistance* was a short piece of piping through which the wire had been previously threaded. Attached to the piping was a further cord used to pull the pipe back up for the next jumper. Holding onto the piece of piping for dear life one would launch oneself into space and hurtle down the wire slide. Adding to the fun and the *foefie* (filthy) part was the muddy landing strip which would be religiously hosed in order to keep a constant supply of slippery mud in which one would laughingly end up.

Climbing every possible tree was another enthusiastic childhood challenge. Gugs and I had yet to find a tree that was not "climbable" for this intrepid duo! One determined tree however saw me losing my hold and plunging to the ground. A plaster cast and sling saw me showing off my broken arm with pride.

Not only was Randolf the bigger house it also boasted a lovingly, tended garden; Peggy's great passion, pride and joy. Whilst Cur turned up her "well-bred" nose at something so mundane such as gardening (we had a "garden boy" to deal with our equivalent) a barefooted Peggy worked endlessly to keep the garden at Randolph a riot of colour with plantings of antirrhinums (snapdragons), irises, gladioli, dahlias, cannas, poppies, portulaca and many other plants. Adding to the cacophony of were endless old, gnarled msasa trees and pergolas festooned with climbing purple and rust-coloured bougainvillea or swathed in golden shower creeper (a plant with a dubious namesake).

I remember vividly Peggy's horrified expression on being told by Cur about the slipshod manner in which Injima the "garden boy" had "clipped the lawn" (he would squat, patiently clip with lawn with a large pair of garden shears; no lawn mower for him).

"I tell yew Peggy," said Cur with a grim smile, "hed grate, grate grand-father Louis been here he would have given the useless kaffir a good *sjambokking*!" Having experienced Cur's enthusiastic use of a *sjambok* she obviously believed in what she preached.

It was through Peggy I was introduced to the joys of *The Young Elizabethan,* a children's magazine brought out in 1953 to celebrate the coronation of Elizabeth 2nd and other childhood "Svengalis" such as the intrepid Enid Blyton, the mischievous Richmal Crompton, the gung-ho Arthur Ransome and an incredible book, *The Swish of the Curtain* by Pamela Brown which sowed the seed for my never-ending interest in the theatre. The conclusion is obvious; from a very early stage I was destined to become an avid reader and to this very day I consume paper backs with a ferocity. Three or four a week is about average and to prove the point one only has to see my weekly spend with Waterstones Books on King's Road, Chelsea, where the ever obliging staff make sure RA has his "weekly fix" as it were.

Needless to say Cur was not at all impressed by the new queen, her elaborate coronation (as endlessly shown at the local cinema) subjected to a dismissive sniff followed by a cryptic "I wouldn't mind *her* job instead of mine!" Try beating *that* for arrogance combined with ignorance.

*

A never-forgotten young read was Helga Moray's bodice-ripper set in - believe it or not - the days of the disgruntled *Voortrekkers*. How my school friends and I sniggered over Katie's "breasts like melons" and Paul's naked body "browned but for a narrow strip of white about the lean buttocks"! (If only Cur and Him could have been like these two god-likes!) Later in my teens I was to see Hollywood's version of this searing epic starring Susan Hayward and Tyrone Power. Not even the fact *Untamed* was presented in the new wide screen technic of Cinemascope, the film - and its two stars - proved to a great disappointment and sorely lacking in Katie's "melon-like" breasts and Paul's much anticipated "white strip".

In 1953 and at Peggy's insistence Him and Cur took Ian and me to Bulawayo for "an experience of a lifetime", the Rhodes Centenary Exhibition. A glittering occasion to celebrate a hundred years of Colonial rule and opened with much heraldry by Queen Elizabeth the Queen Mother. I truly believe if it hadn't been for Peggy's persistence the two of us would have missed out on the historical occasion.

Cur, having deigned to attend the Exhibition "only for its more "cultural events" and despite repeated claims of being "a devotee of classical music", a performance by the Halle Orchestra in the obsequiously named *Theatre Royal* was happily overlooked in favour for the *Variety Show* with George Formby being the main attraction. At the impressive age of thirteen I regarded Formby as an embarrassing irritant but revelled in the dazzling Madame Zizi, a two foot tall blonde bombshell of a marionette created by Frank Mumford and based on Lana Turner and Gypsy Rose Lee; her "curvaceous" figure dressed in trademark pink Schiaparelli. Madame Zizi - billed as "sex on strings" - proved equally as memorable to Helga Moray's *Untamed* Katie!

Who could have believed even the most fearsome lion skin-draped and dried snake festooned witchdoctor had he - at such a tender aged - foretold of my future befriending a living Czech version of Madame Zizi in the form of the equally glamorous Ivana Trump.

In the fifties the only form of live entertainment in Southern Rhodesia was the radio, with *Radio Lorenzo Marques* and *The Federal*

Broadcasting Service - based in the capital Salisbury - being the only sources available. How one used to enjoy huddled over "the wireless" to listen in to *Dick Barton Special Agent* or - when popular music began to take a hold of one's ever expanding interest - *The LM Hit Parade*; a "must" on Sunday evenings. Little did I know several years on I was to become "The Golden Voice of Teenage Half Hour" broadcast live from Bulawayo!

One of my happier Gwelo memories was joining the queue (a breathtaking six at the most) outside Archibald and Kingston, Gwelo's one and only bookshop to buy the latest Enid Blyton; especially her "Adventure" series with fondly remembered titles such as *The Island of Adventure* and *The Castle of Adventure* plus the other six. Unknown to innocent me I was introduced to my first "dyke" in *The Famous Five* series; the "butch" George.

At this early introductory stage family-wise I feel it necessary to once again mention my "home grown" brother "hatched" in remote Umtali, a small town close to the Mozambique border, a mere year and five days before my overseas emergence. Unlike most brothers (or so I've been led to believe), elder brother Ian and his little brother (me) would grow with the "brotherly love" between the two of us tantamount to the "love" between a mongoose and a cobra: big brother Ian being the cobra and me the "battling for survival" Rikki-Tikki-Tavi (aka the mongoose). I wouldn't go so far as to say we disliked each other; see it more of a case of completely ignoring one another's existence.

If, at the time of publication big brother Ian is still alive I would strongly suggest he bypasses my book for it *does* contain many never-forgotten moments.

At the time of writing big brother is very much alive and well and living in Australia with - from what I have managed to glean - a devoted wife, a twin son and daughter and a horde of grandchildren. From a family photograph inadvertently spotted on Facebook while checking on a publicity blurb for one of my latest tomes the smiling group appear to be - literally - living off "the fat of the land". Following a brief meeting with Margaret his wife some forty years back, I remember my sister-in-law being the proud possessor of an atrocious South African accent so God knows what their offspring and subsequent grandchildren sound like with their Australian accents and grandmother's "infusion" combined!

While elder brother devoted himself to boy scouts (not to be misinterpreted I hasn't to add!) and achieving the Queen's Scout Award, he also became a first class sportsman with rugby and swimming his favourite sports, I went off at a totally different tangent. However, before one "veers off" an accolade is due and though I say it myself, big brother Ian became a diver of Olympic standard but in those days in remote, stultifying Southern Rhodesia, such qualities were never recognised.

As elder brother Ian continued his capitulations to the wayward demands and healthy outdoor passions of Baden-Powell (no relation to Peggy nota bene!), I continued to escape from the strict confines of isolated Gwelo via the magical world of books until one morning - a morning I still remember as vividly as if it was yesterday - when I saw my first Pelham puppet in the shop window of Meikles store in First Street; Gwelo's answer to Bond Street or Rodeo Drive!

Forget the impact of seeing Madame Zizi (the equivalent of being hit by a thunderbolt or love at first sight!), this was heaven on two crossed sticks! Come hell or high water I simply *had* to have the slumped wooden figure (a marionette or puppet created by an English manufacturing company named Pelham Puppets) and, to my immense surprise, Him and Cur presented me with my "passion" a few days later. I promptly joined the Pelham Puppet Club and became a Pelpup (with frequent letters to the legendary Pelpop!) and if I say my life changed literally overnight, I wouldn't be exaggerating. Along with my books, the enthusiasm and encouragement from Peggy to "look, look, look, explore life and enjoy all around" my new puppet friends saw my childhood going into orbit. (Or "Obit" - depending on how cynical one wishes to be!)

By this stage of the exciting proceedings we had moved from "Noakie's House" to a much more impressive property owned by a wealthy widow named Elsie Childs. Mrs Childs' establishment was far grander than Randolph (Cur could not stop purring and preening) boasting a tennis court and several acres of thirsty lawns, a magnificent rose garden and a bountiful orchard which saw me and Gugs along with Ian and his gang having an endless supply of guavas, oranges, peaches, paw-paws (papaya), mulberries and loquats to gorge on.

Lining the driveway like a battalion of tall, dark soldiers were two rows of bushy conifers. At the time and a minor claim to fame was my ability to climb to the top of the first conifer and move from tree to tree until I had worked myself down the whole row of swaying sentinels. I would then shin down the last tree, scuttle across the drive and climb the first conifer in the opposite row and work my way back to where I had started. Ian was my only challenge and boasted he could work his way along the driveway and back knocking at least ten minutes off my time. The length of the driveway was comparable to that of at least three tennis courts so the amount of trees we traversed must have been at least a hundred. I distinctly remember how sweaty, itchy and exhausted I would find myself after this "fir" marathon but goodness, the fun I had.

It was inevitable Cur would fall prey to the glittering lights and glitterati inhabitants of glamorous Gwelo. Without so much as a whisper Him succumbed to her demands a house *in* town being the call of the day and without any further ado we moved from the splendour of "Mrs Child's House" to a "suitable house in town". To give Cur her due, the benefits of "the move" were apparent. Ian was able to indulge in his sport and me in my hidden talent as a puppeteer! At the tender age of twelve "the young Puppet Master and his puppets" were the talk of the town and in great demand for birthday parties. Added to which I gave frequent puppets shows at home; entry to one of my shows costing a tickey (3 pence).

A keen fellow puppeteer was "Miss" Patricia Pretorious whose widowed mother, Minnie (all thanks to her ownership of Southern Rhodesia's only flour mills) proudly bore the mantle of being the richest woman in Gwelo; hence the prefix "Miss" when addressing her youngest daughter! A photograph of Miss Patricia and the young Puppet Master, each clutching the control bar to a puppet of their choice, even appeared in the weekly *Gwelo Times*.

"Miss" Patricia (small and dumpy like mummy) boasted an extremely elegant and glamorous older sister named Val. Gwelo's social event of the year (perhaps even the decade!) was the wedding of Val to dashing David Barbour (a Gary Cooper lookalike) whose father "Old Man Barbour" owned Barbours, Salisbury's answer to London's Fortnum and Mason. Val and David would go on to become great friends and I would always arrange to "catch up" with them on any visits to this once wonderful country.

A hereditary gift from Him for which I am grateful was his talent for painting and on order to escape Cur's never-resting waspish tongue, he would take himself away on "painting trips" where he would spend many happy hours capturing the stunning beauty of the varied Rhodesian countryside in endless watercolours, the majority of which were framed and proudly displayed in the houses occupied by Him and Cur. Needless to say the scenery for the sets for my puppet theatre were fairly spectacular as were the imaginative props. Who else could fashion a grand piano out of a piece of plywood and strips of cardboard? Who else could assemble a witch's cauldron out of a dried gourd set atop a fire of crumpled red crepe paper covering a small torch? Who else could take a dried pumpkin skin; mount it on a set of giant cotton reels and paint all in gold thereby creating Cinderella's coach? Who else but the young Puppet Master of course!

Manipulating the puppets and immersing myself in all the colourful characters "on stage" gave me a confidence I would be blessed with for the rest of my life - no matter *what* the situation. This "confidence" and the wonderful world of my books saw me with a growing independence: an independence which would see any future contact with my fellow humans clinically approached and cautiously monitored. In far-removed Rhodesia I had no great friend or friends - acquaintances yes - and if it *did* come to a friend, animal, vegetable or mineral, I would have placed my trusty Raleigh bicycle as being the most loyal.

*

An essential part of one's childhood was one's pet albeit a dog, cat, parrot whatever. I somehow acquired a wonderful mongrel duly name Miffy. At a wild guess Miffy's ancestors could have been a mixture of a Lhasa Apso (distinctly African as opposed to Tibetan!), a Jack Russell and a Scottish terrier and I loved her with a passion. Miffy, my puppets and my books became the mainstay of my existence. Even at this tender stage I knew I was "different" and to be "different" in Colonial Southern Rhodesia was tantamount to having the plague. "Being different" was something you did *not* advertise and a further inducement to become a loner and a dreamer lost in the safety net of make believe.

Aided and abetted by my puppets I revelled in my roles as a prince, a princess (I was extremely versatile!), a villain, a South Sea belle, a witch or even a drunken Scotsman in a kilt. When operating a puppet I *became* the character. To my great delight Pelpop presented me with two puppets of my choice; the puppets being the prize awarded for a play I'd written and which appeared in the *Pelpup Magazine.* Needless to say it was Miffy who had to sit patiently listening to me reading bits of my play out loud for her approval.

Without any warning or tangible excuse Cur suddenly decided Miffy had "to go"; her unwarranted reasoning a selfish claim it was easier whilst living "out of town" to keep a bitch on heat away from potential paramours, whereas in testosterone-infused Gwelo it would be nigh on impossible. In other words Miffy had to "go" and "go" she did - within a day. Adding insult to tremendous injury the woman simply instructed the cook to give my hallowed pet to an associate of his irrespective of who the man was or where he lived. So much for Cur's claim of being kind to animals and children. Later I was informed by the tactless cook Miffy, after refusing to eat had starved to death. In other words the poor little dog, pining for her "little master", had simply given up.

Here the seeds of "it's too good to be true; too good to last" were viciously planted and unfortunately are still flourishing to this very day. Hence my pessimistic attitude to life in general and the fact I only once ever entrusted myself and my feelings to one other person: a person who will remain unchallenged until the day I die. A person who is never far from my thoughts and whose photograph sits alongside my computer as a never-ending reminder of the word "magical".

Despite Cur's hallowed persona she did herself no favours by allowing her offspring to attend the local "Government schools" which no doubt saw a tremendous saving in school fees and a tremendous boost in the sales of gin. Gugs and Ligs were destined to go on to pastures new in far-off South Africa (Gugs to the stately St. Annes in the then Province of Natal - now KwaZulu - and Ligs to Michaelhouse, an equally select establishment for boys). I suppose one advantage of this free schooling could be the fact one was taught from an early age to "rub shoulders" with all sorts. This would stand me in good stead when dealing with workmen and other trades people later on but at the time it was a hideous, tortured experience and one not easily forgotten or forgiven.

At school one was inevitably branded with a nickname (nine out of ten times both cruel and denigrating) and I, because of my then sticking out ears, was promptly dubbed "Rabbit" as opposed to my given name Robert!

It was at this stage tragedy struck! To everyone's amazement Roger Powell was offered a position with a Johannesburg-based mining organisation and within a matter of months the Powell family moved to South Africa. I was stunned by Peggy's sudden departure which somehow was momentarily forgotten in the excitement of Him also gaining a promotion and transferred to what Gugs in her letters (we corresponded frequently) dubbed "gay Bulawayo".

An understatement if ever there was seeing in those innocent days Gugs would not have been aware of the term "tongue in cheek"!

To give the place its due, Bulawayo proved to be a soothing balm for two heart breaking incidents; namely the deliberate murder of Miffy (Cur's heartless betrayal of a much loved, innocent pet to an unknown African family) and the departure of my beloved Peggy for distant Johannesburg. Even today these two particular factors are vividly remembered.

After the move to "gay Bulawayo" I would spend hours cycling solo on my faithful Raleigh bicycle to such "romantic spots" as the local Hillside Dams and the more affluent suburbs where I would take great delight in surveying the different styles of various homesteads; suburbs with the pretentious *soubriquets* of Hillside (where we lived), Burnside, Kumalo and the original "Suburbs" itself where certain residents were considered almost "worthwhile" by the superior Cur!

Architectural styles were varied from thatched homesteads to magnificent granite constructed residences set atop granite hills known as *kopjes.* Palatial Tudor, Dutch-gabled or even French château styled residences and sprawling bungalows sat incongruously amidst smooth, Lincoln green Kikuyu lawns complete with dazzling blue swimming pools. It should be remembered Southern Rhodesia, in its heyday, was a veritable Valhalla and literally a "goldmine" with its endless fertile, agricultural acres and vast mineral resources. Tobacco, gold, precious stones and asbestos being the call of the day.

It was through these endless "sightseeing bicycle rides" a further passion was brought to the fore; a passion for architecture leading to a curiosity as to what the interiors of this kaleidoscope of varying styles could offer. The influence of Peggy, these endless cycle rides (an introduction to "another fantasy world") along with my daily "fix" of books (by now I had discovered the delights of Beverley Nichols, E.F. Benson and Agatha Christie) added to my determination to move to the magical sounding England from southern Africa as soon as I could. Like Dick Whittington I firmly believed I would find the streets of London literally "paved with gold" and on arrival in this faraway, magical city of dreams I would make a name for myself by doing "something artistic". Surprisingly enough, despite my great interest in the theatre as shown through my puppet shows and enthusiasm for amateur dramatics, I never once considered acting as a career. Instead I began to buy a selection of breathtaking design magazines from Etherton's (Bulawayo's answer to Foyles) with the glossy American *House Beautiful* being the most revered.

Through *House Beautiful* I was introduced to and mesmerised by the likes of Frank Lloyd-Wright (his Kaufmann house, Fallingwater, still vividly imprinted in my mind), Le Corbusier, Mies van der Roe and Eero Saarinen along with interior designers Sister Parish, Albert Hadley and others. Little did I realise at the time another Lloyd - David Lloyd-Lowles - would change my life forever.

School was another "rough and ready" Government Secondary establishment named Milton Boys High; the highlight of my time there playing the role of Miss Gossage in John Dighton's *The Happiest Days of Your Life.* Enough said.

*

A definite high point of my Bulawayo years - in addition to the solo sightseeing bicycle rides - was being invited by John Wright the puppet maestro, to sit backstage for a performance when his touring company, John Wright Marionettes, visited Bulawayo. The invitation had come following a letter I sent to the great man himself prior to his visit. In my letter I expressed my unfailing interest in the magical world of puppets and if I there was a chance I could meet him I would be "over the moon". I sat transfixed through the group's production of *The Little Mermaid.* An evening never-to-be-forgotten.

Regular visits to Southern Rhodesia from Johannesburg-based Brian Brooke Theatre Company saw Bulawayo treated to a rip-roaring production of Sandy Wilson's *The Boy Friend* and a veritable eye-opener to a mesmerised young boy who revelled in every moment of the toe-tapping, magical "madcap" show. Little did I know my wide-eyed admiration for the dashing Bobby Van Husen in the famous dance number *Won't You Charleston With Me?* would lead to me becoming fully involved with the dancing, prancing Bobby not only in South Africa but also in China!

Another major "happening" was joining an amateur theatrical group, The Hillside Young Players, which saw my forte for playing "character parts" coming to the fore. Whether it was the vindictive Mr Throstle in *Berkeley Square* or the tap dancing Jerry Winterton in *On Monday Next,* I was always first up for the role. Our director was an earnest man named John Cobb who secretly lusted over the charming uber-butch Bill Cordell whom he would always cast in the leading roles. I meanwhile lusted over a Tony Law and a David Crozier, two boys at Milton School. Needless to say this was feeling heavily repressed and would remain stifled until I entered the hallowed precincts of Rhodes University where, unfettered, this latent Phoenix soared as well as "rose" (literally) from the ashes. Apart from their good looks and charm I also remember Crozier and Cordell each boasting a pair of magnificent right-angled "sticking out" ears which I saw as some sort of weird sympathy towards my own matching "affliction". (This was one of the first matters dealt with when I was able to afford the operation by having London's leading plastic surgeon, Mr Robin Beare, firmly pin my embarrassing "Dumbos" back.)

Excruciatingly conscious of my protruding ears I had been aware of a simple operation for rectifying this. Despite the comforting photographs of Prince Charles arriving at Gordonstoun in 1962 where his ninety degree-angled ears can be clearly seen, I was still determined to have mine "flatter than flat" (I had reached the staggering age of twenty three). In 1965 the long-awaited operation took place and I will never forget the moment I dived into a swimming pool and was able to sweep my wet hair back against my head without feeling at all self-conscious. Later photographs of the Prince show *his* ears set back at an acceptable forty five degrees as opposed to their former right angles. As far as I recall this momentous "pinning of the Prince" received no publicity whatsoever.

A chance meeting with Prince Charles in the mid-eighties resulted in my eyes being surreptitiously drawn to his still impressive set of "jugs".

William (Bill) Cordell became a firm friend and Bill's mother, a charming, highly intelligent woman named Mai (a surrogate Peggy) with whom I remained in contact through letters and a several rare "long distance" phone calls. However Peggy would remain *numero uno* until her death in the 1973.

They say there is always one Mr Chips (read schoolmaster) in one's life who is never forgotten. My Mr Chips was a Mr Tickner the English teacher at Milton School who introduced to my philosophy for life by insisting I read George Bernard Shaw's 1903 masterpiece, *Man and Superman*. I am sure Mr Tickner's awe-inspiring gesture was unintentional but never-the-less a prime example of shooting oneself well-and-truly in the foot. From the moment I read two sentences passed between Bob and Jane I was hooked with Jane's comment becoming my mantra for life.

BOB: I'm so discouraged. My writing teacher told me my novel is hopeless.

JANE: Don't listen to her, Bob. Remember, those who can, do; those who can't, teach.

Today I still wonder if benign Mr Tickner ever fully aware of what he told me to read and absorb or, more importantly, even read *Man and Superman*!

Not fully satisfied with Jane's comeback I added a few words of my own; the result being:

Those who can, do; those who can't, teach or preach.

I am always amused by the so-called elite who review books, shows and plays. If this isn't a glaring example of those who can and those who can't, I rest my case.

As for the preachers of this world I throw up my hands in horror. A staunch atheist I have no time whatsoever for those who believe or pontificate - pun most certainly intended - and anyone guilty of either failings I simply dismiss. Life ever after? The majority of the world's population is already guilty of acute boredom. Imagine an eternity of this gross self-indulgence.

*

In the then Southern Rhodesia one was able to attain a driving licence at the age of sixteen. I passed my driving test on my sixteen birthday and whenever I could I would borrow Cur's celadon green-coloured Morris Minor which I promptly (for no particular reason) christened Jennifer. Natty Jennifer soon took over from my faithful Raleigh bicycle all thanks to Cur becoming too fraught at the idea of having to cope with Bulawayo's heavy traffic.

Jennifer became a highly popular member of The Hillside Young Players and promptly joined in the numerous picnics arranged amidst the ravishingly beautiful Matopos Hills (renamed Matobo), an area of granite kopjes (hills) and wooded valleys with tumbling streams some thirty five miles south of Bulawayo and accessible by the usual, pothole-enhanced "strip road"; this being a set of parallel tarmacked eighteen inch-wide "strips" crudely set on a suitably cleared width of raw, cleared veld or *bundu*. Meeting an oncoming car or overtaking a car required a propensity for "give or take" and considerable skill! Cecil Rhodes, the founder of Northern and Southern Rhodesia, who died in 1902 is buried in the Matopos Hills. His grave - set atop an immense kopje personally chosen for his eternal resting place and named "View of the World" - is marked by an impressive bronze plaque mounted on a double-layered plinth of carved granite.

A daring prank carried out by several discerning pupils was to indecently drink a lager whilst *lounging* on the great man's grave. Something Mugabwe and his cronies would no doubt cheer! I am happy to say none of our group were guilty of this blasphemy! Instead we would happily drive with several passengers in our respective cars to the area, select a random spot, park and spend the day rock climbing, swimming or generally lazing about followed by a sumptuous picnic of sandwiches (usually sliced beef or egg mayonnaise) washed down by gallons of orange squash. Key "players" making up the group of frolicsome teenagers included such fondly remembered names as Pat Collison, Helen Minter, "Gorgeous George" McClean, Sally Jensen, fabulous Pauline Webb, Rob Apps and the aforementioned Bill Cordell.

Through John Cobb, the energetic founder of the Hillside Young Players, the group was introduced to the delights of Michael Flanders and Donald Swann whose LP record *At the Drop of a Hat* I listened to again and again. No doubt Cecil Rhodes would have been somewhat astounded by our lusty rendition of *Mud, mud, glorious mud* from *The Hippopotamus Song* while standing toasting each other round his grave. (No lager toasts this time nota bene but with orange squash instead!)

*

Prior to attending university I was determined to try my hand at journalism and after a brief interview I found myself employed as a cub reporter on *The Bulawayo Chronicle.* As if such an accolade was not enough I was invited to take part in several junior broadcasts for the FBC (Federal Broadcasting Corporation). This "taking part" eventually leading to even greater heights as   presenter of "Teenage Half Hour" and described in the Arts Section of *The Bulawayo Chronicle* as *The Golden Voice of Teenage Half Hour*!

Usurping all was a consignment taken on behalf of the newspaper; a visit to the extraordinary world of Operation Noah. The late nineteen fifties saw the completion of the massive Kariba Dam built across the mighty Zambezi River thus linking northern and Southern Rhodesia. The construction of this largest man-made lake on the planet led to thousands of former bushland being flooded and thousands of animals at risk and while every effort had been made relocate the Tonga people living in the danger zone, it was up to a man, Rupert Fothergill, to ensure the wellbeing of the animals under threat. Operation Noah saw the physical rescue of over six thousand animals including elephant, rhinos, lions, leopards, zebra, antelopes, warthogs and more. Many more animals "made their own way" but the human response was enormous. It was also a tremendously emotional experience and I am extremely proud to have not only witnessed but taken part in Operation Noah.

In my children's book, *Four Zimbabwean Adventure Tales*, Operation Noah is avidly described in the tale *The Adventures of Lucy the Baboon & Charlie the Cheetah.*

Apart from writing several articles about Kariba and Operation Noah and a year spent with *The Bulawayo Chronicle* I decided a career as a reporter was not for me so did what the majority of young people did in order to delay the undertaking of a final profession or a life of selected drudgery, I opted for the usual "treading water". In other words "marking time" by going on to university while contemplating one's (at the time) distant future career. The university of my choice was the much lauded Rhodes University. Dubbed "The Oxford of South Africa" Rhodes is situated in the city of Grahamstown set in the lush, hilly region of the Eastern Cape. It was at Rhodes Univeristy the RA butterfly finally emerged to spread (amongst other things) its glorious wings.

RHODES, RHODES, GLORIOUS RHODES! THE "OXFORD OF SOUTH AFRICA" WITHOUT THE DREAMING SPIRES

The small city of Grahamstown in the Eastern Cape Province is home to Rhodes University, founded in 1904 and named after Cecil Rhodes (likewise Northern and Southern Rhodesia). Originally dubbed "the city of Saints" Grahamstown boasts a magnificent cathedral along with a plethora of churches (approximately forty in number). It is also considered as *the* centre of arts in South Africa.

I arrived at this "seat of learning" after a hot, sticky (totally platonic) three day train journey from Salisbury (the top rung of Cur's ladder) where Him and Cur had subsequently moved to during the latter part of my time with the *Bulawayo Chronicle.*

I am a firm believer in first impressions and on stepping down from one of the grimy passenger coaches pulled by a smoky, coal-fired locomotive, I was completely won over by the sight of the high, forested hills engulfing the small university town with further viewings of the aforementioned cathedral and the landmark Drostdy Arch leading up the impressive, red roofed main university building. With its impressive clock tower designed by Herbert Baker along with the Arch and surrounding buildings, my enthusiasm for my home for the next three years was virtually irrepressible.

I was not best pleased at finding myself having to share a cramped room for my first year with a rather dull, extremely straight student studying for a degree in chemistry. The person was *so* serious, *so* studious and *so* straight it is here - and only here - I had to admit to a temporary "craft" moment until Mr Chemistry Student's name - Rob Summers - suddenly came back to me. Fortunately the campus offered so many exciting paces in which to spend one's time which meant I hardly ever saw the temporary Mr Anonymous aka Mr Summers.

After the initial excitement of settling in, getting one's bearings and meeting up with the various Professors who would be giving us our first year lectures, it was time to "meet and greet". At first I was both uncommunicative and cautious with the myriad of strangers rushing hither and thither before finally starting to converse with one or two students attending the same lectures as myself. Among the "chosen few" was an elongated, bespectacled, dark-haired young man named Nigel Vermaas and a dank-looking, corduroy-jacketed, buck-toothed, perpetually frowning gentleman called Lance Salway soon to be named (at his insistence) Tallulah. Unfortunately Lance's bohemian appearance could not justify an overpowering aura of BO which was resolved fortunately sooner than later by a discreet talking-to and a suggested daily usage of Mum Rollette!

I often wondered if Lance ever understood the muttered aside "Tallulah's *very* ZaSu today!" ZaSu being a play on the outlandish name of ZaSu Pitts, star of many silent films, and a mischievous reference to Lance's *armpits*. In all fairness to Tallulah and the vast majority of males in the fifties and early sixties "mum" was literally the word as far as deodorants, aftershaves and colognes were concerned; the alternative being a strong smelling soap bearing the macho name of Lifebuoy. As for an aftershave the only one available appeared to be Old Spice (if you were daring enough!)

(Years later I would be sharply reminded of Tallulah's "ZaSu days" on a number of sweaty occasions; once when dancing cheek to cheek with Edward Montagu of - amongst others - vintage car fame at a "boys only" party in Bryanston Square, and again while dancing with Rudolf Nureyev but *not* on the stage at The Royal Opera House, Covent Garden I hasten to add!)

Nigel and Lance would become great friends and in time both would go on to greater things: Nigel becoming a celebrated broadcaster in South Africa and Lance a successful writer of children's books.

Matters took a major turn at the notification of a forthcoming production of *King Lear* in Port Elizabeth, a major city on the Indian Ocean some eighty miles south of Grahamstown. Nigel, Lance and yours truly eagerly put our names on the list of the wannabe audience and on the great day found ourselves seated in the back of a converted lorry as opposed to a coach for the journey to Port Elizabeth and back. Among the group of excited theatregoers was a vibrant, glamorous, dark-haired young woman and her dashing, blond male companion (a veritable Gina Lollobrigida and Leslie Howard) named Shirley Ritchie and Alan Dashwood. Talk about another case of love at first sight! (Apologies Peggy and Madame Zizi!) Shirley would go on to become a high-powered judge in London with Alan not only becoming a judge but receiving a knighthood to boot. As with Nigel and Lance, a lot was still to happen before such illustrious tidings.

I can truly say the night of *King Lear* saw the birth of "The Ritchie Set"; a group which would not only shock the more conventional students at Rhodes but give rise to a combination of envy and extreme jealousy. Unlike the majority of students Shirley lived in a small block of flats away from the campus and it was here the newly-formed set would gather, day in and day out. Though not quite in the realm of Bernie Eccleston, Shirley's father James came a close second in the way he overwhelmingly indulged his brilliant lawyer-to-be daughter! Shirley was without a doubt the most generous "hostess with the mostess" and her non-stop parties becoming the talk (and scandal) of the campus.

Soon to join the Ritchie Set was a tall, gangling, rather vague young man named Humphrey Knipe (Humphrey would go on to become an acclaimed writer and producer of porn films in sunny California!) and a suave charmer named Ollie Anderson (no relation) whose endless string of girlfriends would have made Casanova pale into insignificance. Because of this extraordinary "turnover" in ladies I - along with one or two others - firmly believed Ollie a "closet" gay (if we were mistaken Mr A, I can only apologise for myself and the others for this gross misdemeanour) and trust he eventually found his cloud with a silver as opposed to a pink lining.

Another new member and a rival to Dashwood for the deepest bass voice on the campus was the devastatingly handsome Hamish McLeod who lived in Mbabane the capital of exotic-sounding Swaziland, a small landlocked monarchy in southern Africa.

Shirley would glide about the campus like a female Pied Piper with the Ritchie Set eagerly following in her neat, high-heeled footsteps. With her nipped-in waist and billowing skirts resting on seemingly endless, starched petticoats Shirley was considered the epitome of fashion. Given the fact she was also very tall, sported a sensational bosom, wore her hair in a beehive and adorned her lustrous large brown eyes with an excess of mascara, the overall "Ritchie effect" was "eye-catching" to say the least. Add to this an infectious laugh and a wonderful sense of humour and who could ask for anything more? How we adored her and how we enjoyed worshipping at her exquisitely shod feet!

Before the question arises the answer is "yes" with members of the fairer sex very much part of the Ritchie Set. Among these was the twittering "Little Glen" a fussy, bustling soul), "Windy" Wendy and "dry wit" Gillian MacGillivray otherwise known as "MacGillicuddy" to name but a few.

Last but not least among the "panting" males was Ian "Bubbles" McCausland, a whimsical young man who tentatively dated Little Glen before casting her aside claiming she was "frigid" due to her "continued" resistance of his amorous advances. Little Glen, to give the young lady her due, continued happily twittering despite the slight while Ian went on to become a school teacher sporting the added laureate of "confirmed bachelor" thus intimating Little Glen's resistance may not have been a case of "Oh Bubbles, keep your hands off" after all.

Although the aforementioned characters may have sported a few eccentricities nobody could compete with a bumptious, five foot nothing Quasimodo-lookalike named Julian Craggs. Julian was somebody else who would go and make a name for himself in the arts; this time in Canada before settling in New Orleans in 1971 where he happily (or unhappily) resided until his death in 1992.

Shirley and Alan were always extremely loyal to Julian and as you will read, he became a stalwart friend to the extent we shared a flat in Kensington during our early days in London.

Days rushed by with lectures becoming almost incidental amidst our hectic, enchanted lives. True to form I joined the Dramatic Society (Shirley and Alan were already members) and promptly auditioned for any one of the numerous parts in Alan's planned production of *The Agamemnon* by Aeschylus. Alan was majoring in Greek among other equally erudite subjects and with his blond, matinee idol looks and deep, *basso profundo* voice made an inspirational director for such a cumbersome play. I was given the role of "messenger"- or bearer of ill-tidings - which involved learning several pages of an impassioned, opening soliloquy. Quite a formidable task!

Two years later Alan's sonorous *The Agamemnon* would be totally usurped by a production of Sandy Wilson's *The Boy Friend.* Apart from myself no other member of the Ritchie Set with theatrical aspirations considered the light-hearted musical worthy of their talents. I naturally auditioned for the plum part of Bobby Van Husen "The rich, good-looking American staying at the Hotel Negresco!" and landed the role with little or no competition. Needless to say my Charleston number stole the show!

Despite sitting through endless painful productions of Gilbert & Sullivan operettas as performed by the Gwelo and Bulawayo operatic societies all had been forgiven on seeing the Brian Brooke production of *The Boy Friend* during a tour of Southern Rhodesia. The fun-filled, toe-tapping show saw the start of my love for stage musicals along with my devotion to the spectacular warbles pouring forth from Hollywood. It took no time at all for the musicals of Rodgers and Hammerstein, Rodgers and Hart, Jerome Kern and Stephen Sondheim's *West Side Story* to become firm favourites.

Nowadays when it comes to West End musicals I will happily support any production by Cameron Mackintosh whereas anything associated with Andrew Lloyd-Webber I avoid like the proverbial plague. Works by the man remind me of the winners of the Booker Prize. Boring with a capital B and once bitten, twice *very* shy. If asked to name a major British musical maestro the name Lionel Bart immediately springs to mind.

In addition to the Dramatic Society I became a member of the Debating Society which witnessed *The Golden Voice of Teenage Half Hour* happily re-emerging to take part in many a heated debate. Here Lady Luck seemed to enter the ever-developing picture and, much to my delight, I discovered a hidden talent for witty quips and sharp one liners (the latter more scathing than kind) and soon became known for my acerbic repartee. *Stekel* the university newspaper described me as "the Noël Coward of the campus" and who was I to dissuade them? In my final year I would become chairman of the Society.

Because of the glamour involved (little did I realise the ensuing pain and effort) I took up the energetic sport of fencing and became a positive *maestro* regarding my thrusts and parries.

Apparently my thrusts and parries - as with my earlier bouncing up and down on a pogo stick - were something to be reckoned with and like riding a bicycle, inherent skills not to be taken lightly!

It was at Rhodes - at the astonishing age at eighteen - I had my first sexual encounter; a veritable replay of Deborah Kerr and Burt Lancaster in the (at the time) scandalous *From Here to Eternity.* In this version Burt was a brawny theological student named Geoffrey with the unfortunate surname of McMinn. "Blessed" with a strident voice (a boon for future congregations no doubt) Geoffrey was a prime example of the term "sesquipedalian" or user of long words. If he could substitute a ten letter word for a similar word containing four or five, he would promptly do so. For example, instead of saying someone was simply imaginative, Geoffrey would describe the person as being polyphiloprogenitive! A walking Thesaurus if ever there was!

Geoffrey ("call me Geoff") "picked me up" after one of our debating evenings. Aiding and abetting his burly Burt Lancaster looks was the irresistible attraction of a gleaming motorbike: a sure-fire way for getting a "yes" in response to the meaningful suggestion of a "moonlight picnic on the beach with just us - away from it all". The selected venue was a beach close to Cowie, a small seaside resort set alongside a small river of the same name. "The Cowie" as it was known would become a great venue for future picnics and numerous "away days".

Riding pillion and clutching onto Geoffrey's muscular midriff for dear life, we raced through the night in what seemed a matter of minutes before reaching our destination. Having constructed a roaring fire from bits of driftwood and dried scrub Geoffrey - to my great delight - wasted no time before the much longed-for "attack". After few moments of lying next to each other while gazing at the flickering flames, a mug of wine of in our hands, he suddenly gave out a lusty cry and leapt upon my seductively prone frame. With a lot of panting and fumbling of fly buttons (at the time trousers didn't have the convenience of zips) we energetically wanked each other off. On the many similar tussles following Geoffrey would sonorously proclaim whereas he approved of "correlative masturbation" indulgence in "the ultimate intimacy" was definitely not one of his "habitudes".

"I'll occasionally subject myself to the delights of fellatio but never will I allow myself to effectuate the intimate intimacy" was a much repeated mantra. God forbid the word "fuck" should ever pass his sculpted lips.

I have no idea what became of "substitute Burt" but "substitute Deborah" lived to tell the tale. If Geoffrey is still alive and kicking (or in

"Geoff speak" "cognizant and calcitrating") with luck he will not be reading this.

*

If we were not meeting at Shirley's flat - a rare occurrence - we would congregate in the university *kaif* - or café - where endless Coca Colas or coffees would be quaffed and a mountain of the *kaif's* de rigueur toasted cheese sandwiches (dubbed "toasted cheeses for Jesus") would be greedily consumed while we put the world to rights. It should be remembered in the late fifties South Africa still rigorously supported apartheid which meant all the students at Rhodes were white. The numerous residences dotting the campus were cleaned daily by an army of *ousies* (black maids) and boys (black men) which saw all students literally not having to "lift a finger" where the cleaning of their rooms or laundry was concerned. Meals were served by white jacketed waiters in a series of cavernous dining halls allocated to various residences. The mere fact this way of life was taken for granted still causes me acute embarrassment. However, it must be remembered this was the manner in which we were brought up. An imperious attitude and way of life where those who were not "us" were there to do our bidding and woe betide those who did not adhere to our wishes.

*

The frustrating situation of Geoffrey ("call me Geoff") being a case of "all lust but no thrust" was resolved by - of all people - Julian Craggs who appeared hell bent on instigating the deflowering of his friend! Julian, who lived in glamorous Johannesburg (the City of Gold) as did Shirley and Alan, had become involved with a local bohemian group involving several artists, writers and actors, one of whom I simply "had to meet". This *outré* set revolved around a large, hirsute woman going by the exotic name of Valda Blomberg and my first introduction to a bona fide "fag hag". Despite the fey young men surrounding Shirley none to my knowledge - apart from myself and Bubbles - were gay and therefore the term "fag hag" would have been a misnomer. Having set the sinful scene I was invited by Julian to spend a short end of term break at his home in Sandton where he lived in great style with his parents George and Elizabeth.

George and Elizabeth Craggs turned out to be two of the most outrageous snobs one could ever come across (this dubious accolade eventually usurped by Cherry Moorsom a woman I would later meet in

45

London). Speaking in strangulated voices the affected couple soon let you know *nothing* was good enough for the two of them with Julian seen as nothing more than a wretched inconvenience as opposed to a revered son. After a few days staying with the Craggs's I soon let Shirley and Alan know Julian deserved a medal; if not several rows of them.

"He'll be *mad* about you, Rob!" prophesied Julian with a superior expression. "Mark Jules' words!" ("Rob" or "Robbie" being the call of the day with "Robin" only emerging after my arrival in London). The "deflowerer" of his choosing was a wiry blond actor, a doppelgänger for Jean-Claude Van Damme, named Ian Kennedy and drily billed by Julian as ideal for the role of "Rob's *night* in shining *amour!*"

Meeting Ian saw a much lauded misquote bandied about between Julian and myself. A case of "Once ridden, no longer shy" saw my subsequent behaviour more in keeping with my schoolboy nickname "Rabbit" rather than the boring "Rob" or "Robbie". Like all rabbits, this deflowered "Rabbit" simply couldn't get enough! Forget the Burt and Jean-Claude lookalikes. The two quickly replaced by a stream of even more eager lusts and thrusts.

Through Johannesburg's gay grapevine in which I soon found myself happily entwined I was given several names to "look up" on my return to Salisbury for the forthcoming Christmas vacation or "long vac". Meanwhile Julian's original "deflowering" saw me caught up in a glamorous, new world involving further members of the acting fraternity. One such luminary was the devastatingly handsome Jon Whitely and a leading member of the already much lauded Brian Brooke Theatre Company. Through Jon I was introduced to Heather Lloyd-Jones, Brooke's brightest star. I fell head over heels in platonic love with the effervescent Heather on first seeing her in the Brian Brooke production of *Irma La Douce.* Heather eventually married the choreographer Frank Staff and to my delight the happy couple settled in Grahamstown, her hometown. I took great pride in being seen out with Heather in the gossipy, university town and see it as an honour to have become a true friend of this vivacious and very dear person.

In Johannesburg I was also introduced to a group of discreet gay businessmen and various other professional types. I developed a close friendship with a smooth-talking Swiss company executive named Haylett Regenass and his tight circle of friends including an extremely pompous Geoffrey McMinn doppelgänger with the sibilant surname of Spofforth.

Other friends of Haylett were the debonair Lesley Smith and his flamboyant boyfriend, Erik Eikenboom. Contrary to the belief all gay men seek out "pretty boys" or their handsome equivalents I, like many other younger gays I knew, preferred the company of more robust, corpulent types. No doubt a psychiatrist would immediately put this down to a father fixation and he could have been right. My preference being a man's man as opposed to a giggling, gilded lily!

Enter a rugged, young Russell Crowe lookalike (or in the late fifties, a young Errol Flynn) named David Shaffer who I believe ended up living in California with my substitute, a young man named Hardy (a second Hardy "substitute" appears later). David was the "flavour of the month" - literally - and in my third year at Rhodes a photograph of him held pride of place on the desk in my room.

Adding a dash of colour to the business sector of "Joburg's gay set" was a highly neurotic, effete young man named Colin Fletcher, a dead ringer for today's Julian Clary. Colin worked for a PR company and was always busy organising "events" and even busier "falling in love". A gargantuan theatre buff Colin would frequently refer to Leslie French, an English actor who visited Cape Town on a yearly basis on behalf of the Maynardville Theatre in order to direct a work by Shakespeare. He would also mention French's partner, David Lloyd Lowles; a successful London-based businessman and another frequent visitor to Cape Town. Needless to say Colin firmly attached himself to the Johannesburg members of the Ritchie Set.

*

Sadly I had to tear myself away from all the City of Gold's glitter and travel back to Salisbury to spend the rest of the "long vac" (and similar vacations) in the strained company of Him and Cur. Big brother Ian would also make an appearance.

Him's appointment as Chief Government Mining Engineer and subsequent transfer from Bulawayo to Salisbury saw Him achieve the pinnacle of his profession. True to form Cur made sure they invested in a property worthy of Him's new status. The result was a magnificent house in Avondale, one of city's most exclusive suburbs. In the late fifties, early sixties, a hallowed American magazine, *The Saturday Evening Post*, featured Southern Rhodesia in one of their editions. In the article Salisbury was billed as one of the most vibrant and beautiful cities on the planet with

Southern Rhodesia itself seen at the time as "The breadbasket of Africa". With its gleaming skyscrapers, immaculate lesser buildings, colourful garden squares and wide streets lined with purple flowering jacaranda trees the place really was Shangri-La.

A characteristic of the jacaranda trees - or their equivalents - were the uniform bands of white lime-wash applied to the base of the tree trunks as a deterrent to termites which would have otherwise eventually destroyed the trees by building their clay dwellings around the bases. Another colourful and highly original feature dominating the centre of Salisbury was Cecil Square (now Africa Unity Square) laid out in the design of the Union Jack with plantings of red cannas and white and blue irises representing the colours of the former flag.

Jon (Whitely) on learning I lived in Salisbury made certain I met the city's gay glitterati which resulted in even more rabbit-like behaviour with the local television stars and then some! I became firm friends with the erudite Jerry Wilmot and the dazzlingly good-looking Geoffrey Atkins whose daily appearance on RTV, the local television channel, had the majority of female viewers in a swoon and a few select male viewers doing the same (and maybe a bit more!). I am happy to say I was soon to enjoy the pleasure of "a bit more". Jerry had a house close to *Maison* Anderson which saw the faithful Jennifer toing and froing yo-yo-like between the two establishments.

Among the new friends in Salisbury was "a blast from the past" in the form of elegant Val Barbour, elder sister of former childhood puppeteer of Gwelo days, "Miss" Patricia Pretorious. Val and David had built a striking house in the neighbouring suburb of Borrowdale and I soon became a regular visitor. The house - a combination of Frank Lloyd-Wright meets Le Corbusier - sat elegantly amidst gnarled msasa trees and undulating Kikiyu lawns. Because of its striking architecture the house became a main topic of conversation among Salisbury's so-called elite. An additional talking point was the Scandinavian-inspired interior; a vast change to the usual mahogany claw-and-ball three piece suite with matching coffee and side tables typical of so-called upmarket Rhodesian interiors!

Val, a "no nonsense gal" who flew her own aeroplane, played golf to the standard of a Gary Player and given birth to two daughters was surely an example to all her female contemporaries as to what a modern woman could achieve. Furthermore she remained completely besotted with David and vice versa. David was certainly one of the most charismatic men one could ever wish to meet (as well as being a total testosterone-infused dish) and I was a privileged to call him a friend.

Val's aunt, Vi van Wyk, was a mirror image of her sister, Minnie "Midas" Pretorious. Both were widows; both were short and plump and both strutted their tiny, well-upholstered frames like a pair of proud pouter pigeons. Vi had two sons, Bennie and Pieter. I was convinced the effeminate Bennie with his high sing-song voice was gay (he also had a penchant for flower arranging) whereas blustery, rugger bugger Pieter most certainly was not. However, during one of our rare conversations elder brother Ian repeated a previous conversation held with the questionable Bennie. According to Ian the prissy, posturing Bennie had "fucked a girl *so* hard she'd fallen off the bed!"

My response? A cynical "Oh yes?"

Vi van Wyk, was great fun and a marvellous hostess. I would spend many happy evenings (when not fraternising with Wilmot and company) being entertained and dining with the family in their charming, Dutch-gabled house. So much so a scathing Cur suggested I may as well "move in".

A name causing a ripple of excitement through gossip starved Salisbury was arrival of a young man named Benedict James Colman ostensibly sent out to Rhodesia by his family in order to join the BSAP (British South African Police); the real reason for young Mr Colman "being sent to the Colonies" never truly explained. Several years later Ben would become a mega, fun and beloved friend and a director of RAD my interior design company.

Meanwhile the endless days of hot, grimy, sweaty train journeys from Rhodesia through the Transvaal, the Orange Free State and finally the Eastern Cape became a thing of the past all thanks to the loyal Jennifer. Cur no longer acknowledged the plucky Morris Minor so I was happy to take her under my wing. I find it hard to believe Jennifer and self would make the eleven hundred mile journey from Salisbury to Grahamstown travelling at an average speed of 50 mph and think nothing of pulling up along the roadside for a snack and if it was night time, an hour or two's "kip"; the possibility of being robbed or attacked never crossing one's mind. Something unheard of in today's climate.

Having made the three day journey alone on more than one occasion I soon realised a passenger or two would be far more pleasant. Added to companionship was the factor it would see a saving on the cost of the petrol with the bill split between two or three. Naturally the extra bonus for the lucky passenger - or passengers - of enjoying "Rob's amusing company" en route was never mentioned.

Someone who became a regular "passenger" was a jolly, buxom blonde named Mary Bellamy better known as Belle. Belle would eventually go on to marry Michael Etherton, a fellow student and hanger-on from my Bulawayo days. (Michael's parents being the owners of the bookshop responsible for my introduction to Frank Lloyd-Wright et al.) With the buxom Bellamy on board the days of simply parking and "having a kip" changed to staying with friends of Mary's "en route". Needless to say, despite the financial gain, I still hankered for the days I travelled alone.

Rhodes was a university of two distinctive moods. One moment the campus seemed caught up in a hedonistic, carnival spirit before suddenly wrapping itself in a cloak of oppressive silence as everybody entered a state of hibernation whilst "swotting" or "cramming" for exams. Venues varied from our private rooms, the library or Shirley's flat where she and Alan would be concentrating on their law exams and the rest of the Ritchie Set on whatever faculty they had selected. My main subjects were Fine Art and English so I got off rather lightly!

Despite the brevity of my initial stay with Julian I was able to catch up with magical Peggy Powell and proudly introduced her to Shirley, Alan and Julian. As expected my new university friends were enchanted by Peggy with the feeling happily reciprocated by this enchanting woman being adopted as a literal mascot by the discerning Ritchie Set! Peggy was in her element since their move from Gwelo and obviously revelling in the many opportunities Johannesburg had to offer. Not only was she able to pursue a former love for tennis but went on to become a top trophy winner for her exclusive tennis club. Peggy was able to indulge in another favourite previously "designated to the back burner"; namely bridge.

Back in Grahamstown an unexpected, major transformation was to take place following a regular outing of the Ritchie Set to one of the local cinemas where we sat enchanted through Blake Edwards' wondrous *Breakfast at Tiffany's*. Within days of having seen the film Shirley had taken up smoking via an elongated cigarette holder while all the male members of the Set took to sporting unbuttoned cardigans and George Peppard razor-sharp partings in their usually tousled hair. In other words, a complete bunch of wallies with even the corduroy-clad Tallulah sprucing himself up with a dash of bay rum liberally applied to his former neglected personage. Much to our amusement the Ritchie Set found themselves virtually adopted by the University's most eccentric couple, Professor Jakes Ewer and his crop-headed pipe smoking wife, Griff. Ewer was somehow connected to the "discovery" of a rare prehistoric Coelacanth off the coast of East Africa. Apart from this "fishy" claim to fame he was best remembered for his outlandish plummy voice - a combination of Noël Coward meets Vin Diesel meets Christopher Lee - which I would have thought would have resulted in any self-respecting Coelacanth swimming for cover. Jakes Ewer's voice once heard was a voice never-to-be-forgotten.

A highlight of my final year was an invitation from the University of Cape Town Dramatic for the Rhodes Dramatic Society to take part in a "Best Student Drama Competition". Despite *Breakfast at Tiffany's* heady influence the play selected was the suitably sober (and depressing) *On the Frontier* by W.H. Auden and Christopher Isherwood. The final choice left to Dashwood the erstwhile director of *The Agamemnon* and Professor Guy Butler, Head of the Department of English. Needless the "strolling players" were dominated by the Ritchie Set resulting in a fun-filled two day train journey from Port Elizabeth to Cape Town.

Cape Town proved to be spectacularly beautiful and a touch decadent with the Ritchie Set taken to see a drag show - a first for all - performed at a questionable club in the vicinity of the insalubrious Cape docks. We all sat mesmerised as Denise, a giant black drag queen dressed à la Carmen Miranda, shimmied and mimed his way through a recording of the Brazilian Bombshell's hit song, *Chica Chica Boom Chic* and several other throbbing numbers. None of us had ever seen the likes of Denise before which made her the talk of the Ritchie Set for several days. In comparison to the giant waves made by drag queen supreme Denise, *On the Frontier* failed to raise even a ripple. From a competitive point of view and in glaring contrast to the overall fun of our visit the entry by the Rhodes University Dramatic Society proved to be nothing more than a resounding flop. Needless to say no one was surprised by the result seeing our enthusiasm for the play in question had been nothing more than tepid from the start.

Undeterred I returned to Salisbury where I announced to Him and Cur I would be "relocating" to Johannesburg after my graduation where a

Mr Regenass had guaranteed me employment until I had saved up enough for the fare on one of the many Union Castle ships toing and froing between Cape Town and Dick Whittington town. As promised Haylett saw me employed as a "coordinator" (read "male secretary-cum-general layabout") in a friendly office as well as organising a small studio flat for me in the bohemian suburb of Hillbrow.

In 1961 Jeremy Taylor, an English teacher based in Johannesburg became an overnight success and cult figure with his tongue-in-cheek ballad *Ag Pleez Deddy*, a brilliant spoof on a gang (group is too polite a word) of children en route to a local Drive-In cinema. The record sold more copies in South Africa than any single by Elvis Presley. I was fortunate enough to attend one of Mr Taylor's shows and can truly say *Ag Pleez Deddy* must surely be one of the truest depiction of fifty-sixties South Africa ever and I strongly recommend the reader Google *Ag Pleez Deddy* and view Jeremy Taylor singing his mischievous song. Whereas the audiences applauded Jeremy Taylor while laughing at his lyrics I, for one, saw his acerbic words as a true portrayal of the country's cultural backwater along with the proverbial writing on the wall and the ensuing chaos following the eventual establishment of the ANC (African National Congress) under the corrupt leadership of President Jacob Zuma.

True to form I continued to enjoy "living it up" in the City of Gold while scrupulously setting aside as much as I could in order to seek out the *other* golden city; namely Dick Whittington's London and its streets paved with gold. Mission accomplished I duly boarded *RMS Pendennis Castle* on a sunny May morning bound for Southampton, England. The year was 1962, I was twenty two years old and boasted the grand sum of £17 discreetly tucked away inside my jacket pocket.

Prior to my departure Haylett contacted two close friends in London; a John Tillotson and a Peter Carter who he assured me would be an "unparalleled introduction" to London's exclusive gay set. Julian by this stage was already studying at RADA and insisted I rent a room in a flat he'd taken somewhere "in W8". Having no idea as to the importance of a London postcode I simply said "yes" and looked forward to staying in the mysterious locale. Knowing Julian and how fastidious he was whatever the situation, I assumed all would be more than satisfactory and of course it was, with the mysterious sounding W8 turning out to be nigh on perfect.

In contrast the two weeks voyage to Southampton turned out to be a veritable nightmare. Having gone for the cheapest possible fare I found myself sharing an inboard cabin with three strangers, two of whom decided to be sea sick for the whole trip. Undiscouraged and perhaps with a soupçon of inherited *Voortrekker* spirit, I spent most of the fortnight sleeping beneath a lifeboat on one of the decks. Despite the setting the opportunity to "search for the golden rivet" never arose nor did I ever hear a cry of "*Hello* sailor".

*

Julian was waiting at Waterloo to welcome a beaming Robert-cum-Rob-cum-Robbie who couldn't quite believe he had finally arrived in the city of his dreams. Not only was he in London being met by a friend; the intrepid adventurer also had a place to stay. My only worry - and something which would need to be dealt with as soon as possible - was my worldly worth. Apart from a suitcase containing clothes and toiletries the only money I had with me was the aforesaid seventeen pounds sterling which meant once I was settled in my new home I would urgently need to find some sort of temporary job to tide me over. A sure-fire lesson in the value of money.

I vividly remember the magical date of my arrival in London: a sunny June 6th 1962 or, as I would later quip, "RA'S very own D-Day the Sixth of June"!

Julian - as was his wont - immediately took over. With a smug expression and looking even more Quasimodo than before he announced loudly in his newly acquired RADA voice, "Today we're taking a taxi but from then onwards travel will be by tube - I'll introduce you - or by bus." On Julian's lordly instructions the cab driver drove us sedately across Westminster Bridge (as opposed to Waterloo Bridge, immortalised by a distraught Vivien Leigh!); past the Houses of Parliament and Big Ben; along Birdcage Walk and around the golden Victoria Memorial with me noting to my acute disappointment the grim, grimy façade of Buckingham Palace. With Julian and the cab driver both giving running commentaries we proceeded along Constitutional Hill to Hyde Park Corner where I was dazzled by the towering, balcony festooned Hilton Hotel dominating the legendary Park Lane. On Julian's insistence I followed the direction of his endless pointing and managed to catch a glimpse of the world-renowned

Harrods store before we veered off to the right and entered the start of Kensington High Street.

I stared in wonderment at the domed Albert Hall and gazed in disbelief and the over-ornate Albert Memorial. In his new RADA voice Julian loftily acknowledged Kensington Palace, adding grandly, "PM is a virtual neighbour". In the next breath he pointed out Derry and Toms', another landmark London department store. Not giving the taxi driver the chance to elaborate Julian went on to describe the rooftop garden - "at least an acre in size with endless gazebos and fountains" - when suddenly the cab braked and made a deft left turn into Abingdon Road. "Number ninety one you said?" questioned the driver chirpily.

"Absolutely, cabbie!" replied Julian patronisingly as we drew to a halt outside a row of imposing white-fronted Georgian-style houses; my home for the next two years. Our landlord and owner as Julian duly informed me was a dark-haired, rugged actor named Clive Cazes. Clive and his partner, a glamorous actress named Anna Sharkey, occupied the three upper floors of the house with the ground floor and basement housing two flats.

"We have the garden flat," Julian grandly informed me as he skipped nimbly across the small paved garden fronting the house, his words tailing off as he disappeared down a small flight of steps and after a moment's pause briskly opened a red-painted door. Lugging my battered suitcase I gamely followed my sprightly so-called landlord and found myself standing in a long, narrow passage with two doors set into the right hand side wall and a steep narrow staircase attached to the left. An opaque glass-fronted door throwing a dim light stood as the end of the passageway with a similar glass-fronted door viewable at the top of the stairs.

"We share the kitchen with the two boys above," announced Julian throwing open the door to display an old fashioned, white-tiled kitchen. "The bathroom and loo - which we also share with the boys - is at the top of the stairs. Loo, in case you're wondering, is the word we use over here for toilet. We have a rota for when the bathroom is free. The time allocated for you will depend on your work schedule." Taking a deep breath Julian turned back to the second door. "This is your room," he said in a sepulchral voice as he reached for the door knob. "Unlike mine at the front which overlooks the steps; your room overlooks a small courtyard. Lucky you!"

The bonus courtyard turned out to be a dark, dismal paved area approximately ten foot square sporting a defeated-looking rose bush in a red-painted tub. Obviously a design attempt at bringing the red of the front door through to the back of the flat.

"I call this the garden room," said Julian in all seriousness, "and as I told you, the rent - all in - is two pounds a week and I would like a month's rent in advance."

"But of course," I graciously replied placing my suitcase on the stained hair-cord carpeting. Reaching inside my jacket I took out my wallet and plucked out eight one pound notes, leaving me a grand total of £11 to tide me over until I could find a job; temporary or otherwise.

"Thanks Rob," said Julian with a wolverine smile as he pocketed the money. "Now how about a cup of coffee before you unpack. Milk? Sugar? Oh, and when you use the communal coffee jar *do* remember to mark down how many spoons you use! The same applies to sugar. We have our own milk bottle in the fridge plus the use of the bottom two trays. Obviously we split any housekeeping costs."

Over our mugs of instant coffee (courtesy of the communal jar) Julian went on to inform me of a laundromat "several doors along" and an Express Diary "with a slot machine from where one can buy cartons of milk, butter and rather tasteless pork pies."

Leaving me to "settle in" Julian bounced off on "an errand or two" while assuring me he would be back.

Left to my own devices I quickly unpacked before settling down in a lopsided armchair next to a scarred desk. Adding a touch of glamour to my dismal room was the ceiling papered in a garish trellis design of tortured red roses. "Now I can see why it's called the garden room," I muttered, "and with my rose spattered ceiling plus his nibs out there dominating my courtyard in his regal red tub I'll be truly living in my very own Kew Gardens!"

On his return Julian - still relishing his role as "Rob's guide to London" - announced it was time for me to taste my "first pint in a typical English pub" which saw us dutifully making our way to the Scarsdale Tavern in nearby leafy Edwardes Square. After a tentative sip of my "first pint" I took a vow there and then not only would this be my first pint but also my last. Pushing the pint glass towards Julian I said firmly, "You have this; I'm going to get myself a glass of wine."

As we had always downed vast quantities of cheap Cape wine back at Rhodes I couldn't quite understand Julian's switchover to what I considered nothing more than a tepid, bitter swill. Giving him a wry glance as he happily finished off my discarded pint as I likewise sipped from my glass of house white, I put down his enthusiastic quaffing of the lukewarm as practice for "getting into character" for one of the roles assigned to him while studying at RADA.

The next day (the day after my arrival) I made a telephone call which would change my life.

ROBERT BECOMES ROBIN

Marking a firm tick on the pad next to the telephone (another Julian instruction) and placing my finger in the dial I made my first ever London phone call. On hearing a pompous voice bellow "Hello? Who's this?" I replied nervously, "May I speak to Mr John Tillotson please?"

"John Tillotson speaking," came the imperious answer. "Again; who's this?"

"Er . . . Mr Tillotson, the name's Robert Anderson." I managed to stammer, "Er . . . Haylett Regenass . . . er . . . from Johannesburg said I should call you."

"Ah yes!" boomed the voice, "The Golden Boy! Welcome to London young Robert. Now, when can you come to dinner? You free this evening?"

Stammering "Yes I am, Mr Tillotson," I received the brusque reply, "The name's John and the address is A6, The Albany. Say seven thirty as I have arranged to have a drink with a Mr Coats at A1. After a drink or two there we can then go on to dinner. I look forward to meeting you Robert. Haylett has nothing but glowing words to say about you!" With that new friend "John" put the phone.

A6 Albany? I hadn't the remotest idea where this was or what it was but the all-knowing Julian was quick to explain. "The Albany? *Very* smart, Rob! It's on Piccadilly just after Fortnum and Mason and next to the Royal Academy. Not much can top that!" Taking a sip of coffee (two teaspoons of instant coffee granules and two heaped spoons of sugar scrupulously noted down) he continued in what I assumed was now a Regency buck's drawl, "It's an eighteenth century building - or buildings - containing a number of *very* exclusive bachelor apartments. Lord Byron used to live there and I believe Terence Stamp, the actor, now has a place in the same exclusive establishment. A somewhat bizarre occupant I would have thought when considering the term 'exclusive'." Taking a further sip of his by then lukewarm coffee Julian added snootily, "I trust you have a suit to wear?"

Wearing a blazer, white shirt, purple and silver Rhodes tie, navy trousers and black shoes I set off on a Number 9 bus (Julian's directions once again) and keeping a keen eye on the various landmarks I jumped off outside the Royal Academy. Tentatively asking a well-dressed passer-by if I was anywhere near "the Albany" and answered with a haughty "You're right in front of it", I walked through an archway into a large courtyard dominated by a three story building flanked by a pair of lesser buildings on either side. I was greeted by a very lordly, uniformed porter who pointed towards a covered walkway which I was soon discover led from the Piccadilly entrance all the way through to a rear door opening onto Burlington Gardens. "A 6 is second on the right," I was told and giving the imposing man my idea of a casual "Thank you my good man" type smile, I walked jauntily towards flat Number 6. Giving the vaulted walkway and surrounding buildings a quick onceover, it was a case of instant love. *Maybe I could even live here one day?* I thought. *I may not be Lord Byron and I am most certainly* not *Terence Stamp but who knows who or what I will eventually be or become? If not a poet or an actor this import from sunny SR simply has to become a someone or somebody in what he eventually pursues.* (Little did I realise at the time how right this wannabe oracle was in his presumptuous prediction!)

From a quick mental picture based wholly on his voice and bluff manner over the telephone, John was exactly as imagined; a towering, hugely portly man and a doppelgänger for any of James Gillray's cruel caricatures of the gluttonous George 1V. A6 Albany turned out to be an exquisitely decorated two room apartment (called "sets" as I was soon to learn) with John's enormous frame totally alien to such delicate surroundings. As if reading my thoughts John quickly assured me A6 was "merely a bolthole in town" whereas his main residence, The Hall, was near to the village of Kimbolton in Herefordshire. I was offered a dry sherry by my affable host and then told "Chop, chop; time to go and say 'good evening' to Coats in A1."

"Coats in A1" turned out to be Peter Coats, a tall, elegant, well-groomed gentleman whose breathtaking apartment overlooking the front courtyard had once been occupied by "the bad Lord Byron", an Anglo-Scottish poet and leading figure in the Romantic Movement. The high-ceilinged drawing room with its lofty, elegantly draped windows, a marble mantelpiece and a flickering fire, a blending of mahogany Gainsborough armchairs with brocaded upholstery, a pair of carved, painted fauteuils covered in faux leopard skin, comfortable damask sofas and a magnificent fringed Aubusson carpet formed a stunning background for its lord and master. I sat mesmerised by Peter, an erudite sparkling man resplendent in a dinner jacket and sporting a pair of even more sparkling diamond cufflinks. To this day I remember staring at Peter and thinking, *Goodness! I've never seen a man wearing diamonds before!* Several years later I had to admit not even Liberace with all his glittering jewellery had quite the same impact on me as "the Coats' cufflinks". A comment which reduced Peter to peals of laughter when I later informed him of my reaction.

Peter was a well-known writer and garden designer plus gardening editor for *House and Garden*. He had also been the lover of diarist Chips Channon, their affair leading to Channon's divorce from Lady Honor Guinness; the latter going on to marry a Czech airman! After cocktails at A1 (martinis as opposed to sherry) it was on to the Caprice restaurant for dinner. I sat enthralled by the sheer glamour of it all. For me the old-fashioned interior with its plush red velvet banquette seating, crystal chandeliers, platoon of black-jacketed waiters and the elegant diners was reminiscent of the film *High Society*, seen at the drive-in cinema outside Bulawayo in 1956.

Julian was still awake when I returned to Abingdon Road around midnight and sat agog at my recap of the evening's events. These were described in great detail (perhaps even with some elaboration) over several mugs of Ovaltine (his treat with no counting of spoonfuls on this particular occasion). The scene of an amorous John Tillotson making a lunge at me, losing his balance, tumbling from the sofa and breaking a small antique side table in the process was *not* revealed.

Two days later I contacted Peter Carter, the second name of "must meets" on Haylett's list. *Could this Peter ever match up to A1 Albany Peter?* I pondered; Peter Coats being an almost impossible act to follow.

Peter Carter resided in a charming duplex in Eaton Place, Belgravia; an impressive street lined with grand, white stuccoed houses designed and built by Thomas Cubitt in the 1820s, the man responsible for building most of Belgravia. Like Albany, it must be remembered this was all new to me and my ever active mind kept reeling at these unimagined, unparalleled sights. Where Peter Coats's much sought after luncheons reigned supreme,

Peter Carter's dinner parties would soon prove to be the evening equivalent. (Little did I know at the time but several imposing doors down I would eventually design an apartment: an apartment which would be my "open sesame" to California.)

Poor Julian. Although living at the same address I hardly saw him apart from the occasional late night catch-up over a mug of Ovaltine or the odd, snatched cup of strong coffee (three spoonfuls) before rushing off to deal with our various tasks for the day.

To my surprise and delight I promptly found part-time employment teaching English at a nearby language school, The Linguists' Club School and School of English at Niddry Lodge, a genteel, somewhat dilapidated Georgian house set on a patch of land now occupied by the Kensington and Chelsea Town Hall. Niddry Lodge was an unexpected delight and I had great fun teaching there. Faced with several nationalities who would sit and look at their teacher with a terrifying expectancy I would say laughingly, "I am not going to bore you with grammar and such today. Instead we are going to talk *freely* among ourselves - albeit the latest film you've seen or something you may have read - and I will correct your pronunciation and grammar as we go along!" Strange as it may seem my tutorials became highly popular and I was asked to take on extra classes. An added bonus was Niddry Lodge being a mere ten minute walk from Abingdon Road.

True to his word John - a few weeks later - invited me to spend a weekend at The Hall, Kimbolton. Prior to this and during our second dinner à deux John cheerfully declaimed "Robert is much too sober a name for someone as pretty and sparkling as you! From now on I am calling you Robin!"

On my arrival at Hereford Station I was met by John in gleaming Bentley. "Welcome to Kimbolton Robin!" he boomed as I stepped down from the second class carriage. "Welcome to The Hall!" With a gracious smile the newly christened Robin duly slid onto the luxurious, leather passenger seat of the Bentley; the reborn Robin and expensive lifestyle finally erasing the last vestiges of Him and Cur.

The weekend proved to be great fun and apart from a few de rigueur fumbles without the company of a broken side table or two, John could not have been a more perfect host. Kimbolton Hall, a lavish William and Mary-styled house was a treasure trove of antiques and paintings, all of which were proudly introduced and detailed by John. The day after my arrival

John announced we wold be entertaining some young men from the local university (this turned out to be Cambridge) some thirty miles away. One of the young men, a smiley, dark-haired Australian, Brian Ketterer, would go on to become a lifelong friend. Brian would also become an eminent and revered name in cancer research. Brian lived at the with a temperamental young man called Peter Hurford who could well have been Mr Shakespeare's inspiration behind Cassius's "lean and hungry look". My first meeting with Peter when visiting Brian at their apartment in South Kensington consisted of a series of poisonous glares followed by a cacophony of slamming doors. More about the posturing Peter and his other irritants later. Brian would always to refer to him as "Pamela", later elevated to "*Lady* Pamela". A tongue-in-cheek title with which one could only but agree.

It was also through the buffoon-like, blustery, genial John I would meet the person who - apart from Peggy Powell - was to become the most important person in my life. The person who can never - and will never - be forgotten or replaced as long as I continue to breathe this planet's polluted air.

John had been invited to a grand buffet supper given at private house in Montpelier Square, an exclusive enclave in prestigious Knightsbridge comprising a large number of impressive, white stucco-fronted houses built in the 1830s. John suggested we met at the given address. I happily caught the now familiar No 9 bus and nipped off at the stop by the Knightsbridge Barracks. Though having the relevant details enabling me to find the house in question I hailed an approaching taxicab and grandly announced my destination, "49 Montpelier Square!"

"Yer sure guv?" questioned the bemused cab driver pointing to a nearby side street. "Yer'll find Montpelier Square's just down there. First turnin' to the right an' a few yards on!" None-the-less I insisted on being driven so as to arrive in style. Having paid the still-chuckling driver I momentarily glanced in the direction of a couple emerging from the wisteria-festooned next door house (No 51 to be exact), my glance quickly changing to a double take on recognising Leslie Caron, star of the 1953 film *Lili* in which Mel Ferrer, her co-star, played the lovelorn puppeteer Paul who finally manages to express his true love for Lili through his puppets! However, the laughing man accompanying her was *not* puppeteer Paul but her husband stage director Peter Hall; a fact I would learn later.

Thinking wryly, *Your grand buffet supper John will have to be mega grand in order to compete with catching a glimpse of* the *Leslie Caron!* I was greeted cheerily greeted by a thuggish young man sporting a domestic uniform of sorts and obviously the doorman or trendy sixties-style butler waiting by the open door to the adjacent house. Giving me a cheeky grin the young man ushered me into a fussy, hideously over-decorated, marble-tiled entrance hall brightly lit by an enormous crystal chandelier and a phalanx of crystal and ormolu wall lights. Pointing to a wide staircase the questionable doorman or butler (since when did a butler wear black leather trousers and high heeled boots with a dinner jacket?) announced in a rough, East End accent, "Up there, guv!"

"Up there" saw me entering an even more elaborately decorated drawing room filled with an assortment of happily chatting gentlemen from all age groups. John had obviously been keeping a watchful eye out for me and on spotting me hovering nervously in the doorway announced loudly to nobody in particular, "Aha! The blond young man from South Africa!"

Taking me by the arm he added pompously, "Come and meet your hosts" as he steamrollered me though the suited ensemble to where a mischievous, white-haired, twittering, elfin little man was holding court. "Eric, I'd like you to meet Robin!" boomed John, "The golden young man I was telling you about!"

Eric turned out to be Eric Crabtree, founder of Cresta Fashions and the man whose claim to fame was he "created Hardy Amies". A total contrast to Eric was his lifelong partner, Rex Tancred Warren, a society doctor and a positive Goliath to the Eric's dizzy diminutive David.

"Oh babeee, babeee! Welcome!" trilled Eric, his buckteeth glinting in the twinkling light of yet another chandelier. Squinting up at John he added shrilly. "John dear, if you can ever find him, you simply *must* introduce this *heavenly* young man to Sexy Rexy!" before turning his attention back to his former, enthralled audience. (Sexy Rexy I later realised was Eric's pet name for his dithery, dandruff-festooned doting doctor lover.)

John gestured I should join him on one of a pair peach silk-covered sofas facing each other alongside a marble fireplace of desperately climbing cupids. "Goodness, another cupid!" exclaimed a deep, fun-filled voice, "Where have you been hiding him John?" I glanced up at the speaker who was leaning with both hands of the back of the opposite sofa and staring with me with a pair of twinkling grey eyes topped by a set of impressive bushy eyebrows. Added to which the owner of the deep, fun-filled voice was certainly one of the handsomest men I had ever seen.

"Ah David!" boomed John, "I take it you haven't met young Robin?"

"No," replied David with a warm smile, "I haven't had the pleasure but now I have!"

"Robin meet David; David meet Robin," instructed John.

Murmuring "hello" shyly and receiving a warm "hello Robin" in reply any further conversation was halted by John suddenly hefting his vast frame from the sofa and announcing, "Eric's signalling for us to make our way downstairs so I take it dinner - or the buffet - ha ha! - is now being served!"

Adding zest to Rex and Eric's Montpelier Square house had been the deployment of several interior designers-cum-decorators of "the moment" with each assigned a particular room to decorate in his or her personal style (hence the flamboyant mishmash to the interior!). The opulent drawing room was the brainchild (I use the term lightly) of Kenneth Villiers, a neurotic decorator whose modest office was based in Sloane Street close to Sloane Square. Kenneth also owned a small cottage close to Henley-on-Thames which - unbeknown to me at the time - would play a major role in my life. Kenneth was also responsible for the entrance and stairwell along with the drawing room and as I said to myself his fussy style would have made the frivolous Monsieur Jean-Honoré Fragonard look severely censored. The dining room was the work of David Hicks, the study by Tom Parr and other rooms by the likes of Colefax and Fowler and the legendry Mrs Monro (the latter two names also responsible for Eric and Rex's luxurious bedrooms). It was then the thought struck me! *But of course! It was so obvious! I can do better than all this! This is what I want to do! I'm going to become an interior designer!*

Up until then I had happily been biding my time teaching at Niddry Lodge and making vague enquiries regarding a similar post at some minor public school where I could teach either Art or English; or both. My evening at 49 Montpelier Square promptly scotched all that. I was going to become a major player in the word of interior design and *no one* was going to stop me!

Antennae bristling I happened to hear through the informative gay grapevine (read cocktail party circuit) about a South African antique dealer-cum-decorator who owned a shop in Pont Street, Knightsbridge was on the lookout for a salesman stroke assistant. *Bingo*! I thought. With my spell at Niddry Lodge drawing to a close and my plan to get a foothold in the world of interior decorating why not meet this "fellow" South African (despite Scotland being my birthplace!) and if all worked out, why not stay with him for a year or two whilst gleaning everything I could about decorating, the world of antiques (at the time totally foreign to me) and equally as important, the multiple trades involved in the exciting new world.

I resolutely telephoned the number I'd been given and spoke some frail, elderly queeny-sounding man who introduced himself as Pip. Pip informed me the owner of the establishment, The Kent Gallery, was away for several weeks but he would be delighted to make a provisional appointment for me to meet "Roland". Never doubting I would be promptly accepted for this tantalising post I was still obliged to find and alternative source of income to tide me over the coming weeks plus the Christmas holiday.

"Why not Harrods?" suggested the ever-informative Julian over a late night Ovaltine. "They always take on a temporary number of extra staff to cope with the Christmas rush. A lot of my fellow students at RADA do this during the run-up to Santa's descent down those endless flues! Ha! Ha!" (His words exactly.) Taking a sip of Ovaltine he added superiorly, "And you cannot get grander than Harrods!" Such a comment would not be applicable today with the shop no longer the proud holder of any Royal warrants.

"Well, if you say so," I murmured without enthusiasm. The idea of working in a department store prior to entering the aloof world of interior design (I much preferred the term "interior design" or "designer" to "interior decorator") not being what this "inevitable rising star" had in mind.

My six weeks as a salesman in the Harrods "Christmas Toy Fair" turned out to be the greatest of fun; my other part-time colleagues on the shop floor a mixture of languorous, hung-over debutantes and spotty, testosterone-infused ex-public schoolboys along with the older long-serving staff who regarded us "interfering temps" with obvious disdain. Two matters I dealt with literally from day one was the advantage of an enormous staff discount on any purchase within the shop and even more importantly, the commission gained from one's personal sales. Combining the experience gained from my stint on *The Bulawayo Chronicle* along with my "reign" as *The Golden Voice of Teenage Half Hour* and chairmanship of the Rhodes University Debating Society mere members of the general public didn't stand a chance.

A magical moment during my various days of captivating sales patter saw me cautiously approached by an obviously foreign lady wearing a lopsided beret along with a tightly belted black trench coat and dramatically waving an evil-looking woollen octopus clutched in her gloved hand. Having asked the price in a low, sultry voice she added a throaty "I vill 'ave 'im" and stood waiting patiently while I deftly wrapped up her purchase. It was only later one of the excited older staff informed me my customer had been the legendary Marlene Dietrich! Am I perhaps the only person in existence to have sold Miss Dietrich an octopus?

A year later I was among the rapturous audience at The Prince of Wales Theatre for a concert given by the sultry, sexy legend. Titled *The Legendary, Lovely Marlene* and with a dashing Burt Bacharach accompanying her on the piano all I can say is the show could best be described as uber-camp! And when one thought it couldn't get even more camp than a collection of tents (forget a mere row) Miss Dietrich again stole the show by stumbling and falling down on to the stage when taking yet another curtain call. Unfazed by the mishap a smiling Marlene slowly but surely pulled herself to her feet by holding on to the curtain with one hand while blowing kisses with the other. Not even the suave, beaming Burt could compete with such a final curtain.

As I said to myself on the bus taking me back to Kensington, "Sorry Madam Zizi, I realise I feel in love with you at the Rhodes Centenary Exhibition back in 1953 but tonight, exactly ten years later you've been well and truly usurped by the legendary, lovely Marlene!"

My stint at Harrods coming to an end and duly armed with my discounted purchases (a suit, two shirts and a new pair of brass buckled black loafers) I was ready for my scheduled meeting with the decorator-cum-antique dealer, the keeper of the gate to my new word: the mysterious "Roland". Feeling a million dollars in my new suit, shirt, Rhodes tie and brass buckled loafers I was ready for my interview with the "man of the moment". Arriving promptly at nine o'clock I was welcomed by a smirking, self-assured, beady-cum-shifty-eyed plump little man into the hallowed realms of the black and white-fronted shop.

"Aye em Rrroland Spillane en welkim to the Kent Gai-llery," he announced in a clipped South African accent; the salutation delivered through a fine spray of spittle. The accent immediately (and horribly) reminiscent of Cur at her "refeened" best. Over the de rigueur mugs of Ovaltine I would later describe Spillane to Julian as an extremely nasty looking pop-eyed boiled fish, reeking of an equally nasty cologne and dressed in an immaculate but much too tight suit "with - *quelle horreur* - cuffs on the sleeves!" For some reason the latter causing more of a snigger than Spillane's overall appearance.

Spillane's background remained an enigma; his dropped hints of a superior family back in South Africa (a further unpleasant reminder of a similar "Cur" scenario) obviously an elaborate cover-up to his being a bona fide *domkop plaasjapie* (farm boy) or oik from outside some remote *dorp* (settlement).

While I would not flatter Spillane by categorizing him as "evil" he *can* be categorized as being an utterly spiteful and prime he-bitch. An inveterate snob and name-dropper this odious excuse for a human was a figure of derision in whatever guise he chose to present himself. If I learned *anything* from my few months with Spillane it was how *not* to speak to trades people and how *not* to be venomously unpleasant no matter whatever the situation. The days at the Kent Gallery were nothing less than a nightmare but I was determined to "*dazzle* and bear it" while praying fervently something else in this field of work would come along. Again, all thanks to the gay grapevine, it most certainly did! Spillane took a fiendish delight in demeaning the various tradesmen. Ostentatiously sniffing while standing in close proximity to one young workman the leering man had the temerity to squeak, "Aye don't know who it ken be who iss smelling like thet. If it's who aye suspect it is he should learrn to sheve his armpits en *alweys* use a deodorrrant like aye do!"

The thought of the blancmange-like Spillane naked was bad enough, but the thought of him with shaven (sheven) armpits and reclining in a languid pose reminiscent of Modigliani's *Sleeping Nude with Arms* was sufficient to send one rushing for the nearest toilet!

*

Away from the trials and tribulations of The Kent Gallery matters could not have been more golden. A dinner party given by the charming Peter Carter in his Eaton Place apartment saw my second introduction to the twinkly-eyed, dashingly good looking, chunky, hunky David Lloyd-Lowles and the cementing of a love story which will continue for as long as I draw breath.

On telephoning the next day to thank him for dinner I was informed by a chuckling Peter I had "an admirer" but the admirer (David Lloyd-Lowles) - and I quote - "is hesitant to contact you Robin seeing he is A, much older than you are and B, what would a good-looking young man like you see in the likes of him?"

"See in him?" I exclaimed. "Why Peter, I'm *besotted* by him!" I gave a small, forlorn laugh. "I would have thought my gawking at David Lloyd-Lowles before, throughout and after dinner couldn't have been more obvious!"

"Well then we'd better do something about," replied Peter with a chuckle, "hold on a second while I have a word with George." (George being a hunky South African living with Peter but who Peter insisted wasn't "remotely gay". An assertion which caused considerable amusement among his gay friends.) George's advice was straightforward; Peter would call David and suggest he invite the "besotted" Robin to dinner. Once Peter had performed his *Dear Abby* duties it was then up to the "older" David to contact "the good-looking young man" in question. Which - thank goodness to whoever or whatever may be up there - David Lloyd-Lowles did and thereby hangs a masterful tale.

(From now onwards David Lloyd-Lowles is referred to as DLL.)

Meanwhile Peter, charming as always, promptly invited me to another dinner party where one of the guests, a wizened, bald, sun-bronzed elderly man of indeterminate years had been seated on my right. Bob - full name Robert Pelham-Borley - lived in Agadir (hence the leathery tan) and proved to be an absolute delight. His quicksilver, acerbic wit and numerous tales revolving around the plagiarized adage "souk and ye shall find" keeping the dinner guests in fits of laughter.

On Bob asking me what I was presently "doing" along with any "plans for the future" I may have had in mind, I briefly mentioned my aspirations as an interior designer along with the unfortunate first "stepping stone", namely the dreaded Spillane and the nightmare of being the dogsbody - even whipping boy - at his stultifying The Kent Gallery. Staring contemplatively at me for several seconds Bob suddenly barked, "But you simply have to meet John and Seccotine for John is most *definitely* the person you should be working with." He continued, bald pate nodding knowingly. "If you wish to learn anything or everything there is to know about the glamorous yet tricky, hard-working world of interior design John is the answer. John could be your *Open Sesame!*"

"Who is John?" I asked, my mind racing.

"John is John Siddeley *the* interior designer of the moment and Seccotine is my name for Jacqueline, his ultra-chic Swiss wife." Bob gave a wolverine grin. "And before you ask I happen to be seeing John tomorrow. I'll tell him about you and suggest he gives you a call. If John *does* meet you and you pass his and the Seccotine test you may find your way into the world of *real* interior design faster than you could have ever anticipated. Do you have a telephone number?"

I immediately gave Bob the telephone number at Abingdon Road and, as an afterthought, one of the several numbers at The Kent Gallery. The rest of the dinner passed in a blur, my mind churning over with the name John Siddeley and the Mata Hari-sounding Seccotine. Naturally I couldn't wait to tell DLL all about Bob and his promised introduction to Siddeley. (I should explain by this stage I was seeing DLL on a regular basis and an early morning telephone call from him was now de rigueur.)

Having been invited to dinner (thank you Peter and George) I had duly explained and then gone on to show DLL I did *not* find him nor his company dull. Instead "young Robin" found whatever the Lloyd-Lowles persona had to offer totally and utterly elevating!

In addition to the early morning phone calls and dinners *à deux* these breakfast meetings were my voyeuristic glimpses of DLL which led to his delighted comment, "I saw you yesterday morning Robble and the morning before and I cannot tell you how flattered I am!"

(It had taken only a few intimate get-togethers before DLL began calling me "Robble" and me referring to him as "Beesle" or "Bees".)

"Oh," I replied with a sheepish grin, "and there I was thinking how invisible I was!"

"No dear Robble, not invisible at all! Furthermore I love you being totally and utterly *visible!*"

After our initial telephone conversations and several dinners I had taken to catching an early bus to Green Park and then walk towards Hay Hill where DLL kept a pied-à-terre. Adjacent to Hay Hill was a mews where DLL would park his car overnight. On arrival at the mews I would hide behind one of the other parked cars in order to watch this magical man settle in his car before driving setting off for his office in George Street. A sixties equivalent of a twenty first century stalker no doubt! This sounds like a desperate teenage crush but to me meeting DLL surpassed any such crush and I could honestly say I had finally fallen totally and utterly in love and to my amazement found myself being totally and gently loved in return.

It was at one such breakfast two days later restaurant I mentioned Bob Borley and his promise to mention me to John Siddeley.

"John Siddelely?" exclaimed DLL, "But that's wonderful Robble. I know Bob Borley and if he says he'll be speaking to Siddeley rest assured he will."

"I take it you must have heard of this John Siddeley?"

"Heard of Siddeley?" echoed DLL, "Why, he must be one of the best - if not *the* best - of interior decorators in town. He's there among the top names such as Bannenberg, Inchbald and Hicks."

"But will Siddeley call *me*?" I pondered.

"I am sure he will," came DLL's comforting response. "Meanwhile there's this marvellous old lady I'd like you to meet so I've invited her join us for dinner at The Empress." (The Empress - a firm favourite of DLL's - being a five star restaurant off Berkeley Square and close to Hay Hill.)

Dinner with Peter Carter had been on the Tuesday and as a result of Bob P-B's comments I was on tenterhooks especially as Siddeley's hallowed call could come through to The Kent Gallery. Came the Thursday and when the coast was clear - Spillane having left for a meeting with "darling Carly" aka Carla Thorneycroft, wife of a Peter Thorneycroft a politician and two names Spillane would drop with alacrity - I tentatively asked the doddery Pip if had ever heard of John Siddeley. Pip - who I would have described as a woebegone Bob Cratchit from Dickens' *A Christmas Carol* - stared back at me, his watery eyes widening behind his horn-rimmed glasses. Throwing up his hands he uttered with a small, tremulous cry, "John Siddeley? But he's *wonderful*! Not only a brilliant designer he's also *so* good-looking!" Furtively looking over his drooping shoulder he added in a conspiratorial whisper, "Why are you asking me about John Siddeley?"

"Oh, someone mentioned him at a dinner party the other night," I replied nonchalantly having learnt after working a few weeks with Spillane never ever to talk about one's private life. Initially I had mentioned my dinners with John Tillotson and Peter Carter, my exposé leading to Spillane's sneering putdown in his refined South African accent, "Yew sound just like a blerry rrrent boy!"

"Hmm, I see," murmured Pip with a knowing look. "A word of caution Robin; I wouldn't mention John Siddeley or anyone else of his ilk to Roland. I am sure you understand why?" His reference being to an unfortunate, earlier incident which had succeeded in adding considerable "grist" to Spillane's "mill" regarding my various social engagements.

This followed an invitation from DLL to join him for an impromptu dinner at *La Tour d'Argent* in Paris. It was planned I'd take the seven o'clock Air France flight to Orly (forty minutes and with the time difference I'd be arriving earlier than when I left). We would have dinner and I'd stay with DLL at the George V, take the first flight back the following morning and be back in time for the nine o'clock opening at The Kent Gallery.

Needless to say DLL suggested breakfast "somewhere on the Left Bank" and on his insistence I telephoned The Kent Gallery to explain why I wouldn't be at work until the following day. Fortunately Pip answered the telephone but when I walked in a day later you would have thought I'd burned the place down. I remained silent during Spillane's rant while simultaneously repeating to myself, *It's only temporary Robin so stick it out! It's only temporary and you, Spillane, are even lower than your own shit and you can't get any lower than that!*

Despite DLL having assured me "Bob P-B." would not let me down his words, though comforting, did little to dissipate the growing tension. Meanwhile the aforesaid elderly lady who had been invited to join us for dinner and introduced simply as Winnie turned out to be the legendary hostess, Winnifred, Countess of Portarlington who lived in magnificent splendour in a vast manor house named Earlywood near Ascot, plus an elegant mews house in Belgravia. During the dinner it was arranged DLL and I would drive over to Earlywood for lunch the following Sunday.

Thursday began as did every other day with Spillane having his early morning gripe about all and sundry and then having a go at me because the fabric samples, swatches and books needed tidying (the section was immaculate) added to which showroom looked like a "rrrubish tiep" along with anything else he could conjure up for a further unwarranted whinge.

"Ferr-ther more aye hev Lady Elsa Bowker coming in for a coffee en to look at some sampils of dayed shantung end thet means the showrroom must be emeculate for her Ladyshep's visit."

I had no idea who Lady Bowker was but from Spillane's pirouetting and fussing she could have well been the Queen Mother.

"Thank God for Elsa Bowker," I informed Julian later for it was during her and Roland's coffee and shantung meeting the "selected" telephone rang. I grabbed the phone before Pip could reach it and said breathlessly, "The Kent Gallery . . ."

"Mr Robin Anderson please," said a friendly tenor voice.

"Speaking," I cautiously replied.

"Can you talk?" asked the voice, "If not say 'not really' and I'll call back later."

"Er . . . yes and no," I replied glancing though to where Spillane, having heard the phone ring, had paused mid-sentence and looking through to the office section of the shop.

"John Siddeley. Bob's told me about you. Lunch, one o'clock" - he named a small French restaurant in Sloane Street on the opposite side to Harvey Nichols - "near to you and easy to find."

"Er . . . see you there," I stammered.

"Perfect," said Siddeley and hung up.

Leaving Elsa Bowker to contemplate the dyed shantung samples Spillane minced fussily into the office. "Who was thet?" he asked querulously, "was the call for me?"

"It was for me Roland," I replied quietly, "nothing important."

"Aye hev told yew taime end taime again aye will *not* hev you rrrecieving personal calls durring business hours!" came the snarled reply.

"Sorry Roland, I'll make sure it doesn't happen again . . . er, I think Lady Bowker wants to ask you something . . ." I muttered while hardly able to restrain myself from shouting, "Beesle he called. John Siddeley called and I'm seeing him for lunch *today!*"

John Siddeley was already seated at a banquette in the cosy Marcel Restaurant when I breathlessly arrived. DLL had already described him as "silver-haired and very good looking" but I was quite unprepared for the dashing, silver-haired, six foot plus man (a combination of Cary Grant and his lover Randolf Scott) who stood to greet me.

"The brilliant Robin Anderson I presume?" he said in a playful, tenor voice while proffering his hand. "A glass of wine or is a lunchtime drink *verboten* by the dreadful Roland Spillane?"

What a charmer, I thought reciprocating the smile, *Pity about the mouth.* (Siddeley's mouth akin to a small, mean red slit in an otherwise flawless face.)

Siddeley soon made sure I was relaxed and not at all on my guard. "I assume you only have an hour including travelling time," he said with a mischievous smile, "so I suggest we order a main course and if there's time, cheese or a dessert. The *moules marinier* is a speciality; that's if you like clams," he added tactfully.

Not quite knowing whether I would or would not I decided to be safe and settled for a mundane veal escalope.

Siddeley went on to say Bob had mentioned my name on the off-chance there was an opening in the business where he was sure I could be of use while learning about the world of design, plus the fact he was convinced I would eventually prove myself to be "a great asset" to John Siddeley Limited! Bob had also mentioned my interest in theatre and theatrical design. The latter I simply put down to Bob embroidering the facts.

I kept glancing discreetly at my watch.

"Right," said Siddeley, "you'd best be getting back to the Kent *Galley* slave ship and yes Robin, I'd like you to begin working with us as soon as possible. (I've never forgotten Siddeley's "working with us" as opposed to "working for me".) I expect you'll have to give a week's notice so how about Monday week." Said as a statement and not a question. He added with a dazzling smile, "Come along for a drink this evening around six thirty. I'd like you to meet Jacqueline my wife (again, no pompous "Mrs Siddeley") and some of the team. Oh, and by the way, the team call me JS and your starting salary will be a thousand a year plus luncheon vouchers."

One thousand pounds! I nearly fell off my chair (£1,000 in 1962 being the approximate equivalent of £21,000 per annum in 2017). Spillane's "generous" salary being a humble £15 per week or in today's calculations, £720 per annum.

I literally danced my way along Sloane Street back to Spillane's rechristened The Kent Galley.

"Yew're late!" spat Spillane as soon as I walked through the door. "Yew're only meant to hev en hourr for luncheon and yet yew hev been away for en hourr en twenty minutes at least!" He added malevolently, "This means yew will now hev to come in on Saturday to make up forr it; even though yew do not normally werk on a Saturday."

"I won't," I replied, swallowing quietly.

"Won't what?" spat Spillane.

"Be coming in on Saturday," I continued calmly, "In fact I'm handing in my notice as of now."

Spillane's repugnant, reptilian face turned various shades of pink, white and red before settling for a deep bruised purple. "Wha . . . what did yew jest sey?" he screeched.

"I just said I'm giving you a week's notice," I repeated emboldened by John Siddeley's enthusiasm and DLL's reassurances.

Spillane's reaction was even more volatile than I could have imagined.

"Yew ken get out *now*!" he shrieked, his portly frame quivering with a combination of indignation and fury. "Get out now yew piece of Rrrhodesian rrrrubish!"

"Rhodesian rubbish?" I repeated, "Far better to be a piece of Rhodesian rubbish than a gross *plaasjapie* and a *moffie*!" The references being two of the most insulting Afrikaans terms I could conjure up in the heat of the moment: a thicko farm boy and a raving queen.

"Get out! Get out!" shrilled Spillane. "Get out! Get out yew whore; yew piece of scum! Get out!"

"What about my wages?" I said turning Pip and deliberately ignoring the apoplectic, purple-faced, quivering Spillane. "Pip?" I said firmly to the elderly man who sat eyeing his hysterical business associate with unconcealed delight. "Pip," I repeated equally as firmly, "I'm owed for this week plus I was prepared to serve a week's notice but from what you have just witnessed, my services are no longer require."

"I'll deal with it," murmured Pip eyeing Spillane sceptically as he staggered huffing and puffing like a demented pufferfish back into the main shop. "And yes Robin, I think it best you leave now!"

My last sighting of Spillane saw the odious bug-eyed little man gasping and snorting heavily as he lay slumped on to a gilded Regency-style armchair covered in a typical Spillane dyed shantung.

As I said to DLL over a quick celebratory drink prior to my meeting the mysterious Seccotine and other members of the Siddeley team, "Honestly Beesle, to say r-r-ridiculous R-r-roland was incandescent with r-r-rage is putting it mildly. I don't know if you know what I mean by a fish called a barbell? It's an extremely ugly freshwater fish with a preference living in the mud or slime at the bottom of a river or pond. Well that's *exactly* the image Spillane conjured up. A defeated barbell finally landed on a garish green riverbank by this ecstatic fisherman after a year-long battle!"

True to his word Pip made sure a company cheque including payment for an additional week arrived at Abingdon Road two days later.

"FROM NOW ON IT'S JS"

I arrived at Maison Siddeley on the dot of six thirty. John and Jacqueline lived in grand penthouse apartment set atop a large, redbrick mansion block in Queen's Gate close to the Albert Hall and Hyde Park. John Siddeley greeted me warmly before leading me into the sitting room where a small group of people stood chatting happily.

"Attention everybody," said Siddeley laughingly, "I'd like you to meet Robin Anderson. Robin will be joining us at 195 next week." He then went on to introduce me personally to each of his guests. "Ah, and here she is," he added with a proud smile.

When it comes to style, beauty and charisma three woman immediately spring to mind: Jacqueline Siddeley, Margaret Duchess of Argyll and the actress Brit Ekland. Margaret Argyll would become one of my greatest and most dear friends. I have been privileged to meet many other beautiful women but these three remain the most memorable. (I hasten to add I have not forgotten my dear Peggy Powell. To me Peggy was a catalyst, a guru - years before gurus became fashionable! - and still remains a wonderment.)

Jacqueline, a petite Romy Schneider lookalike, swept into the room (I remember her entrance most vividly) a vision in black Balenciaga and greeting her guests a smile which could have easily launched the legendary thousand ships.

"You must be Robin," she said in a deliciously lilting, lightly accented voice. Proffering a tiny, elegant hand she added with a further enchanting smile, "I'm Jacqueline, welcome to the team."

Taking in the smiling group and the dazzling figure of John and Jacqueline Siddeley I said happily to myself, *Now* this *is what it's all about.*

Forget Spillane and all his shit for this *is the world to which I now firmly belong.*

"See you on Monday," said Siddeley with a warm smile and shaking my hand as I was leaving.

"You will indeed Mr Siddeley," I replied.

"From now on its JS as opposed to Mr Siddeley," said Siddeley.

"Thank you for a marvellous evening, JS," I answered. The "JS" confirming my feeling of wellbeing and belonging. As I would bitterly say later, "Just how naïve *is* gratitude?"

When asked by DLL to describe the Queen's Gate apartment I went into overdrive. "I only saw the entrance hall and the sitting room but it is *fabulous!* The colours are intrinsically cream and apricot but used in such a way that the whole place positively *glows!* There was a handsome, white marble fireplace; some comfy looking sofas in a creamy, silk-like fabric; antique Louis XV1 *fauteuils* upholstered in an apricot jaspé fabric (proving some good had come out of my time spent at The Kent Gallery after all); several torchères holding wonderful Chinese - I think - lamps; fabulous cream curtains with apricot tie backs . . . goodness Beesle, I'm quite out of breath!"

*

The showrooms of John Siddeley Limited at 195 Knightsbridge boasted an elegant marble tiled reception area with silk papered walls leading to a vast showroom and a set of hidden office areas; one for JS; one for Reg the office manager and Mrs Ziegler the accountant; one for Alan and Trevor the architects and a large, open plan office for the rest of the staff. Adjoining the main office area were a series of shelving units and cupboards holding fabric and wallpaper samples, fabric swatches, wallpaper books, trimmings, ropes and tassels. All in all a veritable Aladdin's cave.

195 was an imposing, grey-fronted office block overlooking the Hyde Park Barracks. Visitors would find themselves crossing an impressive courtyard before gaining admission via the imposing main reception area with its uniformed porters.

Following JS's instructions I arrived half-an-hour ahead of the nine o'clock start of business and introduced myself to Reg the showroom manager; a nervous, pimply-faced young man dressed in an ill-fitting Burton suit whose overall demeanour didn't quite fit in with the glamorous surroundings. *Reg?* I thought evilly, *Unfortunate name there Reg. With your decrepit appearance I would have thought you more a manky veg than a managerial Reg!*

The main showroom was truly magnificent with its vast floor covered in ivory V'soske sculpted carpeting and two L-shaped "conversation areas" along with a breathtaking display of wonderful lacquer and brass furniture courtesy of Parzinger, New York. Tall windows overlooking the private car park for the building were elegantly covered in full-length translucent silk curtains topped by half-drawn, braided Roman blinds in (as I would soon learn) trademark Siddeley apricot. I was soon to learn John Siddeley Limited also owned a small boutique on the corner of Harriet Walk and Harriet Street, off Sloane Street. The boutique was a treasure trove of exclusive and exotic "goodies" ranging from glassware to lamps cushions, throws and rugs. The items cleverly sourced by JS through his contacts in the States and the Far East.

Reg first showed me my desk followed by an introduction to a small, state-of-the-art kitchenette before leaving me alone with a mug of instant coffee and my whirring thoughts. *This is it*, I kept thinking, *Robin this is it; the start of something big!* At nine o'clock precisely various members of the JS team appeared. I was cheerfully greeted by the people I'd met the previous week at the impromptu drinks party given by JS and Jacqueline. One person who completely ignored me as he sashayed his way through to the back offices was a sanctimonious-looking youngish man with an exaggerated quiff of dark hair and a rather prominent nose which immediately made me think of an anteater! *Now I wonder who that is,* I thought. *One of the architects perhaps?* Reg also introduced me to Fiona the receptionist; a tall attractive, typical *Tatler* front cover-looking type of girl. I was somewhat taken aback when told our receptionist's full name was Fiona Bowes-Lyon and she was related to the Queen Mother. (One up on Spillane and his "Elsa, Lady Bowker"!)

"JS usually arrives a few minutes after nine," Reg confided in me, "You can see him park his car - it's a brown Alfa Romeo - out there." The "out there" accompanied by a vague wave in the direction of the windows overlooking the private car park. "He starts the day by discussing work progress in general with Paul Bevan his associate designer."

"Oh," I said genuinely surprised, "I thought there was only Mr Siddeley?"

"Let me put it this way, Mr Bevan handles the less important clients," replied Reg tactlessly.

Ah yes, I thought, *the snooty anteater who just flounced through.* "And his office is where?" I asked politely.

"He shares an office with JS," replied the all-knowing Reg.

"I see," I murmured, returning to a design magazine I had found neatly placed on a console table in the main showroom; my immediate thought being, *As I said to DLL its almost too good to be true and here, I fear is the first hiccup. There's always one bad apple in the barrel and I have a strong feeling Mr Bevan - who obviously thinks he's heaven on a stick- could well be it!*

"Fuck!" said an imperious female voice, "Fuck bloody fuck!"

I looked in amazement at the soigné, impeccably dressed young woman sporting a vast cloud of lacquered hair, whose opening words seemed to leave the others in the immediate vicinity unperturbed.

"Oh," she said on noting me sitting gaping at her, "You're the new one; Robin is it? I'm Maggie, Maggie Sherston-Baker. Welcome to John Siddeley Limited. Now where the *hell* did I put that fucking piece of paper?"

Talk about being star struck! Maggie may have not equalled a Jacqueline, a Margaret or a Britt looks-wise but certainly made up for it with her marvellous, warm personality and poise. Added to which she was the greatest of fun, had an acrid wit and what was more appealing, *nothing* but nothing seemed to phase her. Maggie also boasted a spectacular bosom and took a fiendish delight shaking this at a blushing Reg whenever he tried to talk to her about her petty cash vouchers or anything to do with expenses. She was also a brilliant and patient teacher when introducing me to the horde of fabric samples and sample books. "Upholsteries here; damasks over there; silks on those shelves there" and so forth. Her knowledge proved to be formidable and she was only too happy to come to one's rescue when a fabric decided to more elusive than usual.

As anticipated JS arrived and parked in his designated parking space in full view of our windows.

"Don't pay any attention if he ignores you," remarked Maggie with a wry smile, "He'll eventually come and say 'good morning' but first of all we have to do 'the office walk'." She gave me a sardonic look. "I always refer to this two-faced scenario as the calm before the shit hits the fan!"

"The office walk" saw JS arrogantly enter the premises of John Siddeley Limited, stride past Fiona, stride through our office, stride past Alan and Trevor the two architects, murmur a "good morning" to Mrs Ziegler and acknowledge Reg with a cursory nod before disappearing into his office and slamming the door shut behind him. Having viewed the day's post, any new messages and after a brief tête-à-tête with the sanctimonious Paul, JS would reappear, greet everyone with a cheerful "good morning" as he headed for the kitchenette. Another day in the wonderful world (later a question mark) of John Siddeley Limited had begun.

Initially I accepted JS as a top designer, a marvellous raconteur and best of all as a man who took no prisoners. Obviously at times he could be impetuous, tyrannical and a walking time bomb but always a perfectionist - or so I initially thought - and when needs be, extremely fair. If you were wrong you were wrong and it had to be put right. If you were right, you being right was acknowledged and duly praised. However - as previously said - just how naïve *is* gratitude?

After a few weeks I began to appreciate Maggie's sardonic attitude to the wonderful world of John Siddeley Limited (her dubbing it "John Siddeley *very* limited") and soon realised how wrong my fanciful expectations were turning out to be. Whereas Roland Spillane was openly bitchy, vicious and vindictive, John Siddeley covered his bitchiness, viciousness and vindictiveness with a hidden flair for *exterior* as well as interior design. The perfectly designed "exterior" exuding charm and empathy and the complete antithesis to his real "interior" self.

"What gives with JS and Bevan?" I asked Maggie a few weeks later.

"Ex-boyfriend? Ex-lover? Who gives a fuck?" came a typical Maggie reply accompanied by a mischievous grin and a predictable shaking of her spectacular bosom.

Talk about being thrown into the deep end! Within days JS had introduced me to whole new world of trades people and suppliers. I met Mr Adams (known as "Fanny") the elderly owner of Norrington & Adams Limited, the *crème de la crème* of curtain makers; Mr Eric of Percy Bass

Limited, a top firm of upholsterers; Mr John Skellorn of Skellorn Carpets plus endless fabric and wallpaper suppliers totally foreign to Spillane and The Kent Gallery. I was also introduced to building contractors along with specialists in furniture restoration, manufacture and paint finishes. In other words the A to Z of interior design.

*

As this particular section deals intrinsically with my "JS days" my private life will be vividly detailed (read exposed) in other appropriately titled sections I feel it important at this stage to let it be known my days at Abingdon Road were coming to an end. After only a few months I found Julian becoming increasingly tiresome in his role as a flat mate along with his attempts to "discover his true self" via a never-ending array of lady friends or obvious Arthurs-cum-Marthas type gentlemen cluttering up the communal kitchen in the morning. As were Simon and David from upstairs who were also put out by Julian's "am I or aren't I?' stream of guests.

A chance conversation with the owner of an exclusive children's clothing boutique in Walton Street en route to a meeting with Mr Eric at Percy Bass Limited saw me agreeing to "take a look" at a small studio she owned in Rees Mews, close to South Kensington Station. On viewing the studio the next day - a small windowless room illuminated by a substantial skylight with a kitchenette and miniscule bath room positioned above a garage with access to via a steep, narrow staircase alongside - I immediately informed the elegant landlady, a Mrs Hone, I would take it. On handing me the keys Mrs Hone assured me the studio was "very quiet" and my immediate neighbour was an artist who - like his work - was "rather weird" but someone "who kept to himself".

A few years later I would have gross misfortune of meeting Peter Hone her son, a young man sorely lacking in any of his mother's charm. Hone owned the flat below me in Ladbroke Square and for the first three to four years the flat remained (blissfully) unoccupied and then, much to my surprise, he moved back in. Talk about the neighbour from hell! Overnight the tranquillity of living at No 5 became a thing of the past with Hone's penchant for playing loud, eerie music until the early hours. On tactfully being asked at two o'clock in the morning to please, turn the volume down his response was a sneered, drawn-out "no". The saving grace to this decidedly unpleasant young man's attitude was the fact I was in process of moving to a stunning penthouse apartment overlooking Hyde Park, thus leaving Mr Hone to upset the poor unfortunate moving into my former flat. Later I saw in some magazine this charmer owned a remote country bolthole *sans* indoor toilet facilities. To use a well-worn phrase: "No comment".

I excitedly informed DLL about my new abode - no rosebuds on the ceiling but a large skylight instead! A few weeks later I laughingly informed DLL of a strange happening the night before.

"I was in bed reading and enjoying my newfound solitude," I said, "when suddenly - on hearing a noise from the vicinity of the skylight - I glanced up and got the shock of my life for there was this strange-looking man lying spread-eagled across the skylight peering down at me!"

"Good Lord Robble!" exclaimed DLL raising a bushy eyebrow, "What happened next?"

"I gave a yell and jumped out of bed - starkers of course." I gave a laugh. "Perhaps that's what chased him off; the sight of me starkers!"

Reaching for a piece of toast (we were having an early breakfast at the Chelsea Room, The Carlton Tower, which was to become a regular occurrence before setting off to our various businesses) I added nonchalantly, "I don't know what happened to 'Victor the voyeur' but a minute or two later there was an almighty crash so he could have either have fallen through one of the skylights next door or slipped off the roof."

Years later I would learn my peeping Tom had been George Dyer, a petty criminal from the East End peering down at me minutes before crashing through the next door skylight and ending up in Francis Bacon's studio. The then unknown artist being my next door neighbour. Bacon had given the bewildered burglar an ultimatum. "You've got two choices. I can call the police or you can come to bed with me." Dyer chose the second option. Not only did he go to bed with the artist he stayed on and was Bacon's lover until his death in 1971. For reasons known only to himself George Dyer committed suicide in Paris on the eve of Bacon's retrospective at the Grand Palais.

DLL's reaction to the skylight incident as straightforward. "You need your own flat Robble. And a car." A week later I was the proud owner of a spanking blue Hillman Imp and three weeks later the proud owner of a charming, one bedroom apartment overlooking leafy Ladbroke Square in the so-called "somewhat dicey" Notting Hill Gate area.

At the time Maggie lived with her mother, stepfather, sister Jane, brother Robert and great friend Valarie in a large, rambling apartment off Kensington High Street so it was obvious I would become her regular mode of transport or - as she succinctly put - "a fucking relief seeing I won't have to rely on Ronnie (Sir Ronald Leach, her stepfather) for my fucking wheels!" Maggie and I became close friends. Not only did she completely accept the gay scene she positively revelled in it. I refused to refer to Maggie as a "fag hag". She was too individual and too aloof for such a slight. She became hugely popular within my select circle of gay friends, one of whom she would eventually marry.

A new sensation at the time was the opening of Danny La Rue's, an uber-stylish club set in Hanover Square in the heart of Mayfair. Danny La Rue's was named after the owner, a drag artiste extraordinaire. Maggie and I were regular patrons visiting the venue at least once or even twice a week where we'd twist or bop the night away bumping shoulders with the likes of Princess Margaret and Twiggy prior to watching Danny's glamorous, witty drag show; a show filled with songs, dancing and sophisticated sketches bubbling with wicked repartee. Danny became a firm friend along with other members of his enchanting troupe; among them the diminutive Ronnie Corbett.

What I always admired about Danny La Rue was the way in which he kept his drag persona strictly for the stage. On meeting him in private life he was a charming, kindly, unassuming silver-haired gentleman who could have easily passed for your friendly bank manager. Paul O'Grady, aka the outrageous Lily Savage is another such person. Unlike today when most drag queens one has the misfortune to meet appear to be more camp *off-stage* than *on!*

*

One morning, having dutifully collected and deposited Maggie at the showroom and parked the car, I was greeted by JS who said with a theatrical sigh, "Can you be ready in ten minutes Robin as we're meeting two new clients who've bought a property somewhere near Guildford. We'll need at least an hour to get there."

The "new clients" turned out to be the actor Peter Sellers and his new wife, the Swedish actress Britt Ekland. Sellers received us warily; his whole persona shouting "paranoia" before summonsing the new Mrs Sellers. (I've already mentioned my impression on first meeting Britt Ekland. Words such as "stunning", "exquisite" or "ravishing" did not do her justice and even Monsieur Roget of *Thesaurus* fame would have been "at a loss for words" in expressing how beautiful she was.)

JS went into a huddle with Sellers who kept muttering and mumbling about various terms and conditions. I kept catching snatches of "won't be taken for a ride", "will I like it?", "what if I *don't* like it" and so forth while Britt, having served us coffee, suggested I take a look at one of the rooms in the basement.

"I would like to turn this into a fun bar," she announced in her sultry, accented voice.

"A bar?" I said brightly and thinking to myself, *Be charming as well as witty Robin, after all it's not everyone who can claim they advised Britt Ekland on her private bar!* "Ah yes," I continued almost doubling up with laughter at what I was about to say, "a bar; I can see it now. I spy with my artistic blue eye a series of Chianti bottles holding red or black candles and dribbles of wax ; festoons of fishing nets holding the odd spangled starfish here and there, and" - I couldn't resist a mischievous chuckle - "the *pièce de résistance*, a cheerful octopus sitting on the bar waiting to welcome your guests!" (Thank you Marlene!)

Giving me a "curiouser and curiouser" type of look Britt Ekland stood staring at the room before saying quietly through her pursed lips, "An octopus? I will have to think about it . . ."

On the drive back to London I nervously told JS what I had said as a joke but appeared to have been misinterpreted. "Well Robin," replied JS nonchalantly, "Having had to deal with Mr Neuroses Incorporated back there, nothing would surprise me."

Mr Neuroses back there? I thought, staring straight ahead, *What about Mr Neuroses sitting right next to me? Talk about the pot calling the kettle black!*

Nothing more came of our visit and the outcome of "Britt's Bar" remains a mystery to this day.

Another JS client was the boxing promoter Harry Levine who left the complete handling of the furnishing and decoration of his new apartment in the exclusive Bilton Towers near to Marble Arch to an enchanting woman named Georgina Halse. Georgina, a tall, elegant redhead would have made any fashion magazine green with envy. I've mentioned Jacqueline Siddeley in Balenciaga and now its Georgina Halse's turn. At our first meeting in the reception lobby of the exclusive block (hence the term "apartment) I stood mesmerised by the smiling woman who rose from a sofa to greet JS and myself; a striking figure wearing a bright green coat and matching dress designed by Hardy Amies. Georgina was warm, funny and one of the most open-minded people I have ever come across and who I am proud to say also became a close friend.

On our second meeting *sans* JS I couldn't help commenting on her luxurious, knee-length mink coat. "Ah," Georgina replied with a throaty chuckle, "Not only a luxurious mink coat but a mink coat with a secret; Germaine's secret." Stooping graciously Georgia lifted the hem. "Now *full* length coats are de rigueur for the evening and as I really didn't want *another* mink what does one do? Easy. Simply *zip on* the extra length and hey presto, my knee-length becomes full-length!" How could one *not* fall in love with Georgina!

"And who's Germaine?" I asked.

"Germaine Woolf," said Georgina, "She and her husband Cyril are the best furriers in London. You simply *have* to meet Germaine. She'd adore you and vice versa!"

Overall JS's clients appeared to be more of the "have cash to splash" or "if you've got it, flaunt it" category. Probably a sound basis for such a precarious business where competition was rife and - like the length of Georgina's mink coat - wholly dependent on whether you were "in" or not.

However, as time would tell, there was definitely another world out there just waiting for RA.

*

Inevitably Maggie or myself and on occasions one of the "lesser mortals" (a junior member of staff) would stand-in for JS when invited by a worshipful client to a celebratory drinks party to show off their newly decorated abode.

"Can you join me for an hour or so before we meet Peter for dinner?" questioned Maggie. "I've been invited for drinks at the Hymans whose flat - as you well know due to my regular explosions - I've been overseeing on behalf of our illustrious Bored and Master."

The "overseen" Hymans had recently moved into Chelwood House, a new block of much-coveted luxurious apartments in Gloucester Square, Bayswater. Maggie and I duly arrived and were greeted by our gushing hostess who after expressing her disappointment at JS "not being able to join us" insisted we meet another "young person who's also in the arts - ha ha"; his form of "the arts" being more of "the musical variety". We were duly introduced to a dark-haired, sallow young man who looked as out of place among the mainly elderly guests as we did.

"Bloody hell, talk about a fucking cadaver," murmured Maggie in a discreet aside.

After several minutes of strained conversation I was fortunate enough to begin talking to the Hyman's glamorous daughter-in-law leaving a glowering Maggie to the dubious charms of "Mr Cadaver".

On the way to La Popote where we were meeting Peter Leggatt for dinner I remarked waspishly, "I must say Mags you appeared to be somewhat er . . . captivated by Mr Cadaver."

"Exactly," snapped Maggie. "Captivated and bored to death!"

"What was he banging on about then? London's most memorable mortuaries?"

"Almost." She gave a snort. "Some boy band he manages."

"Anyone I may have heard of?"

With a dismissive shrug of her spectacular bosom; quite an achievement while seated in a cramped Mini (by this stage I had exchanged the Hillman Imp for a much more trendy Mini) Maggie added nonchalantly, "Some strange name to do with insects."

Weeks later we learned Mr Cadaver was if fact Brian Epstein and his band of "insects" was called The Beatles.

THE JS-SG SAGA

Two years after joining John Siddeley Limited, JS and his fellow director (Jacqueline) took the decision to transfer the showroom from prestigious 195 Knightsbridge to modest Harriet Walk necessitating in the closing of the former boutique. Apart from not having a reception area and vast showroom the new office premises were as good as before. Fiona in the meantime had left to get married (the whole of John Siddeley Limited being invited to the wedding, a grand affair with the reception held at St James Palace) and as JS wittily quipped, "Saved me the embarrassment of having to sack her!"

"Can you meet later for a drink this evening" asked JS *sotto voce*. The invitation coming as a complete surprise for as far as I was concerned JS had lost all his initial charisma and Maggie, myself and the rest of the team were suitably wary of the man and his unfathomable (and unforgiveable) violent mood swings; something even one or two clients were starting to notice. I remember one woman, Paula Leigh, the vivacious wife of property tycoon and racehorse owner Gerald Leigh, being totally shocked by JS's snapped "Jesus Paula! For Christ's sake stop behaving like some Jewish Joan of Arc" when she chose to question a particular paint sample.

Considering most of his clients were from London's moneyed Jewish elite JS's anti-Semitic comments could be at times somewhat startling. A prime example taking place after a visit to the showroom by a certain Mrs Bernstein, married to some mega TV mogul, who happened to come out with some asinine remark concerning people on welfare. JS's sneered comment following her departure was a scathing "Talk about a pontificating Jewish Mahatma Ghandi in drag and diamonds. She's a fine one to talk!"

Two more JS sniggered comments which spring to mind; one made (naturally) behind the back of a particularly tiresome client, an overly made-up, immensely pleased with herself woman named Lloyd (Lloyds do seem to abound in my recollections!) was a yawned "That one would even make a Rabbi anti-Semitic" and the other - following a particularly harrowing site meeting with a very disgruntled man named Lever - "Remind me to send him some striped pyjamas for Christmas!".

By the time of the move to Harriet Street, Paul Bevan had also "moved on". Maggie and I both assumed Bevan's unctuous presence (plus the fact he may have been an ex-lover) partly responsible for JS's impossible behaviour and we were not at all sorry to see him go. However, as I had hopes of eventually becoming a director of the company and being totally absorbed in my work (which I adored) I was quite happy to play along.

"A drink this evening? Of course JS; where?" Thinking, *Christ, don't tell me it's now my turn to get the chop?* my thoughts were quickly put to rest by JS's hissed follow-up sentence, "The Chelsea Room Bar, Carlton Tower at six thirty; I'll see you there. There's this young Australian I have to meet. The Introduction is through Charles Lloyd Jones, owner of the David Jones chain of shops out there. It's a bore but there we are." (JS had become a firm friend of Lloyd Jones and worked as a design consultant for the David Jones chain in Australia; he and Jacqueline visiting Australia on several occasions.)

A bore? Well thanks for including me! I thought. *Anyway, it's only a drink so meeting up with William and co later won't be a problem.* William being William Davis, a talented young artist and Michael Pitt-Rivers' lover. The "and co" including Derek Collins and Michael Mander (known as Poofty and Madge) and Peter Leggatt; all part of a smart, select circle of contemporaries.

The Chelsea Bar was well-known to me and adjacent to the Chelsea Room Restaurant where I frequently breakfasted with DLL. I arrived a few minutes before six thirty and having order my usual Pinot Grigio from Gino, the affable waiter. I sat down, helped myself to a handful of mixed nuts and casually glanced the half-empty bar, my eyes homing in on a slim, suntanned young man with a positive halo of ash blond hair who sat staring at me in turn. To my astonishment the young man suddenly sprang up from his armchair and skipped nimbly over to where I was sitting.

"Are you John Siddeley?" he asked in a curiously accented voice accompanied by a dazzling smile.

"No I'm not," I hastily replied, "But it er . . . so happens I'm meeting JS er . . . Mr Siddeley; he should be here any minute." I gave a reciprocal smile, though not as dazzling. "You must be Charles Lloyd Jones' friend. The one meeting Mr Siddeley?"

"I am," said the young man flashing another whiter-than-white smile. He stuck out a suntanned hand. "Hi! I'm Stephen. Stephen Gregory. And you are?"

"Robin. Robin Anderson. Good evening Stephen," I replied graciously, "Please have a seat and I'll get Gino to bring your drink over."

"So you work for John Siddeley," said Stephen making himself comfortable in one of the deep, upholstered armchairs. "You must be very good!"

For as opposed to with? Black mark Mr Gregory! I thought; my line of thinking followed by a quick *Lucky you, saved by HMV* (His Master's Voice) on hearing JS's over-excited, "Sorry I'm late!"

"JS!" I exclaimed in exaggerated surprise as if I hadn't seen him for several years as opposed to a few hours. "*There* you are! I've just met Stephen and Gino's about to bring his drink over! Stephen *this* is Mr Siddeley! (I didn't make light of Stephen's *faux pas* in thinking *I* was JS. Far too dangerous!)

The instant rapport between JS and Stephen was obvious. *Fuck knows what* I'm *doing here,* I thought (Maggie's liberal use of the F word was catching), *Talk about being a spare part . . .*

After an hour and more of watching the two sitting in an animated huddle leaving me to my thoughts and another glass of Pinot, a flushed JS suddenly announced he had to leave. "I take it you can you give Stephen a lift to Marble Arch Underground?" he asked as if unaware of my presence up until then.

"Absolutely," I replied, "It's on my way." *And even if it wasn't, I wouldn't have any choice now would I, Mr Siddeley?*

"Good," said JS giving Stephen a long, lingering look. Turning to me he added with a conspiratorial smile, "See you in the morning, Robin. Thanks for coming along. Er . . . and can you settle up with the barman and ask Mrs Ziegler for the cash in the morning."

Don't think about it, I thought, *I thoroughly enjoyed chatting to you and Miss Down Under as well as paying for the privilege.*

Walking towards Lowndes Square where my Mini was parked I asked Stephen which part of Australia he was from as he didn't sound "quite Sydney".

"I'm Hungarian," came the reply. "I came to Australia when all the troubles started back there. My parents are dead." (Later I would discover this flamboyant "war orphan's" parents were alive and well and living in Australia. This type of fabrication being the first of many such "Stephenisms". A colourful tale to suit every occasion.)

Well that explains the strange accent, I thought during the brief silence following his somewhat unexpected revelation, *an accent which JS obviously found made you even* more *glamorous than your first impression!*

Hungarian eh? In other words Hungary's very hungry *answer to a gay Zsa Zsa Gabor!*

"You must be good if you work for John," said Stephen using the dreaded "for" as opposed to "with" a second time since meeting. *John and not JS? I thought evilly, I'm sure if you stick around long enough that will soon change.*

Sitting reflectively as we sped down Park Lane towards Marble Arch he added suddenly, "Just as I'm going to be doing!"

Just as I'm going to be doing? I mentally repeated. Just what the fuck is JS up to? There must be more to this than meets the eye? And what's more, just what is the Charles Lloyd Jones connection?

The following morning JS called me into his office. "I've asked Stephen Gregory to work here," he said brusquely. "Of course Jacqueline has to agree and this is where you come in."

"Me?" I replied innocently. "How?"

"Simple. You call her and say you need an assistant then tell her you've met this young Australian who'd be ideal for the job."

I looked at JS who returned my look, his steely blue eyes unblinking and his tiny slit of a mouth even more mean-looking than usual. "May I say something?" I asked, breaking the brief silence.

"You may," replied JS with a slight twitching of his puckered lips.

"Rosemary, the young trainee. Why don't I call Jacqueline and say I don't wish to go behind your back but knowing how much the business means to her, young Rosemary is more of a hindrance than a help and I know a young man who would be a brilliant asset to the company if he was to replace her. Someone I'd like Jacqueline and you to meet?"

"A perfect solution, Robin," replied JS with a wolverine smile, "and you're right about Rosemary. I'd quite forgotten she even worked here!"

A week later Stephen Gregory joined John Siddeley Limited; his role given the grand title of "Coordinator and Site Supervisor". The same title would apply to another equally as ruthless and unpleasant Australian I was later destined to meet.

By now I had become firm friends with one of DLL's business directors, Anthony Galliers-Pratt, and Angela, his charming, fair-haired wife. Tony and Angela owned a magnificent estate, Mawley Hall, in Shropshire whereby hangs another remarkable "never" tale. Tony was not a John Siddeley fan and was genuinely dismayed at my future plan for continuing working with the man and perhaps - one day - being appointed a director. Tony was not only a director of DLL's company, The Tap and Die Company, but chairman of his own family company, F. Pratt Engineering, whose London offices occupied a vast house in Belgrave Square.

Tony was quick to point out it was blatantly obvious Stephen Gregory would become a director well before I did. JS's infatuation for Stephen was no secret and to say Stephen Gregory didn't take advantage of the fact would have been laughable.

"I want you to meet Alistair Colvin," announced Tony in his affected, high-pitched voice (some waspish queen would eventually nickname him "Decibel". A name which would stick). "What's more the whole of F. Pratt Engineering at 45 Belgrave Square - including the mews house - needs redecorating and I want you to do it. However I must make it quite clear Robin this has *everything* to do with you and *nothing* to do with John Siddeley. Whereas I would be more than happy to work with you through Alistair's company anything involving Siddeley would be a definite no-no. I have already discussed the matter with Alistair and he is more than happy for you to become an integral part of Alistair Colvin Limited as well as responsible for the complete redecoration of 45 Belgrave Square." He added with a smile, "You would have a free reign Robin; *carte blanche* in fact. *But only if you're away from Siddeley!*"

That evening I tossed and turned over my dilemma; my mind racing. *Do I or don't I? More importantly, dare I? And If I do take up Tony's offer would it lead to other projects? Added to which is million dollar question nobody's ever brought up; would I enjoy working with this Alistair?*

The next morning saw DLL and me having one of our cosy, early morning breakfasts at the Chelsea Room. I immediately explained my conundrum to DLL. His reply was succinct.

"Working with Alistair would introduce to a whole new world," he said, "and if I were I'd seriously consider it, my Robble." He added with a twinkle in his eye, "Decorate Belgrave Square as you see fit; no hold barred. Tony and Alistair will certainly allow you to have your work photographed and what's even more important, allow you the credit!" Giving me a loving smile DLL discreetly squeezed my hand. "And knowing you, young man, it won't take long before you're out there. Robin Anderson himself."

Matters came to a head when JS - accompanied by Stephen - returned from a business trip to Bridgnorth near Birmingham and rang in a fury from the airport on finding nobody there to meet them. In fact, why hadn't *I* been there? Having taken a taxi from the airport JS and a pale-faced Stephen duly arrived at Harriet Street. Storming in through the main door JS proceed to throw a tantrum to surpass all tantrums.

A few days beforehand JS had been extremely bitchy to me in front of Georgina Halse at Harriet Street during a meeting regarding the redecoration of her own apartment. It was not long before a tight-lipped Georgina excused herself and left. The same evening as I was about to leave for dinner with William and Peter, the telephone rang. To my surprise it was Georgina Halse who expressed her disgust at the way JS had spoken to me and vowed she would never recommend him to anyone else ever again. Nor would she be using him for redecorating her apartment. "What a pity you aren't working on your own, darling," were her parting words as she gently put down the receiver.

I sat staring at the telephone, Georgina's words still in my thoughts and reminiscent of a comment made by another JS client, a Mrs Silk who had been similarly appalled by JS's attitude towards me when visiting Harriet Street to discuss her new apartment. Mrs Silk, a large, florid woman had been regarded by JS with amusement, her initial visit followed by a typical snide observation, this time a referral to "a Jewish Hattie Jacques". The apartment was part of the newly renovated Georgian Terraces overlooking Regent's Park and little did I know at the time what my working with the motherly Mrs Silk would lead to. I became extremely fond of Polly Silk and went to extra length to ensure her apartment was a success. I remember Polly's surprise - and delight - when she and her husband Robert Silk, a property developer, found me visiting the site on a Sunday to make sure the requested paint effects to the drawing room were exactly as we had discussed; JS never bothering to visited the site. "I'm sure it's all alright," he said blithely, "After all, who taught you everything you know?"

The temper tantrum on his return to Harriet Street saw the lighting of the fuse. "Enough is enough!" I shouted, my reaction causing JS to stop in the middle of another venomous, spluttering sentence. "I quit!" I stormed.

"If meeting you at the airport is more important than dealing with a disillusioned client because you didn't bother to inform any of us what you'd agreed with her, then fine. Otherwise hire a chauffeur. Meanwhile, I quit. I'll complete whatever I'm responsible for and then I'll leave."

I longed to say, "And why was Stephen Gregory with you? As *office coordinator* shouldn't he have been here 'coordinating', in other words driving you to or collecting you from the fucking airport?" but held my tongue.

"Leaving? Leaving?" shrieked JS, a doppelgänger to Spillane and his behaviour five years earlier. "You will bloody well leave now! Get out! Get out!"

An hour later I telephoned Tony Galliers-Pratt. "I've done it," I said hoarsely, "I've quit Siddeley's so when do I meet Alistair and when can I have a look at Belgrave Square?"

Tony gave a whoop. "Wonderful! Let's have a late celebratory lunch" - he named a restaurant - "and meet Alistair later. After meeting Alistair we can then come back to Belgrave Square and I'll give you the grand tour! You can start tomorrow!"

DLL's reaction was simple. "About time my Robble; you're well out of there."

DLL, being the fair-minded, decent man he was, had - on my joining John Siddeley Limited - suggested the firm redesign The Tap and Die Company boardroom for him. The Tap and Die Company being DLL's highly successful business and valued at several million.

"I would like Robin to design the boardroom," he told JS, "as it would be good for him and obviously good for John Siddeley Limited."

"*I* am John Siddeley Limited," came the imperious reply, "but of *course* Robin can have a hand in it."

"So he wants *Robin* to design it, does he?" sniped JS on our return to the showroom. Giving a Machiavellian-like laugh he added spikily, "Well for starters I suggest *Robin* uses this" - he randomly grabbed a sample of bright green silk from off one of the shelves - "and for the walls *Robin* uses *this* ("this" being a snatched book of grass paper wall coverings from which he folded back an uninspiring natural-looking sample). Looking wildly at the swatches of upholstery fabrics he plucked out a garish geometric weave.

"And of course *Robin* simply couldn't resist *this* for the boardroom chairs." JS stood glaring at the crumpled length of silk, the dull grass paper sample and the brightly-patterned weave before adding spitefully, "Tap and Die boardroom well and truly done. Tap and Die? God, talk about a ridiculous name."

"They're the names of various machine tools," I replied in a nervously.

Giving me a disdainful look JS said sneeringly, "Make up a colour board and get those estimates to your fussy friend Lowles as soon as possible. Organise the curtain people, the carpet people - choose a carpet you - *Robin* - think fit etcetera, etcetera. No, make it a depressingly *dark* dull carpet and have the ceiling painted to match."

On receiving the colour board and the estimates along with my description of JS's overall approach to the project, DLL wrote a polite letter thanking JS for his time and enthusiasm but regrettably he would not be proceeding with the redecoration. JS never commented on the outcome.

As if bearing the old proverb "revenge is a dish best served cold" in mind, DLL bided his time before getting his own back following JS's bitchy slight and demeaning comments. At my continued self-promoting suggestions DLL reluctantly agreed to invite JS and Jacqueline ("only because it may be beneficial for you, Robble") to dinner at the Mirabelle, one of London's most exclusive and extravagant restaurants.

As anticipated dinner turned out to be somewhat strained with the atmosphere becoming positively electric when DLL said smilingly to JS "I'd offer you a cigar John but judging from the size of your mouth I would strongly suggest a smaller, less imposing, easily manageable cigarillo."

You could have heard the proverbial pin drop. *Shit!* I thought, *tomorrow is* not *going to be a good day!*

JS sat sulking for the few moments following dinner with DLL and Jacqueline making obvious small talk before saying with a sudden snarl, "Jacqueline it's time to leave. Thank you for dinner *David*. Now if you'll excuse us."

Within a matter of minutes DLL and I found ourselves thankfully alone.

"I think another Courvoisier is called for, don't you?" said DLL with a mischievous smile.

"Courvoisier?" I exclaimed. "Make mine a magnum of Dom Perignon!"

As with his abortive scheme for the Tap and Die boardroom, JS never referred to my "beneficial dinner" with DLL at the Mirabelle.

*

At the end of the sixties a great many people were investing money in various tax havens abroad; the Mediterranean island of Malta being one of the most sought after. DLL, Eric and Rex along with a host of equally shrewd business men soon joined the bandwagon and here again I was able to carry out some private design work for DLL.

"I've bought a property in Valetta - two in fact. They're a couple of typical 16th-century houses somewhat shoddily converted so I thought a bit of my Robble's touch - ha ha - to bring them up to standard. There is also a small cabin cruiser which you again can take a look at. And Robble, this has nothing to do with Siddeley; nothing whatsoever! Do you think you could manage to carry out such a project without the wretched man becoming involved? I suggest you come out for a day or two during your holiday." He gave a wry chuckle. "That's if, of course, Siddeley permits his overworked, under paid and much maligned staff a holiday break."

"Where there's a will there's a way Beesle and come hell or high water, RA will find a way!" I replied giving his hand an affirmative squeeze.

I flew out to join DLL for a few days during my scheduled holiday break, my destination causing JS to say with a sneer, "Malta? But that's where all the package tours and hoi polloi go. Need I say anymore?"

Apart from enjoying DLL's always much-treasured company I planned to take myriads of measurements, make sketches and present him with the two schemes for the houses and the cabin-cruiser. Unbeknown to me at the time DLL had also been viewing properties in Italy and had already set his mind on a semi-derelict 14th-century mountain village in Liguria. The village, a tumbledown collection of stone houses set in the beautiful Cinque Terre Mountains overlooking the small port of Levanto some thirty miles east of Portofino. (On seeing peoples' confusion whenever I mentioned the Cinque Terre I would laughingly explain by saying "It's bang on the knee to the boot of Italy".) Practically the whole of

Dosso (the name of the village) was for sale apart from a couple of houses owned by the elderly headman and a few peasant olive farmers.

"We're lunching with Rex and Eric up at Mdina, the walled city which is quite a drive so we'd best leave around twelve," said DLL as we were having breakfast by the pool at the Corinthia Hotel. At Rex and Eric's alfresco lunch I was introduced to David Hicks who was not only another "in" designer but married to Lady Pamela Hicks, the Queen's cousin.

"If you are free you simply *must* join me for lunch tomorrow, Robin and David," drawled Hicks (from now on referred to as DH) in a vowel choked voice as we were walking back to our various cars, "I have some amusing people lunching whom you may enjoy meeting." (Little did I know at the time how big a part DH's catchphrase "some amusing people" would play in my life.)

Having accepted DH's invitation we joined him and his guests at a small restaurant in Valetta town (the Corinthia Hotel located some distance away at St. Georges Bay, St. Julian's). Two of the guests included a couple who were planning to open a restaurant in St Julian's and extremely excited by DH's design proposals.

"Knowing Mr Hicks you'll be spared the embarrassment of an obvious Maltese theme," I laughingly told them.

"An obvious Maltese theme?" repeated the woman, "what do you mean by an 'obvious Maltese theme'?"

"You know the sort of thing, walls draped with banners relating to the famous Knights of Malta; an extensive use of the eight-pointed Maltese Cross in the fabric and carpet designs (my actual design ideas for DLL's two properties and cabin cruiser) and other local artefacts. Ha ha!" my so-called witty comment resulting in stunned expressions on the faces of DH's two clients and a furious look from the great man himself. Apparently I'd "hit the DH nail" (in this case "the DH design") on its proverbial head. Needless to say conversation during the rest of the luncheon and DH's "amusing people" was somewhat stilted.

Talk about the saying "revenge a dish best served cold". A decade later would see DH spitefully getting his own back. Expressing my annoyance at the designer's behaviour a comment from Ben Colman (more about Mr Mustard later) was typical. "Eek Mumsie! He's now behaving even more queenly than his missus's cousin! I wonder if Her Maj ever sees him as a rival to 'Us'?"

"Not very tactful my Robble but bloody funny," chuckled DLL on the taxi ride back to the hotel.

"So much for originality," I sniffed. "I must say I expected something a bit more innovative from our host."

"We must make sure we ask him to drinks in one of our houses or our boat ("our"? I approved of that!) so he can see how clever he's about to be!" replied DLL with a smile.

In case anyone is at all curious, we never did.

*

DH did eventually invite me to for dinner *a deux* at the family house in St Leonard's table where he seemed to seek some sort of revenge by chasing me around the dinner followed by a great deal of *pinching*! A very strange pattern of events and not quite what I had expected. In retrospect I remember the dining room - like his behaviour - was *most* innovative.

A few months later DH surprised me and DLL by inviting us one Saturday to dinner at Britwell House, his spectacular country home on the Britwell Estate in Oxfordshire. To say Britwell House was a showpiece and at the same time a wonderful family home does not do it justice. The place was magnificent. We were introduced to Lady Pamela, DH's charming wife and all in all enjoyed an enchanting evening. Little did I realise at the time how big a part DH, Lady Pamela and Britwell would play a fun part in my life a few years later.

*

On the evening flight from Malta back to London I found myself seated next to a burly Burl Ives type of American who, proffering a large hirsute hand, introduced himself as "Hi, I'm Ernest, Ernest Hofer. Pleased to meet yah."

So it would seem, I thought coquettishly as I did my best to return Ernest's intense gaze. *Oscar Wilde, eat your heart out!* I thought with an inward grin. *This important Ernest looks as if he could easily give* your *Ernest a run for your money when it comes to winning this fair Gwendolen - or Gwendal if one needs to appear a tad butch - or gender correct!*

"Good evening Ernest. I'm Robin. Robin Anderson," I said in reply.

"I must tell you something Robin," said Ernest in a conspiratorial whisper, "When I saw you checking in I said to myself I wouldn't mind sitting next to that young guy. He looks as if he could be an interesting travelling companion."

I sat staring as importantly as I could into Ernest's unblinking, startlingly blue eyes, "Well let's hope I don't let you down!" I gave a carefree laugh. "Now where's that drinks trolley?"

Armed with "a whisky and dry ginger" Ernest (unasked) gave me a quick whispered summary of his life. Eyeing my vodka with a hypnotic stare I thought sourly, *Don't tell I'm expected to suffer this bloody soliloquy all the way back to Heathrow,* when the words "professor" (his professional title) and "Oxford" suddenly caught my attention. "I take it you mean Oxford England and *not* Oxford Ontario seeing you're American?" I quipped, signalling for another vodka.

"Oxford, England," Professor Hofer replied proudly.

"Oh," I said for want of something to say. "I know nobody at Oxford, only Cambridge. A Brian Ketterer for one. Ring any bells?"

"Brian Ketterer?" exclaimed Ernest. "Why I know Brian; he's studying chemistry. My Oh my, talk about a coincidence." Giving a shake of his large, unruly head he added in a hallowed voice "It's certainly a small, small world" before going on to enthuse about Brian and several of his fellow students. Ernest ended by saying earnestly (apologies for the pun), "Say, like you knowing Brian Ketterer I somehow see our sitting next to other on the same flight as ordained." He turned to look at me with a totally unexpected hangdog expression. "I know it'll be late when we finally get into London," he said sheepishly, "but would you consider having dinner with me? I suggest Mimmo's in Elizabeth Street . . ."

"I know Mimmo's," I interrupted, "its round the corner from my offices in Ebury Street!" Thinking, *Seen as something else ordained, no doubt.*

"I can easily book into a small hotel I know near there and take an early train to Oxford," concluded Ernest; his look now more pleading than hangdog.

Why not? I thought, *if he's a friend of Brian and co then he obviously prefers Gwendals to Gwendolyns!* "I'd love to have dinner," I replied in what I considered a suitably odalisque-like manner, "but instead of Mimmo's and a bed and breakfast hotel why not a similar restaurant, just as good and near to my flat in Ladbroke Square? Furthermore, if you don't mind doubling up you can stay the night. It'll not only save you the hassle of having to book into a hotel etcetera added to which Paddington's easy to get to either by tube or taxi!"

"As I said a few minutes back, I see this ordained," said Ernest still looking earnest and giving my thigh a furtive squeeze.

Later we both lay satiated having experienced several marathons of what a panting Ernest wheezingly described as either "experiencing the ultimate intimacy" (a flash back to wordy Geoff McMinn) or - in more basic terms - "a coupla fabulous fucks".

I saw Ernest several times before he returned to America. I also stayed with him in his delightful house near Amherst, Massachusetts where in addition to endless viewings of the "Ernest 'Excaliber'" Ernest insisted I also "view the unparalleled colours of an Indian summer" and pay a visit to his old alma mater, Harvard.

"And in spite of me *not* being a necrophiliac perhaps you'll also show me Jackson Pollock's grave which I gather is situated in nearby Green River Cemetery?" I asked. (I had first been introduced to Jackson Pollock's work while at Rhodes University and had become an avid fan.)

"Why sure," replied the always affable Ernest. "I know it well and Pollock's headstone is something else. Quite emotive in fact."

The "something else" turned out to be a large granite boulder with a simple inset plaque displaying the artist's name and as Ernest so rightly said, "quite emotive".

I was dazzled and overwhelmed by the autumnal colours for which New England is famous. On our journey through endless glowing woodlands from East Hampton to the Hofer "haven" I couldn't help but say in an awed voice, "I think the best way I can describe all of this is by simply saying its all *very* Grace Metalious."

On seeing Ernest's perplexed expression I added, "Grace Metalious and her bestselling *Peyton Place* with its memorable opening line: *Indian summer is like a woman. Ripe, hotly passionate . . .*"

"Obviously she never met ya hot, humpin' Ernest," interrupted my host. His sniggering comment accompanied by a lascivious licking of his provocative lips.

Later Ernest decided to spend more time in England and subsequently purchased a flat in Brighton. During one of his I return visits to the States I rented the flat as a weekend getaway and enjoyed many happy stays in the attractive seaside town. Like Brian Ketterer, Ernest would become a lifelong friend.

*

Soon after Stephen had joined the company JS asked me if I knew of a flat Stephen could rent. I never knew where Stephen was living at the time but assured JS I would "keep my eyes and ears open". True to my word I left a note for Mrs Edwards, my sprightly cleaning lady, asking her to contact me if she heard of anything suitable on what I termed "the cleaner grapevine". The same afternoon I received a call from Mrs Edwards who excitedly informed me the ground floor flat in the very same building as mine was about to be vacated and would *this* be of any interest? I had never been inside the flat but assumed it to be at least double the size of my own being on the ground floor with ceilings double the height as well. Telling Mrs Edwards I'd call her back within five minutes I raced through to see JS and gave him news. "I said I'd call her back to let her know if you are interested," I told him.

"Where is she?" he snapped.

"My flat," I replied.

"Let me speak to her!"

Within the hour JS and Stephen left to meet Mrs Edwards and view the flat. I was busy working on a colour board when Stephen telephoned. On hearing my voice he said with a triumphant laugh, "Hi neighbour!"

This came as no surprise to Maggie or myself, nor my "elite circle" who regarded the extrovert Stephen with utter disdain; William dismissing him with a laconic "vulgar", Madge and Poofty with a dismissive "is he *really* necessary?" and Peter with a snorted "too much for a white woman,

99

darling!". Through his own contacts Stephen became firm friends with Nicky Armstrong whose boyfriend at the time was Phillip Profumo, brother of John Profumo, the Conservative Member of Parliament caught up in the notorious Stephen Ward (another Stephen!) and Christine Keeler case which led to the eventual toppling of the Conservative Government in 1964. Through Nicky he also became friendly with another Nicholas, Sir Nicholas Sekers - better known as "Miki"- the elderly, flamboyant owner of Sekers Silks. Miki's other claim to fame was his Rosehill Theatre created from an old barn on his country estate near Whitehaven in Cumbria and part of the beautiful Lake District. Before "the frosting" (a result of my resignation from John Siddeley Limited) Stephen and I spent many happy weekends as guests of Nicky's at his small "grace ad favour" cottage on the Sekers' estate.

It was not long before the beady gold-digging Stephen found an additional admirer named Richard Taylor who described himself as a "landowner". A landowner with his fingers in many other lucrative pies, Richard owned (or leased) a dilapidated but charming property, Crouchlands, near to the tiny village of Plaistow in West Sussex. He also held a stake in a racehorse or two. Richard, a short, stocky brown-haired young man (in some ways he uncannily reminded me of Julian Craggs) was the complete antithesis to JS and much to my amazement along with one or two others, Stephen appeared to be devoted to him. Apart from Crouchlands, Richard owned a palatial house in Neville Terrace, South Kensington which saw Stephen flitting between Crouchlands, Neville Street and Ladbroke Square. I am pleased to say once the "frosting" finally thawed I would spend many a fun weekend there.

1966 saw the publication of The Wolfenden Report which legalised homosexual acts between over twenty one as long as these "acts" took place in private. Despite the restrictions of age and venue the aftermath of the Report had far reaching results which made even the highest point on the Richter scale appear redundant. With it "okay to be gay" London was suddenly swamped with trendy "gay friendly" restaurants, shops, books and plays despite the old faithfuls having been around for several decades if not more. Even the West End caught up in the euphoria with a production Mart Crowley's *Boys in the Band* at the Wyndham's Theatre and Kenneth Tynan's outrageous *Oh! Calcutta!* The latter seeing censorship well and truly buried.

Having been introduced to an elite gay circle on my immediate introduction to London I have to be honest and say apart from the openly public stage events any great change was not discernible. I was already familiar with the works of James Baldwin (*Giovanni's Room*), Mary Renault's *The Charioteer* and Michael Nelson's *A Room in Chelsea Square* along with John Rechy's *City of Night* plus Christopher Isherwood's *A Single Man* which meant further novels such as Gore Vidal's highly acclaimed *Myra Breckenbridge* were not exactly earth-shattering. Added to which forays to the Mediterranean fleshpots of Morocco, Mykonos and the farther afield Thailand were par for the course and had been for centuries.

I was to become a regular visitor to Marrakech where I was royally entertained by Yves Saint Laurent and Pierre Bergé in their enchanting villa with its blue and white themed gardens. Likewise Tangiers where I became friends with the flamboyant David Herbert and enjoyed my visits to the exotic Pink House, his equally flamboyant home.

HELL HATH NO FURY AS JS SPURNED

The redesigning of 45 Belgrave Square was a like a fairy tale come true with Tony Galliers-Pratts being the *very* good fairy in more ways than one, two or even twenty three! So much so his "good deeds" were becoming an embarrassment. Tony, already camp, revelled in the sobriquet "Decibel" while becoming even more out of control and camp in his behaviour. As DLL wryly observed, "Dear Tony seems to have gone and tossed his bonnet well and truly over the windmill!" His reference no doubt to the similar, eccentric behaviour of Cervantes' Don Quixote.

Having "seduced" me away from John Siddeley Limited Tony went on in a thwarted attempt to seduce me by other means. He enthusiastically introduced me to his tailors Sullivan and Woolley (now Henry Poole and Co of Savile Row) where I was fitted out with several suits, a dinner jacket and several overcoats as well as showering me with expensive gifts. Among these were a splendid of seventeenth century carved oak chairs to grace my entrance hall at Ladbroke Square, a John Piper lithograph, endless cases of champagne along with extravagant dinners and lunches. Tony was even brazen enough to invite me – accompanied by Angela - on a four day excursion to Barbizon, France, where we would "immerse ourselves among The Impressionists"!

I was becoming more and more concerned by Tony's irrational behaviour; the complete opposite to JS's I hasten to point out! Tony's behaviour was also causing further embarrassment regarding my connection with Alistair Colvin Limited. While I was working on 45, Belgrave Square, Tony would be constantly on the telephone to the office about nothing in particular, so much so Susan Marr, one of the other designers remarked crisply, "Why doesn't he just move in here? Answering the telephone to him time and time again is now getting on everybody's nerves!"

Alistair Colvin's answer to JS's Fiona Bowes-Lyon was Caroline the "pattern girl" - otherwise Caroline, Duchess of Fife - who was equally cryptic.

"Your *persistent* Mr G.P. should at least have some consideration for our poor eardrums when calling!" she would remark with a gracious sniff when handing over the telephone. If she had expected any reaction on the snide "your *persistent* Mr G.P." she was disappointed as I simply chose to ignore the implication.

A suitably chastised Tony stopped calling Alistair Colvin Limited but made up for it by calling me at home around six o'clock in the morning; hovering around whenever I was on site at Belgrave Square and peppering the evening with late night calls to "see" how I was faring.

As the saying goes *Every Cloud has a Silver Lining* with my "cloud" - namely 45 Belgrave Square and its redecoration - approaching completion and the "silver lining" metamorphosing in the form of one Charlie Cottenham or to give him his correct name, Lord Charles or Charles, Earl of Cottenham.

Charlie, an accomplished sportsman and a striking, elegant young man about town had become the proud owner of a large apartment set in a sombre, thirties-type brick building in Cadogan Lane, Belgravia. Some heaven-sent person suggested Charlie should contact Alistair Colvin Limited about decorating this forbidding abode resulting in Alistair introducing Charlie to me. Charlie was a dream client, his requirements being quite clear; "I want the apartment to be way out, fabulous and at the same time comfortable. So will you do just that and perhaps even a bit more please?" His instructions followed by a chuckled, "From what Alistair tells me, such a request will not be a problem for Maestro Robin Anderson!"

Charlie's "way out apartment" without a doubt "put me on the map" by appearing in *House and Garden* (the sitting room given a two page centrespread) and my innovative usage of lights, lighting and colour featured in several "coffee table" type books. Unhampered by the architectural style of the building (unlike 45 Belgrave Square with its restrictive cornices, mouldings and such) I was literally given a selection of different size boxes to deal with as I pleased. To say I *un*-bottled all those *bottled*-up ideas would be putting it mildly! At the time there was an explosion of new ideas and materials on the design scene such as plastics, acrylics, metals, new forms of lighting, stereo equipment, fabrics and coverings including *faux* leathers, furs and metallic wallpapers.

It was in Charlie's apartment I first introduced what would become an RA trademark, colour bands on the ceiling. These were painted in two to three inch wide parallel lines inset from where the wall met the ceiling (Charlie's apartment was devoid of any cornices and had there been a cornice this too would no doubt have been in the colour of the innermost band). I revelled in the praise heaped upon me as a result of this colourful innovation. Imagine my dismay on visiting Cuzco in Peru almost a decade later where staying in a hotel dating back to the mid-16th-century I spotted a run of several rather wavy colour bands painted on to the ceilings to several of the public rooms! On pointing these out I was told by the proud manager the bands were original, hence their unevenness and faded colours.

"Perhaps I'm a reincarnation of Francisco Pizarro come back to check on my colour bands?" I quipped, my comment receiving blank looks from the manager and the receptionist. "Forget it," I muttered, "and anyway, maybe Pizarro was too busy conquering the Incas to dabble in décor!"

Charlie's large, rectangular sitting room was a tranquil haven of yellow, deep blue, ivory and black with a polished chrome-framed fireplace complimented by a nail painting by David Partridge. A large canvas by Sandra Blow, painted in blues and yellows dominated one end of the room and at the other end, a three-sided sofa in yellow set on a special viewing platform for the large, central television. An article by Anne de Courcy in the *Evening News* was headed by the tongue-in-cheek caption *What's yellow, 57 feet long and luxurious? Lord Charlie's sofa!*

Leading from the sumptuous sitting room was the dining room walled in genuine cowhide with metals chairs with alternating seat cushions in blue and yellow. Another innovation was the introduction of "dream screens", a type of hologram which featured in the bedroom and viewable from the large, modern four poster bed with a canopy of blistered steel as opposed to the usual, pleated fabric.

London hadn't seen anything like it since the days Kenneth Partridge stunned the design world with his psychedelic makeover of Kenwood for John Lennon in the sixties.

As Tony had promised any publicity appertaining to any work I carried out while at Alistair Colvin was duly credited to Robin Anderson and nobody else. Further articles on Charlie's apartment appeared in *The Daily Mail* and to my immense surprise I was even a written up in *The Bulawayo Chronicle*! The *pièce de résistance* however was a full-page feature in the New York *Home Furnishings Daily* captioned in bold print, *NOW IT'S ROBIN ANDERSON*.

Aha, I thought, *time to take the plunge and form my own company!*

DLL always said he would help finance me in such a venture but I tactfully explained I would prefer to "go it alone" and *not* go the easy route of having my greatest friend and lover as my sponsor. I was determined to keep my independence and what's more my personality and individuality. I had seen too often what "being kept" could lead to; a prime example being the talented William Davis who literally wilted, personality and talent-wise, under the machinations of his control freak of a lover, Michael Pitt Rivers.

The obvious solution was Charlie Cottenham who, when approached, was as excited about the proposed venture as I was! Poofty (Derek Collins), a successful businessman in his own right, introduced to his wily accountant, Brian Pearl, who proved to be brilliant at helping me set up RAD aka ROBIN ANDERSON DESIGN (London) Limited. Charlie promptly produced the backing (a whacking £1,500!) and all it left for me to do was to find suitable premises.

Lady Luck really appeared to be looking after me. At the time I had been using a small travel agency at 60, Ebury Street owned by a distant relative of Ben Colman's (Peter Lubbock; a grey-haired ditsy old queen) for any holiday bookings. In passing I mentioned to Warren Sampson, one of the directors, my search for a small office, somewhere local to Sloane Square if possible. "Why not here?" suggested Warren, "We have two reasonable rooms and a bathroom upstairs which are doing nothing. I'm sure Peter would have no objection to you renting these. In fact he'd be delighted."

"Done!" I said.

"Good," replied Warren with a cheery smile. "We're delighted. Alison?"

"Bravo!" cried Alison, Warren's gently spoken spinsterish co-director. "We've always wanted someone fun upstairs!"

With mounting excitement I sent off my design for the company note paper to the printers; a bold RAD outlined to form a box above the name of the company with the address and telephone number. At the bottom of the page was my name as managing director followed by Charlie's name and title and Ben Colman's name. I had asked Ben to be a director simply because he had become one of my greatest friends. *Not bad for starters*, I thought, *a lethally ambitious RA, an Earl and the heir to Colman's Mustard!*

News of my company spread like the proverbial wildfire followed by endless messages and telegrams (*nota bene* it *was* 1970!) of congratulations and goodwill. Not all surprising were a number of telephone calls from various suppliers and contractors who had been contacted by a furious JS threatening to close *his* company account should they open an account on *my* behalf! Again a dead-ringer for the spiteful Spillane who, as expected, spewed out sentiments such as "a rrich old man's sponsored pet" and "I ken not wait to see him fail".

My good luck continued! Ned Hoopes, an American friend, on hearing I had decided to "go it alone" suggested I meet a colleague of his, a "rather eccentric but highly efficient character named Bryan Larkin", who was looking for "something artistic to do" and was I interested? I tentatively telephoned Bryan who agreed in a strange falsetto to come along to Ebury Street for "an interview".

I tried not to look too taken aback by the tall, Modigliani-like figure making his way slowly up the stairs for the aforesaid interview sporting what I could only describe as a Jackie O hairdo and wearing a blouson-style shirt opened to the navel, baggy cotton trousers, no socks and a pair of well-worn espadrilles. Even more extraordinary was the battered wicker case clutched in his arms.

"Good afternoon," said the Modigliani "portrait" in a falsetto voice reminiscent of "Decibel", "I'm Bryan Larkin. Allow me to make it quite clear I can't promise I'll stay but Ned says you're quite a pleasant person so I thought I'd come and see for myself."

"Oh," I said, "Oh. Well you'd best take a seat and I'll fill you in on er . . . RAD." I went on to discuss my plans for the company in general plus a starting salary (as guided by DLL). I also asked Bryan if he held a valid driving as I was planning on buying a small Bedford van for the delivery of rolls of fabric, small pieces of furniture and such. Bryan assured me he had a licence and if he *did* join the company he *assumed* the van could be used "out of hours".

"But of course," I replied weakly and thinking, *I see you more as Boadicea in her chariot, hair flying as you race along whipping your horses rather than sitting behind the steering wheel of a small Bedford van! But I like you Bryan and despite your bizarre appearance you seem to be efficient, have an eye - I like the comments you made on my new colour card and details for David's boardroom - plus I think it'll be fun having you on the team.* "I plan to officially open RAD next Monday, February the sixteenth and I would be delighted if you would be here, nine o'clock sharp. In other words, as an assistant and coordinator."

"You mean I've got the job?" rasped Bryan with a quizzical lifting of one carefully plucked eyebrow.

"Er . . . yes," I said, "I'm offering you the . . . er . . . position."

"How extraordinary," he murmured staring around the new office with its neat shelving, desk lamps and Habitat chairs. "Oh well, I'd best be going then See you Monday. Goodbye Mr Anderson and allow me to assure you, RAD will not regret your decision. Thank you."

"It's Robin; and thank *you* Bryan!"

Without further ado Bryan picked up the wicker case and with a gracious nod of his Jackie O-inspired head disappeared down the stairs.

"Who or what was that?" queried Warren having spotted seen Bryan sashaying past his office door.

"*That* Warren," I replied, "is Mr Bryan Larkin, part of the RAD team."

"*Lady* Larkin you mean," tittered Warren. The title was to stick with Bryan becoming known to all and sundry - including several clients - as the one and only Lady Larkin.

The position of a secretary - along with a new contract - was resolved by the ever charming Charlie. Enter Elizabeth - Liz - Anderson (no relation), a fun, charming and extremely capable, violet-eyed Liz Taylor lookalike: the contract being the design for Charlie's latest venture, an exclusive fashion boutique in Lower Sloane Street.

*

I spent the few weeks prior to the nervously awaited "grand opening" setting up the new premises. The top floor at No 60 Ebury Street comprised of one large room with a smaller room overlooking the street itself. John Skellorn happily donated the carpeting and Dennis Paget, a building contractor, constructing a run of vinyl working tops in both rooms and shelving for the sample "room". The newly acquired sample room came from removing the old bath and partitioning off most of the back bathroom while leaving the original loo (toilet) and hand basin and a making a new opening from the main office to the new sample room. Access to the loo was by the original door which lead into a narrow L-shaped corridor.

The roomy sample contained rows of shelves - some with additional hooks for ganging fabric swatches - plus a "kitchen cubby hole" boasting a small fridge, work top for a kettle and shelves for a cutlery tray, glasses and crockery. Washing up was intrinsically done in a bowl with hot water carried through from the loo but nine times out of ten ended up in the basin next door.

Under my directions Dennis positioned the vital filing cabinets under the desk runs. A much appreciated piece of furniture was a large plan chest donated by Bill Kendall, an architect I had met through Alistair Colvin Limited. Bill, a kind, quietly-spoken man worked as a freelance with RAD for several years. Bill had been extremely supportive over some of my startling ideas for Charlie's apartment (the metal bed canopy for one) and I was delighted when he agreed to be part of my team.

RAD (London) Ltd was all ready to go; not only my newly formed company but life in general.

IN THE INTERIM - ONE

Introductions through John Tillotson and Peter Carter never seemed to waver. After meeting Rex and Eric it was inevitable I should meet Ken Villiers the interior designer responsible for the overly fussy drawing room and staircase to their house in Montpelier Square.

"Meet Ken Villiers," said Peter as I entered his South Eaton Place drawing room, a tastefully restrained room much more suitable for a "bachelor gay" as opposed to a glade for a pair of Edmund Spenser's *Faerie Queenes*! A "taste" which unfortunately eluded the dining room.

I shook hand with the affable Ken; a large, balding pink-faced man who immediately reminded me of a jolly Santa Claus *sans* beard; but a Santa with a voice more flute-like than "Ho ho ho!" Another dinner guest was a tall, tanned aesthetic man who was introduced as Derek Adkins "from Hong Kong". During dinner I was seated between Ken and Derek in Peter's claustrophobic dining room which gave the appearance of being doubly wrapped in a garish Chinoiserie wallpaper along with an elaborate pair of ruched, swagged and tortured-looking silk curtains courtesy the labours of hundreds of thousands - if not millions - of silk worms. For want of something to say I said smilingly to the ebullient man, "I er . . . admired your er . . . designs for Rex and Eric's house er . . . would this *charming* room be another of your er . . . triumphs?"

"Yes," came the smug reply, "and how astute of you. You obviously have a very good eye." He gave a sniff. "Unfortunately the sitting room was decorated by Tom Parr and a bit unimaginative if I may be so bold!"

"Not at all," I answered diplomatically. "One couldn't fail to recognise your . . . er . . . *very* distinctive style. And yes, as you say Mr . . . Parr was it? (Ken's jowls wobbled in confirmation) Mr Parr is *much* more er . . . restrained."

"I like your young Robin, Peter!" fluted Ken, "Quite the connoisseur!"

A few days later Ken telephoned and asked if I would care to spend the coming weekend at his "cottage near Henley-on-Thames". "Rex and Eric are staying so you could easily travel down with them and back," he chirruped.

"I'd love to and thank you Ken," I promptly replied, thinking, *Anything to escape another weekend In Julian's company, a weekend visit to the local laundromat, the Scarsdale Arms or the alternatives of a visit to Portobello Road or Speakers Corner at Marble Arch!*

"Good," said Ken, "I'll let Sexy Rexy and Tinkerbell know! Could you give Sexy Rexy a call and make arrangements where to meet and so on? I look forward to seeing you again Robin. Until Saturday then. Toodle-oo!"

At this early stage I had not experienced the delight of a second meeting with DLL. Meanwhile all fun sounding invitations - along with those with a hint of being beneficial regarding the first rungs up the "success" ladder - were happily accepted.

On Saturday morning Rex and Eric duly collected me from Abingdon Road; their car a splendid Bentley complete with a uniformed "butch-looking" chauffeur. I glanced at Rex and Eric resplendent in tweeds (Rex in a discreet houndstooth and Eric in less subtle bottle green and red check) while I wore my faithful blazer and twills; a left over from my university days. A glowering Julian stood watching, arms tightly folded, as we drove off; me treating him to a regal wave.

Digberry, Ken's tiny cottage, sat in wooded isolation at the end of a tree and bramble-infested lane. "No room to turn the car 'ere, sir. I'll 'ave to reverse out," grumbled Mr Butch.

"I'm sure Babee is quite capable of reversing!" trilled Eric in response. With a narrowing of his eyes he added waspishly, "However, before you *do* start reversing I suggest you help carry the bags plus the two cases of wine and case of champagne into Mr Kenneth's cottage. Ah, and here he is! Mine host, the man of the moment!"

Ken appeared in the low-beamed front door dressed in what I assumed to be the correct attire for a country decorator as opposed to a country squire; his outfit comprising a loose lilac-coloured shirt with a canary yellow cravat, red corduroy trousers (I couldn't make out the shoes due to the bottoms of the trouser legs being bunched up festoon-like - obviously a Ken Villiers trademark - around his ankles). "Welcome!" he fluted, "Welcome to Digberry!"

I stood quietly taking in the small, double-storied flint stone cottage with its mullioned windows. *If that contains more than two bedrooms I'll be surprised,* I thought. *Please don't tell me I'm to share a bedroom with festoony Ken?*

The sleeping arrangements came as a relief. I would *not* be sharing a bedroom with Ken but "making do" with the sofa in the tiny sitting room. The sigh was twofold having noticed a small, dilapidated caravan set back among some trees near to the cottage and wondering if, at times, the extra guest had to "make do" with this forlorn-looking facility!

To my surprise I soon discovered the caravan was home to a sullen, thickset youngish Moroccan who was simply introduced by Ken as his "major domo". (In later years when retelling the story I would wryly refer to the young stud as Ken's "major homo" or "MH".) MH apparently spent all his time at Digberry with excursions to London taking place only once or twice a year. To quote the White Rabbit from *Alice in Wonderland,* "Curiouser and curiouser." I questioned several people about Ken's relationship with MH and apart from a few murmured "he obviously likes big, burly Arabs" nobody appeared to be any the wiser.

The weekend proved to be the greatest of fun with an endless stream of young and not so young gays (*Where does Ken find them?* I kept thinking) dropping by for a drink and one or two staying on for a meal. To my great delight I remained "unscathed" apart from one inebriated gentleman grunting in an aside "I'd really love to really fuck you sometime" before searching inside his jacket pocket and adding in a disappointed growl, "Sorry, I don't seem to have a card. Another time perhaps?"

Ken turned out to be a most affable and generous host with him and MH serving up the most delicious meals. Needless to say the wine and champagne flowed nonstop.

A MINOR DIVERTISSEMENT

Rex and Eric turned out to be a combination of Baloo and Tinkerbell with their never-ending invitations one of which saw me finally having passionate sex with my first black man! Despite growing up in Africa the idea of "having it off" with a black man never occurred (to me anyway), plus it was literally unheard of. I can remember most clearly Cur and her friends' outrage when Seretse Khama, President of Botswana, married Ruth Williams, a white English woman back in 1948. Racist jokes abounded; "Seretse and Ruth and their planned little coffee Khamas" being an example. The word "Khama" being a play on the Afrikaans word *kamer* meaning a room. In other words a place serving "white coffees" or black coffees with a splash of milk.

"Babee we're now taking you *out* for lunch on Saturday," chirruped Eric over the telephone.

Good, I thought, *the fabulous, fun La Popote I trust?*

"A great friend Peter Pollock who owns a farm (my heart sank) and his friend, Paul Danquah, an actor" - Eric gave a trill - "he starred in that wonderful film *A Taste of Honey* - have invited Sexy Rexy and I so, as we've already invited *you* to lunch it would be great fun if Babee joined us! Peter has already said 'yes'!"

Peter Pollock owned a farm near Flaunden in Hertfordshire. We duly arrived to be greeted by the affable Peter and his *black* actor friend, a beaming, testosterone-infused Paul Danquah.

Wow! I thought, *"Wow! It's never really crossed my mind before but you, Mr Danquah, you are one hell of an attractive chap!* (Yes! In the nineteen sixties we did indeed use the word "chap" as opposed to today's "guy".) *Plus I wonder if it's true what they say . . .*

Sitting alongside the swimming pool was Peter and Paul's houseguest, a bright, smiley young woman with what I would later describe to an amused DLL as "Mrs Tiggy-Winkle features". The lady turned out be Rita Tushingham, Paul's co-star in *A Taste of Honey* filmed in 1961. (Decades later I would meet Rita again under less amiable circumstances.)

Peter spent several moments bringing Eric and Rex up to date about his great friend, an unknown artist named Francis Bacon who had also - or so I gathered - been living in Peter and Paul's flat in Battersea. "Francis has moved out. He's leased a studio in Reece Mews, a rather smart mews in South Kensington."

"Perhaps we can meet up in London, Robin?" suggested Paul positively oozing s-e-x as we were saying our "goodbyes".

"I'd like that very much er . . . Paul," I giggled; a tad coquettishly.

"Give me your telephone number and I'll give you a call," replied Paul with a cheeky wink.

Three days later Paul telephoned and invited me to the Battersea flat for dinner. Needless to say I paid no attention *whatsoever* to any former Southern Rhodesian or South African taboos!

Peter and Paul (as did many gays) eventually moved to Tangier where I was fortunate enough to meet up with them again; Peter having opened the highly successful Pergola Bar and Restaurant on the seafront.

Another arresting young man met through Eric and Rex was a tall, blond, athletic Tab Hunter lookalike named Donald Stephenson. Donald claimed he was a descendant of Robert Stephenson, the engineer responsible to *Stephenson's Rocket*, the first steam engine to be built. Having experienced Donald's "rocket" on several occasions I was quite happy to authenticate Donald's claim to fame.

Thanks to Donald I was introduced to his delightful doctor Patrick (socially I hasten to add) known, rather insultingly as "the clap doctor". Adding further insult to injury was Patrick being "blessed" with unfortunate surname of Woodcock. Patrick was a popular figure in a select gay circle and it was at one of his much sought-after dinner parties I met the legendary Noël Coward who - on being told by Patrick I had recently arrived from South Africa - greeted me with a pompous, "Good evening dear boy; *alles sal reg kom!*" which translated from Afrikaans means "everything will be alright".

I can only assume Mr Coward must have mistaken me for one of Patrick's "after hours" patients as opposed to a dinner guest! In retrospect I expect a fan would have found the Maestro's so-called greeting to be "terribly, terribly funny."

END OF DIVERTISSEMENT

"How was your weekend?" questioned a scowling Julian, his attitude more RADA Spanish inquisitor than a flatmate.

"Fine," I replied nonchalantly.

"It would be most appreciated if, for *once*, I was included in one of these frivolous forays," he continued sneeringly, "After all, not only did I ensure you had accommodation on your arrival in London but I have also sacrificed valuable RADA time showing you about."

My response was to give my landlord a warm smile and hand over a bottle of wine. "For you," I said. "As you can see you are *not* forgotten!" my remark and gesture being greeted by a harrumph; the bottle being taken immediately into his room and the last I saw of it.

The invitations continued to swarm in and I was soon caught up in a whirl of cocktail parties and dinners. Rex and Eric introduced me to a charming new restaurant, La Popote, in Walton Street, Chelsea. Little did I realise at the time La Popote would become (as Christopher Hunter, the dashing manager so rightly described it) "a way of life".

Feeling slightly guilty about Julian and his gripe of not being "included" I suggested the following Saturday we begin by having a light pub lunch (on me) at the Stock Pot in King's Road before spending the rest of the afternoon "people watching" while strolling down the colourful thoroughfare. The King's Road thronged with gorgeously garbed people. Flower power, punk, hippie or even soberly dressed like the two of us, London was enjoying a fashion explosion and I had arrived in time for the gathering tempos making up the swinging sixties.

"Hello there!" called a laughter-filled, light tenor voice. Startled, I turned staring in the direction of "Hello there", my eyes being drawn to a smiling, fair-haired charmer sitting behind the steering wheel of a blue Aston Martin convertible. "Can I offer you a lift?" continued "Hello there". "Maybe find a spot for a cup of coffee?"

"Er ... I'm with someone," I called back.

"Lucky someone!" replied "Hello there". "Next Saturday perhaps?"

Damn Julian and his wanting to be included! I thought as I quickly glanced around at the animated, psychedelic crowd, "But he seems to have disappeared?"

"Better jump in then," suggested "Hello there" leaning across and opening the passenger door, "There's a highly popular coffee shop near Sloane Square. I suggest we try our luck there!"

"Hello there" turned out to be Anthony Ward whose family owned a giant pharmaceutical company. Anthony would go on to become a longstanding friend.

*

"And where did you get to?" demanded Julian when I telephoned latish the next morning to apologise for "vanishing".

"I bumped into an old friend from Rhodesia," I murmured, "and one thing led to another."

"Will you be back in time for a visit to the Scarsdale?" came the piqued reply.

"No," whispered Anthony stretching luxuriously alongside me in the king size bed. "We're out to lunch."

"Sadly not, Jules," I said smiling into the phone, "Er . . . Alan, Alan Richards is meeting friends for lunch and I'm invited."

"I thought he was from Rhodesia?" sniped Julian.

"Rhodesians still have friends," I quipped, "Take me for example." There was a heavy silence. "It's his parents, they're also here on a visit," I said adlibbing wildly. "I'll catch up with you later."

Before Julian could respond I hung up.

"A late, lazy lunch I think?" suggested Anthony as we sat sipping Bloody Marys in the spacious, state- of-the-art-kitchen in Anthony's elegant Greet Street (Mayfair) apartment. "I suggest the Connaught Grill. They do a very good chateaubriand for two there!"

Anthony Ward epitomised the term "elegant man about town". He was also an inveterate gambler. Anthony introduced me to Aspinall's where Lady Luck again proved to be lurking in the shadows and to my utter delight I won an unbelievable £100. "You must have my winnings," I told an equally delighted Anthony, "after all I'm only here because of you!"

"Not at all," came the laughing reply, "put it down to your untapped expertise!"

Several days later I met Mrs Edwards, Anthony's chirpy, highly efficient housekeeper.

"If ever I need someone to look after my flat - or apartment - it would most definitely be you, Mrs Edwards," I jokingly told her.

"You only have to ask, Mr Anderson," replied Mrs Edwards seriously.

*

Anthony Ward called a few weeks later.

"I'd like you to meet a charming couple I know," said Anthony, "David and Georgina Ryott who live in St. John's Wood. They're having a party on Saturday and I thought you may like to come along?" He gave a gentle chuckle. "I'd also like you to meet Donald, Donald MacLeary. Someone I've been seeing quite a bit of recently."

"I'd love to, Anthony," I enthused; the thought of meeting a straight couple for once being somewhat of a novelty in my hectic gay social whirl.

David and Georgina owned a large, Georgian-style house with a delightful garden (this would play an important part later in the section headed *The French Erection*). Anthony duly introduced to Georgina, a somewhat patronising, matronly young woman dressed in a full-length red evening dress further complimented by her auburn hair which tumbled in a magnificent mane down her elegant back. Georgina eventually went on to change her hairsytle for a mere bob and a style of dress suggesting the red number could only have been a one off! (Further explained in *Caribbean Capers.*)

"How lovely to meet you Robin," she murmured greeting me with a condescending smile. David her husband, a flamboyant, arm waving Charlton Heston lookalike was also introduced by the ever attentive Anthony. *If you're not gay Mr Ryott,* I thought with an inward snicker, *then neither am I!* (David Ryott being referred to as DBR from now onwards, the B representing his middle name Bradford; the city of Bradford once the centre of the English textile industry. A somewhat pretentious choice I would have thought.)

"Is your friend Donald here?" I murmured eyeing the other guests and seeing if I could guess which of the milling young men could be the mysterious "I'm seeing quite a bit off recently".

"No, he'll be joining us after his performance enthused Anthony with a proud smile.

"After his performance?" I repeated, "Why, is he an actor?"

"No, he's one of the leading male dancers with the Royal Ballet at Covent Garden," replied Anthony. "As I've already told you, his name's Donald MacLeary."

"Oh," I said, my knowledge of male ballet dancers being limited to Rudolf Nureyev.

"Meanwhile come and meet Mrs MacLeary, Donald's mother. She's staying with me at Green Street."

I met DBR and Georgina's eldest daughter Henrietta who had been allowed to stay up for an hour "no longer" to enjoy the party. Her two younger sisters, Portia and Emma, were restricted to huddling on the stairs and peering at the "grownups at play" through the staircase balusters. DBR and Georgina hailed from Yorkshire. Georgina's maiden name was Armitage, making her a member of the Armitage-Shanks Company famous for their bathroom fixtures and plumbing supplies. Georgina's mother Mildred Armitage - a harridan I was unfortunate enough to meet - turned out to be the most outrageous snob rivalled only by her son-in-law and another equally supercilious woman named Cherry who appears later.

A much-repeated story concerning Mildred was her insistence the name Armitage be removed from the inside of any toilet bowls within the Armitage residence. As one builder is reported to have said; "Obviously the miserable old cow doesn't go in for the idea of people *genuinely* shitting on her!"

I got along amicably enough with Georgina but not so amicably with DBR who proceeded to become more arrogant (if possible), more camp and loud as the evening progressed. Added to which he seemed to spend an inordinate amount of time subjecting various young men attending the party to endless "arms around the shoulders" and a lot of back slapping. *Surely Georgina must know?* I kept thinking.

Much later I was introduced to Donald MacLeary, an athletic pouting princess if ever there was one. Anthony made it blatantly obvious he was besotted, enamoured, star struck or whatever with the handsome young dancer. Towards the end of the party Anthony surreptitiously asked if I could give Mrs MacLeary a lift back to Green Street. "Of course!" I replied sweetly casting the preening Donald surrounded by a group of adoring fans what I considered my best poisonous look.

Eventually Donald and I became firm friends and he and Anthony welcomed as regular visitors to Hedgerley, DLL's country house. DLL adored Donald and also adored another close friend of mine, an American named Ralph Enz. I am happy to say this adoration was equally bestowed on Anthony's Donald and Ralph's Donald (Donald Scheldrup) so how could I possibly be jealous?

An added surprise was to discover Donald lived close by to my flat in Ladbroke Square. With Donald a neighbour I did what Mrs Edward's (Anthony's housekeeper and Donald's cleaner) had suggested and duly "asked". Within days my flat at No 5 was subjected to the first of many sparkling cleanings.

Towards the end of my first year in London I received a letter from Shirley (Ritchie) who, having gained her LL.B was on her way to Europe where she would be spending a few months in Paris and Germany "to get an understanding of the language" before arriving in London in order to pursue a career in law. Shirley would also be linking up with Alan (Dashwood) from Rhodes and another contender for a career in law. I was looking forward to seeing the two of them but had to confess any enthusiasm for resurrecting the former Ritchie Set had cooled considerably. Another major event has also taken place; I had also met DLL for a second time.

I am not at all sure how Peter and George organised the invitation but I received an early morning call prior to my leaving for Niddry lodge. "Is that Robin?" said the warm, clear tenor voice.

"Speaking," I said cautiously and thinking, *it can't be?*

"David Lloyd-Lowles speaking. Er . . . we met again at Peter Carter's the other evening."

"*And* at Rex and Eric's before that!" I squeaked, blushing furiously. "Er . . . fun evening at Peter's, wasn't it?"

"Great fun," agreed DLL

So go on then! I thought, *get on with it!*

"Robin, its short notice and I don't know if you'd be interested but I have a few friends dining with me this evening and if you're free, perhaps you'd like to join us?"

"I'd *love* to!" I almost shouted followed by a more subdued, "David, I'd love to."

"Splendid!" came the jovial reply, "There's a restaurant - the Empress - situated at the top end of Berkeley Street which runs between Piccadilly and Berkeley Square. If you could manage to get there by eight o'clock, even better. If you ask for me - Colonel Lloyd-Lowles - they'll show you through to the private dining room where we'll be."

Colonel Lloyd-Lowles? I thought. A private room? How grand! And another chance to see the dazzling David despite being a last minute infill!

"Er . . . Robin?"

"Yes, David?"

"Are you sure you can manage to make your way there?"

"Yes; I'll take a Number 19 bus and jump off at the Ritz."

"Ah, I can see you're getting to know London's most important landmarks," replied DLL with a warm chuckle, "I am very much looking forward to seeing you again, young Robin."

"Me too David . . . I mean I look forward to seeing *you*, David; not me!" I stammered into the silent receiver. *"Yes!"* I whispered punching the air with my fist, "Yes!" Whispers as opposed to shouts as I simply had no wish having to deal with a prying and sulking Julian again.

*

"Ah yes, Mr Anderson; Colonel Lloyd-Lowles is expecting you," said the immaculately groomed maître d', "if you would please follow me sir."

I was led past the rather dull-looking main dining room restaurant through to an impressive-looking closed mahogany door on which the maître d' briskly knocked before showing me in to a second reception and dining area where a group of people stood talking animatedly.

All men? I thought, now there's a surprise Colonel and no wonder your dinner party's in a private room as opposed to the main restaurant!

My reaction on seeing DLL was as expected. A rapid increase in my heartbeat followed by a second and a third. This further sighting of the handsome, smiling man with his bulky frame and aura of *bonhomie* I knew - without a second doubt - DLL was destined to be a major factor in my life.

Having been introduced as "newly arrived from South Africa" I found myself seated - to my delight - between the author Beverley Nichols (his books had become favourite "escapisms" back in the rapidly receding Bulawayo) and a charming, moustachioed military-looking man named Julian Frisby who I was later informed owned a large "stockbroker Tudor-style house in Guildford". DLL's "guest of honour" and the main purpose for the dinner was an arrogant, large, loud-mouthed businessman, Mic Sandford, who lived in Italy. As I was again later informed Mic Sandford's offices were based in Rome where he resided during the week in a magnificent apartment overlooking the ruins of the *Teatro de Marcello*. Weekends were spent at *Il Bacio,* his spectacular sixteenth century overlooking Florence.

A particularly glamorous guest was a dark, brooding, gypsy looking young man with the unlikely name of Tony Hutt (*How very un-gypsy,* I thought" *Surely a Carl or a Heathcliff instead of a mundane Tony Hutt?*). Thanks to Julian's proud murmurings I was soon to discover Tony was Julian's "friend" who, when not visiting Julian in Guildford, lived a bohemian existence doing "a variety of things" in "remote Islington".

DLL's three remaining guests were a bluff, hearty and decidedly drunk Cyril Butcher (Beverley's partner), an embarrassingly fey, bespectacled man, Dudley (a doppelgänger for a gay tapeworm), who kept staring at me with disapproval and "tut-tutting" audibly with a distinct shaking of his sinuous head and a frail young Irish redhead called Breffni Henry. The demure Breffni sat silently throughout dinner, his very unsmiling Irish eyes fixed firmly on his dinner plate!

I wonder what Miss Leprechaun's doing here apart from looking decorative? I thought waspishly. *Oh no, it can't be? What if he's David's other half?*

Apart from a curious glance at the odalisque Breffni I sat pondering who I had replaced as the mysterious "at the last minute" guest. *Another Breffni perhaps or, God forbid, another 'Miss If Looks Could Kill' Dudley?*

Dinner ended with Mic Sandford saying brashly, "You must bring Robin to stay at *Il Bacio* David, I'm sure he and Mouse would get on." His loud, unexpected comment followed by Dudley's hissed rebuke, "I think *Leslie* may have something to say about *that,* Michael!"

It suddenly clicked; I *knew* where I had heard the name Lloyd-Lowles before. It was back in Johannesburg where Colin Fletcher during his endless name dropping of Leslie French the English actor and his annual productions of various works by Shakespeare at the Maynardville Theatre, would inevitably mention his wealthy English businessman partner David Lloyd-Lowles.

I glanced at the group making ready to leave. *Oh well,* I thought despondently, *now I unfortunately remember Colin's interminable adulation regarding Maynardville, Leslie French and David Lloyd-Lowles this really can only be a severe case of 'Much Ado About Nothing'. Just wait until I tell Julian. Talk about having the last laugh!* I gave a self-pitying gulp. *David Lloyd-Lowles is spoken for; Julian Frisby has his gypsy; Mic Sandford has his odd sounding Mouse; Beverley's got his slurring Cyril . . . which leaves 'Must Be Avoided At Any Cost' acidic Mistress Dudley or the beautiful Breffni who is not my cup of tea at all!*

Having sulkily thanked DLL for "a memorable dinner" and said my "goodbyes" (Dudley deliberately turning away when spoken to) I stalked off in order to catch my reliable Number 19 bus. *So much for my pipe dream of a few hours ago,* I thought as we rumbled around Hyde Park Corner, *Oh David, dear lovely cosy David, why did there have to be someone else?*

*

By this stage Shirley had arrived in London. Excited at the thought of seeing her again plus hearing her (hopefully) indiscreet exploits during her brief sojourns in Germany and France, we arranged to meet "at the Stockpot" on the coming Sunday for a cheap and cheerful lunch. Shirley was emphatic neither Julian nor Alan would be joining us. "I have *stacks* to tell you!" she cried, "none of which Craggs or Dashwood would approve!"

To my surprise and chagrin (after all he had been two timing innocent me!) DLL telephoned early the following morning apologising firstly for calling so early and secondly for subjecting me to such a "heavy dinner party".

Ignoring my pathetic protestations about the dinner not being "heavy at all" he surprised me even more by saying, "If you happen to be free on Sunday would you like to come down to the country for lunch? Just us; no surprise guests I promise!" The latter comment accompanied by a warm chuckle.

"I would have loved to," I replied, "but I can't." *Oh shit*, I thought, *he'll immediately think I'm playing hard to get?* I quickly went on to explain about Shirley, our closeness at university and her subsequent arrival in London along with the fact we'd arranged to meet for "a gossipy lunch on Sunday."

"Why not invite Shirley?" suggested DLL. "If she's a friend of yours she must be fun. Do you want to call her and then call me back?" He gave a further chuckle. "You'd be travelling down by train and as the journey takes an hour you've plenty of time for a gossip!"

Shirley said an immediate "yes" (I had already told her about DLL but not about the latest developments). I promptly called DLL back with the good news and dutifully made a note of the instructions for getting there; namely the Piccadilly Line from Earl's Court to Uxbridge.

We were both hugely excited at our pending venture into the English countryside but not nearly excited as Shirley was with her latest purchase; a pair of high-heeled, knee length, trendy black, high heeled leather boots and the current rage.

A smiling DLL was waiting for us at Uxbridge Station accompanied by a panting, tail wagging liver and white Cocker Spaniel. After warmly welcoming us DLL went on to introduce Shirley and me to Borgie who, as DLL went on to explain, was named after a river in Scotland, famous for its salmon fishing. Talking excitedly - DLL and Shirley were already chatting away as if old friends - we clambered into David's dark green MK10 Jaguar, Shirley firmly ensconced in the passenger seat and me in the back with my new best friend Borgie! Leaving the busy motorway near to the turn-off for Gerrards Cross we drove on for a few miles through the wooded countryside before reaching the start of a leafy, country lane. "Here we are," announced DLL as we approached a pair of gleaming white painted gates fronted by a small, neatly trimmed lawn boasting a white painted flag pole. "Welcome to Hedgerley!"

Busily chatting to our host we entered a long, low ceilinged corridor and following DLL, made our way directly into a cosy study with a cheerful, crackling fire, a brightly patterned chintz-covered sofa, two comfortable-looking leather armchairs and an enormous, leather-topped desk. I sat bedazzled by DLL; so much so I didn't pay much attention to our arrival and my surroundings apart from thinking, *A lovely room but a bit small for a sitting room. More cottagey than anything else with maybe a bedroom or two above. Rich businessman Colin? Oh well . . .*

DLL dutifully offered us drinks from a collection of decanters set on a large drinks tray. "Sherry or something stronger?" After a few minutes Shirley was happily instructing a bemused DLL on the pros and cons of ladies boots while I sat quietly fondling Borgie's ears and thinking, *At least it's a free lunch if nothing else* and *Jesus Shirley, I'd quite forgotten how you can go on once you get the bit between your teeth!*

A motherly, bustling woman knocked lightly before entering and saying briskly, "Lunch is served, Colonel."

"Thank you Mrs Horsfall," DLL replied. "Drink up," he added. "If I remember correctly we're starting with cheese soufflés and Mrs Horsfall would never forgive us if we allowed them to collapse!"

The dining room situated at the one end of the long, entry corridor proved to be an eye-opener with two walls filled with David's collection of colourful ceramic furniture rests of which there were literally dozens lined up on a series of shelves. (For the record, the soufflés did *not* collapse and the lunch plus wine was sublime!)

During lunch DLL gave us a brief history of the cottage (I was right!). Dating back to the fifteenth century it had been originally used as a hunting lodge and its claim of fame was its ghost who appeared with alarming regularity on a specific night. "But not tonight," said DLL with a chuckle, "as we have nobody staying in the ghost's favourite room!"

(My chilling experience with the infamous Hedgerley ghost can be read in my collection of short stories, *006+6+6 Volume 2 - A Tudor Tale*.)

"Right; coffee and liqueurs!" announced DLL rising from his chair.

"Coffee and liqueurs it is!" yodelled a well-fortified Shirley as she teetered from the dining room in DLL's wake with a tail-wagging Borgie and me in tow.

Still following the narrow corridor which now veered to the right we entered a small vestibule before proceeding through a high arch leading into one of the most enchanting rooms I had seen to date. On our arrival I had failed to notice a matching double storied wing to our left which had been designed to cleverly blend in with the original cottage. Later, on closer observation, I would note there had been two substantial additions (or wings) built; one to house DLL's extravagant bathroom and dressing room above a state-of-the-art kitchen and the other to house the splendiferous drawing room in which we were now standing.

The far wall facing us boasted a splendid carved pine mantelpiece with a cheerfully burning log fire and a feature to end all features, a recessed mullioned window centred above the fireplace! The first half of the spectacular room soared the full height of two floors and was reached by a staircase leading to a book-lined gallery and an en suite guest room. On a future visit I would learn the majority of leather bound books lining the gallery were embellished with magical fore-edge paintings. A fore-edge painting being the skilful technique of painting a scene on the front edge to the pages of a book, the artwork or "painting" only viewable when the pages are fanned out.

The walls were painted in a soft apricot "drag" effect with furnishings in lime green (not the glaring acidic green as suggested by JS for the Tap and Die boardroom), burgundy and tapestry weaves. Several Impressionist-style paintings and glowing pieces of mahogany and satinwood furniture completed the warm, eclectic picture. A row of Gothic-styled windows and a pair of matching doors opened on to a paved terrace bedecked with stone tubs chockablock with flowering shrubs.

"David, this is *fabulous*," I breathed.

"*Fabulous!*" echoed Shirley taking a hefty sip of Drambuie.

"I'll show you the garden after we've finished our coffee," suggested DLL, "then we're on to see Eggy, my brother-in-law, for tea before I take you back to the station."

One side of the beautifully presented garden with its glowing flowerbeds (reminiscent of dear Peggy and Randolf) was bordered by a ha-ha obviously there to keep out the cows seen grazing contentedly in the neighbouring field.

"And what's over there?" demanded Shirley pointing at a long, tiled building as she teetered dangerously on her high heeled boots while gamely clinging to the glass containing the remnants of her Drambuie.

"An outdoor dining room, kitchen and changing rooms serving the swimming pool," explained DLL. "We spend most of summer, come rain or shine, out by the pool."

We, being Madam bloody French I suppose? I thought uncharitably. *But despite the hovering spectre of Little Leslie Sunshine Hedgerley becomes more attractive by the minute!*

Eggy, Vice Admiral Eric Longley-Cook, turned out to be a charming, silver-haired man who seemed utterly mesmerised by the shrieking, Drambuie-infused Shirley and her boots!

"So what did you think? I asked Shirley as we collapsed onto the banquette seating in the train.

"Think? I think David's quite, quite divine!" carolled Shirley.

"So do I Shirley," I grinned in reply. "So do I!"

*

With my stint at Niddry Lodge coming to an end I quickly adapted to my role of "Super Salesman" in the tinselly Harrods Toy Fair "Will he or won't he?" I kept asking myself. The million dollar question being an invitation from DLL to spend Christmas alone with him at Hedgerley. Unfortunately this was not forthcoming following DLL's matter-of-fact announcement he would be spending the coming festivities in Cape Town.

All was not lost however thanks to an out of the blue telephone call from Kenneth Villiers. "I have a couple of friends staying for Christmas and if you don't mind sleeping on the sofa once again, you're more than welcome dear Robin to spend the holiday with us?" he fluted.

Julian, much to my relief, had been invited to stay with "*the* most amusing friends" and Shirley with friends equally as entertaining which saw me under no obligation to spend any time with either.

Ken's houseguests included a rather withdrawn misery named Alan Davies who had something to do with television and his nondescript friend who also worked in the media. Two other couples joined us for a splendid Christmas Day lunch served by MH looking somewhat ludicrous wearing a pink crepe paper crown, a sweater decorated with a jolly Santa's face and a pair of worn jeans displaying what could only be described as Santa's most challenging chimney combined with a burgeoning sack of toys.

It came as no surprise I spent most of my time thinking about DLL and wondering what he and friend French were up to. By this stage I had done my homework and learned more about the mystery man I now regarded as a major rival. Leslie French had originally been a child actor, singer and dancer whose heyday appeared to have been in the twenties and thirties. He also appeared in the Old Vic and the Open Air Theatre in Regent's Park where he was noted for his roles as Puck in *A Midsummer Night's Dream* and Ariel in *The Tempest.* I was suitably stunned on discovering the dreaded Leslie had been the nude model for the statue of Ariel which decorates the façade of the BBC's Broadcasting House. Some rival!

My venture into the unexpected, spiteful atmosphere of The Kent Gallery saw my mind focussing with some alarm on the unintended world I seemed to have landed myself into. Having envisaged endless days of learning the ins and outs of interior design and assembling a basic knowledge of antiques, I found instead a world of ugly slights and spitefulness with Spillane having no idea of how to advise or encourage a person in either field; the man appearing to inhabit a world of hatred and self-hate. The only saving grace during my stay at The Kent Gallery was Pip Pelham, the kindly, general dogsbody-cum-accountant who appeared to act as a constant buffer between Spillane, me and the various tradespeople.

However - as they say - difficult though it may be one should give credit where credit's due and it was through Spillane I had the good fortune to meet Charles Ribon, a wealthy American living in Paris, who was voluntarily visiting Spillane (something I found hard to believe). Charles had wandered into the showroom where he announced with a soft lisp he had arranged to meet Spillane before going out to lunch.

"Ah yes," said Pip quaveringly, "Roland's running late Mr Ribon, so if you wouldn't mind waiting . . ."

"Of course," replied Charles, "I'll take a seat in the showroom." He glanced over to where I was making myself look busy by rearranging the pattern books for the umpteenth time. "Hello," said Charles proffering a delicate hand, "I'm Charles Ribon; and you are?"

Charles and I were soon deep in conversation about South Africa and Southern Rhodesia when repellent, roly-poly Spillane breezed in. "Oh Charlie!" he mewed, piggy eyes narrowing, "There yew are! Sorrrie aye em late en how naughtie of yew to be talking to mai staff when they should be werking!" Before Charles could respond Spillane loudly announced they simply "hed to flay" in case they "lost their tabil".

Several hours later the two returned; Spillane puce-faced and elocuting more than ever with a decidedly uncomfortable and nervous-looking Charles obviously desperate to escape from his host's endless ear-splitting shrieks of laughter. Making sure I was within hearing Spillane flashed me a malevolent glance as he came to the end of a particularly barbed recitation finishing with "so I hed no choice but to mek do with a wet behind the eerrs *Rrrhodesian* es decent staff is impossible to faind these deys".

After a smirking Spillane had excused himself to go the "the little boyz rrroom" Charles - obviously unaware Spillane had been overheard - lispingly announced with a benevolent smile, "You must come to Paris as my guest one weekend, Robin. In fact, I've already suggested this to Roland and he readily agreed."

Spillane agreed for me to go to Paris as Charles' guest? I thought. *But of course, not only is Charles immensely rich (Bolivian silver) he's also a great friend of Henri Samuel, the famous French interior designer Spillane's always banging on about. No doubt Madame Defarge imagines my going to Paris with his so-called blessing will show him to be a benevolent, caring employer as opposed to the pond slime he really is. However, in vino veritas and his tactless comments a few minutes ago show he's probably forgotten Charles's invitation.*

"While you were downstairs I told Robin about you agreeing with my suggestion he should come to Paris for a weekend so Tom and I can show him the sights," lisped Charles when a puffing Roland reappeared.

"Oh yes! A lovely idea of maine don't yew think, Rrrobin?" trilled Spillane, licking his thin lips lizard- like with his pink, pointed tongue.

"Oh yes Roland; a lovely idea and thank you. I'd love to. Most unexpected and *so* kind."

*

Charles turned out to be an impeccable host and Tom, his "buddy, buddy" American" friend (a professionally "resting student"), a total charmer. Both were determined I should see all the sights, enjoy a show at the Lido (a hint of things to come!) and enjoy dinner on a *bateaux mouche* as Paris slowly drifted by. Charles and Tom also introduced me The Louvre and Leonardo da Vinci's "must see" Mona Lisa. My first reaction on seeing the much lauded portrait was a muttered "God, it's so *small!*" and second, "Forget her famous so-called mystical smile; she looks so *dull.* More of a *moaner* than a Mona."

I much preferred Caravaggio's rumbustious boy bitten by a lizard. Not dull and more of a camp screamer than a moaner!

Charles had previously arranged a small lunch party in his beautiful Avenue Foch apartment designed by the aforesaid Henri Samuel where I was now the unexpected guest. Among the other guests was the writer Graham Greene and a shrewish-looking woman named Jeanne Stonor who apparently irritated Green by her constant claims they were having an affair! The only two things I can remember about Graham Greene was how tall he was and how dull whereas the only two things I can remember about Jeanne Stonor is how short she was and how *dull.* Years later when dining with Margaret, Duchess of Argyll, I happened to mentioned meeting the couple at Charles Ribon's lunch in Paris, Margaret's quick riposte had been a witty, "Jeanne Stonor having an affair with Graham Greene? Why, she couldn't even have an affair with her husband!"

As expected, Spillane's behaviour following my "prrresent of a trrrip to Parrris" was appalling with non-stop hissy fits, insults and tiny tantrums following one another at breakneck speed. *I must get out of here,* I kept thinking to myself and at the same time, *but where?*

Again, it was all very well meeting people through the likes of Peter Carter and Rex and Eric but I really needed to meet some people of my own age. Of course I could have rung Julian Frisby's "gypsy" but bohemian Tony wasn't exactly what I had in mind. Anthony Ward was a charmer but then again his social world of gambling and gentlemen's clubs was totally alien to my limited world of antiques and design.

DLL by this stage had returned from Cape Town and to my immense delight become a firm fixture in my life with endless weekends spent with him and Borgie at Hedgerley and fun meetings in London along with regular breakfasts at the glamorous Chelsea Room at the Carlton Tower Hotel overlooking Cadogan Gardens. During the heady year when I found myself spending more and more time with DLL there followed second somewhat ill-fated visit to Paris leading to a further series of explosions from the seismic Spillane.

I would be wrong if I said I hadn't met up with any people of my own age (apart from Craggs) for there were meetings with Shirley and Alan but no young people actually living in London. All this was soon to change all thanks to Christopher Hunter's magical La Popote. After my win at Aspinall's Club (again my thanks to Anthony Ward) I decided it was time to "paint the town" but with who? Then it came to me, why *not* Julian Frisby's gypsy Tony? Not only was he dark, dashing and devilishly handsome he would also be the perfect complement to blond, lissom me! Without a doubt we would be one of the most glamorous - and hopefully *talked* about - couples in the restaurant . . . (!)

Tony accepted my dinner invitation with alacrity. "I was going to call you," he cheerfully lied, "but I imagined you'd be *far* too busy to want to meet up with an old roué like myself!"

Old roué, I thought, *you can't be more than thirty?*

Tony suggested we meet at The Enterprise, a pub in Walton Street and "a stone's throw away" from La Popote. "See you there around seven thirty?"

"Seven thirty," I said before adding grandly, "I'll reserve a table for eight."

"I thought it was going to be just the two of us?" quipped Tony.

"Just the two of us at eight," I solemnly replied, no doubt leaving my dinner guest trying to work out whether I'd got the joke or was just a simple Colonial after all.

The subsequent evening turned out to be pure and utter magic. "At last the golden boy returns!" carolled Christopher dancing over to greet us as we entered the atmospheric, candlelit, purple-coloured restaurant with its giant ceiling hanging of pink and purple paper flowers. "And not only returns but brings his very own Arabian prince with him!"

Noticing my surprise at his warm, flamboyant greeting, Christopher added with a further carolling, "We all thought that wicked fairy Old Mother Crabtree and Doctor Faustus must have spirited you away after showing you off a few weeks ago but here you *are*!" (I would never forgot Christopher's warm welcome that evening; the first of endless dozens.)

"I'm seating you *here*!" he announced leading us to a centrally positioned, purple-covered banquette faced by a pair of spindly gold chairs.

Whisking away a *reserved* sign he pulled out the table covered in a pink linen table cloth resplendent with purple linen napkins and a glowing candle (the table obviously reserved for dining VIPS!). "A glass of champagne; on the house, Mrs A?" suggested Christopher.

Mrs A? I remember thinking. *Who on earth is Mrs A?*

"I didn't realise I was having dinner with a star?" whispered Tony teasingly giving my knee a furtive squeeze, "Julian was right after all."

Julian right after all? I thought, flushed with excitement by Christopher's exuberant greeting and now Julian's mysterious compliment.

"Right about what?" I asked reaching nonchalantly for my flute of champagne.

"You're obviously going to be a 'somebody'. David Lloyd-Lowles' words as well before you arrived the other evening! What is it you do? Julian thought an interior designer perhaps?"

"Yes Tony," I replied modestly, "an interior designer in the making, ha ha!"

"Tony *dahling*! What on *earth* are you doing here so out of place in the middle of sophisticated civilisation?" brayed a voice.

"Barry!" exclaimed Tony quickly rising to his feet in order to give the pink-faced, silver-haired Liberace lookalike a delicate kiss on his subtly made-up cheek, "And in answer to your question I'm the guest of this charming young gentleman; Robin Anderson! Robin, Barry. Barry, Robin."

"You must be a very rich young man if you can ask *him* out!" brayed Barry flashing a mischievous, whiter-than-white smile. "I'm here with the Leggatt and a few other jaded souls; join us for a drink after you've finished dinner." Said as a statement and not a question. Giving me an arch look and raising a perfectly plucked eyebrow he added with a further braying, "On me of course. Knowing Mr Hutt here you probably wouldn't have had any money left *anyway*!"

Perhaps they're all thinking Tony's my handsome, paid for escort for the evening? I thought proudly. *And as I'm too young to be Tony's sugar daddy I wonder what else they could be calling me? His* very *young fairy godmother perhaps?*

Tony continued to regale me with wild tales concerning Morocco (they made Kenneth's MH look not much of a MH after all!) and his "sexploits" in India with Goa being a "must". He was interrupted on numerous occasions by strangers (to me) stopping by our table to say "hello". One couple in particular couple, a smiley, blond, pock-marked American named Ralph and his tall, lean, auburn-haired Australian companion with matinee-idol looks named Don striking an immediate chord. I gave Tony a discreet, sideways glance, *God, and there I was Tony thinking* you *were the best looking guy in the room? Forget it; Don whoever wins hands over!*

"Mrs Griggs says ready when you are!" called Chris dancing over to the table "She's ordered champagne; Dom Perignon would you believe? Madam must have won the pools!"

There was a sudden hush within the busy restaurant resulting in Christopher making a deft pirouette in order to face and greet the cause of the abrupt silence.

"Margot!" he trilled, reaching for the petite woman's velvet evening cape, "And Rudi! How absolutely *superly* lovely to see you!"

"It's Margot Fonteyn and Rudolf Nureyev," I whispered excitedly as Christopher - manipulating the cape as if he was a toreador facing a snorting bull - finally handed it over to one of the waiters. This was followed by a similar performance involving Rudolph's full length black mink coat.

"Yes, they hang out here quite a lot," replied Tony nonchalantly. He took a sip of the house white before adding matter-of-factly, "Everybody who's *anybody* sooner or later (he gave my thigh a definite as opposed to furtive squeeze) comes to La Popote!"

Thanks to DLL I had already sat enchanted through several performances by the Royal Ballet at Covent Garden starring the legendary Nureyev and Fonteyn. What used to add to the glamour of every performances were the seemingly endless curtain calls the pair received from the rapturous audience and the stage itself ending up a foot deep in tossed roses, bouquets and programmes

We quickly moved to join Barry and "the Griggettes" as Tony billed them where I immediately found myself caught up in a completely magical and over-the-top world of camp and more camp: black drag Denise in Cape Town a very far cry from the Griggettes and La Popote!

Shrieked comments such as "Miss Hartnell almost had a *heart* attack at the sheer size of him" and "As for Mother Crabtree and her penchant for licking guardsmen's boots - a proper Miss Nugget on all fours if you ask me!" appeared to be never-ending. I sat dazzled for at last I had found the world I wanted to be in and share. As I later said to DLL, here the witty fast flowing non-stop bitchy asides and jibes were said in jest and therefore quite harmless; unlike Spillane's sickening spat venom. As far as I was concerned Eric would have chortled with fiendish delight at such a comment, as would have Norman Hartnell.

It was almost two o'clock in the morning when we stood on the pavement saying our "goodnights". Among the last to leave were Ralph and his dishy Don. After chatting for a few minutes Ralph, drawing me aside so we were out of earshot of the others, suggested I meet him and Don back at La Popote the following Saturday for lunch. I immediately accepted.

"How about breakfast in Islington?" suggested Tony as we waved off Barry and his friend; the two having somehow managed to stumble into a waiting taxi.

"Why not?" I replied with a grin and feeling deliciously decadent at the thought of breakfast in licentious Islington. With a gypsy!

"With luck there may be a night bus from Hyde Park Corner," said Tony. "It isn't that far a walk."

"Why not take a taxi?" I said grandly; the wad of money in my breast pocket obviously burning the proverbial hole. "After all it's not every day - or night - one gets invited to breakfast in Islington!"

*

"You went home with Tony Hutt?" gasped Ralph when we met for lunch the following Saturday, "But he's got a black cock?"

Despite Ralph and Don's questioning looks I chose to remain schtum.

*

Peter Leggatt, one of Barry's dinner companions, had also suggested the two of us should meet up again. Dark-haired and a bit run-of-the-mill as opposed to good-looking - plus a bit on the beefy side - Peter had kept us entertained with the trials and tribulations of a mysterious "Lady Dee" and her whippet. "Like two peas in a sod!" he quipped. "Skin and bone but never alone!"

"Let's meet on Monday if you're free," he suggested. "You're Pont Street I think I heard you say so I suggest the Queen's Head in Tyron Street, off the King's Road. You can't miss it. Would around sixish be okay for you?"

I assured Peter "sixish" would be fine.

Talk about a successful evening, I kept thinking. *Not only have I met some really fun people, they're also incredibly nice!*

The Queen's Head was situated on the corner of Tryon Street and to my (delighted) surprise Anderson Street which in turned linked the King's Road to elegant Sloane Avenue. Looking at the row of small terraced houses lining Anderson Street I made a Scarlet O'Hara-like vow, "One day I am going to buy No 10. Robin Anderson residing at No 10, Anderson Street would be quite a coup, *n' est ce pas?* (The latter said in tribute to my two visits to the city of "Ooh la la").

*

Peter was standing chatting amiably to an extremely fey, blond young man dressed in a pale blue flared jacket, floral-patterned shirt, beige flared trousers and buckled shoes. Apart from being a study of sartorial elegance the young man stood surveying the other drinkers as if he, quite literally, had a highly pungent smell under his decidedly *retroussé* as opposed to aquiline nose.

"Ah Robin! Here you are!" Peter called jovially, "Come and meet William; William Davis better known as Lady Dee!" *Ah, the famous or infamous Lady Dee of whippet fame,* I thought immediately calling to mind a smutty schoolboy rant of "whip it in; whip it out; wipe it!" Looking at the smirking Lady Dee it was hard to resist a snigger. *I very much doubt if her ladyship here has ever* whipped *it in her preference being for a big, butch and brutal someone else to definitely whippet in, whippet out and wipe it!*

On my being introduced Lady Dee gave a faint sneer of acknowledgement before continuing to stare superciliously at the colourful, boisterous scene around us.

"You must forgive Lady Dee's standoffish attitude," murmured Peter with a mischievous wink, "but ever since people have started telling her she's a dead ringer for a young Edward, Prince of Wales, she's become even more grand than grand!"

"Despite *looking* like a younger Prince of Wales I would have thought more of a whippet Wallis!" I quipped, my sharp reply catching both Peter and myself by surprise. *Wow!* I thought, *one up to you Robin and long may it continue!*

"I ordered a bottle of white wine, a rather passable Sauvignon Blanc," said Peter, "Would you care -for a glass or would you prefer something else? William - Lady Dee - is having a martini."

Now there's a surprise? I thought sarcastically. "Thank you Peter, a glass of wine would be great."

"Ah, and here's Jeremy, Jeremy Benstead" laughed Peter as one of the more vitriolic and decidedly vindictive "Griggettes" from Saturday night appeared. Peter and I, along with Jeremy, stood chatting animatedly about Saturday evening and making various comments about the extrovert drinkers around us.

"My turn," I said interrupting Peter as he was about to order another bottle of wine. I turned to the still staring Lady Dee. "William? Another martini?"

Whether it was me referring to William by his correct name as opposed to the ridiculous Lady Dee, I received a surprised glimmer of a smile. "I wouldn't say 'no' to another of their questionable martinis, thank you Robin," he replied turning his full attention to me (Peter was back to chatting with Jeremy), "Peter tells me you're a designer."

"A designer in the making," I laughed, ruefully thinking, *But not if the odious Spillane has anything to do with it.* "And what do you er . . . do, William?" thinking wickedly, *Apart from not whippet it, whippet out and wipe it!*

"I'm an artist," William replied taking a disdainful sip of his questionable martini.

"Oh?" I said, "And what medium do you work in? Watercolours or oils?"

From them on I could do no wrong with William positively blossoming. *You really are quite pleasant once one gets through all that la di dah flam,* I thought taking another sip of wine.

"Dinner!" announced Peter, "where shall we go for dinner?" The answer was unanimous! Half an hour later we were being greeted by a smiling, prancing, dancing Christopher. "Mrs Leggatt, Mistress Benstead, Lady Dee and Mrs A all here on a Monday?" he carolled, "Bring on the marines, the tambourines and any other 'marines' you can think of! Welcome you extravagant band of pilgrims! Welcome to La Popote!"

*

Dinner passed far too quickly and on my return to Abingdon Road I was suddenly plunged into a deep, dark depression. *So near and yet so far,* I thought. *If it hadn't been for Anthony's win at Aspinall's the other week* (I was still finding it hard to accept the fact I had personally won a hundred pounds) *I could never have invited Tony Hutt to La Popote and thanks again to Anthony's win I was able to stand a round of drinks and pay my share for dinner tonight.* Dolefully preparing a mug of Ovaltine I murmured to the silent kitchen, "However, Anthony's win isn't going to last forever; talk about having to grin and bear it . . . Damn!" I added banging down the spoon on the Formica countertop, "Pull yourself together Anderson! Whatever it takes I'm bloody well going to make it in the world of interior design and if spitty, shitty Spillane has to be the first step, so be it!"

The sight of William Davis' handsome, petulant face suddenly came to mind. "However, not rich in the way Lady Dee, William Davis or the Prince of Wales as he - or she - sees himself or herself as rich," I confided to the silent kitchen. "I have no more desire to be a kept bum boy than fly to the sodding moon!"

After dinner Peter couldn't wait to tell me about William being the notorious Michael Pitt-Rivers' toy boy or *poule de luxe*! (In 1954 Pitt-Rivers, Lord Montagu of Beaulieu and Peter Wildeblood had been charged with "conspiracy to incite certain male persons to commit serious offences with male persons" or "buggery" with all three receiving jail sentences.) "Either Lady Dee is very shrewd or else very stupid seeing Pitt-Rivers is a total control freak. At the end of the day, what Michel Pitt-Rivers says Lady Dee bloody well does and woe betide Her Ladyship if she doesn't. It wouldn't surprise me if, in a few years, Pitt-Rivers didn't make lady Dee give up her passion for painting."

Lying in bed and staring up at the barely discernible rosebuds on the ceiling I chided myself for being such a misery. "Look how lucky you are to have found David," I murmured, "and let's face it, even if he *did* offer to keep me I'd most certainly refuse. I want David to love me for me and me alone. Love me for what *I* achieve on my own bat and whatever I *do* achieve will be wholly down to me, the former Robert now the new Robin and unfortunately for the likes of disapproving, four-eyes Dudley, a 'star' in my own right'."

Before I drifted off to sleep I couldn't help thinking of darling Peggy and what *she* would have said. No doubt something of the stiff upper lip variety such as "Look on the bright side, Robert! Always look on the bright side!" or, if I was truthful. "Aargh Robert! Aargh!"

*

Even more determined to "look on the bright side" and "go it alone" I decided it was time for a definite a plan. A strategy which would see the former "Rhodesian and Rhodes Robert" now candidly graduating as the new "Ruthless Robin" with - if needs be – one or two or even more poison-tipped arrows!

"Don't join them, bloody well *beat* them!" I kept repeating to myself en route to another "Spiteful Spillane" day. My plans for the coming weekend were clear (unless, of course, there was a last minute invitation to Hedgerley). Dinners "yes" but lunches "no".

The first Saturday saw the new "Ruthless Robin" splendid several blissful hours revelling in the endless delights of the Victoria and Albert Museum. Whereas I will always remember the impact of first meeting Jacqueline Siddeley, Britt Ekland and Margaret, Duchess of Argyll and the three women's breathtaking beauty, the impact on viewing the Victoria and Albert Museum could easily have been the "material" equivalent.

In my colourful life I have seen many, many places of note; met many wonderful people and experienced many moments of awe but only a few stand out.

Material wise I most certainly rate the Victoria and Albert Museum followed by the sheer impact of walking into my first ever Jumbo jet- a Pan Am flight bound for New York - where I joined sixteen other passengers in the cavernous tourist section. In the early seventies package holidays were virtually unheard of which made flying even Tourist Class a delight! It may sound a ridiculous claim but it really was a reaction never to be experienced twice and therefore never forgotten.

From an architectural point of view the top slot must surely go to the Taj Mahal seen at sunrise as opposed to the much overrated "by moonlight". Quite wonderful. Second place must surely be the exquisite, rich red Torii Gate at the Itsukushima shrine as it stands reflected in the placid Inland Sea, some two hundred metres offshore the city of Hatsukaichi in the Prefecture of Hiroshima, Japan.

*

"Tell me about Winnie Portarlington?" I said to DLL as he, I and Borgie drove towards Earlywood, Winnie's palatial house near Ascot in Berkshire. This being my first visit DLL quickly briefed me about our Winnie, Countess of Portarlington, Portarlington beef (Australia), her reputation as a former society hostess and her eclectic style. The brief résumé followed by the curious comment; "Winnie's also mad about pugs; as you'll see by the silver."

Earlywood and Winnie most certainly lived up to their reputations when it came to style. I was fascinated to see an extensive use of plain sisal carpeting in the grandest of the rooms; but sisal carpeting adorned with cleverly positioned priceless Aubusson, Persian or Bokhara carpets and rugs. The furniture was equally as mixed with Biedermeir, elaborate Boulle work and fine Georgian pieces living happily together and embraced by a vast collection of towering Chinese lacquer screens. Nor was there any shortage of stunning paintings, bronzes and objet d'art and objet trouvé. However the pièce de résistance had to be the implausible figure of a giant, stuffed grizzly bear standing guard by the tall double doors leading to the main drawing room!

David Hicks would wax lyrical about Winnie Portarlington and her style and it was obvious where he got his inspiration for the use of sisal in many of his interiors. Several decades on I would take this a stage further where, with the help of a brilliant artist Colleen Berry, I would produce a hand-painted Aubusson-style sisal carpet for the study in Sally Burton's elegant Georgian town house along with a hand-painted, flower bedecked sisal stair carpet.

"Winnie's mad about pugs? A bit of an understatement don't you think?" I said laughingly to DLL as five, plump, yapping pugs bounded down the wide granite steps to greet us. Clambering from the car I bent down to pat a particularly snuffly, bug-eyed pooch while Borgie energetically began to sniff the curly tail end of another with the remaining three dancing, yelping and yapping around DLL's feet. "But what on earth do these five demented firecrackers have to do with silver?" I added glancing up at him.

"Patience Robble; patience," chuckled DLL heading up the steps to where an elderly butler, resplendent in his immaculate morning coat, stood waiting to greet us.

Winnie "received" us in a cosy, decidedly feminine study walled in a soft, terracotta-coloured toile du Jouy; the same print used again for the curtains and upholstery. It was start of an instant love affair between Winnie and me (platonic of course) when she said in her croaky voice, "If any of the puggies decide to jump up onto your lap and you don't mind - please note they're quite entitled to do so!"

A few minutes later I was trapped on a sofa with *two* pugs vying for the most comfortable position on my lap; a large glass of wine in one hand and my other hand gently fondling a very put out Borgie's ears as he sat on a priceless Persian rug gazing mournfully up at me.

Sitting down to lunch the mystery of the silver pugs was instantly solved. Three place settings had been arranged at the one end of the beautiful mahogany dining table which could have easily catered for twenty. Each setting comprised of the traditional silver cutlery (knives, forks and spoons) and a cluster of glasses with the addition of a silver pug pepper pot, silver salt shaker and a silver bow-legged pug carrying a mustard-pot. In competition to Bruno the bear guarding the entrance to the main drawing room each place setting was guarded by a pair of solid silver pugs.

Golly, I thought (I hadn't met Maggie by this stage so my somewhat bland vocabulary had still to be taken over by an infusion of four letter words), *should Winnie ever entertain twenty for dinner there would have to be twenty silver pepper pugs, twenty silver salt pugs, twenty silver mustard-pot carrying pugs and forty guard pugs. A hundred pugs in all!* I gave a small snigger having suddenly noticed the two sets of silver candelabra had a number of silver pugs frolicking around their bases. *Plus their puggy friends lifting their legs against the bases to the candelabra!*

"What a fabulous old lady," I said to DLL as we sailed down the drive (Borgie having promptly moved from his usual position on the back seat and lying defiantly across my lap), "and what a fabulous house. I can't thank you enough David for introducing me to such a special friend and lady."

"And Winnie's only the beginning Robble; only the beginning," replied DLL with a warm smile.

In addition to Eggy (Eric Longley-Cook) who had been married to DLL's sister, Dickie, I was also introduced to a niece, a reserved, red-headed young woman called Freya and her hail-fellow-well- met husband Christopher. Freya and Christopher were always excruciatingly polite on meeting me but it was obvious I was regarded not only as an intruder on Leslie French's territory but also as "one of those conniving young queers who can only be around for what he can get out of poor David".

Another supposed relative I could never work out was the glamorous Pepe Stratton who lived in a large Georgian house overlooking a forbidding private lake near "somewhere in Berkshire". Pepe didn't seem to do much except smile a great deal in a superior fashion.

After meeting the frigid Freya, the backslapping Christopher, the irrelevant Eggy and the supercilious Pepe, I kept thinking, *They're obviously only putting up with me because I'm with 'their' David and they dare not upset* King *David because - hopefully - he will be remember them in his Will So, okay, I'm an interloper but, unknown to them, an interloper who has no plan whatsoever of 'loping' off. Ever! But the million dollar question, what do they genuinely think of Leslie French and how genuinely do they accept him? Talk about a bunch of twenty two-faced arseholes!*

*

Several days later I had an "out of the blue" phone call from William Davis inviting me to dinner. I duly arrived at his apartment in Hornton Street opposite Niddry Lodge my former place of employment. While teaching at Niddry Lodge I had often noticed the imposing terracotta-coloured house opposite the school. I was soon to learn Michael Pitt-Rivers occupied the main house while William lived in the spectacular top floor apartment accessed by a private staircase leading up from a small walled garden with its own private entrance. Little did I know that within a few months I would be an "almost" neighbour following my move to Ladbroke Square.

As long as he isn't expecting me, of all *people to whippit in, whippet out and wipe it dinner could be fun!* I thought.

William had booked a table at the Caprice, another prestigious restaurant positioned behind the Ritz and noted for its illustrious clientele. My second surprise (the first being the invitation) was finding William the greatest fun; bitingly amusing and to coin a well-worn phrase, "the two of us got along like a house on fire" or as Peter Leggatt later wittily put it, "Two dizzy queens putting the world to slights!"

William was the proud owner of a Morris Oxford Estate and it was with great, wine-infused gusto, we drove on to La Popote for a nightcap. (No breathalysers in those halcyon days - or nights.) "Good heavens!" cried Christopher in greeting, "Lady Dee and Mrs A *together*? Now there's a marriage made in camp heaven!"

"Don't you simply *love* being rich?" giggled William opening his wallet and showing a heart-stopping array of one pound and five pound notes (Ten pound notes were still to be printed.)

Courtesy of Pitt-Rivers, of course! I thought bitchily followed by a mellowing, *What the hell? One day I'll be doing the same; only more discreetly and with my* own *money!*

The more I got to know William the more I began to realise apart from his camp carolled "Don't you simply *love* being rich" repeated *ad nauseam* his personal life was not the proverbial bed of roses he claimed it to be thanks to the extremely prickly Michal Pitt-Rivers. A man previously described by Peter Leggatt as a control freak.

I was invited by William for a weekend at Tollard Royal, Pitt-Rivers' elegant country house in Dorset, where I was suitably stunned at the complete change in the usually flamboyant Lady Dee. Gone was the dazzling butterfly as scoped on the London party scene and in its place a very timid, dull chrysalis giving no hint as to what colours lay in store on "hatching".

Conversation between William and Pitt-Rivers seemed to be a series of snapped "Bud (his nick-name for William) do this" or "Bud, don't do that" and I was horrified at seeing William, the dazzling young man about town, reduced to nothing more than a put-upon William: a simpering concubine.

A welcome relief to the strained weekend was lunch with society photographer Cecil Beaton at his home, Reddish House, near Broad Chalke in Wiltshire where Pitt-Rivers and Beaton seemed to spend the whole of lunch gleefully dissecting all and sundry. Later I was intrigued to discover Beaton, a bi-sexual, included among his female paramours the acerbic actress Coral Browne who in time would become a dear friend.

For all his posturing William - in between flaunting Pitt-Rivers' wealth - was a talented artist: a talent which was stifled and never allowed to flourish due the machinations of his domineering, sanctimonious "lover". (The term "lover" in inverted commas being deliberate.)

Unfortunately I have been privy to several such relationships. Perhaps, as with the others, William-cum-Lady Dee enjoyed being submissive and ordered about. A role I would never have auditioned for no matter how glittering the awards or rewards.

*

"Is there only this instant muck? Don't you have a coffee grinder?" asked an imperious female voice from the direction of the kitchen.

Oh no, I thought as I descended the staircase having spent my allocated time in our shared bathroom, *Not another of Julian's wretched 'I still can't decide whether I am or not' overnight lady friends from RADA?*

"No, there's only instant," I said as I rudely pushed open the flimsy, frosted glass kitchen door.

"Oh, and who are you?" demanded an overly plump, tousled brunette wearing one of Julian's Turnbull and Asser shirts.

"Robin Anderson. The other person who lives here," I snapped. "And you are?"

"The mystery woman," came the equally sharp reply followed by an imperious, "I won't bother with your instant coffee, thank you. Instead Jules will simply have to take me out for a civilised breakfast somewhere else instead." She eyed me disdainfully through a pair of mascara-smudged eyes. "I take it there *is* somewhere civilised round here?"

Not giving "mystery woman" the courtesy of a reply I stormed into my rosebud haven muttering in true new Ruthless Robin form, "Out to breakfast? With your figure madam you should be on a strict diet instead!

141

And as for *you* Julian, you with your bloody 'trials and errors', as soon as I can manage it I'm out of here!"

Meanwhile the trials and errors at The Kent Gallery showed no signs of letting up either. Apart from my two visits to Paris each day appeared to be similarly lacking in inspiration and boringly predictable. Spillane arrives. Spillane spits spite. Day progresses, Spillane bitches. Come the evening and thanks to my many new introductions, life sparkles.

Among the continuing "sparkles" were Peter Carter's always enjoyable dinner parties at his elegant South Eaton Place duplex. Among the never-ending of glamorous guests I met was the doppelgänger to Al Pacino's *Scarface*; a cynical American best described as Charlie B who having whispered in an aside during dinner he'd "like to run barefoot through my hair" went on to do so several hours later back at his lair in a luxurious but dull apartment in Harley Street.

Next morning I was introduced to Charlie B's flatmate, a cheerful, chunky, curly-haired Scotsman named Ian Marshal and (as I would soon learn) Scotland's answer to Casanova in a kilt. Referred to affectionately by his many friends as "the Marshallene" Ian became a close friend and was a frequent visitor to Hedgerley where he would proudly show off his latest paramour. Among the many I met through Ian - and there were *many* - was the actor Alan Bates (*Women in Love*) plus Peter Wyngarde of *Jason King* fame. Ian remained a close friend up until his untimely death from AIDS.

Ian also introduced me to Russell Rhodes who truly epitomised the charming American living abroad. A dashing Clark Gable lookalike, Russ had lived in Paris for several years before moving to Lowndes Square in London where he resided and entertained in great splendour aided and abetted by a sour-faced French housekeeper nickname "Misery Marie" specially "imported" from his former French apartment. While I enjoyed many luncheons and dinners with Russ during his sojourn in London my attempts to become a stand-in for Vivien Leigh never materialised; our relationship being one of friendship without any of Margaret Mitchell's anticipated huffing and puffing. Apart from being a major player in the complex world of advertising Russell also wrote several novels, two of which, *The Herd* and *The Styx Complex* I have in my "bookcase for specials".

Whenever I visited New York I would make sure I contacted the dashing Russell (Clark Gable) Rhodes who sadly died in 2010.

The advent of Bob Pelham-Borley (I see my meeting with Bob as an "advent") was to lead to two immediate mega changes in my life. My introduction to John Siddeley and a flat of my own in Reece Mews. A third mega event was DLL's insistence I move to yet another flat; this time a flat *sans* threatening peeping Toms and questionable skylights. Added to which I would need a car, not only for toing and froing between the new apartment and John Siddeley Limited plus - as DLL so rightly surmised - it would see a tremendous saving on those "return fares to Uxbridge"!

What a year it would turn out to be, and what changes. A proper flat of my own overlooking leafy Ladbroke Square, my own car and, to top it all, a dream job in the particular profession I so coveted. A dream job which, sadly, would eventually disintegrate into another Spillane-like nightmare.

5 LADBROKE SQUARE

Much to my amusement the building next door to No 5 was an old people's home which years later, would be gutted by a fire and quickly bought by some beady property developer. Today the refurbished building is considered one of the most prestigious (and expensive) blocks of flats in the whole of Notting Hill Gate.

My flat in Ladbroke Square became the first of my "dream homes" (little did I know thirty years on I would feature in a television series of the same title). Sitting snugly on the second floor (third floor in American "speak") *Maison* Anderson comprised of a small entrance hall with a spacious coat cupboard and smaller storage cupboard. To the left of the tiny hall was a bedroom and a sitting room; the two rooms sharing a tall, wide window overlooking the seven and a half acres verdant garden Square. I was fascinated to learn Ladbroke Square was originally a racetrack before being turned into gardens in the middle of the nineteenth century.

To the right hand side of the small entry hall was a bathroom and toilet; the bathroom boasting a crude gas-fired water heater which turned itself on and off at the opening and closing of the hot water taps. (At the time had no idea as to the significance of this archaic detail.) Next to the bathroom was the kitchen the narrow window overlooking a tree infested mews and, to my great amusement, the local police station complete with a large lantern with its blue lamp. Beyond the police station was the

Bayswater Road. Cross over the busy thoroughfare and you were in elegant Campden Hill Square, a much sought-after Kensington enclave. Had I been able to see *over* the hill and further I would have been able to view the former Niddry Lodge and William's apartment!

"Right Ruthless Robin," I said staring at the shabby interior, "it's all yours and for all those snide bitches waiting in the wings to have a laugh at my expense *I* plan to have the "last laugh" so let's do something truly unique!" Having studied the four areas I planned what I would like to do and having set myself a miniscule budget, I designed the first of many RA'S.

I was amazed at the generosity of the various tradespeople I had met within my first few months working with JS. At DLL's insistence I moved into his splendid "bachelor apartment" in Hay Hill, Mayfair (also Lesley French's "resting place" whenever he was in London) for two weeks while the flat was being decorated. The dull, beige sitting room was repainted in a rich pumpkin yellow with white woodwork and ceiling. On either side of the door two splendid shelving units were built and finished in white. The bedroom was papered in a burgundy and black drag finish (again with white woodwork) and a burgundy-painted ceiling. The bathroom was papered in a golden grass paper and the kitchen (in order to "bring the flat together") was a replica of the bedroom scheme. The door to the sitting room was scrapped and the three remaining doors were faced with mirror and drilled to take the impressive brass and rosewood swirl doorknobs.

Carpets? No problem.

"Let me see what cut-offs we have in the workrooms?" pondered John Skellorn, his "pondering" leading to a white carpet in the sitting room; a burgundy carpet in the entrance hall, bedroom and bathroom. For the kitchen John Skellorn put me in touch with a colleague who in turn supplied a white Amtico floor tile thus "bringing" the sitting room into the kitchen.

Not to be outdone "Fanny" Adams insisted on donating a pair of full-length, wall to wall, lined and interlined, French-headed white linen curtains for the sitting room and a splendid Roman blind in a burgundy and white stripe fabric for the bedroom. I used the same fabric for the handsome, fitted bedspread. Throwing caution (and budget) to the wind I ordered a severe, rectangular dark brown, faux leather bedhead and matching bed valance to complete my "dream fuckery" as Maggie so eloquently put it!

I obviously must have been back in favour with Lady Luck for "out of the blue" Jo Kanarek, one of JS's clients, asked me if I needed a bed as she and husband Brian had recently ordered a new one! "Yes please!" I said; thus ending up with an imposing queen size bed.

I promptly chucked out most of the furniture which came as part of the flat with the exception of a mahogany tallboy, a small mahogany desk and two small dark wooden bedside cabinets. The chest of drawers and two cabinets remained in the bedroom and the desk I repositioned to the left of the fireplace which fortunately had a plain wooden mantelpiece which I painted black.

Through another JS introduction, a cheerful metal worker named Ben West, I ordered a simple, low, X-frame table base in blistered steel which served as support for a large sheet of clear plate glass. In other words, a simple but stylish coffee table.

The kindnesses continued with Vic Furzer, an upholsterer, who agreed to supply a modern, square arm-style sofa at a ridiculously low cost. The sofa was duly covered in a striking Bargello print run off especially for me (another favour) by Martin Battersby at his Sphinx Studio in Brighton. Needless to say the colours printed on to the white linen background were black, brown, burgundy and pumpkin yellow.

In the kitchen, along with the existing fridge and gas stove, I introduced a pair of chrome A-frame bases found in a second hand furniture shop in Lots Road, on which I placed another substantial piece of plate glass for the top. Two white wire Bertoia style chairs with black, padded seats completed the setting.

To my immense surprise JS and Jacqueline suggested a housewarming present; their suggestion leading to a feeling of acute embarrassment as to what I *could* ask for! A set of glasses? A bedside lamp? It was Maggie who, in reply to JS's "what do you think he would like from the company as a moving in present?" (I was away from the office at the time) had drawled in her laconic voice, "Would like? What he *really* needs JS are two modern chairs to go on either side of his sofa. Rather like those two we originally supplied for Mrs 'Tiddlypops' and which she promptly rejected! You know who I mean? That miserable old bitch in Chelwood House. The one with the bad nose job!"

"Good idea, Maggie," replied JS. "The rejected ones. Where are they?"

"With N and A, I think?"

All thanks to Maggie's quicksilver thinking I became the proud owner of Mrs 'Tiddlypops" rejected chrome and brown leather Norreklit chairs.

*

"You *have* to meet Derek and Michael," said William during another of his "don't you simply *love* being rich" dinners: this time at The Ivy in St, Martin's Lane.

"*Poofty* and Michael," corrected Peter.

"Whatever," said William, "I'll arrange a little get-together; Derek has some sort of secretarial agency and Michael's simply rich. Something to do with paints - hee-hee - rather like me! Now, how about another bottle of The Widow?"

*

A few weeks later at Rex and Eric's lavish Christmas "bash" given at their home in Montpelier Square; the already over-decorated house even *more* decorated for the festivities with festoons of sparkling tinsel, elaborate garlands, reams of twinkling fairy lights and a glittering Christmas tree with a - surprise, surprise - fair on top, I was introduced to the dazzling Benedict James Colman.

"Ben Colman!" I exclaimed, staring at the smiley, burly blond young man, "BSAP Salisbury?"

"Eek!" replied Ben ("Eek" I soon discovered being a favourite expression of his), "How on earth did you know *that*?"

"I lived in Southern Rhodesia, in Salisbury, before I came to London," I replied matter-of-factly to the smiling charmer, "You caused quite a stir with rumours rife; some scandal perhaps?"

"Maybe, maybe," chuckled Ben. "Robin was it? (I gave a nod) Let's get another glass of this highly toxic punch and I will tell all!"

Rex and Eric had invited a small group to stay on for a late dinner and I was delighted to find myself seated next to the effervescent Ben. By the end of evening I felt as if I had known the irrepressible Ben forever; the real "brother" I never had. The sporty, thuggish, somewhat "thicko" Ian being more of a mean son of a bitch (literally!) and a bully to boot.

Ben was fascinated to hear I worked with John Siddeley. "Eek Robin! That poisonous closet queen? Don't be mistaken for you are very obviously no fool but as Alexander Pope wrote, *Fools rush in where angels fear to tread*! Be wary. Rather you than me!"

I was captivated by Ben and to my delight the feeling was reciprocated. At the time of our meeting Ben - despite being gay - was vaguely involved with a tense, over-hyped American girl with the strange sounding name of Kiki Botty. To quote one acidic young man whose advances had been firmly refused by the magnetic Ben, "It's all because of that stick insect American Botty bitch! God, if ever I get hold of her she'd get a kicking up her damn 'botty' all right!"

"Do you drive?" asked Ben.

"Yes, I have a car," I replied.

"What make?"

"A Mini."

"Pity," murmured Ben and left it at that.

As he was about to leave Ben gave a cheery smile and pressed a card into my hand. "Give me a call and let's meet up again. The sooner the better."

*

Like a ripple on the surface of a pond the Robin Anderson circle of friends kept evolving. Suggesting Peter join Maggie and me for dinner at La Poule Au Pot in Pimlico, a Maggie favourite, the three of us had gone on to Danny La Rue's nightclub in Hanover Square for an ocean of nightcaps and fun. Maggie was a lively dancer with the two of us only leaving the miniscule dance floor when it was time for the cabaret. However our behaviour didn't appear to have upset Peter who, when we returned to our table, was laughing and chatting with the couple at the next table. Maggie and I greeted the familiar looking woman and her companion with a smile and a nod. "I *know* I've seen her before," I said quietly to myself. "Maybe at some cocktail party?"

On leaving the tiny woman gave us an icy smile. "I *know* that face," I said to Peter, "any idea who she is? Seeing you three so heavily involved it almost looked as if Maggie and I were interrupting a *ménage à trois*!"

"What?" exclaimed Peter with feigned alarm, a mischievous smile appearing on his pleasant face, "A *ménage à trois* with the Queen's sister? That would never do!" The couple being Princess Margaret and an anonymous male escort.

*

I called Eric at his office (Cresta Fashions) to thank him for a "fabulous evening" and a "fun dinner", adding with a laugh, I did so enjoy meeting Ben Colman. Great character!"

"Divine babee isn't he?" trilled Eric. "Do you remember Digberry? Ken Villiers' little cottage where we all stayed a few years back?"

"I do indeed, Eric. I also spent my first Christmas in England there!"

"Well, dishy Ben bought it from Ken and I must say he's done wonders with the place." Eric gave a squeak. "Or *had* wonders done with it! He's built on a lavish extension as well as installing a swimming pool! You simply *must* get him to invite you down!"

Assuring Eric I would do "just that" I sat staring at the telephone. "Shall I? Shan't I?" I muttered staring at the silent phone. *Shall I? Shan't I?* I sat pondering my thoughts interrupted by Stephen (Gregory) breezing into the office.

"Morning everyone!" he crowed. "You look as if he spent the night on top of you (this to Maggie who was sitting next to me going through her check list for the day) and *you* don't look much better (this directed at me) especially when you see how beautiful *I* am!"

"Obviously you haven't looked in a mirror recently," replied Maggie crisply.

"Only a pillow!" I added bitchily.

"Jealousy will get you nowhere!" yodelled Stephen blowing the two of us a sloppy kiss before hefting up his Louis Vuitton briefcase (a gift from his loving employer no doubt) and retreating to the basement office he shared with Mrs Ziegler.

"He must be spending a fortune in taxis," murmured Maggie.

"Read petty cash," I growled as I immersed myself in my own check list for the day.

"Have you asked him if he'd like a lift with us? With you, I mean? After all he *does* live below you?" she replied.

I gave her a glare. "Separated by one floor, one flat and two ceilings, you mean? But you're right; it's so silly seeing I dash past his front door every morning. I *have* mentioned it to him Mags - on several occasions - but he always offers up some lame excuse like not wanting to be of any trouble or else he's off somewhere else prior to making it to the office."

"Leave it to me to have a word," she replied, "Plus it could be fun. Rather like Macbeth's three witches riding to work in your Mini instead of on a broomstick!"

"More likely three bitches!" I quipped.

Half an hour after we'd been subjected to "the walk" and JS's growled "good morning" Stephen came bounding into our office, a broad grin on face. "In case either of you are about to ask my heavenly body to lunch I can't!"

"Well consider yourself a failure seeing *these* two even *more* heavenly and exquisite bodies had no intention whatsoever of *asking* your much abused and once-upon-a-time heavenly body to lunch. Had we Robin?" chortled Maggie.

Curiosity getting the better of me I said as matter-of-factly as I could, "Who's the unlucky person?"

"He's lovely, he's good looking and he's *rrich*!" laughed Stephen jangling a gold bracelet adorned wrist (in the sixties bracelets, chains and medallions were de rigueur among the trendy, fashion conscious men).

"Is he still capable of walking or does he need a wheelchair?" quipped Maggie; Stephen's unattractive avariciousness already well-known around the office.

"The lucky person," continued Stephen with an even broader grin - if possible - "the *extremely* lucky person is none other than Mr Mustard himself! Ben Colman, heir to the Colman mustard fortune! So say 'hello' to Mr Mustard number two!"

"Number two being the operative term," snickered Maggie.

"Ben Colman?" I gasped, thinking, *But how and how bloody unfair!*

"Yes Robin. He says he's met you."

"He did?"

"He did. When he dropped me off after we met at a dinner last night he asked me if you didn't have a flat at No 5 as well." Stephen gave a cackle. "He also said apart from being bossy you were also very witty!"

Witty I can understand. I thought grudgingly, *But bossy? Where the hell did that spring from?*

"Ah yes, It must have been during our witty-cum-bossy conversation," I replied spikily. I remembered having mentioned to Ben I lived in Ladbroke Square next door to an old people's home to which he had laughingly replied, "Eek! I take it you aren't planning on moving for a year or two!"

"What's more he's asked me to his country house for the weekend," crowed Stephen; his words driving a Dracula-like stake right into my Turnbull and Asser covered chest.

Half an hour later I was getting ready to leave for a meeting when the phone on my desk rang.

"Can you get that please, Mags?" I called, "I'm running late for the licentious Lloyd and you know what a cow she is!"

"Robin! Hold on!" called Maggie, "I think you'd better take this! It's your friend and Stephen's newest, *greatest* friend Ben, Mr Mustard!"

"Good morning Robin!" sang Ben (*God, even his* voice *is smiley!* I thought), "Ben, Ben Colman or Mr Mustard as I heard the lady cry! I'll be quick as I'm sure Mr Siddeley doesn't take too kindly to his slaves receiving personal calls." He gave a mischievous chuckle. "Are you by any chance free this coming weekend and if you are, would you like to drive down on Friday - I remember you have a car - and stay until after supper Sunday? Unless of course you're an early bird like me and prefer to leave at sparrow fart on Monday?

"Why Ben I'd *love* to!" I crooned.

"Eek! That's great!" sang Ben, "I've also invited your neighbour and business associate Stephen Gregory and as you'll be driving down could you give him a lift?"

Not would you but could you, I thought cynically. *In other words you need a bloody chauffeur for your weekend screw, Mr Colman! Plus what's this 'business associate' shit?*

"Of *course* Ben," I seethed, "I'd only be too delighted to *run* Stephen down!"

"Thanks! I'll give you a call later - you gave me your home number the other evening - and give you directions."

"I know where it is," I said sullenly, "Digberry isn't it? Ken Villiers' former cottage. Eric told me."

"Eek!" cried Ben, "How clever of Old Mother Crabtree! So, Friday then around seven thirty? Be warned, the traffic out of London can be somewhat nightmarish. See you Friday then. Byee . . . Oh! And Robin, it's very informal." He gave a chuckle, "Stephen seems to think as you're - I quote - 'so grand' - unquote - you'd probably expect us to dress for dinner! Byee!"

Stephen seems to think? Stephen bloody seems to think? I inwardly stormed, *Oh, and I wonder if dear Stephen seems to think it'll be a weekend fuckee orgy for him and Ben as well?*

"Ben called," I said casually to Stephen on my return to the office after two hours of listening to the garrulous Lloyd woman banging on about her oafish husband, equally oafish son and how wonderful they all were; JS's schemes and any minor problems more-or-less overlooked.

"I know!" yodelled Stephen, "he's already called me! You're driving me down to the estate!"

Driving you down to down to the estate? I thought wickedly. *Driving you yes, but as for an estate Stephen Gregory, be prepared to be disappointed! Very!*

*

To be fair Stephen could not have been a more pleasant - and fun - passenger. The added fact he had asked whether he should "bring anything" such as a cake (a *cake*?) endeared him - but only slightly - to me!

"Why don't we take down a couple of bottles of wine?" I tactfully replied, "In fact I need to stock up for myself at Oddbins so I can easily get three more bottles of Sancerre. As for a cake? I'm sure Ben will find you sweet enough!"

"Wow!" I exclaimed on drawing up in the new, neatly raked, gravelled parking area at the end of the leafy lane. "Talk about a major change!"

What had once been a humble, double-storied claustrophobic flint stone cottage now boasted a lavish new double-story extension completely dwarfing the original. This I soon learned housed a magnificent drawing room and above this, Ben's lavish bedroom, bathroom and dressing room. All the windows to the original cottage had been replaced with gleaming white, Gothic-style frames while the front of the building was faced with a neat white trellis entwined with well-trained, colourful rambling roses. (Flashback to the rosebuds decorating the ceiling in Abingdon Road!) A wide footpath of York stone led from the parking area across a narrow, neatly clipped lawn to the gleaming blue-painted front door. At the sound of the Mini's crunching arrival the front door slowly opened.

"Who's that?" questioned Stephen warily eyeing the tall, cadaverous grey-haired man, resplendent in butler's uniform who had appeared in the open doorway.

"Good evening gentlemen," warbled the tall, thin stooped man as he shuffled slowly towards the car, "I'm Tatchell, Mr Colman's butler; allow me to divest you of your cases and show you to your room."

I stared at an equally startled Stephen. "Butler?" I muttered, "I thought we weren't supposed to be grand?"

"I think we can manage thank you er . . . Tatchell. However, if you could take the box of wine - I'll just open the boot - that'll be er . . . great."

Tatchell, giving a wobbly nod, continued shuffling forward until he finally reached us and the Mini. Stephen and I watched nervously as he grappled gamely with the box holding the three bottles of wine and a bottle of Courvoisier brandy before finally hefting it against his tiny paunch. "If you gentlemen would kindly follow me," he wheezed. As suggested, Stephen and I, clutching our small holdalls, followed Tatchell into the enlarged and refurbished hall leading to the new drawing room and former sitting room of the cottage.

I was about to introduce ourselves when Tatchell announced in a louder warble, "You two gentlemen are in the Trellis Bedroom and Mrs Colman is in the Pink Bedroom."

Mrs Colman? Stephen and I looked at each other in alarm.

"He said nothing about his mother coming down?" hissed Stephen looking suitably distraught.

"What on *earth* is Ben up to?" I muttered, "I, for one, certainly don't wish to spend the weekend holed up with his mother!"

"Nor me," murmured Stephen.

"Aah! They've arrived!" cooed a high-pitched, camp voice. "Welcome! Welcome!"

Now what? I thought eyeing the small, portly, rosy faced, gnome-like figure, resplendent in a pristine white chef's jacket plus black and grey checked trousers, as he emerged from the former sitting room.

"Good evening gentlemen, I'm Hector, Mr Colman's chef."

Chef? Whatever next? I thought, *A bloody welcoming brass band?*

"Good evening er . . . Hector. As I er . . . was about to say to Tatchell, I'm Mr Anderson and this is Mr Gregory,"

"Of course, Mr Anderson and Mr Gregory. Mr Colman sends his apologies at not being here to greet you but he's running late and won't be arriving until around ten o'clock."

"And Mrs Colman?" I asked.

"Mrs Colman?" repeated Hector looking confused.

"Yes, Mrs Colman. The butler er . . . er . . . Tatchell's just told us we're in the Trellis bedroom and Mrs Colman's in the Pink bedroom."

"Oh *no* Mr Anderson!" tittered Hector. "Trust Tatchell to get it all wrong. Mr Colman said Mr *Gregory* is in the Trellis room and Mumsie - *not* Mrs Colman - is in the Pink room."

I looked at the three faces staring back at me.

"What?" I said.

"Ben called you Mumsie!" shrieked Stephen, his face breaking into a grin. "Hello Mumsie!"

"I don't wish to appear disrespectful, Mr Anderson," said a perplexed-looking Hector, "But I think Mr Gregory could be right and you are - as Mr Colman said - Mumsie! As yes, come to think of it Mr Colman's very words were 'and Mr Anderson or Mumsie - he appears to be a bit bossy where we're all concerned - better have the Pink bedroom'!"

The name was to stick. At five minutes to eight on a cold November Friday evening I became known as Mumsie to Ben, Stephen and other members of the exclusive Colman circle.

*

"Good morning," crowed a smiling JS as he proceeded with "the walk" on the way to his office. "Morning Mumsie!" he added as he swept through the open doorway.

"Mumsie?" echoed Maggie, "Who the fuck's Mumsie?"

"You're looking at him," I replied sheepishly. "Unfortunately - no thanks to Ben Colman - it appears I was well and truly christened 'Mumsie' over the weekend!"

"Was it a pretty christening - *Mumsie*?" asked Maggie with a chortle; her question accompanied with the usual shaking of her shaking of her (today) Biba-covered bosom.

Jesus Benedict James, I thought, *see what you've now gone and started?*

"Very pretty!" yodelled Stephen causing us all to jump; his silent entrance in the wake of JS having gone unnoticed. "What else could you expect with *me* being there?"

"How *was* the weekend with your new friend and Stephen's new best friend?" asked Maggie once Stephen had descended to the bowels of the office to join Mrs Ziegler.

"My weekend with our new friend was non-existent," I replied with a wry smile. "My weekend with *Stephen* however was a weekend with Stephen and Stephen's rhetorical question, 'Money, money, money, how can I make more money'? As for Benedict, he eventually arrived accompanied by a very thin and highly camp young black man called Sylvester whose claim to fame - as I was later told by an enthusiastic Ben - was several appearances as a dancer in Top of the Pops!"

"And?"

"And? There really isn't an 'and'! Ben and Sylvester promptly disappeared upstairs where they remained for the weekend, Hector leaving or collecting trays of food and bottles from outside the bedroom door when

154

required." I stared at Maggie's incredulous expression. "Yes Mags that really was *it*!" I gave a snicker. "Apart from Hector saying, eyes wide, 'I did happen to get a glimpse of what the young man had hanging between his legs, Mumsie, and I swear - on Tatchell's miserable life - at first he was having fun with one of the empty wine bottles'!"

"Goodness!" drawled Maggie, "lucky Benedict!"

"In fact, Stephen and I drove back yesterday afternoon immediately after lunch; again without our host making an appearance!" I gave Maggie a knowing look. "And before you even begin thinking of asking Maggie *dear,* yes, as well as Hector and Tatchell, Ben *also* introduced me to Sylvester as Mumsie! Satisfied?"

Ben telephoned me later on Monday evening. "Eek Mumsie, sorry about all that! To make amends, can you make dinner one evening this week? Wednesday or Thursday? Wednesday? Great. Brooks Club, St James at eight?" He gave a cheerful laugh, "And Mumsie?"

"Yes Benedict?" I replied cautiously.

"No Stephen and *no* piccaninnies!"

I was delighted to find Ben and I were the only two for dinner. I was also delighted at being invited to Brooks, one of London's most esteemed gentlemen's clubs. Ben proved to be even more entertaining and enchanting (if possible) than our first meeting at Rex and Eric's Christmas "bash".

When I mentioned the unexpected presence of the Afro-haired, willowy Sylvester, Ben happily confided in me his penchant for young black men.

"Goodness," I quipped, "joining the BASAP in Southern Rhodesia must have been like heaven on a large liquorice stick for you!"

"Eek Mumsie, it was!" replied Ben with a mischievous grin, "Pure heaven and there were a *lot* of sticks or - better still my - favourite. Big black truncheons!"

Ben also told me - much to my surprise - he and his brother Anthony were adopted, "My real dad being a policeman," he said before adding wickedly, "hence, perhaps, my hankering for a different type of policeman! A beaming black Bobby as opposed to your usual Dixon of Dock Green!"

The next weekend I was back at Digberry (DLL was away in Italy). To my relief Stephen had not been invited. "I have Rex and Eric coming to lunch on Saturday along with William and a chum of his . . ."

"William?" I repeated, "William Davis?"

"No, William Gloucester," replied Benedict matter-of-factly, "and on Sunday we're invited to lunch by Jane and Michael Colston of dishwasher fame." He gave a chuckle, "So no tiresome voluntary washing up and once again Mumsie, no piccaninnies!"

"Ooh Mumsie, imagine?" squeaked Hector with an excited wiggle of his portly frame, his plump moobs (man boobs) shaking in spectacular rivalry to Maggie's, "I just hope His Royal Highness enjoys Hector's game pie!"

"I, of course, will be offering Mr Colman's esteemed guest - and you too Mumsie, of course - a Kir Royale prior to serving Hector's *princely* fare!" added Tatchell sonorously, not to be outdone.

This was to see the start of many such weekends at Digberry; so much so DLL couldn't resist saying somewhat sourly, "So which Forty is it to be this weekend? The A40 or the M40?" The M40 being the exit road from London for Henley and the A40 the exit road for Gerrards Cross and Hedgerely.

At this stage another important addition had joined what I deemed the RA, BJC Digberry Detachment. A smooth talking charmer named Richard Reynolds; the three of us becoming almost inseparable with holidays in the South of France and several memorable weekends in Paris. One particular weekend taking place during the period Ben mischievously described as "Mumsie and the French Erection" which is detailed in full later.

With his heavy, thickset frame, dark wavy hair, brooding looks and lethal financial brain, Richard was a compelling presence.

"Eek! Rather like Marlon Brando in *The Godfather* - only younger!" had been Ben's first impression and - typical Ben - after a few more get-togethers Richard was promoted (or demoted) from Godfather Richard to the more relaxed Uncle Richard! As I would discover to my severe cost several years later the ostensibly charming Richard would finally reveal his true colours making Brando's original ruthless Godfather pale into insignificance.

Christine Gallois, a key player in the French Erection sequence had invited me to a private dinner at Maxims the famous Parisian restaurant. It so happened Richard and I had planned a weekend in the city and would be staying at the Ritz. A break for me from my usual routine of staying with Christine's son Michel, a well-established star of the Lido.

"Christine, Michel's 'muzza' has asked me to some glamorous dinner *sans* sonny boy," I said to Richard, "so why don't I see if I can get you invited as well? Christine, for some bizarre reason known only to herself, thinks RA divine and I am sure she would love to meet any friend of mine. Before you ask Michel is spending a few days in Grenoble where he and some friends will be skiing."

"Sounds great," said Richard adding wryly, "Plus we both need a break from Benedict."

Richard, like myself, had been watching Ben's increased drinking with growing concern. Richard was also convinced sessions with "Charlie" were becoming a regular feature of Ben's day. I had to agree with Richard who concluded his observations by saying, "While you and I Mumsie never say 'no' to a drink we do say a resounding 'no' to drugs and long may we continue to do so!"

The one thought that never crossed our minds was the fact Ben Colman, an heir to part of the Colman Mustard fortune would ever find himself with financial problems. In retrospect we should have realised Ben's lavish lifestyle plus the money showered on the "Ben toys" would sooner than later have an effect on even the deepest of a so-called "bottomless pit".

I promptly telephoned Christine who was only too delighted to have *Monsieur* Reynolds at her dinner party. "'E *et* Papa Gallois should get on well togezza as zay can spend za evening discussing za high finance." Michel's father from what I could gather being the owner of a newspaper empire.

Ben did not appear to be at all put out by the fact he wasn't included in the weekend break.

"It's not like some wild weekend in Amsterdam or Berlin," I went on to assure him. "We're er . . . holing up at the Ritz and apart from a dinner party at Maxim's and - weather permitting - a stroll round Montparnasse we'll be back before you've even realised we've been away."

"Dinner at Maxim's and holing up at the Ritz?" replied Ben. "Sounds rather lavish to me?"

"Did you hear the latest sexploit concerning Michael Razzer?" interrupted Richard quickly changing the subject.

Among Christine's guests whom I knew were her husband, elegant daughter Madeline and her partner Bernard plus another four couples I had never met. Christine made a great fuss of Richard and I was amused to see he was placed on her left.

We were about to start on the main course when the general conversation in the restaurant was broken by a strangulated "High team! I'm not too late am I?"

Benedict! Not only in person but also a very drunken Benedict wearing what could best be described as an outmoded Sergeant Pepper-style jacket, a tortured dinner shirt with a skew-whiff bowtie and a pair of half-zipped black silk trousers.

I looked at Richard in horror whose look of abject horror easily outdid mine.

"Mumsie!" crowed Ben, "And Uncle Richard! Now where's the French Erection's mummy?"

"Christine er . . . forgive me . . . us," I stammered as Richard and I rose simultaneously from our chairs. "This is Ben, Ben Colman a great friend of ours." I gave Richard and anguished glance. "We had no idea he'd er . . . be in Paris," I added lamely.

"*Monsieur*," cooed Christine unfazed, "I am Christine Gallois an' as you are za friend of Robin *et* Richard I trust you will be joining us?"

What? I thought. *Christine are you* mad?

"*Enchanté Madam*," slurred Ben as he lurched forward to greet his hostess. "*Enchanté*," he repeated shakily proffering his hand. "*Merde!*" he yelped as he stumbled and crashed face downwards on to the lavishly set table.

Highly embarrassed Richard and I bundled Ben from the restaurant.

"Tell me you're not staying at the fucking Ritz?" growled Richard as I valiantly attempted to hail a passing taxi.

"Eek! Too grand for me," giggled Ben. "I'm at the Travellers Club on the Champs Elysées."

The Ben saga didn't end there. On arrival at the Travellers Club we escorted Ben into the tiny, wrought iron cage of lift and pressed the button for the relevant floor.

"Are you sure you preshed the correct button?" hiccupped Ben tapping blindly at the control panel. "Eek" he chortled as the lift drew to a shuddering halt.

Fifteen minutes later we found ourselves rescued and back on terra firma with a giggling Ben back in his room. We returned to Maxim's in time for the sweet course.

Richard and I never made Montmartre but lunched with a bubbling Ben at a bistro of his choosing instead.

*

"I have one of my directors and his wife, Tony and Angela Galliers-Pratt coming to dinner on Wednesday and if you're free Robble, perhaps you'd like to join us?" said DLL at one of our tongue-in-cheek "business breakfasts. "Tony's a bit of a repressed screamer but quite harmless. I'm also on the board of directors to *his* company; F. Pratt Engineering."

Must I? I thought, *a boring company director and his wife? Though knowing Beesle and his mischievous remark 'a bit of a screamer', it may be quite fun. Plus I'm not doing anything on Wednesday . . .*

"Sounds fun Beesle; thank you. Tony and Angela you say?"

"Yes, Tony and Angela Galliers-Pratt. They own a magnificent house, Mawley Hall, up in Shropshire. Play your cards right and you may even be invited to stay!"

*

I see what you mean by a repressed screamer, Beesle, I thought staring at the sleek, seal-like man who stood to greet DLL and myself as we walked into the foyer of the Empress.

"Good evening Angela; good evening Tony," said DLL jovially. "Are we late or are you two early?" he added leaning forward to give Angela a chaste kiss on her proffered cheek.

Grace Kelley out and about with Rudolf Valentino, I thought eyeing the two. *An extremely* brilliantined *Rudolf Valentino and if I'm not mistaken, a touch of the Max-ine Factor?*

"No David, Angela and I were early having dropped by the Redfern Gallery en route," brayed Tony in a voice which immediately reminded me of *Francis the Talking Mule.* A comedy film about - you guessed it - a talking mule and a big hit in the fifties. He gave another bray before continuing in an extraordinarily high-pitched vibrato, "We took the liberty of ordering a bottle of *The Merry Widow.* I trust you approve? Ha! Ha! Ha!" His ear-splitting shrieks of "Ha! Ha!" causing several heads to turn.

"So much nicer than Dom Perignon don't you agree?" squeaked Angela, a study of expensive elegance in a pale yellow dress which I later learned was a creation by the fashion designer Hardy Amies; a favourite of HM The Queen. She gave me a quizzical smile. "And you must be Robin. David has told us *so* much about you!" adding with a girlish giggle, "You're from Darkest Africa I hear?"

"Yes!" brayed Tony proffering a fleshy pink manicured hand and showing part of a pristine cuff weighed down by a heavy gold, monogrammed cufflink. "A rarity I believe? Ha ha ha! An interior designer from Darkest Africa. Did you design a lot of thatched huts? Ha ha ha! And did you find it difficult to find your way out due to the dark? Ha! Ha! Ha!"

Jesus, I thought, *no wonder you wept? Added to which what gives with Ha Ha's breath? Talk about a leading member of the Halitosis Choir!*

I looked at DLL in horror at his suggestion we went to our table. *Don't tell me it's only us four?* I thought, *Angela, Mrs G-P I can cope with but as for hubby? I wouldn't be at all surprised if all the wine glasses on the table shatter before we've even had a chance to use them!* Giving DLL a sideways glance (I was sure he was deliberately ignoring me) I turned my attention back to Tony waxing lyrical about the food at a rival restaurant to DLL's beloved Empress. "*Dee*-licious!" he brayed, "Positively *dee*-licious!"

Don't tell me he carries on like this at either his or David's board meetings? I thought with a snicker, *Talk about a demented parakeet and not only demented but a demented parakeet on heat!*

"You must bring Robin up to Mawley for a weekend," brayed Tony as we were bidding each other goodnight.

"Yes! It would be *such* fun!" squeaked Angela, "A weekend in the spring when all the daffodils are out! Mawley looks *so* divine amidst all the daffodils!"

William Wordsworth eat your poetic heart out, I said to myself. "I'd love to!" I said to Angela.

I could hardly wait until the two were out of earshot before saying in a disbelieving voice, "Jesus Beesle, I see exactly what you mean!" Placing a hand on my hip and adopting a Mae West slouch I added with a Mae West twang, "Honey, that screamer ain't repressed; that repressed screamer's *possessed*!"

DLL telephoned the following evening. "You were obviously a hit with Angela and Tony, Robble dear." He gave a deep chuckle. "Despite it being February and Mawley is *not* basking among 'a host of golden daffodils', Tony has suggested we drive up to Shropshire weekend after next. How does that suit you?"

"Surprising enough Beesle I am not all that keen on daffodils," I replied, "so a weekend not having to play at being Wee Willie Wordsworth sounds - to quote the *other* Galliers-Pratt - *divine!*"

*

Mawley Hall even without the daffodils must surely be described as one of the most beautiful houses in all England. Built in the mid-eighteenth century in stands in an elegant park and was bought by Tony Galliers-Pratt in 1962 and since then has been lovingly restored and maintained.

DLL and I duly arrived after a smooth, three and a half hours drive from London to Cleobury Mortimer, a small, ancient market town and on to nearby Mawley Hall where a beaming Tony, accompanied by a serious-looking butler came out to greet us. Within seconds our cases had been deftly collected from the boot of the MX10 and whisked away as if by David Blaine himself.

During our journey DLL had waxed lyrical about the marvellous restoration work having taken place under the auspices of Tony. DLL was particularly taken by the magnificent plaster mouldings and cornices in the vast entrance hall. He also took great delight in describing the unique balustrade (or handrail) to the main staircase, this having been carved in the form of a rippling serpent with its open-mouthed, hissing head the showpiece atop the main baluster.

Apart from ourselves there were two other houseguests, a plump, jolly woman named Shelagh and her balding, bespectacled husband named John. Years later I would discover how much the likes of Shelagh, Countess of Lisburne and her cronies disliked RA, blaming me for Tony's eventual and complete "bonnet over the windmill" behaviour in the eighties and nineties. I never had any further contact with Tony from the time I broke off all ties with Alistair Colvin Limited in 1969. The real culprits - comrades in arms would a better choice of words - behind the "freezing" being a coven of over-the-top queens headed by Barry Grigg and Tommy (Kitty) Kyle, former boyfriend and heir to Gussy Perrier's "ever effervescent fortune" as one wag so eloquently hissed it.

"Just the six of us!" brayed Tony, "Much more fun! Much more cosy! Ha! Ha! Ha!"

We all dressed for dinner which was served in a cavernous apricot-coloured dining room where the serious-looking butler looking even more serious and accompanied by a dour Nanny McPhee lookalike silently served us. Prior to changing for dinner I was amused to find my small suitcase unpacked and my dinner jacket, shirt, bow tie, trousers, socks and black patent evening shoes neatly laid out for me. Causing another somewhat rueful smile was discovering DLL's bedroom and my bedroom were at opposite ends of an extremely long corridor.

Next day Tony drove us over to visit Michael Severn, owner of Quadrant Furniture, at Shakenhurst his country house. Michael specialised in acrylics, the new and very "in" style at the time. I was mesmerised by the variety of items Quadrant was producing. These ranged from console tables, coffee tables, dining tables, obelisks, trays and more. You name it and Michael seemed to be producing it.

I had already met Michael and his lovely wife Rachael in London. Sadly Rachel died following a long, painful battle with cancer. I will always remember Rachael for her dramatic Ava Gardner-like looks, wonderful warmth and glorious sense of humour.

"It's all stunning Michael," I told him as I stood surveying the gleaming acrylics, "absolutely *stunning* and one day, I promise, I'll be ordering several - if not lots - of your unique pieces. Mark my words, Michael! Mark my words!"

It was during an after-lunch stroll to "have a peek a peek at the new folly" Tony suddenly brought up the subject of John Siddeley. "Dreadful man! Quite dreadful!" he brayed, "And very restrictive, I'm sure."

"Not exactly my favourite person," agreed DLL.

"Okay, he's difficult but I enjoy working there," I said with an edge to my voice, their comments certainly hitting a nerve.

"You should be working under your own banner! Under your own name!" brayed Tony, after which he let the matter drop.

*

Meanwhile Tony's continued interference in my life was quickly becoming an embarrassment.

"Holy fuck!" explained Maggie as a green uniformed delivery man from Pulbrook and Gould, the Royal florist, appeared at the Harriet Street office carrying an enormous basket (forget a mere bunch) of red roses. "Who on earth can those be for?"

"Jacqueline obviously," I murmured, not really paying much attention.

"More likely for Stephen," said Maggie with a mischievous giggle.

"Someone call my name?" yodelled Stephen appearing at the top of the stairs leading down to his and Mrs Ziegler's office.

"We think this extravagant basket of red roses is for you!" said Maggie teasingly.

"Or Jacqueline," I repeated nervously.

"I really *do* think they're for me," said Stephen in all seriousness. "From Phillip, Phillip Profumo. I had dinner with him last night!" (Phillip - as already mentioned - being the brother of John Profumo, the MP involved with Christine Keeler and subsequently blamed for the collapse of the Conservative Party.)

Tart, I thought, *and where was Nicky during this wine and roses dinner?* (Nicky Armstrong supposedly being Phillip's lover at the time.)

"Who are they for?" Stephen snapped at the delivery man who stood eyeing him and Maggie in turn.

"Mr Anderson," squawked the man. "Mr Robin Anderson. Is there a Mr Robin Anderson 'ere?"

"Are you *sure* you don't mean Mr Gregory? Mr *Stephen* Gregory?" barked Stephen, a look of pure fury on his face.

"No, it definitely says Mr Robin Anderson," growled the delivery man looking decidedly peeved. "'Ere, Look for yerself!"

"That's me," I said through gritted teeth while silently seething. "Thank you so much. Where do I sign?"

"Who'd ever want to send *you* roses?" muttered Stephen spikily.

Having signed the delivery book I took the vast arrangement from the scowling man and handed it over to Maggie. "Please accept these Mags; no questions asked," I murmured, "Plus I'd like you to have them. Give me a sec to grab hold of the attached card.

"So who's sending *Mumsie* red roses?" spat Stephen, his voice filled with spite.

"Actually they're for Maggie," I replied blithely, "Er . . . Peter Leggatt wanted them to be a surprise so that's why he sent them care of me!

"Who's Peter Leggatt?" snapped Stephen.

"My fiancé," said Maggie with a shake of her splendid bosom and an even more spectacular shaking of the basket of roses still clasped in her arms; little realising at the time how those two risible words would come back and haunt her.

"You're getting married?" yelped Stephen.

"Yes, but nobody's supposed to know yet," drawled Maggie getting into the act. "So Stephen dear, for *once,* could you try and keep *this* particular piece of news a secret?" She gave a sniff. "In other words, keep your fucking trap *shut!*"

"I won't tell a soul," adopting a suitable "my full lips sealed" expression, "not even JS!"

"*Especially* JS," warned Maggie, "He's the last person I'd want to know." Catching my warning look and discreet nod in Stephen's direction, she added in a syrupy drawl, "You *know* what JS is like. If he hears I'm engaged - secretly or not - he'll immediately want to throw a party for me. After all, *you* Stephen - of *all* people - know *just* how generous he is!" Her remark followed by a pointed look at Stephen's glistering new gold wristwatch.

"Does Peter know?" I quipped as Stephen hurried back downstairs no doubt to inform JS of Maggie's "secret".

"Of course not *Mumsie*," drawled Maggie. "It's a secret. Even from him!"

*

"Tony, Tony, thank you for the roses but please, *please* do *not* send anymore flowers or gifts of any sort to Siddeley's as it will only cause unnecessary grief."

The "gifts" referring to the endless cases of wine and champagne being delivered to Harriet Street. Undeterred Tony had his secretary contact Mrs Edwards (now my cleaner) in order to arrange a convenient time for his chauffeur to meet her at Ladbroke Square where champagne, wine and the occasional Fortnum & Mason hamper could be delivered instead!

"That wretched man!" Tony brayed over the telephone, "Now listen Robin and listen well, it's high time you met Alistair Colvin and what's more, this evening is as good a time as any!"

After much humming and hawing I reluctantly agreed to meet the mysterious Alistair "at No 45, Belgrave Square at six thirty on the dot" having informed Tony I could not be late for a dinner party at Albany given by a new face, Adrian Pryce-Jones, a friend of Ben's.

*

Meanwhile Tony's ongoing generosity seemed to know no bounds.

"I simply *have* to drop into Sullivan & Woolley, my tailors," he brayed after a particularly liquid lunch on his part, "perhaps you wouldn't mind sitting there while I have a fitting?" I have a feeling the whole venture must have been a set-up for at the insistence of Tony aided and abetted by one of the geriatric tailors I ended up being measured for a suit. A few weeks later when calling by for a fitting I discovered three suits waiting for me to try on; the fabric for the other two having been selected by Tony and his "tailor in crime".

The Marshallene, a dapper dresser himself, did his best to encourage me to switch allegiances and try out Douglas (Dougie) Hayward the trendy "in" tailor on Mayfair's Mount Street. However, after a few suits from Dougie's emporium I returned, cap in hand, to Sullivan and Wooley where I found myself duly introduced to young, apprentice tailor named Parker.

Sullivan & Woolley was bought out by Henry Poole & Co in 1980 and today Phillip Parker - the young apprentice - is now vice-chairman. I am happy to say the unique quality of Henry Poole remains unchanged some fifty years on.

Another "TGPG" or "Tony Galliers-Pratt gift" as I took to calling the seemingly endless flow was a membership to Annabel's, the exclusive Berkeley Square set up by Mark Birley in 1963 and named after his then wife, Lady Annabel Vane-Tempest-Stewart. I had the great pleasure of entertaining Peggy at Annabel's on a rare visit to London to see her daughters. Eventually Margaret, Duchess of Argyll and I would spend many a happy evening in this exclusive haven indulging in an after dinner glass of champagne or three.

*

Bach home after my meeting with the much-lauded Alistair Colvin (who turned out to be an amiable, bespectacled giant and not at all "interior designer-ish") and subsequent alcohol-infused dinner with Adrian Pryce-Jones, I lay tossing and turning regarding my dilemma, my mind racing. *Do I or don't I? And more importantly, dare I?* I kept asking myself. *And if I do take up Tony's offer would it lead to other projects? And of course the question nobody brought up; would I enjoy working with Alistair and vice versa?*

A week to the day an ashen-faced Maggie handed me the telephone. "You'd better talk to Mrs Fox," she murmured, "she's after blood. *Anyone's* blood"

"I don't bloody well believe it!" I snarled, slamming down the telephone after listening to a non-stop five minute rant from a hysterical Mrs Fox interspersed by snarled interruptions by *Mr* Fox. Taking a deep breath I sat staring at Maggie. "Not only did JS bugger off to Bridgnorth day before yesterday with bloody Stephen, he never let *any* of us know of a meeting between him and both Mr and Mrs Fox this morning. Or did he? Mags?"

"Not a dicky bird," drawled Maggie.

I asked the two junior members of staff plus Trevor and Alan if *they* had been informed of any such meeting, my question being received with a negative response from all four.

"Fuck, double fuck!" I stormed, "This is so wrong and so *fucking* unfair!"

Several hours later Maggie, on answering the telephone, turned to me and said nervously (so unlike her), "That was JS in a *supreme* temper tantrum. Something about you not being at Heathrow to meet him and Stephen off the Birmingham flight and the two of them having to take a taxi."

"Tough shit!" I snapped, "I somehow think dealing with Mr and Mrs Fox and their completely justifiable complaints is perhaps a tad more important than JS and his bloody bum boy having to take a fucking taxi!"

An hour later an apoplectic JS exploded into followed by a smirking Stephen and all hell broke loose.

RAD

At 8.30 a.m. precisely Bryan swept up the stairs and ended up standing in a balletic pose in the doorway to my office (dubbed a few weeks later as "RA's orifice" by a caustic Bryan and a snickering Liz), one espadrille-clad foot pointing forward and the other forty five degrees sideways; the wicker case from his first visit clutched to his orange and white striped, rumpled blouson.

"Coffee?" he rasped, "I always begin the day - phase one, two, three or even four - with a stimulating cup of steaming, ambrosial coffee!"

"Er . . . good morning Bryan," I replied crisply, "and thanks; that would be great. There's a jar of instant in the kitchen cupboard and a bottle of milk in the fridge."

"How do *you* like it?" he called from the main office where I heard a crash as the wicker case landed on the L-shaped desk top.

"Black please. *Strong.* So I suggest four heaped spoons! Ah, and here she is!" I added cheerfully as Liz crept slowly up the final run of stairs, "The one and only Liz! Secretary to the wannabe er . . . stars!"

"That'll be *three* coffees then," cawed Bryan from the sample room-cum-kitchen, "and Liz - or secretary to the stars as I heard you named - should you wish to add milk it's here at your disposal. Plus" he added with a combined cawing and a croak, "I spy with my blue, beady eye two bottles of a rather palatable Sancerre to which I have now added a third bottle of not quite so palatable Safeways plonk." A few seconds later Bryan appeared in the doorway bearing three steaming mugs balanced precariously on a thin, wallpaper sample book in lieu of a tray; Liz meanwhile having made herself comfortable on the spare chair in my office, no doubt in anticipation of a coffee without milk.

"You must be the Liz I heard our elegant task master greeting a few moments ago," rasped Bryan, "and goodness, aren't you a beauty? Renoir meets Liz Taylor!" (Liz and I gaped at the beaming Modigliani-like figurine, his Jackie O hairdo looking slightly more *Struwwelpeter* - or Shocked-headed Peter - than before.) "I'm Bryan, Bryan Larkin, potential right hand to my new lord and master." He handed Liz a mug of coffee as if presenting her with a jewel-encrusted chalice. Within seconds he had reverently placed a mug on my desk. Leaning the wallpaper book against the door jamb he slowly raised his mug in a pose reminiscent of the Statue of Liberty. "To RAD!" he announced in a quavering voice, "and all the best for the future!"

"To RAD," I said, swallowing the lump which had suddenly appeared in my throat.

"To RAD," repeated Liz, "and er . . . Bryan, whilst you're still on your *very* elegant feet would you mind *awfully* fetching the bottle of milk and a spoon please? Perhaps even in your potential right hand? And talking of spoons, if there's any sugar about this Liz Taylor wouldn't say 'no'."

The first day *ever* at RAD had begun.

I sat looking proudly at my team of two while my team of two sat (Liz) and stood (Bryan) staring quizzically back at their managing director. The first to break the silence was Liz.

"As much as I'd like to," she said with a mischievous smile, "I really *can't* sit here like a figure in an Impressionist painting, Robin - thank you Bryan, I *loved* the way you described me - so what would you like this Renoir-cum-Liz Taylor-cum-secretary to do?"

"What I'd like you to do to begin with Liz is start making an inventory of all fabric swatches hanging in the sample room so far. More are being delivered later today along with a few more wallpaper books - or trays as Bryan seems to see them! Ha ha ha!"

"Oh great," said Liz in a feigned or genuinely pained voice, "cataloguing sample swatches; just what I need."

Ignoring Liz's comeback I continued in what I considered a suitably authoritative manner. "When Bill Kendall turns up - he's the architect and should be here around half-tennish - could you and Bill check out the plan chest please? Not that we've any plans - apart from a few copies of Charlie's new boutique *to* sort out - ha ha ha! Oh, and despite the early hour would you also offer Bill a glass of wine from the ever expanding RAD cellar."

"*Now* you're talking," giggled Liz. "Oh, good morning," she added looking through to the landing.

"Good morning," replied Warren Sampson, "I just popped up to wish you all the very best of luck for your first day and the many more to follow!"

"Good morning again, Warren," I called (I had dropped by to say "good morning" to Alison and Warren earlier), "You haven't met Liz, Liz Anderson - no relation! - our secretary." Giving Warren a sly wink I said loudly, "I think you met Bryan when he was here last week."

"I did indeed!" said Warren with a chuckle.

"Bryan and I are about to go out . . ."

"We *are*?" rasped Bryan from the other office.

"About to go out," I continued, "so why don't you and Alison join us, the team, at around twelve for a celebratory glass of wine to toast the future of RAD?"

"Good idea RA," replied Warren and like Mumsie to a select few, RA became my name for the majority. Calling "see you later" he went back downstairs.

"You said we were about to sally forth on a mission?" rasped Bryan as he suddenly materialised in the doorway.

"We are indeed, we're on our way to have a look at Charlie's new shop . . ."

"Our first telephone call!" cawed Bryan on hearing one of the two lines starting to ring. "Leave it Liz, I'll get it." Not giving Liz a chance to react (she was still sitting in my office clutching the remains of her milky, sugary coffee) Bryan disappeared à la Rudolf Nureyev with a great bound back into the main office. "Robin Anderson Design," he crooned on picking up the phone, "How may I help you?"

"I take it that must be one of the chosen?" said a cheerful voice, "Tell Mumsie its Ben and she's to come along to Jack Barclay in Sloane Street where her new chariot awaits! It's parked on the pavement; with me!"

"Good Hades!" rasped Bryan from the main office, "An almost dirty phone call from a Ben for a Mumsie whose new chariot awaits outside Jack Barclay in Sloane Street! Whoever this Mumsie *is* her presence is required *tout de suite!*"

"What?" I exclaimed jumping from my chair and racing into the other office. Snatching the telephone from Bryan and ignoring his indignant squawk at such effrontery I said angrily, "Benedict, Mumsie. What's this about a new car?"

"Eek Mumsie! Keep your knickers on! Charlie and I decided our investment - I stand corrected, *Charlie's* investment - cannot be seen driving about in a mundane grey Mini so we ordered you a new one!"

"But . . . but . . . but . . ." I stammered.

"No buts Mumsie!" reprimanded Ben, "Simply stop flapping and get Lady Larkin to chauffeur you round to J Barclay's so you can collect your new executive motor. It's the very latest Mini Cooper, its black, has quarter light windows - very smart - a Webasto sliding sunroof, a radio and an extra luxury, a car telephone - your call sign 'Green Seven Six'!" He added with his trademark squawk, "Eek! And in case you become *too* famous you've got tinted windows to protect you from all those prying eyes!"

"But Benedict," I replied weakly, "we haven't even got a client as yet . . ."

"What?" cried Charlie snatching the telephone from Ben, "You've got my boutique for starters so along you come Mr A, collect your car and then you can drive us to Foxtrot Oscar where the three of us can have the first of our many directors' lunches!"

"Eek! And another thing Mumsie," chortled Ben taking the telephone back from Charlie, "Leave your old Mini here - Lady Larkin can take a taxi; take it out of petty cash - as I've organised this to be traded in for a small Bedford van. With RAD painted on the sides of course!"

"Er . . . Benedict . . . *dear* Benedict," I replied sarcastically, "is there anything left for me to do with my new business apart from declare immediate bankruptcy?"

"Eek Mumsie! As I've already said - and Charlie agrees - untwist those knickers, come to lunch and then do what we all know you do best. Start designing!"

*

"Robin Anderson Design" I crooned in a smoother, more grownup rendering of *The Golden Voice of Teenage Half Hour.*

"Is that Robin?" questioned a high-pitched, affected woman's voice.

"Robin Anderson speaking."

"Oh Robin, its Barbara Eppel here. We met while you were working with John Siddeley. I've never forgotten how kind and clever you were when helping my mother, Mrs Silk, with her flat in Clarence Terrace, Regents Park."

"Of *course* I remember you Mrs Eppel!" thinking, *Ah yes, the attractive, highly-strung, dark-haired young lady so enthusiastic and appreciative of my design ideas!*

"First of all Robin, I called to wish you the very best of luck with your new venture - I sincerely mean it (added with a squeak and an affected laugh). Secondly, I have a friend I'd like you to meet. She lives in Portland Place along from the BBC building (*Eek!* I thought, doing a Ben, *Where little Leslie French, disguised as Oriel, lurks above the main door!*). I appreciate it's short notice but Lita, Lita Young my friend, is one of those people who once they've set their mind on something there's no holding him or her back!" said Barbara followed by a trill. "Is there any chance you could meet us day after tomorrow at, say, ten o'clock?"

"I'd *love* to Mrs Eppel. May I know where?"

"At Lita Young's flat," Barbara replied and having given me the address added with an affected squeak, "Oh Robin, I'm really *so* looking forward to seeing you again!" She gave another high-pitched squeak, "Mummy and I never stop singing your praises! And it's Barbara by the way."

Barbara Eppel would prove to be one of my most stalwart supporters and apart from designing two magnificent homes for her and Leonard (her husband), I also designed two sets of offices for Arrowcroft, Leonard's successful property development company. Little did I realise - again all thanks to Barbara - I would also achieve one of the most prestigious design contracts of my whole career.

*

Dressed in an immaculate Sullivan and Wooley suit (later to become Henry Poole Ltd.), a Michael Fish shirt with matching "kipper" tie, de rigueur Gucci loafers and an off-white Jaeger trench-coat draped over my shoulders, I pressed the entry buzzer for the address supplied. Five minutes later I found myself seated in the study of a spacious apartment with a cup of coffee and facing three young ladies - Barbara Eppel who had greeted me at the door before leading me into the study and making the introductions, Lita Young and Sandra Weiner.

Whilst Barbara sat nervously smiling I realised I was being thoroughly scrutinised by the other two; Lita Young in particular. On being introduced I was immediately taken by Lita's vivacious personality, her flashing eyes, her Helen Shapiro bee-hive hairdo, saffron-coloured shift dress and two-tone shoes by Chanel. *She fabulous!* I thought, *And not only fabulous but also, I'm sure, great fun! In fact, all three are but out of the 'Three Little Maids' Lita is definitely the winner!*

"I'll show you what David and I - David's my husband - would like you to design for us," announced Lita. "Let's leave Barbara and Sandra to their coffee while you come along with me!"

Obediently following the diminutive "call me Lita" - a veritable miniature powerhouse - I was shown "Karen's bedroom" (Karen being the eldest daughter), "Judith's bedroom" (Judith being Karen's younger sister), the dining room and the master bedroom suite. "We'd like you to design these areas to begin with," said Lita with a bright smile. "However, it's the dining room and master bedroom we'd like you make that bit extra special."

I returned to Ebury Street in a state of euphoria. Charlie and now Lita Young all in my first week? Why did I ever doubt the Phoenix-like *sans* ashes RAD?

It didn't stop there. The following week Georgina Halse telephoned to congratulate me and offer her best wishes. "I would like you to meet a great friend and character, Germaine Woolf," she said in her husky voice, "the furrier of magically lengthening fur coats fame. She'd like you have a look at their showroom in Upper Grosvenor Street, Mayfair, plus her apartment." Georgina gave a chuckle. "I showed her the *House and Garden* photographs of your friend Charlie's apartment and she was immediately hooked!"

Germaine Woolf, a small, vibrant woman dressed in simple black, her dark hair dressed in a simple chignon, epitomised the word "chic" and she too would become an extraordinary catalyst in RAD's continuing success. Through Germaine I was introduced to Herty Massey, a thin, blonde woman whose husband Harry owned the prestigious Milestone Hotel facing Kensington Palace in addition to a mind-blowing portfolio of other prime London properties. Apart from designing the penthouse suite in the Milestone Hotel Herty introduced me to a shrewd looking personage named Doris Morrison who, at first, appeared to be a dream client by giving me carte blanche regarding the refurbishment of her palatial home in elegant Abbotsbury Road, Kensington. 0

I was even more delighted when Doris invited me to Jerusalem to design a newly built house in Pinkus Street, the Rose Garden but not at all delighted when, on arrival, I was told I would be staying with a friend of hers and his family in their flat as opposed to the King David Hotel where she would be. Needless to say I did *not* stay with her friend and his family but insisted on being taken to a decent hotel instead. *Not* the King David! I ended up spending the night at the Mount of Olives Hotel situated atop the historic mount. Adding insult to injury was being told by the listless barman there were no olives for the requested, much-needed very dry martini.

"No olives?" I exclaimed, "But we're meant to be sitting on a wretched *mountain* of the effing things!"

Next day I returned to Tel Aviv and took the first available flight back to London. Obviously Doris Morrison did *not* pay for my hotel. Fortunately I had my return ticket which I was able to change. My brief sojourn in Israel left a very bitter taste indeed and I found the atmosphere of general animosity of the place something I had no wish to experience ever again. This and an overwhelming reminder of Salway, Montagu and Nureyev combined - a constant presence wherever I went - did nothing to help one's olfactory organs. Oh how I longed for a sudden attack of what they call olfactory fatigue! Whereas I would always remember India as smelling of curry and shit Israel would always be associated with the malodorous ZaSu.

Prior to the disastrous and to my mind insulting visit I had spent considerable time working on the designs for the house from the plans supplied by the Jerusalem architect so all in all, apart from an actual visit to the site, beady Doris Morrison was ready to go. I never heard from her again nor did I wish to. For the record RAD never bothered to invoice her for the balance of my fee. However I was informed by someone who later visited the finished house it was "fabulous".

A few days later I bumped into Peter Dudgeon, owner of a prestigious design and furnishing company and happened to mention the whole Israel fiasco including the name of the client.

"Doris Morrison?" exclaimed Peter. "Good God Robin, if only I'd known; speaking from bitter experience I would have warned you to steer well clear of her. I wouldn't touch the woman with a barge pole; even a germ-infested one!"

It seems as if Doris Morrison, hell-bent at proving herself the personification of abhorrent, was unknowingly a comedienne when it came to being worldly-wise. I have no idea how the subject came up but Bryan could hardly wait to tell us on his return to the office (this obviously occurring before the Jerusalem fiasco), "Did you know?" he rasped pouring himself a large glass of Pinot Grigio, "according to Doris M, unlike the majority of Englishmen - amongst who it appears to be rampant - there are apparently *no* Jewish gays? None at all!"

"Perhaps Mrs Einstein in drag has never heard of Rabbi Lionel Blue, Stephen Sondheim or Leonard Bernstein?" I replied with a syrupy smile. "But then why should she? Despite being Abbotsbury Road's answer to Metro Golda Meyer I very much doubt if Doris Morrison would ever find herself being invited to mix in such contaminated circles."

"Imagine *Copacabana* without Barry Manilow?" chortled Liz.

"Or *Hans Christen Anderson* with Danny Kaye and *not* RA!" yodelled Bryan, "Though even with a stretch of my extremely fertile imagination, a bit before your time Liz *dear*!"

"Bad luck Bryan!" I chortled, "Dastardly Doris wins the day. Danny Kaye wasn't gay!"

"Oh no?" rasped Bryan. He gave a snigger, "See it as *my* deliberate mistake; to coin one of your beloved phrases!"

"Touché douché!" I replied.

"Explain?" demanded Liz as she topped up our glasses.

"RA the other day at Maison Wasserman, Janet W asked our lord and master if he was quite sure the bright purple banding in the conservatory was correct. 'See it as my deliberate mistake Janet,' replied RA, "and a test for you! Of *course* it's a bit bright but that will make sense once you see the upholstery'. Janet said she had, in fact she still had a sample and as far as she could remember there was no purple in the pattern. None whatsoever! 'Of course not,' said RA as cool as the proverbial cucumber. 'The purple will be introduced in the piping to the upholstery and scatter cushions'."

"And?"

"And?" echoed Bryan, "After we left RA calmly said 'shit, a bit of a balls-up there. Here, take this paint chart with you. That's the purple I told Jim to use. Best get on to Sekers and match a stock silk to it but before you do, ring Percy Bass and tell them to hold *all* the piping as this has been changed from green to purple. The same applies to the scatter cushions. Instead of *eight* in green there'll now be four *purple* and only four green.' RA then gave a laugh and said to me, 'That's how you resolve a mistake by turning into a *deliberate* mistake'!"

"Talk about food for thought," replied Liz giving me a knowing look. "How wonderful to go through life knowing you can do no wrong!"

*

Herty never mentioned the Jerusalem fiasco. Instead she introduced me to another "great friend" of hers and the dreaded Doris Morrison; Estée Lauder. Here again I was subjected to what we, in the office, referred to as "the Herty Hex"! On meeting Estée Lauder I took the liberty of saying working with her would be a pleasure, to which her chilling response "not a pleasure, a privilege" saw me backpedalling as fast as fast as my Gucci loafers would allow. Maybe the Doris Morrison saga could have had something to do with it but I never heard anything more from Estée Lauder.

While RAD was working on Doris Morrison's house in Abbotsbury I had to give credit to Bryan who supervised the project throughout with an almost frenetic devotion. Bryan never broached the subject regarding my short, sharp visit to Jerusalem but I did know he continued to visit this devious, unpleasant woman albeit for drinks in the evening after a day at RAD or a more relaxed dinner.

Compared to the Doris Morrison I knew, Bryan's Doris Morrison appeared to an extremely good fairy as opposed to a hideously wicked witch.

In retrospect the difference between Herty and her two "great friends" was Herty's overwhelming kindness and generosity. When I telephoned Herty at the apartment in Cannes to say her "gold disc tiles" specially fired by Franco Pecchioli in Florence, had arrived and looked "fantastic" her response was equally enthusiastic.

"These I must see," she cried, "so why not fly out with a sample and stay the night? This means I can also invite you for a spoiling 'thank you' dinner."

I duly flew out with the sample tile, lunched with Herty in her stunning apartment in Cannes, stayed the night at the Martinez Hotel and flew back the next morning. QED. It goes without saying Herty "loved" the sample.

Herty adored Ben having been introduced to him at a chance meeting in Burkes where Ben and I were having lunch and Herty and a lady friend happened to be sitting at the next table. So much so that he was invited to several dinners at the Milestone and in Cannes.

"Surely she must realise Ben's gay?" commented Bryan on hearing Ben had been a dinner guest at the Milestone several nights previously.

"No doubt she sees him as delicious handy window dressing and nothing more?" replied Liz.

"*Randy* window dressing you mean," rasped Bryan. "After all from what I've been told once upon a time - before Anna Sewell entered the picture - there *was* the slotty Botty!"

"Anna Sewell? Slotty Botty?" questioned Liz.

"Ignore him Liz, he's only being more pestiferous than usual," I said giving a grinning Bryan a pained look. (The word "pestiferous" an unexpected flashback to Rhodes and Geoff-cum-Burt Lancaster McMinn no doubt.)

"Pestiferous? *Moi?*" cawed Bryan. "Never. Paragon yes but pestiferous? *Pas sanglante probablement*! And before you ask again Liz, Anna Sewell was the author of *Black Beauty*, a tale concerning an extremely well-hung black stallion. Now *there's* a surprise! " Giving a toss of his Jackie O style hairdo he added smugly. "And for the unenlightened the French stands for 'not bloody likely'!"

Like the ever-increasing ripple of my social life, the ever-increasing ripple of RAD successes continued to ripple. Added to which Germaine and her continued introductions to potential new clients appeared to be without an end. "You must meet Freda and Eddie," she announced which resulted in RAD designing an elaborate, oriental-themed duplex above the Scotch House in the heart of exclusive Knightsbridge.

"You must meet Raine and Marvin," she insisted, thus securing the company a contract for refurbishing a spectacular apartment in Chester Terrace; another of the elegant Regency-style conversions overlooking Regents Park. Raine quickly became known in the office as *Reign* (Bryan's doing) due to her "even more regal than the proper Queen's" behaviour; the nickname resulting from a meeting arranged between Raine, Bryan and myself at Blanchards, an exclusive decorators showroom in Sloane Street. The meeting, scheduled for eleven o'clock, saw Bryan and me arriving some ten minutes ahead of the appointed time.

Having dropped me off in Sloane Street, Bryan drove off to park my Mini. On the dot of eleven Raine's dark green Bentley drew up outside Blanchards impressive entrance. Wondering where Bryan had got to I watched with growing amusement the pantomime taking place outside as a solemn-faced, uniformed chauffeur, complete with peak cap, made a great show of opening the rear door of the car before Raine graciously stepped out. Half expecting the overdressed woman (a Woolf fur on a summer day perhaps?) to regally wave at a bemused passer-by (she didn't) I moved forwards to greet her as she made her grand entrance.

"What kept you?" I hissed as Bryan finally joined me. Meanwhile Raine was busy nodding graciously as Mark Aldbrook, son of the owner, stood talking to her about a piece of furniture she appeared to be admiring.

"You won't believe this," Bryan rasped, his hand shielding his mouth, "but having parked in Lowndes Square I noticed a dark green Bentley parked on the corner of Harriet Walk - almost out sordid Siddeley's, your old stomping ground - and who should be sitting in the back but our client." He gave a snicker. "Fascinated, intrigued, whatever, I stood saying to myself, 'I know RA and yours truly couldn't believe the affectation on our first meeting with Raine but it isn't? It *can't* be? I checked my watch and a *minute* before we were due to meet regal spelt *R-e-i-g-n* (he mischievously spelt out his version of the name) obviously instructed the chauffeur it was time to move on - she must have done a recce beforehand - which meant the car drawing up in front of Blanchards as the clock struck! Talk about delusions of grandeur."

Naturally Bryan's tongue-in-cheek "regal Reign" was to stick.

After Bryan's denouement I had no alternative but to let him have all future dealings with the regal Reign. Needless to say the two got on famously, so much so I said to Liz over a de rigueur glass of lunchtime wine (Bryan was at yet another meeting with regal Reign), "Give it another week or two Liz and I'll have to bow to his nibs when addressing him and you'll have to curtsey!"

"But only should His Royal Nibs deign to acknowledge us!" commented Liz holding out her glass for a top up.

Whereas Germaine rode high in the "introduction to new clients" stakes, regrettably not all Georgina's introductions would be as successful as her introduction to Germaine. It was through Georgina I was introduced to a favourite eatery of hers; the opulent and over-decorated Walton's in Walton Street. On arrival we were effusively greeted by the obsequious manager, a short, bearded young man who, if he'd been a shorter, could have easily passed for the actor *José* Ferrer in his role as the stunted Henri Toulouse-Lautrec in United Artists 1952 film *Moulin Rouge.* Ferrer was subjected to an incredible makeover by United Artists' makeup department; the illusion of his dwarfism further helped by walking on kneepads. The manager's name was Malcolm Livingston who required no encouragement whatsoever when it came to getting down on *his* knees. More about the Lilliputian Livingston later.

*

A much sought after prominent "rich American living in London" on the social scene was the silver-haired, silver-tongued Johnny Galliher whose house in Chester Row (a five minute Gucci-shod stroll from Ebury Street) was a talking point with his clever use of colours and eclectic collection of furniture and objet d'art. I had met Johnny several times and been to lunch at Chester Row. He was a great friend of Ben's and unbeknown to me, Ben had arranged for Johnny to view Charlie's apartment. After the surprise visit Ben couldn't wait to tell me what Johnny had said, "Eek Mumsie, Johnny was suitably stunned. Stunned and highly impressed!"

"Robin Anderson Design, good morning. Bryan speaking. How may I help you?" rasped Bryan in his strange falsetto on answering the telephone.

"Help me?" repeated an imperious voice with a slight Australian twang, "Maybe, maybe not," followed by a sharp, "and as that's *not* Robin Anderson . . ."

"No, this is Bryan Larkin, Mr Anderson's assistant."

"Well then 'No, this is Bryan Larkin Mr Anderson's assistant', if Mr Anderson *is* there I would like to speak to him!"

"Of course," snapped Bryan, his Jackie O feathers obviously ruffled (I could hear Liz giggling in the background), "and may Bryan Larkin, Mr Anderson's assistant dare ask who's calling?"

"Oh, getting ratty are we?" said the voice followed by a nigh-on fiendish cackle. "You'd best tell him its Coral Browne a friend - or maybe an *ex* friend - of Johnny Galliher. It all depends on the sheltered Mr Anderson."

"Coral Browne?" yipped Bryan, "Oh, please hold on a second *Miss Browne* whilst I put you through!"

"You do that dear," twanged Coral Browne. "Hold on a second?" she repeated loud enough for me to overhear from my own office. "Put me through? Sounds as if you have very large premises, dear: large, *expensive* premises!"

"It's Coral Browne," said Bryan with an excited hiss appearing as he suddenly appeared in the doorway. "I've put her on hold . . ."

"So I heard," I replied drily.

"Okay if I put her through? Ooh, this is *so* exciting!"

"Who's Coral Browne when she's at home?" I added uninterestedly as I continued checking an estimate sheet.

"Who is Coral Browne?" rasped Bryan, his voice moving up an octave (if possible) in indignation, "Only one of our greatest actresses; Shakespeare being her forte!" Apparently forgetting one of England's greatest actresses was on hold he added vehemently, "Didn't you see *The Killing of Sister George*?"

"Oh? I don't recall Shakespeare having ever written something with such a title . . . ?"

"*The Killing of Sister George*," repeated Bryan tremulously (or it could even have been reverently), "in which she appeared with Beryl Reid and Susannah York. She played the glamorous lesbian from the BBC!"

I thought that was Leslie French, I thought bitchily, *but no, my mistake, a glamorous dyke he ain't!* "Now you mention it does ring some sort of cracked bell," I replied with a patronising smile and giving an inward snicker as Bryan literally deflated in front of me. "Well go on then, put her through. I'm sure one of England's greatest actresses won't take too kindly at being eternally on hold."

"*Shit!*" squawked Bryan immediately withdrawing his Medusa-cum-Jackie O like head from the doorway. "Bitch," I heard him mutter to a bemused Liz (she secretly enjoyed the daily sparring between Bryan and myself), "one Coral Browne is worth a *million* rich, bored Yente housewives! Take it from one who *knows!*"

"Try telling *that* to your Shylock friend, Doris Morrison!" sniped loyal Liz loud enough for me to hear.

"Good morning Miss Browne," schmoozed the adult version of the former *Golden Voice*, "and what an unexpected pleasure! What can I do for you?"

"Bitch! Double bitch!" yodelled Bryan from next door.

"Interesting background noises," came the crisp reply, "as for helping me Mr Anderson - I take it *that* is Mr Anderson I'm speaking to on long distance? - I'm not at all sure yet; it depends. I was talking to Johnny Galliher the other evening about a facelift to me flat and he gave me your name. He says you're very good which means you must be expensive and from what that strange sounding assistant of yours said about sending out a fucking search party to find you (I was soon to learn the F word was an integral part of Coral's technicoloured vocabulary) your premises must be somewhat extensive which also means pretty fucking expensive!"

I looked at the telephone in my hand, my mind racing. *Quite an opening line or even a soliloquy Miss Browne and as for the use of 'fucking' twice in one sentence, I thought that was Maggie's prerogative?* "Ha ha, Miss

Browne," I replied with a chortle, "Al depends on what you er . . . *deem* expensive!"

"Well you'll soon *deem* well know, won't you Mr Anderson?" cackled Coral not to be outdone. "So when can you come and see me flat? I live in Eaton Place - Johnny says your office is near to Chester Square; *very* expensive that Chester Square! - so you're quite close." There was a distinct pause before she said in a matter-of-fact voice, "So when, dear?"

"Would be free later this morning Miss Browne?" I replied, "I did have a twelve o'clock appointment but it's been cancelled . . ."

"Oh, so they must have received their estimates I take it?" interrupted Coral with a further cackle; her Australian accent even more pronounced. "Flat 3, No 15 South Eaton Place. See you on the dot of noon, dear. Goodbye."

"Ooh!" Bryan sang raspingly on re-entering my office, "RAD meets Miss Coral Browne at noon?" He struck a balletic pose and fluffed up his formidable hairdo, "A bona fide star at last! A total *coup* Robin. A genuine first for RAD!"

"I *have* worked with Peter Sellers, Britt Ekland and Christopher Plummer to mention but a few," I reminded him loftily.

"Yes, but *not* through RAD," rebuked Bryan pursing his lips and giving me a disapproving look. "*Not* through RAD."

*

"Come in dear, unlike her mother she won't bite," twanged Coral bending gracefully to stroke the yapping, bug-eyed Chihuahua cowering at her elegantly shod feet.

"How do you do, Miss Browne," said The Golden Voice (down an octave) as I proffered my hand.

"Miss Browne is doing very well, thank you," replied Coral with a faint twitching of her perfectly painted lips, "and whether we end us best friends or warring enemies you'd best call me Coral and I'll call you Robin. So come in dear, no need to remain in the lift. As I said, she won't bite (another cackle) she leaves that up to me!"

I followed Coral into a large sitting room chock-a-block with what I wittily later described to Liz, Bryan and Bill Kendall as endless "VVSC" (Vile

Victorian Schmutter Clutter), a look I found so many clients guilty of pursuing.

"Coffee?" asked Coral, "or a glass of wine? I'm going to have a large *goblet* of wine in order to fortify meself as to what you may suggest to do with me flat!"

"A glass - or goblet - of wine would be great thanks . . . er Coral," I replied with what I considered a rakish smile.

"As long as you don't start seeing fucking double when it comes to any figures!" barked Coral before sweeping back into the entrance lobby and then the kitchen. "I won't be a moment. The bottle's already uncorked!"

Well, well, at last I meet up with the legendary Coral Browne, I thought my mind still whirring at my first impression of the imperious, elegant actress with her Nefertiti, sculpted features, her beautiful face topped by an elegant, terracotta silk turban complementing the sleeveless green shift dress she was wearing. And of course, the aforementioned elegant feet in black Chanel flats. *This project could be great fun or - to quote you, Coral Browne - 'a fucking disaster'!*

I made a quick recce of the large, high-ceilinged room with its two large windows overlooking Eaton Place and Peter Carter's apartment! *One or two really good paintings, pity about the frames,* I thought, *but take a look as these!* "These" being an impressive collection of sphinxes in all shapes and sizes battling for space on virtually every table surface available.

"These are incredible, Coral," I enthused as my client-to-be made her entrance clutching two enormous pewter goblets of wine, the Chihuahua still hovering at her feet and still yapping.

"What are incredible, dear?"

"Your collection of sphinxes Coral. Absolutely mind-blowing!" (A typical Liz expression when talking to Bryan about goodness knows what.)

"Sit," Coral replied handing me a goblet, "but not *there* dear otherwise you'll squash me fucking cat!"

Having avoided squashing the "fucking cat" I perched myself on an uncomfortable, overstuffed, Victorian mahogany framed chair.

"Yes, me sphinxes," continued Coral from where she sat on an overstuffed, Victorian-style sofa facing me, the Chihuahua silent at last and cowering shakily on her lap, "They're to be the main feature of the room." She gave a dramatic sweep of her free hand (the other clutching the goblet), "As for the rest, get rid of it! I want a complete *new* look! We've men on the fucking moon and everybody who's anybody is heading for fucking outer space," - she paused to take a sip - "and that's where I want to be; in space, in a fucking space ship along with me collection of sphinxes!"

"No problem, Coral," I replied, "RAD aka Houston will make sure the blast off and subsequent journey into outer space goes smoothly!"

"Blast off?" murmured Coral eyeing me over the rim of her goblet, "Sounds more of a bumpy journey than a smooth one!"

"Let me assure you Coral there will be *no* bumps," I said with a smile, my mind going into overdrive as I envisaged a pair of Michael Severn's acrylic pyramids subtly spot lit from above and from the softly lit opaque, acrylic bases below.

"Go on," said Coral bending her graceful neck to give the trembling Chihuahua a gentle kiss on its head. "Stun gun me."

"Accompanied by your many sphinxes I see you as a future queen of the Nile; a *modern* Egyptian future queen as you float along more spaceship than any other type of ship . . ."

"Hmm," interrupted Coral, again eyeing me over the rim of her goblet, "A future queen of the Nile floating along in her fucking spaceship? Doesn't sound *nearly* as much fun as an *old* queen *going down* the Nile on a *felucca*, does it dear?" The two sentences said with a deadpan expression.

"No, I suppose it doesn't," I replied lamely. *RA of RAD you're being pathetic,* I thought admonishingly, *Pull yourself together. At once!* "But then again Coral, I don't think going down on a felucca would be nearly as rewarding as going down on the whole *Milky Way* accompanied by your many sphinxes and a couple of acrylic pyramids! A challenge but think of the outcome; the *end* result?"

Try that *little lot for innuendoes Miss B!* I thought taking what could my last gulp of wine before I was told to felucca off.

"Ha ha ha! Hee hee hee!" cackled Coral rocking with laughter and almost dislodging the Chihuahua which began to spasm violently at the unexpected seesawing of its mistress's lap. "I love it dear, I *fucking* love it! Me, in a space suit - Jean Muir will have a fit - in a space ship surrounded by all me fucking sphinxes as I go *down* on the whole fucking Milky Way? What a thought? What a blowjob! What a *challenge!*" She gave me a wide smile. "What a clever, conniving *and* clever young man you appear to be, dear. Don't allow anyone to pull the cashmere over *your* eyes, do you? *Very* clever and worryingly so." She gave a snicker. "Let me assure you this probable new space age queen shudders, positively shudders when she thinks of the feluccing costs!" This last witticism followed by more cackles of laughter and a choked, "Another goblet dear?"

"Then there's the rest of the flat," said Coral once the laughter had subsided and our goblets replenished (the whimpering Chihuahua having obviously decided to seek sanctuary in another part of the potential felucca), "Remember, I will need some sort of a dining area in *this* room . . ."

"Easy Coral," I cut in, "two white acrylic console tables which can be moved together to form a table for eight!"

"Love it dear, so clever, as long as I don't have to call in a couple of fucking removal men every time I decide on inviting people back here for fucking dinner!"

"The acrylic tables won't have to be *carried* Coral. All you'll have to do is *push* them and they'll *glide* or slide across the carpet to meet and form a perfect table!"

"You've an answer to every fucking thing, haven't you dear?" purred Coral. "Now, up on your Gucci loafers, grab your goblet and follow me."

I dutifully followed Coral around the flat (the yapping Chihuahua again in tow) and back to the sitting room.

"So dear," said Coral again ensconced on the sofa, the Chihuahua back on her lap and a refilled goblet in her hand, "When do I next see you accompanied by the shocks?"

"Same time next week?" I suggested brightly. "However, I will have to have pretty free access to the flat over the next few days for measuring up and estimating purposes. The presentation cards appear to be fairly straightforward. Fabric samples are minimal but there will be several photographs and of course my idea for those two magnificent windows."

"And what would your idea for my magnificent windows be, dear? Or must I wait until next week for yet *another* fucking shock?"

"Think ancient Egypt, think Anthony and Cleopatra," I replied, quick as a flash, "and thinking of Anthony, think Roman blinds but Roman blinds with a space age look. Roman blinds made of canvas and slats of mirror with an inset band of green taking up your carpet colour. A matching colour band will also be applied to the ceiling and to draw one's eye away from that simple but very wonky cornice. A band of *mirror* set slightly below running the perimeter of the room. I will also put the two new sofas on recessed *mirrored* plinths so when you walk into the room the sofas will give the impression of floating. A pair of green and white fellucing sofas as it were."

I took a deep breath and mentally crossing fingers continued embroidering my scant knowledge of Ancient Egyptian culture. "And for the entrance hall, Coral, why not a chequerboard effect with *appliqué* panels of *coral* - ha ha - and the selected green on an ivory lacquer background to the cupboard fronts and the walls? After all the game of chequers or *mancala* as it was then called . . ." I gave a light, disparaging laugh, "please forgive me if I'm not one hundred percent with the name - would have been happily played in the palace and other such noble establishments.

"As for your bedroom? A touch of Madame de Pompadour meets the Queen of the Nile perhaps?" I reached for a sample of fabric Coral said she had spotted in "some fucking arty farty fabric boutique" and for some "fucking reason known only to Jack Shit" bought the whole roll "for a possible fucking future use". "Seeing - as with your carpet - you already have this coral, green and black paisley design there is no earthly reason - ha ha! - why we shouldn't put it to good use. In fact your purchase couldn't be more fortuitous."

"Really dear. Does this mean I get a major discount as it now appears *I'm* the one designing the fucking place?" interrupted Coral with a further cackle.

Ignoring the dig I continued breezily, "While I appreciate it's basically a paisley design it's a design which could easily be a doppelgänger to a length of hieroglyphic writings! I suggest we wall the room in the fabric with goblet-headed, coordinated curtains, upholstery and bed treatments. Your bed - or sleigh bed to give it its correct name - bedecked with an Egyptian type corona, side drapes and a covered with a sumptuous white fur throw!"

Goblet-headed curtains - geddit? Beat that *for a punchline,* I thought. *And as for a corona or crown, Egyptian or otherwise plus an acre of fur - faux or otherwise - the glitter ball dear Coral is well and truly in your court!*

For once Coral Browne was rendered speechless.

Strike while the iron is hot, RA, I said to myself, *strike while the iron's very hot!* "To expedite matters Coral do you mind if I use your phone?" I asked.

"Help yourself dear," said Coral weakly, "help yourself while I sit here quietly and *digest.* And do help yourself to another goblet dear as I'm sure all this inspirational work must have given you a thirst!"

I rang Bryan. "Bryan, I'm still at Coral's . . ."

"Oh, so its Coral now, is it?" rasped Bryan followed by a raucous giggle.

"I need to meet Bill Kendall here a.s.a.p.," I said ignoring the giggling interruption. "Coral doesn't mind early morning or early evening meetings which should suit all admirably. Of course I'll need to meet everyone involved which means the likes of Dennis Paget, Sander Zarack from Sander Mirror and Fanny from N and A. I'll also need to meet Phil whatshisname the picture framer I used for Charlie's paintings as there are numerous rather stunning works of art to be reframed . . ."

"More feluccing money," interrupted Coral giving the startled Chihuahua a resounding kiss on the head before taking another sip of wine.

"I've arranged to meet Coral a week today with *all* estimates," I continued brightly, "so chop, chop Lady L; chop, chop! I'm about to leave and should be back in about twenty minutes. See you then."

"Lady L?" rasped Bryan, "And *whom* may I ask is this Lady L?"

"Three guesses *Mr* L! Now get organising! I'll be back in the orifice within the half hour."

"*Orifice?*" repeated Coral with a lewd cackle. "I didn't realise you were quite so *dedicated* to your profession, dear!"

*

Bryan, aided and abetted by the luscious Liz, went onto overdrive and all in question agreed to me at Eaton Place and carefully selected times throughout the Friday.

"Now we wouldn't want Dennis Paget getting into Fanny's way or vice versa, now would we? A veritable tangle of tapes and tempers, *n'est-ce pas*?" rasped Bryan.

"Great, and well done team!" I beamed.

"What about Johnny?" demanded Bryan with a petulant caw.

"Johnny? What has Johnny Galliher to do with Coral's estimates?" I retorted.

"Not Johnny *Galliher*," rasped Bryan with a theatrical rolling of his eyes, "Johnny *Skellorn* of carpet fame. Surely Coral requires the present carpet replaced?"

"No she does not, and if it *was* going to be replaced I would have already said so," I replied brusquely, "the present carpet is exactly the colour I wanted and Coral is more than happy with my choice."

"Please *don't* call me Madam Arcati," hissed Byran with a toss of his Jackie O and adding sibilantly, "Despite *Madam* Arcati being slightly more preferable to Lady L."

"Lady L?" giggled Liz.

"A puerile name dreamed up by puerile people!" rasped Bryan sashaying into the sample room-cum-kitchenette. "Coffee anyone seeing I *don't* have to call Johnny *Skellorn*?"

*

Coral sat silently sipping from her goblet as I explained the various design boards with their fabric snippets, photographs and my sketches. Having received a solemn nod and a murmured, "So far so good dear, I'm very impressed", it was time to go through the accompanying estimates. Running through the individual quotes in a soothing monotone, I finally held up a sheet of paper showing the various totals and the final total or "grand total" as Liz had typed.

"If we're to go ahead Coral RAD will require a fifty percent deposit of the . . . er . . . grand total plus a starting date. Of course - depending on the starting date - I must point out some of the items; for example the reframing of whatever paintings you - we - decide to keep may not be ready in the time frame you stipulate . . ."

"Makes sense," murmured Coral patting the shivering Chihuahua once again ensconced on her lap, "Go on, I'm all ears."

"Plus the two sofas seeing these are not of your standard design and will therefore require special frames in order - ha ha - to help you and your guests get that *floating* feeling!"

"Instead of the *sinking* feeling I'm experiencing at the cost of it all," said Coral with a wolverine smile. She pointed at the photograph of a Wassily chair. "*Very* stylish dear, in fact I must congratulate you. It's all quite magnificent!"

"Why thank you Coral!" I exclaimed, genuinely delighted at her words of praise.

"Don't get *too* fucking carried away dear," cackled Coral reaching for her goblet, "you haven't even started - never mind finished - me flat as yet!"

"Surely you mean we haven't even got a *starting* date in order to calculate a *finishing* date," I replied craftily.

"Ooh-err!" camped Coral, "Whose been sleeping in the knife box? Now let me see . . ." Dumping the indignant Chihuahua on to the treasured carpet she then peered into her handbag which had been lying on the sofa next to her. Taking out a neat, leather-bound diary and a pen she quickly flicked through the pages. "Ah, here we are! I'm away filming from" - she gave a date - "until" - she gave another date - how does that suit you?"

"It's brilliant, Coral," I said breathing a discreet sigh of relief as the time before her departure would be giving us several unexpected weeks grace in which to process the acrylics, organise the mirrors, the bedroom curtains, seam up the bedroom walling and get the upholstery well underway. I took a well-deserved sip of wine. "What's more RAD can happily assure you we'll begin the site work the day after you leave and welcome you back to your ready and waiting spaceship apartment."

"Good," replied Coral followed by an evilly cackled, "As long as that doesn't mean ready for *blast off*!" She tapped a numbered page with a red finger nail, her other hand reaching again for the pen. With an exaggerated, theatrical flourish she drew a large X on the otherwise blank page. "X marks the spot!" she said with a sinister "horror maestro" Vincent Price-like chuckle, "That's the fucking day I move back in with me, cat, me dog and me lawyer!"

A few days later Coral called the office and having asked a swooning and mentally genuflecting Bryan how his day was going, was clicked through to me. "No need to panic, dear, I haven't changed me fucking mind despite me sleepless nights!" crowed Coral. "Still love your designs; still loathe your estimates but the reason for calling is to mention an actress friend I'd like you to meet. Her name's Jill Melford and she lives in Chester Row next door to your friend and my probable downfall, Johnny Galliher." She gave a chuckle. "In addition to the stage, television or films, Melford revels in the offstage role of Lady Leon - her former husband is a baronet - which I suppose helps when making a reservation or impressing shop assistants! And when she's not acting - does she ever stop? - Melford's also *decorator*. Need I say anymore? Anyway, I thought the two of you should meet as I'm sure you'll get along. I've suggested Jill give you a call and if it turns out you've nothing in common you can at least discuss *exorbitant* estimates!" With a further chuckle-cum-cackle Coral hung up.

"At least she didn't say *fucking* quotes?" I muttered with a snigger.

The following day Jill Melford rang resulting in Bryan adding a serious attack of the vapours to his growing repertoire of reactions. "Its Jill *Melford*," he rasped appearing ghoul-like in the doorway. "I've put her on hold. Shall I put her through?"

"Jill Melford?" I murmured questioningly, "Ah yes, Coral said she may ring. She's an actress I believe?"

"Actress?" squawked Bryan his eyes widening (I swear he dyed his lashes), "You should have seen her in *What the Butler Saw* in which she starred with Coral!"

"Well I didn't have the immense privilege; unlike some," I replied with a chilling smile. "None-the-less, you'd better put her through."

"Bitch!" hissed Bryan returning to the main office, "Bitch! Bastard!" His daily mantra being greeted with giggles by the always entertained Liz.

"Good morning Miss Melford?" I crooned, "Coral said you would most probably be calling."

"Probably calling?" said a throaty contralto in reply, "See it as more of a life or death threat if I didn't!" Not giving me a chance to respond Jill

Melford added with a chortle, "Which means we have no alternative but to meet so what are you doing for lunch tomorrow?"

"Er . . . meeting you perhaps?" I said with a touch of *The Avengers* Patrick McGee.

"Divine darling," came the gurgled reply. "I understand you know the address; No 15, next door to the old American queen. One o'clock. Look forward to our sparring!"

Without the benefits of Google and the internet I had no idea what to expect on meeting Jill Melford but it was nothing compared to how we did meet. Deciding on *not* giving Bryan the pleasure of asking for a description of my about-to-be hostess I set off jauntily the next day on my literal blind date. Chester Row, an offshoot to Elizabeth Street and Chester Square (where Bryan parked the RAD van and I parked my mini-hearse), is a narrow street flanked by neat, double-storied early 19th-century houses along with a sprinkling of boutique-type shops and the popular Duke of Wellington pub. My first sighting of Jill Melford (for it *was* a sight) saw me stopping mid-stride and staring open-mouthed at an exceedingly glamorous redhead sitting on the front steps to No 15 while attacking a lobster with a hammer.

"Jill Melford?" I asked tentatively, the grown up version of *The Golden Voice of Teenage Half Hour* momentarily forgotten.

"Darling you must be Robin," she said - a statement not a question - glancing up from under an errant red curl, "are you early or am I late? Forgive me whilst I give this fucker another bang or two - he's an integral part of our lunch - and then we can go inside, say 'how do you' or whatever turns you on and more importantly, organise a welcome drink and introduce you to Liz, my business associate."

Need I say with such a meeting and greeting it could only end up as a case of love at first sight?

The lunch with Jill and Liz (aided and abetted by several bottles of chilled Chablis and three perfectly hammered lobsters) turned out to be a triumph. Jill - a double for a young, sultry Lauren Bacall and known to all as simply Melford, a habit I immediately acquired - and Liz Williams, ex-wife of Brook Williams, Emlyn Williams' son, having me in peals of laughter regarding the various antics of their great friend Liz Taylor and other

Hollywood luminaries. Swearing undying love to the two ladies I swayed my way back to the office.

"Some lunch," rasped Bryan making a great show of studying his wrist watch (he also carried a fob watch on a chain kept tucked away in his jacket pocket), "just as well *we* at the office don't believe in the saying 'while the cat's away the mice will play'!"

"Ha bloody ha!" I snapped, "Maybe you should also try remembering the saying 'bite the hand that feeds you'!"

"Talking of which," said the ever practical Liz, "would you like another glass of wine as I'm positively *dying* for one as, I am sure, is the always industrious Bryan!"

To my disappointment and to all concerned Coral was adamant about not having the flat photographed by several eager magazines.

"What? And give the fucking taxman an idea of what I may have spent on me fucking Nile Delta? Sorry darling, but the answer is no; a great big fucking no!"

Unbeknown to Coral I did manage to take some photographs but, true to my promise, they have never appeared in any magazine. (The only photograph ever to appear was a shot of the sitting room which can be seen in Rose Collis's fabulous biography of Coral Browne titled *This Effing Lady.* I have taken the liberty of using a similar photograph here.)

AN EVENING SEVERAL MONTHS LATER

"Now Hedgerley looks as if it's about to become a refuge of the past and though Benedict is more than generous with his invitations to Digberry, I really would *so* enjoy a country retreat of my own," I said in a self-pitying tone of voice to Liz during one of our regular "well that was quite a day, wasn't it?" evening glasses of wine.

"Strange you should say that," murmured Liz as she reached for a cheese straw (courtesy of the petty cash and the corner grocery shop), "Daddy was only saying last weekend how one of the cottages on the estate has become vacant; the tenants, a vet and his wife - or something like that - emigrating to Canada. Would you like me to have a word? I can't promise anything . . ."

"Would you?" I eagerly replied.

"I've just *asked* if you'd like me to *ask*," Liz drawled with a rolling of her Elizabeth Taylor-like violet eyes, "Honestly, *some* people . . ."

But you asked me if I wanted to you to ask and I've just asked you to do what you asked me? I give up, I thought giving her a baleful stare.

"A country squire no less?" rasped Brian refilling our glasses. "More sartorial extravagance I suppose what with tailored plus-fours and a Rupert Bear-type scarf?"

"Unlike you with an Isadora Duncan-type scarf!" I retorted. "However, as you drive a common-or-garden RAD van opposed to a Bugatti it's highly improbable you'll *ever* be strangled by your Marks and Sparks scarf caught in the rear wheel!"

"No need to be witchy-bitchy," rasped Brian reaching delicately for the last cheese straw.

"Manners maketh man," murmured Liz, "but then I suppose *that* doesn't count here." She nodded in the direction of the sample room-cum-kitchenette. "There's another packet in there, greedy pig!"

"Takes one to know one!" yodelled Brian. *"Petunia!"*

"Petunia?" questioned Liz.

"Petunia Pig of Mickey Mouse fame!" simpered Brian heading for sample room, *"Not* that you'd have the remotest idea!"

"At least you didn't say sow," sniped Liz.

"No I didn't, did?" rasped Brian striking a balletic pose in the doorway. "Cow!"

"I may be a cow but you a bull? Never!" retorted Liz. "A bullshit yes but a bellowing bull? Don't make me moo!" She gave me a dazzling smile. "Please excuse my French RA but I'm sure you've heard worse!" She reached for the telephone. "While dear Bryan *brutally* and *savagely* tears open another packet of cheese straws let me call my father and see if the cottage is still free. If it is and you'd like to have a look at it, why not come down for lunch on Saturday? We live in Surrey approximately halfway between Lingfield and East Grinstead." Liz gave a mischievous smile, "Unless you're planning on joining Ben at Digberry after all?"

"Definitely not this weekend, Liz," I replied with a snort. "Dear Benedict's got what I call one of his *Afro* conventions teeming with hysterical, camper than camp screaming Sylvesters so RA is keeping well out of the way!"

"Good," said Liz starting to dial, "Let me speak to Daddy."

*

"It's perfect Captain John!" I enthused having spent an energetic half hour looking over the enchanting 16th-century cottage set in the overgrown garden to one of the farms making up the Liz's family's estate, along with and several acres of impenetrable woodland. Barely visible through a thicket of oak saplings and brambles were several disused pigsties (flashback to Randolph) which provided a further catalyst for my enthusiasm. "And if the er . . . terms are agreeable I'd love to rent it for, say, a minimum of five years." I treated Liz's father to what DLL called my "*cunning*-lingus" smile. "I appreciate you *will* take into account the undisputed fact I will, among other things, be redecorating the cottage and reorganising the garden?"

"Let's return to the house and discuss all over a large drink," replied Captain John Anderson, a tall, bluff, genial man; the house being Wilderwick House, a large, rambling white-painted Georgian-style edifice.

Liz, who had remained at Wilderwick House, came bounding out of the front door followed by her younger brother James and a tumble of dogs. "Well?" she said as she stood staring at the pair of us, hands firmly on her hips, "What's the verdict? Guilty or not guilty?"

"Apparently oi'm now one of yer ever so 'umble tenants m'Lady," I replied, doffing an imaginary cap.

"Wonderful!" cried Liz moving forward to give me a hug. "Now come and meet Mummy. She's heard only *censored* things about you so don't you *dare* let down your devoted, fibbing secretary!"

Ha! I can see where you get your looks from, Liz, I thought on meeting Lady Gillian, Liz's mother. *Daddy's okay but Mummy, Lady G, is a violet-eyed Madonna in country gear!*

Lunch was a cheerful affair joined by Liz's elder sister Sarah and a friend who was staying the weekend.

"I really look forward to you moving in to the cottage, Robin," said Lady Gillian as we all tucked into a delicious game pie, "it's such a *pretty* cottage and such a waste leaving it lying empty; or half empty seeing it *is* more or less furnished."

"Likewise Lady Gillian, and it couldn't have come at a better time." I replied with a warm smile. "I see no reason why Liz should have mentioned it but I am presently in the process of buying an apartment in Albion Gate, a vast thirties block near to Marble Arch and overlooking Hyde Park." I paused before speaking my favourite line of the moment. "In fact I've just signed the lease!"

"Albion Gate?" echoed Captain John, "I know the block in question." He gave a chuckle. "All I can say is business must be good! Ha! Ha! Ha!"

"All thanks to Liz and co," I replied modestly, "but, as I was about to say, Albion Gate is to have a whole new look; RA today and RA tomorrow as it were. This means selected pieces from Ladbroke Square will fit happily into their new home at the cottage." I gave a light laugh. "The sofa, covered in Martin Battersby's vibrant Bargello print will look fantastic in the beamed sitting room and blend perfectly with those two, splendid Mahogany framed Victorian chairs I'll be inheriting." *Thank Christ they're covered in a drab, olive velour and not at all offensive,* I thought as I gave my host and hostess a disarming smile. "I'll also be bringing down a large plate glass coffee table, a small desk and several pictures and prints. Anything I don't use can always be stored in the large basement storeroom at Albion Gate." I gave another smile. "Apart from the pieces mentioned and items such as bedlinen there's really nothing else needed for the cottage which makes it even *more* of a surprise, the place being - literally - fully furnished."

"Goodness gracious," exclaimed Lady Gillian, "I can hardly wait to see all these new, special effects!"

"What will you do with the small room next to the sitting room which *isn't* furnished?" questioned Liz. "The room with some sort of former oven?"

"It'll make a perfect cosy TV room, Liz," I replied with a condescending smile. "I'll get a couple of large beanbags, make sure there's a *vast* drinks tray and Bob's your uncle!" I raised my wine glass in a toast. "To the cottage!" I cried.

"To the cottage!" chorused the others.

On my first weekend in the cottage I decided to trim the ivy bunched about the heavy wooden lintel above the low front door. "Good heavens?" I muttered, "A name of sorts burned into the wood."

I clipped energetically away at the tough, errant tendrils. "This looks like an M and next to it an O and then another O . . ." clipping away furiously I quickly uncovered the name branded along the top of the door. "I *love* it!" I shouted, "I simply *love* it!"

Standing back to admire my handiwork and the exposed name I burst out laughing. "M-o-o-r-h-a-w-e-s cottage!" I finally managed to gasp, "Not in a thousand years did I ever dream I'd be living in a place called Moorhawes or - as no doubt my *dear* friends will call it - *More Whores*!"

*

Two of John Siddeley's clients were a glitzy couple, Raymond and Sybil Zelker, the founders of the Polly Peck fashion chain. While still working at John Siddeley Limited I had helped supervise the interior work to Raymond and Sybil's flashy penthouse in a new building facing Portman Square close to Selfridges and busy Oxford Street. During one site meeting with the Zelkers I had been introduced to their attractive younger daughter, a no-nonsense type named Liz. Miss Zelker did not appear at all interested in the new apartment but was always charming on the few occasions we did happen to meet.

Almost a year and a half after launching RAD the office received a call from a Liz Levin.

"Liz Levin?" I repeated to RAD Liz who had put the other Liz on hold, "Who the hell's Liz Levin when she's at home? Better put her through."

"Robin?" said a not at all familiar voice, "First of all, congratulations on setting up your own company; you were *wasted* at John Siddeley. It's Liz Levin but you'll only know me as Liz Zelker; Sybil and Raymond's daughter."

"Liz . . . of course . . . thanks for the congratulations. How are you?"

"Great thanks and even *greater* now I've got hold of the man himself! Danny and I - that's Danny Levin, my husband - have just bought our first flat and who else could we ask to design this but Robin Anderson? Danny saw the article on your director Charlie's flat and was - as I told him he would be - totally hooked!"

"Why thank you, Liz," I murmured with faux modesty.

"The flat's in a block on Bayswater Road near Marble Arch and overlooks Hyde Park. We're both very excited about our new home." There was a tentative pause. "When do you think you could meet us there?"

"How about this evening? If I come via Park Lane it's literally on my way back to Ladbroke Square."

"This *evening*?" Liz gave a yelp of delight. "That would be fantastic! What time?"

"Six thirty okay?"

"Couldn't be better," enthused Liz, "it's in the first big grey block facing the Park as you come from Marble Arch. Danny can wait for you in the lobby by the porters' desk and then bring you up to the flat. Oh Robin, this is *fantastic!*"

*

Liz and Danny proved themselves to be that rare phenomenon; perfect clients! Both knew exactly what they wanted from the flat and from me; our initial meeting leaving the three of us in a mood to total euphoria. Liz and Danny had been enthusiastic about my preliminary suggestions regarding colours, window treatments and placing of furniture. Danny was adamant on keeping an Arco floor lamp he possessed and I said, without hesitation, "It will look brilliant in the sitting room; a curved elegance!" whereas Liz's main concern was cupboard space.

"No problem," I said pointing to one long vacant wall, "that wall is simply *crying* out for a vast cupboard run and, depending on the final choice of fabric, I'll incorporate part of the fabric design into a raised motif to the front of cupboard doors. I'll look at fabrics tomorrow and get what I feel you would be happy *sleeping* in sent over to you. If one - I'll send three suggestions - is to your liking I'll have Bill Kendall, my architect, draw up a plan of a typical cupboard front with its applique moulding for you." *What's the betting Lady Larkin falls for Danny?* I thought with a snicker, *and when I tell him of Danny's fondness for long, curved things there'll be no holding the rapacious Lady L!*

After we had finally agreed on the designs and estimates Liz, Danny and I were sitting in the empty flat on three foldup chairs having a celebratory glass of wine when I gave a start and said, "How clever of you to find such a flat. Not only is the block so fabulously well built; look at the position; look at the view? All you see are trees and parkland and - apart from Basil Spence's ghastly phallic skyscraper the other side of the Park - you really could be in the country!" I took a sip of wine. "I wouldn't mind finding something similar: a series of cubes handled as we are doing here and as I did for Charlie." I gave a wry laugh. "It would be a designer's heaven!"

"Why not speak to Joe the Head Porter?" suggested Danny, "He and the rest of the porters are one hundred per cent *au fait* as to what goes on in this block and its twin next door."

"Maybe I'll do just that," I said and promptly did.

"There's only a top floor flat or penthouse as some people call it," Joe the foreign-sounding porter informed me. He flashed conspiratorial gold capped grin. "I have the keys. You wanna have a look?"

With apologies to Caesar and his immortal quote: "I came, I saw and I was conquered!"

Liz and Danny's Albion Gate flat featured prominently in British *Homes and Gardens.* (Anne de Courcy again.) Whereas blue, yellow and ivory were the predominant colours used in Charlie's stunning "bachelor pad", Liz and Danny nestled amidst deep chocolate, red, green and ivory colours for the various backgrounds, upholstery and soft furnishings. A perfect setting for their eclectic collection of furniture ranging from Danny's prized Arco floor lamp to Liz's stylish introduction of 16th -century oak pieces.

My Albion Gate penthouse featured prominently in *Architectural Digest,* the American bible of Interior design (this being my second appearance in the prestigious magazine.) However my penthouse was not the first of my endeavours to appear in *Architectural Digest.* Re-enter Lita Young.

*

"It's Mrs Young for you," announced Liz. "Shall I put her through?"

Lita? I thought. *Surely there's nothing left at Portland Place that needs redoing? Unless of course it's an effing complaint.* I picked up the receiver. "Lita! How are you? This *is* a surprise."

We exchanged pleasantries before Lita said, "Remember the flat you did for Barbara's mother?"

"Yes," I replied cautiously, "The flat I worked on while I was with John Siddeley."

"Do you remember the large Terrace before Clarence Terrace, the one still to be redeveloped?"

"Most definitely," I replied. "Why?"

"David and I are thinking of buying an apartment there and we'd like you to have a look at it with us before we make a final decision."

"Great!" I said being acutely aware of the impressive, redevelopment taking place within several of the glorious Regency Terraces overlooking the Park. "When were you thinking of us having a look?"

"Could you possibly meet us later today?"

Dear Lita, I thought, *another apartment in the massive Regent's Park development? Why, I'd meet you and David at midnight if necessary!* "For you and David, Lita?" I said breezily, "Any time!"

"Is five o'clock too late?"

"Five is fine. Shall I meet you there?"

"Meet us outside. It's York Terrace West, the newest redevelopment directly behind Madame Tussauds.

*

"The flat is on two floors," announced Lita as the three of us entered the relevant freshly plastered main entrance lobby.

"Two floors?" I repeated, "Sound impressive."

"It is!" said Lita excitedly.

We spent a good half hour exploring the shell of the apartment which, like the rest of the impressive Terrace, was still in an acutely raw state. I gazed with typical designer's delight at the challenge. Overshadowing an impressive drawing room and an adjoining study or library area with their elegant, double-height sash windows with views over the Park was an inner, double storied, oval shaped stairwell with the rudiments of an oval shaped staircase. Despite the walls being in a plastered finish and the basic concrete steps supporting a crude, wooden handrail, the impact was immediate. *Fabulous*, I kept saying to myself, *Fabulous and what potential!*

In addition to the drawing room, study or library the extraordinary inner stairwell and a perplexing split entrance hall, the ground floor also contained a cloakroom, a large dining room, an extensive kitchen and utility area, a shower room and a room which could either be used as staff quarters or a further utility room. Upstairs there were for bedrooms and four bathrooms.

"So Robin, what do you think?" asked David Young.

"Buy it," I said without hesitating.

A few days later I had a meeting with the architects responsible for this particular section of the redevelopment. "While the downstairs layout seems fine - though I have expressed my thoughts regarding the two small cheek-by-jowl entrance lobbies to Mr and Mrs Young. I mean, why wasn't it simply formed as one?"

One of the architects mumbled some vague response but as David and Lita hadn't appeared fazed by my query I left it.

Lita insisted on an exact replica of the dining room I had designed for their flat - or apartment - in Portland Place. This involved four large angled cupboards and a series for full height arched mirrors edged in brass.

"However the upper floor requires several major changes (I chose to ignore the indignant glances shared between the two men), the main change being one of the front bedrooms, the matching rear bedroom and the two internal bathrooms are now to be incorporated into one master bedroom with an adjoining dressing, bathroom and shower area. Your greatest challenged will be to design a run of *curved* cupboards to follow the inner oval wall of the stairwell. Added to which this will be mirrored in a large, curved double vanity unit with floating mirrored cabinets suspended above." I gave the two bug-eyed architects a conciliatory smile. "I have also repositioned the bath and sketched in an area for Mr Young's walk-in shower. And in spite of your obvious misgivings gentlemen, let me assure you this finished master bedroom suite can only be a one off."

"Anything else?" asked one of the men tersely.

"Apart from transporting the Portland Place dining room to Regent's Park I think that's about 'it' for the moment; apart from my earlier question about the entrance lobby or lobbies which is still bugging me." Ignoring the additional glares from the architects I continued breezily. "The other two en suite bedrooms stay as is and the small room set between what will now be the new master bedroom suite and one of the daughter's bedrooms will be turned into a small study for Mrs Young. I will let you have details of my suggested wall unit for Mrs Young's study within a day or two."

The major structural changes dealt with along with any built in units, it was time to deal with the interior design. As before, David was happy to leave this to Lita and me. However, one item the three of us did discuss was whether or not to have a fireplace with decorative mantle in the drawing room. As there were no chimney flues incorporated throughout the development (gas log fires were still virtually unheard apart from the States) it was decided to overlook such a traditional enhancement and go for something "different" instead. The "alter ego" or alternative I came up with as opposed to a traditional marble mantle housing a fire screen and (God forbid) an electric fire, was a tall, eight panel screen covered in silk and decorated with dome headed brass nails in a geometric design inspired by one of the fabrics used for part of the window treatments and part of the upholstery.

The fabric, finished in what I can only describe as a "geometric Bargello" of various greens ranging from emerald to acid and blended with ivory and taupe was used to form three upholstered, deep cut out *back* pelmets to the three soaring windows. The same fabric was also used for the covering of two comfortable armchairs. Three sets of curtains made in ivory ribbed silk with extra deep pinch pleat headings along with inset borders of rich green were hung *in front* of the back pelmets described. The sofas were covered in an ivory, green and stone damask with hints of maroon, the maroon coming into its own on a pair of maroon silk-covered Louis VX style armchairs. The walls were finished in a drag effect (ivory, upon deeper ivory with a hint of stone) and the elaborate cornice picked out the colours of the damask to the sofas. More "picking out" was detailed in the finish to the heavy dado rail and the extra deep skirting. At this stage I had already been complimented on my lighting (Charlie Cottenham's apartment and my Albion Gate penthouse having been featured in two major design books detailing lighting and special lighting effects) and made sure all the pertinent features in the drawing room were either pinpointed or washed with light. This did not mean the large room was devoid of any table lamps as several were introduced to give an additional warmth and overall glow to room.

In contrast the study-cum-library was dramatically finished in red, ivory and black with one walled filled with ebonised bookshelves and cabinets.

The most spectacular decorative effect was the inner black and white marble staircase with its curved walls covered in a breathtaking Art Deco style black, ivory and silver wallpaper and a spectacular modern chrome chandelier hanging from the domed ceiling. Knowing how fastidious Lita was about everything used for the interior I arranged for the two of us to visit the prestigious Yubido Lighting showroom where I made her lie down on the floor and gaze up at the chandelier in order to get a better idea as to how the gleaming unit would look soaring above her!

It was David and Lita's spectacular apartment which would appear in *Architectural Digest* (March/April 1973) prior to my own Albion Gate penthouse overlooking Hyde Park (*Architectural Digest* November 1974) snidely referred to as "RA's very personal wet dream" by Lady L aka Bryan.

My Albion Gate penthouse could not have been more different and was further proof I refused to be stigmatised as a one style designer. If you wanted a traditional "feel" to your décor I was more than happy to accommodate this up with distinct touches of RAD and which I dubbed "updated trad."

An earlier visit to the Temple of Knossos on Crete and the vibrant use of terracotta, cerulean blue and black throughout the building had firmly lodged itself in my mind; this along with the mirror-like impact of the placid surrounding Mediterranean Sea. Prior to "signing on the dotted line" for the purchase of the apartment I made sure I would have permission to break down the majority of the inner walls forming a series of box-like rooms. Permission granted and the apartment finally mine I proceeded to have most of the inner walls removed so as to create a spectacular sitting room with two sets of floor to ceiling high double doors on either side of the original fireplace wall; the double doors leading to the master bedroom which comprised of a further lobby leading to an open dressing room and a luxurious bathroom.

The sitting room was reached via a long entrance corridor tiled in glistening black floor with the walls and ceiling lined in a series of black, silver, terracotta and blue bands running both vertically and across the ceiling to give a tunnel-like effect. Adding to the tunnel effect were a pair of full height mirrored doors opening into the extra-large sitting room. To the immediate right of entry corridor there was a small state of the art kitchen. Beyond the kitchen was a tall rectangular opening to the dining room (I was determined to entertain "at home" as opposed to my usual forays to a restaurant) which also housed a "window" looking into the sitting room. Leading off from the dining room was my study plus a shower and guest cloakroom.

I had the sitting room walls and ceiling finished in matt black with two vertical wide mirrored panels set at either end of the vast room, the four sheets of mirror linked together by two extensive runs of mirror panels fixed to the ceiling. The inner panels to the walls between the four vertical pieces contained the only colour in the otherwise black room; namely terracotta. The effect of the two parallel reflective bands soaring as if into infinity amongst their black surrounds was stunning to say the least. The dining room was finished in a lacquer the same terracotta used between the mirrored panels on the sitting room ceiling.

The sitting room hosted an impressive off white L-shaped sofa unit set on a recessed mirrored plinth, three imposing square, off-white upholstered stools (again on mirrored plinths) and four chrome-framed Wassily chairs with off-white canvas upholstery. In the dining room I had an impressive chrome and black dining table with six Knoll Warren Platner dining chairs upholstered in a cerulean blue tweed. The wall containing the "window" to the sitting room was fitted out with glass shelves on which I was happy to display numerous artefacts I already owned or planned to collect on any future travels.

In total contrast to the reception areas I walled the bedroom in panels of beaten steel, including the backs of the floor to ceiling high doors while the bed and bedhead were covered in a vibrant green suede; the green taken from a colourful Joan Miró lithograph; a previous birthday present from DLL. From day one I made it clear I had no intention of being a typical "younger friend" showered in endless fripperies (if you can all a Cartier watch a frippery) but wouldn't say "no" to something "sensible" should any sort of "spoiling" be on the cards!

(As a result one of my many Christmas presents from DLL saw me the proud owner of two further lithographs, one by Henry Moore and one by a Sandra Blow, the latter caustically referred to by Bryan as "RA's never-ending blowjob".)

To emphasise the green I had a fully grown Ficus tree (otherwise known as a Weeping Fig) installed in front of the off-white curtained window. Any carpeting used was an off-white Berber and the windows to the sitting room shielded by wide, vertical off-white panelled blinds. Lighting was by adjustable spots throughout with the exception of the bedroom which boasted adjustable spots on vertical tracks.

According to hearsay an apoplectic Siddeley, on seeing David and Lita's flat featured in *Architectural Digest*, had simply binned the magazine whereas, on seeing my own apartment appearing in the prestigious magazine several months later had given a cry of pure fury before tearing the relevant pages into tiny pieces and binning the magazine.

*

While all seemed to be going from strength to strength in the world of RA the general feeling in England - London in particular - was the total antithesis. Plagued by social discontent (the miners' strikes) and the city being randomly bombed by the IRA the world of RA was akin to living in the proverbial ivory tower. However, this does not mean one was completely oblivious to what was going on. I have to admit - shamelessly and selfishly - one's response was not all that sympathetic. On having to endure London being subjected to three day power blackouts my sympathy was not with the miners. Instead I decried the inconvenience of it all seeing Liz, Bryan and I were unable to use our *electric* typewriters added to which, with the random IRA bombing of London with targets ranging from offices to cars and virtually anything else, post boxes were also avoided.

This led to the added inconvenience of Liz or Brian not allowed to risk posting any letters (some of which had to be hand written due to the power cuts) in the local post boxes. Liz would dutifully deliver any mail to the main post office in Sloane Square on her way home where all the staff were constantly on red alert.

Georgina Halse, who had become a great friend and lived in neighbouring Campden Hill Square (by this time I had moved to Albion Gate) was at home the night the IRA placed a bomb under the car of

Conservative MP Hugh Fraser. Early the following morning, a neighbour, Professor Gordon Hamilton-Farley out walking his two dogs spotted a strange looking device poking out from under Fraser's Jaguar and on stooping to take a closer look inadvertently set off the device. The explosion killed the Professor, his two dogs and completely destroyed the car. Five days before the Campden Hill bomb Walton's Restaurant in Walton Street had also been subjected to an IRA bomb, the bomb killing two people and severely injuring twenty six. Georgina had introduced me to Walton's and it soon become a favourite of mine. Through my frequenting of Walton's I soon became acquainted with both the owner and the restaurant's manager; the latter already briefly mentioned and an acquaintanceship best forgotten: but only after the lurid spilling of the beans!

Despite the continuing "winters of discontent" which seemed to apply to the early seventies business could not have been better for RAD and, as I was soon to learn, for Woolf the Furriers! At the intrepid Georgina's suggestion I duly rang the mysterious Germaine Woolf. I have previously described Germaine as a small, vibrant woman dressed in simple black, her dark hair dressed in a smile chignon, but I have yet to describe our first meeting and subsequent machinations.

"Ha! You arrive on time," said Germaine, her small dark eyes studying me shrewdly, "come, follow me." Her instruction followed by a quick pirouette before tapping her way briskly into the impressive but tired-looking first floor showroom overlooking Grosvenor Street in elegant Mayfair. *Have I a choice?* I thought following the small, busy, ferret-like figure. "You take coffee?" she asked in a croaky staccato.

"Please. Black, no sugar."

"Good! That is why you are so slim," she said. "Darling sit." The word accompanied by a small, bony finger tipped with deep red finger nail pointing in the direction of a drably upholstered, *faux* Louis XV chair, "I'll get us each a coffee and I'll also fetch Cyril." She gave a brief, discoloured smile. "Mr Woolf, my husband."

Sitting with a cup and saucer perched precariously on my Doug Hayward covered knee I sat staring at Germaine and Cyril Woolf who sat staring back. *They're exactly like Heckle and Jeckle,* I thought with an inward grin (Heckle and Jeckle being the witty, over-the-top talking magpie heroes created by Paul Terry for Terrytoons), *only which one's Heckle and which one's Jeckle? Both have impressive beaks but then I have a feeling Germaine* wears *the bigger beak if not the trousers!*

"What did Georgina tell you?" asked Germaine (her voice *definitely* a croak thus confirming my Heckle and Jeckle association). "What did she tell you about us?"

"She said you were great friends," I replied diplomatically, "and had been talking to her about giving your elegant salon a facelift"- I gave a light laugh - "Georgina's expression, not mine - and perhaps I was the person who could help you."

"Yes?" This from Germaine.

Yes? What do you mean by your questioning yes? "So here I am." Taking hold of the cup and saucer I set it down carefully on the polished parquet flooring before making a great show of looking around the cavernous room slowly and thoughtfully. "Very elegant," I murmured, "but the cornice and the mouldings to the walls - as with the dado rail and the panels below - are sadly ignored whereas they should be allowed to make a statement; but a statement that *flatters* your furs, not overshadows them."

Germaine sat staring at me for a moment or two before turning to Jeckle aka Cyril. "This young Robin, he is good, huh?"

"Very good," clacked Cyril in timorous reply.

"Good," croaked Germaine. "Sit or walk around. Have another cup of coffee. Think and then come back to me and Mr Woolf with your ideas. Georgina tells me you charge a designer's fee (*Good on you Georgina!* I thought) and if we agree to your designs you will then submit your estimates. (*Even better plus there'll now be a lavish dinner for you at Walton's, dearest Georgina!*) Should we agree, how long?"

"That will depend on my specialist painter Mrs Woolf. I will have to bring him to the showroom and discuss the various colours and toning I plan to use. Some of the mouldings will be wiped or even stippled. It all depends on my feelings when I discuss the final details with Jim, the painter." I patted the chair on which I was sitting. "I have the perfect fabric for your chairs and the two matching gilt framed sofas so when I come back with Jim for estimating purposes I will also being along Fanny . . . er . . . Mr Adams to measure up the furniture and if any extra stuffing to the chairs and sofas is necessary, he will advise me and include this in his quote."

"Good," croaked Germaine, "Georgina said you were very efficient. She said with you there is no *merde!*"

"No *merde,*" clacked Cyril nodding his dark, sleek head.

"Good; very good," I replied before I could restrain myself. I gave the two my brightest smile. "A letter will be in the post to you tonight with my suggested fee along with an invoice for the requisite deposit and, if all is agreeable, I will be here early next week with Jim Coull my specialist painter and *Mr* Adams regarding the upholstery."

"Good, Robin, very good," croaked Germaine, "and please call me Germaine. Mr Woolf is Cyril."

"Good, very good," clacked Cyril, "and now I must get back to the workrooms."

I longed to say "Good, very good" but funked it saying "I look forward to seeing you both again next week" instead.

The fee accepted and the deposit cheque duly deposited I had Bryan accompany to the site meeting with Jim and Fanny.

"*Bonjour* Madam," rasped Bryan on being introduced to Germaine, "*un plaiser de vous recontrer,*" before lapsing into a tirade of French, whatever he was saying accompanied by high-pitched giggles and a lot of arm waving.

She's off, I thought sourly, *and Christ knows what she's sprouting. Probably suggesting the showroom should be done in nipple pink with gold and lilac mouldings.*

"What's he on about?" muttered Fanny.

"Better be sure he's not letting slip any trade secrets," murmured Jim, his words being more profound than any of us realised.

"If you *don't* mind Bryan, we have work to do," I said sharply.

"Oh, *pardon mois!*" rasped Bryan giving Germaine a pained smile before sashaying over to join us.

Later that afternoon I received a phone call from Germaine.

"What's she want?" I muttered to Liz who had put her hold, "Christ, I was there for at least an hour after Jim and Fanny had left . . . better put

Madam through. Yes, Germaine, how may I help?" I asked on hearing the cautiously croaked "Robin darling?"

"That man Larkin," continued Germaine, "please do not send him or bring him here again. Cyril and I admire you and know we will love your schemes but we do not wish to have to deal with your assistant. Please see he does not visit our showroom ever, *ever* again." She added sharply, "We will see you next Wednesday at ten o'clock. Kiss, kiss!" With the "kiss, kiss" still resounding in my ears Germaine hung up.

"Well, well" I murmured, "That was a tad unexpected and I wonder what the hell sparked off *that* little reaction? Maybe Bryan was a bit too familiar prattling away in French as if he was an old chum? Okay, no site visits for Bryan but then, apart from me checking on Jim and checking on the furniture at the factory, no other site visits should be necessary."

I had a flashback to similar complaint from Coral Browne regarding Bryan. "That old queen Larkin," she snapped, "I don't want him anywhere near me flat: ever!"

"Dare I ask why, Coral?" I murmured in response.

"Dropped some photographs of himself through me fucking letter box, darling. And if fucking *mugshots* would have been bad enough *these* happen to be of Lady fucking Larkin *starkers*!"

"Shit!" I said.

"Not shit dear; starkers." Coral gave a sigh. "Best you just tell him quietly dear that Miss Browne would prefer it if he didn't come a courting! The old queen'll know what Miss Browne means."

"Have you er . . . got rid of the larking Larkin in all is gory glory?" I asked.

"Got rid of them? Of course I've fucking well go rid of them and from the noise its making me fucking toilet's been having a hard time swallowing him!"

When I tactfully suggested to Bryan he "cool it with Coral" I was relieved to find he accepted my request without question and - if I was not mistaken - was acutely embarrassed by the fact Coral must have brought up the subject of the nude photographs.

Due to the amount of work coming through I had had several talks with Liz and Bryan about taking on another assistant. Liz had mentioned a friend who she described as "ultra-stylish and super chic". "Why don't I arrange for Vanessa to come round on evening so the two of you can meet?"

"Why not?" I replied.

"She's not having the van!" rasped Bryan.

"Maybe she'll have a van of her own?" I chuckled, "I rather like the idea of two RAD vans zooming around the fleshpots of London."

The glamorous, elegant Vanessa de Lisle joined the company two weeks later and proved - as Liz had prophesised - "a boon to RAD". I loved her being there as did Bryan, Liz, Bill and all the various tradespeople who worked with her. When it came to the clients there was no doubt whatsoever. Vanessa ruled okay! About a year later I found myself alone with Vanessa in the office. It had been another long active day and we were sitting enjoying a much-needed glass of wine; Vanessa waiting for Liz who had "popped along to Justin's for a few bits and pieces for dinner" and me waiting for Bryan to return from a meeting with a client who, unlike Germaine and Coral, obviously enjoyed her meetings with him.

"Can I say something, Vanessa?" I said tentatively, "and please don't get me wrong but I feel you're wasted here. No," I hastily added on seeing her shocked expression, "I'm not saying you should leave - God forbid, I'd ever say such a thing - but seriously you should be doing something in *fashion*; not interior design." I gave a smile. "Look at you. Straight out of a fashion magazine. You always look a million dollars, even on a tacky, dusty building site."

"But I *love* working here," replied Vanessa.

"And we love having you here," I said in return, "but think about it!"

"*J'arrive!*" came a rasped yodel as Bryan came puffing up the stairs, a pile of fabric swatches and the de rigueur wicker case clasped in his arms, "And what did I tell you? Lily simply loves, loves, *loves,* all my suggestions!"

*

A few weeks later an apologetic Vanessa announced she had decided to enter the parallel cutthroat world of fashion. The enchanting young lady would eventually go on to become the Fashion Editor of *Vogue* and a legend in her field. "Vanessa's Van" as it was known sat forlornly in a garage before being repainted and sold to an elderly friend of Bryan's who "dabbled" in antiques.

The work on the Woolf's showroom proceeded without a hitch. According to Jim Coull Germaine was in raptures with the new look, Cyril was enraptured with the new look and all their customers "bloomin' overwhelmed".

"Now you come and look at our apartment," commanded Germaine. Having vaguely described the present decor she went on to mischievously finish by saying I would find the apartment a challenge and a *"vraie douler dans le cou."* (A real pain in the neck.)

Cyril and Germaine lived in one of the rambling top floor apartments in Bickenhall Mansions, an impressive Victorian mansion block overlooking Marylebone Road; the flat characterised by its red brick exterior and tall gables. During the course of World War 11 the elaborate property had been home to the British Special Operation Executive, an arm of the intelligence services.

Germaine's demands, were - as she put it - *"i'impossible"* to which I blithely replied "my dear Germaine, when it comes to RAD *nothing* is *i'mpossible!"*

Undeterred by my words of wisdom Germaine continued with what she considered her so-called impossible demands. "I want the most chic and unusual dining room. Cyril and I entertain a great deal and there is nothing more flattering than inviting a client to our home - but only *after* the contact has been secured! The same mood - *le même humeur* - applies to the sitting room and corridors. The entrance hall must *tres, tres chic* with a hint of the showroom. *D'accord?"*

Assuring Germaine her requests would be dealt with and the results "truly *fantastique"* I returned a few days later with the initial designs, all of which were greeted with delighted cries of *"fantastique"*, *"merveilleux"* and "bravo".

The design for the dining room not only stunned Cyril and Germaine, it also stunned their guests as they sat cocooned within a glowing, red lacquer shell; the shell severed by the tall window dressed in a waterfall effect of glimmering brass chains. Lighting was by cleverly positioned brass uplighters focussing on the gleaming walls and directional spots set inside a large plate of beaten brass fixed to the ceiling and reflecting the exact size of the new modern plate glass and brass Albrizzi dining table. Two spots illuminated the centre of the table with eight other pin spots lighting each place setting. All lighting throughout the newly decorated rooms was dimmer controlled. Germaine already possessed a set of Regency style black and gold dining chairs which were reupholstered in a black and lacquer red Regency stripe velvet. An added plus to the apartment were the gleaming parquet floors throughout; the gleaming floor of the dining room, the red lacquer walls and matching ceiling with its inset of beaten brass all helping in creating the cocoon effect.

The entrance hall was replica of the show room and finished in cream and taupe. To give an added illusion of grandeur I introduced a lowered ceiling in order to introduce a central, oval-shaped dome to accommodate an elegant crystal chandelier adapted to house elegant, flickering electric candle-style lights. The stylish sitting room with its impressive white marble mantelpiece, three sofas and pair of Regency style armchairs was decorated in cream, taupe and lacquer red with accents of bronze green.

After the initial success with the apartment's reception areas I ended up redecorating Cyril and Germaine's large, airy bedroom. Again, cream and taupe dominated with accents of deep chocolate and turquoise. One of Germaine's prized possessions on display in the bedroom was a threefold, small fretwork Oriental screen, the pattern of which I adapted for the design of the bedhead; an elaborate full height unit upholstered and outline quilted in a magnified version of the screen. The same exaggerated pattern was again used to form a fretwork proscenium arch to the large window with curtains in the same fabric as the upholstered bedhead and cover.

"I'd *love* to see Germaine's apartment," rasped Bryan from the doorway where he stood in typical ballet pose, a glass of wine clasped firmly in his hand. "So tell me RA, when's the grand opening?"

"The grand opening's already opened, Lady L," I advised with a chuckle.

"Oh?" came the querulous response, "And why wasn't I there?"

"*I* was," cooed Liz from the main office, "It was *tres, tres manifique!*"

"Traitorous wench!" I called out followed by a further chuckle. "And you weren't there Bryan simply because you weren't invited." *Shit*, I thought, *no need to be quite so unfeeling towards poor Lady L.* "Remember

Bryan, we can't win them all. Take mother Machiavelli Morrison for example? Whereas she *loathes* Robin Anderson as far as she's concerned, Bryan Larkin can do no wrong!" (I had heard on what I called "the Herty grapevine" Doris had invited Bryan to lunch soon after the Jerusalem fiasco and the two had become as thick as the proverbial thieves. I also knew Bryan had been quietly advising Scottie Morrison, Doris's husband, on the redecorating of his company offices.)

As if to save Bryan any further embarrassment Liz cooed again, "I thought it all quite divine, especially the dining room. You'd *love* the dining room Bryan which looks *exactly* like some very upmarket brothel!"

"Thanks a lot loyal Liz!" I called, feigning indignation.

"Good heavens Liz," rasped Bryan, "I never realised you were an expert on either upmarket or *downmarket* brothels. Speaking from experience are you?"

"Slut!" shrieked Liz.

"Takes on to know one!" simpered Bryan in return. "More Pinot anyone?"

*

Germaine had grown increasingly curious regarding my private life and the way I spent my weekends were of special interest. By this stage I was spending most weekends at Moorhawes with occasional forays to Digberry and even less visits to Hedgerley. Meanwhile DLL was in the process of selling his successful Tap and Die organisation and concentrating on the Italian property complex he was busily redeveloping. This saw DLL spending more time abroad with Hedgerley left in the care of the loyal Horsfalls. Much to their dismay Leslie French had taken it upon himself to take up a new starring role, namely Lord of the Manor. I don't think anyone was at all surprised when the Horsfalls eventually handed in their notice leaving DLL no alternative but to put his beloved Hedgerley on the market. Although this had been his intention in no way did he realise how soon he would have to set about the sad task.

It was at this stage Ben announced he would be putting Digberry on the market (the cottage was bought by pop star Kenny Lynch, best known for his 1962 hit *Up on the Roof*). "It's become too much, Mumsie," he explained. "I intend to get rid of the bolthole in Eaton Square and buy something more elaborate. Eek! Give you something to do for once! Ha ha!"

Georgina (Halse) had been introduced to DLL when he and I accidently bumped into her and a friend during the interval at the theatre one evening. DLL and Georgina got along famously and during the second interval DLL had drawn me aside and said *sotto voce*, "I know Georgina's been a great ally, Robble, so would you like to invite them to join us for dinner? By the way, she's very glamorous and great fun and I can see she obviously adores you!"

Georgina and friend happily accepted DLL's invitation which saw the four of us enjoying a laughter-filled dinner at the Mirabelle. Georgina must have mentioned our impromptu dinner to Germaine and more importantly, expressed DLL's fondness for me and vice versa.

Several months later I met up with Germaine and Cyril at an elaborate dinner given by Freda and Eddie Cowan at the Dorchester. "Germaine!" I cried air kissing her lightly on the cheeks, "What a lovely surprise!" After complimenting each other on how well we looked I added cheerfully for want of something to say, "Have you seen Georgina recently? We're about to begin work on her charming penthouse apartment overlooking Campden Hill Square."

"Yes," purred Germaine fixing me with a beady look. "I know, you know," she added with a croak. "Georgina didn't actually say so but I know, you know!"

"Know what?" I asked, my mind racing. *Don't tell me Georgina's actually gone and told you I'm gay and have a devoted very rich and much older lover? In other words her charming RA's not only a designer but also an old man's poule de luxe? No wonder Germaine looks so triumphant and so pleased with herself!*

"Know what? Know what?" cackled Germaine in her very own Heckle (or was it Jeckle?) way. Giving a twisted smile she leant forward and whispered conspiratorially, "I know this David is your father!"

*

Moorhawes continued to delight with the added plus of entertaining the occasional houseguest or guests for the occasional weekend. I had become extremely fond of my "other" Anderson family with Liz, Lady

Gillian and Captain John always the most welcome of visitors. A regular and highly popular guest proved to be none other than Peter Coats. Peter thoroughly enjoyed his weekends at Moorhawes; so much so he took to inviting himself! Peter described the cottage as "an enchanting, fun haven" and I could only agree!

"*Quelle horreur!*" I cried, raising my hands in mock horror when DLL suggested both he and Leslie paid a visit.

"We'll drive down for lunch," DLL continued, "and, if it helps, I can ask Breffni. He'd love to come along. And before you say something rude about the poor young man, remember he's a great admirer of yours, Robble!"

"You mean Breffni in lieu of Leslie?" I said wickedly.

"Now, now Robble," replied DLL as if speaking to a truculent child, "Leslie would be flattered to be asked plus it would be a very worthwhile move if I may say so?"

After a telling pause I said brightly, "Right then! Lunch it is! Me, you, Leslie and the buoyant Breffni! I'll also ask the Ryotts; DBR and Georgina. They're always saying they'd like to see Moorhawes and, if they're free, the three Andersons. Lady G, Captain John and the luscious Liz." I made a rapid, mental calculation. That leaves us one short. I know, let's leave little Breffni for another *very* distant time." *Not that there'll be another time,* I thought with an inward snicker.

"Eight for lunch?" mused DLL, "that's quite a gathering. Are you sure you can handle that? We wouldn't want to impose on you . . ."

My look said it all. *So what do you call the French Letter? A heavenly aspiration?* "No imposition at all," I added sourly. "If I can cope with the likes of Coral Browne and Madam Woolf, luncheon for eight will be mere child's play."

The dining room in the cottage (I had added a pair of bright yellow, black and terracotta paisley pattern curtains to the room and given the walls a light coating of terracotta emulsion) housed a cumbersome thirties style mahogany table. With the addition of several extra leaves discovered in an adjoining cupboard the table could comfortably seat twelve.

Always an early riser I was up well before six o'clock and after a steaming mug of strong black coffee I set the table, moved the drinks tray from the television room to the entrance hall and set out eight tumblers (no flutes) for the welcoming Bucks' Fizzes and began organising the lunch. As a starter I had brought down a large smoked fish pâté from Justin de Blank and for the main course a large Shepherd's Pie with a creamy, mashed potato topping. For vegetables I seeded and sliced plump, red peppers along with sliced fennel. These I placed separate roasting pans and sprinkled liberally with coarse black pepper and drizzled with virgin ("virgin" *nota bene*) olive oil. The sweet course was simple and another cheat; eight small tubs of strawberry ice cream. Voila!

Lunch turned out to be a great success. Almost at zero hour I had telephoned Georgina earlier prior to them leaving London and suggested they may like stay the night. "Simple sups," I said to Georgina, "a pizza from the local shop, a salad and a *very* runny Brie to follow."

"We'd love to Robun! (Robun being the name bestowed upon me by the three Ryott daughters). Sounds delicious!" cried Georgina into the phone.

"Sounds good to me!" brayed DBR in the background.

"Please try and arrive before the alternate witching hour of twelve noon, Georgina," I added in a sepulchral whisper, "as I really don't wish to have face prissy, patronising Leslie French alone! It'll be bad enough having to be polite to him throughout the whole time of his brief regal visit!"

"We'll be there by eleven thirtyish," replied Georgina with a light laugh. "And I can hardly wait to meet this *bête noir* of yours!"

To my extreme annoyance DLL and Leslie were first to arrive followed by the three Andersons and lastly by DBR and Georgina who claimed they had gotten lost while trying to find Moorhawes.

A smirking Leslie graciously handed me a blue ceramic jar shaped like a beehive. "Your very own little honeypot *dear* Robin," he simpered slyly. "Or *Christopher* Robin should you know a Winnie the *Pooh* to share it with."

"The only Winnie *I* know is Winnie Portarlington who would probably take umbrage and being dubbed a 'poo'," I replied lightly, "Which reminds me, I *must* ask Winnie to dinner when she's next in town. I know she'd simply *adore* La Popote."

"I've never *been* to La Popote," said Leslie with a pout.

"What a pity," I trilled, "though not a honey pot it's a veritable *potpourri* of fun!"

Everybody dutifully "oohed" and "aahed" about the food and appeared to thoroughly enjoy themselves with Georgina going to the top of the class for her diplomatic handling of Leslie French.

"An enchanting young woman," said Leslie on leaving, "a positive breath of fresh air!"

"Wonderful my Robble," said DLL giving me a great bear hug. "I'm always *so* proud of you!" he whispered, "The cottage is quite magical: almost as magical as the person who lives in it."

"That was great fun, Robun," said Georgina, "now, who's helping you with the washing up?"

"Nobody," I laughed, "I'm not that grand; *yet*! So why don't you and the Dada (Dada being the Ryott girls name for their father) help yourselves to more coffee and liqueurs while I get to work."

"Nonsense," admonished Georgina before adding - much to my surprise - "We'll help ourselves to another liqueur and then we'll *all* get to work!"

With the dining room and kitchen cleared and the washing up all done we settled ourselves in the sitting room when, to my delight, DBR and Georgina asked me if I would be interested in designing the entrance hall, stairs and drawing room to the house in Clifton Place. I immediately said "yes" which led to a cheerful discussion involving their likes and dislikes taking up right up to pizza time.

One of my personal RA design favourites was the geometric half-drop design for Charlie Cottenham's London apartment; the format being a half-drop repeat of an H motif on a contrasting background. To achieve the most vibrant effect I would suggest a tight woven Brussels weave as opposed to normal wool but it would be up to the client to make the final choice of texture. Whereas Charlie's carpet had been woven with a yellow H linked with black on a blue background, I chose terracotta, black and navy for the Ryotts' entrance hall and imposing staircase, the colours again being incorporated in the walls and ceiling.

Soon after he had sold both Digberry and his flat in Eaton Square Ben gave me a call. "Eek Mumsie!" he announced excitedly, "I've found *the* most sensational top floor flat - or apartment as the agent called it - of immense character in Cadogan Gardens for you to design!"

Knowing Ben's taste I proposed an "updated trad design and then some".

Ben's only input was a cheery, "Eek Mumsie! They've never been on display before but I have about a hundred silver mustard pots I'd like displayed" (flashback to Coral and her sphinxes) and "Promise me you won't forget my toy train either!"

Mustard pots and a toy train? Another flashback. This to the childish rhyme, *Easy peasy, lemon squeezy* and the saying, "Now, now, *Benny Wenny, don't cry about it, learning how to add fractions is easy peasy".*

Without a doubt the colour mustard would also predominate but in a subtle manner so as not to be too unpalatable!

"I like Charlie's carpet," commented Ben. "By the way Mumsie, Hector and Tatchell were bowled over by their new surroundings." He added mischievously, "Though Tatchell did say having to serve dinner to his lordship's guests 'seated inside a cow's udder' would certainly be a first!"

"Seated inside a cow's *udder?*" I replied with feigned indignation, "Should you ever be one of his lordship's guests at a dinner I suggest you discreetly moo to dearest Tatchell the cowhide covering the dining room walls comes from the most beauteous of Argentinian cows fed only on the best alfalfa!"

I had momentarily forgotten Ben's suggestion to Charlie (on selling Digberry) he perhaps would like a chef and butler team to take care of him. To give Charlie a "taster" he invited Charlie to the cottage for lunch in order to see Hector and Tatchell "at work". Hector - always titillated by a title - produced a stunning Earl Grey rum and sticky toffee pudding while Tatchell (for some reason known only to himself) sported a dazzling red, white and blue striped waistcoat. Charlie was hooked and invited the two to take over the running of "my London apartment as soon as Mr Colman releases you!"

Ben's new "playpen" in leafy Cadogan Gardens occupied the complete top floor of a converted, 19th-century red brick Flemish-inspired gabled building.

"Eek Mumsie, a penthouse like yours but - unlike yours - a penthouse with reservations!" said Ben with a chortle.

The architect responsible for the conversion had skilfully incorporated the original staircase belonging to the house for exclusive access to the top floor apartment while creating a new, smaller entrance lobby and staircase to serve the two apartments below Ben.

Mustard pots and a toy train, I thought before saying out loud, "Surely there can be nothing better for displaying the pots than a pair of Coral-type acrylic pyramids?" I gave a chuckle. "As for Benny Wenny's chuff chuff, why not a railway siding at the foot of Master Mustard's beddy weddy?"Ben also admired what he termed "Charlie's hieroglyphic carpet" leading to the half-drop H design being recoloured using mustard yellow, tan and black.

With the contents of Digbery and Eaton Square combined Ben ended up with an impressive collection of framed drawings, prints and paintings, all of which I used for an eclectic display covering the walls of the three tiered staircase. Directional spots were inset to the ceiling and attached to the wall to illuminate these. "Never again," I said to Bryan after he and I had spent a whole day aided and abetted by two patient carpenters positioning and hanging the collection.

"Never again," I would repeat a few days later having polished and positioned ninety plus silver mustard pots in two towering acrylic pyramids in the newly decorated sitting room.

Ben's sitting room set in the steep gabled roof resting on a set of low walls contained a pair of French windows leading onto a small terrace with stone balustrades. Within a couple of days the terrace was soon a riot of colourful flowers and shrubs which had been transplanted into a selection of the stone urns and planters.

Two long, comfortable cream-covered sofas formed an L-shape embracing a large plate glass topped table with a beaten X-shaped brass base. Sitting at either end of the L-shape were a pair of illuminated opaque white cubes holding the two acrylic pyramids Illuminated from above and below, ensuring the silver pots glittered and sparkled. Heavy cream silk curtains with mustard and gold rope ties and tassels graced the French windows. A pair of gilt-framed Louis XV tapestried armchairs faced the elegant sofa area. To compliment the furnishing the gables and walls were finished in mustard coloured glaze lightly sponged with black to convey an antique finish. A set of twenty four map prints in gilt frames were literally stuck to the sloping gables above the two sofas (more mutterings of "never again").

All the skirting, door frames and doors throughout the apartment were finished in a rich mahogany veneer; the same veneer used on the base of the marble-topped vanity unit and the bath panels in the bathroom. I also installed a mahogany dado rail with mahogany panelling below and the haphazardly sloping walls and ceiling papered in an exaggerated black, mustard and gold French cane patterned wallpaper from Osborne and Little. *Pièce de résistance* was the toilet hidden within an antique mahogany armchair with a lift-up French cane seat. (A tribute to Mildred Armitage perhaps?)

There was also a small study boasting a Regency mahogany desk, leather desk chair and two olive green leather club chairs. Holding centre stage as it were was another "Ben toy"; a large globe on which he'd pinned small flags showing parts of the world he had visited.

"You've still to visit Dosso!" I quipped, "So get your flag ready!"

The bedroom featured a large steel-framed four poster bed designed by Alessandro Albrizzi whose original shop in Sloane Square is now under the name Albrissi; a double "S" replacing the double "Z". The fitted bedspread in bright green suede (the colour taken from Ben's enormous Hornby model train) was overlaid by a giant size panel of raccoon fur. The model train sat at the end of the bed on a low, extra-long, cream-coloured square edged console table. Two mahogany military chests served as bedside tables complimented a handsome mahogany tallboy next to the dormer window.

Martin Hunt, RAD's newly appointed architect, somehow managed to sneak in (or accommodate) a small, walk-in wardrobe. RAD's housewarming present for Ben was a pair of two brass angled Billy Baldwin wall lights for the bedroom duly positioned above the chests. In the seventies no such lights were available in England so I arranged for the pair to be sent over from New York. Ben was highly chuffed with his house warming gift from RAD. Photographs of Ben's apartment featured in several editions English *House & Garden*.

*

"I expect Ben's launch party will be subject to an all-male guest list?" quipped Liz.

"So astute is the lovely, outcast Liz Anderson," rasped Bryan.

"So sad *you* won't be on it either. Lady L!" retorted Liz swinging back to continue with her typing.

"Stupid stuck up cow," hissed Bryan.

"Better a stuck up cow than a Taurus the Bullshit," cooed Liz with a camp flutter of her eyelashes.

"Taurus the Bullshit?" Bryan raised a badly plucked eyebrow. "Far too original for you Liz dear. Well if *I'm* Taurus the Bullshit you must be Liz the Laconic seeing you hardly ever move your shapely arse unless it's to make yourself a coffee, Bloody Mary or a Mimosa!" He gave Liz a glare before adding prissily, "And as you're being so brilliant in casting aspersions see if you can work out *this* little gem."

"Try me." hissed Liz, her eyes narrowing dangerously.

Bryan leaned back against the worktop and folded his arms, "Okay Miss Clever Clogs, Miss Smarty Pants, Miss Know-all or whatever turns you off; here goes . . .

'Elizabeth, Elspeth, Betsey and Bess

They went together to seek a bird's nest

They found a nest with five eggs in

They all took one and left four in.'

Explain that little lightbulb if you can!"

"Idiot," trilled Liz, "it's obvious. Seeing Elizabeth, Elspeth, Betsey and Bess can only be the lovely me of *course* I'd have left the other four eggs to hatch or whatever. Honestly Lady L. Have you *never* thought of growing up?"

"Now now children," I said soothingly, "please remember in RAD we are all *nice!*"

"Try telling *that* to the marines!" cawed Bryan.

"You wish!" chortled Liz.

"*Definitely* wine time," I interrupted sharply, "without the H that is!"

*

I stood smiling smugly as I watched Ben greeting what appeared to be a never ending line of guests. Snatches of "it's all thanks to Mumsie", "It's great, isn't it?" and "isn't she a clever old thing?" could be heard uttered by a delighted Ben. Fashionably late Diamond Lil dressed from top to toe in denim eventually deigned to make an appearance.

"Diamond Lil!" I exclaimed. "A veritable vision in denim," I added as he graciously proffered a limp hand in greeting as if expecting some sort of Papal kiss. "Love the ring," I said, my eyes fixated on his ring, a large a sapphire surrounded by diamonds. "Fabulous sapphire."

"What else does one wear with denim?" pouted Diamond Lil before swanning off to greet our host.

"Uh-oh," I muttered on hearing a muffled crash on the lower stairs followed by a few muffled "fucks", "bugger it" and "shit"!

A grinning American businessman friend, Jack Davis (known as "Uncle Jack") duly appeared supporting a tousled colleague somewhat the worse for wear.

"Hi gorgeous," drawled Jack, "I was able to bring along my friend after all." He gave the swaying man a shake. "Edward, this is Robin. Robin this is Edward; Edward Albee."

Ah yes, Mr Albee of Who's Afraid of Virginia Woolf *fame, I thought. Ben did say he could possibly be one of the many.*

"Good evening Edward; evening Jack." I nodded towards the doorway of the sitting room. "Ben's in there with another forty or so kindred spirits. There's a bar set up in the kitchen plus two extremely harassed waiters serving drinks in general." (Ben having "borrowed" Hector and Tatchell from Charlie for the occasion and Christopher Hunter having loaned "Welsh" Hugh from La Popote to act as barman.) "If you need a seat for Edward manhandle one of the guests from a sofa or chair. I'm sure they'll be delighted!"

"Will do," drawled Jack steering Edward in the direction of the sitting room.

"Riccardo!" I cried on seeing a beaming Richard Reynolds appear on the staircase. "And Little David? Great to see you!" Little David (apparently he wasn't "little" at all) being a charming young black man Ben had recently introduced to Richard.

"Fabulous staircase, Mumsie!" chuckled Richard. "Sorry we're slightly late but you know how it is . . ." Giving Little David a playful nudge he added *sotto voce,* "The Little One caught decided to join me in the shower and . . ."

"And things got out of or - better still - in hand. No need to elaborate Richard." Ignoring Little Richard's squeaked "Naughty Mumsie!" I continued cheerfully, "It all appears to be going great guns.

There's quite a crowd already with even more expected . . ." my words cut short by a thunderous crash coming from the sitting room followed by a series of startled yells.

"Christ! What on *earth . . .* ?" Richard began.

"Don't tell me but I have a very nasty suspicion!" I replied dashing into the sitting room where I was greeted by the sight of Edward Albee lying flat on his back among some fifty mustard pots and various sections of the former, upright acrylic pyramid. I glanced to where Ben was standing shaking with laughter.

"Eek Mumsie!" he managed to gasp, "Seeing your expression I don't think its Virginia Woolf poor Edward should be afraid of!"

An embarrassed Edward was helped to his feet by two concerned guests. "I'm *so* sorry Ben," he kept repeating, "Somehow I just *seemed* to bump into your charming, family heirlooms!"

"No need to worry, Edward," replied Ben with a mischievous grin. "It'll give Mumsie something to do later! She always enjoys playing 'too old to cut the mustard'!"

In no time at all Tatchell helped me resurrect the pyramid (*sans* mustard pots) while a tut-tutting Hector collected the errant pots together and placed them in two large bin bags. "For Mumsie to play with tomorrow!" he quipped.

The rest of the evening passed without further incident.

On saying "goodnight" to Ben, a sobered up Edward turned to me and said with a wink, "If it's any consolation to you, Robin. I don't think you're at all too old!"

"Eek Mumsie," said Ben as he watched Edward and Jack cautiously descending the stairs, "who knows, maybe there'll be a rival to Virginia Woolf after all? However, it can't possibly be called *Who's Afraid of Robin Anderson* because we *already* know the answer to that. We *all* are!"

*

The extraordinary "surprises" Ben appeared to produce never failed to amaze me. "Mumsie, say hello to Lionel," he said one evening on introducing me to a hairy little man standing examining one of the pyramids of pots.

"Lionel?" I asked staring at the uninspiring rather shabby looking person, "Lionel who?"

"Lionel Bart!" chorused Ben before breaking into a strangulated *"Oliver! Oliver!"*

Unlike DLL who epitomised the terms *Il Colonnello* or a tall, upright, somewhat portly English gentleman and therefore my "ideal" match as it were, I would also find myself overwhelmingly attracted to the complete opposite, namely men who were short, thickset and hirsute. This usually meant they would also be bald or balding. Think Bob Hoskins and yes, I do mean it, Danny DeVito but in name only; the two not being gay. Another short "fun fur" on my list was Irving Rapper of *Now Voyager* fame. An "all revealing" *vignette* about Bette Davis's Svengali comes later.

Lionel Bart could easily have stepped into any of these gentlemen's shoes. I found Lionel to be charming, self-effacing and without doubt one of "gaydom's" nicest success stories. After half an hour during which Lionel and I wickedly "knighted and blighted" (depending on how you looked at it) most of the giggling, gossiping, posturing and preening queens gathered for another of Ben's "fun evenings" I turned to my delightful companion and said, "Lunch tomorrow Lionel if you're free?"

"Sounds fun," smiled the little man. "And yes Mumsie, I'd love to."

"Brilliant!" I replied, "But only on condition you call me Robin as opposed to Mumsie!"

"Sounds even more fun," said Lionel with an even bigger smile. "And yes Robin. I'd love to!"

I saw Lionel on several occasions and can only repeat what I've already said, Lionel Bart was most certainly one of "gaydom's" nicest.

"Eek Mumsie!" grinned Ben on seeing the rapport between Lionel and myself, "Talk about the Colonel and the clown! As Uncle Richard so rightly says, 'Mumsie certainly keeps us guessing'!"

In hindsight Ben and Richard could not have been more accurate for if you lined up the likes of a DLL, a Nicholas Eden, an Anthony Ward, a Charles B or a Tony Hutt next to a line-up of a Lionel Bart and a Bob Hoskins or Danny DeVito lookalike, the contrast would be startling to say the least!

*

Another wild fortnight spent with Ben in St. Tropez saw us spending a great deal of time with another of Ben's new finds, a rugged, brash, loud-mouthed American named Thomas (Tom) W. Murphy whose claim to fame along with a substantial fortune was his ownership of a "trotter" (horse) called Laverne. Not only did Laverne trot admirably but he also proved to be a super stud resulting in a series of lucrative stud fees for his garrulous owner. Hence Murphy building the most ostentatious of villas overlooking St. Tropez. The villa, set along from the exclusive Hotel Byblos, being aptly named Villa Laverne.

On this occasion two of Tom Murphy's guest were a couple from New York, a doppelgänger for Danny DeVito positively *drenched* in thick, unruly, whorls of black hair and his alcoholic other half known simply as Briggs. The hirsute troglodyte was named Sandy Sandson, a teacher at the Montessori School. From the moment Sandy and I locked eyes the wicked deed could be taken as done. He and Briggs became great friends and I would see the two whenever they passed through London or when I visited New York. Poor Bryan. On one occasion having been roped into dinner at La Popote to make up a fourth he was left to the drunken wiles of Briggs while Sandy and I went on to dance the night away at Yours or Mine, a gay disco in Kensington.

"How *could* you RA?" rasped Bryan the following morning as he clutched a much-needed Screwdriver (orange juice and vodka). "And as for Brigg's breath . . . forget it!"

"You were only meant to sit and have another drink or two, not go to *bed* with him," I replied with a snicker.

"Ever tried to shake off a very drunken limpet?" cawed Bryan. I laughingly shook my head. "I thought not," he said glowering, "otherwise you'd be even more than overtly sympathetic!"

*

"Peter Coats for you," carolled Liz as I stood in the kitchenette preparing two mugs of instant coffee.

"I'll take it here," I said placing one of the steaming mugs onto Liz's worktop and reaching for the telephone. "Peter, good morning! This is indeed an honour; a call from the erudite Mr Coats before ten in the a.m.!"

"It's about dinner tonight," replied Peter with a chuckle. "Whilst appreciate it's a bit of a cheek could you possibly manage one other?"

"One other as in guest? Surprise me before I say yes."

"An actor friend named Barry Justice. I don't think you've met him?"

"No, not to my sordid, worldly knowledge," I replied. I added with a chuckle. "For a dreaded moment I thought you were about to suggest the even more dreaded 'I've a porcelain complexion' Tony Pawson should he be in town!" (It was rumoured the eccentric Tony Pawson had gone through the painful process of having all his facial hair removed by electrolysis.)

"As if even *I* would dare suggest such a clashing?" laughed Peter. "So is Mr Justice permitted to attend?"

"Absolutely Peter. Up until now there were only four guests plus yours truly." It was my turn to laugh. "I *was* considering inviting Peter Stiles but he will now have to wait."

"I can assure you Mr Justice is *far* more entertaining than the lumbering, oafish, social climbing Mr Stiles," sniped Peter. "See you around eight us usual?"

"*Perfezionare*," I replied.

I turned to Liz who was sitting sipping her coffee while peering at a copy of the *Daily Mail.* "Does the name Barry Justice ring any bells?" I asked, "Apparently he's an actor?"

"*Barry Justice!*" shrieked Liz almost spilling her coffee, "Barry Justice as in Barry Justice the dishy, dastardly Burgo Fitzgerald in *The Pallisers* now on television?"

"If you say so," I murmured blowing on to my coffee.

"I *do* say so and he's *divine!*" Liz gave me a schoolmarm-ish look, "Oh no, don't tell me . . .?"

"Yes Liz, I'm afraid so plus he's coming to dinner tonight!"

*

A beaming Peter arrived at Albion Gate on the dot of eight with a smiling Barry Justice in tow.

Goodness, I thought as the evening progressed, *I can see what the lovely Liz meant in between swoons for you, Mr Justice are not only a dish but an extremely charming and amusing dish at that. Nor would the description 'sex on legs' go amiss!*

As he and Peter were leaving Barry suddenly spun round and planted a hearty smacker on my lips. "Lunch tomorrow?" he said, his eyes twinkling.

"Why not?" I laughingly replied. "Do you know The Tent in Eccleston Street?" The Tent being literally round the corner from the RAD offices.

"Know it well. One o'clock suit you?"

"Suits me fine!"

"My, what a matchmaker I am," quipped Peter giving me a backward glance as he and Barry entered the elevator.

Barry and I began meeting on a regular basis with our developing friendship leading to Coral coming out with one of her typically lethal quotes (on this occasion to Melford who wasted no time in repeating Coral's remark to several others ensuring it would get back to me sooner than later).

"Robin's seeing Barry Justice?" Coral had questioned, a wicked glint in her eye. "But I was told Boozy Barry was only interested in fucking old ladies? Oh dear, what *have* I said?" Her crack "Boozy Barry" never registering at the time.

On being asked if he knew of Jill Melford "the actress who had appeared in *What The Butler Saw* with Coral Browne" Barry's reaction was even more acerbic.

"Jill Melford?" he cried, "Of course I know Jill Melford. Ghastly woman." He raised a much-practiced eyebrow. "Calls herself an actress, does she? Good God, from what I've heard the woman couldn't act her way *into* a brown paper bag never mind her way out of it!"

"She also dabbles in interior design . . ."

"I would have thought dribbles or *defecates* a more appropriate description," replied Barry spikily.

Ouch! I thought. *Best not to suggest a get-together involving these two. Never ever!*

Much to Liz's delight Barry was a constant visitor to Moorhawes and we spent many a gassy Sunday luncheon with the Anderson family over at Wilderwick House.

Leafing through a copy of Bryan's *Harpers & Queen Magazine* I found lying on his desktop I spotted an article on the opening of a new, luxurious hotel on the little-known Caribbean island of St. Lucia. I read the article several times before coming to a decision. *Why not?* I thought. *I need a break and as I've never been to the Caribbean and if this La Toc Hotel is as good as it promises to be . . . Furthermore, I'm sure Barry - if he accepts my invitation - would prove the impossible by looking even* more *handsome with a tan!*

We flew direct from London to Barbados where we had a stopover of several hours before taking the "island hopper" (a small eight seater) on to Castries, St Lucia's tiny airport. Prior to leaving for St. Lucia Barry and I invited to another of Peter's delightful lunches. Among the other guests was David Hicks who insisted I contact Oliver Messel, the interior and set designer, who lived on Barbados.

"What's more," DH said on being told of our stopover on the island, "I'll call Oliver and suggest you and Barry take a taxi over to Maddox, Oliver's enchanting house. He'll know doubt ask you to lunch. Both of you will *adore* Oliver and vice versa!"

As anticipated Oliver Messel promptly invited us to lunch.

"If La Toc and St. Lucia can match this I'll be as happy as a pig in shit!" announced Barry with a mischievous grin in between gulps of this third rum punch.

"As opposed to a 'pig' in clover?" replied Oliver waspishly.

"Or even a 'pig' in the Caribbean?" I added giving Barry a reprimanding look.

Lunch was served on a veranda overlooking a verdant lawn which sloped downwards to a small private beach. Maddox was a pure reflection of Oliver's rich, theatrical designs and a positive treasure trove for new ideas. I was particularly fascinated by one of the walls on the veranda where we had lunch. Oliver had covered the terracotta coloured wall with a variety of white painted picture frames; each frame containing a mirror. The result was a wall of sparkling, reflected garden and seascapes and a feature I copied for the garden room at The Grove, the dower house I would eventually lease from David Hicks. (The Grove being a glorious Georgian house on DH's spectacular Britwell estate.)

I sat watching nervously as an already rum-infused Barry began downing glass after glass of wine, his words beginning to slur and his eyes adopt a vacant look.

"Fanny Cradock and Johnnie were also on the flight out," he suddenly hiccupped; the reference made to Fanny Cradock the flamboyant celebrity cook who appeared regularly on television with her hen-pecked husband, Major Johnnie Cradock during the sixties.

"What fun!" trilled Oliver spearing a segment of his fruit salad.

"Say Oliver," added Barry with a lopsided leer, "what's the difference between a jogger and Fanny Cradock?"

"The er . . . difference between a jogger and Fanny Cradock?" repeated Oliver. "I've no idea . . . Barry. You'd better tell."

"One's a pant in the country," guffawed Barry, "while the other's a . . ."

"I think Oliver can work out the *punch*-line himself, thank you Barry," I interrupted sharply.

"Er . . . yes, I'm sure I can," chirruped Oliver looking decidedly uncomfortable. "Coffee anyone?"

Bidding farewell to Oliver we returned to the airport and boarded our flight for St. Lucia. To my delight La Toc Hotel proved to be exactly the magical place *Harpers & Queen Magazine* promised it would. Determined to see more than one island I arranged for two weeks on St. Lucia plus a week visiting the neighbouring islands of Martinique and Trinidad.

I was completely overwhelmed by an evening visit by canoe to the Caroni Swamp on Trinidad where on sat watching the sunset and the endless flaming Scarlet Ibis flying in to roost on the numerous small islands dotting the swamp. "It looks like flaming Oxford Street at Christmas," slurred Barry taking a swig from his ever vigilant hipflask.

"Are you sure you don't mean Delirium Tremens Street?" I replied sarcastically. My comment receiving a further glared - by this stage - cross-eyed response.

During our final week on St. Lucia - apart from a drive to Soufriere where Barry and I tested out the hot, sulphur baths; a legacy from the former volcano - I found myself spending more and more time in the company of the other guests at the hotel while my guest lay slumped out on a sunlounger accompanied by never ending rum cocktails; our intermittent conversation reduced to nothing more than a cool minimum.

Aware of my enthusiasm regarding the luxurious hotel development the charming manager, gave me a private viewing over one of the luxurious bungalows being built in the grounds of the tropical paradise.

"They are scheduled to be in operation by the end of the year," he informed me during our walkabout.

"And if I wished to rent one or even two over Christmas?" I enquired nonchalantly.

"Obviously we could come to a special arrangement," came the smiling reply.

My mind whirring at the thought of inviting a select group of friends to spend Christmas in the Caribbean I made my way to the bar where, having ordered a rum punch from the barman, a tall, lean, serious-looking black man named Albert, I sat drawing up a list of potential guests plus an approximate costing of the whole exercise.

"I will have to hire one of the hotel's Mini Mokes, if not two," I muttered, "plus check the possibility of chartering a boat for a few days beach hopping."

"Excuse me Suh," said a deep bass voice.

"Yes Albert?" I replied glancing up.

Albert stood staring down at me before nervously clearing his throat. "Forgive me for the intrusion Suh but I have to tell you I have been watching you since your return to the hotel a few days past. I find you very handsome and elegant Suh, and I would be honoured if you would allow me to romance you from behind."

After my initial surprise at Albert's totally unexpected declaration I replied to his somewhat startling request as gently as I could, "Thank you for your kind words Albert," I said with feigned shyness, "but as you know I am travelling with a friend and he would be most upset if I took you up on your charming invitation."

"I am saddened to hear that Suh," murmured Albert. "For now I will have to replace Suh with my hand."

*

"How as your trip?" asked Liz on entering the office.

"Beware Liz, be very beware for methinks our illustrious Lord and Master is a tad pissed off," rasped Bryan handing her a Mimosa. "Here, have one of these as we help him drown his sorrows. From what I gather Bergo didn't er . . . do *justice* to all dose islands in da sun."

"Very funny Lady L!" I snapped. "But you're right. However, I can't fault St. Lucia and will venture back but this time making sure I am *not* accompanied by Mr Alcoholic not at all Anonymous!"

After the Caribbean debacle my meetings with Barry became more and more sporadic. In a moment of weakness I suggested he joined me for a weekend at the Cipriani in Venice. The weekend proved to be even more of a disaster than one could have possibly imagined. Instead of spending three days exploring this glorious city Barry spent the three days holed up in the hotel room under the beady eye of a doctor brought in by the management.

The doctor's instant verdict? "Alcohol Use Disorder".

"That young man's more trouble than he's worth, darling," said Margaret Argyll on being told of the disastrous Venetian venture.

"There many more fish in the sea," said the Marshallene no doubt speaking from experience. "Take it from me, when one door closes another most certainly opens!"

Six years later I was telephoned by a distraught Peter Coats who informed me Barry had shot himself.

*

"I know that look," I snickered eyeing Liz, "Don't tell me Lady Larkin's finally pregnant or something equally as mundane?"

"No he's not," snapped Liz, "And nor am I! Nor is what I'm about to tell you 'mundane'. In fact, for me it's both embarrassing and sad." Seeing my curious expression - I immediately thought something dreadful scandal had befallen the other Anderson household - she took a deep breath and said softly, "Daddy's about to call you. It's about the cottage. He's been busy interviewing a new manager for the estate."

"Which means the new manager will need a place to live," I said cutting in. Not a question, simply a statement.

Liz let out a sigh. "I'm so sorry RA."

"Double chins up Liz, it's not your fault . . ."

"I have *not* got a double chin, thank you very much!" retorted Liz, her violet eyes flashing.

"Oops, my deliberate mistake!" I gave a chuckle. "If you cast your mind back Captain John did say when discussing terms of rental there was always a chance he would require the cottage back and we agreed on three months' notice should the situation ever arise." I gave her a reassuring smile. "See what Captain John's about to say as something more fortuitous than a disaster. Moorhawes has been the greatest fun but I haven't really been giving the cottage the attention it deserves. Over the past year not only have I been spending virtually every second weekend in Paris but there are my endless visits to Dosso as well. I'll be sad at saying goodbye to magical Moorhawes but to be honest Liz, see it more as a load off my Gucci adorned shoulders."

Inwardly I felt an overwhelming feeling of relief at Liz's so-called sad news seeing the cottage had become more of a liability than a getaway haven. While I delighted in the glamour of Albion Gate there were visits to Dosso and last but not least, the latest addition of a chalet, *Belle et Sabastian* the Alpes Maritimes north of Nice. With regards to the latter all is revealed in the section titled The French Erection!

As for the few items originally organised for Moorhawes I knew of several people who would only be too happy to take these off my manicured hands.

IN THE INTERIM - TWO

Ben telephoned literally bubbling with excitement over the latest "Ben toy".

"It's Ben," announced Liz, "I can't quite understand what he's babbling on about; something about a new toy?"

"No doubt a giant, black dildo," rasped Bryan in the background (Ben's addiction for young black gentlemen now common knowledge).

"Jealousy is so ugly in an ageing, frustrated queen," I snapped reaching for the phone and calling out "Thanks Liz. Put him through."

"Mumsie!" cried Ben, "Change in plan. Instead of you driving down to Digberry, I'll be along to collect you from Ebury Street around four. I take it you've already got your Dorothy bag in the car?"

"Yes . . . but . . .?"

"Good. You can leave the car parked in Chester Square over the weekend as before."

"I was planning leaving *here* around six as I usually do plus I still have several bits and pieces to finish up." I let escape a small sigh of exasperation. "Why the urgency? Is something wrong?"

"No, nothing's wrong Mumsie; so be a good old grandmother and I'll see you around four. Byee!"

Now what's our Benedict up to? I pondered. *Oh well, let's wait and see. At least he didn't mention a passport!* It was not unlike Ben to suddenly suggest an away weekend in Amsterdam, Paris or Cannes.

"So tell me," I said hefting my small case on to the back seat of Ben's Rolls-Royce and sliding into the passenger seat, "Why the big mystery?"

"Wait and see, Mumsie! I know I mentioned it to Liz but maybe not to you; it's the latest Benedict toy!" chortled Ben as we set off in a completely alien route instead of the usual M4 exit for Henley. He gave me a mischievous sideways grin. "You know Stan's been busy first scything and clearing the undergrowth to the field backing on to the pool house?"

"Yeees," I replied cautiously as we glided over Battersea Bridge and thinking, *just where the hell are we going?*

"Well now he's spent the last week perched on the motor mower mowing the remaining stubble."

"*Mowing* it? But why?"

"You'll see 'why' in about ten minutes," came the cheery reply.

Ten minutes later we drove into the car park to the Battersea Heliport.

"What on *earth* dearest Benedict are the two of us doing sitting in *your* Roller in the parking lot of the Battersea bloody Heliport?" I asked.

"Eek! No questions, Mumsie!" chortled Ben, "Simply grab your bag and follow me your Uncle Benedict!"

"*Yebo Baasie!*" I replied giving Ben a mock salute. "Whatever the white *Baasie* says!"

"All ready for you Mr Colman," called out a smiling, middle-aged man dressed in a neat overall as making his way towards us. Proffering a hairy hand he greeted Ben with a hearty handshake. "Hello sir," he added cheerfully greeting me with a similar, enthusiastic handshake. "I'm Dave, one of the mechanics. This way please, gentlemen."

"What do you think?" questioned a proudly smiling Ben as we approached the small Bell 47 Helicopter perched dragonfly-like on a landing pad.

"What? Of that miniscule glass bubble claiming to be a helicopter? Jesus Benedict . . . Please don't tell me . . . ?"

"Eek! Yes Mumsie! It's the new Ben toy I just told you about!"

"A *helicopter*?" I exclaimed, "Since when have you had a pilot's licence?"

"Oh, for several years; since Southern Rhodesia in fact," came the nonchalant reply. "So some on, clamber aboard. It's time for take-off."

"So *that's* what Stan's been sweating over for the past couple of weeks, a landing pad for Digberry's latest?"

"Clever old thing, aren't you?" chuckled Ben, "Now, make sure you're strapped in Mumsie and put on your earphones. Great. So let's fly!"

"Do you know the way?" I shouted into the small mike attached to the side of the earphones.

"No need to shout, Mumsie!" replied Ben with a sideways glance, "I can hear your dulcet tones loud and clear. And yes, of course I know the way. We simply follow the M4!"

*

Flying from Battersea Heliport to Digberry and back became a regular weekend commute along with the occasional car journey when extra items deemed necessary for the house required transport down. In Nettlebed, the village closest to Digberry, we relied heavily on the village shop owned by Stan's jolly wife, Brenda. Needless to say Brenda's shop must have been seen by the locals as a bit of an enigma with its stocks *foie gras*, pastas, selection of wines, brands of exotic sauces and canned goods, mixes and more; all as requested (read demanded) by the pernickety Hector..

Several months after my introduction to Ben's newest toy, DLL suggested - as the weather forecast had promised a sunny weekend - Ben and I fly over for Saturday lunch. It was one of the few occasions DLL's "blast from the past" and Rottweiler-like hanger-on Leslie French was "in residence" and when Madame Defarge French was "in residence" I made sure I stayed away. In other words DLL and I would see each other as often as we could but when Leslie was back in England this could become a problem; something I soon learned to accept. This meant any weekend spent at Hedgerley in the presence of the French Letter was more of a pain and a strain resulting in me refusing most of DLL's invitations. As I said rather sourly to Ben, "I suppose the original, aged Ariel-cum-Puck-cum-Madame Defarge has a claim of sorts on David seeing they *did* start living together a whole *nine* years before I was even born!"

"David's invited us over for lunch on Saturday," I said to Ben during one of our frequent telephone conversations, "He and the French Letter are planning an alfresco lunch by the pool" - I couldn't resist a derogatory sniff - "It'll probably be filled with Ariel-Puck's preening actor friends and you can bet your bottom dollar the ghastly Heather Thatcher will be staying!"

"Eek!" exclaimed Ben, "You mean the old dyke who wears a monocle?"

"Bingo!" I replied, "Madam Monocle accompanied by a coterie of corpses!" I gave a chuckle, "No, I tell a lie. David did mention ginned-up Jimmy Myers, owner of the Old House at Windsor, would also be joining them. Jimmy and his latest thuggish obviously well-hung paramour. A Tim something or other. Tim Testosterone knowing Jimmy!"

"Why not?" said Ben. "Jimmy's great fun and really Mumsie, I'm sure David wouldn't have suggested we come over unless there weren't one or two other worthwhile souls there." He added softly, "Plus Mumsie, you know David treasures every chance he has when it comes to seeing you."

"You're right, Mr C," I said with a sigh, "Hopefully the French Letter will keep his snide asides to a minimum."

"Hopefully," replied Ben. He gave a chuckle. "Eek Mumsie! Promise me you'll make sure I'm about when you eventually *do* let *fly* at Leslie the French *letter* French!"

*

Saturday dawned bright and clear which saw Ben and me sitting by the swimming pool while having a leisurely breakfast of croissants, brioche, fruit and Buck's Fizz served to us by the ever genial Tatchell.

"It should only take us about twenty, twenty five minutes," remarked Ben setting aside the Ordnance Survey map, "and if I remember we should be able to land in the field across from the ha-ha at the end of the main garden. Last time we were at Hedgerley the field was home to a lot of cows so the grass should be well cropped!"

"As long as we don't land on a cow or two!" I quipped.

"Now, now, Mumsie! No need to be quite so bitchy about Mesdames Defarge French and Thatcher!" laughed Ben.

"Ha ha and *ha-ha*," I said reaching for my Buck's Fizz, "as well as being bang on I was about to tell you David suggested the same thing; the real McCoy cows having been moved to another field."

Asked to arrive (or land) around o'clock we took off from Digberry at twelve thirty on the dot.

"Knowing Madame Defarge French and her penchant for floral displays," I said into my headphones, "what's the betting we'll have to forage amongst the equivalent of the Chelsea Flower Show to find our place settings, never mind our wine glasses or anything to eat."

"Spoken like a true, devoted rival!" chortled Ben, "Eek Mumsie, maybe Leslie could even find himself lost in his tribute to Kew - or, as *you* said - the Chelsea Show!"

"Chance would be a fine thing!" I replied spikily.

*

"Thar she blows" Ben's voice crackled into my headphones on our approach to Hedgerley. On reaching the surrounding fields and woodland to the house we hovered tentatively above the suggested landing pad. "Very colourful," he added peering down from our Perspex bubble, "and judging from the row of garden umbrellas, lunch is obviously by *la piscine*! Plus I can make out David and some of the guests - I can see Jimmy! - standing round what appears to be a large drinks table."

"Something I wouldn't say 'no' to under the circumstances," I replied somewhat petulantly.

"Now, now Mumsie; *behave*!" admonished Ben with a chuckle. "Plus you're too aged and wily for Madam Defarge to drive you to drink. Now hold on while I'll prepare to put us down in the field."

"Look," I said sourly glancing down at the small group of guests, "they're all waving led by little Rumpelstiltskin French himself!" I gave Ben a mischievous, sideways glance. "Why not give Madame Defarge French the fright of her tedious life and *dive bomb* the little turd?" I grinned, not for one minute expecting him to take me seriously.

"Whatever Mumsie wishes!" cried Ben suddenly changing direction and instead of descending we veered sharply to the left, whirling our way to where DLL, Leslie and their guests stood waving dutifully in anticipation of our landing. On seeing the helicopter change from hovering above the field to banking sharply and heading towards the pool, DLL's waving changed from welcoming to frantic, his actions soon taken up by the other guests with all arms flailing or pointing in the direction of the field.

"Talk about jazzing up the locals!" I laughed, "I mean, just *look* at Madame Defarge? She's positively *jumping* for joy at our impending arrival! Beat *this* for a flying entrance: *Ariel*!"

"One quick dive and then we'll land," chortled Ben as the helicopter hovered momentarily above the pool area before zooming downwards. "Eek!" he added as the four garden umbrellas caught up in the strong downdraft from the rotor blade took to the air.

"Shit," I muttered as two of the umbrellas ended upside down on the frothing surface to the pool.

"Fuck!" cried Ben taking the helicopter sharply upwards.

"Double fuck!" I added on glimpsing tablecloths, crockery, cutlery and several elaborate flower arrangements join the two umbrellas in the turbulent pool.

Ben glanced at me as we hovered again over the correct landing area. "What do we do, Mumsie?" he yelled, "Stay and face the music or head back to Digberry?"

"Stay and face the Handel!" I quipped.

"Ha ha!" laughed Ben, "Very droll Mumsie. *Handel* the situation whilst facing the *water* music? Ha ha! Right, let's do just that!"

Ben and I sat inside the helicopter waiting for the rotor blade to stop.

"Here comes the welcoming party or execution squad," muttered Ben as DLL and another figure having scrambled through the ha-ha began picking their way towards the silent copter.

"At least Beesle's not with Madame Defarge," I snickered. "And if she *had* been we wouldn't have been able to differentiate between her and the cowpats!"

"No, no cowpat," chuckled Ben, "but good old Jimmy Myers who not only looks pissed but looks as if he's *pissing* himself laughing!"

"Unlike Beesle . . . David," I said grimly, "who looks pissed off!"

"Hello there!" yodelled Ben quickly removing his headphones, pushing open his door and jumping out. "Eek! Apologies David but I didn't realise we were quite so near!"

"Liar!" I murmured as I repeated Ben's movements on my side. "Talk about an *ethereal* entrance!" I called as I jumped out; the innuendo not lost on Ben who promptly burst into giggles.

"Well Mr Colman and Mr Anderson," said DLL as he stood regarding us with a stern look, "I have no idea what Mrs Horsfall had in mind for lunch but with luck she'll be able to *squeeze* something edible from what she and Mrs Jones manage to rescue from the pool. Now I suppose you two gentlemen - particularly after your unprecedented display of aerobatics - would like to partake of a welcome drink?" He gave a hint of a smile accompanied by a soft chuckle. "When you said you'd be flying over for lunch I didn't realise you mean flying over the *actual* lunch!"

"None of us did," interrupted Jimmy Myers, a cheerful tall, grey-haired, ruddy-faced man who miraculously was still clutching his drink despite the hazards of crossing the ha-ha and dodging the cow pats. "However, despite the umbrellas and table fiasco, what a starter; if you catch my drift? Ha! Ha!"

The four of us picked our way across the field dodging the cowpats ("Not *quite* what the Guccis ordered!" quipped Ben), scrambled through the ha-ha and slowly approached the other guests who stood watching us silently. (Thanks to Horsfall and Mr Jones the umbrellas - two still dripping - were already back in position and the two men were busy helping their respective wives with the salvaging of the lunch and table settings.) Suffice to say remnants of Leslie's flower arrangements had been piled up on the pool edge or left floating in the pool; a scene somewhat reminiscent of an Esther William's aqua ballet.

I stopped mid-stride as a puce-faced Leslie French bustled towards us.

"Now, now Grum," DLL began (the name Grum being his term of endearment for Leslie and a play on Shakespeare's odd ball Grumio in *The Taming of the Shrew*) only to be interrupted by Ben's cheery, "Sorry about that!"

Stepping nimbly between Leslie and myself he continued breezily, "Hi! You can only be Leslie French? I'm Ben, Ben Colman the rather errant

241

pilot of yon chopper, I'm afraid!" Proffering his handed he added disarmingly, "I've heard *so* much about you and Maynardville, Leslie; all from two great friends of mine who live in Cape Town. You may know them? Lettie and Hennie du Toit? Du Toit as in Du Toit Sugar?"

I looked at Ben in amazement as a totally enchanted Leslie having shaken Ben's hand promptly took him by the arm and with a coquettish giggle dragged him off in the direction of a monocle wearing, lilac-clad Heather Thatcher and two other theatrical-looking types.

Needless to say Leslie chose to ignore me throughout the luncheon plus I had a feeling my remark to those seated at my end of the table - "I would have thought one of the things David and Leslie would have had in their enchanting garden would have been a *water* lily pond" - was not at all well received.

Adding insult to injury was Jimmy's slurred reply, "But Robin dearest, surely you must know David's a closet waterlily and Leslie his water sprite!"

On the flight back I couldn't wait to congratulate Ben on his diplomacy in defusing what could have been - for DLL - an embarrassing situation. "Who are these Du Toit people and how on earth do you know about Maynardville?" I asked.

"Eek Mumsie!" chortled Ben into his headphones, "Those Du Toit people are as much a mystery to me as they are to you! I don't *know* any Du Toits! As for Maynardville, you mentioned Madame Defarge and her connection with the theatre out there some time ago." He gave a grin. "No doubt when fondly charmingly reminiscing about the old bat!"

"Whatever the reminiscences you were bloody brilliant!" I gave a snicker. "So much so I think Madame Defarge now has the hots for you and unless I'm mistaken, the old crone was openly panting in her pantaloons!"

"Eek Mumsie!" yelped Ben as we prepared to land, "At times you really *do* know how to scare the shit out of a person!"

I telephoned DLL later to thank him for lunch and apologise yet again for our chaotic arrival.

"Next time you and Ben come along to lunch or dinner I suggest you drive," responded DLL with a chuckle. "Much safer! I can't have my Robble falling from out of the sky!"

A year later to the day we were invited to Hedgerley for dinner. Instead of flying it was a case of driving from London to Nettlebed via Hedgerley. Ben had recently changed his sedate Rolls-Royce Silver Cloud for the latest Ben toy, a sleek black Corniche convertible. On our arrival he took great delight in saying to DLL, "Eek David! As guaranteed, no wind damage this time; apart from Mumsie's hair!"

Four hours later Ben and I were in the Casualty Department at Stoke Mandeville Hospital following the Corniche flipping nose to tail several times on the M40 on our journey back to Nettlebed (Ben claiming he swerved to avoid "something in the road"). Miraculously our injuries were not life threatening. The most chilling memory of the accident was Ben and I being informed by one of the police officers had we been wearing seatbelts we would have both, without doubt, been decapitated. The car, needless to say, was a write-off.

Typical Ben. For several months after the accident he would mischievously introduce us as "Hi! I'm Tarzan Ben and this is Mumsie Jayne!" The reference being to muscleman Micky Hargity (Tarzan Ben) ex-husband of blonde bombshell Jayne Mansfied (Mumsie Jayne) who found herself decapitated in a road accident en route from Biloxi, Mississippi (read Hedgerley) to New Orleans (read Nettlebed) in 1967.

"Twice bitten now *very* shy and from now on we travel separately," I said to Ben. To prove a point when Ben and I travelled to New York a few months later, I flew courtesy of the newly formed British Airways and Ben via Pan Am. This would be my third visit to New York. Prior to this I flew out to meet Ben in the South of France where Ben had rented a *cave* - (literally a luxuriously converted cave with *all* amenities located above St Tropez) from an eccentric Englishman named Francis Byrne and known among the smartest gay set as another "leader of the Halitosis Choir" which speaks for itself. (Donald Trump would have had a hey-day talking to Messrs. Galliers-Pratt and Byrne on TV!)

The following year would see a virtual repeat performance with Ben no longer a caveman but residing in an eyesore of a modernistic villa in St Tropez itself, close to the Byblos Hotel while Richard Reynolds and I settled for the five star comforts of the Martinez in Cannes. Among the hotels clientele was Diamond Lil. It was inevitable Richard, Ben (who had driven over from St Tropez for the day) and I would be asked to join Clive (Diamond Lil) for a "sparkly" luncheon.

"I thought of Eden Roc darlings," crooned Diamond Lil, "away from the hoi polloi and of course the food's *quite* divine."

Needless to say when it came to Diamond Lil's persona dress code see it a case of "diamonds *shall* be worn."

"I'm surprised the Lil hasn't been dragged to the bottom of the pool considering the number of diamond brooches he has pinned to that very itsy teeny weeny silver lurex bikini," I remarked drily to Ben as Clive with suitable shrieks for the benefit of the very able-bodied life guard, cavorted camply in the pool.

"Eek, don't exaggerate Mumsie!" scolded Ben, "maybe if he was wearing a few more bracelets and an anklet or two, but unlikely today with only a minor Fort Knox worth of his usual sparklers enhancing his questionable tan!"

Richard had been offered the use of a speedboat from one of his London business associates which saw me and Richard setting forth a few days later to rendezvous with Ben and David Hicks. DH was staying at the family holiday house in Port Grimaud (a marina created in the 1960s on the nearby marshes to the Bay of St. Tropez; a pastiche of Venice with French "fishermen" style houses as opposed to palaces) and had arranged to meet us. One look at our boat as we chugged into the private dock resulted in a horrified cry of "you can't be seen in *that*!" from DH. Without further ado we transferred to DH's gleaming Riva and set off to collect Ben from St. Tropez. DH introduced us to an unbelievably good-looking American who was staying with him.

After a few minutes in the young man's company Ben duly dubbed him "Fred von Mirrors".

"Eek Mumsie," chuckled Ben, "have you noticed how young Frederick (his proper name) never stops looking at himself? Poor David hardly gets a glance into the boat mirror!"

Another David who had latched onto us was a journalist named David Harvey described by Richard as a "typical Ben waif or stray". However it did not take long before the "waif and stray" proved himself to be a major rival to the posturing, preening Fred when it came to the vanity stakes. Harvey was the boyfriend of William Clarke, a diplomat and former press secretary to Anthony Eden. The two resided in a cluttered, tumbledown 18th mill house in Cuxham, a small village near Watlington in Oxfordshire.

Several years later David Harvey and William Clarke would become neighbours of mine. In spite of Richard and my endless taunting Ben remained a loyal supporter of Harvey and it was none other than the primping Harvey who arranged for Ben to move into the mill some twenty years later when Ben became seriously ill and took care of Ben until the day he died.

After a morning spent zooming along the coast and stopping now and then for a quick plunge into the sparkling sea, Ben insisted on treating us to lunch at the exclusive Club 55 on Pampelonne Beach where "the Mirrors" and Harvey found themselves in ogling heaven due to the endless admiring and lewd glances the two kept getting from men and women alike.

"Take it from me Ben," I murmured as Fred struck another provocative pose in spite of being seated, "if they ever sell tickets for when the mirror cracks - or preferably shatters - I want to make sure I'm first in the queue! The guy's *unreal*! And as for your friend 'don't take the piss as I know I'm sheer bliss' Harvey, I sincerely trust he's only seen and rarely heard on the very occasional holiday!"

"Now, now Mumsie, don't be such a wicked old crone," replied Ben with a chortle. "Why, we *all* know you'd simply love to be the mirror in Fred's powder compact and an itchy, bitchy little crab inside Harvey's Speedos!"

*

Having stoutly claimed I would never travel by "the same means" as Ben again this was never to last. A year later saw the two of us making our way towards Digbery in Ben's helicopter.

"Thar she grows!" chortled Ben as we approached the field of mustard yellow rapeseed adjacent to the field Ben used for landing. "Only five more minutes to martini time, Mumsie!" Giving me a grin as we hovered over the mustard yellow carpet his expression quickly changed as the rotor blade suddenly cut out, the sound of the blade becoming more of an exaggerated swishing than the usual thrumming. "Shit," muttered Ben instead of his usual "Eek!" into his mouthpiece.

I glanced down at the glowing field of rape blooms below. "Tell me you planned this?" I managed to gasp into my mouthpiece as the helicopter began a downward spiral.

"No Mumsie . . . I swear . . ." came the grunted reply as we landed with a massive thud, bouncing up and down wildly on the skids as if on a trampoline before coming to a stop in what appeared to be a yellow whirlwind as the rape flowers were ripped from their stems due to the still twirling rotor blade and sent flying helter-skelter in all directions.

Ben and I sat staring at each other in stunned silence before breaking out into guffaws of relieved laughter.

"Eek Mumsie!" Ben finally managed to splutter, "Now you'll *never* go anywhere with me ever again; not even it boasts a bar!"

To Ben's great relief the helicopter - like its pilot and passenger - appeared to be undamaged and the cause of the rotor blade cut-out due to an "overlooked electrical fault". Needless to say I flew time and time again with the intrepid Ben despite his much-repeated quip: "As to be expected Mumsie took the impending rape sequence in her stride!"

"At least you had the decency *not* to say I'm too old to cut the mustard when push comes to shove," I replied acidly when first hearing Ben's decidedly corny comment.

*

A few months following the opening of RAD I was invited to a dinner party by another of Peter Carter's dinner party. Among the guests was the brilliant wit and raconteur Peter Coates whom I had previously met through John Tillotson.

"Ah yes," I smiled on being introduced, "How could I ever forget meeting you Peter; the first man I ever met wearing diamonds."

"Why? Was there ever a second?" laughed Peter, his eyes twinkling.

"Yes indeed," I replied with a smile, "and he was positively *dripping* in diamonds. Have you never come across London's very own Diamond Lil?"

"Diamond Lil?" questioned Peter.

"A very beautiful young man - pure Oscar Wilde's Bosie - name Clive Mackay-Kemp." I gave a light laugh. "The only person I've ever seen have a Securicor van turn up at a restaurant with an array of trinkets from Cartier or some other Bond Street jeweller for him to view."

"Good heavens!" exclaimed Peter, "You can't be serious?"

"I most certainly am. Extremely serious," I replied. "Furthermore Diamond Lil - having first apologised to his startled guest for the intrusion - proceeded to snap open the assortment of cases spread out on the adjoining table. Solemnly appraising each sparkling piece in turn he finally closed three cases and announced to the stony-faced guard, "I'll keep these three. The rest can be returned." The whole scenario - taking no more than a few minutes - breathlessly watched by the other mesmerised diners; myself included."

"Good heavens," murmured Peter

"There's more," I said mischievously, "with Diamond Lil saying breezily to his decidedly dull guest, 'Where was I? Ah yes, Cannes. I'll be staying at the Martinez for the summer. So much more fun than the Carlton if you catch my drift? And won't this diamond pendant will look positively *dreamy* pinned to the front of my Speedos?'"

"Good heavens," said Peter for a third time, "Talk about an extremely bizarre and *very* different second!"

As we were leaving the dinner Peter said cheerfully, "Robin, if you're free next Wednesday come to lunch. Twelve thirty. Apartment A1."

"I remember it well Peter and thank you. Yes, I'd love to," I replied. "Look, I have my car, can I give you a lift back to Albany?"

"I was planning a quiet, after dinner stroll back but if you wouldn't mind . . . ?"

"I don't mind at all, I'm parked over there," I said pointing to the Mini.

Peter's luncheons became almost a fortnightly "happening". I use the word "happening" because all Peter's luncheons were exactly that: a "happening". Guests were invited for twelve thirty and on arrival were introduced and given a welcome drink by Peter before being ushered downstairs to the basement dining room with its circular dining table set for six or eight. Lunch was prepared and served by a silent, dapper little man called Briggs. *Eek*, I thought as I watched the efficient Briggs deftly pour the wine and skilfully serve the food, *Hector and Tatchell could certainly take a few pages out of your cookbook, Mr Briggs!*

Peter's guests never ceased to amuse or impress - or both! – with every luncheon giving the impression of being a "one off".

"Any future luncheon will have quite a challenge if it's to outdo *this* one," I would murmur each time I left Albany (Peter insisting we all left promptly at two thirty), and sure enough the next luncheon appeared to do just that. Surpass its predecessor!

It was at one of Peter's earlier luncheons I would meet one of the most elegant, witty and beautiful women on the planet who in turn, became (next to DLL followed by Ben) my greatest friend and confidante. A grownup Peggy and therefore another Margaret; Margaret, Duchess of Argyll.

On being introduced I remember most distinctly Margaret's amazing eyes, her flawless complexion and beautiful, beautiful face. She was impeccably dressed in Hartnell, her grey dress enhanced by an exquisite diamond brooch attached to the left shoulder. Having been introduced Margaret continued her conversation with another guest whilst I continued chatting to Peter.

At the time the talk of London's theatre land was all about the latest play on at the Mermaid Theatre. "If you haven't yet seen it Peter . . ." I began.

"You simply *must!*" interrupted on of the guests.

"As I was about to say," I added nonchalantly, "it so happens I have three tickets for next Thursday. A 'thank you' from a grateful client . . ."

"May I be so bold Robin as to suggest I make up the third?" cut in Margaret, "Unless, of course, you've already asked someone else?"

"Er . . . no . . . and I'd be . . . er delighted er . . . Your Grace."

"Margaret please," replied Her Grace with a dazzling smile.

"Er . . . Margaret. With er . . . dinner afterwards - at Burkes?"

"I *love* Burkes," came the melodic reply. I was hooked.

I had heard endless stories about Margaret, her scandalous divorce and, naturally (or unnaturally - depending on one's point of view), the famous photograph produced in evidence of Margaret supposedly giving a blowjob to a mystery man whose (proper) head was not depicted. All this I took with a pinch of the proverbial salt as from day one of our meeting I could not find fault with this delightful person. Margaret epitomised the words "glamour" and "style" to which I will also add the words "ethereal", "charming" and "extraordinarily kind". She also had an amazing wit; sometimes caustic (as shown by her comment regarding Graham Greene and Jean Stonor).

Margaret and I would dine at least once a fortnight plus enjoy the occasional lunch. One lunch in particular springs to mind; the lunch I organised at Walton's a few days after the restaurant had been bombed by the IRA. A group of us, including Margaret, sat defiantly at a table in front of the window (temporarily replaced and covered with a mesh screen) through which the lethal bomb was thrown.

To quote Margaret, "Never bow, kowtow or give in to anyone".

Margaret lived in great splendour in one of the few privately owned houses overlooking Grosvenor Square and the American Embassy. A charming and generous hostess an invitation to one of Margaret's sparkling soirées was eagerly sought after. Another regular guest, an *uber*-privileged guest, was Louis; Margaret's raffish French poodle. I once offered to take Louis for a walk and was well and truly dragged around Grosvenor Square.

"God knows how you manage to take him for a walk," I said to Margaret, "he'd make Ben Hur's chariot look sluggish!"

"Darling Robin," replied Margaret with a twinkle in her eye, "perhaps it's because you simply don't have the Argyll touch!"

*

Whereas Peter Coats' luncheons were a meeting place for Duchesses, Countesses (Maureen, Countess of Dudley. The former Rank starlet Maureen Swanson) and royal connections (another Bowes-Lyon), Peter Carter's dinners continued to be a meeting place for dashing sexual encounters. One such dinner saw me introduced to a typical TDH (tall, dark and handsome) American made even more TDH by a tantalising scar gracing his otherwise unblemished face: the previously mentioned it was the intriguing Charlie B of running "barefoot through your hair!" fame who in between "running barefoot" through my hair (a regular athletic enterprise) found time to introduce me to the Marshallene. Soon after we'd met Ian moved from the elegant apartment he shared with Charles B to a house in Chester Row, a few doors along from where Melford used to live and where Johnny Galliher still had his house. I was told the house in Chester Row belonged to an "incognito" American friend and Ian was merely the house sitter but who knows? Ian eventually moved in with an equally "incognito" farmer "somewhere near Bath" but that's another story.

Ian seemed to have a never ending stable of lovers passing through the door of Number 48, Chester Row (a sure case of the stable door never bolted) and several became personal friends whereas one in particular, didn't. Namely a slight blast from the past, Brian Ketterer's the Lady Pamela (aka Peter Hurford). Ian became besotted with Peter and part of this particular saga unfolded to both their detriment when I invited Ian - not Peter - to visit me in Dosso. A case of *Bella Italia* becoming *Dramatica Italia*.

From what I could glean from one of his many admirers, Ian worked in some minor travel agency (not unlike Peter Lubbock Ltd.,) and lived, all expenses paid, courtesy of the phantom landlord whom nobody ever met. Part of the arrangement saw Ian having to cope with as many of the landlord's friends passing through as well as his own queue of seemingly endless lovers. There was always a friend of the friend staying and at times these constant visitations must have been somewhat humiliating and a strain. As one vicious so-called friend was heard to bray, "It must be utterly dreadful for the poor darling having to act as housekeeper-cum-ladies maid and occasional arse aperture to all those stopover queens!"

To my knowledge Ian rarely entertained unless it was on behalf of the mysterious American for one of his visiting friends, meaning an all-expenses-paid situation. At one of his rare personal gatherings at the house Ian took take pride in introducing me to a tousled, jowly dark-haired man who looked vaguely familiar. "Robin, you must meet Alan," he said in his soft Scottish burr.

It suddenly clicked, the actor Alan Bates and long-time lover Peter Wyngarde. Surprisingly enough Ian had brought Peter Wyngarde to Hedgerley for lunch so I was fascinated to meet the former "other half". Despite being married Bates also had a passionate affair with Olympic ice skating champion John Curry. I found the actor charming to talk to. However our conversation was soon interrupted by an excited Ian dragging Alan off to meet another "must".

Prior to the re-entry of the Lady Pamela, Ian had taken to excitedly announcing the arrival of a new stallion in his stable, an American named Kurt Ross. Kurt (soon to be known as Kurty babes) - an amiable giant and owner of a successful New York Public Relations company - appeared to be besotted with everything English. This included the Marshallene despite him being Scottish. I was delighted to be first in inviting Kurt to Covent Garden; a venue he was eager to visit. While he "oohed and aahed" over the lavish English Baroque design and the red and gold interior, he promptly fell asleep during the overture to *Giselle* and remained asleep until the interval. Clutching a champagne flute in a giant, hirsute hand Kurt blamed his "dozing off" on his jet lag (he had taken the overnight flight from New York). Returning to our (very expensive) seats he promptly went back to sleep thus missing the whole of the second and final act. When asking Ian if Kurt had said anything in particular about his "introduction to Covent Garden" I was subjected to a deluge of rave revues. According to Ian, Kurt had "never seen anything like it", adored "the dinky bar", thought the décor "reminiscent of a glorious brothel," and last but not least, "Christ, despite being a group of *feygeles* weren't those the guys well hung?" Kurt, I would soon discover, took a great delight in expressing his Jewishness with a sprinkling of Yiddish words and phrases.

"In other words he loved it," said Ian with a chuckle.

For some inexplicable reason Kurt professed a hankering for the works of the Victorian artist Edward Burne-Jones and became an avid collector of the man's drawings. On one of my later visits to New York I was suitably impressed by the number of drawings on display in his apartment.

I invited Ian and Kurt to Moorhawes for the weekend and duly arranged a dinner party for Saturday night which included the three Andersons and a local couple. On this occasion Kurt did *not* doze off and he and the Lady Gillian got along famously. The following day saw the arrival of Shirley and her husband, yet another Robin, Robin Anwyl (they had married a couple of years earlier). Kurt could not quite believe Shirley was a lawyer - "she's so *glamorous!*" - but thought Anwyl "a tedious, arrogant arsehole, a *momser* and more-than-likely a closet *faygala*". Enough said.

It was during the lunch Shirley beamingly announced she was pregnant, her news leading to Kurt saying seriously, "Great news Shirl! I shall certainly be sending you a congratulatory gift from New York!"

I never found out whether a gift from New York ever materialised but I was told by a New York associate Kurt had been spotted wondering around FAO Schwarz clutching a giant giraffe.

Kurt was always fun to see when I visited New York and I enjoyed staying in his stylish Park Avenue apartment where, for some strange reason, the doormen would refer to me as "Your Lordship". A case of Kurty Babes telling porky pies about his "ever so English" visitor perhaps? Like the final destination of the FAO Schwarz giraffe, this is something I would never know.

It was around this time Ben, who had remained in contact with Stephen Gregory, announced the young fortune seeker had suddenly decamped to New York. Siddeley as expected, was not at all happy about the city of Big Ben being swapped for the city of the Empire State. At this stage Richard Taylor had not appeared on the scene.

"Apparently he's staying with a friend of Siddeley's which says it all," grinned Ben. "Eek! Talk about a rehash of *Et tu, Brute!*"

Another ex-paramour of the Marshallene was Nicholas Eden, the devastatingly handsome and son of the former Prime Minister, Sir Anthony Eden. Nicholas (Earl of Avon) who served under Margaret Thatcher was openly gay; a fairly remarkable state of affairs at the time. In conjunction with a friend, Malcolm Johnson, he opened a highly successful gay restaurant in Ifield Road, Fulham named (surprise, surprise) Eden's. Nick was not one to withhold his charms judging from a long queue of admirers waiting patiently for a table. To my delight I was one member of the queue whose "queuing" was not in vain. Someone soon to put an end to Nick's "spreading of the Eden charms" was - and I joke not - Brian Ketterer's former Peter Hurford aka the Lady Pamela. (Further revelations appear in the *Bella Italia!* section.)

Ian Marshall was extraordinarily anti a future friendship which developed between myself and PR guru Liz Brewer and her husband John Rendall, a stance he refused to back down on. "Them and their unsavoury arrangement with that man de Savary for example," was all he would mutter. Despite asking Ian to explain "their unsavoury arrangement" the Marshallene remained silent so I took whatever he was hinting at as idle gossip.

Re-enter Coral Browne!

*

Due to an invitation to dinner one Saturday I decided to spend the weekend in London and was planning on a lazy Sunday, the highlight being lunch at La Popote with Richard Reynolds and a few others.

"Sunday lunch at La Popote should see the rest of Sunday written off," I said to Richard.

"I second that!" came the cheerful reply.

Sunday morning saw me lounging on the sofa with *The Mail on Sunday* when the phone rang. *Strange?* I thought seeing most people would think I was at Moorhawes. *Better answer, just in case.* "Hello?"

"Robin?" said a strange sounding voice (as if the person was speaking through cotton wool), "Darling is that you?"

"Er . . . yes . . . excuse me, who's speaking?"

"It's me - or what's left of fucking me - Coral! Coral Browne!"

"Coral? Sorry dear, I didn't recognise your voice. You sound" - I gave a snicker - "as if you're trying to speak with something *very* strange in your mouth!"

"Ha ha effing ha!" came the muffled response. "It's because I *have* no fucking face, never mind a fucking prick in what's left of me mouth seeing I've just been fucking fried under a fucking hairdryer!"

"You've been *what*?" I exclaimed. "Did you say you've just been er . . . fried under a *hairdryer*?" I couldn't resist a snigger, "Albeit a fucking one?"

"Your heard me! Furthermore it's me fucking something birthday and here I am, ignored apart from being fucking fried!"

"First off all Coral dear - dare I say it as you've just been fried? - happy birthday despite the apparent culinary disaster but perhaps if you could let me have a few more details . . ."

Coral went into a torrent of muffled expletives and some sort of explanation. The setting was a hair salon in Knightsbridge for the filming of her particular cameo part in *Theatre of Blood* starring Vincent Price and a cast of well-known English actors including Coral, Diana Rigg, Harry Andrews, Jack Hawkins and blonde bombshell Diana Dors among others. Vincent Price played a frustrated actor called Edward Lionheart who decides to take vengeance against all those who dared criticise him. Coral, revelling in the role of Chloe Moon an acerbic critic, is energetically "cooked" under a hairdryer having been placed there by Vincent Price disguised as an extrovert gay hairdresser sporting a giant Afro wig!

"It sounds as if Miss B is in need of some TLC," I quipped. "So why don't I call by the hairdressing salon where you're filming with a fortifying bottle of The Widow and we drink a birthday toast or two?" (The Widow being my reference being to Coral's favourite Veuve Clicquot champagne.)

"You'd better bring a couple of straws as well so I can stick them through this fucking piece of gauze covering me fucking face!" came the muffled reply followed by a camp, gargled, "Me face, me face. Oh me lovely face!"

"I need the address Coral. You said a hairdressing salon in Knightsbridge?"

"Yes dear; I'd suggest you avoid the place like a dose of the fucking syph but I need the champagne." There was a strangulated sound. "The place is like the leading actor; fucking awful! Nothing but a melange of stripes, mirrors and more stripes . . ."

I quickly cut in with a name.

"Clever you!" said Coral. "How did you guess? Place must have had you in fucking fits!"

"I designed it."

There was a brief pause before Coral went into overdrive. "But it's *lovely* dear. So original. So *brave!*"

*

"I've come to see Miss Browne," I said to a nervous young girl standing by the door to the salon. "The name's Robin Anderson."

"Ah yes, the bearer of birthday gifts," murmured the girl giving me a timid smile. "Miss Browne is the person sitting solo over there. Be prepared for I am sure you won't recognise her."

"It's that bad?" I said with a conspiratorial chuckle.

"It's that bad," said the young girl wryly. "Rather you than me!"

I approached the hunched-up figure sitting in a chair set well away from the main group of people enjoying what I assumed was a break in filming.

"Jesus Coral," I laughed. "Talk about a bad hair day. Happy birthday dear and yes, I can see why straws must be sucked!"

"Very fucking funny," came the muffled reply. "Now gimme!" I stared at Coral whose hair was concealed by a flesh-coloured skull cap with random tufts of singed hair. However it was her face which explained my expletive and comment. Coral literally had no face. Due to skilful makeup Chloe Moon (her character in the film) had been well and truly broiled with one eyeball hanging down a cheek and the other looking heavenwards. There was no sign of a mouth apart from a crinkled slit or designated aperture for the straw. (Flashback to a former employer.)

"Where's your co-stair or nasty hairdresser, Mr Price?" I asked.

"Over there," muffled Coral followed by a loud slurping sound. "Over there," she repeated giving a nod of her tufted pate towards the group gathered at the back of the salon.

"Ah yes," I said, "I didn't recognise him for a moment in that ridiculous Afro wig."

"Yet you fucking well managed to recognise fucked-up me!"

"Only because the young lady at the door pointed over to where you were sitting," I replied diplomatically. "Er . . . apart from him frying or roasting you, how are you getting on with Vincent Price? He's obviously very popular with the cast and crew."

"Ridiculous old queen," Coral managed to say, "Talk about bees around a fucking honeypot!"

A few weeks later I was stunned when told by Melford Coral and Vincent Price were getting married.

Next thing I knew Coral's original sleigh bed (dubbed "Coral's *slay* bed" by Bryan) was being replaced by a king size bed and could I arrange for "some sort of cheap patterned tat to replace the paisley spread - I'll keep the fucking throw" as the former spread was now "too fucking small and I ain't paying a fortune for any more fucking paisley." Pausing for breath she added mischievously, "I didn't have the face to order a *queen* size dear when in the shop," she gleefully informed me, "especially as the sales assistant was so obviously a rival to our dear Maj!"

Coral would eventually move permanently to Los Angeles. In our many fun-filled telephone conversations one in particular saw me collapsing into even more fits of laughter than usual.

"He's not only sold the fucking Roller and is in the process of buying another house; he's gone and replaced the Roller with a *Camper* and the new house is situated in fucking *Swallow Drive*! Can you imagine anything more mortifying? Me associated with Vinnie, a camper *and* a swallow?"

It was inevitable Coral and Vincent would become known in Hollywood as Mr and Mrs Horror. Despite the title they were one of fickle Hollywood's most popular and sought-after couples.

*

Unbeknown to DLL I was about to meet another hero and heroine of my "informative years.

"Some fun people coming to lunch on Sunday, Robble," he announced at one of our Carlton Tower breakfasts. "I've invited a particularly charming lady who's a writer . . ."

"Can't be Enid Blyton as she's just popped her clogs," I interrupted with a laugh.

"No, not Miss Blyton," chuckled DLL, "but a lady named Helga Moray and a gentleman - a touch of poetic licence there! - called Beverley Nichols."

"Helga Moray the author of *Untamed*?" I exclaimed. "I don't believe it? A highly entertaining and educational influence in my otherwise innocent life. I'm one of her greatest fans!"

"I've also asked Beverley Nichols and Cyril Butcher his longstanding lover; both of whom you've met."

"Ah yes; my first grand dinner with *Il Colonnello* at the Empress," I said with a smile. "I didn't mention it at the time but I've read several of Beverley's novels; *Death to Slow Music* and *The Rich Die Hard* for starters and as you well know - from personal experience - not *all* people from South Africa are philistines!" Somehow I managed to stop myself from adding, "Even those who've had to suffer the French Letter in full fig at Maynardville!"

"Helga's driving down with Dudley and obviously Beverley will be coming along with Cyril."

"Cyril the *butch* and Bev his bitch," I quipped. Helping myself to another croissant I waved the pastry at DLL. "A longstanding case of *croissant neuf* no doubt?"

"That dear Robble," replied DLL with a chuckle, "was *quite* terrible!"

*

Had I not known about or, better still, never read *Untamed*, I would never have believed the delicate little old lady sitting next to me was the author of the searing bodice ripper which so enthralled as well as mesmerised us smutty schoolboys. A dead-ringer, doppelgänger or body double for the widow of the FO bigwig and her "craft" moments.

"Having be brought up in South Africa I simply *loved* your novel *Untamed*, Miss Moray," I schmoozed.

"Oh, I'm so glad," came the squeaky reply, "and do call me Helga. Miss Moray makes me feel positively ancient!"

Beverley Nichols turned out to be the balding, delicate, fey figure I remembered from dinner and a perfect foil to the giant, bumbling Cyril Butcher. *A very ancient David and his Goliath or Abbot and his Costello*, I thought wickedly.

"So what did you think of your literary heroes?" asked DLL as we sat having another brandy once the guests had finally left.

"Looking at Helga you'd firmly believe *nothing* - and that includes butter - *ever* melted in her mouth! And as for bonny Beverley I'd forgotten just how fey he was." I gave a snicker. "Why Bees, next to him even the Beverley Sisters would look butch! Butch; butcher. Geddit?"

"So charming, my Robble," murmured DLL pouring himself another Remy.

*

"I think it's time I paid a visit to New York," I announced to Liz and Bryan, "Not only will it give me the chance to visit the showrooms of people like David and Dash, Brunschwig and Fils and Van Luit plus I'd also like to see the Parzinger showroom . . ."

"And the Empire State Building no doubt?" rasped Bryan no doubt thinking, *With any luck the tyrannical bitch will decide to jump!*

"And Bloomingdales," carolled Liz. "Everybody who's anybody visits Bloomingdales!"

257

"Hush minions and let me consult the oracle," I said with a bright smile as I began flipping through the appointment book on Liz's desk. "I think the first week of September could be good added to which it's close to my *very* jubilant birthday. Therefore not only a business trip but a much deserved birthday treat for this hardworking soul." Ignoring Bryan's cynical sniggers and Liz's snorts I continued cheerfully, "So, while you're opening a bottle of Pinot Lady L in order for us to toast my latest brainstorm, I'll quickly nip downstairs and tell Alison and Warren the exciting news. Imagine, a request for return ticket to New York first thing on a Tuesday. What a way to start your agency's day!"

"Hip hip hooray, while the slave driver's away the slaves will play," crowed Bryan.

"Or pay," sniped the wily Liz. "Remember your slut-ship; don't care was made to care!"

"Back in a few minutes," I cooed giving the two a twiddle of my fingers.

"Make haste with vino Bryan!" I heard Liz cry as I leapt nimbly down the stairs to annoy Alison and Warren in their Peter Lubbock Travel office.

*

"Ah, you must meet Kenneth Jay Lane, *the* jeweller," said Peter Coats on hearing my plan.

"Ah, you must meet Billy Baldwin," said David Hicks another guest at Peter's luncheon.

With the legendary Billy Baldwin and Kenneth J. Lane already on board how could I possible lose?

"Mumsie you should really look up Stephen," announced Ben. "Despite your dislike of John Siddeley, Stephen and you were very close and had a great deal of fun together so don't be a silly old girl and give him a call when you arrive. In fact I have a small package for Stephen and if you would be so kind and if you wouldn't mind, perhaps you could give this to him; for me?"

"After such a *subtle* hint how could I possibly even *think* of saying 'no'?" I wryly replied.

An ardent fan of Kay Thompson's *Eloise* it was inevitable I should choose to stay at the Plaza.

The day of departure soon arrived and I was graciously driven to Heathrow by a triumphant Bryan.

"You're really here to make sure I *do* catch my flight, aren't you?" I said laughingly.

"Damn right!" rasped Bryan, "Plus Liz had threatened to have my guts for garters if you *don't* make your flight!

NEW YORK, NEW YORK

I flew to New York courtesy of Pan Am and will never forget my amazement at the size of my first Jumbo! It was like walking into an aircraft hangar, never mind a plane! On arriving at JFK I was directed to a Pan Am gaudily painted *Happy Helicopter* (the copter having a bright, smiling face gracing the fuselage) which ferried arrivals from the terminal to the heliport on top of the Pan Am building, fifty eight floors above Park Avenue in New York itself. (In 1997 a not so happy helicopter fell from the roof killing five people; the accident resulting in the cancellation of any further flights.)

What an entrance! What an arrival!

It took only a glimpse of the fabled city from my lofty viewing point for me fall totally and utterly in love with Mr Sinatra's "New York! New York!" This saw the beginning of a love affair with the Big Apple which will last until my exit from Planet Earth.

Having checked into the Plaza (another overwhelming case of love at first sight) I made my way to the Oak Bar and savoured my first New York dry martini, straight up. Bliss! I had decided on no special plans for my first evening in anticipation of the legendary "jet lag" and after several elevating martinis took myself for dinner at another New York legend, namely Trader Vic's; a staggering restaurant decorated in an over the top mishmash of Hollywood meets Samoa. After a delicious platter of "genuine" South Sea delicacies accompanied by two floral-enhanced Mai Tais I decided my unsteadiness could only be due to the threatened jet lag therefore a breath of fresh air and a brief constitutional before going to bed was the only answer to cure my sudden loss of balance. Gliding (read tottering) from the

Plaza I made my way down Fifth Avenue and homed in on Tiffany's, the catalyst for the Ritchie Set over a decade ago.

Gazing groggily at the low key window displays I decided it really was time for bed and returned to the hotel. "After all it is almost *eight* in the morning in London," I murmured as I switched off the bedside lamp. My last thoughts being of Lady Larkin, Courvoisier in hand (courtesy of the well-stocked mini bar), piloting a Pan Am Happy Helicopter.

Up and about a few hours later I scribbled a note for "things to do today" before going downstairs for breakfast. On returning to my room I called Billy Baldwin, Kenneth Jay Lane and somewhat reluctantly, Stephen Gregory who was staying with a friend of John Siddeley.

"Mumsie!" yelped Stephen, "Where are you? Don't tell me you're in New York?"

"Yes," I said. I added smugly, "I'm here for a few days on business. I'm staying at the Plaza."

"But you must join us for lunch!" exclaimed Stephen. "I'm lunching today with an ex-boyfriend of JS's and my host Paul" - he gabbled the surname - "somewhere near . . . hold on (I could hear more gabbling in the background). If you *can* join us we're heading for a place called Joe Allen's. The concierge at the hotel will be able to give you directions." There was what they call a pregnant pause. "Mumsie. You *must* join us! I insist!" Stephen's enthusiasm was contagious and before I could stop myself I found myself agreeing to meet him and the ex-boyfriend at twelve thirty.

With details for Joe Allen duly noted I left for my second (and definitely more sober) taster of First Avenue, my first stop being an actual *visit* to Tiffany's. Walking out into the dazzling sunshine (having only been in New York for a few hours I was already convinced *everything* dazzled) I stopped mid-stride and stood smiling idiotically at the row of horse-driven carriages waiting patiently in an orderly line outside the Plaza next to a luxuriant-looking Central Park. *Fab!* I thought. *Fucking fabulouso!*

I began to make my way along Fifth Avenue. "But everything's so *massive!*" I murmured. "The buildings are massive, the streets massively wide and, after London, all the cars - especially the yellow cabs - appear massive. In fact the whole place is simply marvellously massive!"

I spent a happy hour browsing around Tiffany's and treated myself to a pair of the jeweller's iconic ball-end cufflinks before finally emerging and hailing a cab. Reaching for the door handle I slowly enunciated my destination (horror stories concerning the vagaries of New York cab drivers relayed by previous visitors firmly fixed in my mind) before sliding onto the backseat.

"Saay, ya must be from Engeland?" nasalised the driver - a Danny de Vito lookalike with hair - turning to stare at me through the mesh screen separating us.

"Yes I am. Absolutely. Spiffingly. Super. What?" I replied with exaggerated enunciation.

"Wowie!"

We took off with squealing of wheels which saw me thrown back in my seat before the driver braked suddenly. *Fuck*, I thought, *don't tell me this one thinks he's a reincarnation of Steven McQueen in bloody Bullitt?*

"Ya look kinda grand," continued "Danny" glancing at me via his rear-view mirror, "so I suppose ya must know Queenie?"

"Queenie?" I replied. "Oh, you must mean Her Majesty The Queen?"

"Yeah, like I said. Queenie."

"No, I don't know *Queenie* personally," I quipped, "but I know quite a lot of her relatives - or rivals!"

"Wow!" said "Danny", his bushy eyebrows almost disappearing into his hairline. "Does that make you a prince or a somethin'?"

"A somethin'," I replied more Mata Hari-like than mysterious.

"Here we are Your Whatever-you-are-ship," said "Danny" still eyeing me in the rear-view mirror. He twisted round, his nose dimpling against the wire mesh. "That shoulda been twelve dollars but I'll charge ya ten." His nose reminiscent of a red waffle he added with a yellow and gold toothed leer as I pushed a ten dollar note through the slot in the screen, "Can I have ya autograph then Your Whatever-ship? "I ain't got a book but this scrap of paper should do."

"Have you a pen?" I asked loftily as I reached for the piece of paper which looked suspiciously like a much used table napkin.

"Pen? Why sure. Here."

Taking the battered ballpoint I wrote with a flourish: *Prince Igor.*

"Wow!" said "Danny" for a second time as he glanced at the name (his eyebrows no longer visible), "Wow! Wow! *Wow!* Why *thank* you Prince Igot! It's been a real pleasure!" Muttering a further "Wow!" "Danny" roared off with a further squeal of tyres.

Stephen, on spotting me entering the restaurant, gave an energetic wave from where he and two men were sitting. "Mumsie, you made it!" he crooned, "Come and meet Paul (again he gabbled a name) and Donald Cameron the designer associated with Tommi Parzinger!"

Ah yes, the fabulous lacquer pieces of furniture synonymous with Siddeley's former showroom, I thought, eyeing the smiling, twinkly-eyed man dressed in a loud Harold Lloyd style mustard and black check suit, his smiling face sporting a jaunty, Salvador Dali-like moustache complete with waxed, curled ends. *Goodness Mr Cameron, you look fun?* I continued thinking. *Plus I* adore *the moustache!*

"Sit next to Donald, Mumsie," instructed Stephen, "but no touching!" He grinned at a bemused Donald and a seemingly uninterested Paul. "Mumsie, my aged mother is a wild, wild woman," proclaimed Stephen with an evil grin. "She not only steals *clients*; she also steals lovers!"

I gave Stephen and angry look. "I don't *steal* clients, Stephen *dear*, I simply *lure* them away with my towering talent. And as for stealing lovers, perhaps my comment regarding clients *also* applies!"

"Ladies! Ladies!" interrupted Donald with a laugh. "I've heard of handbags at dawn but never nails at lunchtime! So, let's change the subject and order ourselves a drink before we look at our menus?"

From the moment of my arrival the talk over lunch appeared to be divided between Stephen and the Gabble (I never did learn the man's surname) talking nonstop with each other while Donald and I chatted amiably about Tommi Parzinger and Billy Baldwin (Donald was delighted I was lunching with Billy the next day at Le Cirque) among others. Surprisingly enough Donald seemed to know all about RAD. "Stephen tells me your company's a great success," he confided, "In fact he says you're the toast of the town!"

"He *did*?" I replied, my disbelief evident in my voice.

"He did indeed," said Donald *sotto voce*, "which is why I was somewhat taken aback by his bitchy comment earlier."

Lunch abruptly ended with the Gabble suddenly demanding "the check".

"What are you doing later?" asked Donald as we headed for the door.

"Having dinner with a certain DC, I trust?"

"Good, I was hoping you'd say that," came the beaming reply (I swear I saw the waxed ends of his luxuriant moustache curl even more). "Let's say cheerio to Stephen and Paul, grab a cab and head back to the showroom where you can meet Tommi. I can give you my address etcetera one we're there."

Donald's apartment on East 51st Street was a mixture of the bizarre and the brilliant. Bizarre for a vinyl-covered armchair with part of its stuffing deliberately poking out and brilliant in the way such a bizarre item blended in perfectly with the gleaming, lacquer Parzinger drinks cabinet and tables, the squidgy, uber-comfortable sofas and encompassing, plain plaster walls.

I questioned Donald about his relationship with John Siddeley to which his only comment was - and I quote - "He's a weird one that John; he really is." On asking Donald to elaborate as to what he meant by "a weird one" he appeared reluctant to do so and changed the subject.

Donald Cameron, along with Peggy, Ben and especially DLL (Beesle) are the four people never far from my thoughts. Donald, a charismatic Canadian also proved from day one to be a loyal and caring friend. However, nobody could, or ever will, match DLL who, to me was and still is unique.

I have to confess my room at the Plaza saw very little of me as most of my evenings were spent with Donald. Through Donald I met Tom Hubbard, a fellow designer. On the one evening Donald was dining with clients, Tom very kindly invited me to join him and some friends for dinner. Here I was introduced to Nat La Mar, a smooth talking, extremely attractive African-American who has also become a lifelong friend. I soon learned Nat lived with an Englishman, Christopher Adlington, who I had met back in London where he was associated with the London branch of an American fabric house.

Nat and I immediately hit it off. *This is someone I'd really like to keep in touch with,* I thought. Promising to "keep in touch" I managed to speak to Nat several times before my return to London and it was not long before we met up again all thanks to my unquenchable thirst for New York, New York.

*

The only way to describe Billy Baldwin on first meeting him would be as a charming, mischievous pixie! A tiny man (but a tiny man of steel) Billy not only entertained me to a delightful and delicious lunch at Le Cirque but also showed me over his latest project; an impressive duplex overlooking Central Park. He also presented me with a signed, glossy "coffee table" table book *Billy Baldwin Decorates* which today sits with other "coffee table" books containing designs by a certain Robin Anderson; the books placed in the howdah set on the back of a handsome, carved elephant. Guarding these precious tomes is a jaunty gent in a large, colourful painting titled *Carnival*; a gift from the South African artist, Lee Molenaar.

Kenneth Jay Lane, the jeweller, a dashing Alain Delon lookalike, proved to be delightfully entertaining and great fun. Kenneth introduced me to his collection of skulls which sparked of a new - perhaps hidden - interest. My present day collection of skulls range from a Damian Hirst diamond encrusted skull lookalike, bookends and several granite skull doorstops! However, without doubt, it's Miss Abel Mabel Mortis who proudly bears the title of *Most Elegant Skull Supreme.*

Ken is perhaps best-known for his dazzling Duchess of Windsor Collection inspired by the chunky costume jewellery originally created by Cartier for the diaphanously thin Duchess in the 1940s and '50s. I certainly wouldn't be telling a "porky pie" (white lie) when - on viewing Ken's collection of grinning skulls - I couldn't help thinking. *Good heavens, a ghoulish get-together of Duchess of Windsor wannabes no less!* followed by a grisly flashback to the long-forgotten vision of the dead mine boy lying on his stomach while grinning up at the relentless blue African sky.

*

The days seemed to whiz by.

"This time tomorrow you'll be back in London," murmured Donald sleepily as he lay gently stroking my forehead.

"I'll be back before you know it," I replied softly. Pulling myself up into a sitting position I gazed down at Donald. "Mr Cameron," I said, "You are, without doubt, one of the kindest, loveliest men one could ever wish to meet; no, make that *blessed* to meet."

"After what you've told me about David I take that as a massive compliment," came the tender reply.

"Talking of David," I continued, "I take it you will also be visiting Europe in the not too distant future (Donald had mentioned the possibility of a visit to Stephen at our introductory luncheon) and as I've already said, you simply have to come and stay with us at Dosso."

"In the guest room?" replied Donald with a chuckle.

"In the guest room," I repeated. "Better still the guest room in my very *casa, Casa Robino Bello* which, when translated can only refer to its captivating owner. It's going to be rather like a French farce, Italian style, with me flitting between *Il Colonnello* and *Il* Camerono!"

"Tart!" said Donald giving my hand a squeeze.

"As I've already said *Il* Camerono, I've fallen in love with New York" I gave a light laugh - "especially with what New York offers *design*-wise so I have an idea I'll be back here before you've even considered a trip across the Atlantic!"

*

I returned to London where I was met by Heathrow (no Siddeley-like dramas here) by a smug Bryan who greeted me with a rasped "Welcome back RA and before you ask RAD did *not* collapse in between your endless 'is everything okay?' phone calls during you short absence. The lovely Liz didn't run off with dishy Dennis Paget and I haven't been seduced by any one of note. All in all, it's been as calm as the proverbial millpond."

"Aha, but maybe the calm before the storm," I replied with a feigned smile.

"You're absolutely right and how remiss of me to forget," muttered Bryan turning on the ignition of my Mini. "The Met Office did say they were anticipating a hurricane which seems determined to make its way across the Atlantic. Hurricane Anderson I believe?"

*

Liz welcomed me back with a hug and a large Buck's Fizz.

"Any vital messages?" I asked as the three of us settled ourselves comfortably in the Liz and Bryan's office.

"One or two new enquiries," replied Liz. "A Mrs Lemos for starters. I checked her out and checked her out and yes, she *is* part of the shipping family, a Mrs Stapleton and Mr Clive Mackay-Kemp known to those in the know as Diamond Lil."

"Diamond Lil?" I exclaimed. "What does *he* want? Surely he must realise I'm an interior designer and *not* a jeweller or a furrier?"

"Furrier?" questioned Liz.

"Surely you've heard our esteemed boss say Lil not only looks like an illuminated Christmas tree but a glittering Christmas tree set in the middle of a mink farm?" cawed Bryan. "A case of sparklers and furs galore."

"I'll make Diamond Lil my priority call *after* we've finished our drinks," I said, "but first things first; any news on your flat, Liz? I trust you'll be brave enough to ask RA for a few free, *gratis* and for nothing ideas or touches?"

"God forbid!" exclaimed Liz.

"What a grotesque thought," rasped Bryan, "free touches by RA? Ugh!"

"Hello RA! Welcome back!" I sang. "It's obvious you've been sorely missed!"

"Naturally - or unnaturally - there's a 'welcome back' message from Ben," giggled Liz, "I left in on top of everything else in the folder on your desk. He and Richard are expecting to see you for lunch at Brooks." She gave another giggle. "As Ben so rightly said, jet lag would never *dare* intrude on your return!"

Dear Mumsie, I read, *Uncle Richard and self are expecting you for a 'welcome back' lunch at Brooks, I p.m. today. We expect to be told all! No holds barred! Love, Benedict.*

"Ben first to say 'yes' and *then* Diamond Lil," I muttered.

After confirming lunch I dialled the number Liz had been given by Diamond Lil.

"Yes?" came the imperious reply; the phone being snatched up after half a ring.

"Clive its RA. I've literally just got back and seeing it's you, you're my first call."

"Good!" said Clive without so much as a "how's yer father". "I'm thinking of buying a townhouse and would like you to have a look at it. So when?"

"Not today Clive as I've literally just flown in from New York."

"How very exhausting," said Clive with a snicker, "I would have taken a plane."

"Ha ha! So not today seeing both me and my arms are a tad tired."

"Tomorrow?"

"Let me check the week's diary with Liz and I'll call you right back." I gave a chuckle. "As yet I haven't had a chance to sus out the appointments she's bludgeoned one into!"

"Fine," came the brusque reply. "Oh, will you be at the Redmile launch tonight?"

"Yes indeed. I wouldn't miss it for all the silver palms in Hawaii!"

"I'll no doubt see you there. Er . . . you free for dinner?"

"Unfortunately not, I'm dining with William Davis aka Lady Dee."

"How unfortunate and how unappetising," purred Clive, "I take it you'll have a good book tucked inside your evening bag?" He hung up.

The opening of Anthony Redmile's spectacular new showroom in Sloane Street predictably attracted a large gathering of London's self-proclaimed "glitterati" and what I called London's "Nescafé society". Almost acceptable but not quite.

I arranged to meet William at the venue. On arrival I was welcomed by two giant, Mandingo-lookalikes clad in extremely "dieted" silver lamé loincloths and silver Roman gladiator type sandals. Each of the young black men held a large silver tray encrusted with semi-precious stones, each tray bearing brimming silver gem-encrusted goblets. Taking one I stood staring in amazement at the scene in front of me. To enter the first showroom one walked through a tunnel (or guard of honour) of elephant tusks, each tusk mounted on a massive silver gem encrusted base. Once through the tunnel of tusks the stunned guests found themselves inside a cavernous black painted showroom bristling with objet exclusive to Anthony Redmile.

Towering silver palms trees, shields of giant tortoise shells on silver plinths, screens of ostrich eggs, ostrich eggs on silver mounts, consoles and other tables made of seashells, ostrich and crocodile skin, wall mirrors framed in silver antlers and much, much more were set out in a dazzling display. At one end of the first showroom (there were three such Aladdin - or Redmile – type caves) I homed in on an enormous wooded Dodo bird standing proudly in spot-lit glory.

"Darling! Despite you having flown in from New York earlier I simply *knew* I'd see you here this evening," cooed a familiar voice.

"Darling, I wouldn't have missed Anthony's *opening* for the world," I replied giving Margaret Argyll a light kiss on her porcelain-like cheek.

Margaret, elegant in black, gave a vague gesture at the glittering surroundings. "What a queer man this Mr Redmile must be?" she said conspiratorially. "And why this strange obsession with ostrich eggs? Perhaps you can explain?"

"Not really Margaret, unless Mr Redmile has some sort of affiliation with the Ooh Aah bird as opposed to an ostrich," I replied drily.

"Ooh Aah bird?" blinked Margaret.

"A bird that lays large ostrich sized eggs and when doing so caws or croaks 'ooh' followed by a relieved 'aah'!"

"Do not, for one second Robin darling, think I am going to respond to *that* with an 'aah, I see'," replied Margaret with a playful smile

"Darling!" yodelled a familiar voice, "I say this simply *has* to be the campest opening since *Kismet*!" added Diamond Lil as he cleaved his way through to animated guests to where Margaret and I were standing. He gave Margaret a dazzling smile. "Isn't this *fun*?"

"I take you know each other?" I muttered. "Oh," I said noting Margaret's blank look. "Margaret this is Clive; Clive this is Margaret." (A key factor of Margaret's incredible charm was her ability not to stand on ceremony when meeting the friend of a close friend.)

Diamond Lil gave Margaret another dazzler of a smile. "Lovely to see you, Margaret dear!"

"Likewise, Clive," replied Margaret giving Clive a smile which easily outdid his two dazzling ones. "Not only fun but so gay!"

"I suppose you could say that," replied Diamond dryly. "Especially Mutt and Jeff greeting the guests with those goblets of hemlock or whatever?" He peered at the buoyant guests around us. "I wonder where our host extraordinaire could possibly be lurking?"

"Unless that's Mr Redmile trying to climb that unfortunate Dodo bird over there?" observed Margaret.

"Goodness Margaret; where?" said Diamond Lil gazing vaguely around the crowded room.

"There! Almost right in front of us!" I cried pointing to the Dodo bird and a thin, bearded figure, his arms akimbo as he attempted to retain his balance while sitting astride the massive carving.

"What on *earth* is he doing?" asked Margaret. "Not trying to compete with your Ooh Aah bird I trust?"

"Attempting to hold a drink in one hand, the Dodo's neck with his other and clinging on for dear life I expect?" I replied with a chuckle.

"Whee!" came the cheery cry barely audible through the general cacophony of strident voices, "Whee I'm a pixie . . ." the word "pixie" tailing off as the intrepid adventurer lost his balance and plunged to the floor covered in a blanket of faux silver-coloured grass.

"Goodness," murmured Margaret craning her elegant neck in an attempt to see if the young man was in need of help. "I can't make out if he's simply lying there or what? What was it he called himself? A pixie?"

Talk about déjà vu, I thought with an inward smile, *Billy Baldwin sans beard but not sans alcohol!*

"As you've just seen Margaret dear, you can't take a pixie anywhere these days," tittered Clive.

"Especially if *pixie-lated*!" quipped Margaret.

"Dreaded cabaret if I may say so?" sniffed Diamond Lil not to be outdone. He added in disbelief. "You won't believe it but the pixie-lated pixie is actually attempting to take a bow!"

"Well I never," remarked Margaret. She gave Clive a gracious smile. "Do you think there's a chance of finding another Mutt or Jeff, Clive dear, as watching all these flying fairy folk is thirsty work?"

(I would later learn the bearded pixie was none other than Anthony's canny accountant, a young named Bob Miller and a former employee of the legendary financier and property magnate, Charles Clore.)

I left Margaret and Clive presumably discussing each other's jewellery and made my way to where William was talking to gallery owner Roy Miles and a tall, thuggish-looking young black man.

"Did you see the fall from grace? The bearded figure atop the Dodo bird back yonder?" I said in greeting.

"No, I was too busy talking to William about his latest work," boomed Roy. He glanced at his scowling companion. "This is Troy. Apart from his sour expression he's actually quite nice." Roy nodded to where Margaret and Clive were standing deep in conversation. "I see you've been chatting up Diamond Lil and the Duchess?"

"I have indeed," I replied. Giving Roy a tight smile I turned to William. "Shall we go? Peter and the others will be wondering what's happened to us?"

*

"I take it you and Roysie Boysie aren't exactly the greatest of friends?" giggled William as we walked towards the junction of Sloane Street and Pont Street en route to La Popote.

"Not quite topping my list of arseholes to avoid," I replied, "but climbing rapidly. But then, he's good at climbing any ladder, no matter how rickety." I gave William a sidelong glance. "However, if he's thinking of giving you an exhibition - better sooner than later - I'll make sure he returns to the bottom of my list. But only temporarily!"

"Exhibition or no exhibition you've now whetted the Davis appetite so come on RA, spill the Heinz; why don't you approve of Mr Miles?"

"It'll have to be quick," I said as we turned into Walton Street, "and it involves Roy and the one and only Coral Browne."

"I love it already!" giggled William.

"It all stems back to a cocktail party given by Roy not at his gallery but at his apartment in Ennismore Gardens a year or so ago," I began.

*

"Roy Miles on the blower for you!" trilled Liz. "Shall I put him through?"

"Roy Miles?" I murmured, "What on earth can the world's most unsubtle gallery owner want with me? I've already said I'd drop by his cocktail party this evening on my way to dinner at Johnny Schlesinger's. Better put him through, Liz."

"Robin dear!" boomed Roy, "And how are we this merry morn? (It should be noted Roy, following his introduction to several of the Royals, took the opportunity of using the royal "we" at the slightest provocation.)

"*We* are doing well and I trust 'we' is also well?" I replied with a feigned laugh. Not waiting for Roy's reply I added brightly, "To what do I owe the pleasure of a call from Roysie Boysie?"

"Tonight; you *are* coming, aren't you?"

"I've already said so, Roy."

"And if I remember correctly you did mention going on to dinner at Johnny's?"

Johnny's? I thought, *that's a bit bold, even for you Roysie!* "If by Johnny you mean Johnny Schlesinger, then yes."

"We heard from another guest Coral Browne may be going?" Roy added smoothly, "We also heard clever you did wonders with her Belgravia apartment?"

"There's a rumour."

"And not a false one we're sure!" boomed Roy; his comment followed by a loud, phony laugh. "Miss Browne - Coral - as we're sure you must know is a much sought-after lady of the moment after her *magnificent* performance as a dyke in *The Killing of Sister George.*" There was a slight pause. "We were wondering if there was any chance of you persuading her to join your good self for a drink at Maison Miles before you descend on Maison Schlesinger."

Bloody mind reader, I thought, *or else he automatically put two and two together seeing I'd more than likely be giving Coral a lift.*

"As I'll be ferrying Coral to and from Johnny's I'll suggest it to her ..."

"Please do," Roy cut in, "We'd be delighted to see you both plus I know our guests would *so* much meeting the star of the moment!"

Star of the moment. Coral would love that little bon mot! "It's entirely up to Coral," I said firmly, "so I can't promise she'll agree ..."

"We are sure that with your persuasive powers she won't be able to refuse," came the guffawed reply. "Seven thirty would be an ideal time for you both to make you entrance." Roy hung up.

"Gloria Gallery?" exclaimed Coral when I told of the invitation, "You mean Miss ex-hairdresser Miles who's more regal than the real Queen?" She gave me an arch look which didn't bode well. "If, as you say, it's 'on root' we may as fucking well drop by." Coral gave an unnerving cackle. "Saves me opening another bottle of Sainsbury's best!"

"You've arrived!" boomed Roy as he glided across the over-decorated sitting room to greet us. "Welcome, welcome Miss Browne. A delight and a privilege! Welcome, welcome RA!"

"Call me Coral," said Coral with twisted smile. "Most queens do." The remark seemingly sailing unnoticed over Roy's "poofed and bouffed" lacquered head.

Shit, I thought, *we'll stay for one drink and then we're leaving before the party witnesses Miss Browne unleashed!*

"Excuse me Coral," I muttered, "I've just spotted someone I've been trying to get hold of ..."

"Don't worry about me dear," said Coral with a serene smile, "I'm sure I'm going to be having a lovely time treading stagnant water before leaving."

Ten minutes later I glanced across the animated crowd where, to my acute dismay, I saw a very bad tempered-looking Coral sitting bolt upright in the middle of a gilt framed sofa; an awe struck young man perched either side. Without hesitation I moved over to where Roy was loudly proclaiming about his latest "find" (obscure, well-endowed Russian artists being his current forte). "Jesus Roy," I hissed grabbing hold of his arm, "You specifically asked me to bring Coral Browne and now you appear to be totally ignoring her and from the look if it, Madam is not at all pleased!"

"We have? Oh dear, how remiss of us. Where *is* Miss Browne?"

"In purdah over there bookended by two vacuous little queens!" I snapped. "And if they haven't actually *bored* her to death as yet, the situation is imminent!"

"Do excuse us," said Roy giving his taken aback guests a syrupy smile, "duty calls." Spinning round he made a great show of approaching Coral, his arms outstretched wide. "Coral!" he boomed, "We wondered where you'd gotten to and *there* you are! A veritable rose between two thorns!"

"Yes Roy dear," glowered Coral, "and I'm waiting to see which one has the bigger prick."

Not giving Roy the chance to respond Coral rose majestically to her feet and said in a voice accustomed to being heard in the back row of the stalls, "Robin dear, it's time we were fucking on our way. *Not* that Johnny Schlesinger's dinner party for Ava, Harry and me could ever hold a dildo to *this* fucking party when it comes to excitement."

*

"Hence Roysie Boysie Miles not being flavour of the month for several months following and even today he *still* leaves a nasty taste!"

"I imagine Roysie Boysie *always* leaves a nasty taste," snickered William. Stopping midstride he gave an exaggerated shudder. "Ugh! The thought of the Miles paintbrush near *any* palette - ha ha - would put any *artiste* off his stroke."

"From what I've heard Ted Heath would disagree and *he's* an *artiste* albeit a con *artiste*," I replied spikily. Ex-Prime Minister Ted Heath being a regular visitor to Roy's Mayfair gallery.

"Touché RA!" said William with a trill. "Though a Christine or Mandy our Roysie is definitely not!"

*

"I can hardly wait to hear what Diamond Lil wears to a meeting on a building site," chirruped Liz as I was about to leave for my eleven o'clock meeting with Clive.

"Think denim overalls with mink trimmed shoulder straps," rasped Bryan.

*

I duly returned to the hallowed precincts of Ebury Street.

"Sorry to disappoint you Liz. Despite Bryan's prediction no sign of a mink trim anywhere. Our potential client appeared wearing a dark jacket, dark roll neck and dark trousers." I gave a placatory smile. "However, not to disappoint you, the Lil *did* have a large diamond broach pinned to the roll up of his roll neck; a matching broach to one of the lapels of his sober-looking jacket plus enough diamond rings and bracelets to decorate Tiffany's Christmas window."

"Now Madam Liz has had her voracious appetite well and truly sated perhaps a tad more serious?" rasped Bryan. "Apart from our new victim's 'wardrobe of the day', what about the project or, in layman's terms, the house? A potential Hugh Heffner horror or what?"

"More Mother Hubbard and her cupboard," I quipped. "It's one of those dull, dark brick townhouses built in the thirties. Thanks Liz . . ." I reached for the proffered Screwdriver and took a welcome swallow before continuing. "The client's main concern was whether Dennis Paget could or couldn't manage to insert a two-way mirror inside the cupboard and relevant wall between his bedroom and the guest bathroom. In other words a clandestine view of the room with a view!"

"Room with a view?" questioned Liz.

"Another word for loo or, in this case, the bathroom," I replied with a snigger. "And apart from a two way mirror, nothing else really. No mink covered sofas or coffee tables with diamond studded legs. Zilch."

"But we *do* have a room with a poo!" croaked Bryan.

"I would thought a cock-a-dribble-do more in keeping?" I replied with a wry smile.

"*Definitely* time for Screwdrivers all round," murmured Liz gathering up our empty glasses.

"Seriously RA, what *did* you think?" questioned Bryan tossing his Jackie O and adapting his "I'm a serious designer" face.

"Honestly? I think it's a passing fancy and what's more I very much doubt we'll hear another peep from Diamond Lil regarding London's potential answer to Fort Knox."

We never did.

Due to the number of what I considering bona fide projects pouring in I was secretly relieved at the ensuing silence and as expected, when I next saw Clive there was no further mention of property.

A few weeks on from what Bryan described as "a peek at Diamond Lil's version of *Rear Window,* ha ha!" (his reference to the 1954 Alfred Hitchcock thriller starring Grace Kelly and James Stewart) Liz could hardly wait to fill me in about Ben's latest paramour who she had met on one of Ben's impromptu visits to the office. "His name's Noddy," gushed Liz, "and he simply has to be the handsomest parrot on the planet!"

"A parrot?" I exclaimed. "I know our Benedict has a hidden *feelthy* fetish or two, but a parrot? Tell me you're not pulling my plonker?"

"His name's Noddy,"continued Liz ignoring my crude reference, "and let me assure you RA if *I* was a lady parrot, Ben's Noddy could ruffle my feathers at any time!"

I immediately telephoned Ben. "Houston, we have a problem," I said sonorously, "My Liz has gone and fallen head over stilettoes for your handsome Noddy!"

"Eek Mumsie!" laughed Ben, "That explains a lot! I thought Noddy was repeatedly squawking 'his' when in fact he's been repeatedly squawking *Liz!*" He gave a chortle. "Added to which he's gone right off his favourite sunflower seeds!"

After a few minutes prattle Ben hung up but not until Noddy had squawked "good morning" over the telephone. I buzzed Liz. "Liz, have you got a minute?"

"Screwdriver on its way!" came the cheery response.

"I wasn't actually referring to a Screwdriver," I said acidly. "We need to discuss a 'Welcome Noddy' present."

After a giggled discussion I telephoned Dennis Paget. "Mr P its Robin Anderson. RAD has a very special, top secret commission for you. Brace yourself and here goes."

The *Daily Mail* proudly gave an update on the shenanigans of playboy "Mustard Heir Ben Colman" and his latest acquisition, a handsome Macaw named "Rodney" (his given name); the news snippet referring to his *"splendid mahogany perch and silver plated seed tray designed by interior designer Robin Anderson"*.

Ben later informed me Noddy was "delighted with his perch, the ensuing publicity and squawks his thanks".

In between my never-ending projects I managed a fun break in New York with Christopher Hunter and his Texan friend, William Moody Junior. William (call me Bill) invited us to stay at the family mansion In Houston. Bill's pride and joy was a black Lincoln Continental with a pair of gold steer horns replacing the usual emblem on the car's hood. Houston was hot and humid and passed in a daze of barbecues, dinners and a sea of lethal milk punches. Bill introduced to a great friend simply named Petty. I never discovered whether Petty was his nickname, Christian name or surname but when it came to the Texas longhorn department petty he most certainly was not.

There was endless talk about me returning to Houston to do "some decorating" for Bill but looking back it was obviously the milk punches talking and I heard no more.

"Typical," I sniped one evening at La Popote. "Nothing more than cowpats in the Texan sky!"

"Now, now Mrs A," yodelled Christopher, "No need to be so *petty!*"

I accepted Christopher's invitations with an almost fiendish delight seeing one would always be guaranteed an outcome *extraordinaire.*

"You free tomorrow evening Mrs A?" he would yodel over the telephone (the evening varying) followed by a details of a cocktail party, dinner or event.

One evening I was invited to join Christopher "and Lee" at the opening of some show in the West End. Having no idea who Lee was I could not have been more delighted when introduced to Liberace resplendent in a diamante encrusted dinner jacket and sporting even more of the real

McCoy than Diamond Lil. Accompanying "Lee" was a genial Scott Thorson who - apart from nodding and smiling - appeared to spend the whole time guarding Liberace's discarded mink coat.

It was around this time a new restaurant appeared as if daring to usurp La Popote from its exalted place in London's gay firmament. Set in a Knightsbridge mews and named AD8 after April and Desmond the two owners', the restaurant caused a certain buzz all thanks to one owner in particular. The uber-glamorous April Ashley one of the first much-publicised "sex changes" of the early sixties. April certainly had no rival when it came to being the most glamorous "hostess with the mostess" on London's fickle restaurant scene. A genuine show-stopper the elegant, towering April in her dazzling outfits accompanied by an even more dazzling wit was much sought after and people thronged to meet the living legend.

Needless to say when Christopher, Lee, Scott and I arrived at AD8 later for dinner there was a near riot. As I wittily informed Ben the next day, "I've heard of clash of the Titans but I can assure Perseus and Hades had *nothing* on April and Liberace in the clash of the sequins".

*

"You'll never believe who's on the phone," said a smiling Liz from doorway to my office.

"Betty Ford wanting me to redo the White House now that hunky hubby's booted the nefarious Nixon out?" I quipped.

"Neither hot nor cold," chortled Liz, "though you almost had the continent correct!" She gave another giggle. "No, not bouffant Betty but your bête noir, Mr Stephen Gregory."

"Stephen Gregory? But he's meant to be in America? Apart from that minor discrepancy why on earth is he ringing me, of all people?"

"As I said, you *almost* had the continent correct!" replied Liz with a chortle. "And in answer your second question why don't you simply ask him? Give me a sec and I'll put him through."

"Stephen Gregory back in London? Wonders never cease," I muttered as I picked up the receiver. "According to Richard Reynolds Stephen's friend - the other Richard, Richard Taylor - told him Stephen would be in the States for at least six months."

"Putting him through," trilled Liz.

"Morning Stephen," I said cheerfully, "this *is* a surprise. When did you get back?"

"This morning." There was a moment's pause. "Er . . . Mumsie are you free for lunch?"

"I could be," I replied cautiously, "Though it would have be a quickie as opposed to a catch up due to a three o'clock meeting."

"Shall we meet at Mimmo's at one o'clock?"

"See you there," I said replacing the receiver. I sat staring at the blustery rain spattering against the window. "Curiouser and curiouser," I murmured. "Obviously someone or something has gone and got your liberal knickers in a twist. No doubt all will be revealed over a glass or two and a pasta."

"Enjoy your lunch," trilled Liz as I was about to leave. She nodded to her office window. "Nasty out there. I take it you have a comb seeing the gale out there is sure to play havoc with the RA wig!"

"Tart!" I called back over my shoulder as I skipped nimbly down the stairs.

*

"You're back early?" commented Liz as I appeared windswept at the top of the stairs.

"Only because bloody Stephen did a no show," I grunted from the tiled vestibule to the cloakroom as I shook out my umbrella and hung up my rain spattered trench coat. I entered her office. "I don't suppose anyone's called? Someone from Siddeley's?"

"Not a dicky bird." Liz nodded at the rain buffeting and spattering against the window. "Talk about a tsunami." She gave a giggle. "Maybe he's been blown away à la Mary Poppins and her brolly."

I was in the middle of checking a builder's specification when Liz buzzed me on the intercom. "It's Mrs Edwards your cleaner. She says she's calling from Stephen's flat. She sounds in a right old state."

I picked up the phone. "Yes Mrs Edwards?" I said brusquely.

"Oh Mr . . . Mr A . . . Anderson," stammered Mrs Edwards, "It's Mr Gregory. There's been a terrible accident." There was a painful pause. "He's . . . he's dead."

I later learned Mrs Edwards - also responsible for looking after Stephen's flat - had arrived at her usual time, let herself in and was surprised to hear the shower running. Assuming Stephen must have returned from the States earlier than expected she went about her chores with the intention of leaving the bathroom to the last. After about an hour she realised the shower was still running. Concerned, a perplexed Mrs Edwards nervously tapped on the door calling softly, "Mr Gregory, its Mrs Edwards. Are you alright?" Getting no reply she tentatively tried the door handle and finding it unlocked, slowly opened the door where upon she was immediately hit by a strong smell of gas despite the bathroom window being partly open. To her horror she saw Stephen lying in the bath, the shower running full blast on to his inert body partly hidden by the shower curtain. After her initial shock Mrs Edwards called the local police station a few blocks away from Ladbroke Square.

When seeking further information I was informed Stephen's death was "an unfortunate accident" all due to the gas fired boiler for the hot water. As with all the flats at No 5 both the kitchens and bathrooms relied on these units and their open pilot lights which would ignite the gas ring beneath the water tank when the hot water tap was turned on. Apparently Stephen had turned on the shower, stepped into the tub and drawn the shower curtain. It was assumed a freak gust of wind had blown out the pilot light and as the water was still running the gas kept pumping; the poisonous fumes eventually causing Stephen to collapse and be killed as a result of his continued inhalation of the lethal fumes.

As I said to Ben and Richard (Reynolds), "Sorry I don't buy it. Surely Stephen must have realised something was wrong when the hot water started to run cold?" My question was never answered and a verdict of "death by misadventure" recorded.

"Eek! The real problem will be dealing with bloody JS," said Ben in a worried voice.

"Tell us about it?" muttered Richard (Reynolds).

John Siddeley's reaction on being informed about Stephen's unexpected demise was as expected. A scene of embarrassing, selfish grief surpassed by an even more spectacular performance at the Crematorium which would have made Callas proud. None of the mourners could believe their eyes when a sobbing Siddeley suddenly leapt from the pew and flung himself across Stephen's coffin as it made its way towards the "final curtains" (a Ben-ism) leading to the incinerator. A few quick-minded souls managed to get hold of Siddeley and lead him back to his seat among the startled mourners: Jacqueline-stroke-Seccotine included.

"Christ," hissed Richard (Reynolds) in an aside to Ben and me, "And in front of Jacqueline. The man's nothing more than a shameless idiot."

"Thank goodness Mumsie for your much-needed bit of light relief earlier," chortled Ben. "At least you caused a giggle or two for a few of us."

"More than a giggle; a minor uproar," chuckled Richard (Reynolds) referring to an earlier incident where having been called in at the last minute to be a pall bearer, I teetered along desperately holding on to Stephen's coffin. Because of the varying heights of the pall bearers (including the six foot something JS and the diminutive Richard Taylor) the wobbling coffin was seen as if about to slide forward or keel over on to its side.

Knowing Stephen's avaricious nature and fondness for jewellery I could not help myself saying in what was obviously an impressive stage whisper as we shuffled past Ben and Richard (Reynolds), "Who said the avaricious bitch wouldn't take it all with her? Fucking coffin weighs a ton!"

The end of the Stephen Gregory Saga was the scattering of Stephen's ashes in the grounds of Crouchlands, the farm belonging to the other Richard, Richard Taylor, Stephen's erstwhile lover.

Ben, Richard (Reynolds) and I were present for the solemn occasion as was John Siddeley. This time the light relief was supplied by Richard Reynold's flavour of the month (a "flavour" which was to last many years), Little David, a charming, young black man who for want of something to do prior to the big event, decided to clear out the debris to the fireplace in the sitting room before replacing the kindling and wood.

Clutching a dustpan and brush Little David timidly entered the study where we were sitting and said in all innocence to Richard Taylor, "What do I do with these ashes, Richard?" His question resulting in another mega weeping, wailing and gnashing of teeth by a self-pitying Siddeley.

"Makes you wonder whose next on the list," I said to Richard and Ben when we met for lunch two days later. "Talk about dropping like flies; first Barry Justice and now Stephen. I thought the deal with Him upstairs was three score years and ten?"

"Eek! Well as the saying goes, only the good die young."

"Good at what?" quipped Richard Reynolds.

*

Among the guests at one of Peter Coats always entertaining luncheons was David Hicks who greeted me warmly. During the course of conversation Peter remarked, "So sad you had to give up your charming cottage, Robin. Surely you must those delightful weekends away from it all?"

"Well there *are* the weekends in Paris plus my ruin in Italy - now known as *Casa Robino Molti Domani* - could even be completed in time for the twenty first century," I replied drily.

"A country retreat?" interrupted DH homing into the exchange. He gave a smile. "Well, should you ever be interested in renting another getaway I could have the perfect place for you at Britwell; namely The Grove."

"That's most kind of you David," I replied with a light laugh. "But as I've just said I seem to be spending most weekends abroad which means a country retreat is simply not on the cards at the moment." I took a sip of wine. "However I'll keep it in mind and who knows? If it's not The Grove which sound rather grand, maybe something else?"

A YEAR LATER

"The Terrible Trio" as Bryan described Ben, Richard Reynolds and myself were having one of our regular dinners at Brooks Club. Richard was full of enthusiasm over the "job supreme" he had been offered by some City firm. "Who know Mumsie, there could even be a new punter of two for you in the offing."

"Great," I said with a light laugh, "The more the merrier."

"But," said Ben giving Richard a conspiratorial glance, "there's something Uncle Richard and I have been discussing."

"Yes," interrupted Richard. "RAD." He sat allowing his comment to sink in before saying, "Why RAD when life could be much simpler and less of a financial burden should RAD become RADC."

"RADC?"

"Robin Anderson Design Consultant," replied Richard.

"But I'm already a design consultant as it were; only I call myself an interior decorator," I said in a puzzled voice. (So much for a fun dinner!)

"We're not saying you're not," insisted Richard. "What we're saying is while your main talent should be focussed one hundred percent on your designing a vast amount of your *valuable* time is worryingly spent collecting monies on behalf of your numerous sub-contractors."

"Now wait a minute Richard, RAD is *my* business and when push comes to shove it has nothing to do with you or Ben," I said heatedly.

"Please Mumsie, hear me - us - out," soothed Richard. "Take your builders for example. Why are you funding them on behalf of the client when they could be invoicing the client direct and paying *you* a percentage of their contract? In fact, *all* the contractors, no matter what they supply, could be invoicing your clients on a pro forma basis. Your contractors aren't fools and are well aware of the fact if it wasn't for *you* they wouldn't be getting these lucrative contracts in the first place. Come to think of it, not only should they be paying you a percentage but an introductory fee as well? The beauty of all this is, in addition to introductory fees from the various contractors you, working as a consultant, charge a specialist fee. Your fee as a design *consultant.*"

I stared at my two smiling friends. "Go on."

"Do you really need those many offices?" asked Richard. "Okay, you started with two rooms at the top of 60, Ebury Street but now you're renting a further *two* floors - Peter Lubbock must love you - and for why? You certainly don't need the space seeing all your appointments are either on site or the clients' existing home or office. You are known for sussing out any new fabrics and such by your constant visits to the various showrooms and nine times out of ten you are given a preview of the latest ranges before anyone else.

"Let's face it RA, Ben and I know damn well you're at the office by seven thirty each morning making up to date check lists for your staff and writing endless specifications for the various contractors. Surely it's up to them to take down the required details and present *you* with *their* specifications for *you* to okay? Think of the time and the paper work you would save yourself?"

I sat speechless.

"We know how much you're paying the likes of Lady Larkin, Les Gabriel and the rest," added Ben, "plus the balls-up Les made when supposedly supervising the entrance floor tiling to Angie Danziger's house in Cheyne Row is well known. What's more the contractor was adamant Gabriel's instructions were contrary to yours when you visited the site and *still* the Aussie arsehole wouldn't listen. And who had to pay for this to be remedied? RAD. In other words Mumsie, it came out of *your* pocket."

Allowing no let-up Richard once again took over. "Wages for those two and the other two girls, your architect, bookkeeper, secretary and general running expenses form a hell of a commitment each month. Added to which, whether the client's money comes through or not you now are responsible for VAT payable on *any* orders."

"So what are you suggesting is I close RAD and go it fucking alone?" I said spikily.

"Yes and no," replied Richard. "All you need is a part-time secretary and an efficient answering service like the one I use."

"So no office, no front and literally a one man band?" I snapped.

"You have a perfectly good study at Albion Gate which, let's face it, is never used," said Ben. "In fact Mumsie, should you ever consider what we suggest Uncle Richard and I worked you'd be saving a fortune in outgoings. In turn your personal income would increase accordingly. You'd be making a fortune."

"Sounds to me like going back to the beginning," I replied sourly.

"No Mumsie . . . er . . . RA," insisted Richard, "The beginning was exactly that; the beginning. Now you're an established name." He added exasperatedly, "Look at your list of clients for fuck's sake! Not many designers can claim to have clients as prestigious as yours." Flashing me a conciliatory smile Richard said softly, "Mark your Uncle Richard's and Uncle Benedict's words; you'll never regret it."

"But what about the likes of Les, Lady Larkin and the others?" I said. "Liz, as you know left to take up a post on *The Spectator* and was replaced by Sue but there's also young Gordon; the new kid on the block."

"A bitchy birdie tells me the 'loyal' Lady L has something called Morrison up her voluminous sleeve," chuckled Richard. "As for Les 'balls-up' Gabriel, no doubt he'll simply bugger off back to Australia."

"Best place for him of you ask me," muttered Ben.

"As for the new 'kid on the block' simply see him as another millstone," sniped Richard. He added with a wolverine smile. "And I can assure you Mumsie, don't have to worry about Sue. If you ever decide to go ahead with what we suggest she would be more than welcome to join me in my new venture." He gave a chuckle. "No need to look so pissed off Mumsie. It's only a suggestion."

"Merely food for thought, Mumsie, "quipped Ben, "merely food for thought. And talking about food, why don't we order?"

*

I hailed a cab, clambered in and gave the driver the address in Ebury Street, my mind whirring over what we'd discussed. Despite my reaction to the unexpected luncheon topic I had to admit the idea of not having to act as a designer-cum-bank had its appeal.

"I've enough on my overflowing plate at the moment," I murmured as I climbed the stairs to the office, "and like Scarlet O'Horror I'll put all on hold until after St' Lucia. After all, tomorrow *is* another day!" My witty comment accompanied by a wry smile.

"Good lunch?" rasped Bryan.

"As always." I looked at Sue, a Farah Fawcett lookalike and Liz's glamorous blonde replacement. I was sad to see the uber-loyal, fun loving Liz go but quite understood her need for a more serious career change and was delighted to hear she'd been headhunted by *The Spectator* where she would reign as Arts Editor for some twenty three years.

"The Archaic Angel out?" I asked. The Archaic Angel being Bryan's tongue-in-cheek name for Les Gabriel.

"Seeing Linda Lemos and then on to Norringtons."

"Right. And Gordon?" (Gordon being the latest addition to the RAD team.)

"With Les."

"Showing him the *rapes* no doubt," rasped Bryan. "Or so the Archaic Angel wishes."

"Now, now Lady L, be nice." I turned my attention back to Sue. "Have the two of you divinities decided anything as yet regarding our great Christmas get-together?"

"Bryan and I thought lunch next Wednesday instead of dinner," replied Sue.

"We'd all *love* to go to Burkes Club and gorge among the rich and infamous," rasped Bryan.

"Take it as done. Sue can you do the necessary and give Burkes a ring," I murmured, my eyes fixated on Bryan's garishly patterned shirt.

"Anything wrong RA?" Following my gaze Bryan glanced down at his midriff. "Something dribbled down the front of my latest from the local charity shop? Shouldn't be for unlike the Antipodean Angel Gabriel I don't dribble my drink."

"No, apart from the pattern there's nothing wrong with your top Lady L. I was simply checking your sleeve."

*

"Darling it's Georgina, Georgina Halse."

"Georgina!" I exclaimed, "What a lovely surprise. How are you?" I added with a chuckle. "I take it all is well in Halse Land and the Big Bad Woolf is as bad as ever?"

Georgina gave a throaty laugh. "Germaine remains Germaine darling which means she's even badder; if that's at all possible!"

"My lips are sealed."

"But darling, my reason for calling. Harry and I dined at a delightful new restaurant last week. Walton's in Walton Street. Do you know it?"

"Never heard of it," I replied with a chuckle. "I'm sure you're well aware the only restaurant of note in Walton Street for artistic souls such as yours truly is La Popote."

"So why not remove your sparkling blinkers for once and let me invite you to a pre-Christmas dinner at Walton's; that's if you happen to have a free evening in the run-up to Christmas, of course." Georgina added mischievously, "Darling, and as for the décor you'll either love it or loathe it."

"Now you mention it I have glanced at the place when driving past and have to admit I do have a tendency to accelerate."

"Touché darling! Give me a call and hopefully we can make arrangements for you to park instead of pass."

"*Et* touché you too Mrs Halse! And to *really* stun you, if you're free this very evening I could be all yours."

"Really? That's wonderful darling. Robin Anderson foot loose and fancy free? I can hardly believe my luck!"

"C'mon Georgina, an evening with you sounds far more fun than an evening with a man-eating shark at the Kensington Odeon!"

"A man-eating shark sounds much more fun than dinner with me, darling!" said Georgina with another throaty laugh.

"Nonsense Mrs Halse! How could the film *Jaws* ever hope to compete with the likes of *Jaw*-gina Halse?" I cried.

"Darling, that was quite terrible," replied Georgina with a snicker. "Back to business. I'm having drinks with friends literally round the corner from the restaurant so let's meet there at eightish?"

"See you there, *Jaw*-gina!" I said hastily replacing the receiver.

Despite Georgina's misgiving I was full of admiration for the lavish grey, yellow and ivory décor plus the unique touches of polished chrome tiebacks and poles for the lushly draped silk moiré curtains which matched the wall covering, chrome table lamps and a floral centrepiece of Kew Garden proportions. Leading off from the marble-tiled entrance with its limed oak armoire serving as a bar and it modern chrome reception desk was a second dining room walled in black mirror.

Not only was I full of praise for the opulent décor I was also intrigued by the beaming dapper, somewhat obsequious bearded and moustached midget maître d' introduced by a smiling Georgina simply as "Malcolm" whereas "mixed-up, mercenary, manipulative, materialistic Malcolm" would have been much more appropriate.

BELLA ITALIA

"It's such a relief Beesle," I said gazing at DLL who was sitting at his desk browsing through various papers, "but I still can't believe how vindictive JS is being. Why, he's even outdoing the wretched Roland and that in itself is a *mega* achievement!"

"Forget about him, Robble," murmured DLL, "You're now involved - all thanks to Tony - with Alistair Colvin Limited". He gave me a shrewd look before adding conspiratorially. "And knowing you as I do, young Robble, I have a feeling your time spent with Alistair could also be somewhat limited. Meanwhile, have a look at these."

"These" being a stack of crudely drawn layouts and photographs of what appeared to be a derelict hillside village nestling amidst vine-covered hills dotted with twisted, spindly trees. "I don't know if it's at all possible for you to take a few days off next week . . .?"

"Absolutely! My role with Colvin's is part-time so, for once, your Robble is Gucci foot loose and fancy free!" I reminded him from where I was lying on the sofa, a copy of *Portnoy's Complaint* on my lap.

"Good," replied DLL, "I was hoping you'd say that." He nodded at one of the photographs I was holding. "As you know I've been negotiating a property deal in Italy?"

"No, not one hundred percent Bees." I tapped the photograph with a finger. "Is it one of these houses? They look somewhat dilapidated."

"No my Robble," chuckled DLL. "Not *one* of the houses; almost the whole village apart from one or two stalwart locals who tend the surrounding olive groves."

"You've gone and bought almost a *whole* mountain village?" I gasped, sitting bolt upright.

"Yes Robble; and I'd like you to join me out there next week; maybe come up with a few ideas? Rumour has it you're a dab hand at dealing with rundown properties even though these may be slightly older than what you usually deal with."

I sat staring at DLL. "But that sounds fabulous, Beesle! Your very own village! Am I correct in thinking it's somewhere in *Bella Italia*? You've mentioned Italy and this photo - *all* the photos - look very Fellini *Eight and Half.* The scenery that is!"

"Spot on Robble! It lies east of Genoa and if you remember your schoolboy geography, approximately on the knee to the boot of Italy at the start of a picturesque mountain range known as the Cinque Terre."

"Does the village, *your* village, have a name?"

"Yes indeed, Robble. It's called Dosso."

"I take it that's *not* Italian for dosshouse?" I quipped.

*

We flew to Genoa the following Wednesday. Having hired a car at Cristoforo Colombo airport DLL and I drove through part of the ancient maritime city before taking the coastal road bound for Portofino; a multi-coloured, 14th-cenutury picture postcard seaside town nestling between the steep hills.

After a quick lunch at a charming little restaurant, a stone's throw from the Hotel Splendido, I found myself already head over Gucci heels in love with *Bella Italia* despite having only been in the country for a few hours. Well-fortified by a delicious seafood pasta and several glasses of Pinot Grigio, we continued along the coastal road before finally reaching the Bracco Pass (*Passo del Bracco*) where were forced to queue behind a long line of cars and their irritated occupants trailing behind a giant lorry as it laboured its way up the winding road. Eventually DLL took an exit to the right marked Levanto.

"Talk about a giant switchback," I commented as we began the steep descent towards the seaside town, "this even makes the term 'hairpin bend' appear obsolete!"

"Today I'm taking you via the scenic route," announced DLL as he manoeuvred the hired Fiat 124 around a particularly sharp bend, "whereas next time we'll take the highly illegal shortcut."

"Illegal short cut? What does that mean?"

"We drive through the old disused railway tunnels which follow the coast. Saves having to deal with the Bracco Pass plus it saves a considerable amount of time unless you have the misfortune to meet an illegal oncoming lorry!"

"What happens then?" I asked with a grin: not believing a word.

"As he's bigger than you, you diplomatically reverse until you reach one of the ventilation bays facing the sea and draw in there."

"You're joking of course?"

"No joke Robble. We'll use the tunnel route on our return to Genoa. With luck we may even meet a wayward lorry or two!" replied DLL with a chuckle.

(In the years to follow this was the route I would always travel by car. Nine times out of ten I would take the *Rapido* from Genoa to Rome and get off at Levanto. On the rare occasion a journey by car *was* deemed necessary I would hire one at the airport.)

"We'll be staying in Levanto for the next few nights. We won't be seeing Dosso this evening - I can point it out for you - but head up there first thing in the morning. So an early start, Robble."

"And this evening?" I asked. "Anything planned apart from a calorific pasta dinner somewhere?" I gave a snicker. "Somehow I don't think Levanto is known for its wild night life."

"We're having dinner with Helene and Jacques Malan a South African couple now living here. They played a major part in the negotiations; Helene as a translator and Jacques concerning the never-ending legal angles." DLL gave a warm smile. "Jacques can be a bit long-winded but I think you'll warm to Helene." He added mischievously, "Helene's very elegant and apart from being fluent in Italian she claims she has, quote, 'a flair for interior design', unquote."

"Great," I muttered, "that's all I need; a fucking Richard Brinsley."

"Charming as always, my Robble. May I ask what you mean by a 'Richard Brinsley'?"

"A rival; as in R.B. Sheridan's *The Rivals*."

"Oh, very droll, Robble," chuckled DLL. "Though on meeting Helene you'll probably change Richard Brinsley to Marlene Dietrich."

"Marlene Dietrich? Don't tell me your translator with a flair, the enigmatic Helene Malan is actually Marlene Dietrich in mufti?"

"What a clever Robble you are!" came the laughing reply.

Jacques and Helene were exactly as DLL had described them. Jacques was tall, rapier thin, balding, ponderous elderly man (he immediately reminded me of humourless Roger Powell; dear Peggy's husband) and Helene really *could* have passed for Marlene's long lost twin.

We dined in a charming little restaurant highly recommended by Helene. DLL kept giving me amused glances as Helene waxed lyrically what she visualised and planned to "create" within the first house (DLL's house) to be refurbished. "I call it my 'pampered peasant' look," she said self-effacingly in her strong South African accent. "Or Helene Malan's 'Heavenly Haven'."

"I simply *love* your ideas Helene," I replied cuttingly, "particularly your idea for the main salon where you make the fireplace - or *central* focus as you put it - *off-centre* so it looks central to the doorway when viewed from the entrance hall, despite it looking completely cockeyed when - seconds later - you're standing in the salon itself!"

"I still think I'm rrright!" snapped Helene in a perfect parody of Roland Spillane.

Several weeks later I was stunned when DLL broke the news of an impromptu visit by the French Letter to Dosso.

Impromptu my arse! I thought, *David and he must have made the arrangement weeks ago!*

Naturally Leslie was introduced to Helene and on been regaled by an indignant Helene as to my comments ridiculing her siting of the fireplace promptly sided with the wretched woman. The end result being what I would always refer to the off-centre fireplace as "Lesley and Helene's lop-sided leer".

"I know, Robble, I know," said DLL in a placatory voice when seething with indignation I asked why "them" and not "me"? "But at times some things are best left unsaid."

"At least you didn't say 'let sleeping bitches lie'!" I snapped.

"That's my Robble!" chuckled DLL. "He always has to have the last word!" He looked at me seriously. "There's something you should know about Helene . . ."

"You mean she can't see properly?" I sniped.

"Ah, so you noticed? How astute," murmured DLL giving me an admiring look.

"Noticed what?

"Helene suffers from Kalnienk vision."

"Which is *what* exactly when Signor Kalnienk's at home?"

"Promise not to laugh, wicked Robble. In layman's terms, Helene suffers from tunnel vision."

"No wonder she thought wherever she positioned the fucking fireplace was perfect!" I gave an evil grin, "Perfectly fitting into what she thought was the bigger picture when all she was seeing was a miniature! Sorry," I added contritely, "That was cruel and I apologise. What you've just said explains a lot. I noticed how Jacques literally steered her into the restaurant and back out again when they met us for dinner. How on *earth* did she manage to make her way around Dosso? Those steep, cobbled streets are lethal."

"The trusting Jacques. He literally never leaves her side when they're out and about." DLL gave a smile. "Fortunately Signora Malan is well known and well liked in Levanto so they're always on the lookout for her and very caring."

"Now I feel a total shit," I said. "Poor Helene. But she should realise its *totalmente sbagliato* to contradict a genius!"

"Totally wrong to contradict a genius Robble? Goes to show what a *donna coraggiosa* our Helene seeing I could never do something so *tialmente sbaglaito* and dare disagree! You know *whatever* you say is your demand."

On my next visit to Levanto I was delighted when Helene confided she found Leslie "most unsuitable for David's reputation and for Dosso". Her words uttered in a sinister voice; her narrowed eyes focussed partly on my face. "The villager's do not understand *Il Colonnello's* (DLL's name amongst the locals; DLL having been made a Colonel during the War: a fact I discovered after my first dinner at The Empress) relationship with the *strano ometto* (strange little man) whereas they all see you as *suo figlio*. His son!"

(Smacks of Germaine Woolf and *her* claim!)

I was only at Dosso once when Leslie was also "in residence" and I couldn't believe how out of place he looked.

"It was like the grand finale with dismal Dirk Bogarde in Visconti's *Death in Venice*," I said waspishly to William during one our "don't you simply *love* being rich" dinners. "Only when it comes to the mimsy French Letter it could only be a case of *Death in* Little *Venice*." (Little Venice being a pleasant, tranquil canal area close to the not so pleasant or tranquil Paddington Station.)

"I think you flatter him," snickered William spooning a large dollop of caviar on to a sliver of toast. "I would have said *stench* in Little Venice!"

"Something the French Letter wouldn't even have even noticed seeing he *epitomises* any French stench," I said giving an exaggerated sniff.

"Rather you than me," murmured William beckoning the wine steward for a refill.

"What you and Michael must do," I said (Michael being the aforementioned Michael Pitt-Rivers and William's lover-cum-Maecenas), "is come and stay for a days when it's just me and David at Dosso. You could bring your paints for not only is the village stunning to look at; the views from the *Casa Padronale*, the main house, overlooking the mountains, the vineyards, neighbouring villages and of course the blue, blue Mediterranean."

"We must," agreed William taking a dainty sip from his replenished champagne flute. "Give me some dates and I'll speak to Michael."

You do that, I thought, *but I very much doubt if you'll have any success because where the two of you are concerned what Michael says, William does.*

Whereas whatever Whipped Whippet William says goes in one ear and out the other!

Peter Leggatt and I had often discussed William's relationship with Pitt-Rivers (wittily dubbed "The Pits" by Peter). "Michael Pitt-Rivers is a control freak," he would repeat sonorously, "you and I call William Whipped Whippet William and mentally the poor guy is exactly that. Whipped. When Lady Dee - William - is in the Pits's company he literally cowers like one of those wretched dogs the Pits surrounds himself with at Tollard Royal. His answer to Sandringham."

"In other words a rival queen but with whippets as opposed to corgis!" I laughed, smearing the last portion of the caviar onto a piece of toast.

*

The redevelopment of Dosso proceeded slowly but surely with DLL spending more and more time in Italy. His first priority was the completion of the *Casa Padronale*, off-centre fireplace and all. *Casa Padronale* was positioned at the apex of the village nestled in a V-shape amidst tumbling vineyards and olive groves. The house consisted of a large, galleried downstairs *sala* with two enormous windowed arches opening on to a large, paved terrace overlooking the verdant valley and the distant, sparkling Mediterranean.

Visitors would have to climb a series of steps leading from the small cobbled piazza before coming face-to-face with an impressive, studded wooden door opening into an impressive double height hallway with an open staircase leading to the upper level and a similar staircase leading down to lofty galleried *sala* below. Both the stairs and the floors throughout were finished in shiny black slate tiles of varying sizes. All the walls were finished in a lightly textured plaster and painted a flat white. A large dining room with an arched ceiling was set to the right-hand side of the main hallway along with a rustic, country-style kitchen. Leading off from the sitting room housing "Lesley and Helene's lop-sided leer" was a further terrace (part of the roof to the downstairs *sala*) overlooking the large paved terrace below.

The upstairs section was made up of DLL's en suite bedroom, a double guest suite, a single bedroom with the use of a bathroom across the landing plus a smaller en suite bedroom ostensibly for the French Letter.

Meanwhile the sale of Hedgerley had finally gone through which meant various items being shipped out to Italy. I was surprised at how well the majority of selected items blending in with their new surroundings. Like *Il Colonnello*, they had no problem in adapting with DLL's collection of furniture rests looking completely at home in the downstairs *sala*.

A small building adjacent to *Casa Padronale* soon became the guest house or *cassetta* and much to Lesley's chagrin, more-or-less my domain. The tiny property boasted a downstairs reception room, small entrance hall and a kitchenette. Upstairs housed a small bedroom and a shower; the steep staircase leading directly to be bedroom. From a small terrace outside the sitting room a series of narrow steps led down to the main terrace of the *Casa Padronale.*

*

Sadly DLL's devoted Borgie was never to enjoy Dosso. Having lost my devoted Miffy all those years ago I could understand DLL's hesitation in finding another dog to replace his faithful friend. But all was to change.

Driving back up to Dosso following a particularly boisterous lunch with Helene and Jacques I called out to DLL to stop the car.

"Over there!" I said, pointing to the roadside, "That bundle of sorts. It looks as if it could even be some sort of small animal. A small dog or even a young goat. Surely it can't have been hit by another car? As far as I know, apart from Isidoro and maybe Carlo (one of the few remaining villagers) we're the only ones who've driven along here today." I gave a frown. "Surely they would have stopped and checked if either had thought he'd hit something?"

"Unless he didn't notice," replied DLL. "C'mon Robble; we'd best take a look."

The "bundle of sorts" turned to be a dog; not a "run over" version but a dog who was fast asleep.

"Pooch!" I called, briskly clapping my hands, the sound causing the sleeping mutt to open one eye as if checking the source for the intrusion. "Pooch!" I repeated in a sharper tone accompanied by a louder clapping causing the small dog to scramble up on to all fours, his scraggly tail giving a few tentative wags.

"Now there's a handsome fellow if ever there was," chuckled DLL eyeing the small, scruffy animal who appeared to be a mishmash of a Fox, a Cairn and a Jack Russell terrier; Italian version!

"*Very* handsome," I agreed with a grin. "Do you think he's a he ... yes, pooch *is* a he," I added noting the pert bubble beneath his tail, "What's more, do you think he's a stray and if so, can we keep him?" I gave a laugh. "After all is said and done the one thing missing from *Casa Padronale* is a fearsome guard dog exactly like our handsome friend here!"

"I don't see why not?" replied DLL with a smile. "As you rightly say, *Casa Padronale* could well do with fierce guard dog and this fine fellow looks as if he'd fit the bill! Let's see if we can get him into the car. We'll introduce him to Isidoro and Joanna and take it from there."

The scruffy animal needed no encouragement to jump nimbly into the car and sit panting happily on the passenger seat. "If you don't mind," I muttered, hefting him up and putting him on my lap, "this is *my* seat!"

"All set?" said DLL.

"All set," I replied as we drove off. "*Fuck!*" I cried a few moments later.

"What?" exclaimed DLL slamming on the brakes.

"His nibs here!" I retorted, "He's literally crawling with fucking fleas!"

Thanks to a beaming Isidoro and a cooing Joanna a thoroughly bathed and defled pooch joined the two of us on the upper terrace where we were enjoying the sunset and an evening. Me with a glass of wine and DLL his whiskey.

"So what do we call him?" questioned DLL gently stroking the dog's muzzle. I was slightly miffed to note the pooch had headed straight for *Il Colonnello* and without a moment's hesitation jumped sprightly up on to his lap.

"Seeing he's such a *handsome* pooch, why not name him after some Italian signor equally as handsome?" I suggested, "Some glamorous *historical* figure? Someone like Adonis? On second thoughts no. I can't quite see you traipsing the surrounding hills and dales Beesle shouting, 'Adonis! Here boy'!" Taking a sip of wine I added whimsically, "If you *really* wish to bestow a worthwhile name on our new friend why not a play on Alexander the Great sometimes known as Paris?"

"Alexander is on a par with Adonis and not ideal for shouting to the hilltops." DLL gave a deep chuckle as he gently patted the small dog on his furry head. "However, if we go for an *Italian* Paris, in other words a *Pariji*, I would have no problem with shouting for an errant *Pariji* while hiking through the Cinque Terre!"

"Nor would the locals!" I said with a smile, blowing the pooch a christening kiss.

With DLL's decision to live permanently in Italy changes to Dosso were soon apparent. Apart from the *cassetta*, a total refurbishment of two larger houses was soon completed. One of the houses being promptly bought by a charming English family named Thompson and the other by a rich Milanese. A major plus for the village saw the creation of a proper gravelled parking area leading down to the village plus improving the steep, narrow cobbled streets wending their way through the stucco-fronted houses. Slowly but surely the derelict houses began to blossom in true Cinque Terre colours. *Casa Padronale* was dressed in terracotta, the *cassetta* in a lime green, the Thompson's house in yellow and the Milan house in cream (nicknamed the *Malan* house by me due to the house being on two levels resulting in a lopsided look). If Helene ever picked up on the double entendre she never let on.

Through Jacques and Helene's introduction DLL had become friendly with an American and his Spanish wife (supposedly a retired Flamenco dancer) who rented the badly renovated local *castello* overlooking the small harbour serving Levanto. Dick, the American claimed to be an author. Try as we did we were never able to find out Dick's surname and despite Helene's claim he had "endless best sellers" under his Gucci belt, she was unable to supply the missing link. I simply referred to him as *Castello* Dick and his wife as *Castella* Castanets. He had also become friendly with Giuseppe and Giovanna the local *Barone* and *Baronessa* who lived in a nearby *palazzo*, even more crumbling than the *castello*. Giuseppe, a Rosanno Brazzi lookalike was a great charmer and roué while Joanna, a doppelgänger for Sophia Loren with a touch of Mother Earth-cum-Mother Theresa was adored by the local community for her good works and genuine compassion.

DLL also invested in a motor launch (bought through a contact of the Malan's) which I promptly dubbed *Titanic Secondo*. Though not of Riva quality the boat was adequate enough for ferrying DLL and his guests from

Levanto to the Cinque Terra ports of Monterosso and Vernazza for lunch. Pariji was always invited on these outings and would stand proudly on the bow, his muzzle pointing firmly into the wind and his tail pointing proudly to the stern. Needless to say the restaurant owners in either port always had something special for *Capitano* Pariji.

The surroundings to Dosso proved to be another delight. DLL, Pariji and I spent many happy hours following the seemingly endless small footpaths twisting their way through the carefully tended vines and olive trees. During summer the hillsides became a magical, multi-coloured carpet of wildflowers. Here I have to make a confession. When staying alone at Dosso alone (DLL being back in England or elsewhere) I would use the opportunity for inviting one or two friends to stay. A particular treat would be a short, slow ramble through the hills supposedly to "work up an appetite" prior to one of Joanna's sumptuous lunches. Accompanied by Pariji and a small rucksack containing several bottles of iced prosecco, a bottle of vodka, grappa and the requisite number of plastic tumblers, we'd find a shady spot and make ourselves comfortable before quenching our thirst with a Russian White Bear cocktail Italian style; prosecco, vodka with a dash of grappa. It wasn't unusual for a canny Joanna despatching Isidoro in order to summon us for lunch. All due to RA and guests having dozed off having downed several lethal Italian *Bevanda Orso Biancos* (White Bears). Joanna would always make sure we were all back at *Casa Padronale* before putting the final touches to her tasty dishes.

While DLL didn't disapprove of my *Bevanda Orso Bianco* walks he did disapprove of the subsequent *Bevanda Orso Bianco* forty winks. "Just as well you have the fearsome Pariji to guard you my Robble," he would say in a sonorous voice. "Imagine the scandal should you be carried away by some rampant, hirsute *bandito*! All joking apart, a drunken White Bear 'forty winks' is not at all good for *Il Colonnello's* handsome *figlio's* image!"

"At least they're not forty White Bear *wanks*!" I had quipped on more than one occasion to which DLL's replies were either a sardonic "you do surprise me", "as I've said before; there's a *thirst* time for everything!" or "Lucky for you loyal Pariji believes in keeping schtum!"

DLL's endless love, kindness, humour and generosity knew no bounds.

"You do realise my Robble you have free run of the *Casa Padronale* when I'm not here," he announced one evening as we sat enjoying and after dinner drink on the upper terrace; a snoring Pariji obviously not keeping a lookout for whatever fearsome guard dogs are mean to look out for.

"Thank you Beesle, that sounds absolutely wonderful. I know several enviable souls who would jump at the opportunity of a few days in *Bella Italia*. The Marshallene for one." I took a sip of grappa. "Come to think of it I would like to invite Lady Dee - William Davis - and Michael Pitt-Rivers to stay for a few days; but only if you're here. You know Michael, don't you?"

"Yes indeed; though he's more of acquaintance than a friend." There was followed by what I could only describe as a very pregnant pause. *Oh dear*, I thought, *someone else who doesn't see the Pits as flavour of the month. A bit like Lance's distantly remembered 'ZaSus' perhaps?* "When were you thinking of asking them?"

"It would have to be sometime in September, Beesle. Not only is it my birthday on the thirteenth - geddit! - I also know Lady Dee and Michael are planning a trip to Venice around September time so why don't I suggest they combine a visit there with a visit here?"

"Why not?" replied DLL without much enthusiasm. "Simply let me know." He added mischievously, "And talking of birthdays, Pariji and I have already decided in your present."

"I *loathe* Bulgari," I grinned "*Loathe* Valentino. *Loathe* Gucci so surprise me!"

"How about your own *casa* here in Dosso?" said DLL with a gentle smile. "*Casa Robino Bello* sounds just right to us."

"*Casa Robino Bello*?" I cried. "I love it! I simply love it!" Springing to my Gucci shod feet I moved across to where DLL was sitting and enveloped him in a warm hug. "*Grazie* Beesle," I murmured. "Love you and thank you."

"In the morning I suggest you take a look at three possible *Robinos*," said DLL with a chuckle.

"Are one of the suggested properties by any chance the tumbledown wreck a few yards away from the Thompsons?"

"It most certainly is," replied DLL, his eyes twinkling. "Pariji and I *thought* that would be the one you would plumb for seeing nobody in their right mind would take on such a challenge."

*

The next morning I spent two ecstatic hours clambering among the ruined walls of the future *Casa Robino Bello.* My enthusiasm must have infectious when one took into account Pariji's non-stop tail wagging and excited gruff barks (or maybe something to do with Joanna's special Pariji treats tucked inside the holdall containing my drawing pad, pens, pencils and measuring tapes). My ensuing plan was to rebuild the outer walls to double their original height in order to create a large studio-like space containing a spacious sleeping loft. A modern galley kitchen, shower room and loo would be sited beneath the sleeping area leaving me with what the French Letter would sniffily describe as "a cavernous room barely capable of containing that so and so's swollen head!"

The main wall facing the tumbling vineyards, olive groves and sparkling Mediterranean I envisaged as mainly glass and formed from the largest sliding doors available. These would open on to a small terrace. On the side wall facing the loft, galley kitchen and shower I envisaged a modern, floating gas fire along the lines of those uber-stylish Italian Aeris hanging fireplaces you see today.

"In addition to *Casa Robino Bello* Pariji and I are also including a budget," said DLL with a chuckle when I joined him for lunch. "However, judging from you initial sketches I can see it's going to be tight. *Very* tight!"

"When can I start work in *Casa Robino Bello*? By 'start work' I mean when can I have a preliminary meeting with your site foreman and better still, with Guido your architect?"

"Why not directly after lunch?" smiled DLL, "It so happens both are on site this afternoon having spent the morning dealing with another property."

"Would you mind?" I asked excitedly.

"Put it this way," chuckled DLL, "They're already expecting you. As I explained to them I couldn't see you concentrating on anything else this afternoon."

How right he was as from that moment onwards Robin Anderson and *Casa Robino Bello* became well and truly conjoined.

*

Lady Dee and Michael duly visited us in September as arranged; William/Lady Dee the proud possessor of two Louis Vuitton suitcases and

Michael the nonchalant owner of a battered, well-travelled suitcase from Asprey.

"Better Asprey than 'Swag'!" I quipped once William and Michael had gone upstairs to "freshen up".

"Now, now Robble," chuckled DLL. "Behave!"

"I'd better check what Lady Dee plans to stun us with at dinner," I suggested. "Not that I would even *dare* attempt to compete!"

Back in London kaftans for men were all the rage and considered de rigueur for many private dinner parties one deigned to attend. Having been to one such dinner party where not wearing kaftans another guest and myself stood out like the proverbial sore thumb. Once bitten I invested in what I considered a suitably stylish maroon and black striped kaftan. "Smart and not too queeny," I told myself. Knowing William's penchant for dressing in the latest fashion trends and introducing one or two ideas of his own for "that extra zip", I had taken the precaution of bringing my "one and only Ali Baba" with me in anticipation of William/Lady Dee "strutting his stuff".

Sure enough Lady Dee, sparkling in a silver and purple sequin kaftan made his entrance *sans* trumpets into the salon prior to dinner. Having been told by William his planned outfit for the evening I gamely wore my "smart and not too queeny" in a futile attempt to make him feel "more comfortable". Needless to say DLL and Michael were the epitome of style in their navy blazers, cravats, gleaming white shirts and dark trousers. To my surprise William (I alternate between William and Lady Dee knowing the latter is taboo with Michael) claimed to be a stranger to White Bears and therefore a total novice when it came to the Italian version. With wide-eyed glee he downed glass after glass and by the time we sat down to dinner he was decidedly drunk. In between further gulps of the lethal potion he began a great deal of sequinned arm waving à la Shirley Bassey causing the walls of the dining room and a wildly blinking Isidoro (attempting to serve) to sparkle like glitter balls in some disreputable disco.

Our very strained dinner completed we adjourned (Lady Dee staggering) to the *sala* below and on to the adjoining terrace for a nightcap. By this time I could see from Michael's expression he was furious with William and from his ferocious glances in my direction held me responsible for "Bud's out of order condition" (Bud being Michael's pet name for

William). Without any warning Lady Dee - his arms now definitely more Don Quixote's windmill than Miss Bassey - leapt from his chair chanting in a weird falsetto, "I'm a firefly! I'm a firefly!" before plunging down the stone steps leading into the olive grove below.

"Bud *get back here immediately!*" roared Michael storming over to the stone balustrading. The response to Michael's furious demand being a carolled "I'm a firefly! I'm a firefly" followed by a distinct thump as Bud/William/Lady Dee collided into a very old, gnarled and extremely solid olive tree.

*

The next morning a stern-faced Michael accompanied by a sheepish William announced "a change in plan" and their immediate departure for Venice.

"No need for me to ring for a taxi, Michael," replied DLL his eyes twinkling, "as Isidoro would be more than happy to drive you down to Levanto. Sorry you've decided to cut your stay short. Robble and I were looking forward to taking you and *Bud* out on the boat and to Monterosso for lunch."

Being charitable neither DLL nor I commented on Lady Dee's bruised forehead and black eye. Nor did we mention the fact their three day visit had lasted less than twenty four hours.

I have no idea whether Michael forbade Bud/William/Lady Dee from having anything more to do with me but after his "firefly exhibition" at Dosso our once close friendship slowly faded.

"I think no more White Bears Italian style for any future unsuspecting guests Robble," chuckled DLL.

"And definitely no more kaftans," I added with a smile. "Or saris!"

"Saris?" questioned David.

"In case Peter Leggatt comes to stay. He's about to take up residence in India on behalf of the company he works with." I have a snicker. "Madge and Poofty are already referring to him as Rita Raj so no doubt a sari could have been on the chapati!"

A few months later Peter dropped a bombshell worthy of several megatons. "I'm getting married," he blithely announced to a stunned

Madge, Poofty and me. "Murmurings from the company I work for indicate they prefer their directors married as opposed to a bachelor gay - ha ha!"

"So who is she? This victim of what your company prefers?" snickered Derek. "A mail order bride?"

"It's Maggie," replied Peter with a deadpan expression.

"Ha! Ha! Very funny Peter," I said sneeringly. "Pull the other one. First of all you couldn't act the role of a happily married man; not even for all the tea in China or, in this case, India!"

"I've already asked her and she's said 'yes'," came the defiant reply. "We'll be getting married at the Chelsea Registry office in two weeks' time followed by a private luncheon in the River Room at the Savoy. I trust you three will be there." A statement; not a question.

After a moment's silence Poofty asked perkily, "Who on earth will you have as your best man? Obviously it's not one of us?"

"Lady Dee of course," said Peter.

"Lady *Dee*?" I squawked. "Now you *must* be joking?"

Peter Leggatt had never been *more* serious and to say the luncheon at the Savoy was a strain was putting it more than mildly. Sir Ronald, Maggie's stepfather, looked furious while Bobby Leach, her mother, simply looked bewildered. Hopefully the "blushing bride" had no idea her newly wedded husband, his best man and myself had ended up enjoying an energetic bout of drunken rutting on his stag night: a far cry from Peter's more sober get-together with a few work colleagues and friends "not in the know".

A year later neither Poofty, Madge nor myself were the least surprised when told Peter and Maggie had gone through an amicable divorce.

*

"Talk about leaving in a cloud of dust," I remarked as I stood on the terrace watching as Isidoro's car disappear from view. "Hopefully Lady Dee doesn't attempt a replay of her firefly frolics in Venice otherwise the poor cow will find herself dumped not only on the Bridge of Sighs but also on a *Bridge Over Troubled Water*!" My comment causing DLL to shake his head in mock despair. "I wonder if the Pits knows Peggy," I continued unabashed, "William would have adored to meet her." This particular Peggy being DLL's special Peggy, the legendary Peggy Guggenheim.

"I was thinking the same thing," murmured DLL looking up from the outdoor table where he was going through some papers. He gave a smile. "However, I'm sure you'll soon find out."

"Well Lady Dee's the loser if he doesn't," I replied. "And from what I know about the Pits their visit to Venice will make that of Signori Bogarde and Visconti completely *carnevale* in contrast!"

DLL and I had visited Peggy Guggenheim on several occasions at the Palazzo *Venier die Leoni,* her home situated in the *Dorsoduro* on the Grand Canal. I always found Peggy G (like Peggy P) the greatest of fun and the fact she was devoted to her pet dogs - all Lhasa Apsos - endeared her even more to me (the Lhasa Apsos with their long fur and squashed faces resulting to flashbacks to Miffy all that time ago.) When Peggy G died in 1979 I heard she was buried in the gardens of the palazzo next to her beloved pets (4 in all). The plaque above the list of her pooches endearingly reads: *Here Lie My Beloved Babies.*

Peggy G happened to be staying at *Casa Pardronale* during one of my impromptu weekend visits.

"It's almost seven o'clock and this is something you simply have to see for yourself," said DLL with a discreet, whispered aside. "What's more it's been part of Peggy's evening routine since her arrival."

On the dot of seven o'clock the telephone rang and without even checking with DLL Peggy G picked up the telephone and began crooning lovingly in Italian to whoever was calling. I gave DLL a questioning look as I quietly mouthed. "Who the fuck . . .?"

"The pooches," whispered DLL, "Peggy calls them - or rather they call Peggy - in order to say goodnight to each other."

After some ten minutes of billing and cooing Peggy G softly replaced the receiver.

Eyeing Peggy G I asked mischievously, "Out of curiosity Peggy, how do the dogs manage a cumbersome thing like the receiver?"

"Oh the butler holds the telephone to their ears so they can hear me," replied Peggy G with a "what a silly question" type of bemused smile.

Apart from Venice DLL and I were frequent visitors to Florence. DLL, always the diplomat and knowing I wasn't a fan of Mic Sandford would always suggest we stay at the Excelsior on the handsome Piazza *Ognissanti.* On one such occasion and during an evening meander through the neighbouring streets I spotted a white marble memorial plaque with the letters QMP carved above the head of a serene-looking cherub or *putto.*

"Look Bees," I cried pointing at the plaque, "a perfect portrait of Quimp!"

"Quimp?" questioned DLL.

"Our newly adopted son, of course!" I replied with a loving wink. "His name inspired by the letters QMP which, if my constantly improving Italian lingo serves me well stands for *questa, memoria pose* or 'may his memory remain'."

"May they indeed dear Robble; may they indeed," whispered DLL giving my hand a gentle squeeze.

A few months later I received a handsome photograph of the Florentine Quimp specially commissioned by DLL. Quimp was duly framed and hung in one of my apartments but sadly lost in between one of the moves. Undaunted I was happily able to reinstate (I won't use the word "replace") Quimp in the form of a bronze statuette. He now resides in great luxury alongside the computer in my Chelsea apartment.

*

I spent a many blissful days with DLL at Dosso. Leslie French was rarely mentioned although Helene couldn't wait to tell me there had been a major set-to between him and DLL over my newly acquired property.

"I mest sey I was very surprised to hear yew'd actually bought the property," she told me. "I would hev thought it would hev been a prezzie. After all, everyone around here think's yew's David's son."

If that's what Beesle's telling them, then good on him, I thought, *and fuck you French Letter along with all those fucking nosey-bloody-parkers and shit stirrers you claim to be your friends!* As you may have gathered I was somewhat annoyed by the situation.

*

As DLL's had suggested I went on to have various friends to stay. Helene and Jacques loved meeting what Helene described as "all those colourful *volk* yew know, Robin. *So* amusing, *so* original en so charming I could hug them to bits!"

Yes, if you could see them to catch them, I thought evilly.

Among the first of these "amusing", "colourful" and "charming" guests to visit was Ian Marshall, aka the Marshallene who, as expected, asked if he could invite his latest paramour.

"But of *course*," I replied full of bonhomie. "The more the merrier!"

It was fortunate the Marshallene was unable to witness my expression (we were on the phone at the time) when he cheerfully announced, "His name's Peter Hurford." In other words the dreaded Lady Pamela and Brian Ketterer's bête noir.

As I said to Ben later, "Had the Marshallene's Lady Pamela been a fucking mountain climber instead of a social climber she would have made Everest appear a mere pimple."

"Eek Mumsie!" said Ben with a chortle. "I can tell deep down you really enjoy Her Ladyship's agile mountaineering company but are too stubborn to admit it!"

It was arranged Ian would fly to Genoa and take the train to Levanto where I would meet him while Peter, who would be visiting friends in Rome (*Friends?* I thought, *they must be desperate*) would take the Genoa bound *Rapido* two days later and leave the train at Levanto.

The day of Peter's impending arrival saw the Marshallene unable to sit still, his jittery toing and froing making the boisterous Pariji appear the epitome of calmness. Due to the Marshallene's growing agitation at the idea we could be late for the northern equivalent of Cleopatra's entry into Rome we arrived at the station an hour early. While I spent the hour in the Station Bar chatting happily to one of Signora Basso's sons an anxious Ian paced the platform as if willing the train to arrive.

The *Rapido* pulled into Levanto Station on schedule. After a few minutes the train pulled away without a single passenger alighting from any of the carriages.

Squawking like a demented turkey the Marshallene raced alongside the departing yelling "He *must* be on it! Peter! Oh Peter!"

Doing my best to hide my delight at Peter's "no show" I led a sniffling, bewildered Marshallene into the Station Bar where I made him down a large Stock brandy before we journeyed back to Dosso. We had barely entered the *Casa Paronale* when an excited Isidoro announced "Signor Hereford" (*An apt slip of the tongue*, I thought) had telephoned and would call again within ten minutes. The Marshallene, hovering over the phone, snatched it up at its first ring.

"Heartbeat!" he cried, "What happened? Where *are* you?"

Heartbeat? I thought. *Whatever next? Precious penis plunger?*

From Ian's cries of "How could you!", "Silly *silly* Peter" and other snatched bits of dialogue I gathered Peter had been asleep when the train pulled into Levanto station and only woken when the train drew into Sestri Levante, a few stops before Portofino. To his dismay he'd been told there were no returning trains until early morning.

"Tell him he'll simply have to catch an early train - can he at least give us a time? - and we'll collect him." I snapped while simultaneously thinking, *Serves the stupid queen right!*

"We can't *leave* him there!" cried a distraught Marshallene. "Not there when he's so near and yet so far!" (Christ!) "Can't we go and fetch him?"

Fetch him? I thought. *Slaughter him more likely!* "Where is he?" I asked, "I *heard* something about Sestri Levante but somehow I don't think geography is quite his (Heartbeat's) forte."

"He's in a hotel next to the station," snivelled the Marshallene in reply.

"Tell him to stay there. Tell him *not* to move one iota and we'll be there within the hour."

I doubt if Ian would ever forget the drive to Sestri Levante in order to fetch Peter nor the two of them the return journey to Dosso.

Ignoring the usual way via the Bracco Pass I raced the Fiat 124 Stirling Moss style through the disused railway tunnels skirting the coast. Fortunately we met no oncoming traffic and were back in Dosso within an hour and a half. It goes without saying the emotionally exhausted couple were *so* overcome by the evening's events they had no alternative but to immediately head for the sanctuary of their bedroom.

I sat silently seething as I ate part of the dinner Joanna had left for us. I couldn't be bothered to reheat the main course simply making do with a salad and some cheese along with a welcome bottle of Barolo: a sympathetic Pariji being treated to a cheese plate of his own.

The two lovebirds having deigned to appear for breakfast sat billing and cooing while practically ignoring their host. The mating calls, giggles and girlish shrieks continued throughout the day until we journeyed down to Levanto for a dinner party given by Helene and Jacques. Helene, traitorous bitch (although her "tunnel" vision may have had something to do with it) thought the Marshallene "a lovely led" and Peter "verry elegent end *so* attetched to his frrend".

Yes, I thought, *Attached today, despatched tomorrow and may God bless* all *who sail in her!*

Two months after what I would always refer to as "the Marshallene's tunnel of love experience" an exuberant Ian invited me to Chester Row so I could meet the new "love of his life" and solemnly vowing this one was "for keeps".

Meanwhile Peter Hurford would go on to find a more elevated partner in the manly form of Nicholas Eden 2nd Earl of Avon. To give Peter his due he remained devoted to Nick until Nick's untimely death in 1985.

*

"Georgina Ryott on the phone for you," chirruped Liz over the intercom. "Are you in, out or not available as you sit pondering beautiful design thoughts?"

"You mean perched on my beautiful butt pondering even *more* beautiful thoughts," I replied with a chuckle.

"Hideous thoughts more likely," trilled Liz not daring enough to place my beautiful butt in the same category.

"Georgina Ryott?" I murmured, "I wonder what she wants. No doubt to tell me how sorely this flavour of the month was missed at her dinner the other evening."

"Screwdriver?"

"As long as that isn't a substitute for 'screw you' a Screwdriver would be great."

I picked up the receiver. "Georgina, what a lovely start to another busy day in the world of RA. Again, my apologies for having to cancel dinner the other evening . . ."

"That's not the reason I'm calling Robun," came the simpering reply, "It's something totally different. If I remember correctly won't you staying at *your* David's lovely house in Italy in a few weeks' time?"

"Four to be exact."

"And David's house is where?"

"A place called Dosso near to Levanto."

"Levanto?"

"A small seaside town east of Portofino in the province of Liguria," I replied simultaneously thinking, *Why the geography lesson and sudden interest Georgina dear?*

"Sounds fun," trilled Georgina. "It so happens David and I will be in Italy around the same time - we'll be staying with friends near Sienna - and we thought maybe a visit to David's house . . . what did you the name was?" She gave a girlish giggle. "Dosso? Losso?"

"Dosso is the name of the village Georgina and the *house* is known as *Casa Padronale.*" I replied loftily. I added mischievously, "However, seeing David owns the whole village there would be little chance of one getting lost." After a prolonged silence I said somewhat querulously, "You still there?"

"Yes indeed Robun. I was just looking for Levanto in our *Philip's World Atlas . . .* ah yes, found it!" She gave another simper. "As you so rightly said, east of Portofino. Hmm, I can see no problem and yes, we'd love to come and stay for a few days."

But you haven't even been invited? I thought.

"Will David be there?" she continued blithely. "Such a *delightful* man!"

"No, he'll be in South Africa."

"How unfortunate. He and *my* David get on so well with each other . . ."

That's news to me, I thought, *seeing Beesle thought DBR a bit of a prick when first introduced to the two of you at Covent Garden and even* more *of a prick when I invited the two of you to Hedgerley for lunch. He also questioned my original description of a glamorous you suggesting I'd really meant* un-glamorous!

"Give me a few minutes to have a word with *my* David and I'll call your secretary back as I know *you're* busy . . ."

"Call Liz back?" I questioned.

"Yes. To give her the dates we could visit you at *Casa Padronale* which we now know is part of the *village* which in turn is named Dosso! Lovely to talk to you Robun and David and I look forward to seeing you in *Bella Italia!*" Giving a giggled "Byee!" Georgina hung up.

"Talk about jumping the gun," I muttered staring at the silent phone. "Oh what the hell. Why not?"

*

Standing on the upper terrace I spotted the Ryott's dusty hire car slowly making its way along the bumpy, hillside track leading up to Dosso. I assumed the car could only have been theirs seeing the only other cars travelling to or from Dosso would have been Isidoro's tiny Fiat *Bianchina* or Carlo's dilapidated APE pickup truck.

Calling for Isidoro and Pariji to join me I took my time making my way up the steep, narrow cobbled street leading to what passed for a car park set above the tiny hillside village. Reaching the top level of the street I spotted a confused looking DBR and Georgina slowly climbing out of their car.

"Hello!" I called coming into view. "Welcome to Dosso!"

"Oh my goodness, Robun!" cried Georgina breaking into a relieved laugh, "For a moment we thought we'd come to the wrong place. Now I realise Dosso is the pretty village we could see from the road."

"Dirt track!" sniped DBR.

"From the *road*," repeated Georgina, "which means we're now parked *above* which explains why we couldn't see any discernible buildings." She gave a giggle. "I must say Robun it was a great relief to see you rising - literally - like a Phoenix from the edge of the er . . . car park."

"Clearing," said DBR pettily.

"I never thought of myself as a Phoenix," I replied, deliberately ignoring DBR's snide asides. "Once again, welcome to Dosso. This splendid young man next to me is Isidoro, our major domo while the extraordinarily, handsome young man busy sniffing your foot Georgina is Signor Pariji, master of all he sniffs!"

"Naughty Pariji," tittered Georgina as Pariji gave her bare ankle a further sniff and a tentative lick.

Jesus Pariji! I thought with alarm, *whatever you do please do* not *lift your leg and piss on Mrs Ryott!*

DBR and Georgina were enchanted by the narrow cobbled street leading down to the small village square

"Must take a few photographs for the old album, what?" brayed DBR stopping midstride. He plonked down his holdall and fumbled for his camera.

"You have three days for that," I chided. "Let's get you settled in before we start any sightseeing."

"There's nothing like the present!" came the reply, "Dosso may be fourteenth century but can we be guaranteed it won't suddenly decide enough is enough and collapse even more over the next day or two? What? Ha! Ha! Ha!"

Having waited somewhat impatiently while Yorkshire's answer to Cecil Beaton took at least a dozen shots of the picturesque street we finally reached the tiny main square with its dilapidated, peeling church and two houses in the process of being refurbished. "Welcome to *Casa Padronale*," I said proudly.

Georgina stood resignedly at the bottom of the steps leading up to the magnificent carved front door while DBR took at least six photographs of his beloved and the *porta d'ingresso*. I am sure we would have been held up for at least ten more shots if a beaming Joanna hadn't decided to open the aforesaid front door!

On entering the airy, elegant main hall Georgina turned and said breathlessly, "Dear Robun, knowing your taste and David's taste we knew it would be quite something but this is, literally, out of this world!"

After introducing DBR and Georgina to Joanna I showed them up to their suite. "Twin beds as requested," I said smilingly, "and the small cupboard by the door to the bathroom houses a fridge with mineral water - still or sparkling - white wine, vodka etcetera. The two decanters on top of the cupboard hold whisky or sherry." I gave a light laugh. "So if you feel you need a sharpener before facing your host you don't need to ask."

"Or need to face your host *ever*! What?" brayed DBR. "Ha! Ha! Ha!"

I never knew whether Mr Yorkshire immortalised the drinks cupboard and the decanters or not. However, I have my suspicions.

I introduced the Ryotts to the Malans and Giuseppe and Giovanna our token Baron and Baronessa along with *Castello* Dick and his clicking, clacking wife, the glamorous *Castella* Castanets. With Pariji at on the bow of the Riva and accompanied by the Malans I took the Ryotts to lunch at Monterosso and Portofino whilst the *Baron* and *Baronessa* invited us for dinner: a pizza served on silver plate in a vast dining room decorated with tattered wall tapestries. In addition we went on several walks among the vine covered hills surrounding Dosso; yours truly armed with a canvas holdall containing all the ingredients for our White Bears, Italian style. Needless to say DBR kept on photographing all and sundry as if commissioned by *National Geographic* to fill several editions of their prestigious magazine.

A gushing Georgina promised to make all their friends "green with envy" when telling them about their stay with "lovely Robun" at Dosso.

A few days later after Isidoro, Joanna, Pariji and I had posed for several group photographs we finally waved the pietistic couple goodbye. Returning to *Casa Padronale* I had a fortifying White Bear before collecting the car and with Pariji acting as chaperone, bodyguard or whatever his choice of role for the day, coasted down the winding road to Levanto. My plan was to call on Signora Basso hoping to purchase some truffles as well as restock the *sala* and guest room bars. I would also be collecting the de rigueur three day old copies of *The Times,* the *Daily Mail* and the *Express* from Levanto's one and only *giornalaio.*

"*What* a handsome fellow!" I heard a feminine voice cry.

Glancing over my shoulder I saw two couples - obviously off the beaten track tourists - patting and fussing over Pariji who, being a total tart, was revelling in all the attention.

"Is he yours?" asked one the women.

"He is indeed," I replied flashing my most charming smile. "His name's Pariji and yes, as you can see he *is* the most handsome pooch in all of Levanto." I gave another whiter than white smile. "I'm Robin, Robin Anderson. I take it you're English. Are you staying in Levanto or just passing through?"

"Only here for the day," replied the first young woman. She proffered a delicate hand. "Hello, I'm Joanna, Joanna David."

"And I'm Gawn, Gawn Grainger," said one of the men shaking my hand. The other couple following suit.

"I was about to have a glass of vino at the small café over there," I announced. "Care to join me and Pariji? Pariji I hasten to add is teetotal and has to make do with a mundane bowl of water. Rest assured, Tommaso the owner always has his special bowl ready for him!"

"Do you live here?" asked Joanna once we had made ourselves comfortable at one of the outside tables.

"Not fulltime unfortunately. However I do try to visit as often as possible."

"I take it then you have a house in Levanto?" suggested Gawn.

"Yes, a house," I said proudly. "But not in Levanto." I pointed in the direction of the encompassing hills. "If you look up to your left you can just spot Dosso, one of the little villages where my house is. It's the village which looks rather like an upside down triangle." I added excitedly. "Have you plans for lunch?"

"Er . . . no, not really," replied Joanna.

"Then why not join me for lunch up at Dosso?" I suggested. "It'll give you a chance to look around an authentic fourteenth century village which a friend of mine bought and is in the process of redeveloping. David's house, *Casa* Padronale, is where I'm presently staying and where we'll be lunching. My own house is still at the *very* ruined stage."

"That really is so sweet and very kind of you," replied Joanna with a smile. She looked at her three companions. "Shall we?"

At Gawn's and the other couple's enthusiastic "Yes please" and "Yes, we'd love to" I promptly excused myself and raced into the main café where

I asked the genial Tommaso if I could use the telephone and rang the other Joanna.

"Joanna!" I said excitedly, "I know I said I'd have a salad for lunch but I've met up with four friends here in Levanto and invited them back to Dosso which means there will now be five of us. Can you organise a pasta or something and as I am phoning from Tommaso's café I can easily get some *prosciutto* from Lorenzo at the delicatessen . . ."

A cheerful Joanna assured me lunch for five would not be a problem. Having calculated we would be back at *Casa Padronale* "within an hour and a half" I went back to join Parji and my newly acquired guests.

I soon discovered the four were all actors. A few years later Joanna married Edward Fox the actor. Edward and Joanna would become parents to Emilia, a glorious, elegant lady and one of my favourite actresses. Through Jill Melford I would later meet Edward's first wife, the actress Tracy Reed. Tracy and her glamorous daughter Lucy (known as "Juicy Lucy") became firm friends and in the eighties I spent many a fun weekend at Tracy's country house in Oxfordshire. A surefire catalyst to these fun weekends was the name of Tracy's country haven. I took great delight in telling people I would spending the weekend with friends at Old Pyles and Baby Pyles. Old Pyles being the name of Tracy's comfortable sixteenth century thatched, timbered house and Baby Pyles the name of the equally comfortable guest cottage.

One Christmas I invited a particularly outrageous group to stay at Dosso (DLL dutifully spending the "Season of Goodwill" with the French Letter in sunny South Africa). Heading the guest list was Christopher Hunter, the dashing manager of La Popote. Accompanying Christopher was Raynor Power, the glamorous manageress of La Popote's upstairs bar (woe betide the ignoramus who dared to refer to her as "the barmaid!") along with the cherubic David Flynn, a young Australian waiter working at La Popote and ostensibly travelling under Christopher's well-exercised wing. Christmas wouldn't be Christmas without a touch of the bizarre coming down the chimney and nothing could have been more bizarre than my two other guests, a wealthy, slow talking American named Sam Crocker and his choice of festive cheer, a remarkably handsome "resting actor" named David Hilton who seemed to be in a constant trance while preparing himself for his next fantasy role of a wannabe guru. "Guru David" as I dubbed him and the drawling Sam would spend hours chanting and meditating ("or mutually masturbating" to quote the wicked Miss Power) among the frosty olive trees.

Raynor's pièce de résistance was her regular early morning yodel "Is it time yet for a gin?" from the sanctuary of her bedroom before preparing herself for another day. On being answered by a cheery "Yes, if you come and get it!" Raynor would then join the rest of us for a late breakfast. By this time Pariji and I would have driven down to Levanto for the papers and after an espresso at Tommaso's café, replenish Raynor's daily gin infusion plus any other alcohol that needed replacing (Sam and Guru David obviously found vodka an able stimulant to their meditations) and purchase any groceries Joanna required for her kitchen.

Meanwhile Christopher teased a delighted Helene unmercifully; Raynor flirted outrageously with the beaming Basso boys and waiter David kept bursting into grappa-induced tears because he was "homesick for the folks back in Aus".

Armed with hipflasks we all attended church on Christmas Eve in an adjoining hillside village and spent Christmas Day with Giuseppe and Giovanna. I was delighted to note lunch was a delicious suckling pig as opposed to the usual pizza on a platter. I reciprocated by holding a dinner party two evenings later where *Castello* Dick made a drunken pass at Raynor causing an equally drunken *Castella* Castanets to throw an almighty clacking fit. A quick thinking Christopher and Giuseppe had no alternative but to physically restrain the flamenco fury from attacking her husband while a startled Raynor had to be tranquilised by another gin *nota bene* and not wine. Poor Helene missed all the fun as she was focussing in the wrong direction whereas Sam and Guru David sat viewing the debacle with benign - or maybe divine - expressions on their placid faces.

*

Progress on *Casa Robino Bella* appeared to be non-existent despite me having finalised the plans and building specification with Paulo the architect what I deemed "aeons ago".

"The so-called work on the house would make a Mogadon look like Speedy bloody Gonzales," I said sarcastically on meeting Guido outside Signora Basso's shop. Guido, having no I idea what I meant by a Mogadon or Speedy Gonzales, explained in broken English and a series of frenetic hand gestures he had been instructed by *Il Colonnello* to concentrate on the two houses currently being worked on and *si adatta* (fit in) my house when he could. Here I had to bite my tongue seeing *Casa Robino Bello* was a gift and a very generous gift at that.

Looking back time spent at Dosso seems more like a glorious, technicoloured fairy tale (no pun intended) and made even more memorable for it was here, in this magical space, I had never seen DLL/Beesle looking so happy and content. During all my travels - and I have travelled extensively - I have never seen or experienced anything that can compare with the moments spent with the irreplaceable *Il Colonnello* at this veritable Shangri La.

A casual *Il Colonnello*. The one and only BEESLE aka DAVID LLOYD-LOWLES in sunny St. Lucia. 1976.

PEGGY POWELL striding out in typical *"Aargh Bungo! Aargh!"* mode.

DONALD CAMERON. A Canadian charmer and friend extraordinaire.

Never too *young* to cut the mustard. Dazzling BEN COLMAN

"The Golden Voice of Teenage Half Hour". FBC (Federal Broadcasting Corporation), Bulawayo, Southern Rhodesia (now Zimbabwe), 1955.

THE RITCHIE SET - Rhodes University 1960. (Left to Right) ALAN DASHWOOD, SHIRLEY RITCHIE, RA, LITTLE GLEN and LANCE (TALLULAH) SALWAY.

RA and "TALLULAH" SALWAY.

ROBERT BECOMES ROBIN. London 1962.

The sitting room 5 LADBROKE SQUARE. My first London home.

MOORHAWES COTTAGE - an inherited name. My first country pad.

MOORHAWES COTTAGE – a cosy "away from it all".

BELLE ET SÉBASTIEN Valley – Alpes-Maritimes

The interior - CHALET BELLE ET SÉBASTIEN - un erreur grave (no pun intended) all thanks to THE FRENCH ERECTION.

Not quite From Here to Eternity. An "offshoot" to the chalet and the anticipated last resting places. Even the best-laid plans go astray.

DAVID LLOYD-LOWLES in his role as Master of the
Worshipful Company of Girdlers, London. 1964.

General view of DOSSO with glorious
Casa Padronale in the forefront.

RA at DOSSO, Cinque Terre, Liguria, Italy. 1972.

ALBION GATE PENTHOUSE - Two views of
the sitting room overlooking HYDE PARK,
1972.

The master bedroom at ALBION GATE with   The dining room at ALBION GATE all set for
Monsieur LIDO keeping tabs on anything   a typical fun "dishing the dirt" dinner.
untoward.

RA as Guest Speaker,
AN EVENING WITH ROBIN
ANDERSON, Royal Festival Hall.

BEN COLMAN - The sitting
room showing three pyramids
(of six) housing BEN's collection
of silver mustard pots. Cadogan
Gardens. 1974

BEN COLMAN - Study - Cadogan
Gardens. 1974.

RA with MARGARET, DUCHESS OF
ARGYLL at an event obviously not
exactly mind-blowing.

Advert for the launch of PARK WEST. London, 1979.

IN MEMORY OF MARGARET. RA'S tribute to the
legendary DUCHESS. A host of admiring males and
a skull (read head) originally named DOUGLAS later
renamed DUNCAN. REDCLIFFE SQUARE.

Drawing room of RA'S second country home showing the "after" to ANDY WARHOL'S admired "before". 1975.

"Feluccing fabulous!" CORAL BROWNE'S Egyptian-inspired "VINNIE" (VINCENT PRICE) trap, Eaton Place. London. 1972.

General view The Colonnades, THE ROYAL ALBERT DOCK, Liverpool.

A show flat, THE ROYAL ALBERT DOCK. Liverpool. 1985.

RA'S Chelsea apartment
REDCLIFFE SQUARE, London.
The entrance hall. 2017.

REDCLIFFE SQUARE - The main corridor of covers. 2017.

REDCLIFFE SQUARE - The sitting room
showing MISS ABEL MABEL MORTIS and RA'S
splendid red lacquer "coffin" table. 2017.

REDCLIFFE SQUARE - The sitting room
looking towards the second corridor of
covers. 2017.

REDCLIFFE SQUARE - The Black Hole of
All "Schmutter" aka RA's study where it
all happens. The handsome fellow on the
couch is named DEDDY in keeping with
RA's collection of contented skulls. 2017.

REDCLIFFE SQUARE - RA at his desk In The
Black Hole of All "Schmutter". 2017.

THE FRENCH ERECTION

Robin Miller called inviting me to dinner at his small, terraced house in Ripplevale Grove, Islington. (Tony Hutt of the "black cock" territory!) "David and Georgina won't be there," he added with a girlish giggle, "it's a 'Boys Only' evening!"

Despite having now met Robin several times as well as supporting his musical, *Dames at Sea,* by seeing the show at least five times, I could never enthuse over him the way the Ryotts did but remembering Georgina's penchant for "names", why not? I never quite knew what to make of the tall, giggly, girlish Robin (Peter Leggatt had previously dubbed him "a *very* poor man's Noël Coward") but, as I said to myself, "It's only dinner and who knows? There could be one or two interesting guests worth meeting; maybe even a prominent name from London's theatreland."

*

"And of course - as I *must* have already mentioned" - gushed the other Robin in his strange falsetto as we entered the chintzy, cluttered sitting room - "my guest of honour this evening is the singer Michel Gallois who is about to appear in cabaret at the Savoy!"

So what's he doing here for dinner is he's 'currently appearing in cabaret at the Savoy'? I thought acidly. *Plus the fact I've never even heard of him.*

"Let me introduce you as you may not know everybody - or *any-*body," simpered the other Robin addressing the small, claustrophobic room. "Everyone this Robin Anderson and in turn Robin please meet John and Tony, Robert and Simon, Alan and of course, *Monsieur* Michel Gallois!"

Smiling and nodding in turn at the five strangers - John and Tony looking like a couple of well-fed bankers or estate agents playing at "being casual"; Robert and Simon looking like Don Quixote and Sancho Panza *before* the windmill scenario and Alan whose whole bug-eyed persona screamed "kinky" - I ended up staring at the "guest of honour" lounging on sofa; a long-legged, dark-haired Heathcliff lookalike (as played by a *young* Laurence Olivier) who regarded me lazily through lowered lids. *"Enchanté,"* said Michel Gallois in a deep, rich, right from the balls baritone voice.

Get you Mr Matinee Idol looks! I thought. "Good evening," I said.

"Robin's the interior designer I told you about," simpered the other Robin. He turned to me, "Michel's mother is also a designer - though not a *professional* like you, of course!"

"How interesting," I murmured thinking, *Shit! Don't tell me I'm expected to talk to Monsieur I'm the Bee's Knees on Legs all evening about his interior designer mother? Next thing we'll be talking about another type of pet. Maybe Monsieur Bee's Knees has a dog?*

As anticipated, the other Robin placed me next to Gallois for dinner. *Thanks Robin, this is all I need,* I thought glancing sideways at the handsome, almost beautiful profile on my right. "Er . . . you must find it very comfortable staying at the Savoy," I said for want of something to say to the brooding young staring somewhat disdainfully at the other guests.

Michel Gallois slowly turned his handsome, beautifully coiffed dark-haired head and gave me what could easily have been interpreted as a long smouldering look, "I do not live at za Savoy," he replied with a sex-infused accent, "I live in za Maida Vale."

"Maida *Vale*?" I exclaimed, "But I thought you were about to appear in cabaret at the Savoy?"

"I *am* appearing at za Savoy but I live in za Maida Vale wiz Hardy, my loverr." "Lover" said with what I swear was an exaggerated Eartha Kitt-like purr.

"Ah," I replied breezily, "and here I was thinking you - being a *French* cabaret star - would automatically live in Paris where - again - I would have thought all the action is."

"I do live in *Paree*."

"Of course! *Paree* Maida Vale as opposed to *Paree* France," I quipped, thinking, *Robin Miller, judging from the way the evening's progressing* you're *going to have a lot to answer for!*

"Do you 'ave a loverr?" Gallois asked suddenly.

"Yes, yes I do," I answered.

"Do you live wiz your loverr?"

"No, we *don't* live together; we see each other when we can."

"Zen 'e cannot be your loverr," said Michel Gallois dismissively, "loverrs should always live togezza."

So where's Maida Vale Hardy if loverrs should always be togezza? I thought.

As if reading my mind, Monsieur of the Matinee Idol looks aka Monsieur Mr I'm the Bee's Knees said in a new, soft velvety voice, "My Hardy, 'e comes to collect me later wiz Sidney,"

Siddeley? I thought with a start. "Siddeley? Did you say Siddeley?"

"*Non.* Sidney; 'e is my dog."

This is uncanny, I thought with an inward snicker, *didn't I just say to myself he'd probably start talking about his pet dog?*

"And what does Hardy do?" I asked politely.

"'E is za window drezza at za Harvey Nichols," came the deep, mellifluous reply.

Great, a French cabaret star, a window dresser and a dog called Sidney. Not quite a gossip columnist's wet dream Monsieur Gallois, but then one never knows . . .

"Ah!" exclaimed Gallois, "I zee 'e comes but' 'e is early; *non?*" He rose to his feet uttering a sultry "Cherie" in the direction of the doorway where a frail, nervous figure stood peering timidly into the smoke-filled dining room, half the guests having brought their unfinished cigarettes in with them. "I must go," announced Gallois to the startled other Robin about to serve the first course. "*Excusez-moi,* but now I leave." Slinking his way around the cramped table he greeted Hardy with a light kiss on the lips (I immediately thought of Nelson and his final "Kiss me Hardy" request) before turning to mutter a few words to our host. Without a backward glance Gallois grabbed Hardy by the elbow and propelled him from the smoky dining room.

"Isn't he wonderful?" breathed the other Robin (most definitely not this one), "So charming and so *handsome!*"

And so bloody rude, I thought, *"simply walking out of your dinner party like that.*

"I wonder if he's got a big cock?" said bug-eyed, kinky Alan, obviously one of the more practical guests.

"I wouldn't know!" trilled the other Robin followed by a girlish giggle, "But I wouldn't mind finding out!"

After a few more giggles and ribald remarks concerning Monsieur Gallois genitalia the other Robin announced solemnly, "Naturally we must *all* attend his opening night at the Savoy two weeks on Wednesday. I'll book a table shall I?"

"What's Gallois doing living with Miss Harvey Nichols in London?" I asked the other Robin once the conversation was more-or-less back to normal considering the somewhat quirky guests, "Surely, profession-wise he'd be better off living on Paris?"

"I don't understand it myself," simpered the other Robin, "but Michel seems quite happy toing and froing between the two cities. It's *so* romantic; a true *love* of two cities as it were!"

"Hey, maybe Miss Hardy Harvey Nichols is the one with the big cock?" suggested the ever-practical bug-eyed kinky Alan with a leer.

*

I telephoned Maggie the following morning.

"Mags, you free next Wednesday?" I asked.

"Why, you planning an orgy?"

"You wish! Seriously, I was at a dinner party last night and met this French singer, a Michel Gallois. He opens at the Savoy next Wednesday and I thought we'd get a few chums together and go along for dinner and a dekko? I'll see if Peter's free. Let me explain . . . Robin Miller, our host - he wrote *Dames at Sea* the show I dragged you to at least three times - suggested he organise a table but I have a feeling it's a case of *very* small doses when it comes to Mr Miller. A bit too 'luvvie' if you catch my drift? The man positively *drips* with 'luvvie-ness'!"

"I'd *luvvie* to!" replied Maggie. "You call Peter and I'll see if Valerie's free. We could also ask David and Victoria?"

"Jesus Maggie; David Ashton-Bostock and Robin Miller? It'll be a bloody 'luvvies' convention!"

"Don't be nasty!" chastised Maggie.

"Nasty? *Moi?*" I cried with feigned indignation, "Never! And as for the *moi*, it must be Monsieur Bee's Knees rubbing off on me!"

"Monsieur Bee's Knees?" retorted Maggie, "Who or what on earth are you talking about?"

*

The six of us duly arrived at the Savoy for Michel Gallois' opening night. I was greeted coolly by Robin Miller who no doubt had taken umbrage at being told I wouldn't be joining his table but making up a table of my own. However he did thaw when Maggie waxed lyrically about *Dames at Sea.*

"*Our* Robin simply *insisted* I see the show and I'm so glad he did!" she drawled, "I really loved it! So much so I insisted my mother and step-father take a party along to see your enchanting show!"

"Your mother and stepfather?" cooed the other Robin.

"Sir Ronald and Lady Leach," came the offhand reply. The mentioning of the two titles causing the other Robin to give a giggle and bend a knee (or perhaps perform a modest curtsey).

"Promise to come back stage and meet the cast should you decide to come and see the show again. Perhaps *your* Robin may insist on bringing you a second time?" The other Robin turned and looked at me coolly. "Such a lovely young lady, your Maggie. Joyce Blair and Blayne Barrington would simply *love* to meet her!" In other words, you, Robin Anderson are *not* invited backstage!

Michel Gallois was good. In fact, he was very good.

"What a performance," moued David Ashton-Bostock prissily, "And *so* good-looking!"

"Divine," said Victoria in her high plummy voice,

"Super Robin, really super!" enthused Maggie, "I didn't quite know what to expect but it was a lovely show and as for Michel's voice; it's magnificent!" She gave a twiddle of her spectacular bosom, "In fact his voice gave me goose bumps all over!"

"Aha! And here he is, the man of the moment," I said as Gallois appeared in the dining room accompanied by a smirking Robin Miller.

"I didn't see the Miller sneak out?" I muttered to Maggie, "Obviously he enjoys the limelight; even if he has to steal it!"

"Don't be unkind," hissed Maggie, "Furthermore, Michel Gallois *is* Robin Miller's friend; not yours!"

"Touché," I muttered.

Michel, having been introduced to Robin's guests murmured to the other Robin who in turn gave a nod; the two turning and crossing over to our table. "Michel," said Robin pointedly, "this is Maggie."

"*Enchanté Mademoiselle,*" said Michel reaching for Maggie's hand and giving it a theatrical kiss.

"And this is Valerie," I said as a giggling Valerie proffered her hand, "and this is Victoria." A tittering Victoria doing the same. After being introduced to Peter and David, Michel turned his attention back to Victoria while Maggie and Valerie appeared to gently drift away.

"He didn't offer to kiss *my* hand," hissed Peter.

"Nor mine," sighed David. (Whereas I knew Peter to be camping it up I had my suspicions David most certainly wasn't.)

"Perhaps he didn't find either of you *enchanté* enough?" I said with a chuckle.

"Did he actually say good evening to you?" asked Peter. "Somehow I don't think he did?" he added with a chuckle before moving nimbly to join Maggie and Valerie.

"You're right, he didn't," I muttered to nobody in particular, "rude bugger!"

Michel Gallois suddenly turned to face me and said in his deep, rich voice, "Robin, your friends are enchanting an' we mus' all meet again!" He nodded to where Peter, Maggie and Valerie stood in a huddle whispering. The two of us giving a start as Maggie suddenly uttered a loud, unladylike shriek.

"Yes, we must," I replied wondering what could have caused Maggie's outburst.

"Or you could come to us," called Victoria in her high debby voice from where she had joined David; the two of them looking as if their invitation was an offer too good to refuse.

"Thank you Mademoiselle, zat would 'ave to be in za two weeks' or *trois semaines,* after I finish at za Savoy," said Michel in a patronising voice. "Er . . . where does you live?" (Michel Gallois from now onwards referred to as Michel.)

"Victoria," said Victoria.

Yes, and I am sure Hardy could easily manage to bring you and collect you from David and Victoria in Victoria, I thought bitchily.

After what appeared to be an eternity of polite chit chat Peter sidled up to me, "I think a restorative nightcap at La Popote is most certainly on the cards," he hissed, "but *sans* the Victorians!"

"Hear! Hear!" I whispered in reply.

A few minutes later Maggie, Valerie, Peter and I clambered into my Mini.

"So tell me," I said as we zoomed down The Mall towards the bona fide Queen's discreetly floodlit London residence, "what was so funny back there? The three of you could hardly contain yourselves from laughing out loud."

"It's Monsieur 'I'm so pleased with myself' Gallois," said Peter as the three burst out laughing once more, "He wears a toupee!"

*

"Robin? Michel," said the voice.

Michel? You must mean the one and only Mr Bees Knees Michel Gallois? I thought. *What the fuck do you want and what's more, how the fuck did you get this number?*

"Robin Miller 'e gave me your numberr," continued Michel as if reading my thoughts.

"Oh? How charming of him," I said sourly. "So, how can I help you Michel? If you wish to talk to Maggie it would be better I got her to call you as JS - Mr Siddeley her boss - doesn't approve of personal calls to the office." I gave a snicker. "Plus I'm sure her office number is something Robin Miller *doesn't* have lurking in his little pink book."

"Leetle pink book?" questioned Michel. "What do you mean by zis 'leetle pink book'? *Non*, I wishing - er *wish* - to talk with you." ("Wish" pronounced with exaggerated correctness.)

"*Avec moi*?" I replied camply, "Well, here I am!"

"Maybe you would care for za *le déjeuner* er . . . za lunch today?"

"Lunch today? Sorry Michel but lunch today or any day this week is not possible."

"Hmm, *oui,* yes, Robin Miller did zay you was always verry busy. So when?"

When? Never preferably! "Er . . . let me have your telephone number Michel and I'll call you back once I've checked my office diary." I gave a light laugh. "I never quite know what Liz may have organised. So, your telephone number, please."

Michel repeated the number in his deep, rich vibrato. *Jesus*, I thought, *Monsieur Gallois can even make a Maida Vale number sound sexy!* "Thanks," I said, "now I must dash. You only got me at home seeing I'm waiting for my painter. Otherwise I would have been at za - I mean *the* office."

"I know! I know!" crooned Michel, "Zo za lady Liz zed!"

*

"Talk about an *alarmer* charmer," trilled Liz, "Monsieur Gallois' voice got me all a quiver!"

"Doesn't say much for your experience of stimulation," I quipped.

"Experience?" rasped Bryan from his work area, "Didn't you realise - or know - RA when it comes to stimulation our lovely Liz is, in *real* life, the mysterious author of the bestselling *Tales of the Twat*?"

"And for *that* crass remark Lady L, you can damn well mix your own Mimosa!" snapped Liz making her way to the kitchenette.

"See that as a truly *black* mark against you Bryan," I chuckled. "It'll take at least one brioche and one *pain au chocolat* from Justin de B and then some to make up for your slanderous remark!"

*

"He's called again, Monsieur Gallois," announced Liz sometime later. "A knee trembling thrice within the hour."

"Talk about storming the Bastille," said Bryan giving Liz a sly look and fluttering his blatantly tinted eyelashes. "Perhaps this Monsieur Gallois sees himself as the French Sir Percy Blakely and wishes to help rescue RA from all those rampant English clients!"

"Did he leave any message?" I asked, deliberately ignoring Bryan who had started to hum *Le Marseilles* while supposedly checking the estimate he was currently working on.

"Yes; would you be free for lunch on Monday."

"And you said?"

"I said I very much doubted as it was the third Monday of the month and every third Monday is the day you have your wig done."

"You didn't actually say *wig*?" I replied aghast.

"Oh *merde!*" exclaimed Liz followed by an unladylike giggle. "I'd forgotten about the revelation at the Savoy!"

"So discreet our hallowed secretary," crowed Bryan. "So tactful and so utterly reliable when it comes to in-house confidences!" He gave a snort. "No doubt she's also let slip to dreamy Dennis Paget he's referred to as 'pendulous Paget' inside the sacred precincts of RAD because of the obvious pendulum *cock* within his jeans?"

"Really Lady L," I began, "at times . . ."

"I know I know," Bryan cut in, "my eyes are bigger than my *longing* - geddit?"

"You can forget RA's earlier comment for starters seeing *that* little *bon mot* deserves at least a *week's* supply of brioches, *pain au chocolat* plus a couple of bottles of vino," trilled Liz, "So get out there Bryan boyo; get out there and get buying!"

"Bryan *boyo*?" rasped Bryan. "I'm a laddie not a paddy if you must know!"

A laddie? Surely you mean a lady? Christ on a bike, I thought, *don't these two* ever *stop?*

"Is that with an 'I' and an 'E' or with a 'Y'?" chirruped Liz.

"Oi you two! Enough!" I snapped. Giving Liz a feigned smile I added nonchalantly, "Anything else?"

"No," snapped Liz as she started to type.

Oh shit, I thought, *they're only sending each other up as we all do.* "Perhaps you should have told him we could have met for lunch in gay Paree," I said with a chuckle. "After all it *is* where I go for my three weekly wig trim! Ha ha!"

"Ha ha! Ooh la la!" tittered Bryan. "Mr G in gay Paree? We'll simply have to wait and see!"

*

When working with John Siddeley we were subjected to his regular "I really shouldn't" routine - or what Maggie called "JS's monthly" - when the smirking man would fly to Paris in order to have his hair cut at the elegant salon of *Alexandre de Paris* on Avenue Matignon.

Soon after the launching of RAD I was sitting discussing JS with Fanny Adams and Alf Baker in their offices at Norrington & Adams. Alf was in a state of high dudgeon following a call from JS advising them not to open a trade account with RAD "or else".

"Stuff him!" snapped Alf. "In a matter of a few weeks I'd say you've given us more work than he has over the past few months! Bossy sod." Reaching for his mug of tea he added with a chuckle, "Just as well you haven't tried to make an appointment with that frog hairdresser of his; he'd probably ask them to scalp you!"

Have my hair cut in Paris and maybe by the legendary Alexandre no less? Well why not? I thought. On my return to the office I put through a Charles Ribon (we'd kept in touch despite Spillane's continued venomous tirades against me) and asked him for the name of his barber as I had no desire to ape JS to the extent of making a provisional appointment with *Alexandre.*

"Oh, you must and can only go to my divine Jean Pierre!" cooed Charles. "Make an appointment with Jean Pierre. Better still, allow *me* to make the first appointment for you. If you make it earlyish and if you can spare the time, let's have lunch afterwards as I would love to see you." He gave a titter. "I hear via the strangulated *green* grapevine you're becoming a great success? Well done. I always told Roland you were non-containable!"

Having decided on having all future haircuts carried out by the suave Jean Pierre, I agreed to join Richard (Reynolds) on his latest venture of French lessons at the Berlitz School in Oxford Street. At this stage Richard and I had been talking about going halves on a small villa near to St Tropez which seemed to make sense as we all seemed to congregate there for the summer. Our teacher was a voluptuous young French woman named Madame Hughes. Richard appeared to get a kick in dropping his "H" and greeting her with a patronising *"Bonjour Madam 'Uge,"* whenever we arrived for lesson. Not to be outdone Madam "'Uge" retaliated by greeting Richard with a wolverine smile accompanied by a *"Bonjour Monsieur Rrreynard"* and greeting me with a beaming *"Bonjour Monsieur Robin; concepteur merveillieux!"*

*

"What the hell?" I muttered on turning to the sanctity of my office. Checking for his number in my notebook I dialled Michel.

On hearing the deep, "'Allo, zis is Michel. Oo is calling?" I replied caustically, "I hear you called again. You don't give up do you?"

"Give up? What is zis 'give up'?"

"I mean calling me at least half a dozen times within the same morning."

"Zo, you don't want to see me?" came the surprised reply. "Why iz zis? *Everyone* one wishes to see Michel Gallois!"

Oh piss off you arrogant prick, I thought. "I'm delighted to hear that Michel," I sniped. "Oh, you'll have to excuse me, my client has just walked in," I added glancing at Liz in the doorway clutching the promised Mimosa. "I'll call you back during the week."

"So I'm a client as well, am I?" questioned Liz arching an eyebrow. "Talk about an overworked, underpaid Girl Friday!"

"Thanks for the drink, *client*," I quipped. "Now shoo as I have to think beautiful schemes for lovely Mrs Katz."

"The VAT Mrs Katz?" asked Liz with a giggle.

"The very one."

"Well, don't forget to add the vital VAT!" said Liz with a toss of her chestnut locks, "Now that she's all geared up an' jes rarin' to go!"

*

The introduction of Value Added Tax (VAT) in 1973 had been the cause of widespread confusion among members of the general public. One of our clients, a charming Austrian woman named Ann Katz asked me to explain the whys and wherefores of this new intrusion to our lives. (Like some of my more likeable clients I had asked Mrs Katz to call me RA).

"Tell me, RA, vat is this V-A-T?" asked Mrs Katz spelling it out in her heavy Austrian accent.

Jesus, I thought, *think, RA think. One thing you don't want to do is confuse the ever lovely Mrs K.* "It's really quite simple Mrs Katz. VAT is a new tax to er ... cover *vear an' tear*!"

"Ah yes, of course RA! Vear an' tear!" repeated Mrs Katz with a satisfied smile.

*

Out of curiosity combined with a soupçon of l-u-s-t (after all he was extremely good-looking and positively oozing with testosterone and Gallic charm) I telephoned Michel the following day and suggested dinner as opposed to lunch. "Will you be bringing Hardy?" I asked sarcastically.

"Hardy? *Non. Pourquoi?*"

"Oh, it's simply I thought the two of you were more-or-less conjoined but no matter." *Oh Christ, now he's going to ask what I meant by conjoined!*

"What do you mean by zis 'conjoined'?"

Ignoring the question I suggested dinner at the inevitable La Popote.

After dinner I asked Michel if he would like to come back to the flat for a nightcap. (I was still living at No 5, Ladbroke Square at the time.)

"Zo, you want me to go to za bed wiz you, eh?" came the deep reply. (If a voice could be deadpan this would be it.)

"If you zay zo" I replied, equally as deadpan.

*

Michel thought the flat "*inhabituel*" (unusual), my bed "verry nice, *très comfortable*" but the zebra-patterned pillowcase and sheets "*très vulgaire*". He also wanted to know the identity of the man in the framed photograph on the tallboy in the bedroom.

"David, my part-time lover," I teased, "seeing we don't actually live together."

"'E looks old enough to be your fazza," came the snide reply.

"Just as well he's never likely to become your true *faux pas* then," I replied drily.

"*Faux pas*? Vhat do you mean wiz zis *faux pas*?" asked Michel looking suitably bewildered.

"Your French stepfather," I quipped.

There was a moment's silence accompanied by an even more bewildered look. "I ask about your loverr, not your stepfazza," came the testy reply.

"Yes, and as I said the photograph's of David; my part-time or full-time lover depending on which way you look at it."

"Does 'e know you make za love wiz za uzzer guys?" asked Michel.

"I am sure he does," I swiftly replied. *Don't tell me France's answer to Vic Damone is allergic to both my bed linen and David playing voyeur which means maybe I won't get him into bed after all?* I thought. *Oh well, as he'd most probably say, c'est le vie!*

"Zo it za okay we make za love?"

"Okay by me and I'm sure David understands; a lover alone . . ." I replied in a martyred tone (I didn't dare say "loverr").

"Okay zen. We make za love." (In retrospect I have a feeling his response was crooned as opposed to spoken.)

While Hardy the erstwhile lover seemed to have been firmly placed on the back burner, Sidney the whimpering whippet most certainly was not: Michel's attitude being one of "love me, love my dog". So much so it soon became a case of "and Sidney came too" with matters coming to a head when Michel suddenly announced he was returning to France for a week while Hardy was spending his two weeks annual leave in Benidorm. The unexpected news coming out of the blue three days before Michel's departure.

"You will look after Sidney, eh?" said as a statement and not as question.

"But of *course*, Michel. I couldn't think of anything more edifying," I replied through gritted teeth. The word "edifying" resulting in another session of having to explain "zis edifying".

Compared to shivering Sidney Miffy (my childhood love and companion) had been a lioness and the thought of the neurotic whippet spending a week with me was alarming to say the least. *Fuck!* I thought, *not only a nightmare but what if something happens to shivering Sidney? Knowing my luck he'll probably get run over or savaged by another dog!* I suddenly had a brainwave. *The Ryotts!* DBR and Georgina knew Michel and Sidney plus they had a massive garden for him to play in. Leaving Michel's question unanswered I gave Georgina a call.

"Of course Sidney can come and stay," she enthused, "the girls would love it!"

"Would it be alright if I brought him over on Friday evening?" I asked.

"Absolutely Robun and of course you'll stay for dinner?"

"Love to Georgina," I said in a relieved voice. "So expect me, Sidney, his basket and some toys around seven if that's okay?"

"Perfect. And it makes sense Sidney stays with us as he'd only get in your way."

So all I have to do is have shivering Sidney at the office for the Friday, I thought smugly. I gave a laugh, saying out loud, "I can't *wait* to see Liz or

Lady Larkin's faces when asked to take our neurotic guest 'walk about' so he can do his shivering business!"

My mind flashed back to my murdered Miffy (as far as I was concerned Cur had murdered the little dog when she coldly got rid of the poor animal all those years ago). "When I think of Miffy," I muttered, "I picture a *proper* dog as opposed to an inbred, neurotic animal like shivering Sidney."

To my surprise Sidney had never been to Moorhawes. "Sidney is za city dog, 'e doesn't like za country," announced Michel when first invited to the cottage. "'E much prefers to stay in za Maida Vale wiz Hardy!"

*

Weekends in particular when spent with Michel at Moorhawes proved to be more catastrophic than calming. One Saturday morning in particular springs to mind when, on hearing strange voices emanating from the sitting room, I came downstairs to find Michel talking to two young boys perched on the sofa.

"What is going on here, Michel?" I asked angrily. "Who are these two and what are they doing here?"

"Zey came asking for za drink of water . . ." Michel began.

"There are no drinks of water here," I snapped pointing towards the door, "So will you two please leave. *Now.* No Michel!" I thundered, "Don't you *dare* interrupt! They're leaving! Go on you two, Go! Get out!"

Glaring at me the two young boys slunk silently from the sitting room. Inwardly fuming at Michel's irresponsible behaviour I followed them through to the small entrance hall and out on to the lawn where their bicycles were lying and stood watching until they had pedalled off. One of the youngsters turning to shout "bloody pouf bastard" before they disappeared from sight.

"You monsterr!" yelled Michel as I re-entered the sitting room, "You evil monsterr . . ."

"Shut the fuck up!" I bellowed not giving him a chance to continue. "Jesus Christ Michel, what the *fuck* were you thinking by inviting two young boys into an isolated cottage where two guys are? Added to which one's just called me a 'pouf bastard'." I stood glaring at him. "I wouldn't be at all surprised if the police don't turn up within the hour and *arrest* us for being fucking child molesters!"

"I am not like zat!" retorted Michel, "*You* are my loverr!"

"That makes no difference you idiot. Think how it *looks*?"

"You English 'ave za sick thought all za time," sneered Michel. Giving me a look of total disdain he added with a shrug of his muscular shoulders. "Now I need za glass of wine. Spending za time wiz you iz making me what zay call za alcoholic!"

"Yes, and fetch me a glass as well, if Monsieur *doesn't* mind," I replied sarcastically. "Ah, the telephone. That could either be the police or my call to Italy."

"'Ow can you speak to your loverr zere when I am *'ere*?" hissed Michel from the doorway.

"Simply by picking up the telephone," I snapped. "Now if you'll excuse me . . .'"

*

A scowling Michel noisily returned carrying two glasses of wine, one of which he noisily banged down on to the coffee table accompanied by a loud "Your wine an' I hope you do za choke on it!"

"As opposed to your cock?" I replied feigning surprise while covering the mouthpiece.

"Buggerr - feelthy buggerr!" hissed Michel, "You an' zat old loverr of yours! But one zing I *do* know, you will *never, everr* have anuzza loverr like Michel Gallois! "

Oh no? I thought. *Try going to bed with Kenny Partridge.* Nobody *could be a better lover than our Ken!*

Giving a toss of his artfully coiffed head (a rash gesture considering his supposed secret) Michel stalked from the sitting room into the entrance lobby and out into the garden.

Michel's jealousy towards DLL - rather like Topsy in *Uncle Tom's Cabin* - simply "just grow'd". One evening we were lying in bed watching television (*Armchair Thriller* was a favourite of his) when he suddenly

342

growled, "'Ow can zat old man be a better loverr zan me, eh? I am young an' strong but 'e is za antique!"

"Really?" I replied querulously, "You've obviously have never heard of Lord Brockhurst from *The Boy Friend*. Well *he* sings *'one never drinks the wine that's new, the old wine tastes much nicer'*!"

"What 'as za tasting of za wine 'ave to do wiz your old, ugly loverr?" snapped Michel, "Now I will speak no more and watch za television."

"Good idea," I replied reaching for the glass of wine on the bedside cabinet. "Ugh," I said on taking a sip, "too young for my taste therefore it must be about your age."

"You English are all mad," muttered Michel.

"At least you didn't say *merde* which shows you secretly love us," I murmured giving him a light kiss on the cheek.

"But only za zometimes," came his rumbled "deep from the balls" reply.

*

Michel's reaction on first viewing Albion Gate was the complete antithesis to his first impression on seeing my Ladbroke Square apartment; *inhabitue* (unusual) being replaced by *fantastique* and the extra-wide low bed covered in green suede described as *très sexy*. To my immense surprise he insisted on giving me a moving in present which turned out to be a large oil painting of himself dressed in a harlequin costume. *Hmm*, I thought uncharitably, *an Oh so subtle way of moving in with me no doubt?*

Not wishing to cause affront to Messrs Joan Miró, Moore and Picasso whose lithographs hung in the sitting room I coquettishly suggested we hung the portrait above the bed. "So when you're not here I will have the comfort of knowing you're here looking after me," I murmured demurely.

"Ha! 'An 'e will also see if your old loverr 'as been 'ere an' tell me," replied Michel with a deadpan expression.

Apart from weekends spent at Moorhawes, Michel would never stay overnight but return to Hardy and Sidney in Maida Vale during the early hours; an arrangement I found ideal.

DLL, it should be noted, never failed to be amused by my endless renderings of "its hell with Michel" or "the Brynner from gay *Paree!*" and was completely philosophical about my dalliances.

"I know you love me Robble but you're a very good looking young man plus we live separate lives so I expect you to have a 'pink ticket' which is not only fair but totally natural."

The term "pink ticket" I later discovered was a phrase conjured up between David and the French Letter several decades earlier to make for such allowances.

"You're so *naughty* Robble! Poor Michel!" DLL would chuckle on hearing the latest dramatic saga concerning *The Paris Erection.* (Ben's nickname for Michel.)

One episode remained secret and occurred while I was still living in Ladbroke Square. Michel had been given a set of keys to the flat and would have great fun leaving "surprises from your loverr" for me. These surprises ranged from flowers to boxes of chocolates and a never-ending supply of croissants, all of which would be promptly taken to the office. The flowers and chocolates shared between Liz and Alison (in the travel agency below) and the croissants devoured by the staff of RAD and any visitors.

I had returned to the apartment after a dinner party and having taken off my suit, put the jacket on a hanger and the trousers in the Corby trouser press, I kept staring around with an uneasy feeling (and distinct impression) something was missing. After a few moments it dawned on me: DLL's photograph which held pride of place on the tallboy was nowhere to be seen. *Bloody Michel!* I thought reaching for the phone and dialling his number.

"Er ... hello?" said a sleepy voice.

"Can I speak to Michel Gallois please; I know it's late but I need to speak to him."

"But he's asleep," came the plaintive reply.

"So fucking well wake him!" I shouted.

After a few background noises Michel screamed into the phone, "'Ow *dare* you rring me an' zwear at Hardy!"

"Screw Hardy," I said through gritted teeth, "what have you done with David's photograph?"

"I destroyed it! 'E is not your loverr! I *am*!" screeched Michel.

"You can bloody well fuck off Michel and don't ever show your face here again. You can drop off the keys to the flat with Georgina (Michel drove his own French version of a Mini, namely a left hand drive) and if you *don't* I'll not only change the locks but also report the matter to the police! I've said it once and I'll say it again you bloody piece of ignorant French *merde*. Fuck off!" I slammed down the receiver.

*

It must have been around mid-afternoon the next when Georgina telephoned the office. "Robun," she purred, "I have your keys. Poor Michel is very upset and I do think you have been a bit hasty and harsh in your actions, if I may say so?"

"No, you may *not* say so, Georgina!" I snapped. "Sorry dear, I can't talk as I have a client here."

"Simply a thought Robun," cooed Georgina, "simply a thought. Byee!"

"Fucking interfering do-gooder!" I muttered. "And before *you* start lecturing *me*, Georgina dear, look at home before you look abroad as the saying goes! If you think that flamboyant hubby of yours is ruler straight, think again! Really fancies the young lads does your David! You only have to see how he ogles your daughters' boyfriends!"

A few minutes after Georgina's call Liz buzzed through. "You'll never believe it," she cooed, "but its Michel Gallois for what can only be the *tenth* time today!"

"Tenth time?" I echoed, "Surely that's a tad exaggerated even for Miss Elizabeth *Hans Christian* Andersen!"

"A tad perhaps?" laughed Liz. "Shall I put the *fairy* tale through?"

Ouch! I thought with a snigger, *is nothing in the offices of RAD sacred?* "Out of consideration for your poor eardrums perhaps you'd better," I replied in a resigned voice.

"You must forgive me!" crooned Michel before I had a chance to respond by saying "I told you not to call". "You must forgive me," he repeated, "for as your loverr I have za right to be jealous! If you do not forgive me it means *you* do not love Michel Gallois!"

"I maybe *lust* Michel Gallois,"" I quipped, "but when it comes to *lurve. . ."*

"So you wish to see me again?"

Should I be flattered? I thought, *or shall I go on behaving like a spiteful old queen? Best to be flattered I suppose? After all, it was only a photograph which can easily be reprinted.*

"I'm busy this evening but how about a late dinner tomorrow? I have a late business meeting." (I didn't dare say I was going to a cocktail party given by Richard Reynolds.)

"Zo," said Michel triumphantly, "you *do* love Michel Gallois!" and promptly hung up.

*

I lay in bed staring at Michel as he slept, his handsome profile gently illuminated by the glow coming through the window from the streetlight outside. *Dare I?* I thought mischievously, *Come to think it is too good to be true.* I moved closer to Michel, my eyes fixated on his luxuriant, impeccably waved hair. *As they say, it's now or never so let's make it now.* Having decided on the momentous move I tentatively reached over and gently took hold of a few glossy strands between my fingers. *It feels like hair which of course it is but something is definitely not quite right!*

I gave a start as Michel suddenly mumbled in his sleep. I lay staring at him for a few more minutes before saying softly to the silent room, "So c'mon RA, time to stop *wondering* about it. Ask him!" Which I did.

*

I sat facing Michel while the waiter cleared the plates before placing the cutlery for pudding course on the table. As soon as the man had moved away I took the plunge.

"I simply must compliment you on our hair, Michel. It's always *so* perfect even after we've made *amour fou* (wild love) as you describe it." I gave a light laugh. "So perfect it could almost be a wig."

Michel's response was a deep, smouldering look as he softly in his deep, rich baritone, "As you are now my loverr for everr an' everr I will tell you; my 'air, he is what we call in the French *une perruque*. I am za bald on za top." The smouldering look became more intense. "My fans mus' never know an' you *mon amour* mus' never tell." Regardless of the diners next to us he grabbed my hand as I was about to reach for my wine glass. "As my loverr you too mus' understan' you will neverr, everr see Michel Gallois *sans sa perruque*! It is forbidden!"

"Absolutely," I said pulling my hand free. "It will be our secret. My lips are sealed. The truth about your wondrous hair will never, ever be shared with another soul. You have my word."

"*Merci, mon amour.*" Michel's sculpted lips took on a playful smile. "You zay your lips are sealed but later zay can be unsealed for za kissing; *non?*"

Having sworn myself to secrecy I couldn't wait to tell DLL the latest in the Michel Gallois saga which I duly titled *The Wig and I.* In fairness to Michel I never revealed my findings to Maggie or Peter.

*

Two days later Michel called during office hours, something I had repeatedly asked him not to do unless it was an emergency such as the President of France wanting a date. This, naturally - or unnaturally - having led to a puzzled "but I don't know za President Pompidou?"

"It's Michel," said Liz stifling a giggle, "he says it's very, *very* urgent."

"Now what?" I muttered, "Maybe Sidney or Hardy is in the middle of giving birth; *nothing* concerning bloody Monsieur Gallois would surprise me! You'd better put him through Liz and *do* try to stop giggling!"

"*Mon amour?*"

"*Oui?*" I replied thinking, *In for a penny, in for a pounding!*

"I have za very bad news an' I do not know if you are strong enough to 'ear zis?"

"What?" I asked. "It's nothing to do with your family is it?"

Michel and I were due to fly to Cannes in three weeks' time to meet "my muzza" and stay in the family's recently acquired "château" outside Grasse. Along with "muzza" (Christine) I would also be meeting his two sisters, Natalie and Madeleine plus Madeleine's "loverr" Bernard. During his planned time away Michel had again made arrangements for Sidney to spend the break with the Ryotts in St. John's Wood.

"Non cherie mon amour, It iz za Lido in Paree, zey want me for za star of za new show! I 'ave to return to Paree *tout suite!* Zis means we will have to delay our *vacanses!"*

Delay our holiday? I thought? *Thank you God! That deserves a multitude of Hail Marys, inshallahs or whatever else turns you on!*

"I will call you back when you 'ave - as they zay - recovered," Michel added sonorously. "Until zen, *au revoir mon amour!"*

"Forget gutsy Gene Hackman's *The French Connection,"* I said gleefully to my empty office. "Seeing it's now RA destined to star in *The French Erection!"*

*

Michel telephoned from Paris several weeks later. "I have found za *grande apartement* on Rue Michel-Ange *(Michel-Ange? Where else?* I thought). It is *très très élégant* but it needs my loverr's touch!" he added with a deep, mellifluous chuckle.

Plus some RA expenditure no doubt? I thought malevolently.

"So when can you come an' have za look?"

"Does Sidney like it?" I asked, determined not to commit myself to an extra visit in addition to my regular trips to see Jean Pierre, my barber.

"Sidney 'e is not 'ere. 'E 'as gone to live wiz my muzza in Lyon."

"Lyon as opposed to the château?"

"'E travels between za two."

*

The second floor apartment on Rue Michel-Ange contained a fair-sized entrance hall, an enormous reception room (or *salon* as Michel preferred to describe it) with French doors opening onto a narrow balcony; a large bedroom, comfortable bathroom and kitchen.

"How clever of you to find such an attractive apartment, Michel." I said as I dusted myself and adjusted my trousers after a quick, fumbled christening fuck on the dusty *salon* carpet. "It must have cost a (about to say "bomb" I quickly swapped the incendiary word for one of lesser impact) a lot."

"I don't know, my fazza, 'e pays for it."

That figures, I inwardly sniggered, *not only a poof de luxe Monsieur G, but a poof de luxe with - perhaps - a smattering of incest!*

"Hmm," I murmured as I stood surveying the main room, "I don't object to the taupe-coloured linen covering the walls - we could use that as a foil for some rather dramatic colours - while the taupe-coloured carpet can be seen as another blessing in taupe disguise."

"What do you mean by za disguise?" questioned a frowning Michel.

Shit, or should that be merde seeing we're now in la belle France? I thought. "I mean as a complimentary colour, Michel," I said bristling. "Now, as your *designer*, may I go on?"

"You see?" crowed Michel, "zere you start. We make za love on za floor an' zen you wish to argue!"

"I am not *arguing* Michel, I am trying to design a beautiful *salon* here for you and me to enjoy . . ."

"Ah *bon*," said Michel flashing his flawless (and no doubt expensive) "I'm a starr! I'm a starr!" smile. "An' while you design I will go to fetch za champagne to celebrate za start of our new way of za life in za gay Paree!"

Gay Paree with only you and me? I thought, "Somehow I see troubles ahead. Beaucoup de mal. In fact I foresee acres of merde hitting the much abused proverbial fan!*

Holding a flute of Dom Perignon I stood staring at the spacious reception room. "Do you have any furniture, any furniture at all?" I asked.

"Furniture? *Meubles?*" snapped Michel, "*Porquois*? Do you think Michel Gallois iz za peasant? I have za *magnifique* furniture!" The word "furniture" accompanied by an indignant spray of Dom Perignon. "I have za chairs, za tables an' more in my present *appartement!*"

"And the upholstery fabrics; the coverings? Are they plain or patterned?"

"I will show you later," said a tight-lipped Michel. "Basically za covers is za *moutarde velours*."

"Mustard velvet and taupe linen?" I muttered sarcastically. "How elevating."

"Why you now zay elevator when you know zere are only stairs?" snapped Michel. "*Mon Dieux . . .*"

I have to admit I was most impressed with the antique pieces Michel possessed and was soon waxing lyrically with my ideas for our Parisian love nest. "Obviously I will have all the curtains, blinds, bedhead, bedcover and valance made back in London," I said enthusiastically. "Plus the *whole* scheme will be worked around your mustard upholstered furniture and the taupe linen wall covering to the sitting room. However, we shall need a painter seeing I must insist on having the entrance hall, bedroom, bathroom and kitchen repainted. The present murky cream colour will never do." I stared at Michel. "Well Michel? Do you know of a painter seeing the cost of bringing one over from London would be prohibitive?"

"*Oui*, I will ask Bernarrd."

"Bernard?"

"Bernarrd Coulon, my sister Madeleine's loverr."

"Great. Once I've selected the various fabrics for the curtains and such I'll let you have a couple of paint samples - or charts - to give to Bernard. Seeing you always seem to be wearing the colour I take it you have no objection to the introduction of blue? *Very* Vermeer!"

"Why should I zay *non* to za blue? I like za colour blue." Michel gave a snigger. "Are my eyes not za blue?"

"I would have said more of a murky grey to be honest," I replied wickedly.

"An' you call yourself *un* designer?" sniped Michel. "Pah!"

Two weeks later I returned to Paris armed with sketches, fabric and paint samples. I was accompanied by Dave Schultz, a dynamic younger member of Norrington & Adams. While Dave busied himself taking relevant measurements and making notes of my planned curtain treatments, I went through my proposed designs with Michel.

Giving me an arch look Michel tapped the cobalt blue paint sample I'd suggested for the entrance hall. "I also like za *chocolat* you show me," he rumbled, "an' you plan to have za blue an' *chocolat rayures* on za ceiling to za *salon, non?*"

"*Absolument,*" I replied caustically. "A *merde* and blue stripe will be sensational. A real tribute to RAD!"

"*Furieux*; you English are all mad, *furieux,*" said Michel with a snort. He turned to Dave who was in the midst of measuring the French windows. "Don't you agree Monsieurr Dave zat Monsieurr RA is mad, completely mad?"

"I *always* agree with my clients," replied Dave diplomatically.

*

Back at RAD the work kept pouring in while in Paris, aided and abetted by Bernard (whom I had yet to meet) the repainting of the apartment as quickly completed including the inset double banding of blue and black (a change to the original *chocolat*) to the ceiling perimeter; the blue being a match to the vibrant cobalt blue of the entrance hall. The same blue was also used on the walls to the bedroom. Drapes to the reception room were in ivory linen with an appliqué border adapted from a mustard, blue, ivory and black geometric fabric made by David & Dash; the border fabric itself being used for the drapes and bedcovering in the adjoining blue bedroom. A faux black leather bedhead and valance completed the scheme. Adding a touch of S & M to the en suite I had the bathroom painted in black gloss with the His and His towels in alternating mustard and blue.

On my third visit to Paris Michel invited me to the Lido where I was introduced to the legendary Miss Bluebell (born Margaret Kelly in 1904 in Dublin, Ireland), founder of the famous Bluebell Girls dance troupe. The show at the Lido was spectacular with Michel earning a standing ovation for several of his songs. I was fascinated to discover most of the glamorous Bluebells were English and I ended up (quite happily) acting as a courier for some of the girls' letters and small packages "for Mum and Dad back home". Robin's "letter and package run" becoming a fortnightly event.

"It's only right," I said to Michel when he complained about the girls taking increasing advantage of "za star's loverr". "First of all it saves them the cost of postage and secondly, it puts *you* in good stead."

Bluebell (as I called her) and two of the leading dancers at the Lido, a virile Frenchman sporting what appeared to be a baseball glove tucked inside his silver G-string and his "topless" partner, a stunning Jessica Rabbit lookalike with gigantic, jutting anvil-like silver, nippled breasts and matching G-string, became regular visitors to the apartment for a drink or a light snack before the show. But not in their stage apparel I hasten to add!

"Only za snack an' a *soupçon* of za wine," Michel would solemnly say. "Rememberr, we are za starrs!"

*

The following spring I finally got to meet "muzza" (Christine), papa and Michel's two sisters plus Bernard Coulon of painter fame. Michel had already told me of Christine's reaction to the apartment on Rue Michel Ange and how she was adamant I should take a look at the château outside Grasse before she went "any fuzzerr with za colourrs." It was arranged I would fly to Nice where I would be met by Michel and driven back to the château. After his highly successful debut at the Lido the "star" was enjoying a short, well-deserved break.

*

"You look like za ghost, *un fântome*," announced Michel as I waltzed out from Customs at Nice Airport clutching a Fendi briefcase and matching holdall.

"Hopefully for 'muzza's' sake *un* friendly *fântome* at that!" I quipped, "Seeing she could soon be making *un fântome* contribution towards the soft furnishings now gracing her son's extravagant Parisian passion pit!"

"*Mon Dieux*! 'E just arrives an' already 'e talks za confusion!" muttered Michel shaking his perfectly coiffed head. Giving me a piercing look (murky grey-eyed or blue-eyed, take your pick) he added with a growl, "Arre you pleased to see yourr Michel?"

"Absolutely, otherwise your Robin wouldn't be here," I said giving him what I considered a coquettish look. I eyed Michel's six foot, two inch frame appraisingly, taking in the beginnings of a golden tan further enhanced by the tight, white T-shirt showing off his muscular torso to perfection and a pair of white linen trousers displaying a "crotch basket" which would have made Nureyev green with envy. "I must say a tan suits you," I added with a smile.

"I look good, *oui*?" came the smug reply. He gave me another piercing look before saying matter-of-factly, "But you? You look like I zed; *un fântome.*"

"Call me Caspar," I quipped following him out to the sun-drenched car park. "And before you ask who Caspar is, he's not an ex-loverr but a friendly ghost!"

His forehead creasing into a puzzled frown Michel gave a typical Gallic shrug accompanied by a muttered, "*Totalement fou!*" He pointed to a daffodil yellow Triumph 2000 saloon. "My muzza's car," he added as if in anticipation of my question. "Za Mini 'e stays in za Paree."

The journey to Grasse saw us making our way through gentle hillsides, groves of pine trees and fields of flowers before reaching the town famous for its perfumeries.

"I never would have expected the actual *air* to be perfumed," I said giving an appreciative sniff. "I take it that's because of the various perfume factories; not only these endless fields of flowers?"

"*Bon pour l'âme, non?*" said Michel, the pronouncement accompanied with a dazzling smile. "Oh *mon amour*, I am zo 'appy you are here. Christine my muzza cannot wait to meet 'er Michel's new English loverr!"

God! I thought with an inward snicker, *Good for the soul or not, am I supposed to present myself as a blushing bride-to-be or else a foppish Englishman; the French idea of Sebastian Flyte? What's more, did Mama Christine ever meet the maiden from Maida Vale, the ever so 'umble Ardy? Somehow I doubt it!*

We bypassed the town of Grasse and a few miles later Michel slowed down before steering the car between a pair of impressive white pillars leading to a pine tree-lined driveway. "Za château," he said proudly as we approached a towering edifice sparkling in the sunshine. I sat staring in amazement at the opulent building ahead. "But its massive Michel," I whispered. "I know you said a château but I never expected *le Petit Versailles!*"

Silly star, I thought evilly, *why settle for the likes of Rue Michel-Ange when I'm sure Papa Gallois would have been persuaded to by the Lido's leading lover with an apartement on Avenue Montaigne with change to spare!*

"You like it, eh?" asked Michel with another dazzling "I'm a starr" smile.

"Like it? I *love* it and that's without seeing what's inside!" I exclaimed. "Oh, and look, isn't that dear little Sidney traipsing over to say 'hello'?"

"*Oui*; an' za uzza dogs! Sidney iz a very 'appy dog now 'e iz in *la Belle* France!" The barbed comment accompanied by an accusatory stare.

"Why, wasn't little Sidney happy in London? After all you did say he didn't like the country." I replied feigning bewilderment.

"'E did not like za *English* country," countermanded Michel, his patrician nostrils flaring, "but 'e loves za French country! Ah, an' 'ere is *Maman* an' Madeleine! 'Allo *Maman*, 'allo Madeleine," he crooned, "come an' say 'allo to Robin!"

At least you didn't say loverr, I thought, *so thank you God or whoever reigns for small mercies.*

It took only one look at Christine Gallois (unless Papa Gallois proved to be devastatingly handsome) to see where Michel got his stunning looks from. I stared at the elegant woman and her daughter as they made their way daintily down the wide steps from the front terrace to greet us. I was struck by Christine Gallois' likeness to Henri Toulouse-Lautrec's portrait of Jane Avril the lead can-can dancer at the Moulin Rouge (but Jane Avril wearing a colourful sarong) whilst Madeleine looked like a young Jane Fonda. *No wonder she's one Jacques Fath's favourite mannequins*, I thought.

"Welcome to Château Gallois, Robin," purred Christine proffering a delicate, perfectly manicured hand. She added smilingly in a heavily accented English, "Michel, 'e nevair stops za talking about you!"

I was soon to learn Christine's grasp of English was sorely limited which saw my former lessons with Madam 'Ughes coming into their own. To say Christine and I got along like the proverbial house on fire (in this case read "château") would have been an oversight; our obvious delight with each other's company leading to Michel saying sulkily after our first dinner, "I zink you love my muzza more zan you love yourr Michel!"

What I "loved more" than Christine was the design challenge the château offered RAD. My first reaction on viewing the grotesque modern furniture which epitomised the term "seventies ugly" bought by Christine to grace the main salon and dining room, was an audible gasp of incredulity which thankfully was mistaken as a gasp of admiration. I stood staring with disbelief at a gigantic orange sofa covered in a crushed velvet which gave the impression of a tortured caterpillar crawling across the cavernous room accompanied by a host of baby green and black crushed velvet caterpillar-like chairs. The only saving grace was all the walls and ceilings, despite a plethora of tortured mouldings, were painted white.

"You like?" asked Christine her sarong-clad frame positively wriggling with pride.

"All I can say is it's very, *very* different," I managed to squawk, "and I can honestly say I have never, ever seen anything like this; ever!"

"*Bon*," said Christine, "zo now you 'elp Christine *avec* za colours for za paint."

Playing on a little practised theory if you *did* make a mistake but think you can gloss over the error and even get away with it then one should casually dismiss it as one's "deliberate mistake." One could take the "deliberate mistake" a stage further by a congratulating the client on spotting the teaser which would then be corrected. If the client remains unaware of the mistake, well and good.

In order not to offend Christine at her appalling choice of furniture and their colour, I stood staring contemplatively at the garish collection before saying with a beatific smile and sepulchral voice, "Your colours, your vibrant colours Christine. Think drama, think spectacle; *think* the Sistine Chapel! Those mouldings to the ceiling cry *out* for colour. In other words I'll make a quick drawing of one many ornamental squares with individual sections treated in your orange and fabulous green with accents of black. In contrast to all the white they will not only *look* sensational but tie the whole room together!"

Later even I had to admit my "deliberate mistake" was never questioned and did, in fact, look - as Papa Gallois put it - "*sensationnel*."

Exonerating Christine from the orange, black and virulent green caterpillar invasion was the spectacular Olympic-size swimming pool set on a lower terrace overlooking the distant hills surrounding Grasse. A hedonistic kitchen, bar and changing rooms completed the luxurious complex with the outdoor area proving a welcome design relief with all the poolside furniture supplied by the prestigious firm Triconfort. With their gleaming white frames and low-key traditional upholstery of blue and white stripes I deemed the overall effect "faultless" and a "welcome relief" to what passed as "top seventies style" inside the lavish château.

Determined to get me away from the clutches of Christine and Madeleine a sulky Michel announced he wished to show me the small village of Saint-Martin-Vésubie nestling in the scenic valley of Gordalasque and part of the Alpes-Maritimes, north of Nice.

"It was zere I starred in za children's television series, *Belle et Sébastien*," he announced loftily.

"*Another* mountain village?" I proclaimed giving him a mischievous look. "Surely you're not suggesting a competitor to Dosso, my Italian favourite?"

"Hah!" came the snapped response. "Michel's village iz farr, farr *supérieur* to za ruin belonging to zat *ancient* loverr you nevair see!"

"Not until late summer you mean?" I sniped. "Right then, Saint-Martin-Vésubie it is, I suppose. After all, who can resist walking in the footsteps of the famous?"

(I later discovered Michel featured in thirteen episodes of the popular series where he appeared as the dashing young Doctor Guillaume. At the time of filming in 1965 his professional name is shown as Jean-Michel Audin.)

As a frequent visitor to the famous Le Colombe d'Or restaurant in Saint-Paul de Vence I was expecting (in a perverse way) for Saint-Martin-Vésubie to be much of a muchness but found instead a considerably smaller village tucked away amidst the towering, snow-capped mountains.

"*Charmant* huh?" said Michel as we drew up outside a small *auberge* where I assumed we would be having lunch.

"Fabulous in fact," I replied staring at the massive snow covered peaks and pine forests surrounding us. *What a contrast to cosy, loveable Dosso with its vine covered hills and olive groves*, I thought. I pointed to the bank of snow running several metres above from where we stood. "What I find quite, quite extraordinary is the definite break where the snowline meets the meadows and the dazzling white suddenly becomes a vivid green. A definite line of demarcation as it were."

"I told you your Michel's Alpes-Martimes iz farr, farr *supérieur* to your old loverr's Italy," crooned Michel in reply.

After a delicious lunch of crudités followed by rabbit in a red wine sauce accompanied by endless glasses of Beaune, Michel suggested another drive along one of the more remote roads leading from the village.

Quelle horreur! Surely my somewhat pissed loverr's not about to suggest an after lunch roll in the snow as opposed to the hay? I thought with an inward grin.

"An' zen we can return to za Grasse."

His comment, "return to Grasse" resulting in a further inward snigger.

As we made our way through the spectacular landscape Michel suddenly braked, his eyes fixated on a crude sign saying *A' Vendre.* Moments after spotting the rough "For Sale" sign myself our eyes were immediately drawn towards a small stone and wood chalet set high above on the steep mountainside.

"*Il est parfait, non?*" whispered Michel. "Za *parfait*, perfect place for za loverrs 'oo wish to be alone; *très très privé!*"

Afterwards I would blame it on the wine ("a Beaune to pick with the Beaune!") as three weeks later I found myself the owner of the aforesaid chalet which Michel proudly christened Chalet *Belle et Sebastien.*

On hearing about my *folie de grandeur* Bryan's immediate reaction was a rasped, "Chalet *Belle* and Sebastien? I would have thought Chalet *Hell* and Sebastien much more appropriate!"

Adopting the attitude of "what's done is done so I'd better make the best of it" I immediately set about organising the furnishings and anything else I considered relevant from a designer's point of view while leaving Michel and an enthusiastic Christine to deal with more mundane items such as cutlery, crockery, kitchen ware, towels and linen. "God forbid the matrimonial bed should appear bedecked in caterpillar orange, black and green sheets, duvet and pillows," I said worriedly to a grinning Bryan and giggling Liz, "then the hills will certainly be alive with the sound of murder!"

Before my return to London Michel and I arranged another visit to what I inwardly cursed and would in future refer to as my dreaded PALP (pissed after lunch purchase). We were accompanied by Monsieur René, a jovial carpenter and handyman recommended by Christine. Armed with a measuring tape, pen and a notepad I quickly sketched out a large L-shaped seating unit for the one corner of the sitting room before measuring the small, wooden framed windows and any other measurements I deemed necessary. The seat and back cushions would all be made according to the measurements given by Monsieur René.

"I just hope Christine's Monsieur René is not as *ridicule* as he looks," I muttered bitchily to Michel.

While Monsieur René stood scratching his head and studying my sketches I spared no time in telling Michel he would have to strike a hard bargain with the French comic Fernandel lookalike or else we'd be sitting *From Here to Eternity* on the wooden floor while he dithered and dallied. I have little doubt Christine ended up paying for the seating unit as this turned out to be a splendid affair with a varnished pine frame and seat with several large drawers for general storage below.

Christine's housewarming (chalet-warming?) present for the love nest turned out to a redundant bed from the château along with a lumpy mattress. "Just as well I'm an Anderson with an 'O' and not an 'E' and we're both bona fide queens as opposed to princesses," I quipped on trying out the bed. My reference to Hans Christian Andersen's story The *Princess and the Pea* going straight across my "loverr's" wigged head.

The rustic feel to the pine clad interior was further enhanced by a small, glass topped dining table and chairs commissioned through Anthony Redmile; the chairs and table base created from reindeer antlers. I found a delightful patchwork pattern fabric which I used throughout for the seating unit, sill-length curtains, bedhead and gathered valance. Adding a further touch of whimsy (or camp) to the bedroom was a sumptuous white fur throw courtesy of Madeleine and the mysterious Bernard who I had yet to meet.

Lighting was by a selection of brass wall brackets which, like the small stove and hot water was run off a small gas boiler; any additional lighting coming from antique style brass oil lamps. The local *avocet* handling the sale assured us we could expect electricity towards the end of the year.

"*Seeing* will see me believing," I quipped in dour reply.

Water was via a single pipe fed from a spring directly above the chalet; the tap having to be turned on at its source in order to fill the water tank inside the chalet when we were "in residence".

"You should feel quite at home," I said to Michel on eyeing the miniscule bathtub. "Judging from the size of the so-called bath a chorus girl's wash is all you can be guaranteed!"

"Chorus girls wash? What do you mean by zis chorus girl?" snapped Michel.

"Pits, privates and feet!" I chirruped, my witticism greeted by a puzzled look and a muttered, "*Fou, complètement fou.*"

I have to admit a stay in the chalet a few months later (and Sidney came too) was more enjoyable than anticipated. We were visited by Christine and Papa Gallois along with "Jessica" and her dancing partner from the Lido. An additional delight to our endless alfresco lunches in the meadow above the chalet was the manner in which we chilled the wine. This was simply done by sticking the bottles up to their necks in the metre high bank of snow where it met the flower bedecked meadow.

It was arranged Madeleine and the mysterious Bernard would be staying for a few days which saw our guests sleeping on the extremely comfortable L-shaped unit as opposed to our lumpy marital double bed. On finally meeting Bernard, a charming Mel Ferrer lookalike, we became great friends and I was delighted when he and Madeleine asked me to design their apartment in the new La Défense business sector of Paris and a forerunner to London's Canary Wharf.

After a typical "meadow lunch" which witnessed several bottles of wine happily retrieved from the "snowbank fridge" I was blearily persuaded into another boozy purchase; namely two adjoining burial plots in the small village cemetery of Saint-Martin-Vésubie. The plan being for the two of us to "lie togezza for za eternity".

*

Back in the real world of RAD work continued to accelerate by leaps and bounds.

"It's almost too good to be true," I kept muttering to Liz, Bryan and Martin. "And though I hate to say it and although we've coping admirably without lovely Vanessa, one's a long time dead so instead of working ourselves into an early grave (the cemetery at Saint-Martin-Vésubie immediately springing to mind; a happening I hadn't dare mention to Bryan or Liz) I have no alternative but to take on an extra member of staff."

Re-enter the Marshallene who just happened to have another discarded lover, an Australian, who surprisingly "happened to know all there is to know about interior design." Cue for Les Gabriel, a dark-haired, craggy Charles Bronson lookalike.

Angela Danziger, a new client, had recently purchased a charming Grade Two listed house use in Chelsea's exclusive Upper Cheyne Row. After introducing Les to the glamorous Angie I left him to oversee the limited building work permitted on such a property. Despite the arrival of Les I found myself still working seven days a week with weekends spent supposedly relaxing at Moorhawes given over to estimates, sketches and estimates. "We need to find yet another genius for the RAD team," I announced a few weeks later as Liz, Les, Bryan and I sat enjoying a de rigueur glass of wine. "However, the million dollar question is who?"

"Who" turned out to be Maggie who suddenly reappeared on the scene without any prior warning.

"Hello there, I'm back in London," she drawled over the telephone. "I'm in the middle of divorcing Peter and I need a job!"

Bingo! Maggie joined RAD he following week. On hearing about my rollercoaster relationship with Michel she had to sit down in order to control her laughter. "I can't believe it," she guffawed. "You involved with the warbling *Monsieur Perouque* and furthermore with a flat in fucking Paris plus a *chalet* in the fucking Alps Marinade, Marmalade or fucking whatever? Well I never!"

"What's more I'm off back to Paris next week and we're driving from there down to Grasse via Lyon. Christine Gallois . . ."

"You mean your fucking mother-in-law!" interrupted Maggie followed by further spasms of mirth and shaking of her spectacular bosom.

"Where Christine Gallois, Michel's *mother* is hosting some glamorous luncheon," I continued glaring at Maggie whose response was a further guffaw of laughter accompanied by a wiggle of her spectacular bosom which I would later refer to as her very own Alpes Maritimes.

*

It was a relief to find the Lyon penthouse appeared devoid of anything related to Christine's invasion of caterpillars in Grasse and turned out to be ditchwater dull instead of dramatically disastrous.

Christ, I've heard of contraceptive décor, I thought, *but whoever's responsible for this fuckup didn't even bother to ejaculate!*

"So where's the so-called guest of honour?" I hissed at Michel as he stood making polite conversation with a drab looking couple who I would take great delight in teasing Michel by referring to the two as "your muzza's constipations!"

"*Elle arrivera à n'importe quelle minute,*" he growled in reply.

"You do realise we could have been nearing Grasse by now?" I hissed back, "But no, instead we had to make this ridiculous stopover ..."

"'Ush! She comes!"

The words were hardly out of Michel's mouth when the door to the private elevator serving the penthouse slid open. On cue, Christine and her guests began applauding as the guest of honour stepped out, her arms outstretched in acknowledgement of their adulation. I stood staring at the diminutive figure wearing a "fun fur" of bright orange mink banded with horizontal strips of black leather and dead ringer for a hyperactive bumble bee.

"It can't be?" I muttered, "La Lollo?"

"*Oui,*" said Michel with a smirk. "Gina Lollobrigida is za guest of 'onourr. Now you are 'appy we stay, *non?*"

Of all the film stars I have met I can still say Britt Ekland is the only one who lived up to - and beyond - my expectations as to what a "star" should look like. Gina Lollobrigida, though glamorous, couldn't hold the proverbial candle to Britt or Margaret, the elegant Duchess of Argyll. Years later I met the legendary Elizabeth Taylor where my reaction was similar; the breathtaking star of *National Velvet* decidedly more a case of *crushed velvet*. A close second to Britt and Margaret would have to be Joan Collins. For some reason known only to Joan we have never "got on" despite meeting at several grand social events, lunches and dinners. Surprisingly enough I first met Joan when I was Margaret's escort to the opening night of *The Last of Mrs Cheyney* in which Joan starred alongside Moyra Fraser and where Margaret and I were invited to join the cast for dinner on stage after the performance.

"Zo, what did you zink of La Lollo?" asked Michel smugly as we finally set off on the last stage of our interrupted journey.

"Okay," I murmured.

"Only za okay?" stormed Michel. "Typical English! If she 'ad been za Julie Christie you would 'ave said she was *fabuleux!*"

"What I can't quite understand," I continued as if spoiling for a fight, "is why you and Christine suddenly switched allegiances?"

"Switched za *what?*"

"Allegiances or loyalties. I would have thought Catherine Deneuve or Brigitte Bardot - being French - would have been a more appropriate choice for the guest of honour?"

"What 'as Deneuve or za Bardot got to do wiz La Lollo?" snarled Michel thumping the steering wheel with frustration.

"I give up," I murmured sinking down as much as I could in the cramped passenger seat. "And instead of thinking lustful thoughts about La Lollo *Monsieur* Lido why don't *you* simply shut up and drive!"

"What do you zink I am za doing, huh? Swimming?"

"At least it would make a change from *singing!*" I snapped anticipating at least an hour's quietude. Much to my surprise my wish being duly granted; accompanied by what could only be described as a deafening silence.

The next day the three of us (Michel, me and Sidney) drove to the chalet.

I must have been fucking mad. No, correction there RA, you are *fucking mad to have even considered buying the ridiculous pile of crap in the first place: never mind the purchase of 'his' and 'his' graves!* I kept thinking as one struggled to light the various lamps and other minor chores in order to get the love nest "up and running".

Matters came to a head the following morning when for no apparent rhyme or reason Michel let fly with a hefty slap catching me on the left side of my face. My suggestion of barbecuing Sidney as a special treat for dinner possibly having something to do with it.

"Right! That's it!" I yelled. "I'm not staying in this godforsaken place a minute longer! You can either drive me to the fucking airport or else I'll walk to the village and either cadge a lift or call a taxi to take me in to Nice."

Anticipating Michel's response I pointed to my briefcase. "As you must surely know by now I never, *ever* travel without my briefcase and am always in possession of my passport, ticket and credit cards so getting back to London isn't a problem. In fact it'll be a fucking pleasure!"

"I will drive you," said Michel shaking with barely controlled fury. "I will zen return to Grasse and pray for za avalanche!"

Bit of a waste seeing you won't be there, I thought acidly and as we set off on another silent journey.

A tight-lipped Michel and a shivering Sidney barely gave me time to exit from the Mini before they zoomed way from the Terminal building.

"Petulant, pouting, posturing pernicious prick," I muttered as I marched purposefully towards the check-in counter followed by a hissed, *"Au revoir Cannes. Va te faire foutre Chalet Belle et Sebastien. Va te faire foutre gay Paree!"* as I walked towards the plane. ("Goodbye Cannes. Fuck off Chalet *Belle et Sebastien.* Fuck off gay Paree!")

*

"Oh my *God!*" screeched Liz on finding me in the office the next morning. "And here we were thinking while Mighty Mouse is away the staff could make hay!"

"Don't tell us there's been a disconnection with the French Erection?" rasped Bryan. He turned to a giggling Liz. "Didn't I tell you Liz it was all pie in the *Alpes-Maritimes* sky?"

"Christ RA! What happened to your ugly face?" twanged Les with typical Australian tact.

"Finally got into his wig, did we?" drawled Maggie.

"Put it this way," I answered drily, "What was once *bidden* fruit - and by bidden I mean endless free advice, soft furnishings along with a contemptible chalet..."

"Plus a cock!" interrupted Bryan with a titter.

"Has ended up as *forbidden* fruit," I said completing my sentence and deliberately ignoring his comment.

After I had finished regaling the team with what Bryan would continue to raspingly refer to as the grand finale of *The French Erection*, I asked him to step into my office while Liz and Maggie prepared the celebratory Mimosas.

"I've half a mind to hand you a set of keys for the Rue Michel-Ange pad and fly you and Les over to Paris tomorrow to clear the sodding place of anything supplied by RAD," I said in a conspiratorial whisper. "You and Les could then hire a small van and bring the stuff back."

"And then what?" questioned Bryan. "Burn it? Dear RA, that's *so* Maid of Orléans. So passé. So *Jeanne d'Arc!*"

"Bitch!" I hissed, "But you're absolutely right. However this won't stop me from putting the fucking chalet up for bloody sale! In fact let's call the estate agent and lawyer over there right away and you can speak to them on my behalf." I gave a snigger. "After all Lady L, you *are* known as a lady of many tongues; French being a favourite!"

*

DLL, on hearing the latest in the Michel saga surprised me by saying, "I can't promise anything dear Robble, but I may have a buyer for you."

Sure enough the buyer - or buyers - he had in mind confirmed the chalet was exactly what they had been searching for. (DLL having given them the telephone numbers for the estate agent and lawyer while I in turn had the lawyer inform Michel the property was no longer mine and therefor out of bounds to him and Sidney.)

When asked by the lawyer who Sidney was Bryan had cheerfully confided in the somewhat taken aback man "Sidney" was "Monsieur Gallois' *petit copain*" or boyfriend.

Within a few weeks Chalet *"Hell" et Sebastien* was a mere "error of the past" and as a sweetener I threw in the two burial plots. I swore to have no further contact with the star or his family (the French Connection-cum-Erection being well and truly disconnected) but did meet Michel many years later on a visit to Paris. I also made contact to verify his role in the television series of *Belle et Sébastien.*

In retrospect Paris for me will never be regarded as the "city of love" despite the Michel saga. Prior to my meeting with "za starr" and through another chance meeting at one of Peter Coats's delightful lunches I was introduced to a tense but charming American named Howard Barclay Railey who lived in Paris with his wife, a fellow American named Suzanne better known as Sue. The couple lived in an elegant apartment on the Left Bank overlooking the Seine and Notre Dame. Howard, somewhat to my surprise, invited me for a weekend in Paris: an invitation which I duly accepted.

After an elegant dinner at a nearby restaurant and over a late night brandy on our return to the apartment we discussed out plans for the next day before saying our goodnights and going to our respective bedrooms. Much to my alarm just as I was dozing off my host suddenly appeared in the guest room declaring his undying love. My honour at stake I did a Maria Marten of *Murder in the Red Barn* fame by loudly declaring (as she did) "no, no, a thousand times no!" or more colourful words to that effect. The situation was saved by an irate Mrs Railey who suddenly appeared in the doorway in her dressing gown and wanting to know what all the noise was about. Needless to say the next day I bade my host and hostess a tight-lipped farewell and returned to the sanctuary of London.

Several years later I spotted Suzanne at the Ritz where she was having a drink with a woman friend (I was there on a weekend jaunt with Richard Reynolds). I waited to see if I had been recognised before greeting her and as expected, Richard and I finished our drinks uninterrupted!

CARIBBEAN CAPERS

Besotted by St. Lucia - as opposed to Mr Justice whose infatuation would be better described as *rum*-sotted - I decided a Caribbean Christmas a "must". Humming "Oh little town of Castries" to a calypso beat I booked an evening telephone call to the manager at La Toc regarding the rental of two of the new self-contained cottages (a reception area, kitchenette, three double bedrooms two bathrooms, terrace and private pool per cottage) for three weeks; the time to include the Christmas Festivities and New Year's Eve. I also organised the rental of two Mini Mokes. With a wry smile I immediately dubbed the villas Villa RA and Villa Melford.

Spending a well-deserved weekend alone at Moorhawes I sat at the dining table accompanied by a large rum punch (to get me in the mood) and note pad whilst I pondered over the people I could, would and perhaps should invite to spend a "Caribbean Christmas" with me. Without hesitation I printed the initials DLL alongside RA at the top of the page. "You Beesle," I said with a murmur, "assuming you say 'yes', will be my guest from the time you leave Italy until your return to Dosso. With luck you'll fly back via London where I can spoil you even more with a dinner or three! Now, who else? I know Benedict will be in Sierra Leone so *he's* out . . . but of course! Melford. She'd be divine plus I've been longing for her and Beesle to meet. Added to which I *know* David will insist she visits Dosso . . ." I gave a grimace. "Obviously she'll drag along the petulant Petal but see it as a case of simply having to grin and bear him! Rather like Michel and Sidney!" I printed out the names Melford (Jill) and Petal (Desmond O'Power). "And if he's free, why not the Incompetent One (our nickname for journalist Richard Compton-Miller) seeing he's not only great fun but he's been more than generous about me in his annual *Who's Really Who* along various articles regarding RAD."

Knowing Richard to be one *hundred* and ten per cent straight I debated whether I should ask him to invite a girlfriend but thought better of it. I was sure he would have no problem in finding more than one very able-bodied island maiden to entertain him during his stay! I remembered DBR and Georgina Ryott mentioning they would be staying with friends who lived on Antigua. "Why not invite them to stay for a day or two?" I muttered. "And even though *my* David thinks Georgina's DBR a bit of a prat he finds Georgina's arrogant view of the world deliciously Mapp and Lucia and a laugh a minute. Added to which DBR would be an idea foil for Petal meaning we can leave those two to bore the pants off each other! Obviously the icing to the rum and raisin Christmas cake would be Coral and Vinnie if they could be lured away from the garish Christmas lights of Rodeo Drive!"

I checked my list. Me, DLL, Melford and Petal, the Ryotts, Richard Compton-Miller (plus half the nubile maidens on St. Lucia no doubt!) and Mr and Mrs Horror (Coral Browne and Vincent Price). "Done!" I said to the empty dining room, "So let's get telephoning. I'll book a call to LA for later but what's to stop me calling the others straight away?"

Melford's response was immediate and enthusiastic. "Darling it sounds divine and yes we'd love to!"

Richard Compton-Miller was equally as enthusiastic. "It couldn't be more fortuitous RA!" he said cheerfully. "I'm already scheduled to travel to the Caribbean to cover an article and visit friends on Antigua so once you confirm the dates I can have my flight altered accordingly. Sadly I can only stay for a few days and will have to miss the Christmas jollies but thank you *so* much!"

The Ryotts regally agreed to bestow a few days of their gracious company on me and my "colourful" friends before venturing on to join some pompous double-barrelled friends also on Antigua for a week or two of name dropping.

Coral, although delighted at my invitation had to say "no". "We're already spoken for dear," she twanged, "But *do* think of us while enjoying all that rum, bum and fucking calypso!"

Two days later I skipped downstairs to Peter Lubbock Travel where I made the necessary bookings for David Lloyd-Lowles, Jill, Desmond and myself. Namely one First Class return to Rome and three Tourist returns to London.

*

"Just think," I said glancing over my shoulder at Melford and Petal sitting in the back of the chauffeur-driven Mercedes, "this time tomorrow we'll be dining in a little restaurant I know in Castries where the soft shell crab and grilled tuna is simply to die for!"

"Maybe I'll skip dinner instead of wasting the airfare," sniggered Petal in response. His witticism followed by a honked "He-he-he."

My eyes fixed firmly on Melford I added crisply, "Our meal accompanied by several carafes of iced plonk; a vital follow-up to all those welcoming rum punches."

"Sounds wonderful darling," replied Melford. She gave a toss of red hair, "I can hardly wait."

"Weather looks a bit dicey if I may say so, sir," announced Tony the regular driver of the car hire firm I used for "special occasions". "They said to expect fog. You're lucky you're getting away before any delays."

"*A foggy day in London town,*" I crooned, "*while in St. Lucia we'll get lovely and brown.*" My attempt as a crooner followed by a look of disbelief from our female companion.

The three of us cheerfully boarded our flight where we sat waiting for take-off. Fifteen minutes became thirty before the captain finally announced that due to fog we he anticipated a further delay during which refreshments would be served. An hour later we were told to disembark.

As the fog densified so did the amount of would-be fliers. Within half an hour the departure lounge was a sea of irritated and frustrated passengers. Undeterred I made myself as comfortable as I could and took out a paperback from my briefcase. Petal meanwhile sat and sulked while Melford sat looking like a woman with a mission; a doppelgänger for Virginia McKenna in *A Town Like Alice* after she realises there's no escape from the Japanese. I had easily finished another chapter when Melford suddenly rose Phoenix-like to her feet and announced dramatically, "This is ridiculous," before sweeping off in the direction of the busy information desk. Completing a further chapter I happened to glance up and saw Melford striding back to where we were sitting; a "cat that got the cream" expression (in her case a complete dairy) on her face. Holding out her hand she announced triumphantly, "Darling, your ticket and your boarding pass please!"

"My ticket and boarding pass?" I repeated.

"No time for questions! Gimme!"

An hour later we are air bound for St. Lucia via Kingston, Jamaica and Barbados.

"You do realise Melford that Jamaica is at least a thousand miles distant from St. Lucia?" I said quietly as we sipped our well-deserved drinks. "Added to which on leaving Jamaica we will be landing in Barbados from where - hopefully - we'll be able to get onto an island hopper seeing no major airlines fly direct from Barbados to St. Lucia's new Hewanorra airport which is on the *southern* part of the island and miles from Castries. In other words your getaway plan could see us arriving *after* the others still held up in London?"

"Nonsense!" came the throaty reply followed by a tossing of her landmark red hair. She took a large swallow of her vodka tonic. "Whatever happens we'll at least be in the Caribbean whilst they, poor darlings, will more than likely still be fogbound - no, make that *Heathrow* bound!" The comment accompanied by another "cat that got the *dairy*" smile.

To make a long detour short we found ourselves held over in Kingston for a further day before managing to board an afternoon flight of Barbados. For a while our attempts to find a suitable flight were *bafan* (Patois for "difficult) but thanks again to Melford and her Oscar winning performance of a lady in distress - Lady Leon no doubt - (I never discovered what she said to the big black mama behind the check-in counter) we were promptly allocated seats on a supposedly full flight due to reasons of "da compassion"!

On board I sat next to Melford leaving a petulant Petal to the charms of another Englishman travelling to Barbados.

"I have a strong feeling we'll be staying in Barbados overnight," I muttered, "and if push comes to shove we'll simply have to charter one of those island hoppers first thing to get us to St. Lucia a.s.a.p." I added ruefully, "If the Ryotts and the Incompetent One have already arrived God only knows which of the cottages they may have plonked themselves in."

Melford took a sip of her rum punch. "When does David arrive?"

"Not until the next week. Two days before Christmas Eve," I replied, "which will give me time to rearrange the others if necessary. I planned on you having the Incompetent One in your cottage while David and the Ryotts shack up with me."

Half an hour into the flight a smirking Petal (*God, hadn't the guy ever heard of facial expressions* plural*?* I thought) unfurled himself from his seat and made his way over to us. "Done!" he announced smugly.

"Done?" echoed Melford à la Dame Edith Evans and her famous "in a handbag?"

"The guy sitting next to me. His name is Devaux, David Devaux, and what's more he not only *lives* on St. Lucia . . ."

"So?" I said interrupting his self-satisfied flow, "How has that 'done' us?"

"David (*David?* I thought, *does this arrogant oik have no shame?*) not only has his own plane but has also offered to fly us from Barbados to the St. Lucia so we won't have to stay overnight after all," said Petal smugly.

"Who's a clever Petal then?" cooed Melford. Giving me a mischievous glance she added throatily, "Now tell me Robin, isn't our Desmond not only a clever Petal but the *prettiest* Petal as well?"

"If you insist," I replied with a grimace followed by a muttered, "Beauty certainly *is* in the eye of *this* beholder."

"And not only a clever and pretty Petal but also a *unique* Petal!" added Petal smugly with a hint of a sneer.

Jesus no wonder you wept! I thought. *And just as well you and Melford are in another habitat. Poor Melford. The very thought of you being under the same roof with Petal O'Power and the Incompetent One sees me becoming more and more riddled with guilt as the seconds tick by!*

On our arrival at the La Toc complex I was relieved to find DBR and Georgina had placed themselves in the twin-bedded bedroom suite in Villa RA and the Incompetent One had taken over the master bedroom suite in Villa Melford. Needless to say he was given short shrift by me and the the villa's namesake leading to the Incompetent One, tail between his legs, hastily shifting his belongings to one of the other guest bedrooms.

*

Several hours later saw the Ryotts, Melford, Petal, Richard and their relieved host sitting on the pool terrace to Villa RA sipping large rum punches in celebration of "finally getting here!" After a quick discussion with Melford it was agreed the promised soft shell crab and grilled tuna could wait one more evening and we would dine in the main restaurant of the hotel

Within minutes the ever-practical, schoolmarmish Georgina began waxing lyrically about the housekeeper responsible for looking after our respective cottages and who Melford, Petal and self were still to meet.

"She's absolutely marvellous," trilled Georgina. "Her name is Mrs Antilles Wilson and, from what I gather, she prefers to be addressed by her fill name." She added with a simper, "Quite a mouthful wouldn't you agree?

"You mean she expects us to call her the full shebang - Mrs *Antilles* Wilson?" I exclaimed simultaneously thinking, *or is that simply a further example of your fetish for double-barrelled names?*

"Oh no, Robun," came the skittish reply, "after I had words with her we came to an arrangement that plain Mrs A.W. will do."

"I doubt if plain Mrs A.W. would even *know* about a mouthful, what?" exclaimed DBR. "More of a European practice don't you think? Ha! Ha! Ha!"

The five of us sat staring at the puce-faced man who seemed unable to stop guffawing at his wit. Catching his wife's look of disapproval DBR added cheerfully. "I don't know about anyone else but talking about mouthfuls I could certainly do with another of these rum punches. Anyone else for another A.W. job? What? Ha! Ha! Ha!"

Early next morning I walked over to the hotel section of the complex for a brief meeting with the highly efficient and friendly manager who had turned a blind eye to Barry's recurring, abusive tirades at the pool bar during our stay the year before. Having signed for the two Mokes and organised a running tab for any additional requests regarding food and beverages, the manager went on to tell me about a "fantastic new restaurant" which had opened since my last visit. "It's called The Green Parrot," he enthused, "and overlooks Castries from where it sits high up on the road to Soufriere."

He gave a smile. "In fact why not give it a try this evening? I'll make a reservation on your behalf. The restaurant is part-owned by a chap named

Black Harry - St. Lucian obviously - who trained as a chef at your very own Claridge's in London, would you believe?"

On being tentatively asked if Albert was still in charge of the bar I was told - much to my relief - he had decamped (the manager's choice of word, not mine) to another hotel on the island.

Black Harry turned out be a deliciously camp black gentleman and as expected The Green Parrot immediately became St. Lucia's stand-in for La Popote.

"Yet another evening without the much promised and much belated soft shell crab or grilled tuna in downtown Castries," I informed my guests who I found splayed round the pool at Villa RA. "But fear not for tonight we're dining at Castries's latest hot spot instead."

"St. Lucia actually *has* a hot spot?" sniped Desmond.

"Several, *excluding* the hot springs at Soufriere!" I snapped back.

"Hot springs?" echoed Petal. "Next you'll be telling us St. Lucia even boast hot tubs?"

"Those too," I replied, "but more baths than tubs and used here by the military on the island during the late eighteenth century." I added imperiously, "If you deign to look at the brochures left in Villa Melford you would have read all about the two volcanic peaks, the Pitons, the hot sulphur springs as well as the battle of St. Lucia"

"Here endeth the lesson," laughed Melford with a trademark tossing of her flaming red locks. "Now who's for a swim?" She rose gracefully from her sunlounger and unwrapped the colourful sarong tied around her waist, allowing it to fall to the floor.

I gave a nervous gulp and cast a nervous glance at the others. Apart from a leering Petal it appeared no one had noticed anything untoward. Here credit must be given to petulant Petal who, for once, held his tongue. Instead of coming out with some crass remark he leapt nimbly to his feet, stooped to collect the discarded sarong and grabbing hold of a startled Melford, steered her through the patio doors into the sanctuary of the sitting room.

"They left rather suddenly, didn't they?" murmured Georgina half opening an eye against the strong sunlight.

"Something about collecting a backgammon board," I adlibbed.

Half an hour later a serenely smiling Melford and a smug faced Petal reappeared (*sans* backgammon board) and I was relieved to note any hint of Melford's former flaming "lower storey" - a one hundred percent colour match to her "upper storey" - had been totally eradicated. A St. Lucian as opposed to a Brazilian no doubt.

Many years later I would write a novella titled *The Burning Bush*; later to become a successful play. The plot revolved a frustrated elderly red-headed actress named Shelagh La Verne and her devious ploy to ensnare a younger lover. One of the more acerbic characters (if possible) spikily refers to the aged redhead and her "burning bush" - his remark accompanied by an equally bitchy observation, "Let's face it, the old bag is so desperate for someone to quench the flames she'd welcome any old hose in her desperate quest!" Needless to say *The Burning Bush* is strictly a work of fiction and any reference to any person alive or dead is purely coincidental!

*

As Benjamin Franklin so rightly said, "Guests, like fish, begin to smell after three days" and l can assure you guests confined to a veritable island paradise are no exception. Although a niggling pain when visiting Dosso it quickly became apparent the Ryotts had erupted into a festering sore. To my barely concealed delight it was the equally festering Petal who took it upon himself to rub the proverbial salt into their wounds. Whereas the newly trimmed Melford swanned about looking a million dollars in an endless array of kaftans, bikinis and sarongs, Georgina appeared to make do with a floppy linen hat, limp-looking frock and sandals while her other half brazenly paraded around in a garish shirt, baggy, rumpled shorts and a pair of dilapidated canvas boating shoes.

"A frump and a dump in a frock," observed Petal on viewing Georgina's outfit for a visit to the colourful morning market in Castries. "A schlock in a smock with no sign of a cock," he sniggered on viewing DBR's idea of Caribbean cruise wear on another outing. Adding insulting he began openly referring to Georgina as "Mrs Ryott from Leeds" and to DBR as "Mr Ryott from Arseholeville": a surefire example of the pot calling the kettle black.

Melford, Petal and I watched in disbelief as "the frump" and "schlock" ended up having a heated argument over the purchase of an enamel bowl from the aforesaid market. True to form a smug DBR kept remarking on his "good bit of bartering, what?" while his wife reverently placed the hallowed utensil in her nondescript canvas shopping bag.

"Maybe a Customs officer at Heathrow will mistake it for a piece if sunken treasure?" suggested Melford.

"Who? Mrs Leeds or Arseholeville?" quipped Petal.

Needless to say the Incompetent One missed the bartering debacle seeing he was too busy ogling the local talent in spite of an earlier "confession".

On our first evening together Melford pointedly asked Richard why he was abstaining from the rum punches or any of the endless other alcoholic drinks on offer. "May I remind you Richard darling its Christmas not Lent!" she crooned simultaneously tossing her flaming locks.

Giving Melford a disdainful glance Richard announced in a sanctimonious voice, "If you must know Melford yours truly is not partaking of any alcohol due to ongoing treatment for an unfortunate dose!"

"Ugh!" cried Melford making a great show of pushing her chair away from Richard who was seated alongside. "Ugh Richard! Ugh!" she crowed in feigned horror. "Unclean! Unclean! Ugh! Keep away! Keep away! Filthy beast! Ugh!" Her theatrics instantly reminding me of darling Peggy and her "Aargh Bungo! Aargh!"

No doubt some of the guests at the hotel must have wondered why one particular group staying in two of the luxurious cottages on the estate would suddenly break up amidst shrieks of laughter and cries of "Ugh Richard! Ugh!" As expected when ordering pre-dinner drinks at The Green Parrot the person buying would to be sure to ask, "Rum punches for everyone and one 'Ugh Richard'?"

While revelling in his nonstop teasing of "Ugh Richard" Petal was to see his comeuppance a few days later. The day before I had chartered a motor launch from Peter Hackshaw, a charming Harry Belafonte lookalike and proud owner of several such boats. The plan was to motor along the coast towards Soufriere before leaving us at one the many secluded golden beaches where we could have a frolic in the waves followed by long, rum-enhanced picnic. Once Peter had set us down he would travel on to Soufriere and after dealing with several appointments in the town, return and collect us on his journey back to Castries.

"We'll be leaving the dock at ten o'clock sharp," I announced to the group as we were saying our "goodnights", "and please remember as we'll be on a boat for some length of time a sun hat and sun cream shouldn't be overlooked."

At nine o'clock I drove to the hotel where I collected the two picnic hampers I had organised the previous evening. In addition to the hampers I had arranged for a large container of ice in which several bottles of wine, rum and "Ugh Richard's" fruit juice (plus ours for the rum punches!) were chilling.

Parking the Moke next to its twin I found Melford, Richard and the Ryotts ready and waiting. I gave DBR a curious look before I realised his pasty complexion was a result of several dollops of sun cream. Georgina, equally as smeared and carrying a furled sunshade, sat staring at nothing in particular. *Maybe if you raised the brim perhaps the tumble of hibiscus bushes could spark of some sort of wow reaction?* I thought maliciously.

"You, Georgina and Richard go ahead," I said to DBR pointing to the second Moke, "and we'll catch up with you."

Giving a thumbs up and a cheesy grin DBR helped Georgina into the Moke while Richard clambered on to the back seat. With a loud revving accompanied by a series of jerks DBR finally began to chug his way towards the hotel and the road leading to Castries.

"Where's Petal?" I demanded as I remained seated in the Moke, the engine idling. "Peter's planning to leave at ten thirty, *on the dot*, and it's already a few minutes after ten, our scheduled time for leaving from here." I couldn't resist adding snidely, "Knowing the Ryotts and the Incompetent One I wouldn't be at all surprised as if they didn't see this as a replay of *A Foggy Day in London Town* and set off for Soufriere without us and picnic hampers."

"Nonsense darling," said Melford with a toss of her head, today turbaned as opposed to tumbling. "They're not quite *that* asinine . . . or are they?"

"Don't count on it," I muttered. "All *I* can say is if DBR takes one more fucking photograph of a fucking palm tree I'll bloody well *deck* him with a cocoanut not at *all* shy!"

"So loveable is our RA," purred Melford, "and look! In answer to our prayers the Blossom arrives. Better late than never!"

"See *that* as purely a matter of opinion," I muttered spikily.

"I missed my breakfast," growled Petal in greeting as he hoisted himself on to the back seat.

"It was all there ready and waiting darling," crooned Melford. "All you had to do was eat it."

Obviously today's excursion is going be the ultimate fabuloso fuck up, I thought wryly. *Beesle oh Beesle, wherefore art thou dearest Beesle?*

Peter Hackshaw and the others were patiently waiting for our arrival and didn't appear at all fussed by the delay. Apart from the two hampers I had in the Moke the launch proved to have a well-stocked bar and our cheerful crew member for the day had already supplied the garrulous DBR with a hefty rum punch while Georgina and Richard demurely sipped on a couple of "Ugh Richards!" In between sips of his rum punch DBR had already found a lonely palm tree to photograph and from the time of our arrival at the dock to our departure Melford and Petal counted a further three shots of the same palm tree, four shots of Peter and his boat along with one shot of the other intrepid soon-to-be passengers.

"Fuck me, who wouldn't want to have shares in Kodak?" I murmured to Melford as we boarded.

"What do you *think* he does with the hundreds of photographs he takes?" she muttered in reply.

"Keeps his fingers nimble by tearing them up," quipped Petal; his comment followed by an exaggerated yawn.

Richard had wasted no time in chatting up two innocent Barbie type tourists strolling along the dockside. In fairness to the poor man he looked highly relieved at having a break from recurring cries of "Ugh Richard! Ugh!"

"No Melford," I hissed on seeing her giving the Incompetent One and the two young woman a mischievous look. "*No*! The poor guy's only looking!"

"As is Mrs Leeds," snickered Petal nodding to where Georgina who sat staring at nothing in particular.

"Probably thinking beautiful enamel thoughts," I replied somewhat bitchily.

After half an hour's chugging along the verdant coastline dotted with endless golden beaches Petal, stripped down to a pair of trunks and wearing a pair of espadrilles, pulled himself to his feet and made his way over to where Peter was standing at the controls. After a minute or two of animated conversation and a great deal of arm waving by Petal, Peter gave what appeared to be a reluctant nod and slowly turned the launch in the direction of a nearby small secluded beach.

"What's happening?" I called.

"I have no desire to join you lot on some godforsaken picnic," shouted Petal in response, "So I've asked Peter to drop me off at a different beach. You can collect me on the way back."

Melford and I sat staring in disbelief at the smirking man.

"Are you *serious*?" demanded Melford.

"As serious as I'll ever be!" came the snapped response.

"What's going on?" questioned Georgina who appeared to have dozed off.

"I must take a few shots of Desmond as he departs," announced DBR reaching for his camera. "Could be the last record of our intrepid Robinson Crusoe, what? Ha! Ha! Ha!"

"Make sure you take something to drink if nothing else," I suggested with some reluctance.

"Don't forget your sunhat!" instructed the resurrected Georgina in her best schoolmarm mode. "Plus you'd better take a sandwich?"

"I am quite capable of looking after myself, thank you," replied Petal sullenly as Peter slowed the launch and pulled in as close to the beach as he dared. "See you lot later," he smirked as Peter helped him over the side and into the shallows. Without a backward glance Petal gave a vague wave began wading towards the shore.

Some twenty minutes later Peter pointed to an inlet coming up to our port side. "I was going to suggest the beach on that inlet ahead," he announced. "It's ideal for sunbathing and swimming plus there's a freshwater spring should you wish to dilute those rum punches," he added with a warm chuckle. "And should you wish to light a fire there's plenty of driftwood about plus I have several boxes of matches on board."

"Would you care to join us, Peter?" I asked.

Flashing a whiter than white smile the big man politely refused again mentioning his various business meetings in Soufriere. "Have no worries," he said with another dazzling smile, "I will be back around four o'clock to collect you and the other gentleman who was so determined at being dropped off at a different beach."

The day could not have been more perfect and the picnic supplied by the hotel proved to be a delicious spread of spare ribs, cold roast chicken, a variety of salads, crispy bread rolls and a pineapple salad swimming in rum. After several refreshing swims, a filling lunch and a conveyor belt of rum punches we were more than ready for Peter's return. We had studiously packed up the two hampers, rinsed the plates, cutlery and glasses while conscientiously bagging up any rubbish. This would be properly disposed of on our return to Castries.

"Better not forget the *rancid* mariner," I said sarcastically to Peter as we set off.

"I don't know about 'rancid'" brayed DBR, "more likely *reddened* if you ask me! What? Ha! Ha! Ha!"

Bet you he bloody well shouts Petal O'Power ahoy or something to that effect, I thought as we approached the beach in question.

"Petal O'Power ahoy!" brayed DBR as we approached the forlorn looking figure standing by the wavelets.

"My God Petal, are you alright?" cried a concerned Melford.

Despite protestations he *was* alright it was obvious the petulant, pouting Petal was not and suffering from both sunburn and dehydration.

As I confided to Richard later, "Why the stupid cunt couldn't have stayed in the shade is his own indaba."

"Indaba?" questioned the Incompetent One.

"Zulu word for business. A flashback to my grotesque Rhodesian childhood," I quipped. "Added to which Peter told him about a spring or two - the island literally *floats* on an ocean of artesian wells - plus the fact there were bananas galore should the idiot feel hungry or thirsty!"

Whether Melford had "words" with Petal later I'll never know but the day following his "fry" and "dry" he appeared a changed man and a one hundred percent improvement on his former self.

As I would later say to DLL. "Taking into account the hundred percent he already had to work on any improvement quoted is negligible!"

A few years later Melford and Petal "split up" as the saying goes. Petal went on to court and eventually marry an intense hypochondriacal ex-actress-cum-interior decorator and after a few years of nuptial nightmares (she confided once in a whispered tête-à-tête "Desmond used to beat me up") they were divorced.

*

Racing round the island in our Mini Mokes we developed a much practiced strategy for Melford and her penchant for "working on the tan" at every possible moment. With the roof canopy of our Moke rolled back Melford would sit it the passenger seat with her sarong pulled back and her feet resting on the dashboard. On approaching a clearing or plantation where workers could be seen Petal and I would cheerfully yodel "Fanny viewing time!" leading to Melford dropping her rapidly bronzing legs while modestly unfurling her sarong in order to cover her shapely limbs and trimmed "burning bush" from any lascivious eyes.

One particular "Melfordism" which to this day still causes one's blood to run cold occurred when the three of us were en route to meet the others at a restaurant in Anse Chastenet, a small resort close to Soufriere.

"Fuck," I said elegantly, "I've just noticed the petrol gauge seems to be all of a flutter. It must be the gauge itself as I made sure I filled up again yesterday."

"Want me to check?" said Melford taking a cigarette from her mouth.

"Would you?" I replied. I nodded to the metal platform between our seats. "That large cap would you believe, is the petrol tank. Simply unscrew it and have a look. I'm pretty sure we're nowhere near empty."

"Hold on," said Melford placing her right hand on the cap and giving it a twist. "Damn," she said, "give me a sec."

Replacing the glowing cigarette between her lips Melford leant forward and grasped the cap with both hands. "Viola!" she mumbled, the cigarette and the ash on the glowing tip wobbling dangerously in her mouth. Without hesitation she lowered her turbaned head and peered into the nigh-on-full tank. "Seems okay" she started to mumble, her words ending in a puzzled "What the . . . ?" as I grabbed the cigarette from between her lips and tossed it over the side of the Moke.

"Christ Melford!" gasped Petal.

"Jesus Melford!" I managed to squawk.

"Oh my God," whispered Melford. "Oh my *God!*"

"Thankfully He must be busy and doesn't need us quite yet," I said shakily as I restarted the Moke.

"No doubt the others would have simply put down our being blown to smithereens as another excuse for being late," suggested Petal with a chortle. His comment seeing the three of us collapsing into shrieks of relieved laughter.

Years later - forty to be exact - the incident was brought up at one of Meflord's delightful alfresco lunches in her Chelsea garden, the two of us admitting flashbacks to the near disaster still gave us "the willies"!

*

"I must say having the hotel prepare the picnic hampers is - to me - a gross extravagance," announced Georgina as we sat having breakfast on the pool terrace to Villa RA. (A breakfast comprised of papaya, pineapple slices, scrambled eggs, grilled eggplant, toast and coffee.)

"Oh? And why is that?" responded Melford, her eyes narrowing as she sat staring at Georgina in her blue and white polka dot summer frock and clumsy white sandals; the complete antithesis to Melford's flowing primrose yellow kaftan with matching turban.

"I see no reason why we cannot prepare our own hampers," continued Georgina unfazed. "We could easily buy *all* the food and drink at the market in Castries and as you well know both the villas are adequately supplied with glasses, cutlery and crockery."

"I think the little woman, Georgina has a valid point there, what?" brayed DBR.

"As the saying goes, 'Look after the pennies and the pounds will look after themselves'," snickered Petal. "Added to which it'll give the two girls something to do."

"I rest my case," said Richard raising his hands placatingly.

I glanced at Melford who sat staring at Petal in disbelief.

"May I make a suggestion?" I added diplomatically. "Why not give it a try and if we're not happy with the experiment as it were, we simply go back to having the hotel prepare the hampers as before?" I gave Melford a conspiratorial glance. "I was going to suggest we have a picnic tomorrow at a rather fantastic beach I visited last time I was here. It's near to the Carrie Blue hotel and in the opposite direction of any previous haunts." I turned my attention to Georgina. "So Georgina, if everyone is in agreement, why don't you and David visit the market later and buy the necessary? We can make a shopping list and then Melford and I will give you a hand with the hampers?"

I sat looking the Ryotts waiting for them to take the bait.

"No need Robun," simpered Georgina. "David and I will not only do the shopping but also prepare the hampers." She gave Melford a syrupy smile. "After all we wouldn't wish to upset Jill's sun tanning programme now would we?"

"Damn right!" guffawed DBR. "Leave it all to the little woman - Ha! Ha! Ha! - and me; St. Lucia's answer to Fanny Craddock and Johnnie Ryott, what?"

Fanny Craddock and Johnnie? I thought remembering my original flight to St. Lucia with Barry Justice. *Christ, talk about déjà vu!*

"And what pray - if I may be so bold - are you planning to use for a hamper or hampers?" asked Melford with a tight smile.

Georgina sat staring blankly at Melford. "Hampers?" she repeated.

"Yes Georgina. For the picnic. *Picnic* hampers," replied Melford with a theatrical rolling of her eyes.

"Why not my old suitcase?" guffawed DBR. "Add a bit of flavour to the goodies, what? Ha! Ha! Ha!"

"I am sure you will be able to find a suitable basket of sorts in the market," I said crisply. "See it as investment for any future picnics we may or may not be catering for."

*

We set off at noon the next day for the chosen destination.

"Gorgeous beach, darling," said Melford approvingly as we drew up alongside the ribbon of golden sand.

A few minutes later DBR and his two passengers drew up next to us.

"We meet again!" carolled Georgina, her nose with its heavy coating of white sunblock a startling contrast to the rest of her glowing face.

"How observant," mouthed the Incompetent One from where he sat; his large frame tightly squeezed on to the cramped back seat behind the two.

I pointed to a cluster of palm and casuarina trees. "That's where we had a barbecue the last time I was here. There's a circle of stones where we can light a fire and further inland stacks of twigs and broken branches desperate to be gathered." I gave a snicker. "Though I doubt if we'll be doing any grilling of that sort today."

"Over there?" barked DBR pointing his camera in the direction I had just pointed.

"Yes David. Over there by that large cluster of trees I was pointing at a few seconds ago," I replied with a grimace.

"Righty-ho! Leave it to us" came the hearty reply. "Leave it to us. You all enjoy your dip - mind the sharks don't bite - Ha! Ha! - while the little woman and I set out a feast for a king! Ha ha ha!"

"Or a raving old queen," muttered Petal.

"Touché," murmured Melford.

"I rest my case," said Richard.

With a throaty cry Melford shed her sarong and swanned gracefully towards the waters' edge.

"Me too!" cried Richard pulling off his shirt and scrambling out of shorts to reveal his bulging Speedos.

"Why not?" I yodelled following suit.

"I think I'll simply sit here and 'do' a Canute . . . see if I can control the waves," called Petal lowering himself on to the sand.

"You do that," I shouted in reply, "but please don't tell the waves to retreat until *after* we've had a dip."

After a hectic half hour of frolicking in the waves (Petal's aping of King Canute obviously a dismal failure) we slowly ambled back to the designated picnic spot.

"Uh-oh," I muttered, "I spy with my beady eye our usually unflappable Georgina looking as if she's now experiencing a *major* flap!"

"As long as they haven't forgotten the rum," muttered Melford.

"Hi Georgina," I called as we approached the distraught looking woman and a smirking DBR. "Everything okay?"

"Not really old thing," brayed DBR, "The little woman forgot to pack any plates."

"No plates?" I repeated.

"No plates. But fear not, I am sure we can borrow a few from that hotel you mentioned . . . the Cordon Blue?"

"Carrie Blue," I replied sourly.

"Hubcaps," said Melford.

"I *beg* your pardon?" squawked Georgina.

"Hubcaps," repeated Melford. "Two Mini Mokes equals eight hubcaps. Royal Doulton couldn't have arranged it better."

To give Georgina and DBR their due the picnic was a masterpiece and the hubcaps - after a rinsing in Petal's stubborn waves - proved to be ideal substitutes for their very distant cousins. So much so they became a stand-in for any future picnics.

Another outing with a difference was a surprise luncheon I organised two days prior to DLL's arrival and the day after the Incompetent One's departure for Antigua.

"You said you had something special for tomorrow," purred Melford as we lay alongside the pool to Villa RA. She gave a throaty laugh. "Considering the way we must have already explored every square inch of St. Lucia Robin darling, I can't think of *anything* that could surprise us!"

"I'm not suggesting *this* island," I said smugly. "I was thinking of lunch at the Yacht Club on Martinique. Definitely a square inch of the Caribbean you haven't explored."

*

The five of us left Castries the next morning in a chartered Cessna for the short flight to Martinique.

"Darling this is too, too divine and so different to the rather wild and woolly St. Lucia," crooned Melford as we sped along in a minibus (hired in advance) from the airport towards Port-de-France, the island's capital.

"That's because Martinique's French and highly civilised as opposed to British and backward," sniped Petal.

"Oh *look*!" squeaked Melford excitedly. "Look! Can you please ask the driver to stop?"

"Yes do!" cried Georgina following Melford's gaze. The two of them literally scrambling out of the vehicle as the bewildered driver drew to a sudden stop before heading off in the direction of a garish looking building.

"I don't fucking well believe this," I muttered to DBR and Petal as we sat waiting.

"That's women for you, what?" brayed DBR.

"A very sorry but very necessary species," sniggered Petal. "He-he-he!"

"About bloody time," I added as we spotted the two laughing and smiling as they exited from the hallowed portals (according to Melford) of Prisunic; each carrying a large shopping bag.

"Am I missing something here?" I sniped as Melford and Georgina made themselves comfortable in the mini-bus, their shopping bags safely stored. "You're here in Port-de-France on Martinique, an island in the middle of the Caribbean, en route to lunch at the effing Yacht Club and yet you *insist* on stopping for an impromptu bit of shopping when spotting a bloody branch of Prisunic? I take it this a regular phobia of yours Melford? A stopover at the local Woolworths on your way to the Ritz."

"I simply *adore* Prisunic, darling!" crooned Melford, "so deliciously tawdry!"

"Me too," crowed Georgina. "Thanks to Jill's beady eye I found yet another delightful blue enamel bowl."

*

To my immense relief the day of DLL's arrival dawned bright and clear with no hurricanes, tidal waves, dormant volcanos suddenly deciding to erupt or any other such evil portents predicted. Knowing his flight from Rome via London would be landing in the late afternoon and the journey from Hewanorra airport would take at least an hour this meant DLL would not be arriving in Castries until the evening. Having the whole day to prepare for this very special event I made sure Villa RA looked its best with bowls of freshly cut orchids placed strategically about the villa and a towering arrangement of red hibiscus branches in a woven basket bought specially for the occasion, waiting sentinel-like in the entry lobby to greet the man of the moment.

Realising DLL would be exhausted from the long haul flight (Rome to London and London to St. Lucia) I made sure Melford, Petal and the Ryotts made themselves scarce and greet a rested DLL at breakfast the next day. Melford could not have been more understanding and surprisingly enough, instead of being his usual petulant self, Petal invited the Ryotts to join him and Melford for dinner in downtown Castries; Richard by this stage having left for Antigua.

To have *Il Colonnello* as my very own guest to be pampered and thoroughly spoilt was a dream come true. *Nothing* was too good for him.

However a definitely chilling incident (but soon forgotten) took place when the six of us were spending the day swimming from Peter Hackshaw's boat in the beautiful unspoiled Marigot Bay. This being well before the inevitable tourist invasion of the then little-known island. Apart from the remnants of the Pushmi-pullyu who appeared in the film *Dr*

Dolittle (the particular sequence filmed in Marigot Bay) we were the only other "creatures" to be seen and had the bay to ourselves.

Access to the boat was via a small ladder hooked to the gunwale where after diving or jumping into the sparkling blue water and swimming and frolicking around one could then clamber back on board.

I happened to catch sight of DLL holding onto the ladder, a look of panic on his face.

"You okay Beesle?" I asked swimming to where he was clinging to the small ladder.

"Sorry my Robble," he gasped, "but I can't manage to pull myself up the ladder; I really can't . . ."

"Blame it on Joanna's pasta!" I quipped taking him gently by the arm. Looking across to where DBR was lazily treading water, his face held up to the sun, I called out sharply, "David I need a hand here please. *Il Colonnello's* not feeling too good!"

Seeing my concerned expression DBR - to give him his due - swam over without hesitation. Within a matter of seconds the two of us with the help of Peter were able to get an acutely embarrassed DLL back on board. Peter and I made sure he was resting comfortably while the ever-practical Melford promptly set to mixing him a reviving rum punch.

"I'm so sorry dear Robble," whispered DLL giving my hand a squeeze as we made our way back to Castries harbour, "I hope I haven't spoiled your day."

"How could you ever 'spoil my day' Beesle?" I softly replied. "As I said, on your return to Dosso go easy on Joanna's pasta!"

The days of fun and sun sped by. Christmas dinner at The Green Parrot was a hedonistic delight of rum punches, champagne and exotic Caribbean cooking with New Year's Eve at the same venue usurped by a spectacular firework display and the energetic nonstop beat of a smiling Calypso band.

On the stroke of midnight Melford - dressed in a flowing white kaftan, her flaming hair held back a gold Alice band - enthralled the diners by suddenly leaping on to the small dance floor and dancing like a possessed Isadora Duncan to the vibrant Calypso beat. Within seconds she was joined by two grinning gigantic Mandingo-like black gentlemen. After a minute or two Melford had most of the diners joining in the fun. Watching the laughing, prancing, dancing revellers I said in an aside to DLL, "If Ben was here he would have experienced several dozen orgasms by now!"

"David!" cried Melford undulating towards him, "I insist!"

Without any hesitation a beaming DLL joined Melford in what I can only describe as a very sedate shoe shuffle compared to her elaborate gyrations.

Two days later the Ryotts left for Antigua with Melford and Petal taking an afternoon flight bound for London.

"Try and avoid a stopover in Jamaica!" I yodelled as I waved goodbye.

*

DLL and I spent a further blissful two days at Villa RA by ourselves. We were emphatic the two days would be purely "together time" spent by the pool where we sipped our rum punches, laughed, played "remembers" and generally enjoyed each other's company. On the day of my return to London DLL was taking the island hopper to Barbados where he would be staying with Oliver Messel for a few days. Before leaving for the main airport at Soufriere I drove with DLL to the small airport at Castries where I was able to give him a long, fond, farewell hug before he boarded the hopper for the short flight to Barbados.

"See you in London on Tuesday for a catch-up dinner!" I called out as a smiling DLL made his way toward the Departure Gate.

*

"Call for you," sang Sue. "Be warned, whoever it is sounds *very* odd!"

"Odd?" I muttered, "How odd?"

"Odd odd and even more odd," replied Sue, "Hysterical in fact. He said - screeched more likely - it was vital he speak to you seeing it is quote - 'most important' - unquote."

"Okay," I said thinking, *Bob? Diamond Lil? A resurrected Rroland?* "Better put Mr Hysterical Odd-double-odd through. Hello?"

"It's David," wailed Leslie French. "He's dead! Dead on that island and it's all because of you, you murdering, selfish b-b-b-bastard!"

*

Numb with shock I somehow managed to replace the receiver. Finally, having managed several deep breaths I dialled Ben's number.

After a few rings he answered with a cheerful "Good morning."

"Ben it's me," I said chokingly. "It's Beesle . . . David. He's dead. Apparently he had a massive heart a day after his arrival on Barbados."

I vaguely registered Ben's sharp intake of breath.

"Stay right where you are Mumsie," he said, "and I'll be over as soon as I can." He added softly. "Meanwhile, may I have a quick word with Sue?"

As if in a trance I buzzed through to Sue. "It's Ben," I managed to croak. "He'd like a quick word."

A few seconds later Sue appeared holding a large Screwdriver. "Dear Robin," she said gently, "I'm so sorry." She gave a tentative smile. "Here, drink this. Ben's instructions."

Within an hour I was ensconced in Brooks with Ben and, much to my surprise, David Harvey.

We drank a silent toast to DLL.

"Ben and I thought you may want to spend a few days at the Mill," suggested Harvey. "I won't be down until the weekend but please RA, see the place as yours should you wish to get away."

"Thanks David but I'll be fine; honestly," I said with a swallow. I gave the two a sad smile. "Thanks Ben. Thanks David. I won't forget your kindness today. Ever."

*

DLL was buried next to Dickie, his sister, in the small churchyard at Hedgerley Green. Ben insisted on me having the use of his Roll-Royce and Pete the Wheel his driver for the day. The small church was packed but due to a holdup on the journey down I arrived late and ending up standing at the back of the congregation. Adding to my general despair I missed half of the service. I was completely ignored by Leslie as he shuffled past me on his way out. Nodding to Freya, Christopher, Pepe, Heather Thatcher, Leslie's sister Joan and other familiar faces among the congregation, I was given the cold shoulder making it obviously apparent the accusatorial Ariel-cum-

Leslie French had wasted no time in spreading whatever additional malicious gossip he could regarding the gold digging murderer Robin Anderson. Considering the fact my considerable successes both financially and career-wise were all down to me and me alone (apart from Charlie Cottenham's initial investment which was paid back within the first year of RAD being in business) I felt it best to ignore such pettiness.

After more rebuffs from former so-called friends I slipped away before the burial itself. As I was climbing into Ben's Rolls-Royce I heard Heather Thatcher say in her carrying voice, "I dread to think how much *that* little trinket must have cost?"

"Ignore them, Mumsie," said Ben on my return to Glebe Place. "They're only jealous. If the truth be known they also realise David was fortunate enough to spend the last days of his life with his greatest love and nothing can change that."

Ben and I were physically blocked from attending DLL's memorial service.

*

Aware of DLL's Italian lawyer I wasted no time in contacting him regarding *Casa Robino Bello.* Knowing I would never visit Dosso again I intended to put the more-or-less completed property on the market. My potential neighbour, the rich Milanese, had always shown great interest in the project and I was aware that finding a buyer among their friends would not be problem. A week later I received a letter informing me there was no official documentation saying the property belonged to me and it was all hearsay on my part. Looking back I realised DLL and I had never got round to the requisite legalities for making my ownership of *Casa Robino Bello* official.

A clear-cut case of *Arrivederci Beesle. Arrivederci Dosso.*

I never heard from Leslie French Letter again; nor from any of DLL's former fawning relatives. In spite of Ben's insistence and no doubt much to the chagrin of the scandalmongers I refused to have any further contact with his lawyer regarding my right to the property at Dosso. In other words a firm finger to the likes of Heather Thatcher et al.

As DLL once said, "You're a power house my Robble and no matter what happens the world will always be your oyster."

As I said to Ben. "Contrary to the jubilations of the French Letter and his vindictive coterie at David not leaving me so much as an ashtray never mind the much looked forward to *Casa Robino Bello*, what he *did* leave me is a Cinque Terre of glorious memories and who - or what - can ever or will ever hope to compete with that?"

TREADING WATER - RAD BECOMES RADC

Grief can be expressed in many forms. To me it should be a private matter and I find scenes of public wailing and tears of anguish (usually more "crocodile" than genuine) variety) essentially attention seeking than soul searching. My stiff upper lip attitude stemming from an early age. No doubt Cur's annihilation of Miffy and Peggy's departure from my life would be happily seized upon by some sanctimonious psychiatrist as two major factors for my lack of empathy in spite of the truth. Namely, the only way to survive unexpected empty voids, endless taunts of "bat's ears", "squeaky voice" and "sissy" was to grin and bear it.

Not only am I acutely embarrassed by such open displays of any type of affection (the exception being DLL but never forgetting Peggy, Ben and Donald)) I also find the liberal use of the cringing term "loved ones" not only causes my skin to crawl but makes me to inwardly shudder.

After DLL's death I found solace (and companionship) in work, work and more work.

"Eek Mumsie!" commented Ben, "At the rate you're going there'll be nothing left in London for you to design!"

Although he never pushed himself Ben was always there and while I appreciated his never-ending support I made sure I left plenty of breathing space between us.

A few months later Georgina Halse invited me to another dinner at Walton's which, as expected, turned out to be the greatest of fun. Georgina had also asked Harry Levine (whose rakish company I always enjoyed) along with Germaine and Cyril Woolf. I was somewhat taken aback when Germaine gave me an unexpected hug and whispered throatily, "I was sorry to hear about your fazza!"

"Good evening Mr Anderson and welcome back to Walton's," greeted Malcolm the midget maître d' as I swept through the door.

"Er . . . good evening er . . . Michael," I stammered. *Ten out of ten for remembering my name,* I thought. *But then that is part of your job.*

Halfway through dinner Georgina began waxing lyrically about my Albion Gate penthouse.

"Why have I never seen your *appartement*?" demanded Germaine, her dark eyes flashing.

"Simply because I'm hardly ever there, Germaine," I replied meekly, "but before we leave let's make a date for you and Cyril to come along and have a . . . er . . . glass of champagne."

"Everything to your satisfaction?" interrupted Malcolm.

Between our murmured appreciative replies Germaine surprised me by saying to the beaming little man, "Have *you* seen Mr Anderson's *appartement*?"

"Er . . . no," answered Malcolm looking mildly flustered, "But from what Mrs Halse tells me it must be quite something."

"Mr Woolf and I are going to see it very soon," added Germaine fixing me with a beady look. "Aren't we, *darling*?"

"I have heard from a couple of our regulars your flat - pardon me, *appartement* - is quite stunning," said Malcolm as I stood waiting while the others collected their coats or paid a visit to the Ladies or Gents The switch to *appartement* accompanied by a smile. At least I assumed it was a smile seeing his beard made some sort of movement.

"These regulars being?" I asked imperiously.

Malcolm reeled off the names of several people who had been to one of my endless cocktail parties as I stood staring back at him. *A veritable Roddy McDowell but with a tache and a beard,* I mused, *plus a decidedly chunky body and perhaps even a twinkly smile.*

"Why not come and judge for yourself?" I suggested. "But *not* when Mr and Mrs Woolf are there! I'm not cruel enough to put you through an ordeal such as that!"

Malcolm came for the suggested drink. Not only was the midget maître d' delightful company he went on to prove himself a sensation in the sack.

Meanwhile Malcom kept on insisting I should meet the owner of Walton's whom he would describe in a deferential whisper as "My boss and a true friend".

"Soon Malcolm, soon," I would reply. "Just give me a day or two."

Like myself, Malcolm was a great film buff and we made many forays to the local cinema where would sit with a "goody bag" containing two thermos flasks of martinis. Eyes glued to the screen we would sip or drinks from a pair of plastic tumblers. Due to Malcolm having be on duty at the restaurant most evenings, our cinema visits usually took in the six o'clock performance. As a result of the earlier attendance these martinis quickly became known as MMs or "Matinee Martinis".

During one Martini Matinee - the selected film being *The Eagle Has Landed* - Malcolm announced in-between sips, "I'm really looking forward to this as I'm a great Richard Burton fan."

"Prepare to be disappointed seeing he's not in the film," I replied a touch sarcastically.

"I'm sure he is," came the emphatic reply.

"Not unless he's playing the part of Michael Caine or Donald Sutherland," I said with a snicker.

The mention of Richard Burton inevitably sparked off a conversation involving Burton and Elizabeth Taylor and the ill-fated *Cleopatra* in which they starred.

"Despite *Cleopatra* being such an atrocious film I'd still love to visit Egypt," said Malcom refilling our MMs.

"Did you see the Tutankhamun Exhibition at the British Museum a few years ago? Nineteen seventy two if I remember correctly?"

"Sadly I missed it."

Three days later I called Malcolm at the restaurant.

"I've been thinking," I said without any preamble. *"You'd* like to visit Egypt and *I'd* like to visit Egypt so if you can get a week off why don't you join me as my guest?"

After rearranging a few appointments in order to consolidate our dates, we duly set off for Cairo.

Ben was bemused whereas Richard Reynolds was neither bemused nor amused.

"Why invite him of all people?" sneered Richard. "I know his ilk; simply out for what they can get." He added with a grimace. "If you're going to start paying for sex you'd be better off finding yourself someone local. Think of what you'll be saving on air fares and hotels . . ."

"Eek Mumsie! Or else travel alone and invest your Egyptian pounds in a nubile Nubian or hunky Arab for any additional pounding!" chortled Ben.

"Let's face it, for someone whose elevator never quite made the top floor, your wily waiter certainly seems to have managed to reach the penthouse on this occasion, hasn't he?" added Richard sourly.

Before our departure for Egypt I had already organised one of my popular "gentlemen only" cocktail parties at Albion Gate. Further to Malcolm's endless references to his "greatest friend" (this "greatest friend being his employer and the owner of Walton's) and how I simply "had to meet him" I finally acquiesced and agreed to invite Malcolm's "King of Kings".

"And his friend?" added Malcolm in a perfect parody of Oliver Twist's "Please sir, can I have some more?"

"His friend?" I exclaimed. "Jesus, Malcolm. It's meant to be a drinks party for a few chums; not a charity event."

Malcolm's employer, a fellow Yorkshireman named Roger Wren and his friend Norman Swallow (*A swallow and a wren? I wonder who's feathering whose nest?* I thought with an inward snicker) did not strike me as particularly illuminating. Both appeared to drink a lot with Swallow becoming increasingly aggressive in his comments regarding the apartment and the other guests. Swallow's crowning glory was an unsteady totter into the kitchen where, to the horror of the busy barman, he unzipped his fly and urinated in the sink. Needless to say such a display did not endear Wren's "friend" to me. On asking the disruptive two to leave I was subjected to a double tirade of slurred abuse by the departing "guests" as they staggered into the lift.

Whereas I was furious with Wren and Swallow I was equally as furious with Malcolm who merely shrugged the incident off with a murmured "these things happen".

Richard (Reynolds) and Ben who had witnessed the minor fracas were less forthcoming.

"Eek Mumsie! Two very unpleasant 'birds of a feather!" quipped Ben.

"A prime example of how you can't polish a turd," sniped Richard. "And I'm not only referring to the two creeps who've just left but to that greedy little gargoyle you insist on accompanying you to Farouk land as well. Talk about a bloody Farouk-up!"

When it came to criticism of Malcolm, Richard would easily come out the winner with additional epithets of an uncharitable nature including such putdowns as "that mercenary midget" or "the skiving Scot". However Malcolm Livingston wasn't the only one subjected to Richard's searing criticisms. On being told there had been some confusion over an order he had placed with one of my suppliers the poor man whose name was Marc Lelliot became a "marked man" and referred to by Richard as "that skid mark idiot" from then onwards. Nor did Jill Melford escape. On hearing Melford introduce herself to some gullible soul as Lady Leon, Richard would in future refer to her as "Malady Leonine".

*

Our first at the Hilton Hotel in Cairo showed Richard's sneering prediction "I know his ilk; simply out for what they can get" to be resoundingly correct and confirmed by Malcolm's sudden disappearance after dinner on the evening of our arrival. On his return to our sixth floor suite a good hour later he greeted me with a murmured "I went for a walk . . . God, it's certainly warm out there . . . Er . . . I'll just have a quick shower and then join you for a nightcap . . ." Without waiting for a reply he scuttled into the bathroom, distinctly locking the door.

Eventually he reappeared wearing one of the hotel's fluffy white guest robes. Deliberately ignoring my gaze Malcolm nervously helped himself to a drink from the minibar before sitting down in one of two chairs facing the sofa in front of the dark picture window. Still avoiding my relentless gaze he stared fixedly at the reflective glass pane behind me.

"Er . . . nice view from up here," he eventually mumbled after a prolonged silence."

"Possibly a tad nicer than the view you had down there," I said spikily. "Unless of course, the view encountered on your so-called stroll had you hand *clap*-ping with delight." My emphasis on the word "clap" saying it all.

Rising from the sofa I added with a hiss. "May I suggest you bag yourself a blanket and a pillow and sleep on the sofa? What's more it'll give you a further opportunity to study the horrendously extravagant view from the comfort of the sofa as opposed to having to view Cairo whilst on your knees."

Not responding to Malcolm's sharp intake of breath I stalked into the bedroom, snatched up a pillow and a blanket from the king size bed and tossed them through the door. Still seething I added in a sarcastic voice, "And if you haven't gone on another walkabout maybe you'd care to join me for breakfast here in the morning. The view should be even more spectacular in daylight."

*

Despite the misgivings resulting from Malcolm's licentious behaviour on the first night of our arrival. Egypt turned out to be more enthralling than any travel brochure or MGM and Elizabeth Taylor combined. We sat mesmerised through the *son et lumière* at the Pyramids and a further light show at Karnak. Whereas I found Tutankhamun's tomb to be a disappointment and hideously claustrophobic my travelling companion did not. We wandered spellbound through endless temples, visited the Valley of the Kings and the lesser publicised Valley of the Queens. From Karnak we took the Hilton cruise boat along the Nile to Aswan. We were informed the number of cruise boats on the river at the time amounted to two. Unlike today when the number of cruise boats on the Nile represents a busy regatta. I couldn't resist sending Coral Browne a postcard of an old man smoking a hookah on a felucca. "Caught in the act" I wrote. "A blowjob *extraordinaire.*"

I was fascinated to find the area surrounding the temple at Abu Simbel covered in colourful rose bushes. Something I never expected to see in the middle of the Sahara Desert. A beaming Malcolm (his beard moved) informed me roses were very hardy plants and thrived in the driest of climates.

"How interesting," I replied sarcastically on being told this somewhat irrelevant piece of information. "I don't wish to hurt your feelings Malcolm *dear*, but unlike Coral's question as to which thorn had the bigger prick, *your* dubious claim to fame is you and your prick merely having the bigger sting as in con trick sting. Correct me if I'm wrong when in saying your personal rose bush is best known to all and sundry as the *Livingston Prickulous Fraudulous Contemptuous*?"

Needless to say my witty comeback resulted in my travelling companion looking even more befuddled than usual.

*

"And how was the pay-as-you-go fuck, the dreaded Livingston?" sniped Richard when I lunched with him and Ben a few days after our return.

"Yes, Mumsie. How *was* this 'buy one but you won't get one free' siren of the desert or midget maître d' as you first called him?" asked Ben giving Richard a mischievous glance. The two obviously having discussed my inviting Malcom to Egypt at some length.

"In answer to your veiled question gentlemen and in answer to Coral Browne's similar query, yes, Mr Livingston most certainly has the bigger prick." I replied somewhat acidly.

After a few seconds silence Ben and Richard burst out laughing.

"Touché Mumsie!" snickered Ben remembering Coral's parting remark to Roy Miles on leaving his cocktail party.

"More like a case of *douché* Mumsie!" guffawed Richard.

"My lips are sealed," I said. My reply leading to more ribald comments and laughter.

"However Richard, to give you and Benedict your dues, when it comes to tact or discretion not even that wily Janus-faced waiter's copious, calculating cock could ever compensate." I gave a self-deprecating snigger. "Talk about being taken for two extravagant, blinkered rides."

"Janus-faced, Mumsie? I love it but an explanation perhaps?" asked Richard with a questioning chuckle.

"Having two faces; one looking backward and one looking forward like the Roman deity Janus," I replied loftily. "In other words a conniving, devious little shit."

*

A few evenings later I bumped into David Hicks at a private viewing at the Redfern Gallery.

"Good evening Robin; you still looking for a country retreat?" he asked. "If so, The Grove is still available. Have you a pen? Let me give you my private number and should you wish to drive down and have a look simply let me know. In fact, if you *do* decide to drive down come for lunch. Pammy would love to see you again."

"She would?"

"Yes indeed, she enjoyed meeting you and David." DH gave a snicker. "Plus she was highly amused when I told her of your predictions for my project in Malta!"

With The Grove it was a case of "love at first sight"; a Georgian-style house set amidst approximately thirty acres of meadows and woodland. DH could not have been more accommodating. A token rent, a substantial lease subject to renewal plus a free rein with any changes to the interior.

"Do whatever you wish, RA" he said with a grin. "Whatever you do I'm sure will become a talking point among the locals."

After a pleasant lunch at Britwell House I returned alone to The Grove for a second look.

"Okay Beesle," I muttered as I stood surveying the large drawing room with its pale celadon green walls and beige carpet (the celadon green courtesy of the former tenants and a contrast to the understated off-white used throughout the rest of interior), "As I no longer have *Casa Robino Bello* to pamper and to spoil, let's get *this* show on the road.

Having taken my time walking around the airy house I decided my main concerns would be the drawing room, dining room, study-cum-television room and a large, sunny room at the rear of the house overlooking an unkempt lawn, a field and a distant barn. The existing entrance hall with its gleaming flagstone floor I decided would require the least titivating.

With DH having overseen a total renovation to the original property the layout and basics could not be faulted. Upstairs the bedrooms and bathrooms (one en suite) required furnishing and little more apart from - if required - a change to the colour of the walls. This meant my input would basically be wall treatments, soft furnishings and whatever else I deemed fit. At the end of the day I was determined any reactions from my guests would be in the more "now I never expected anything like this" vein than a mumbled "nice, very nice".

From the dining room I walked into a small corridor leading to the large, well-planned kitchen complete with a large table and six wooded chairs and leading off from the kitchen, a small corridor serving the back door, a flower room and a utility room. "Nothing needs doing here apart from introducing a dishwasher … and yes, it doesn't look as if there would be a problem plumbing one in," I murmured to myself as I made my way towards the back door.

"*Perfezionare*," I murmured eyeing the paved courtyard partly enclosed by a stable block, an old dairy and several storerooms.

"If at *all* possible it gets better and better," I said aloud as I exited the courtyard and made my way back towards the front of the house. "I don't believe it!" I added with a chortle on spotting a dovecote leaning precariously on its support. "A dovecote indeed? A bit twee RA, even for thee - *n'est-ce pas?*"

A few weeks later Peter Law, DH's macho gamekeeper arrived with a dozen white doves following my tongue-in-cheek suggestion "a few doves flying about wouldn't go amiss."

"They're pretty tame," Peter informed me, "an' apart from feedin' 'em they shouldn't cause ye any bother. I've also brought along a sack of seed. I'll sprinkle a bit around the base an' that should see yer new friends all set."

After a grinning Peter had roared off down the drive in his mud spattered Land Rover I stood staring at my new friends busily pecking at the freshly scattered seed.

"Almost fucking biblical," I muttered, "Peter scattering his seed . . . And yes Peter, they're all decidedly jolly and very cooey wooey but this is The Grove, RA's new home *extraordinaire* where white is not necessarily right so thinking cap on RA; thinking cap on."

The following weekend I returned to The Grove armed with a selection of vegetable dyes and several packets of condoms; the thinking cap leading to me thinking of a *bathing* cap and a brilliant solution regarding my duller-than-dull doves. "Twelve doves makes six colourful couples," I announced to a puzzled looking Peter who had dropped by to see how I was "getting along".

"You couldn't have timed it better, Peter," I told him, "seeing I was about to start dyeing the doves and before you ask, I'm only dunking their bodies, not their heads. Hence the condoms." I gave a snicker. "While you hold a dove I'll quickly unwrap the condom and roll it over its head. Once the head is covered we'll quickly dip the dove in the selected dye. Seconds later we remove the condom and voila! A perfectly coloured dove apart from the head. Here, pop these on."

"Well I never," muttered Peter donning a pair of rubber kitchen gloves. "Well I bloomin' never."

Half an hour later we stood proudly surveying our handiwork.

"So what do you think, Peter?" I asked.

"Bloomin' marvellous," chuckled Peter, "Bloomin', bloody marvellous."

I turned my attention to the doves back to busily pecking at the freshly scattered birdseed. "Two yellow, two pink, two orange, two turquoise, two peppermint and two emerald green; who needs Judy and her rainbow?" I said with a giggle. I glanced at the strutting doves before bursting into a further bout of giggles. "Forget Judy, the Lion, the Strawman et al." I managed to splutter. "With their white hats this lot look more like members of the local Watlington WI than visitors to the Land of Oz!"

"Er . . . best I leave you to it then," muttered Peter. Giving me a curious look he turned and walked determinedly towards his mud-spattered Land Rover.

*

"I've leased The Dower House on the Hicks' country estate," I informed Melford, "and if you're not up to anything illegal or immoral this coming weekend why don't you at Petal come and stay? You'll have to rough it I'm afraid but I have already organised a couple of beds, one king size and one queen size - ha ha - and if you could bring yourselves down along with a vineyard or two, so much the better. In the meantime Ben's loaned me his driver, otherwise known as Pete the Wheel, to help cart down a whole load of stuff - towels, bed linen, blankets, cutlery and crockery etcetera ex-Moorhawes *including* the Bargello patterned sofa - which I wisely put in storage. He's managed to borrow a van from one of his mates." I gave a chuckle. "As you can see Melford, no hubcaps required on *this* voyage."

The first weekend spent at The Grove was, according to Melford, "mad, magical and very special". I had driven down on the Friday in order to meet Pete (temporarily dubbed "the man in the van") and between the two of us managed to set up the master bedroom and what would become known as the Melford Suite.

"It's yours whenever you wish to visit The Grove whether I'm there or not," I told Melford.

"Preferably when you're not," snickered Petal in an audible aside.

Ben's Pete the Wheel laid the kindling in preparation for a fire in the large stone fireplace of the future study. He also brought in a collection of trimmed logs found in one of the outhouses; the logs not placed on top of the kindling but stacked in a neat pile on the stone heath. We positioned the patterned sofa opposite the fireplace with a canvas "producer's chair" on either side.

"*Maison et Jardin* eat your heart out!" I quipped. Aided and abetted by several glasses of wine we placed various items in the kitchen cupboards and drawers, made up the two beds and most importantly, set up a drinks tray in both bedrooms.

Our final effort of preparation was to arrange the former garden furniture from Moorhawes in a neat group on the unkempt lawn (more meadow than mown) opposite the large window to the drawing room. Glasses of wine in our hands Pete and I sat in the study contemplating our handiwork.

"It's going to be smashin', Mumsie," said Pete. "Simply smashin'!"

A somewhat "smashed" RA followed Pete to my new local, the Red Lion, where we had a celebratory dinner.

It was during dinner that Pete tentatively asked if I would be offended if he was "kinda cheeky" and mentioned something which "really ain't any of me business RA but it's really gettin' to me. Really gettin' on me wick".

"No Pete, I don't mind at all," I replied, "If something's bothering you it's always best to spill it out." *Christ, please don't tell me Ben's mistaken; you're not straight and you've fall head over heels in love with Ben!*

"It's Ben . . . er Mr Colman, RA," said Peter in a choked voice. "I'm really worried about 'im. 'E's drinking terribly, RA, mornin', noon an' night and now it's gotten worse. Line after line of Charlie, RA. Mounds of it. Plus 'e's smokin' joints. 'E keeps a bowl full of 'em next to 'is bed; in the sittin' room; the kitchen . . . every bloomin' where!"

"It's the first I've heard of Ben doing drugs Pete; are you quite sure?"

"As sure as I'm sittin' 'ere 'avin' a bleedin' 'eart to 'eart with you RA," said Pete.

"Let me 'ave - *have* - a word with him Pete," I said solemnly. "However, I'm sure it's simply a phase he's going through . . ."

"Some bleedin' phase," muttered Pete. "'E's doin' me fuckin' 'ead in."

I waved Pete goodbye before returning to The Grove for my first night in the latest RA abode. I sat in the study nursing a nightcap and pondering over what Pete had said about Ben.

"I'm sure Pete's making a mountain out of a molehill," I muttered to the set fireplace. "Knowing our Ben I'm sure there's nothing to worry about and if I *do* say something it'll only backfire on poor bloody Pete so best to let sleeping Bens lie!"

Meanwhile DH had arranged for me to meet Bernie" his gamekeeper's wife, who he said would be only too delighted to "look after The Grove" should I need a cleaner. Bernie and I met the morning after Pete and I had arranged the basics. I gave Bernie a guided tour explaining my plans and was delighted by her smiling response, "Is it alright if I start Monday? Them carpets could well do with a thorough shampooing!"

Whenever Sue or I telephoned her, Bernie's guaranteed response on being asked how she was became a standing joke in the office.

"How are you Bernie?" one of us would ask.

"Oh Mr A (or Miss Sue)," she would reply with a theatrical sigh, "I've been on me hands and knees all morning. Never orf them. But it's been worth it. Ever so clean it all looks!"

"I assume Bernie's referring to cleaning the floor?" quipped Sue after her first enquiry to Bernie's wellbeing.

"What else?" grunted Les Gabriel glancing up from his notes, "Honestly Sue, you and RA . . . ?"

"Don't have a go at Sue," I sniped. "For all we know it could have been another example of Mavis talking to her friend Flo outside their workplace in notorious Shepherd Market."

"Mavis and Flo? Shepherd Market? What's that got to do with Bernie when she's at home?" twanged Les.

"Mavis and Flo," I repeated, "two old tarts outside their respective sex pits in Shepherd Market. Mavis says to Flo, ''Ow's business dearie?' to which Flo, whose business establishment is situated at the top of the building responds in an exhausted voice. 'Oi can't complain Flo pet, I've been up an' down them stairs *eleven* times already an' it's not even three o'clock.' 'Ooh Flo,' cries Mavis. 'Eleven times ya say? Oh yer poor feet'!"

"I still don't get it," grumbled Les.

"Think hands and knees, think blowjobs or a worn out fanny," I snapped. "Jesus Les, for an aged reprobate from Down Under you can, at times, be a tad naïve."

"Must you use the word 'fanny'?" said Bryan in a pained voice, "when surely cunt would have sufficed?"

"Now, now, Lady L," I chided. "Not in front of a bona fide lady."

"No need to spring to my defence RA," said Sue in a pained voice. "After all what can you expect from Mesdames Slut and Smut."

"Now *that*," I replied with a chortle, "most certainly deserves a drink. Screwdrivers for you and me Sue with tap water for the children."

*

Leading the way through the back room overlooking the barn to the side of the house where Pete and I had set up the outdoor furniture, I said to Melford and Petal, "You'll have to excuse the knee-high lawn but I've been a tad busy getting the place semi-habitable for the two you. Plus the fact yours truly ain't got round to buying a lawnmower as yet!"

"Darling, I *love* it; simply *love* it!" crooned Melford placing herself elegantly on one of the garden chairs and promptly disappearing from view. "Hello? Somebody?" she cried camply from behind the waving fronds definitely more thigh length than knee length.

"You'll love it even more once you've tried the Pimm's," I said handing her a glass as she reached out her from where she sat amidst the waving grass.

"Talk about Moses parting the waves!" yodelled Melford taking hold of the glass.

"A Pimms from now on to be known as a RALP." I informed her.

"A RALP?" questioned Melford.

"An RA lethal Pimms, of course!"

*

Decorating The Grove proved to be both satisfying and therapeutic. DH turned out to be the most generous and considerate landlord and an always welcome visitor to The Grove. However, he was meticulous in telephoning to see if it was "okay" for him to drop by; his visits usually taking place after lunch on a Saturday when he and the occasional guest would join us for drinks or coffee. I am sure DH enjoyed meeting the eclectic group of people I happily entertained. People including the likes of Hayley Mills, Leigh Lawson (who went on to marry Twiggy), Tracy Reed and Bill Simpson (TV's *Dr Finley* and her husband after divorcing Edward Fox), Bea Greene and husband Richard (TV's *Robin Hood*), Ray Milland, Patricia Medina, Christopher and Gitte Lee, Margaret Argyll, Peter Coats, David Harvey ("Fred von Mirrors" rival and my country neighbour) and RA regulars such as Melford, the Marshallene and, of course, Ben.

During the earlier stages of my decorating I received DH's usual courtesy call - "David here; is it convenient for me to drop by?" - I laughingly assured him he was most welcome as always and he'd find us on the side lawn with our after lunch RALPs or coffees. Having returned to the kitchen to fetch more ice I was passing through the entrance hall when I heard DH's Range Rover crunching to a halt on the gravelled driveway.

*

Before continuing I feel it necessary at this point to bring one up to date with regard to my decorating of The Grove.

The Main Entrance: With its splendid flagstone floor, decorations here were minimal. At the far end of the hall the window now boasted a large lambrequin finished in white Gilford vinyl bound in a terracotta vinyl contrast; the lambrequin framing the towering Ben West sculpture originally commissioned for the Ladbroke Square flat. Adding a gigantic splash of colour and taking up most of the wall to the left of the double doors to the drawing room was a large oil painting by Sandra Blow, one of my favourite artists. A touch of whimsy were four Victorian beech, balloon back farmhouse chairs covered in the same terracotta vinyl as the lambrequin contrast. The pièce de résistance had to be a collection of polished metal Victorian shoe lasts climbing the stairs in single file.

The Dining Room: This I treated as a tribute to the Japanese artist Hokusai, another favourite. Dominating the room with its dark brown walls, Japanese red ceiling, paint work and Japanese red lacquer floor were four antique red lacquer Japanese screens. To further complement the surroundings I had a set of eight Regency style dining chairs sprayed in a matching red and upholstered in the same red velvet as the lavishly draped curtains. Here, the pièce de résistance could only have been the circular dining table of faux tortoiseshell and polished chrome; a replica of the table I had designed for one of my more adventurous clients.

The Study-cum-Television Room: Taking a lead from the lambrequin in the main entrance I had the room painted in the same terracotta as used for the binding. DH had partly fitted out the room with full height bookshelves which, along with the remainder woodwork, I had repainted white. The sofa from Moorhawes now boasted a fitted cover in a wide deep blue and white striped linen with a pair of large comfortable armchairs upholstered in a deep blue tweed. Complementing the blue was a jumbled assortment of blue and white china I'd spotted in one of my forays to Lots Road in out-of-the-way Fulham. (Lots Road would go on to become one of the most sought-after addresses in London with the magnificent Chelsea Harbour Design Centre attracting visitors from all over the world.) The collection contained a mishmash of blue and white patterned plates, jugs, toby jugs, furniture rests, platters, mugs, tureens and in pride of place a splendid blue and white chamber pot.

The Back Room or Garden Room and eventual Pool Room: Remembering Oliver Messel's wall at Maddox covered in a variety of zany framed mirrors I spent several happy hours in Portobello Road market where - in addition to a few more pieces of blue and white china - I bought a boot-load of cheap picture frames. These I painted in a white gloss before carting them along to the Sander Mirror Company where they were fitted with individual pieces of mirror. The finished items were then positioned on the newly painted emerald green walls. Because I was planning for a swimming pool to replace the former back lawn I had the floor tiled in a wild pink, green and white tile manufactured by Franco Pecchioli. A set of white painted wrought iron dining chairs and table with cushions upholstered in a green and pink on white pattern fabric completed the setting.

The Master Bedroom otherwise known as "The Fuckery": In a tongue-in-cheek tribute to Ben I had the room painted in a mustard colour. "At long last I can finally say I'm sleeping with Ben Colman," I quipped. Complementing the mustard was a bold geometric design in mustard, spinach green and burgundy tweed fabric from David and Dash. Not to be outdone by anything down stairs the pièce de résistance to the room was a life size black cast iron pooch snoozing comfortably in front of the white marble fireplace. Another feature to thank DH for!

The Drawing Room: In readiness for its transformation into a Naples yellow and milk chocolate haven with its white ceiling, cornice and woodwork, the drab, celadon green coloured room stood empty apart from the dust sheeted carpet and a couple of stepladders.

*

"Hello!" I called from the where I stood in the doorway clutching the replenished ice bucket.

Replying with a cheerful "Hello Robin" DH turned to give a helping hand to the scrawny, dishevelled figure clambering down from the high passenger seat.

Christ Hicks, I thought, *a human praying mantis no less! Where on* earth *do you find them?*

"Robin, meet Andy Warhol," said my landlord with a Cheshire cat type smile.

Doing a double take I quickly stepped forward and took hold of Andy Warhol's limply proffered hand. "Welcome to The Grove Mr Warhol," I said staring at the living legend with disbelief.

"Andy; it's Andy," he replied in a ghost-like whisper.

"We're all sitting in the usual place on the side lawn," I informed DH. I held up the ice bucket. "In anticipation," I added with a light laugh.

"Here, let me take that," suggested DH reaching for the ice bucket. "I've already told Andy about your er . . . colourful machinations etcetera to some of the rooms so why don't you give him a guided tour and I'll go and introduce myself to your other guests."

"Fine," I replied handing over the ice bucket. Turning to Andy Warhol who stood staring at the busy doves and dovecote as if they were a group of aliens and their spaceship hovering above the neatly clipped lawn, I said cheerfully, "Er . . . Andy . . . if you'd care to follow me . . ."

A solemn-faced Andy Warhol dutifully followed me into the entrance hall where I proudly pointed out the large Sandra Blow painting, the Victorian school chairs, the Ben West sculpture and the row of steel shoe lasts marching up the stairs. All of which he acknowledged with a slight nodding of his blond haystack-like head. *Tell me he doesn't look* exactly *like one of those nodding dogs you see perched in the rear window of those cheapo cars?* I thought with an inward snicker.

Smiling discreetly at my wit I went on to show him the red lacquer dining room, the terracotta study-cum-television room and the garden room. *Forget upstairs*, I thought. *A, I need a drink and B, I don't think Mr Warhol is interested in seeing anything else. Anything at all.*

As we re-entered the main hall Andy pointed to the double doors leading to the drawing room. "What goes on in there?" he asked in another sepulchral whisper.

"Oh, that leads to the drawing room, Andy," I said matter-of-factly, "I haven't done anything to it as yet. The painters are due to start on Monday but please have a look . . ."

I pushed open the doors and ushered him in to the room.

Andy Warhol stood staring contemplatively at the large, shadowy room with its sad-looking celadon green walls and dust sheeted floor. After a long silence he turned to me and said in a conspiratorial whisper. "Now this I like."

A year later, accompanied by Ben, I visited Andy at his studio in New York and found the large complex more quirky than mind blowing. Contrary to what Ben went on to tell everyone I did not say - and I repeat - I did *not* say to the artist, "I'm a great admirer of your work Andy but I must confess now - whenever I see a tin of baked beans - I have a great inkling to fart."

*

During our visit Ben couldn't help asking Andy what he thought about the work of the "new boy on the block" - a certain Robert Mapplethorpe. Andy Warhol's response was a distinct farting noise (I repeat - a distinct farting noise) which would have made a warehouse of baked beans proud.

"Eek Mumsie," said Ben as we searched for a cab in Washington Square, "Obviously Mr Warhol and Mr Mapplethorpe don't quite see eye to eye."

"Or lens to lens," I quipped.

At that stage Mapplethorpe's famous photograph *Man in a Polyester Suit* depicting a gigantic black uncircumcised cock dangling limply from the man's fly had not appeared but several of his startling black male nudes were already known. When the book containing the photograph of the sleeping cock finally appeared I immediately bought a copy for Ben. Ben's reply was a cheerful "Eek, many thanks Mumsie. Pity you couldn't have arranged for Milton Moore, the cock's owner, to *hand* it over to me personally. Never mind, another time with another Milton perhaps?"

I too became a great admirer of Robert Mapplethorpe; something Ben would mischievously remind me of in a most definite "Benedict-like way" a few years later.

*

Sue and Bryan could not stop laughing when told of Andy Warhol's reaction to the room "not blessed with the RA touch".

After the laughter had died down Bryan sashayed across to the kitchenette to prepare "three much needed Screwdrivers" while Sue began to sort through the telephone messages left on the Friday evening and during the weekend.

"This one sounds a goody," she murmured. "A message left by an Arab gentleman on Saturday. He's recently bought a country estate and, having been told of our lord and master's prodigious talent - my words, not his, so please sir can I have a raise? - feels the aforesaid S and M, oops Freudian slip there, I meant L and M, is the only soul who can change an antiquated heap of Tudor hoo-ha into an Arabian Nights type palace. Or words to that effect; my Arabic being somewhat rusty."

"Do Arabs with delusions of grandeur ever sound 'goody' or even good?" I said cynically remembering how one furniture retailer had recently had his fingers burned by a wealthy Arab reneging on the final payment. "Did he happen to mention the whereabouts of this fantasy palace?"

"Somewhere in deepest Sussex as opposed to the Sahara," laughed Sue. "What's interesting is that he mentioned Richard Reynolds who, in fact, was the person who recommended you when he heard the Sheik of Wannabe was looking for an interior designer."

"Did he leave his name?"

"Yes indeed. It's a bit of a mouthful but at least he had the courtesy to spell it."

"Right. Let me give Richard a call and see if the name rings any bells. Preferably not of the alarm type."

Richard's response to my query was a dismissive, "One can never be sure in such matters but as he knows my boss I'd assume everything's above board."

Sue went about arranging a meeting with the client's "spokesperson".

"Why not the client himself?" I asked.

"Apparently he's out of the country and has left everything to his second-in-command," said Sue.

I duly visited the house accompanied by Gordon, the newest member of the RAD team. After several more meetings involving the requisite contractors, schemes and estimates were prepared followed by sketches and colour boards. Two weeks later I made the presentation.

*

"That's certainly a hefty deposit cheque we're asking for," commented Sue as she slipped the invoice into an envelope.

"Ah, but the zillion dollar question," rasped Bryan. "Will he or won't he?"

"As long as his cheque isn't one of the magic carpet kind," quipped Gordon.

Two days later the deposit cheque arrived and project "Sheik of Araby" began.

"It's certainly going to be quite something," I said to Sue after Gordon and I had returned from one of out twice weekly site visits."

"And so it should when you take into account all those glittering sheik shekels," laughed Sue.

"Ah, but remember," rasped Bryan, "all that glisters is not necessary gold. It's only when one has received the final payment can you start counting your chickens."

"Trust our token ladyship to muddle up even the most simple of riddles," I said with a snicker.

*

Having spent the previous Christmas on St. Lucia and still not come to terms with DLL's untimely death I was determined to avoid a festive Christmas at all costs.

By this stage Maggie and Peter had divorced (no surprise there!) with Peter moving to Bangkok in another step up the promotional ladder. When I lunched with him on one of his brief visits to London I had been given an open invitation to come and stay.

Why not take Peter up on his offer and spend a few days in the Far East? I thought. *Spend a few days in Bangkok and Hong Kong and maybe a week in Mitzi Gaynor land getting 'high' on beautiful Bali?*

The idea seeing me discreetly warbling the opening chords to the popular *Bali Ha'i* from the Rodgers and Hammerstein film version of *South Pacific.*

It was great fun to catch up with Peter I Bangkok and see the former Rita Raj enjoying himself in his new role as Missy Bangkok Belle. Peter gave a formal dinner party in my honour, the lavish dinner taking place in a magnificent bungalow befitting his newly elevated status within the company he worked for and *nothing* to do with his new title!

After dinner and all due to the nagging insistence of one particular fey young guest named Jeremy (touches of Lady Dee) Peter reluctantly arranged for us to visit a sex show at some sleazy club in downtown Bangkok. We were greeted with the standard cloak and dagger scenario associated with such dubious establishments by a small shutter opening in the forbidding-looking door to reveal a yellowed, bloodshot slanted eye. Explaining we were a group of "feelthy Englishmen wishing to see the sex show" (Peter's words, not mine) we found ourselves admitted to a dank, dismal bar which I later described to Ben as "pure Somerset Maugham" with the bar's Miss Sadie Thompson transmogrified into our wizened Chinese doorman-cum-greeter who, on closer examination appeared to be not only ancient but "positively oozing with decay".

Clutching our drinks we following our shuffling "Miss Sadie" up a dimly lit narrow staircase and into a dingy room with three wooden benches facing a large uninviting mattress covered in a tatty fabric which could best be described as a "marbleised"; the so-called stage lit by two archaic spotlights hanging precariously from the sagging ceiling.

"Sit! Sit!" squeaked the little Chinaman pointing to one of the benches, "Shlow soon start! Shlow soon start!

I sat staring in disbelief and the frantic happenings taking place on the so-called stage. Giving Peter a sidelong glance I was met by a mischievous wink and a discreet nod in the direction of a wide-eyed Jeremy seated next to our host. In the middle of one particularly energetic coupling involving a sweating Sumo wrestler lookalike grimly holding on to a frantic wing-flapping, squawking chicken the little Chinaman suddenly leapt to his sandaled feet shrieking "Stlop show! Stlop show! English man wanna join in! English man wanna join in!"

"Not true! Not true!" cried a startled Jeremy, "I simply asked for another gin!"

*

I found Bali to be infested by nothing more than groups of drunken Australians; a hint of things to come with the eventual onslaught of mass tourism. Though a beautiful island I had to admit I found the place to be already showing the effects of this careless invasion with litter already beginning to desecrate even the most hallowed of sites.

From Bali I flew on to Hong Kong where I stayed at the world-renowned Peninsula Hotel. As with New York I fell in love with this glowing Pearl of the Orient. A highlight of my stay was an introduction through David Hicks to the charming Charlotte Horstmann, a prestigious antique dealer and owner of one of the most spellbinding shops on the planet.

In retrospect I have to admit my overall reaction to the break as a whole was unfair due to the recurring image of DLL accompanying me never far from my mind and knowing the fun times we would have enjoyed together.

*

On my return to London I soon found myself back in the swing of things. First on the "must do" list was a visit with Gordon to the "Sheik of Araby" site and I was delighted with the project in general.

"A fucking triumph, Gordon," I enthused on entering the house strangely silent due to the last the tradesmen involved having finally left the site. "A fucking triumph and well done you. Unlike the other Gordon not only did you keep your head you also managed to survive this other Khartoum! Ten out of ten for introducing that unexpected stipple of various blues to the master bedroom cupboards. As for your other special touches here and there. Bravo!"

"I was really worried as to you reaction, RA," replied Gordon with a nervous laugh. "I can assure you - and Sue will bear me out - the whole job and the responsibility you put my way has seen me on tenterhooks since day one."

"C'mon Gordon, you *know* it looks bloody terrific and what's more such innovations were exactly what I expected from you. And not only here.

414

Take that Jackson Pollock-like splatter to Mandy L's bathroom for example. She's never been the same since but in the nicest possible way!"

We made our slowly through the rest of the house making a final check of the various rooms.

"As you can see our invisible client could move in at any time," said Gordon proudly. "Asif, his spokesperson or second-in-command, will be here on Monday along with a horde of serfs including a housekeeper, major domo and several maids."

"Hopefully the housekeeper will make sure the place is kept up to the high standard it deserves." I said casting my eye around the sumptuous drawing room. "This looks great, really great. What's more we should have the whole house photographed before it becomes shop or - ha ha - sheik soiled."

"I'll get on to Asif immediately we get back," said Gordon.

"Lucky Asif," I muttered.

"I didn't mean it like *that*, RA," giggled Gordon, his face reddening.

"Much more important, is Araby's final invoice ready?"

"Ready and waiting and if you are happy with what you've seen I'll give Sue the green light *before* getting on to Asif," grinned Gordon.

"Go ahead." I said. "Green it most certainly is and make sure it catches tonight's post. Despite a second substantial payment on account I have a nasty feeling we should have asked for a third payment prior to the final invoice regardless of the fact Araby is a friend of Richard Reynolds' boss. My fault really."

On Monday afternoon Gordon received a call from Asif telling how impressed he was with the whole project. He also informed Gordon the sheik would be "taking up residence" the following weekend.

"I trust you received our final invoice?" said Gordon before hanging up.

"This has already been passed on to the accounts department," replied Asif in what Gordon would later describe as a "suspiciously silky voice".

*

"Any sign of Araby's cheque for the balance owed?" I asked Sue.

"Not a dicky."

"But it's over a week since it was sent," I said sharply. "Please ask Gordon to give that Asif character a ring and see what the holdup is. Christ Sue," I added softly, "we're talking big bucks here. Around seventy grand if I remember correctly?"

"Seventy two thousand, three hundred to be exact," replied Sue (a whopping £577,633.20p in today's terms), *excluding* VAT which sees an additional eight percent on top of the figure I've just given you. In other words a further . . ."

"I get it," I interrupted angrily, my mind racing, "a further five thousand plus. Fucking hell!" (The standard rate of VAT at the time set at eight percent as opposed to twenty per cent today.)

*

"Shit," grunted Gordon giving me a nervous glance, "all I keep getting is a sodding answering machine saying there's nobody available to take the call."

"Have you tried the house in the country?" I snapped.

"Same thing."

"Jesus," I muttered. "This is all we fucking well need. I'm calling Richard."

"It's nothing to do with me, RA," growled Richard when I expressed my concern at not being able to reach either the Sheik or his spokesperson Asif.

"What about your boss?" I said in exasperation, "Surely he must know the whereabouts of the guy? After all he bloody well recommended him!"

"I'll certainly mention it but I'm pretty sure his response will be the same as mine." Richard gave a snigger. "However, when all is said and done and when it comes to mon - or mon-ey - he is not, in any way, his brother's keeper." With a sarcastic "Say hello to Sue for me" he hung up.

Two days later I had a meeting with Marten Bayer, my solicitor. Talk about the proverbial hitting the fan. Adding further insult to injury was finding out the actual owner of the property to be an offshore company registered in the Caymans: the aforesaid company claiming they knew nothing about any contract between RAD and the mysterious sheik. Although we were able to salvage the majority of items supplied I remembered a saying I once heard, "When desperate to sell be prepared for a vast difference between the selling price and the original buying price". How right this foreteller of gloom and doomed turned out to be with RAD failing to recoup nothing more than a paltry twenty percent of the monies owed.

Assuring my deeply concerned and loyal team there was "nothing to worry about" I escaped to The Grove where I planned to spend a solitary, soul-searching weekend. As a result I spent most of Saturday sitting at the dining room table armed with a calculator, a note pad and juggling figures as I went time and time through reams of trade invoices. "Let's be frank RA," I muttered to the silent room, "it's not what you'd like to do but what you *have* to do."

I have always been a firm believer in the mantra "don't delay; do it now" which meant my first undertaking was to telephone DH at Britwell House and ask if could call by for a drink and a "business talk" later that afternoon or else anytime Sunday.

DH arranged to drive over before lunchtime on Sunday. After serving him a large G and T I laid my cards on the table revealing the unexpected turn of events and my sad decision of having to give up The Grove. DH could not have been more understanding and to my immense surprise told me he and Lady Pamela were contemplating giving up Britwill House and moving to The Grove plus they were already planning to discuss such a move with me and hopefully come to some "amicable arrangement".

Although I had been having serious doubts before I now had the feeling perhaps some mystical soul up there could have a liking for me after all!

*

I returned to London the same evening my mind made up. I would close RAD and go it alone. "No longer banker for another fucking wanker," I murmured as I drew up in the side street next to Albion Gate. "From now on it's going be a consultation fee and a handling charge with *all* selected items purchased direct from the supplier on a pro forma basis. This will apply to all other trades such as upholsterers, curtain makers and carpet manufacturers. In other words, if the client doesn't pay upfront, the client doesn't get. So tough shit. But once bitten, once *very* fucking shy."

Sitting in my all black Mini Cooper I stared up at the side of the impressive building and the side windows to my penthouse. "Sorry my friend, you've been greater than great," I added hollowly, "but sadly all good things come to an end. In other words, you and I have no choice but to say goodbye."

Next day I arrived at the office well ahead of the others and by nine thirty had made an appointment to see Brian Pearl, my accountant followed by a later appointment at Albion Gate with an estate agent friend. By lunchtime RAD no longer existed and my Albion Gate penthouse was on the market.

Having made these two momentous decisions I now faced the uncomfortable task of explaining my actions to the RAD team.

"How fortuitous," rasped Bryan, "seeing I was about to hand in my notice *anyway.*" Giving me a disdainful look he unfurled himself from his chair. "May as well pack up now I suppose and, if it's not *too* much trouble I'd like to make a last phone call." Ignoring my startled look he reached for the telephone on his desk and dialled a number. "Hello?" he squawked. "Mr Larkin here, *the* Mr Larkin who's about to join your company as their in house designer. Is Ralph there? Yes, Ralph. Mr M's driver. He's not? No worries, I'll call him later." Bryan turned round. "Once I've put my paltry bits and pieces together I'll leave them downstairs. In the meantime I'll speak to Ralph the Morrison's driver and arrange to meet him here in order to collect my belongings and ferry them over to the offices in Tottenham Court Road. So if you'll excuse me, I'd better get packing. Ha! Ha! Ha!"

While a stunned Sue, Les, Gordon and I looked on Bryan began emptying the drawers to his desk unit and placing the contents in a small cardboard box taken from the pattern room.

After Bryan, box in hand, had sauntered down the stairs it was time to deal with the others.

Les Gabriel's reaction to the closing of RAD was a cryptic, "As long as I get paid along with some kind of compensation I couldn't give a monkey's. Anyways I was planning on going back to Aus sooner than later."

Sue, much to my surprise announced nonchalantly, "Pipped to the post RA seeing I was planning in handing in my notice at the end of the month and taking up my new position as Richard Reynolds personal secretary."

Gordon didn't say much apart from a muttered, "Like Sue I was also thinking of moving on seeing I don't think a career in interior design is quite what I'm really looking for."

Needless to say I was never to hear from Richard nor Sue again. Ben, being the loyal and tactful person he was, made sure he never inadvertently mentioned our former teammate.

Brian Pearl saw to the closing of the company accounts and with the proceeds from the sale of the Albion Gate penthouse (it was sold within a week of being put on the market) I was able to pay off any outstanding monies resulting from the ill-fated "Sheik of Araby" project.

*

With all debts appertaining to Araby cleared I decided to take a short, combined mental and energy boosting break before knuckling down on the new challenges ahead and, most important of all, the replenishing of the seriously violated Anderson coffers.

"So why not do as Coral keeps suggesting and spend a few hedonistic days in L.A?" I said to myself. "What's more there's a bank holiday coming up so I'd only be missing four working days; not that I've ever paid the slightest attention to the term 'working day' seeing - for me anyway - every day is not so much a working day but more of anoyher exciting and creative one!"

Prior to my departure Melford surprised me by saying out of the blue, "Darling, you've had a hellish time so, as an 'enjoy yourself and get yourself together gesture' please accept this." "This" being a neat pile of notes totalling a hundred pounds. To say I was flabbergasted by the unexpected gift is putting it mildly. However, the "gift" ended up with a sting in its tale as to my chagrin I kept being reminded by the likes of the supercilious Cherry Moorsom and Tracy Reed about the *thousands* Melford had given me after "your unfortunate happening". In other words an additional nought to the original two. No   mention was ever made of the many gifts ranging from expensive prints to books and elaborate coffee table books I had literally showered upon Melford in the past. Also completely overlooked was the stunning tortoiseshell and chrome dining table from The Grove along with several sofas, coffee tables, side tables, console and chairs. A few years later I also gave her a pair golden gazelle sculptures brought back from a visit to Bangkok.

From the very first moment Melford homed in on to the pair of gazelle she never stopped saying how much she coveted them and in a moment of weakness (or perhaps having been subjected to a form of "Melford Water Torture" as opposed to "Chinese water torture"), I finally gave her the pair.

As the aforementioned Bob Miller would go on to spikily say (he had never been a Melford fan), "With luck she'll trip over the gazelle instead of the *light* fantastic."

To my amusement Cherry Moorsom never forgave me for giving her "greatest friend Melford" the gazelle. "You know I've always admired them," she said petulantly.

"But what about the wooden sculpture of a rather handsome goat I brought back from India and gave to you when I moved from Scarsdale Studios to my new flat?" I replied.

"I would have much preferred the gazelle," came the muttered response.

"When it comes to being both covetous and ungrateful those two gashes take some beating," sniped Bob on hearing the latest in this "We want, we want" saga.

*

I flew out to L.A. on a Friday and returned to London the following Sunday. Coral and Vinnie entertained me royally and among their many friends, introduced to Bob Hanley, a decorator and set designer whose claim to fame - among others - was having designed the dazzling sets for film version of *Auntie Mame* starring Rosalind Russell as Mame and Coral as Vera Charles, her flamboyant sidekick.

At Bob's insistence I checked out of the Beverley Wilshire hotel and moved to his charming house in Beverley Hills. Bob proved himself to be an amusing, charming and most attentive host. He arranged a private visit to Disneyland where Mickey and Minnie Mouse personally gave me a conducted tour; much to the envy of the other sightseers. Bob also arranged for me to have a personal guided tour of the breathtaking Getty Museum.

Bob and a great friend of his, Wilbur Wright (L.A's undisputed ice cream king) laughed heartily when I regaled them with a tale involving Paul Getty's eightieth birthday party at the Dorchester hotel in London. Organised by Margaret, Duchess of Argyll, not only was I a guest but Margaret had also invited me to come up with a few simple suggestions for decorating the ballroom for the event.

A major topic of conversation in the art world at the time was Getty's extravagant purchase of a major work by the Titian, the famous Italian painter and it was Getty's acquisition of the painting which saw one of the biggest social gaffes of all time. The incident occurred when one of the guest speakers, Ian, Duke of Bedford, coming to the end of his speech glanced across at the lizard-like "birthday boy" and said in all sincerity, ". . . and when looking at Paul tonight I am sure I'm not the only one thinking of more Titians . . ."

"Darling," said Margaret on the telephone the next morning. "When Ian came out with that little bon mot *I* was the one who could have done with a mortician; not Paul!"

As a heartfelt "thank you" to Bob the first thing I did was send him an extra special present to go in a second sitting room he was in the process of adding to his house. Taking into account the highly camp log cabin-cum-rustic look Bob wished to achieve, I bought an elaborate hanging light fitting made from antlers (echoes of Chalet *Belle et Sebastien*) from Anthony Redmile and had this shipped over to L.A.

According to Bob he was "delighted and astounded" by the unexpected gift.

According to Coral "you could have knocked him over with a fucking feather boa!"

An additional highlight to my L.A. visit was a meeting with Paige Rense, Editor-in-Chief of *Architectural Digest*. I found Paige to be a lively, sparkling lovely lady who not only invited me to lunch but chauffeured me back to Bob's house in Beverley Hills where, along with Bob, we sat chatting amiably by the pool drinking Margaritas and watching the sunset over L.A.

During lunch Paige and I discussed various RA projects past and present. Paige was particularly interested in doing a feature on my work to The Grove.

"I had enormous fun doing it up," I told her reaching for my briefcase, "and as you would expect I had a perfectly prepared canvas - read layout - on which to daub a kaleidoscope of my favourite colours which in turn served as vibrant backgrounds for various lovingly collected bits and pieces."

I handed Paige a folder holding a selection of coloured photographs specially taken by the well-known local photographer Julian Alyson, showing interior shots of The Grove plus a photograph so several colourful doves posed (and poised) around the dovecot.

"The rooms are a real potpourri of everything *I* like and *I* enjoy," I explained selfishly pointing to the metal shoe lasts climbing the stairs. "Take the staircase leading up to the bedrooms. A stairway to whatever turns you on perhaps?"

After a few minutes of carefully studying the photographs Paige said the magic words. "We'd love to a feature on The Grove. May I hold on to these?"

"Of course, Paige. And better still, as soon as I get back to London I'll get a set of transparencies expressed off to you."

The transparencies were sent but, to be quite honest, with all going on, The Grove and *Architectural Digest* found themselves well and truly confined to a back shelf.

Several weeks after my return I received a letter from Paige Rense in which she apologised profusely at the magazine's decision not to run the proposed feature on RA and The Grove. The reason? David Hicks was "up in arms" at the effrontery of his property being used as a background for some other designer's "so-called schemes or designs". His indignation perhaps fired up even more when told there would have been no mention of his name in the article.

Taking into account the time difference I called Paige later in the day saying I quite understood her dilemma and not to worry. I have to say I did find DH's reaction a tad unfounded but as I said to a bemused Ben, "A long awaited stab in the back no doubt after my faux pas all those years ago in merry Malta!"

Obviously someone must have mentioned the possibility of the forthcoming feature to DH. In retrospect, had they not, the repercussions could have been formidable. As in the case of John Siddeley another example of "Hell hath no fury as a JS spurned" perhaps? On this occasion, the JS being superimposed by a querulous DH.

During a chance meeting with DH a few weeks after receiving Page's letter I didn't even bother to refer to the incident and vice versa. Despite of what I referred to as The A.D. (*Drammatico Incidente*), DH, I am pleased to say remained a friend until his death in the late nineties.

*

Once again the gods seemed to smiling down on me. Through a contact introduced by Georgina Halse I ended up renting a spectacular studio, part of the Scarsdale Studios, a lavish complex of impressive artists' studios set in a small, private enclave off the Scarsdale Road in Kensington. "Talk about déjà vu," said to Ben, "Scarsdale Studios being literally round the corner from where it all began. Number 91a Abingdon Road."

The large studio was on three levels. A small, ground floor entrance hall with a narrow staircase led up to a landing, a generous L-shaped kitchen, bathroom and the main studio; a towering edifice with a set of enormous, sloping windows. A further staircase wound up to another small landing serving a bedroom which boasted a small terrace positioned on top of the archway guarding the entrance to the main studio complex itself.

The shorter angle to the L-shaped kitchen with its A-frame glass topped trestle table serving as my desk, an electric typewriter (no computers as yet in the seventies), a telephone and a fling cabinet firmly established itself as a perfect work area.

As if ordained the large paintings purchased for The Grove fitted in perfectly. These paintings included the colourful Sandra Blow, two large canvasses by John Hubbard and a painting by Anne Madden. I presented an ecstatic Melford with the chrome and tortoiseshell dining table and in return I found myself presented with a ropey gas log fire for the studio's large stone fireplace which, on a rare occasion, could be seen to bravely splutter and flicker. Much to my amusement Melford would always tell her intrigued guests that *she* had designed the stylish dining table; this from someone whose idea of design - judging from the limited amount of her work I had seen - appeared to consist mainly of a few mirrors, one or two planters and an abundant use of an inexpensive green and white patterned fabric!

In addition to her attributes as an interior decorator (as opposed to a designer) had there had been a cinematic award for "A Tribute To Walter Mitty" performance Melford would surely have been among the nominees. On being told she was starring in *The Greek Tycoon*, a film made in 1978 starring Anthony Quinn and Jacqueline Bisset and loosely based on the relationship between Onassis and Jacqueline Kennedy, Ben and I dutifully traipsed along to the local Odeon to view Melford in her exciting and exacting role.

As Ben so succinctly said during dinner afterwards, "Eek Mumsie! Had we blinked we could have easily missed Madam in the line-up of guests waiting to meet Jackie on her arrival to *The Good Ship Lolly Flop!*" (With emphasis on the word "lolly"!)

I sadly returned the four Japanese screens from the dining room at The Grove to art dealer Johnny (Janet) McCullough on the off chance he would be able to find another buyer. Three weeks later he rang to say he had found not only a buyer but thanks to the revised price on the screens there was even a small commission for me. To compensate for the loss of the four screens I regrouped all the framed mirrors from the Garden Room on either side of the fireplace resulting in a wonderful splintered play of reflected light.

All in all I found the studio an exciting combination of The Grove, Albion Gate and Moorhawes. When asked to describe my new home I would simply say "hectic eclectic".

*

My concerns about "going it alone" proved to be unfounded. Thanks to Lita Young, Barbara Eppel, Anne Katz and a host of other loyal clients it was as if the floodgates had opened. As the three wily ladies had inferred, most people were much happier paying me a generous consultation fee and settling with all the trades people direct. The net result? I was happy and my clients were happy.

Not only did I find myself with a queue of new clients eager to "meet RADC" I also found myself undertaking projects completely alien to the refurbishment of a proper. I have already mentioned

Margaret, D of A's birthday ball for Paul Getty's eightieth and soon on the heels of this "milestone" was a request to create a theme for a popular charity event, The Berkeley Square Ball. This saw me transforming the leafy 18th-century Mayfair Square sans nightingale into a lavish set fit for *Kismet*. Having been a great fan of Vincente Minnelli's colourful film plus having previously entertained Dolores Gray who starred as the sultry Lalume to drinks at Albion Gate, the transformation of the Square to exotic Bagdad in the times of *The Arabian Nights* seemed to me an obvious choice.

Despite the atrocious weather the ball turned out to be a resounding success. Having been forewarned as to a possible deluge "on the night" the organisers and myself made sure there were more marquees set up than usual; the marquees being linked by a pattern of what the American's call boardwalks. I had each marquee tented in a filmy gold fabric (courtesy of Mickey Sekers) and instead of upholstered seating units I used wrought iron garden furniture suitably draped and swagged in a variety of brightly patterned fabrics.

On witnessing the success of the Ball I couldn't help saying to one of the happy guests, "Obviously Dolores Gray knew what she was doing in *Kismet* when she began warbling the hit song *Not Since Nineveh!*"

"Dolores Gray?" exclaimed the guest, "Why I *adore* Dolores Gray! Don't tell me you've actually met her?"

"I have indeed," I replied with faux modesty, "A few of years ago when she came for a drink to my Albion Gate apartment with a couple of show bizzy guys I know."

"And?" said the guest.

"And?" I echoed. "Oh, was she anything like she appears on screen? To be quite honest all I can remember of her visit was her saying what clever hinges I'd used on the full-height doors throughout."

Yes, I thought seeing the look of disappointment on the partygoer's face, *not a word about my fabulous décor but a continual ooing and aahing over the fucking elongated piano hinges instead.*

Another unexpected request was to "introduce an eighties feel" for a ball held in a private palazzo in Venice for a charming friend of DLL's, a wealthy *Principessa Mimi* followed by an unpronounceable surname. To give the *Principessa's* palazzo its due any attempt to enhance the splendiferous building could only be described as "a piece of *torta*" or cake.

Determined not to interfere with the 18th-century interiors I simply introduced a load of carefully positioned uplighters and standing lamps in order to highlight the magnificent *trompe l'oeil* work and tapestries.

To add a touch of RA whimsy I "borrowed" three gondolas, two of which were set up in the ballroom and one in the main drawing room. These I had filled with towering dried branches sprayed gold and bedecked with twinkling white fairy lights. All the Adonis-like waiters (handpicked by the *Principessa* and RA; a formidable task) were blacked up and dressed to look like Blackamoors while the waitresses were draped in virginal white skirts and bikini tops à la a modest Venus de Milo.

Assolutamente meraviglioso! (Absolutely marvellous!)

*

"Is that Robin Anderson Design Consultant?" drawled a gravelly voice.

"Speaking."

"Splendid," said the voice; a delicious combination of Satchmo meets Bacall. "The name's Annie Sunley. Sunshine - my hubby John - and I would like to meet you as soon as poss. We own a house off Eaton Square and having seen David and Lita Young's fabulous apartment overlooking Regent's Park - David is an associate of Sunshine's - we'd simply *love* you to design this for us."

(Annie would go on to become a close friend and when she and Sunshine, heir to the Bernard Sunley building and property empire divorced, I would go on to design two more spectacular houses for her.)

Through Sunshine I was introduced to another property developer named John Law. I was commissioned to design several show flats for "Johnny!" - he always introduced himself as if accompanied by an exclamation mark - who in turn was to introduce me to yet another "property whiz" who had been "completely bowled over by your work, RA!"

Dealings with Annie and Sunshine were never dull and their enthusiasm for my designs knew no bounds. Our meetings were always the greatest of fun and their enthusiasm for my adventurous ideas further complemented by endless flutes of "celebratory bubbly".

Hot on Annie's Manolo Blahnik heels came Barbara Eppel's husband, Leonard, another property developer and owner of the prestigious Arrowcroft Group. I was delighted when I was asked by Leonard to design the company's new offices in Mayfair's exclusive Mount Street.

"Will it never end?" I said to my nook of an office and adding a muttered "I sincerely hope not!" I reached for the jangling phone and was greeted by a cheerful "Robin its Lita" before I had a chance to speak.

"There's a divine couple I'd like you meet," she continued breezily. "Their names are David and Jenny Harris and they've just bought a flat overlooking Regent's Park close to the Zoo. Is there a chance you could meet them - I'll make sure I'm also there - later this week?"

"How about Thursday morning around eleven?"

"I'll check with Jenny and if all's well get right back to you with the address." trilled Lita, "If she and David can't manage Thursday I'll get her to suggest an alternative day and time." With a perfunctory goodbye she hung up.

David Harris, a dapper City type and Jenny his wife a dark-haired beauty who owned a travel agency, could not stop raving about David and Lita Young's Regent's Park apartment.

"Though *our* flat isn't nearly as grand as their duplex I do think, being on the sixth floor we certainly have the better view," said Jenny with a mischievous grin.

A few months after the completion of work to the flat I telephoned Jenny. "Did you know you have a copycat?" I asked her.

"Copycat?" repeated Jenny, "What do you mean?"

"A rather raucous woman named Tootsie," I replied with a snicker.

"Tootsie?" said Jenny sharply. "David and I don't know a woman named Tootsie and to my knowledge no one of that name has ever been here."

"I'm referring to the film Jenny; the new film starring Dustin Hoffman." I said with a chuckle, "Should you and David go and see the film - named *Tootsie* after Hoffman's character - you will also see what I mean . . ."

"Go on," interrupted Jenny somewhat sarcastically, "the suspense is killing me!"

"The sofas spotted in several shots are covered in the same fabric as selected for the two sofas in your place!"

"Wow and double wow," said Jenny dryly. "But sorry to disappoint you Robin, our sofas don't 'do' autographs!"

"Pity," I muttered. "Those fans waiting downstairs *will* be disappointed."

"Such is life, Robin," replied Jenny cheerfully, "but strange that you should telephone for David and I were just talking about you. Could you hold on a minute and I'll go and fetch him." She gave a chuckle. "It's his turn to cook dinner tonight so he's deeply immersed in Robert Carrier at the moment."

"Robin? Hi! I was going to give you are call in the morning as I have another project which I'm hoping you will be able to help me with."

"I'm listening David; I'm listening!"

"I'm now the proud owner of a stud . . . sorry, what's that Jen?" David gave a chuckle. "Jenny has just called out 'not that sort of stud' so I'd better explain." He added with a laugh. "A *horse* stud up at Newmarket in Suffolk. I don't know if you are into horses - oops, Freudian slip there - but my new pride and joy after Jenny I hasten to add - is a horse named Kalaglow. Ring any bells?"

"No David, but before you go any further the answer is a resounding 'yes'. Doing a makeover on a stud sounds like a wet dream come - ha ha - true so how could I possibly refuse?"

"The stud is called the Brook Stud and should you have a free day next week perhaps we could meet up there."

"Give me a second, David, and I'll just check the diary. Did you have a specific day in mind?"

"Friday if you could manage it. This means Jenny could also join us as there's a cottage which will need the RA touch as well as one or two outbuildings."

"Friday it is," I said. "Now, directions on how to get there."

"I'd offer to give you a lift but we'll be leaving on Thursday afternoon so it'll have to be by train if you don't mind."

"Not at all David as I no doubt will be making many more such journeys so fire away."

*

I am slightly jumping the gun here by mentioning Bob Miller who comes into his own in the next section. However, one must bear with me while I describe an incident which took place involving the already mentioned Mr Miller of Dodo Bird and eventual Park West fame.

As soon as I got off the phone to David Harris I called Bob Miller. "Guess what Bob," I said excitedly, "Not only have I just been commissioned to design a stud but a rampant Arab stallion named Kalaglow as well. How about *that*?"

"Do you need an assistant?" quipped Bob. "I can always take a few days off from Louisville!"

"Are you mad? Kalaglow and the stud are strictly in *my* hands," I said with a chortle. "However, if you promise to be bad, very *bad*, I'll make sure you get an invitation to meet all!"

The cottage turned out to be a charming half-timbered building with a comfortable sitting room, dining room, kitchen, guest suite and study downstairs and a spacious master bedroom comprising a dressing room, large bedroom and en suite bathroom upstairs. A distinctive feature of the master bedroom was the heavily beamed sloping ceiling. I found a delightful daisy print (even Jenny couldn't stop "oohing" and "aahing" over the design) and, to her added delight, I had the slopes between the beams painted in alternating colours taken from the fabric.

"Now you've dealt with the cottage there is someone I would like you to meet," said David, his eyes twinkling, "and who knows, he may be even more difficult to please than Jenny!"

"Christ David! Talk about scaring the bejesus out of a person! I'm already shaking in my Guccis at the thought! The name of this terrifying person?"

"The one and only Kalaglow," said David proudly.

"No wonder this stud fees are so astronomical," I said to David as I stood waiting to be introduced to the dashing, dark grey stallion, "what an amazing animal and so polite," the word "polite" following Kalaglow's gracious tossing of his handsome head in acknowledgement of my presence.

"Kalaglow has requested you take a look at his stable," continued David. "Knowing how delighted Jenny and I are with the work carried out on the cottage he is adamant his stable receives the same attention."

"But of course," I replied, "now, if I may have a moment to stand here and look at my new client's rather Spartan stable plus have a few words in private ..."

"Please do," murmured David. "And may I suggest an apple? Kalaglow is rather partial to an apple."

"A good chat?" asked David with a grin when I joined him and a groom a few minutes later.

"Brilliant," I replied, "Kalaglow giving a whinny of approval at the suggestion I decorate his stable in his racing colours." I gave a chuckle. "However he did neigh a mane tossing *nay* when I suggested coloured hoofs to match the décor!"

True to my word I invited Bob to join me on one of my visits to the stud while supervising the work on Kalaglow's stable and several nearby offices. To my surprise Bob and Kalaglow did not appear to see eye to eye with the horse attempting to nip a terrified Bob on his shoulder as they stood warily surveying each other across the paddock railings.

"Horrible horse!" squawked Bob leaping nimbly aside and grabbing hold of my arm as if I was some burly bodyguard.

"Blame it on that yellow sweater you're wearing," I jeered pushing him away. "Don't tell me you're surprised he mistook you for some marauding daffodil invading his turf?"

"And there I was thinking he was smiling at me," sniffed Bob, "when all the time he was *sneering*!" He gave Kalaglow a glare. "And may I say Mr Horrible Horse, if you think I look like a bloody daffodil then you look like a bloody seaside donkey!"

As David had suggested we stay overnight at the cottage Bob and I (Bob having downed several recuperative whiskies and me several glasses of Pinot Grigio) duly walked along to the Red Lion pub for dinner. On Bob's insistence we have "one for the road - maybe even two' - before returning to the cottage we seated ourselves next to the bar where Bob immediately struck up a conversation with a local apparently the worse for wear and whom I swear must have been a close relative to Judy Garland's Scarecrow in *The Wizard of Oz*; even to the hayseeds in his hair.

On my return from a visit to the Gents I found Bob sitting alone, his friendly Scarecrow having decided to stagger off into the night.

"I appreciate you're well-known for you lapses in your lustings Bob," I said with a snicker, "but surely a scarecrow's a tad desperate?"

"At least he was sympathetic when I told him of how I was nearly cannibalised by a horse at the nearby Brook Stud this afternoon," hissed Bob.

"At least you had the decency to say a horse at the Brook Stud as opposed as opposed to a donkey in Tijuana," I replied silkily.

"Bitch!" growled Bob.

"Tacky hayride" I snickered in reply.

Back at the cottage Bob suggested a final nightcap before "hitting the hay"; his comment followed by a combination of hiccups and giggles.

"Did you hear something?" I said a few minutes later. "A crash or something falling?"

"Country noises," slurred Bob. He gave another giggle. "Give me the city anytime; exhaust fumes being so much more attractive than country noises and your bloody country air." He gave a yawn. "Excuse me for a mo while I go and have a pee."

"Meanwhile I'm about to make myself a mug of Cocoa; you game? You obviously need it when one takes into account the *straw* you were quite happy to clutch back at the Red Lion."

"Robin," rasped Bob in a hoarse whisper from the doorway to the kitchen.

"Won't be a sec," I said over my shoulder, "I'm just waiting for the milk to heat up."

"He's here," added Bob in a strangulated voice. "In our bed; in the guestroom."

"Who's here in our bed? *Goldilocks*?" I sniped as I lifted the saucepan from the hob.

"The Strawman from the pub. That crashing sound must have been him breaking the window and now he's spread-eagled on the bed; stark, bollock naked!" His face breaking into a mischievous grin, Bob adopted a somewhat unsteady Mae West hand-on-the-hip pose and added with a drawl, "An' honey, is that a haystack layin' between ya legs or are you jest pleased to see me!"

"You *are* joking?" I said placing the saucepan on the draining board. "Tell me you're joking."

"Unfortunately Robin, I'm not," said Bob who appeared to have sobered up rapidly.

"Jesus Bob, we'd better go and check on our unexpected guest so lead on Macduff!"

Bob and I stood staring at the snoring man.

"Hmm, I see what you mean by a haystack between his legs," I muttered. "Definitely more haystack than hayseed but somehow I think this is a clear-cut case - or in his case uncut - of *not* making hay whether the sun shines or not!"

"Hear! Hear!" agreed Bob nodding solemnly in agreement.

"So, let sleeping haystacks lie," I said softly, "and though it is taking a bit of a liberty, we'll simply have to make do with the master bedroom upstairs.

We tip-toed back to the kitchen and drank our Cocoa, leaving the unwashed mugs in the sink.

Leaving Bob snoring softly I sneaked downstairs to check on our intruder, my mind in turmoil as to what I may discover. Would the young man have burgled or worse still, trashed the downstairs rooms? To my immense relief I found the guestroom intact and the bed neatly made. Imagine my surprise on finding our two mugs rinsed and neatly placed on the kitchen table along with a crudely printed note on a sheet of kitchen towelling. *Sorry bout winder,* I read, *you guys very nice. Did we do anyfink? Love. Ted. XX.*

"Obviously I must be losing my touch, allure or whatever," snickered Bob on reading Ted's note. "I mean if Newmarket's answer to *A Nightmare on Elm Street* can't remember a night - however unfulfilled - in the company of the one and only Bob Miller I may as well give up!"

Maybe a combination of Kalaglow and the Strawman was to blame for, much to the surprise of Steve and Ray his employers, Bob suddenly announced his decision to decamp to the States and spend a few months or more staying with a friend named Frank Messina who lived in Los Angeles. I had met Frank when he was visiting Bob and John in London and as I said to them when introduced to Frank, "Burt Reynolds meets the Marlborough Man? Who could ask for anything more?"

"John will be joining me in a few weeks' time and you should come and visit as well," he said blithely a few days before his departure. (John being his partner.)

"Why not?" I replied cheerfully, "after all it's only a couple of hundred pounds and ten hours plus away from London." After a slight pause I said as tactfully as I could, "Bob, a rather personal question but what will happen to John while you're away?"

"Oh, he'll be quite alright," came the nonchalant reply. "I'm quite sure my half of the bed at Ivor Court won't remain cold for long!"

Joking apart, I had no idea as to why Bob came up with the idea of several months in California but there was obviously method in his madness because it would almost two years' later before I was able to take him up on his invitation.

*

Further reassured by my brimming diary I flicked through the pages until I reached December. "No nostalgia for the Christmas I can never revisit so on to pastures new," I said to myself. "Somewhere *truly* over the top and doubly exotic so why not the land of the Raj and the land of the Taj?

We've done *Bali Ha'i* - not a great success - so why not *Song of India*? A quick call to Alison at Peter Lubbock Travel and heigh-ho, away RA will go!"

My return from India saw a mega change in RA's fortunes. From "treading water" my life changed to a frenzied treadmill along with the formation of a new friendship. Re-enter the mischievous and unpredictable Bob Miller.

*

Previously I had relied on the US Company of David & Dash Fabrics along with H. A. Percheron, a London-based company dealing wholly in French fabrics as sources for my distinctive designs with English companies such as Arthur Sanderson & Sons and Sekers Fabrics used for what I termed "necessary fillers in". All changed following a chance meeting with Johnny McCulloch in the King's Road; Johnny aka "Janet" being the antique dealer who had sold me the four red lacquer Japanese screens around which the scheme for the dining room at The Grove was centred.

Having heard of my various projects it took Johnny only a few seconds after his effusive greeting to ask me who was supplying the fabrics for all my new "excaiting" ventures. On being told "my usual team of tried and true suppliers" Johnny threw up his plump hands in horror and warbled in his affected Scottish accent, "But my dear RA, that will never do! I insist . . . no, make that I *demand* as from now you use *us*!"

"Us?" I echoed, "Who's 'us'? Aren't you still dealing in antiques?"

"Oh goodness me no," crooned Johnny, "I (pronounced "aye") preside over an exclusive fabric house as I've just insisted . . . nay . . . *demanded* . . . from now onwards you order *all* your fabrics through my ("may") company and you'll never look back!"

I stood staring at the large Hattie Jacques (male version) lookalike. *Jesus Janet*, I thought wickedly, *you were bad enough when you had your antique shop but now you've become Queen of the Fabrics you're even more grand; a major achievement to say the least.* "You now supply fabrics?" I said. "So what happened to your shop, Holbein Antiques?"

"Oh, I decided to give up the world of antiques." He gave a shriek followed by a trill. "Too much hassle for a woman of quality!"

"And the name of your er . . . illustrious company?" I asked ignoring the curious glances of passers-by at the corpulent man who stood primping his hair with one hand while waving the other regally in a parody of the real McCoy.

"The company is actually *owned* by a tiresome man named Bernard Thorp; a dilettante who, knowing he needed someone with panache and style to give his organisation a well-needed kick up its slumbering *derrière* simply begged me - and I (aye) do mean *begged* - to come to the aid of the party!" His witticism followed by an ear splitting whoop and more primping and, to my horror, a pirouette.

"You do surprise me Johnny," I said with a touch of sarcasm. "I know exactly who you mean by Bernard Thorp and from what I've heard not only has he one of the most successful businesses around." I gave a light laugh. "In fact I remember meeting Bernard Thorp when he worked with a woman called Nora Tew. Not only a devastating Edmund Purdom lookalike but a total charmer to boot!" (Edmund Purdom best known for his role as the dashing Prince Igor in MGM's *The Student Prince*.)

"Yes, I suppose some people may find him good looking," said Johnny. He added bitchily, "but as they say, beauty is in the eye of the beholder."

"So when can I come along and see your showroom?" I asked. "Or, because of you being so elusive, is a visit by appointment or invitation only?"

"Oh, if you have a minute to spare why not drop by now; meet my team and partake of a glass of wine?"

"Wine not?" I quipped, my mimicking of his exaggerated pronunciation sailing strait over the super salesman's primped head.

"Now I know exactly how Aladdin must have felt," I said to Bernard Thorp after my initial sighting of his large, airy showroom, part of an exclusive studio complex in Burnsall Street off The King's Road. I stood staring in amazement at the hangers of colourful fabrics. "And you say I could have any of these designs printed to my own colouring and likewise the weaves."

"You can indeed, RA," replied Bernard, his dark eyes twinkling. "Added to which, should you want us to supply a fabric or a weave to one of your own designs, we can make up the requisite screens or set up the looms at no extra cost."

God, I now see why you're known in the trade as Bonking Bernard, I thought mischievously. *With those looks and a body that would make Charles Atlas swoon no wonder all the ladies literally 'cum' running just as Janet McCulloch did!*

"Your wine," interrupted Johnny slamming down a tray on one of the work counters. Helping himself to a glass holding the most wine he added loftily. "So, your opinion if you please."

"My opinion?" I repeated giving Bernard a wink. "It's not so much an opinion but a question."

"Oh, and what may your question be?" asked Johnny graciously while completely ignoring Bernard.

"How soon can I open an account?"

As a result of my "bumping into Johnny" I became one of Bernard's most ardent supporters and can truthfully say I never ventured anywhere else. Even today if someone asks me who would I recommend for fabrics I immediately send them to the one and only Bernard Thorp.

TREADING WATER TO TURBULENT TREADMILL

On entering my present London apartment overlooking an elegant Square some fifty metres along from Coleherne Court where a certain Lady Diana Spencer lived before she married her prince, you walk into a red lacquer entrance hall before venturing into what I term the "Corridor of Covers" followed by a further hallway leading to my sitting room, bedroom and study; the latter aptly named "The Black Hole of All Schmutter" due to the all-black décor broken by (among other things) a dazzling collection of white ceramic plates decorated with drawings of male nudes by Jean Cocteau. A vast cantilevered black lacquer bookcase filled with RA titles dominates one wall with the other displaying an equally colourful competitor, a Helen Steele abstract in vibrant reds, yellow and black on a vast white acrylic background.

In answer to the other two prevailing questions, yes, there is a state of the art kitchen-cum-dining room and yes, there is also a large, sumptuous shower room. Colours used throughout are Chinese yellow, Chinese lacquer red, ivory and black. Carpeting throughout is black with the exception of the kitchen-cum-dining room (black stained wooden strips) and shower room (black tiles).

The "corridor of covers" as with its two offshoots is finished in lacquer red with a black ceiling and the aforementioned black carpeting. A perfect foil for the fifty two framed book covers or posters with their shiny black frames and Chinese yellow mounts.

The sitting room is finished in ivory matt with the ceiling graced by an inset perimeter banding of lacquer red and black with a similar double perimeter banding forming a break above the skirting. The tall, massive window overlooks a profusion of extravagantly maintained private gardens. The window wall shows two panels of blistered steel framed in

437

black with a metallic Venetian blind complementing the side panels. A large sofa unit with a black lacquer frame is upholstered in a black on ivory zebra print with the same print used on the two side ottomans. "Carrying" the zebra "feel" across the room and positioned below a large Belmont Spironi canvas is a large rectangular panel of the zebra print in a black lacquer frame. Two black Panton S-shaped chairs separated by a red "severely waisted" geometric cube table is home to an elegant yellow bowl bought on a visit to Beijing and christened "Ming Ting Ding". I am a great believer in carrying features across or through to another room, particularly when dealing with a small space. In order to substantiate this theory or belief the wall facing the window is graced by an enlarged photograph taken of a statue in Prague depicting a badly behaved skull astride a willing participant down on all fours!

I took the photograph during one of the many mini-breaks I enjoyed with DLL visiting the elegant European cities of Madrid, Barcelona, Seville, Berlin, Vienna, Venice and Geneva (which included a cable car ride to the top of Mont Blanc where, clad in a thin summer shirt, cotton trousers and loafers, I was convinced a severe case of hypothermia to be most definitely on the cards!). The photograph which I duly named *Horny Porny Prague* is set in a black lacquer frame with a blistered steel mount "reflecting" the window treatment. Positioned directly above the grinning, copulating skull is a much treasured oil painting by Lee Molenaar, the highly acclaimed South African artist.

The coffee table, centralised between two black Panton chairs, a sofa unit and a further pair of red leather club chairs is in itself a talking point; the table base being a *coffin* as opposed to a usual run-of-the mill frame and automatically christened my "coffin" table. The coffin - finished in red lacquer topped with a large rectangular sheet of plate glass - is home to a graceful John Farnham sculpture, three Mayan heads mounted on steel rods set into clear Perspex bases, a red, black and polished steel and resin Olympic sculpture by Beijing Sino, a large antique bowl from Peru, a large severely battered orange enamel bowl found in a market in Tunis, a piece of the Berlin Wall with its wonderfully coloured graffiti, a pair of elaborate antique metal gaucho stirrups from Argentina, a miniature canvas by Irish artist Helen Steele (I am a great admirer of her work), a handsome python skin lazily lying the full length of the plate glass top, a pair of exquisite, tapered brass Thai funeral jars, a piece of Indian temple window and last but not least, a handsome, grinning skull christened Skully and - not to be outdone - a pair of beautiful wax candle carved in the form of skulls which I purchased in Florence. Two more sit on either side of the television in "The Black Hole of All Schmutter". It's crass and cringingly obvious but the candle skulls simply had to be dubbed "The Blowjobs".

The *pièce de résistance* has to be my elegant lodger, Miss Abel Mabel Mortis, a gracious skeleton who sits regally on a black, severely upright Charles Rennie Mackintosh while surveying her eclectic domain. Despite being a skeleton Miss Abel Mabel remains a devout fashion icon. This is personified by a stunning red and black leather bondage collar with metal spikes, a Christmas present from the local boys and girls in blue.

I refer to the spacious shower room which serves as a shower room-cum-library-cum-art gallery as my "Shower Sanctuary" and a hallowed opposite to the Black Hole of all Scmutter. The term "sanctuary" stems from the eye-catching tribute to Margaret, Duchess of Argyll which includes a magnificent framed portrait of Margaret and her beloved poodle Louis by society photographer Alan Warren. On either side of Her Grace are six framed pornographic drawings by Tom of Finland depicting several outrageously misbehaving male nudes whose mind-boggling frolics and even more mind-boggling appendages appear to be of no interest to the Duchess as she stares stonily ahead. As one visitor wittily quipped, "What's her problem? Surely it should be a case of eyes right or left instead of staring at you in the shower, RA? No wonder poor Marg of Arg looks pissed off!"

A final touch to this shrine-like tableaux is a large, silver skull perched on the silver birch server below. Christened Douglas after the actor Douglas Fairbanks Jr, the supposed "headless man" seen in a photograph presented as evidence in the 1963 divorce scandal involving the Duchess, this Douglas is positioned *below* Her Grace as opposed to being in the more practical (and practiced) "pole" position above.

I could go on with additional details but as this is *not* another boring book on interior design I will spare the reader (if you have gotten this far) the agony. Having said that there is another "design piece" I should mention and feel it would show me a bit of a spoilsport if I didn't give it a mention. In the late seventies I took an archaic paddle steamer down the Amazon River (no luxury cruise boats back then) setting off from the dilapidated riverside town of Iquitos. Stopping off at various remote point I was determined to visit a settlement of the Quechua Indians to see if what I had heard rumoured was true which indeed it was. To show their importance within the tribe certain elevated male members (no pun intended) proudly sported a leather necklace from which dangled a carved wooden penis. In other words the more important your position in the community the bigger your dick! I was riveted by the chief's splendid badge of authority; a magnificent carved cock at least eighteen inches in length. As the proud, posturing little chief stood no more than five foot in his bare, splayed feet, his badge of authority gave the appearance of being even bigger.

In a snickering aside I asked my Indian guide if the chief would be prepared to sell "his badge of honour" to me for a generous amount of "US dollars". After an animated discussion with the little man my guide told me with a sorrowful look the chief was quite happy to sell me his splendid cock but at a *huge* price.

"How much?" I asked.

"Lota dolla," muttered the guide looking acutely embarrassed.

"How many 'dolla'?" I said.

"Twenty dolla," whispered the guide.

"Sold!" I cried in a voice that would have done any Christie's or Sotheby's auctioneer proud.

On my return to England I could hardly wait for the Customs Office at Heathrow to ask if I had anything to declare. Which I had and which I did; the "Goods To Declare" being viewed with guffaws of laugher and a cheerful wave through.

Little Chief Quechua's splendid cock is displayed in the opposite corner to Miss Abel Mabel Mortis.

It's a well-known fact when it comes to indiscretion or "talking dirty" it's the ladies who come out tops! A typical example was the light-hearted banter which took place between Melford and Tracy Reed when I introduced them to the Little Chief's splendid cock.

"I don't know about him," scoffed Melford, "but I can assure you Alexander's got an *enormous* one!" (The reference - or so I assumed - directed at her son.)

"Let me assure you," added Tracy determined not to be outdone, "nothing, but *nothing* could compete with Edward my first husband's willy. It's *enormous!*"

Their definitive comments surely putting the poor Little Chief's former proud appendage well and truly in its place.

Back to Bob Miller and his associated ups and downs. Several years ago I wrote a tongue-in-cheek novel *Bobette - The Ups & Downs of a Total (Male) Tart* which I dedicated to Bob. Bob (hopefully) is lounging in bacchanalian mode on an adjoining cloud to Ben; the two happily discussing the *Ups & Downs of Mumsie.* Apart from the book cover which shows a "yippee-ing" Bob, chalice in hand, atop an extremely jolly Dodo bird, I had MM (Michael Marsden) the illustrator, design a second cover using the same background but instead of Bob astride a dodo it shows Bob quaffing a pint. This spoof cover titled *Bob Miller - A One Off*, is proudly displayed in my corridor of covers.

After Bob's unpremeditated introduction to me at the launch of Anthony Redmile's spectacular showroom I didn't see him until five years when we met under very different circumstances and to this day I still cannot say which one of us had the greater surprise. In the late seventies - having sold Albion Gate for an extortionate profit and terminated the lease on The Grove - I was renting a spectacular studio at Scarsdale Studios, Scarsdale Road in Kensington. Determined to beat "the winter blues" I had treated myself to a lavish tour of India where, apart from the magical Taj Mahal and the Lake Palace Hotel at Udaipur, the overall filth and squalor of the former Land of the Raj appalled me. So much so I was convinced even the Air India plane bringing me back smelt of "shit and curry"! It was a relief and utter delight to return to the pristine sanctity of the Scarsdale studio.

Having taken a long Badedas bath (Badedas being a constantly advertised and highly popular bath *gelee* at the time) I was sitting in the large sitting room in front of the temperamental gas log fire (courtesy of Jill Melford) with a restorative, teak-coloured whisky soda when the telephone rang. *Strange,* I thought, *nobody knows I'm back? What's more it's Sunday evening and I told everybody I wouldn't be back until Wednesday.*

"Hello?" I said cautiously on answering.

"Mr Anderson? Robin? RA? It's John Black. Johnny Law gave me your number. I've been calling for the past few days. Where *have* you been? This was to be my last attempt!"

John Black? What the hell? Ah yes, the mad, flamboyant Ken Dodd-like property dealer friend of Johnny Law aka JL exclamation mark who viewed a couple of show flats I did for Johnny, I thought. *Talk about a bolt from the blue; what the fuck can* he *want? I gave an inward snigger. As long as it doesn't have anything to do with his 'tickling stick'. God! What a thought! Sickling stick more likely!*

"I've been away in India John and literally only got back an hour or so ago."

"*India?*" exclaimed the extrovert property dealer, "Stinks of shit and curry if I remember? Ghastly place. Give me the *Côte d'Azur* any time."

"I couldn't agree with you more, Mr Black," I replied with a hollow laugh, "so, what's the panic?"

"JB please - not Mr Black," came the yodelled reply. "Reason for my frenzied calls is I've just signed a massive property deal with the US company, Gulf + Western, part of which is a sad-looking block of flats - apartments as my American associate prefers to call them - on the Edgware Road close to Marble Arch. I'd like to you there a.s.a.p. How about tomorrow at ten?"

"I'll be there. A block of flats er . . . apartments on Edgware Road you said?"

"Yes. I'll meet you in the main lobby - it's situated on a small private road, Park West Place, *behind* Edgware Road - and we'll take it from there."

"What is it you'll be needing Mr Black er . . . JB? Another show apartment . . .?"

"No, not *a* show *apartment*," interrupted JB, "at least a dozen *model* apartments and six hundred plus standard apartments added to which there is the main entrance hall and several other minor entrance halls, communal areas and a swimming basement pool." He gave a wry laugh. "Should keep you busy for a couple of years."

I met John the next morning as arranged and couldn't resist a snigger at the sight of the dishevelled man with his unruly mop of ginger hair. *My*

God, I'd somehow forgotten just how like Ken Dodd you were, John Black; or JB which you seem to prefer! I thought with an inward smile. Needless to say I was completely overwhelmed at the enormity of the project.

"Something which may interest you RA, when I met G + W's head honcho for Europe - Harold Gootrad who lives in Paris - and put forward your name as designer for Park West, Gootrad announced in a surprised voice that *he* too was about to nominate 'Robin Anderson'. Apparently you met in Annabels'?"

"We did indeed JB," I said with a chuckle. "Harold Gootrad, a tall. Henry Fonda-like character. He was slouched at the bar and the only free stool available was next to him. He was quite impressed by the fact that John the barman promptly produced a flute of champagne without being asked and immediately started chatting. I didn't quite know whether it was a simply a chat-up or pick-up but then Harold - we were on first-name terms by then - asked me for my card and vice versa."

"Well he certainly remembered you RA! So when can you start? It's January now and I'd like the first show flats with the first batch of standard flats ready for a summer launch."

"So, like tomorrow you mean?"

"Like tomorrow," said JB in a sonorous voice. "Plus I suggest you set up a temporary office here in one of the flats - bugger, I mean *apartments* on the first floor - more convenient all round while you redecorate another for your personal use as well as another show *apartment*. Make this a priority. I also suggest you take on Isobel - one of my team - as your secretary seeing she knows the property market like the back of her efficient hand! Part of my team will also be setting up offices in the block under the watchful eye of Tony Aitken, my financial director. Your builders will also need a base so discuss this with Tony when you meet him. Now, let's return to George Street where we can talk about fees and once these are agreed, I will introduce you to Isobel and Park West is yours."

After a very substantial fee, expenses and a deal regarding the purchase of an apartment on the top floor in the main block for myself had been agreed I asked JB if I could have the use of a telephone for half an hour or so.

"There's a spare desk in my office and a phone you can use," said Isobel, a stunning young Piper Laurie lookalike with her tumbling auburn locks and large blue eyes. She gave me a wink. "What's more I'll bring you a glass of wine and leave you to get on with it!"

The first person I called was Steve Edwards. "Good morning Steve or good afternoon. I've got a nice little job for you. Can you and Ray meet me early tomorrow, say eight thirty for an hour or two? Great. There's a small coffee shop on the corner of Kendall Street and Portsea Place off the Edgware Road. It has a striped awning outside. You can't miss it. I'll see you there." (Ray Knight being his business partner in Louisville, their building company.)

*

"So where's this little job then?" asked Ray gently blowing on his mug of steaming coffee.

"We were a bit early so Ray and I had a bit of a stroll around," growled Steve. He gave a grunt. "I said to Ray I bet it was in that block over there (the "over there" accompanied by a coffee-spilling gesture in the direction of Park West). Forget about a flat, the whole fuckin' place looks as it could do with a good going-over."

"Which is precisely what we're going to do," I quipped. "Come on. Drink up. We've ten to twelve show flats plus six hundred plus standard flats - from now onwards referred to as apartments - which require a complete make-over, plus a couple of entrance halls, about a mile of corridors *and* a swimming pool to look at (I tried not to chuckle on seeing Steve and Ray's wide-eyed looks of disbelief). It'll take me at least an hour to show you round and then I'll introduce you to Tony Aitken who will be handling the business side of the project. I've already been shown which apartment I will be using as a temporary office while one of your first jobs will be to decorate my proper office-cum-show flat or apartment as JB feels obliged to call them. After you've met Tony he'll show you another apartment which *you* can use for an office if needs be."

"Bollocks to that," growled Steve. "To me it'll always be a flat; not some fucking poncey apartment."

Steve, Ray and I stood looking at the vast block facing us.

"Fuck me," muttered Steve.

"Bloody hell," murmured Ray.

"Nice little job, isn't it?" I replied with a smirk. "Keep the two of you out of mischief for a year or two."

Two hours later Steve, Ray and I were sitting facing Tony Aitken in his makeshift office set up a few days previously. Tony was a dark-haired, wiry, dapper man with a touch of the Basil Rathbone about him and, as I was later to learn, a keen equestrienne plus a human dynamo at administration. "I've already drawn up several specifications for you fellows," said Tony with a nod to Steven and Ray, "Obviously Robin will be filling you in on the design details. Once the contracts are signed I suggest you start in immediately on stripping out the already vacant flats which are to be modernised and brought up to basic sales standard - the kitchen and bathroom suppliers have already been briefed and will be meeting you sometime on site next week." He turned to me with a smile. "I'm sure you're not really interested in the nitty gritty I need to go through with Steve and Ray so if you need to go and have a look at the flats earmarked as your show flats, we'll meet downstairs later - say in half an hour? - and I'll treat you and these two gentlemen to a 'welcome to Park West' drink across the road at the Holiday Inn."

*

"Fuck me," muttered Steve ("fuck me" I would soon learn being a favourite Steve Edwards expression) after Tony had left us having "a final round" in the bar of the Holiday Inn, "I still can't believe the deal we've just bloody well signed. Thanks a million Robin." He raised a beefy arm. "Here's to you! Cheers!"

"Yes, cheers mate!" beamed Ray. "I still can't believe it either?" he added shaking his dark, unruly locks. "It's a bloody dream job and will keep the lads busy for the next couple of years, if not more!"

"So when do you plan to set an office up on site?" I asked. "I take it you'll still be keeping your office in Wigmore Street?"

"Yea, but I can see us spending most of our time at the site office," replied Steve. He looked at me. "When do you want to see me or Ray in those show flats?"

"Give me a break, Steve!" I replied with a laugh, "I've just got you one of the biggest contracts *ever* so at least give me a day or two before we discuss designs and finishes!" I pointed at their empty pint glasses. "One for the road?"

"Why not?" said Ray.

"Fuck me," said Steve.

I had been introduced to Steve and Ray when I had been asked by Sandra Sherwood the English representative for Sherle Wagner, the American bathroom company, to design one of the show bathrooms for their spectacular new showroom on South Audley Street, Mayfair. The two young men had impressed me with their enthusiasm and professionalism along with their cheerfulness and sense of humour. The difference between the two was startling; Ray a mischievous Donny Osmond lookalike alike and Steve a dead ringer for Shrek. On completing my show bathroom, a concoction of lurid pink and purple waterlilies with a great amount of gold fittings and "bathroom extras", we parted amicably each vowing to keep in touch. On my first viewing Park West and mentally surmising the scale of work involved the name Louisville had immediately come to mind.

"Okay gentleman; we'll meet tomorrow at eight for a general recce. As Tony said you can start ripping out all the kitchens and bathrooms once you have your team organised but I need to walk round the building with you again." I gave the two a smile. "John Black, Gulf + Western and Co? They ain't seen nuthin' yet!"

"Right, eight o'clock it is!" said Ray pulling himself from his chair. "Tony has also asked for a schedule regarding payments so we'll get Bob Miller to set himself up in our site office. It's one of the lesser smart flats on the Norfolk Crescent side. Tony showed it to us earlier and handed over the keys." He turned to Steve. "Can you get Bob to meet us tomorrow?"

"Will do," grunted Steve, "in fact I'm seeing Bob later at Ivor Court for a drink."

"Don't get too pissed," said Ray with a ribald chuckle.

"Bob Miller?" I said, "That rings a bell. An *alarm* bell in fact! You say he's your accountant?"

"Yes, has been for about a year."

"And before that?"

Ray gave a shrug. "Search me. We met him through one of the guys who also has offices in Wigmore Street."

Bob Miller? Bob Miller? I thought. *But of course! The pixelated pixie on the Dodo bird at Redmile's opening!*

Not giving Bob Miller a further thought I took a taxi back to Scarsdale Studios, my mind in a whirl as to what I would be planning for the project as a whole. "Feel free," JB had said, "I want you to give London something never seen before!"

And that Mr Black, is exactly what I plan to do, I said to myself as the taxi pulled up outside the entrance to the studio complex, *as I said the Steve and Ray, they ain't seen nothin' yet!*

The next day and the following days simply raced by. The first day in our temporary office found me busy on the telephone arranging site meetings with the likes of John Skellorn and Bob Christie (a small, independent curtain maker I had been introduced to by Alistair Colvin while working on Charlie Cottenham's flat and the F. Pratt Engineering Belgrave Square offices and penthouse apartment), while Isobel sorted out her office in one of the former bedrooms, organised a small boardroom in another former bedroom and set up the kitchen.

"Robin," said Isobel popping her head round the door as I was busy talking on the phone, "A message from JB; can you pop along to Tony's office when you have a spare moment? I know Martin Hunt your architect's due here at any minute but have no fear, Isobel will take care!" Nodding an affirmative and giving the smiling Isobel a thumbs' up I finished my call, pulled on my jacket and took one of lifts to the fourth floor where Tony had set up his site offices.

"Ah! The one and only RA!" chortled JB as I strode into their reception where he was standing talking to a harassed-looking Tony, "Sorry to drag you away from your designing but a quick question; what are you doing about transport? Isobel tells me you don't own a car at present." He waved an admonishing finger. "Park West can't have its star designer relying on taxis. There're a couple of cars sitting idle back at George Street and one's yours for as long as you need it."

"But that's wonderful, JB," I enthused.

"Great," said JB, "I know Isobel's meeting Karen (one of the other secretaries) back at George Street for lunch - JB knows *all*! - so I'll get her to drive the car back here."

"And I'll get you a permanent parking bay sorted out in the basement garage," interrupted Tony. He gave me a brief smile before turning his attention back to JB and saying in a tense voice, "They're *still* too expensive JB so I'm going to have another go . . . "

Giving JB and Tony a cheery wave I returned to my office where Martin and Isobel having introduced themselves were sitting chatting happily in our so-called boardroom; each nursing a glass of wine with a third glass waiting for - to quote JB - "the one and only RA".

"Some place," commented Martin, "and what a *coup!*"

"Don't tell me," I said, "I keep pinching myself." I gave Isobel a smile. "JB - who claims to know *all* - has kindly suggested you drive back the Mini Cooper that's been languishing in the garage at George Street so the 'one and only RA' now has a set of wheels!"

"Bloody secretary and now chauffeur?" replied Isobel in her broad Scottish accent, "I take it JB - who knows *all* - also realises I expect a *vast* increase in salary!"

"Fat chance!" I laughed.

"Slim chance you mean?" quipped Isobel.

Half an hour later, armed with a batch of preliminary sketches, I was showing Martin around the initial seven model apartments requiring completion for the first sales promotion. "I won't introduce you to the builders today - they've enough on their plate - so let's meet as soon as you've drawn up the units we've discussed." I gave Martin a tight, no nonsense smile. "So, the million dollar question; when?"

"Monday okay?"

"Definitely okay Martin. As early as you wish."

"Eight o'clock sound about right?"

"More than sound about right; it sounds perfect. Many thanks and see you then." I turned to Isobel. "I'm just nipping down to see how the boys are settling in." I gave a grin. "Careful how you drive my car now, you know what they say about women drivers!"

"Fuck off!" said Isobel with a grin, her version of "fuck off" an easy match to Coral Browne's or even Maggie's!

"Jesus Steve!" I said on entering the Louisville premises, "You've only been here a few minutes and already the place looks like a bloody tip! First impressions Steve! First impressions!"

"It's a builder's office," grunted Steve, "not a fucking designer's office!"

"Just as well otherwise I'd be out of a job!" I retorted.

"Now, now," said Ray, "There'll be plenty of time for arguments." He gestured to where a figure was sitting silently next to one of the desks. "Meet Bob Miller, our accountant. Bob, this is Robin Anderson the designer responsible for the whole project."

"*Mr* Anderson and I have met before," replied the dapper, bearded man in a mellifluous tenor voice, "Many years ago at Anthony Redmile's in Sloane Street."

"Ah yes, the launch party," I said with a knowing smile. "The incident with the Dodo bird!"

"I don't know about the Dodo bird *Mr* Anderson, but I most certainly remember one of your visits to the showroom. You were busy selecting one or two pieces for a client. A Mr Loeb if I remember correctly. Murph, Anthony's PA was looking after you," answered Bob Miller in a low voice.

"Ah yes," I replied not having the least idea of the pieces he was referring to, nor the mysterious Mr Loeb or an assistant called Murph. *And what's with the heavy* Mr *Anderson shit?* I thought. "So now you've ended up in the rogues' gallery at Park West? Ha ha! You're going to have your work cut out here, that's for sure!"

"I am quite sure I'll be able to manage, *Mr* Anderson, but thank you for your concern."

I stared at Bob Miller as if I'd been stung. *What gives with the guy?* I thought. *Don't tell me he's nervous I'll let on to Steve and Ray he's gay? What an arsehole!* Before I could stop I found myself saying, "It's Robin, Bob. And if you're free once the boys let you go why not meet me for a drink across the road at the Holiday Inn around sixish?" Not giving the shocked man a chance to reply I did a quick about turn and left.

*

"I'm sorry I'm a bit late and I hope you don't mind but I've asked my friend to join us," said Bob on joining me in the Bar. Giving a nervous smile he sat down in the armchair opposite me.

"No apologies necessary, I've only just got here myself," I replied condescendingly, "I'm sure sorting out Steve and Ray - even at the best of times - must be an onerous task." I added with a slightly irritated look, "Did you just say you've asked someone else to join us?"

"His name's John," replied Bob lamely. "We . . . er . . . live together."

Oh great, I thought, *and bloody lover comes too. Rather like Monsieur Gallois and his Sidney.* "John? How nice," I said crisply. "I look forward to meeting live-in John." I nodded at the hovering waiter. "What would you care to drink?"

"I'd like a 'wikki' if I may," came the almost inaudible reply, "with water and ice."

"Wikki?" I repeated. "I take by 'wikki' you mean whisky?"

"Yes please," replied Bob in a hushed voice.

"Any particular blend of 'wikki'?" I asked sarcastically.

"Dewar's please . . . er Robin. I like Dewar's; so *Scottish!*" The remark followed by a tentative smile and a soft giggle.

Jesus, maybe this wasn't such a good idea after all? I thought staring at the well-groomed young man with his neat moustache and beard, *and who the fuck's this gate-crashing John when he's* not *at home? Some Burt Reynolds or an oafish King Kong lookalike I expect. Shit! You and your big mouth RA!*

For the next minutes we held a strained conversation discussing the many potential problems Steve and Ray's team could be experiencing on site; the gaps of silence more predominant than any conservation.

"He's arrived," announced Bob in a relieved voice.

For a moment I thought he was referring to the second round of drinks I'd ordered desperation to keep the conversation going.

"Heeloo Bob! Heeloo all!" cooed a falsetto voice, "Sorry I'm late but the traffic was *vile!*"

I stared in disbelief at the tall gangly blond, spectacled figure flouncing over to where we were sitting. *Bob Miller's lover?* I thought. *Surely*

450

not? The gate-crashing John - a veritable combination of Sebastian Flyte and Pop Eye's Olive Oil (it takes some imagining) - dressed in a corduroy jacket, an open neck shirt displaying a colourful cravat and neatly pressed chinos.

"You can only be Robin Anderson," announced the camper-than-camp man proffering a long, thin hand. "I'm John Leach. Bobby's told me *so* much about you and here you are at last; in the flesh!"

John Leach literally folded his long, gangly frame into one of the empty armchairs grouped around the small cocktail table. "Yes, you're *exactly* as Bobby described you. A walking advert - now sitting - ha ha! - for *GQ!*" He nodded at my glass. "Is that a martini I spy before me? What a good idea!" John turned to the waiter who was about to set down our second round of drinks. "A gin martini please. Double, straight up and with an olive." He gave me a wide, disarming smile. "Drinks are on me this evening."

"That's very generous of you er . . . John," I said with not quite a matching smile, "but I *did* invite Bob   er . . . Bobby . . ."

"No Robin, no!" interrupted JL, "I'm the unexpected guest so I insist." He leaned back in his chair and, giving me a broad wink, turned to Bob and said shrew-like, "So Bobby dear, how was your first day at *big* school?"

After a few sips of his second "wikki" and with JL sitting next to him the dull, drab cocoon-like Bob, as if skipping the chrysalis stage, literally changed before my very eyes into *Butterfly* Bob (or as I would say to him later "A *Dodo* butterfly Bob!") as opposed to the nervous young man who had appeared earlier. The new Bob turned out to be a manipulative charmer with a mischievous sense of humour, an acerbic wit and a delicious ability to shock!

JL I learned was a top dentist. Like Bob, he too shared an acerbic wit and a mischievous sense of humour. The two soon emerged as one of the most delightful couples one could ever wish to meet. Sadly this was not to last.

Within weeks the three of us were inseparable. Bob became a regular noontime visitor to our splendid, newly decorated offices where Isobel, immediately taking Bob under her wing, made sure his "wikki and water" was always ready and waiting.

Meeting JL at the Holiday Inn became a regular seven o'clock happening. Bob and I would meet earlier and catch-up on the happenings of the day with Bob giving me a comical insight into what was going on within the Louisville offices. By this stage the pressures on the site were immense regarding the amount of people involved and what I, on behalf of John Black and Gulf + Western, was determined to achieve.

"You were *such* a bitch when we first met properly at Redmile's," Bob reminisced fondly as he and I sat enjoying the wind down on such an evening. Giving a mischievous grin he reached for his second "wikki" before adding slyly, "And look at you now; even more of a bitch."

"Only slightly more," I said in mock self-defence.

"Only slightly more?" echoed Bob followed by a chortle fiendish glee. "What about that set to with poor Peter Hardwick this morning?"

"Tell me! Tell me!" carolled JL who by this stage had joined us.

"Poor Pete," Bob continued with relish, "the way Robin bollocked him over some paintwork in one of the show flats." He turned to me with a wicked grin, "What was it you said? Ah yes, I quote; 'Peter' - not the familiar Pete *nota bene* - 'if you *must* insist on using your rancid dick as a paintbrush could you please try *not* to wank off in the middle of the job? If I had wanted a *drag* effect I would have asked for it. Instead I find I've got a fucking unasked-for bit of dragging with an applique *spatter* on top. I want the whole wall repainted and this time instead of using your fucking dick, try using your so-called *proper* fucking head instead and use a fucking roller'!"

"I said that?" I replied in feigned alarm. "Goodness, perhaps I should have simply said, 'It's not really one hundred per cent Pete so I suggest another coat. Thank you' instead?"

"Then you wouldn't be the RA we all love to hate!" quipped Bob taking another sip.

"No, you wouldn't!" agreed JL. "Good God!" he camped, rolling his eyes, "Imagine Robin Anderson *not* bitchy? Impossible!"

*

Bob and JL lived in Ivor Court, an impressive mansion block situated at the top end of Gloucester Place, close to Regent's Park. I didn't know what to expect on my first visit to the apartment but I was more than impressed by the stylish interior; a clever blending of 16th-century oak furniture and stylish modern pieces including a Corbusier black leather day bed and Knoll chairs. It goes without saying several unique Redmile pieces vied for attention amidst the eclectic collection of furniture and objet d'art. A giant turtle shell on a silver mount and a pair of similarly mounted ostrich eggs to name but a few.

In competition with Margaret D of A's Louis, Bob and JL were the proud "parents" of two dachshunds; one a handsome long-haired fellow named Sopworth and his equally handsome companion, a smooth-haired dachshund named Noël (easy to guess the inspiration behind *this* Noël's name!).

Bob and JL employed a lumbering cleaner called Lil (the complete antithesis to Diamond Lil if ever there was) who, from what I could gather, spent more time taking Sopworth and Noël for long walks and picnics in nearby Regent's Park than attending to any household chores. I also learned Lil was known among some of the local lads and the Louisville builders as "Liberal Lil". The reason for this rather dubious sobriquet according to a gleeful Bob being the Lil's unprejudiced parting of the "highly liberal Lil thighs"!

Meanwhile the ongoing saga of Park West continued to dominate my life with each day guaranteed to deliver a new surprise or three; one of the biggest surprises being Steve, the builder who turned up unannounced at my office early one evening.

"Steve!" I exclaimed on looking up at the tentative knocking on the door jamb. "Don't tell me for once a member of the Louisville team is working late?"

"You got a minute, RA?" asked Steve, his eyes avoiding mine.

"Absolutely!" I gestured at the bottle of wine on my desk. "Fetch yourself a glass from the kitchen and join me. Surprise, surprise, for once I'm *not* meeting Bob and John this evening so I'm all yours."

Steve dutifully fetched a glass, poured some wine and sat down facing me.

"So RA," he said eyeing me furtively from under his unkempt eyebrows (a startling contrast to his gleaming pate and clean shaven face),

"I take it you're happy with the way things are going? Happy with Louisville?"

"Of course I am, Steve; otherwise you wouldn't be here; I mean still on site." I gave a feigned chuckle. "You're not here to tell me while I may be happy with Louisville, Louisville isn't happy with RA along with Park West and therefore wish to leave the site, are you?" *Fuck, I thought, maybe the RA temper tantrums are a bit much after all? Maybe I shouldn't have told Trevor the sparks to go and hang himself on one of the exposed cables I found left in one of the cupboards in Flat 6? Or worse still, told him to stick his dick in one of sockets and electrocute himself; unless of course the socket was too big for his prick meaning there'd be no contact with any current!*

"No, no, nothing like that, RA," murmured Steve. He look a long sip of wine, his eyes not leaving mine, before saying in a conspiratorial voice, "You do know, RA, if there's anything, anything *at all* that upsets you on the job you can talk openly to me about it?"

I stared back at the benign Shrek-like figure sitting opposite. *Jesus, Steve*, I thought, *what on earth are you on about and where the fuck's this heading? Your whole team are one hundred per cent as far as I'm concerned and surely you and Ray must surely be aware of my point of view?* "Well . . . er . . . thanks Steve; I'll bear that in mind." I gave him a tight smile. "But, so far so good . . ."

Steve continued to stare.

"Er . . . I'd offer you another glass of wine but I really must finishing checking these invoices for Tony to deal with in the morning so if . . ."

"I'm gay," grunted Steve, "and I wanted you to know so if anyone or anything ever upsets you - *anyone* or *anything* at all - you just let me know."

Not waiting to hear my reply or see any reaction Steve hefted his heavy frame from the chair and lumbered out.

"Gay?" I murmured in disbelief, "Well now Mr Edwards that is something I did *not* expect! And there you are, a Shrek lookalike, more butch than butch, happily married and with a couple of children. I wonder if Ray or anyone else in Louisville knows?" I gave a start. "I wonder if *Bob* knows? Bet he does!"

As expected Bob *did* know and as I was to discover, had been in an "on-off" relationship with the bi-sexual Steve for some time prior to the Park West days.

*

"Any specific requirements for His Majesty today?" quipped JB at one of our weekly meetings.

"Most certainly, JB," I replied, nonchalantly playing with my pen. "The model apartments. What concerns me is all those visitors clomping around once the apartments are open to the general public."

"How can any visitors or potential purchasers be a problem?" questioned JB.

"The damage they'd do - hopefully unintentionally - whilst wandering around the model apartments," I said with a superior smile, "so what I have in mind is a 'you can look but can't touch' approach."

"Meaning?"

"Meaning a deterrent; something like a rope across the doorway to each of the specially designed rooms."

"Good idea," muttered JB.

"But not an *ordinary* rope such as a nightclub entrance sort of rope," I added firmly.

"Okay," grinned JB, "not a *nightclub* type of rope so what other type of rope is His Majesty suggesting?"

"An acrylic *chain* type of rope. In other words a chain made of acrylic links; like the chains they have in Bloomingdale's to keep the hoi polloi out of their room settings."

"I like it! I like it!" enthused JB.

"However, a slight problem JB," I said with a tight smile, "the problem being where does one *obtain* such links? I've already checked with Quadrant and similar sources but none seem to have even *heard* of acrylic chains."

"Well then you'd best see if you have better luck with Bloomingdale's, Mr A?" JB gave a Doddy-like laugh. "I'm sure you could manage a few days in New York? See it as a small 'thank you' for all your fabulous work to date.

I mean it! So set aside a few days and inform Tony so he can arrange your flights and hotel. We usually us the Hilton on any business trips but I expect *you'd* prefer the Plaza?"

"Goodness Mr Black," I said with a simper, "not only a property tycoon but a mind reader as well?"

"Oh, and by the way, RA . . ." JB began.

Uh-uh, I thought, *it did seem too good to be true so here it comes, the sting in the tail; the catch.*

"I've someone new joining the team; he'll be here next week. He's been appointed as Site Coordinator . . ."

"Site coordinator?" I retorted, "What do you mean by 'site coordinator'? I don't need any *fucking* site coordinator interfering with my designs, thank you *Mr* Black!"

"Whoa! Whoa! No, not for *your* side of things, RA!" said JB hastily, "John . . ."

"*Jesus!*" I exploded, "just how many Johns do I *need* in my life?" My comment causing me to inwardly snigger.

"*John* will be liaising with Tony regarding the general running of things . . ." stammered JB, "Er . . . nothing to do with your model apartments or any other design work I assure you. However, should you need any items stored prior to being properly positioned, John will be there to assist."

"How wonderful," I murmured, "John the bloody Balls-up now enters the scene." I gave JB a sharp look. "I suppose I had better trot along and see Tony. Strike while the iron's hot. In fact, if possible, I'll see if I can fly out late Thursday and come back Saturday night which means I'll only miss one working day and be on site Monday morning; bright-eyed and acrylic tailed!"

"So that's it then?" said JB with a deadpan expression. "RA in chains."

I gave a snicker. "I really don't need long. In fact, I've already checked with my contact at Bloomingdale's with regard to stock - I've reserved sixty yards - and once they receive my confirmation they'll have the chain ready for me to bring back. I will also buy one or two decorative pieces which are only available at Bloomie's."

"A prime example of forward planning and a lesson for us all," said JB with a grin.

"A prime example of forward planning for the benefit of *Park West*, JB," I replied. "Nothing to do with RA."

*

The following Monday saw me back on site by six a.m. In fact, I had already done a recce late Sunday afternoon having landed at Heathrow earlier.

"No jet lag?" asked Isobel peering into my office.

"No, no jet lag Isobel dear, but a goody bag for the luscious, lovely Isobel lying on her desk instead!"

"A present?" exclaimed Isobel, "Oh Robin, but you shouldn't have!"

"Shouldn't have?" You don't even know what it is yet!" I laughingly replied.

A few moments later Isobel reappeared clutching a leopard print jacket. "Robin," she said softly and almost in tears, "Thank you so much. It's lovely; absolutely lovely."

"And all the vogue in New York from what I saw!"

"I know, I know," murmured Isobel. "I know and I can't believe it. *All* the girls will be green, simply *green*." Her prediction said in an exaggerated Scottish accent. "Coffee?"

"Wunderbar!"

Half an hour later I stood up from my desk and reached for my jacket. "Lovely Leopard Woman," I called, "I'm off on my rounds." I gave a chuckle. "I told Steve and Ray I wouldn't be back until tomorrow so imagine their *utter* delight when I suddenly appear?"

"Poor buggers," muttered Isobel peering up from the notes I'd left her, "probably die of shock."

"Ah, RA! Welcome back!" called JB from where he and a tall, shadowy figure were standing by the entrance to one of the scheduled model apartments. "Come and meet the newest John on the block! Ha! Ha!"

"Ah yes, the new so-called fucking site coordinator," I muttered on approaching the two men. *Bloody hell!* I thought stopping dead in my tracks, *Talk about a Mr Playgirl centrefold!*

"RA meet JR," quipped John, "or John Rendall to be precise. John's our new site coordinator and is here to assist you should you require anything."

"Ah, the famous RA!" said JB's JR with a distinct Australian twang; his comment accompanied by a dazzling smile. I stared at the burly six foot plus blond, moustachioed, amber-eyed Robert Redford lookalike as he reached for my hand and gave it a hearty shake. "John Rendall or JR as JB's just said. Pleased to meet you." He nodded his shaggy mane-like head towards the partly decorated apartment. "Great colour scheme, RA. JB said you were a genius and I see what he means!"

After such an introduction the newest John on the block could do no wrong. "You *must* come and join me for a glass of wine at lunchtime," I said positively oozing charm. "In case JB hasn't already told you my office - or offices - are on the first floor and to the right of the main lifts. See you about twelve?"

"I'll be there," twanged Rendall with another dazzling film star-like smile.

When I began work on Park West JB had offered me a choice of two cars; a gleaming black Porsche or a black Mini Cooper and as already said I'd chosen the Mini Cooper. One of Rendall's opening gambits on joining me and Isobel for the suggested noonday drink was a self-satisfied, "*So* glad you decided on the Mini, RA, which means I now have use of the Porsche."

A few days later one of the workmen was overheard to say to a mate. "Fabulous Porsche that Rendall bloke drives. Guy must be loaded. Told me it cost a bomb."

I bit my tongue; saying nothing to disillusion him.

*

"Have you met John Rendall, the new site coordinator?" I asked Isobel minutes before the new site coordinator joined us for his "welcome" drink.

"Isn't he a *dish*?" she cooed. "For once JB shown a sense of good taste regarding the people her hires. Present company included!"

I feel it important to refer to another old adage, namely "you can't judge a book by its cover". While I sincerely trust this doesn't apply to *my* books it would certain prove to be true when applied to what Bob Miller cynically described as "the unmasking of Rendall". (I have already given vent to one Colonial, the dreaded Roland Spillane. As with Spillane and his *dorp*, Rendall's emergence from an Aussie backwater named Wangaratta where - rumour has it his family owned a dry cleaning business - was never mentioned.)

"You must meet Lizzie," beamed Rendall nursing a large glass of wine. "Like me she's heard all about all about you from JB and can't wait to meet the famous RA!"

"So let's meet!" I cried. "In fact, why don't you and er . . . Lizzie have dinner with me one evening? Today's Monday so perhaps Wednesday? Come to the studio and from there we'll go on to La Popote. It's a firm favourite of mine. Is Liz . . . er . . . Lizzie . . . your girlfriend?"

"Good heavens no, RA!" twanged Rendall with a further shaking of his shaggy head. He gave a leonine-like grin. "Lizzie's my wife!"

Having downed several glasses of wine Rendall suggested lunch at an Indian restaurant set in the Edgware Road façade of the immense Park West building. Egged on by Isobel I reluctantly agreed. As we swept into the restaurant Rendall immediately asked to see the manager. On introducing himself as site coordinator to the massive redevelopment Rendall went on to say as he intended to be using the restaurant on a regular basis for entertaining VIPs and prospective purchasers he therefore assumed any further visitations would be "on the house" or - as I said angrily to Bob later - "fucking free, *gratis* and for nothing".

Hideously embarrassed I raced through the one course I had ordered before excusing myself. "Duty calls, JR," I cried racing for the door. An hour and a half later I returned to the restaurant and settled the lunch bill. Still seething at Rendall's effrontery I took up the matter with Tony Aitken whose reaction was as expected. I have no idea what JB said to his site coordinator but he never returned to grace the restaurant with the promised VIPs or prospective purchasers.

On asking JB if he'd met Lizzie, the mysterious Mrs Rendall, the reaction was even more Ken Dodd "Diddy" than expected. "Oh she's quite *wonderful!*" he enthused. "A real livewire and a top PR person. Her professional name's Liz Brewer. You *must* have heard of her?"

I had to admit I hadn't and was promptly subjected to JB waxing lyrical about "the golden couple".

In 1969 I was gushingly told, Rendall and a close friend, a fellow Australian named Ace Bourke rescued a lion from the pet shop at Harrods. This led to a book, *A Lion Called Christian*, which followed the lion's rescue and subsequent release back into the wilds of Africa.

"Smacks of Joy Adamson's *Born Free* and Elsa the lioness," I said later to Bob when regaling him with what I could only describe as JB's virtual orgasm while discussing the new site coordinator and his wife.

"The *poor* man's Joy Adamson you mean?" sniped Bob not to be outdone. "Not only did Joy Adamson pip him to the point with her book *and* a film, there was also the hit song *Born Free* as warbled by Matt Monro!"

Years later Rendall and Bourke's book and video *A Lion Called Christian* would appear time and time again on Facebook or in the press. "Talk about flogging a dead lion," quipped Bob on being told of yet another "sighting".

*

Work on Park West progressed by leaps despite the occasional stumble and I found myself spending more and more time on site as Louisville and I worked feverishly in order to have all one hundred and ten percent perfect for the rapidly approaching grand opening.

JB watched - literally - with wide-eyed wonder as the massive Park West's promised "new look" metamorphosed into a reality. After months of dust, debris and seemingly chaotic clutter the shimmering, incandescent butterfly emerged from its former dull, drab chrysalis. On Friday, 9th September, 1979, Park West with its twelve strikingly different model apartments, magnificent entrance lobbies, sumptuous communal areas, six hundred and twenty seven standard apartments (today reduced to five hundred and forty), Olympic-sized pool indoor pool and its two acres landscaped garden officially opened.

The day and night before the opening saw us all on site along with a teams of cleaners, working until dawn seeing to any finishing touches and making sure the last speck of dust had been well and truly dealt with. As for the rumour Bob had "doctored" the endless coffees quaffed throughout the night by cleaners and workmen alike all I am prepared to say is "no comment."

The model apartments provided prime examples of how a standard flat or apartment, albeit a studio or a one or two bedroom unit could be transformed into something special; a one off. I had made sure the décor to each model apartment, irrespective of the size, was both eye-catching and practical and even more important, something to be talked about. Every model apartment was, in JB's own words, a "show stopper". "An exotic riad in Marrakech" to a "magnificent mirrored Manhattan marvel" were just some of the words used in the sales brochure along with the ultimate tease; "Find your dream scheme here at Park West".

When asked how many yards of carpet had been used throughout the project I would say in all honesty, "several miles" and as for gallons of paint, "several square miles".

When it came to discussing specialised paint finishes - "and by specialised I don't mean a dreary drag or a stipple" as I informed Steve and Ray - the two contractors assured me they had "just the guy for the job". Enter a beaming Rod Stewart lookalike named John Wright (another John!) whose father was one of the painters on site. Steve and Ray assured me John (or JW) was "a dab hand at everything" as well as being able to handle "the most difficult of clients"!

JW's first test of this capability occurred as I stood watching Reg and JW senior hanging lengths of specially coloured terracotta and ivory wallpaper in tall, elongated panels mounted along the double height walls of themain entrance lobby and supposedly complementing the dramatic dark brown, terracotta and bronze green geometric carpet.

"Shit!" I muttered as I watched the first strip of paper being smoothed down inside one of the panels. "Shit!"

Close to the carpet the terracotta of the paper was a perfect match but on looking up at the solitary panel the overall effect was totally lost.

"Jesus," I growled to JW who stood nearby watching me; a bemused expression on his face. "When you compare the two together it couldn't be better whereas looking at the paper when up, what should be a lattice effect of terracotta and ivory looks nothing more than a sickly splodge of fucking knicker pink! Shit! Shit! Shit!"

"No prob, Rob," replied JW catching my eye. "Glaze them."

"Glaze them?" I questioned. "What do mean by 'glaze them'?"

"I know exactly what you had in mind but it's the ivory background giving you grief. All they'll need is a heavy terracotta all-over glaze and I assure you they'll look even better than what was envisaged. Look, give a few minutes to mix some glaze and then I'll show you."

Half an hour later I stood gazing up at the gleaming panel of a heavy terracotta tracery floating on its softer terracotta background.

"Fabulous er . . . JW," I said. "What else can I say but glaze away?"

"Take it as done, Rob. I'll have them all finished sometime tonight."

Next day JW came up to me as I stood on the perimeter balcony to the main entrance hall.

"Good morning JW," I said with a smile. "Just admiring your handiwork. It looks really great. Talk about saving the day! Now how about a triple stipple?"

"Anything else?" asked JW with a grin.

"A bleeding drag?"

"Take it as done!"

For the next thirty years I would call on JW (or Bubble Bonce, my nickname for him) to add his magic touch whenever a special technique or effect was required. To give an example of a "special technique" I can refer to the time when wanting a wickerwork effect I had JW finish the walls with a selected base colour before applying a glaze and briskly brushing it with a cross-cum-twirl using a thick, heavy duty yard broom instead of a standard brush. The result? Perfect wickerwork covered walls. Today JW and his charming wife Jan own a fishing farm in France. A subtle difference. I wonder if he techniques the hooks?

As building and decorating works on Park West progressed it was interesting to note the reactions of certain tenants living in the building. Despite a strict adherence to the legitimate working hours during which work could take place there was always the troublemaker who would stomp angrily into JB's office or even mine and complain vociferously about the noise. I dread to think how much time Tony or Isobel wasted while patiently explaining there was "no gain without pain". At the end of the day it would be "well worth it" and they would all "love the new Park West".

"Tell the old cunt to go and fuck herself," I would mutter to Isobel after another visit from one particularly nightmarish resident.

"So use today's version then as opposed to the usual platitudes?"

Glancing up at a giggling Isobel I would come out with my standard response. "You know me better than that. Best you stick to the usual platitudes! 'We apologise and of *course* we will do our best to lessen the noise. Again we can only apologise'. She'd no doubt thoroughly enjoy the uncensored version but the thought of the old cow enjoying herself is the last thing we want on any of our agendas!"

Years later when working on an apartment set in a Grade 2 listed building in Mayfair's Park Street I was confronted by a grim-faced Rita Tushingham who, due to the noise made by the builders demanded, I stop all work forthwith. I calmly suggested she contact the landlords or the client direct as I was only working in accordance with their instructions. In the course of our simmering conversation I gently reminded Miss Tushingham of our meeting many years ago with Peter Pollock and Paul Danquah at Peter's farm near Flaunden. While the memory may have appeased the actress in a minor way it didn't stop Steve and Ray being subjected to endless poisonous glares whenever they crossed paths with the actress.

The first day of sales at Park West was the stuff of legends with fifty percent of the apartments being sold and my diary for the next eighteen months booked solid with appointments to meet a stream of new clients. However, before climbing back on to the thrumming treadmill I treated myself to a well-deserved break to a place I had always wanted to visit. The land of the Samba, Carmen Miranda, Dolores del Rio and more.

One refurbished apartment kept well away from prying eyes was the one included in my deal with JB. As work progressed Steve and Ray as a "thank you" took it upon themselves to decorate "Rob's flat" at no cost. To say I was totally overwhelmed by their generosity simply does not do them justice. JB's expression on viewing the completed apartment was an immediate "Tell me how much you want for the place and if the price is right, I'll buy it!"

JB was overcome by the sitting room in particular with its sepia mirrored walls and lowered ceiling housing recessed spotlights and speakers for an elaborate stereo system. Set within the mirrored ceiling was the large Sandra Blow painting from The Grove, softly washed with strip lights set in the uprights of the mirrored perimeter. "The Vatican may have its Sistine Chapel complete with Michelangelo's frescoes whereas Park West now has RA's pad complete with its magnificent equivalent in the form of what I deemed a vibrant 'Blowjob'. Something the macho Michelangelo - from hearsay - would have certainly appreciated." A tad precious but always well-received.

On the advice of my accountant I decided to give up the lease to the studio and move to Park West. "And should you ever decide to sell you no doubt will appreciate that fact your profit would be virtually one hundred percent seeing the property was a gift as were the furnishings and decorations," he reminded me with a triumphant smile.

I duly moved into the apartment but somehow never felt totally comfortable. As Ben so succinctly put it, "Eek Mumsie! See it simply as another way of sleeping on the job. You began in Bayswater, loved the Kensington studio so why not join ranks with us in good old Chelsea?"

Assuring Ben I would "think about it" I was soon back to hosting small dinners and a stream of cocktail parties in my newest eyrie. Attending one such party was the actor Christopher Lee and his elegant wife Gitte.

"Er . . . Robin, may I have a word," said Christopher beckoning me over.

"You called sir," I replied crossing over to where stood.

"Yes," replied Christopher testily jabbing a long, bony finger up at the small speaker hidden in the mirrored ceiling. "I know it's a thirties-style building, hence the low ceilings, but with your *further* lowering of the damn ceiling I may as well be wearing the speaker as a bloody hat!"

"Perhaps a gentle step frontwards, backwards or even sideways would help solve the problem Christopher," I chided. "What's more, I'm quite sure neither the original architects nor builders ever imagined they'd have a bona fide six foot four Dracula visiting the top floor."

Christopher's reply, accompanied by a haughty stare, was a murmured "It's still too damn low whether I came to visit or not" before moving further into the room and striking up a conversation with Isobel.

*

Liz Brewer and Rendall's enthusiasm over their "new best friend RA - the world's greatest living interior designer" (their words, not mine) - was at first exhilarating but I soon learned the excitement and similar accolades applied to almost everyone they encountered and in most cases, subjected to a limited timescale. Flattering and fickle, it was either a case of "you're in" or "you're out", depending on the circumstances.

At the time Rendall of "joining the team" I was also informed by a bemused JB how Liz Brewer had pleaded with him to give her out of work husband "some kind of job; anything".

Liz was pregnant with Tallulah at the time of our meeting and I was honoured at being asked to be a godfather. Among the line-up of godparents was Dai Llewellyn, brother of Roddy the one time paramour of Princess Margaret. "Roddy the Body" as Liz and Rendall dubbed him was - as we were endlessly told - one of their *greatest* friends. A beaming Rendall took great delight in showing the Body round *his* latest PR project, namely the "multi- million pound Gulf + Western redevelopment of Park West." Needless to say the designer responsible for the whole contract was never introduced. I became friendly with Dai, a great charmer, and used to bump into him regularly at a popular Earl's Court eatery, Balans, in the late nineties and early 2000s.

Rendall and Liz were ruthless in their pursuit of London's rich, famous and supposedly worthwhile souls. One incident which certainly summed this up concerned a dinner invitation from Jill Melford. Rendall, Liz and I had been somewhere for drinks before going on to Melford's house in Chester Row. En route Rendall turned to Liz and said in his now familiar twang, "I do think that other party would be much more worthwhile Liz, don't you agree?"

Liz agreed and the two dumped me outside the house leaving me to explain to Jill why she was two guests short. Rendall and Melford eventually became close friends and as Bob would cryptically say, "Birds of a feather."

Rendall and Liz took over the lease to a rundown house in Cliveden Place, close to Eaton Square which they energetically proceeded to renovate. I was amused to note the remodelled kitchen was a replica of the standard kitchens used throughout Park West where Rendall reigned supreme in his role as site coordinator. I never bothered to check if this had been donated by the enamoured JB or not. Somehow I was not too surprised when a distraught JB informed me his golden couple were getting a divorce. However, I was surprised when Rendall gave me the ultimatum. "You can't have it both ways RA; either you're on my team or my ex-wife's team"

I opted for his "ex-wife's team".

Liz Brewer - like me - is a survivor and survivors make enemies but it's all thanks to Liz that Tally (Tallulah) her daughter and my goddaughter grew up to be the fabulous young woman she is today; a sane, loving and successful person in her own right. Tallulah Rendall is a talented songstress with a wide following in Germany, Australia and the Far East. Tally and I were highly amused by the reaction of Michael Marsden, the artist responsible for my brilliant covers, on spotting a photograph of Tallulah on the desk in my study.

"Is that her? Is that Tallulah Rendall?" he gasped in disbelief.

"Yes," I replied, "she's my goddaughter!"

"But I *worship* her!" cried MM (Magical Michael).

"Have you ever met her?" I asked.

"No," came the laughing reply, "I humbly worship her from a distance."

"Well, we can soon change that," I said smugly, "Tally's got a gig here in London next week so why don't you come along?"

MM duly came along and to his delight was introduced to Tallulah, bought a copy of her latest CD and promised to attend any future London gigs.

Liz and I became well-known for our glossy, highly extravagant dinner parties held in the private dining room at Walton's (RA footing the bill) where, through Liz, we entertained such luminaries as Shirley Bassey and Ivana Trump to name but a few. A charming gesture by Shirley Bassey was her invitation for Tallulah to be the cabaret turn at her seventieth birthday extravaganza with the glamorous Miss Bassey taking a back seat.

Shirley Bassey was a fan of Tallulah's from day one and a low key visitor to several of her gigs. One gig in particular proved to be particularly memorable. This saw Liz, Shirley and me driving to a popular club situated near the end of the New King's Road. Although immediately recognisable Shirley sat self-effacingly through Tallulah's performance allowing her to enjoy the limelight. As planned Shirley, Liz and I were joining friends at Daphne's for dinner after the show. Shirley and I were standing chatting outside the club while Liz went to collect her car parked nearby when we suddenly found ourselves joined by two young lads (urchins being a better description).

"Excuse me Miss Bassey," piped up one of the youngsters, "can I 'ave yer autograph please? It's for me dad!"

"Of course!" acquiesced Shirley giving him a dazzling smile and signing the proffered notepad with a flourish.

"An' me please Miss Bassey!" squeaked the other young boy handing over a piece of crumpled paper.

"An' oo's 'e then Miss Bassey?" asked the first youngster pointing at me.

"He?" replied Shirley with a mischievous smile, "Why, he's Brad Pitt!"

"Brad Pitt?" echoed the second youngster, his eye's widening. "Pull the other one Miss Bassey! 'E's not Brad Pitt. 'E's more likely Brad Shit!"

Thankfully Liz, right on cue, drew up alongside as Shirley and I collapsed with laughter and barely managed to bundle ourselves into Liz's vintage Mercedes.

Ivana Trump I am proud to say remains a great friend. I was delighted when Ivana asked me to design her London apartment followed by her yacht aptly named *IVANA*. The apartment appeared in a BBC1 documentary *The Fame Game* with Liz as the central figure. Thanks to Liz I featured predominantly with shots of my own Chelsea apartment, Ivana's Knightsbridge apartment and in the opening sequence of the programme which took place in the sumptuous restaurant I designed for Thomas Goode Limited in South Audley Street, Mayfair.

Another notable couple met through Liz were Buzz and Lois Aldrin whom we entertained to a fun-filled dinner at San Lorenzo. Unfortunately neither Buzz nor NASSA (unlike Coral Browne) commissioned me to design a spaceship!

Liz and I continued to entertain selflessly, our other "celebrity" guests including the likes of Eamon Holmes, Norman Hartnell, Fiona Fullerton, Angela Rippon, Sebastian Sainsbury, Gloria Hunniford, total charmer footballer Lee Chapman and his lovely wife the actress Leslie Ash, Charles Gray, Harvey and Diana Goldsmith, Lynsey de Paul, Jan and Robert Kilroy-Silk, Sally Burton and many others. Apart from the lavish dinners in the private, upstairs dining room at Walton's another Walton Street restaurant soon appeared on the scene; namely Turner's.

I was introduced to Brain Turner, a popular "television chef" by Bernard Thorp after Brian had approached him with regard to redesigning his restaurant. The original Turner's was a bland affair of beige paint and fabrics with chairs and all other woodwork in simulated ash. "Talk about contraceptive décor!" I said to Brian, "this is not only uber safe it's also uber sorry!" Having made such a pronouncement I went on to produce for Brian what I described as my "Brian Turner meets Johannes Vermeer" look; a combination of cobalt blue, grey blues and yellow. The final effect was stunning. A few weeks later Brian and his charming business associate, Michael Mills, approached me with the idea of RA hosting a weekly fun lunch. I happily agreed. To Turner's delight (and my surprise) the lunches received a great deal of publicity with articles and photographs appearing in the likes of the *Sunday Express, Signature, Impression, OK Magazine* and more.

Obviously I invited Liz to assist in organising the lunches and soon found Miss Brewer taking on the role of the hostess with the mostess, a role I soon terminated when two of her "guests" (total strangers to me) swanned into Turner's and the man - without so much as a "good afternoon" when I greeted the them at the door - handed me his coat and said, "Take care of this and my wife's as well."

Giving him a tight smile I took hold of the two coats and promptly dropped them onto the floor. "I take it you were joining Miss Brewer at my lunch?" I said tightly. The red-faced man managed a nod. "A change in plan," I smiled, "Because as from now you're not. However, allow me to *voluntarily* pick up your coats . . ." - I handed the stunned couple their coats

- "And now please leave as your presence is no longer welcome at *my* luncheon."

I nodded discreetly to Richard Fletcher, the young manager, who was doing his utmost not to laugh, "We're two less for lunch Richard and we're ready to start when you are. Just let me get my bona fide guests seated."

"No, no RA!" trilled Liz, "there're still two more to arrive!"

"I can assure Liz as far as I'm concerned everyone's here so let's sit down shall we?"

Any further protestations from my "hostess with the mostess" were pointedly ignored.

A previously arranged I met up Ben and David Harvey later for a drink. Ben, who had been one of the guests at lunch had obviously mentioned the slight debacle to Harvey who greeted me with a wily "Ah, the man himself! The benevolent donor now demoted to cloakroom attendant!" He gave a chuckle. "At least I didn't say hatcheck girl!"

"Honestly Mumsie," said Ben, "I take it - apart from myself - all those people you were entertaining were there courtesy of Liz Brewer?"

"Not *all*, Ben . . ."

"I don't know why you waste your time with her," interrupted Harvey who had become a major player on the Ben scene. "From what I hear she's nothing more than a case of Miss bloody Me, Me, Me!"

"She has introduced me to one or two new clients," I said defensively.

"Yes, and got you to help out wily-nilly with her effing house," snapped Ben. "That extravagant iron staircase in the garden for starters which 'Bonking Bob' Towler, one of your builders installed for her free, *gratis* and for nothing." He gave Harvey a conspiratorial look. "As I said to David before you arrived, the woman takes narcissism to the nth bloody degree."

"Shall we change the subject?" I said acidly.

At times Liz's rudeness would leave me (to use one of Richard Fletcher's favourite expressions) "gobsmacked".

"Who the fuck does she think she is?" I heard Richard mutter to Willie, another waiter. After a particularly snappish demand by Liz.

"No one I'd like to know, that's for sure!" shrieked Willie in reply.

A few days later I broke the news to Liz. "No more Turner lunches," I announced. "Brian's taking a breather. Maybe a fabulous Christmas lunch but we'll have to wait and see."

By this stage certain journalists had taken to describing Liz as an "expert of etiquette" which was immediately snapped up by Harvey. "Etiquette?" he exclaimed raising an eyebrow. "Surely for want of better word they should have used the term 'excruciate'?"

I can truly say in the nigh on forty years I've known Liz I have never sat down and had a proper conversation with her. As I always say, "I find myself talking *at* Lizzie; never *with* her!" However, in all fairness to the lady I can only refer to the American poet Henry Wadsworth Longfellow and his poem *When She Was Good* which reads:

> *When she was good, she was very good*
>
> *But when she was bad she was horrid.*

Need I say more?

Perhaps Tallulah summed our tempestuous relationship best of all by saying in a bored voice taking me way back to our "Flight of the Angels" scenario, "Honestly RA, at times you and Mummy Liz behave just like an old married couple".

*

One of the many "greatest friends" brought along by Rendall to admire "his grand Park West project" was a lively South African woman named Lesley Lake, another PR person whose claim to fame was helping set up Biba, the famous, eccentric fashion store responsible for introducing the miniskirt to the High Street. Lesley - La Lake to her closest friends - a stylish woman of indeterminate age and a dead ringer for Anna Wintour, the former editor of *Vogue*, was known for her deep, throaty voice and her audacious miniskirts or, as I called them in designer jargon, her "pussy pelmets". Lesley resided in a bijou house set in Kinnerton Street close to Belgrave Square. Her immediate neighbour in an equally bijou residence opposite was the acerbic Irish film director, Brian Desmond Hurst. It was through Brian I met another director, Irving Rapper of *Now Voyager* fame and proud possessor of the biggest pair of balls I have ever viewed, licked or fondled and another of my "exact opposites". Despite my exhausting auditioning for Irving I obviously wasn't enough of a reinvented Charlotte Vale for him as I never got to play a similar role: my type of roll being more of a hands-on experience than silver screen.

Lesley was a generous and brilliant hostess as well as a sublime cook. I spent many happy evenings being entertained in La Lake's all-black basement dining room where wine and laughter flowed. She was also passionate about animals and owned one of the most pampered pooches on the planet, a perky Dachshund named Charlie. In a moment of besotted infatuation (if the two can be combined) I found myself penning an "Ode to La Lake" (its glimmerings no doubt traceable) in honour of this magical person.

If my miniskirts get shorter

Said La Lake, outside her home

I'll have two more cheeks to powder

And a lot more hair to comb!

Lesley was a great friend of Rendall's and to my surprise - and at her insistence - I joined the two of them and Tallulah for a weekend in France as guests of Bernie Cornfeld at his château in France (a hint of things to come for La Lake). Apart from the fact La Lake mislaid her passport resulting in a bout of throaty hysterics (I eventually found this had fallen out of her capacious Biba handbag and was lying forlornly on the floor inside one of the château's Mini Mokes!) the weekend proved to be the greatest of fun with the majority of the time spent alongside the spectacular swimming pool. I was captivated by Tallulah's enthusiasm for her surroundings and in particular her fondness for the various household (or château-hold) pets which included a friendly Labrador, several cats and a severely frowning monkey. Much to my chagrin I was *not* captivated by the attention shown to her by the Adonis-like Jean Pierre, the dashing twenty something son of Justine the cook who caused Tallulah to shriek with endless glee as he threw her time and time again (the muscles of his bronze torso rippling) into the air as they frolicked in the pool.

Jean Pierre gallantly repeated the exercise with La Lake but promptly stopped when the older *femme fatale* once again mislaid another precious possession; namely the top to her bikini!

Zut alors! Poor Jean Pierre - unlike Tallulah, Rendall and myself - didn't know where to look.

Many years later Lesley would be living happily in her very own château in France, Château de Mauprevoir, near Potiers, with her husband the genealogist and former Editor-in-Chief for *Burke's Peerage,* Charles Mosley. Due to Lesley's ill health the couple eventually returned to London and I was saddened to hear of Lesley's death due to an infection. I had spoken to her a few days after the doctors had decided there was no alternative but to amputate one of her legendary legs.

"I either simply give up of make the best of it," Lesley said to me in her wonderful, husky voice.

Several days later she was dead. Charles' death five days after Lesley came as even more of a shock as I had no idea Charles was seriously ill with inoperable cancer. Charles never complained, never explained and made sure he cared for Lesley with love and devotion until the bitter end.

On our return to London I was intrigued to find a message for me to contact a firm of solicitors in Bulawayo, Zimbabwe. "What the fuck?" I muttered on booking a person to person call (at the time one had to book all overseas calls as direct dialling was still a thing of the future). On speaking to the mysterious Mr Holderness I was stunned to be told the Cur had died (I had lost all contact) and much to my surprise had left me a small legacy. The sting in the tail being the legacy was in almost untouchable Zimbabwean dollars; clever Cur and Robert Mugabwe having the last laugh as it were.

"Is there no other way I can spend these 'blocked funds' apart from travelling to Zimbabwe and living it up for a day or two?" I asked Holderness sarcastically.

My sarcasm obviously not registering Holderness replied in a placatory voice, "For starters yew kud pay for eny aer fers to an' from Zim with your funds es long es yew fly Air Zim," he said in a strong Zimbabwean (read Rhodesian) accent. "Infect yew kud use the funds for eny flights to en' from Zim en' if yew want to spend more there iss always Kariba en' the Vic Falls which are good for a jolly!"

Thanking Holderness for this time and disillusioning information I spent the next couple of moments deep in thought. I eventually poured myself a glass of wine and on returning to my desk, picked up the telephone, dialled Directory Enquiries and asked to be put through to Air Zimbabwe. A charming woman dealt with my questions in a calm, efficient way and on being thanked and told I would be calling her back, she replied cheerfully, "My nem is Nadia so pliss ask for me when youse call again."

Casting my mind back to the past few days spent with Tallulah, her father and La Lake, I quietly formulated a plan.

Despite the general exodus of many whites from the former Southern Rhodesia, stalwarts such as John Cobb, Mai Cordell and the Barbours had remained along with two more friends, Ian and April Piercy. Ian epitomised the idea of the "great white hunter" and was responsible for the control of several game parks and extremely lucrative organised safaris under the Mugabwe regime. The Piercy's lived in a sensational, rambling thatched lodge outside Harare (formerly Salisbury); an added feature being a menagerie of animals raging from cheetahs to a baby rhinoceros.

So, I thought, *why not use up some of those blocked funds and treat Tally to a never-to-be-forgotten birthday present? Better still, as her grandparents* (Rendall's parents) *lived in Australia and I had heard her speak fondly of them, why not travel on to Sidney courtesy of QUANTAS and my blocked funds seeing the Australian airline still flew in and out of Zimbabwe?* I saw it as settled but before telling Tallulah I first of all had to clear my proposed present with her parents. Rendall was all for it and why not? A "freebie" to Aus and back via Zimbabwe travelling First Class? Who could possibly say "no"?

After a few scowls and muttered "I don't knows" Liz reluctantly agreed to my goddaughter's birthday present with a difference.

It goes without saying I was also keen to visit Australia plus the fact I had met several Australians from Sydney and was delighted at the thought of seeing them on their home ground.

Two months later the three of us duly checked in at the First Class section at AIR ZIMBABWE counter before setting ourselves comfortably in the First Class lounge prior to boarding one the airline's garishly decorated *707s*. While Rendall lorded it over a few other passengers by the bar, Tallulah and I sat talking about all the wild animals we would be seeing in one of the nature reserves outside Harare as well as a day trip to see the amazing Victoria Falls.

"Can I please have a sip of your champagne RA?" asked Tallulah with a winsome smile. "I have had champagne before." She added in a conspiratorial whisper, "Mummy Liz *always* allows me a sip!"

"Better not let Daddy John see you," I whispered back. "Goodness!" I added, staring at the empty flute, "that was some sip!"

Beckoning a beaming waiter I ordered another flute. Before the waiter had barely set the replacement flute on the small cocktail table Tallulah mischievously treated me to an encore of *Tallulah and the Disappearing Champagne.* Avoiding Rendall's curious glances as we entered the aircraft I cautiously steered my giggling goddaughter towards her seat next to his.

"Have you been giving Tallulah *champagne?*" hissed Rendall with a glare.

"Only a permitted sip or two - like Lizzie sometimes does," I replied nonchalantly knowing any mention of Liz's "dos and don'ts" would lead to Rendall not responding.

Christ, don't tell me he's about to sit next to me? I thought on spotting a portly black man sporting a clerical collar and a purple vest following the simpering air hostess as she sashayed her way towards the empty seat next to mine and directly behind Tallulah and Rendall. *This is all I need; a wannabe bishop or the real McCoy plonking his great arse in what I hoped would be a vacant seat.* Giving the man a smile the hostess made a great show of helping him lower his vast butt into the seat before buckling the seatbelt over his ample paunch.

I was given (or so I assumed) a "gracious" nod by His Grace followed by a loud grunt as he fumbled in an attempt to take a magazine from the pocket attached to the back of Tallulah's seat. After a few more grunts and fumbles he finally managed to extricate one.

With luck that sees Zim's answer to The Purple People Eater well and truly taken care of, I thought evilly. *Better still, get a few glasses of wine and port down Mugabwe's doppelgänger and with any luck he'll snore - and no doubt fart - his merry, smelly way to Zim.*

After take-off and the seat belt sign in turn switched off I noticed Tallulah peering at us over the back of her seat. "Oh," she trilled homing in on the colourful figure, "hello!"

"Hello my child," rumbled His Grace glancing up from the magazine and giving Tallulah a benign smile.

Hello my child? I thought with a snicker. *You can't be serious?*

"My name's Tallulah, what's yours?" giggled Tallulah with a smile more cheery than benign.

"I think you should call him Your Grace, Tally," I interrupted in a solemn voice.

"Hello Grace!" trilled Tallulah, her eyes suddenly widening as she threw up all over His Grace's splendid purple front.

Chaos! Had it not been for his black face I am sure His Grace would have blended in perfectly with his former pristine vest. The dismayed air hostess aided and abetted by a hand waving air steward helped His Grace to another seat next to a prim looking woman. *Why they couldn't have put him there in the first place?* I thought, *Serves the buggers right.*

Tallulah, after a quick sponging by a tight-lipped Rendall and the concerned air hostess, promptly went to sleep (with what could only have been a beatific smile on her angelic face) and woke up when we were preparing to land at Harare. Rendell, needless to say, ignored me for the duration of the flight.

On our arrival at the grandly named Harare International Airport I was delighted to find a smiling Val Barbour there to welcome us. I was not so delighted to discover Air Zimbabwe had mislaid both Rendall's and my luggage whereas Tallulah's case had arrived safely. Assured by a beaming Air Zimbabwe official our luggage would no doubt be on the next flight due in the following day, we were driven by a cheerful Val to Meikles Hotel, Harare's answer to the Dorchester. I had grandly reserved two suites, one for Rendall and Tallulah with the other for myself. On leaving my briefcase in the small sitting room of the suite I went downstairs to join Val and wait for Rendall and Tallulah to join us prior to Val driving us to the house in Borrowdale for an impromptu lunch.

However, before setting off I did insist on a quick visit to "the family firm" (Barbour's) where Rendall selected a pair of trousers, a jacket, a sports shirt and a few toiletries while I went for a rather stylish cream safari suit (after all I had travelled in a Gucci blazer, Doug Hayward shirt, Hermès tie, Sullivan and Woolley trousers and de rigueur Gucci loafers).

For our first evening in Harare I had already organised a dinner for eight at the hotel's luxurious Bagatelle Restaurant. This had been previously arranged through several telephone calls to Val. With Tallulah as my hostess, my guests included John Cobb (a throwback to the Hillside Young Players days) now living in Harare, Rendall, Val and David Barbour, Ian and April Piercy and Merry and Anthony De La Rue (I knew Merry from London before she married Anthony, a partner in some international chartered accountancy firm). At the end of dinner my guests and I were taken completely by surprise as Tallulah boldly approached the black pianist entertaining the diners (a genial Satchmo lookalike) and after a quick, whispered conversation in his ear, began to play a jazzy duet with the delighted man. Not only did Tallulah play, she also started to sing. After several minutes of enchanting cabaret she took endless bows to the ecstatic applause of the cheering diners. A hint of things to come.

We were up bright and early (5 a.m.) for our flight to the Victoria Falls - known by the locals as "The Smoke That Thunders" - on the mighty Zambezi River. Tallulah was fascinated by the wisp of sparkling white, bridal-like veil which appeared to hover over the brown parched landscape (or *bundu* as we approached Victoria Falls airport set approximately eleven miles from the small town of Victoria Falls.

"That whole stretch of mist or 'bride's veil' as you called it is the spray thrown up by the tumbling water," I explained. "The Falls are a mile wide - a bit more than the length of Park Lane - and if you can picture the Hilton Hotel *on* Park Lane, almost as high as the hotel! In other words the Falls you are about to visit are *really* massive!"

"Gosh!" exclaimed Tallulah, her eyes shining. "Wider than Park Lane and as high as the Hilton Hotel? That is *very* big RA! I can't *wait* to see them close up!"

"Plus I have an extra special surprise for you later." I said with a mysterious smile.

"What?" demanded my goddaughter her interest in the Falls momentarily forgotten.

"Wait and see Tally dear; wait and see!" I replied.

"If I *must*," sad Tallulah matter-of-factly peering down through the window at the Falls below. "Goodness RA, they *are* big!"

Prior to lunching at the splendid Colonial-style Victoria Falls Hotel I had organised - through Air Zimbabwe in London - reservations on a morning cruise along the Zambezi River wall above the Falls.

I was amused to find the cruise happily referred to as "our booze cruise" by the elegant young black woman who greeted us on our arrival at the departure point; a primitive wooden jetty set reached by a simple dirt road.

Armed with a glass of wine and Tallulah with a lurid orange *Fanta* drink the two of us sat silently watching the river bank slide by as we chugged along on the large, surprisingly modern motor launch. Rendall, obviously still annoyed by what I would later describe to Bob as "Grace's greeting", had segregated himself from the two of us and was in deep conversation next to the bar with some poor cornered tourist.

"Oh look, RA!" squeaked Tallulah pointing at the passing river bank, "It must be Gucci!"

Gucci? I thought, *what the hell are you on about, Tally? We're cruising along the fucking Zambezi River; not fucking Bond Street!*

"And look, look RA! That must be Hermès and over there, another Gucci or is he a Prada?"

"Tally dear, I take it you're referring to those large logs lying on the river bank?" I said with a patronising smile. "Believe it or not those so-called logs are, in fact, very nasty crocodiles!"

"I *know* that RA!" came the scornful reprimand. "What's more most of those crocodiles - or *logs* as you've just called them - end up as handbags. Mummy Liz and Auntie Niki (Niki Cole a mutual friend and rampant shopaholic) each have one and as *all* crocodile handbags either come from Gucci - or Hermès - or Prada - or - or even Harrods *that's* who I'm pointing out!"

"Silly RA," I said defeated. "Ah, but wait a minute; what would you call *him*?" I cried pointing to the partly submerged head of a large hippopotamus eyeing us balefully as we chugged past.

"A hippopotamus, of course," giggled Tallulah. "*Silly* RA! What else?"

"Er . . . perhaps *Horace* the hippopotamus?" I replied with a light laugh.

"A hippopotamus called *Horace*?" said my goddaughter with a disdainful sniff, "Why on *earth* would you want to call him Horace for heaven's sake?"

"What about another *Fanta*?" I suggested, gesturing towards the disappearing river bank. "I see we're now turning so we must be heading back for lunch." I gave a laugh. "Seeing all these er . . . handbags has given me quite an appetite." (Tallulah's expression at my comment conveniently indescribable.)

Lunch concluded I said smilingly to Tallulah, "You remember the added surprise I mentioned on the flight to the Falls?"

"Yeees RA," replied Tallulah giving me a wary look.

"It's a particularly lovely and *unusual* surprise," I continued nervously. "Or at least *I* think so . . ."

"What *is* it, RA?" asked Tallulah impatiently.

"I've chartered a small plane so we can treat ourselves to what is known as the 'Flight of the Angels'." I gave a bemused-looking Rendall and his frowning daughter a smug smile. "What we *do* is actually fly through the spray along the main gorge to the Falls and hopefully - if there *is* one - under the arc of a rainbow!"

"Oh *per*-lease RA," muttered Tallulah, "not *another* flight."

*

Apart from the grandeur of the Victoria Falls the wild, totally unspoiled setting is an unrivalled plus. Unlike the Niagara Falls which straddles the Niagara River between America and Canada, or the Iguaçu Falls in South America (straddling the Iguaçu River between Brazil and Argentina), the Victoria Falls is surrounded by *bundu* with nothing else to distract one from the awe-inspiring "Smoke That Thunders". Even the barriers set along the edge of the precipitous gorge are made from loosely entwined branches of dried *doringboom* (thorn trees) which exemplifies the feeling anything artificial is strictly taboo.

I still remember my abject horror when viewing the Niagara Falls from the dining room of my hotel while having dinner and seeing the cascading water changing colour due to row upon row of hidden, differently coloured floodlights. Being an intrepid traveller all I can say is "Thank God for *Rennies*!"

We returned to Harare and the hotel where, to my relief, I found our "missing" luggage had duly arrived on the stipulated flight. After our early start and two more "Oh RA, not another!" type flights we joined Val and David for dinner at their *very* dated seventies-styled house. Next day was spent with April and Ian Piercy where Tallulah gleefully rode on the back of Tommy, a gigantic, ancient tortoise, cuddled a baby cheetah, and spent a happy couple of hours feeding a group of very greedy gazelle along with Rodney a rhinoceros and last but not least, helping groom Lulabelle, a most elegant giraffe.

A slight hiccup in an otherwise perfect day occurred during lunch. On commenting on the delicious starter and told by April it was smoked crocodile tail and regarded as a great delicacy I replied wittily, "Goodness, I trust we haven't just eaten a relative of Gucci, Prada or Hermès?" My remark receiving blank looks from the others seated around the table apart from Tallulah who, giving me a pained look said in a reprimanding voice, "*That* RA is what Mummy Liz would call 'in *very* bad taste'!"

"Pun intended Tally I trust?" I quipped not being one to easily accept defeat.

"If you say so RA," replied Tallulah rolling her large blue eyes and reaching for her glass of orange squash.

*

An enchanted and thoroughly exhausted Tallulah was already asleep before being strapped into her seat for the long haul to Sydney.

I *loathed* Australia.

Despite being outrageously pampered at the Sebel Townhouse Hotel (the main instigator being John, the dynamic bartender!), extravagantly entertained by Preston Saywell (whom I had been introduced to in London by Peter Stiles) at the Yacht Club and by a friend of Rendall's who gave an alfresco luncheon for us at her charming beach house, I simply couldn't wait to leave.

Matters came to a head prior to a dinner I was giving as a "thank you" for Preston, Kells (Ray Kelley another Australian I had met in London), a charming woman named Constance Farquharson and a couple I'd met in the Bar at the Sebel Town House. The restaurant (highly recommended by John the barman) overlooked Sydney Harbour and the odd looking, floodlit, Opera House with its iconic "white sails". I was standing there taking in the view while waiting for my guests to arrive when it suddenly struck me how just how far away London was!

Overcome by a wave of panic I managed to survive dinner but not before I announced I was leaving Sydney "on the next available *QUANTAS* flight bound for Harare"! Despite pleadings from Kells, Preston and the others to stay for a few more days, after several frantic late night calls I was able to get a seat on the Air Zimbabwe flight the following day.

"You don't have to worry," I informed Rendall in a brief telephone call to his suite, "When I get to Harare I will make sure Holderness, my solicitor, takes care of your Meikles bill and inform the hotel to deal with him direct. You already have your return tickets." I gave a slight pause before adding without much enthusiasm, "We'll catch up back in London. Give my love to Tally." As with our outward journey the return journey was again via *QUANTAS* with a stopover in Harare before catching the Air Zimbabwe flight for Gatwick.

To give Rendall his due he did introduce me to Rebel Penfold-Russell, the Australian wine heiress, which led to me designing her newly acquired penthouse apartment close to Marble Arch and overlooking Hyde Park. "Great view and great for jogging," twanged Rebel on our first meeting at the property. Her instructions were succinct (always a bonus). "I want the kitchen as part of the main reception and I want a four poster bed!" A very happy lady moved in three months later.

The only glitch revolved around the final payment. Rebel had left all financial dealings with Rendall and for some reason known only to himself, the tiresome man began pussyfooting about when asked to settle the balance owing. By chance I happened to see Rebel in the King's Road a few weeks after she had moved in. We began chatting about the apartment and on being told how delighted she was with her new home I said in feigned innocence, "So there's really no reason for John withholding the final payment then?"

Rebel, suitably taken aback by my comment, asked me as to the amount outstanding and on being told, moved to a nearby table outside one of the endless coffee bars dotting the King's Road, produced a cheque book from her handbag and wrote me a cheque for the balance.

"Sounds as if Australia was a bitter pill indeed!" quipped Bob showing no surprise at my early return, "Perhaps if you'd had a koala with your Daiquiri - I take it they *do* serve Daiquiris in down under? -instead of a Cola things could have looked rosier. I mean you can *cuddle* a koala!"

"Oh, very bloody unfucking funny, Bob!" I snapped, "And for your information I didn't even *see* a fucking koala!"

"Nor I expect, a rampant didgeridoo," chortled Bob. He took a sip of "wikki". "Christ, no wonder you were disappointed!"

*

What I began to refer to as "conveyor belt clients" continued to enter the RA factory and exit having been totally transformed. One particular client to whom I owe my never-ending thanks was Barbara Eppel who seemed to go (effortlessly) out of her way to make sure the conveyor belt was never empty. Through Barbara I was introduced to billionaire philanthropist and world-renowned collector of Islamic art Dr David Khalili and his exquisite wife Marion. The couple commissioned me to design their palatial home in Hampstead's exclusive Ingram Avenue and soon afterwards David invited me to design his private art gallery in Mayfair's Clifford Street.

Along with the plethora of new clients my social life proved to be equally as busy. Alan Davies, the television producer whom I had met all those years back at Digberry (then owned by Ken Villiers) telephoned inviting me to a drinks party. Among the guests I immediately spotted the film star Rock Hudson, currently in England for the filming of *The Mirror Crack'd*, based on the novel by Agatha Christie. Eyeing the gaggle of what I could only describe as *"fawnicating* queens" hovering around the glamorous, genial giant I kept my distance and concentrated on the trials and tribulations of a sibilant, elderly gent whose main problems in life seemed to be the appalling standard of service in shops in general and the rising cost of fuel.

Murmuring "If you'll excuse me while I go and refuel myself" I edged my way from the whinging old soul and headed for the bar.

"I hear you and Alan are old friends," said a melodic, American voice as I reached over to collect my requested glass of wine from the busy barman.

"Many years ago; the swinging sixties in fact," I answered drily glancing up at the owner and did a double-take. *Good heavens!* I thought, *the great man himself!* "Mr Hudson fetching his own drink?" I added for the want of something to say. Giving the smiling giant a quizzical look I continued nonchalantly (and somewhat waspishly), "Don't tell me not one of your circle of admirers never offered to fetch you a refill? How very ungallant of them."

"Put it his way," said Rock with a million-watt smile, "if one of the . . . er . . . gallant gentlemen had offered then I wouldn't be talking to you; would I?"

"That makes sense," I quipped proffering my hand. "The name's Robin . . . Robin Anderson."

"As Alan informed me and I'm Rock . . . Rock Hudson . . . or *Mr* Hudson as *you've* just informed *me.*"

We exchanged pleasantries on how Rock had met Alan, how he was enjoying his stay in England and so forth. From the corner of my eye I was well aware of the poisonous looks cast in my direction from some of Alan's guests. *I realise I'm no George Nader or James Dean but if our talking to each other gets the bitches tongues wagging, so be it!*

Giving a discreet glance at my watch I reluctantly said to Rock I had to leave seeing I was meeting friends for dinner. "I don't suppose you're ever free for lunch what with your heavy schedule?" I added nonchalantly, "But if you are and would like to meet again, that would be great."

"I agree," replied Rock with another million-watt smile. "How about Thursday?"

"Thursday it is! And may I suggest we meet at my favourite restaurant La Popote?"

Near to La Popote and leading off Walton Street is Lennox Gardens Mews housing the popular Toto's Restaurant and a number of small privately owned office units. Stationed in one of the offices was the aforementioned Cherry Moorsom who - in between re-reading her well-thumbed copy of *Debrett's Peerage* - busied herself in helping out with the running of a small travel agency. Due to its location La Popote was a favourite luncheon venue for Cherry and her somewhat "beige" girlfriends.

Imagine my barely concealed delight on seeing her and the girlfriend's reaction when Rock and I walked into the restaurant. We lunched there on several occasions and much to Mrs Moorsom's chagrin I would acknowledge her with a saccharine smile, a murmured "Hello" and nothing more.

As I remarked tongue-in-cheek to Ben, "I can't really see why she should look so pissed off. Apart from being the most handsome man in Hollywood, surely she - of all people - is aware of the fact Mr Hudson doesn't have a title? A slight or blight which would never do!"

Ben's response had been a grinned "Eek Mumsie you're so right! Dear Cherry is so full of it if you tweaked her ears she'd flush!"

I never introduced "Hollywood's Leading Man" to Cherry. Something which annoyed her almost as much as Melford being given the two golden gazelle whereas she ended up with a mere goat!

It was around this time I was introduced to Tom Gilbey, a well-know "master of fashion". Latching on to a passing comment made by one of my clients when surveying a sample of upholstery fabric I had selected for a pair of fauteuils in her drawing room ("I simply adore it but what a waste to only use it on a pair of chairs? Imagine an outfit in the same? Quite, quite sensational.") I immediately thought, *I don't know about an outfit but the idea of a waistcoat could be fun. Better still, should Norma decide on the Missoni-like silk velvet for the two fauteuils . . . ?*

To my delight the aforesaid Norma decided to go ahead with the proposed covering. On placing the order I added an extra yard to the length of fabric which I duly presented to Tom. "I'd like a waistcoat made out this," I explained, "and if you have some jazzy buttons to go with the fabric, so much the better."

Needless to say my arrival at Norma's cocktail party to show off her newly decorated home plus the fact I was wearing a waistcoat to match part of the décor became a major talking point. So much so the question among many of my future clients was which of the room's selected fabric would I be wearing at the flat or housewarming party! Tom went on to supply at least a dozen such waistcoats ranging from a blue, gold and black on white moiré silk leopard skin pattern (Ivana Trump's yacht); a green, sunshine yellow, apricot and purple floral pattern on ivory moiré (Annie Sunley's new house after her divorce from Sunshine) and a sumptuous gold and bronze woven cotton stripe inset with a wider terracotta velvet stripe embossed with a leopard skin motif (Noor Jahan, an exotic Kensington eatery noted for its outstanding Indian cuisine).

Last but not least Tom supplied a waistcoat of busy glittering gold bees woven on to a blue silk background which I used for the extravagant window treatment and bed draperies in the master bedroom (or queen cell) for a client who grandiosely called herself the Queen "Bea". Not that this worker bee was ever required to show off his "carrying it through" waistcoat inside the "queen's cell" I hasten to add. It became a standing joke among the contractors how the Queen "Bea" - with her pursed lips and pained expression - continued to fail dismally in her buzzing attempts to lure the odd worker bee to her personal unsated honey pot.

*

Forget the likes of Annabel's and the Saddle Room: if you weren't seen in the late seventies, early eighties at the outré Embassy nightclub in Mayfair's fashionable Old Bond Street you may as well leave town. Run by a flamboyant Australian named Stephen Hayter - you'd either "love him" or "hate her" - the Embassy was seen not as a gateway to Valhalla but a gateway to a Valhalla extraordinaire. Here guests could happily dance and mingle until the early hours with a never-ending flow of vamps, tramps, drag queens, titles, trash and people simply having fun while nimbly avoiding the empty popper (amyl nitrate) bottles littering the dance floor but not quite so agile when it came to avoiding the odd scattering or leftover line of cocaine on one of the many small surrounding tables. On a raised platform behind the bar four energetic young Adonides in sequinned jockstraps could be seen gyrating energetically to Gloria Gaynor's *I Will Survive* or *I Am What I Am.*

The Embassy was wild, wondrous and because of its prime location and generally well-heeled clientele, a safe haven for all.

Supervising the milling busboys (or waiters) in their cut-off satin shorts was an elderly, flame-haired woman, also in shorts but sporting a sequinned bolero top, who epitomised the term *grande dame* but on this occasion, a *grande dame* with a definite difference! I became great friends with Lady Edith Foxwell and was a regular weekend guest at her elegant 17th-century country house, Sherston, in Gloucestershire. When asked to describe Edith I would laughingly reply, "I don't know if you ever saw the film *The Revolt of Mamie Stover* but if you *did,* Jane Russell - *avec* wrinkles - is Her Ladyship to a 'T'!"

Edith, like Ben, had a penchant for black gentlemen with the Motown singer Marvin Gaye being one of her many paramours. I spent a delightful evening with Edith and Marvin at a favourite eatery of theirs, the modest Pancake House off Berkeley Square. Lady Edith (or "Lady Fuckswell" as the Embassy staff dubbed her) was quite open about her affairs and when in residence at Sherston she would happily introduce her latest black beau to the drinkers in the Rattlebone Inn, her local. To quote a smiling Edith, "Once you've been with a black you'll never look back!"

Not to be outdone Ben was quick on the uptake when being told of Edith's pithy comment.

"Better still, if it involves a black think heart attack!" he chortled. "And by *that* Mumsie, *nota bene* I am *not* being racist but simply paying a humble tribute to the unprecedented size of their yummy willies!"

A comment made by Ben which did surprise me was his reaction after being introduced Bob Miller.

"Your Robert Miller is someone I particularly don't wish to see again, Mumsie," he said. "Had he been the New York Robert Miller perhaps I would have viewed him in a different light." The latter said with a tight placatory smile and a reference to the owner of The Robert Miller Gallery in New York who gave Richard Mapplethorpe his first major exhibition back in 1978

Yet another of life's strange coincidences!

When visiting Sherston I would spend many a Sunday lunchtime with Edith - a popular and much-loved figure and dressed in her standard shorts and a gold lamé top - chatting to the locals while Marvin or the latest in her "ebony stable" (another Edith quote) played darts with some of the men. Let me assure you, when it came to playing darts, Marvin Gaye was one mean player! Marvin went on to be replaced by this brother Frankie who in turned found himself replaced by another equally as charming black gentleman; another Sylvester but not the Sylvester formerly involved with Ben.

However, not all people were as enamoured with Edith's choice of paramours. Having decided to take a weekend break to Venice (I had become a great believer in these convenient short breaks to a variety of European cities) I was sitting at the counter in Harry's Bar sipping the inevitable Bellini when a typical-looking American tourist (sun glasses, camera, sports shirt, chinos and loafers) and his attractive lady friend (or wife) sat themselves down next to me. After a brief pause we started exchanging the usual opening gambits of how wonderful Venice was etcetera before finally introducing ourselves; the man saying nasally, "Hi, I'm Joe."

"Joe" turned out to be Joe Wambaugh, the Los Angeles policeman-turned-author and the "lady friend" his charming wife Dee. Fortunately I had read both *The Glitter Dome* and *The Onion Field* and on saying I knew exactly who he was I wasn't telling a white lie.

I arranged to meet up with Joe and Dee on their arrival in London. Thinking they may enjoy a visit to an *olde worlde* country pub in leafy Gloucestershire followed by lunch with the doyenne of the village in her breathtaking 17th-century home, I made all the necessary arrangements with Edith (I learned to my surprise she was a fan of Joe's) and set off happily with my two guests for Sherston.

Unfortunately Joe was not impressed by Edith's eclectic group of luncheon guests and insisted on leaving with two other equally unimpressed guests immediately after lunch!

Despite the unforeseen hiccup Joe and I have kept in touch. I also sent him a copy of my *Thirteen Tales of Textual Arousal Volume One* which was later incorporated in *6+6+6 Eighteen Tales of Textual Titillation Volumes One and* Two.

At Edith's funeral I was saddened to note there was a single black face amongst the many mourners.

The evening after Edith's funeral I was enjoying a quiet "kitchen supps" with Ben.

"As I've already said I find it quite extraordinary not seeing one black face among the mourners," I murmured in response to his questions concerning the funeral.

"Imagine if it'd been *my* funeral?" said Ben with a wicked chortle.

"A rival to the Black Sea, no doubt," I quipped.

Ben pointed to the book on Robert Mapplethorpe I had bought for him after our visit to New York and catch-up with Andy Warhol. "Have you *ever* had it off with a black man, Mumsie?"

"Apart from a one night stand with Paul Danquah a hundred years ago, no," I replied self-consciously. "Maybe growing up in Africa has something to do with it. A case of coals to Newcastle with no pun intended!" I gave a quiet laugh. "To be quite honest, the thought's never really crossed my mind."

"Pity," muttered Ben. He glanced at my wine glass. "Time for a refill Mumsie and time for you to definitely think again."

One evening about a week later I was sitting at my desk going through a building specification when the buzzer for the front door suddenly went causing to give a start and almost send my glass of wine flying.

"Who the fuck . . . ?" I muttered glancing at my watch. Walking over to door I said brusquely into the intercom, "Yes? Who is it?"

"It's Tony," said a rich, deep mellifluous voice.

"Tony?" I questioned immediately thinking, *Tony Hutt? It can't be . . . ?*

"Tony *who*?" I asked querulously.

"Tony, a friend of Ben's," came the reply. "He said I was to come along and say 'hello' to er . . . Mumsie." There was a pause. "Er . . . is that Mumsie speaking?"

"Oh, he did, did he?" I muttered, my face reddening, "Well Mr Tony, a friend of Ben's whose come along to say 'hello'; whether I'm Mumsie or not I'm rather busy so another time perhaps?"

Jesus Ben, what the hell are you playing at? I thought more in irritation than in anger. *Oh shit! Your waspish comment the other evening. Time to think again.* I gave an audible swallow.

"Er . . . sorry er . . . Tony, I didn't intend to sound so rude so er . . . why don't you come in for a quick drink and then I really *will* have to throw you out as I'm working to a deadline. Er . . . once you're in it's the first door on the right." I clicked off the intercom and pressed Enter.

"Okay Mr C.," I muttered, "let's check out you attempt in making me 'think again'. Whatever this Paul Robeson voiceover turns out to be he certainly doesn't sound like one of your giggly, girlish preferences which you know is definitely *not* for the likes of choosy *moi!*"

On hearing a tentative knocking on the door I jerked it open and found my gaze drawn upwards to a smiling, devastatingly handsome, ebony face towering above me. (I would soon discover my unexpected visitor stood at six foot five or approximately two metres in his bare feet.)

"Hello, I'm Tony," said the young man proffering a gigantic hand. "Please to meet you er ... Mumsie."

"Hello er ..." Tony," I replied, my hand totally engulfed as if in warm, soft black glove. "Pleased to meet *you* too ..."

The best way in which to describe my first impression of Tony would be as a doppelgänger for Robert Mapplethorpe's Ken Moody but with Milton Moore's legendary *accoutrement!* In other words, an ebony priapic god. Sporting a dark blue blazer, a white open-neck shirt and wearing a pair of neatly pressed chinos the young man looked as if he had stepped from a fashion catalogue catering exclusively for the extra-large male. Glancing down at his highly polished shoes I gave a silent gulp. If those weren't a size 16 (European size 49) or more then my name wasn't Robin Anderson or to be more accurate and in a tribute to Robert Mapplethorpe's Svengali: *Robert* Anderson.

Tony, much to Ben's genuine delight (I prefer not to reveal his full name) became my lover plus a respected friend. However Ben was adamant I heed his advice.

"Now Mumsie make sure you don't go and ruin *this* relationship by spoiling the guy rotten and suffocating him with endless presents and disruptive trips here, there and everywhere. Tony has a career as well as his own life so it's best you keep it that way. Meet when you wish to meet but don't push. The big guy seems to think - eek! - the sun, moon and stars shine out of your aged arse which is all you need to know!"

I can truthfully say I never once saw Tony rattled or out of sorts. Not only was he a fabulous lover, he was also kind, considerate, humorous and extremely courteous to my friends. Whenever I did indulge myself in a temper tantrum he would quietly pour himself a drink, pick up a newspaper or magazine and wait patiently for me to calm down. With his innate good looks, charm and obvious sex appeal Tony was an instant hit with my women friends. I am sure had Margaret Argyll met him she would have immediately dubbed the Big T a second "Hutch". "Hutch" being the black American singer who took London by storm in the 1930s; his long-standing relationship with Edwina Mountbatten being an open secret in Mayfair clubs and bars. Hutch would create a stir by arriving at his venues dressed in evening wear and with a white piano strapped to his chauffeur-driven car. (Maybe I should have attached a drawing board to the top of my Mini Cooper!) Tony never professed at being able to play the piano but whether his forte or not, his five finger exercises were certainly of Royal Albert Hall quality. I never discovered if Hutch had been one of Margaret's paramours but it wouldn't have surprised me.

I was fascinated by what I described to Ben as the Big T's "CW fetish" which saw us spending many a morning over breakfast where I would checking my post and making notes while Tony immersed himself in the daily crossword in the *Daily Mail* and over a weekend, *The Mail on Saturday* followed by *The Sunday Times.* He also had a touch of the gourmet in him and would spend many happy hours in the kitchen with the likes of Robert Carrier and Delia Smith. A Big T favourite was his marinated chicken pan-fried in caramelised sugar and simmered in coconut milk. Almost as delicious as the chef! Tony was also a great theatre buff and we spent many enjoyable evenings catching all the West End and out of town shows. Because of Tony's height and broad shoulders I would always try and book seats in the back row of the front section of the stalls in order for the people in the row behind to have the benefit of the space between the two sections; the additional space between the seats making sure those members of the audience seated directly behind us did not have their view of the stage blocked by the Big T's gigantic form!

I genuinely believe Tony and I would have ended up living together had it not been for the dreaded word "drugs" rearing its ugly head and it should have come as no surprise Ben would be the one to make me aware of the developing situation.

"I saw your Big Tony at a party the other night, Mumsie," he told me. "However I feel you should know he wasn't his usual friendly self but extremely aggressive and stoned out of his mind."

"You must be mistaken," I replied defensively. "Tony doesn't 'do' drugs. Why, the Big T even balks at the mention of the word 'poppers'!"

How wrong and how misguided I was.

Tony's downhill spiral into the world of drugs soon became apparent starting with him losing his job with the quantity surveyors he had worked with for the past five to six years. On the few occasions he deigned to meet me I was shocked by his dishevelled appearance and the incoherence of his speech. What made matters worse (and a growing embarrassment) were his frequent requests for money. Nervously referred to as "some pennies" the so-called pennies were always in the region of fifty pounds or more.

After several generous handouts I decided enough was enough and gave Tony an ultimatum; either he checked himself into a rehabilitation unit and quit or else I would quit and never contact him again.

Swearing on endless oaths he would do whatever possible to maintain "our love" a solemn Tony rose from the table in the branch of Starbucks where we had agreed to meet. Avoiding my stern gaze he said nervously, "I promise I will call into Social Services tomorrow . . ."

"I'd be happier if you contacted The Priory," I interrupted, "and of course I'll be more than happy to pay for your treatment but only on condition you really do sort yourself out." I added with an anguished cry. "Jesus Big T, don't throw your life - us - away."

"I promise Robin; I really promise," he replied. "And while I know you would do this for me I must handle it myself." Still avoiding my gaze he added nervously. "In the meantime could you er . . . could you lend me a few pennies to tide me over while I er . . . make the necessary arrangements?"

Knowing I was being an utter fool I duly handed over a wad of notes. "Promise me you'll go along to whatever department you say you're going to tomorrow," I repeated as he withdrew his hand.

"I promise Robin; I really promise," said Tony still not meeting my eye. Giving me a weak, furtive smile he added in a forlorn whisper, "See you."

I never saw Tony again and despite Ben's endless questioning among his many black contacts Tony appeared to have literally vanished. On thinking back to my time spent with Tony or the Big T, how sensible of Ben to have suggested it was time for me to "think again". Tony was such a charmer and such a gentleman I am sure even DLL would have approved.

*

Next on Barbara Eppel's seemingly never-ending "little list" or "Barbara's Mikado" of new clients (a tongue-in-cheek reference to Ko-Ko's *I've Got a Little List* from Gilbert and Sullivan's *The Mikado*) was husband Leonard's latest property venture, the total refurbishment of The Albert Dock in Liverpool: part of Margaret Thatcher's grand vision for the regeneration of England's despondent inner cities.

I flew up to Liverpool with Leonard and on arrival at the site stood staring in disbelief at the vast, derelict property and its rancid, silt-filled inner dock.

"And your intention Leonard is to turn this into a series of exclusive flats, a shopping centre, restaurants, offices and an offshoot of The Tate Gallery, The Tate of the North?" I said in a stunned voice.

"Precisely," replied Leonard. "And I'd like you to take care of the main reception and communal areas to the residential sector which will be known as The Colonnades. I will also require two very exceptional show flats." He added with a smile. "You'll probably have to fly up - or take a train if you prefer it - once or twice a week but I can assure Robin, it'll be worth it."

"I look forward to it, Leonard," I replied enthusiastically, "After all if Liverpool could produce the Beatles let's see what Robin Anderson can do for Liverpool!" My smiling riposte resulting in a puzzled look from my latest client. (The legendary "Fab Four" having first performed at the nearby Cavern Club in 1961. Today the Albert Dock is home to The Beatles Story Museum, Fab 4 Café and a souvenir shop.)

The Albert Dock, a historic Grade I Listed building covering an area of 1.25 million square feet, was designed by the architect and engineer Jesse Hartley. Construction began in 1841 with the work completed four years later. The dock was officially opened by Albert, Prince Consort, husband of Queen Victoria, in 1846. A key factor of the massive construction were the materials used: a combination of brick, iron and stone and therefore completely fireproof.

After its impressive beginning the docks went into a slow decline and were finally closed in 1972. Enter Leonard Eppel and the Merseyside Development Corporation who ten years later would unite in order to breathe new life into the slumbering giant. I had hoped to use Louisville to carry out my side of the contract but Leonard was adamant I work with the onsite contractors. However I insisted on using John Wright for any special paintwork I deemed necessary. Meanwhile, John Skellorn, my carpet supplier, announced he was retiring and introduced me to Doug Williams of the Harrow Carpet Company who I am glad to say went on to supply carpeting to my designs until I decided to call a halt to any more interior design work.

"This should be fun," I murmured as I dialled Doug's number.

"Morning Doug, Robin Anderson speaking. I have a new contract for you involving yet another RA 'special'. Obviously its early days as I still have to work on the pattern but how does a quarter of a mile or so run of twenty seven inch RA special sound to you? Oh, and by the way, that's only for the communal areas: I haven't even thought about the show flats."

A major feature of Jesse Hartley's impressive design was the bold geometric motif used for the handrail to the walkway running the perimeter of the actual marina. I instinctively knew the design, reduced in scale for both the carpeting and any upholstery throughout, would be the perfect answer as well as a tribute to the architect.

A weekly commute to Liverpool for the next five years became a way life with me catching the early morning flight from London Heathrow to Liverpool's Speke Airport (renamed John Lennon Airport in 2002) returning the same evening unless I decided to stay overnight.

The Albert Dock was officially opened by HRH Prince Charles on May 24th 1988. I travelled up to Liverpool for the historic event the day before and was on site in the Colonnades a couple of hours earlier on the great day itself to ensure everything was to my liking. Tut-tutting as I noticed a few pieces of miniscule carpet fluff outside one of the show flats and regardless of my immaculate Savile Row suit, Turnbull & Asser shirt, Hermès tie and de rigueur Gucci loafers, I grabbed a Hoover from one of the utility cupboards serving the floor and began hoovering away.

"Fuck!" I muttered as three figures appeared in the corridor ahead. Giving the men a quick glance as I attempted to steer the hoover past them I said cheerfully, "Sorry gentlemen, I'll have to ask you to step aside for the world's highest paid cleaner. I've Charlie boy dropping by later so no dust is a must!"

"Shit," I murmured glancing back at the three figures continuing their way along the corridor, "I thought he looked familiar despite the pinned back ears! Another case of Dumbo becoming dignified or a Rabbit ravishing!" Later it was confirmed one of the men was Prince Charles having a private view of the project before his scheduled "arrival" by motor launch later.

Ten years on I was briefly introduced to the much-deified Princess Diana at a charity event hosted by Christie's, the auction house, at their salesrooms on King Street, St. James's. My instant impressions on meeting the smiling icon were "Christ, she's a bloody Amazon" followed by "what an enormous hooter!" or "nose" for the unenlightened. On being told of my impressions of the much lauded princess one waspish queen couldn't wait to add *his* first impression on seeing her "in the flesh".

"I know *exactly* what you mean," he said spikily, "Jimmy Schnozzle Durante in drag!"

(As previously mentioned my apartment in Redcliffe Square if literally next door to Coleherne Court where Diana lived before marrying Charles. Despite a time lapse of almost forty years one still gets the odd gaping tourist standing surveying the impressive apartment block. A cult of sorts which totally baffles me.)

In celebration of the special occasion Arrowcroft chartered an aircraft to bring a group of guests from London to Liverpool for the day. Leonard generously suggested I invite six guests. *Numero uno* obviously had to be Ben Colman. I also invited Min Hogg, Editor of *The World of Interiors*, Peter Coats (supposedly representing *House & Garden Magazine*) andJohn Rendall representing *London Portrait Magazine*; a step up from site coordinator on Park West.

Leonard Eppel was certainly not amused when Rendall, bold as brass, inveigled himself into the line-up of special guests waiting to be introduced to Prince Charles. "Who was that man and who invited him?" he demanded later. Fortunately he was interrupted by Nicholas Hai, his son-in-law and one of his directors, before I was forced to explain.

Nicholas, who eventually took over from Leonard as Chairman of Arrowcroft, commissioned a book about The Albert Dock Redevelopment prior to it being sold to a Global investment company in 2016 in a deal worth more than £42 million. In the book there is a photograph showing the Prince being introduced by Leonard to the special guests at the official opening ceremony. In the line-up the smug-looking uninvited guest can be clearly seen.

During one of my earlier site visits to the Dock I laughingly suggested to John Wright he and I combine ideas and enter a canvas for yearly Royal Academy Summer Exhibition held at Burlington House on Piccadilly.

"I see a touch of RA stripes meets JW," I said, "aided and abetted with a touch of Mondrian."

"Sounds good to me, Rob," replied John, "so let's give it a go!"

To this day I am still curious to know who purchased this masterpiece titled *Storm* and their side of the story.

Inspired by the RA Summer Exhibition the other RA decided on a summer exhibition of his own which saw me hiring the Marie Antoinette Suite at the Ritz for a mid-morning "Champagne and Pimms Reception" to which I invited some eighty guests. Among those invited was the legendary Margaret Argyll who arrived with Peter Coats.

"Goodness me darling," said Margaret taking in the glittering throng, her large violet eyes twinkling, "Peter and I were just saying how our indefatigable Robin is full of surprises. Perhaps *next* time it'll be to celebrate his *purchasing* the Ritz!"

*

A fairly exotic "in-betweener" break during the time I was occupied with The Albert Dock was a brief visit to the magical island of Mauritius (Bali eat your heart out). On this snatched occasion my travelling companion was a rugged uber-macho Canadian named Rick Douglas, a friend of La Popote's Christopher Hunter and allegedly one of the smouldering (literally) Marlborough men as featured in the macho adverts. I never got round to puffing on Rick's personal Marlborough but to find a more charming, considerate and amusing holiday guest would be an almost impossible task. Rick proved himself to be the complete antithesis to the manipulative, mercenary Malcolm and Boozy Barry: two very expensive pieces of excess baggage.

I had arranged for the rental of a charming thatched-roofed "beach bungalow" with its own small private tract of golden sand from the elegant Casuarina Club. On our first "beach and burn day" Rick and I spotted a scrawny, exhausted-looking stray dog limping along the shoreline towards where we lay on our beach towels accompanied by a reassuring drinks cooler containing a large packet of chicken sandwiches, ice, white rum and lime juice. The despondent animal, tail between her legs appeared to sport two rows dangling dugs which added to impression of the poor animal being even more worn out.

"The elderly lady slowly approaching us has obviously had more than her fair share of gentlemen friends," quipped Rick in his soft, Canadian drawl, "and don't those pendulous tits prove it! How many litters do you think she's had, RA? A dozen?"

"I think that's a prime example of Canadian chivalry," I replied eyeing the exhausted-looking mutt. "I'd make it at least *two* dozen."

"Somehow I think *this* lady is no tramp - no tramp at all - but simply a lady who needs a little TLC," murmured Rick breaking off a piece of his sandwich and gently proffering the tantalising titbit.

Eyeing Rick warily the lady under discussion cautiously approached the small portion of sandwich Rick was holding and in a flash, dashed forward and before we had time to blink, wolfed it down before turning tail and slinking away. Two days later Delilah (we'd instantly named her after the seemingly appropriate Tom Jones song *Why, why, why Delilah?* in tribute to her drooping dugs) was lying under a Casuarina tree close to our usual spot as if waiting for us. (Rick and I having been to Port Louis the day before.)

On hearing Rick's cheerful "Good morning again, Delilah," the elderly pooch rose shakily to her feet wagging her tail weakly in reply. "I was hoping to see you again," Rick continued with a dimpled smile, "and seeing how much you enjoyed that chicken sandwich day before yesterday I made one especially for you and for desert I've brought you small chocolate bar."

On this occasion Delilah didn't grab the sandwich but accepted it graciously. Even more noticeable was the fact she chewed on the sandwich instead of wolfing it down. I don't think Delilah had never eaten chocolate before and if a dog's eyes could widen in surprise, hers most certainly did. Giving Rick an adoring look and a further wagging of her scrawny tail she sniffed appraisingly at his beach towel before settling down on it and promptly falling asleep. Next day Delilah was accompanied by two more mutts and by the end of the week our adopted family - all of distinctly Heinz 57 parentage - numbered six.

Rick, charm personified, coaxed a dewy-eyed Delilah in joining him for a swim and in his new role as Pied Piper of Mauritius soon had the other five dogs joining in.

"This is not only becoming serious," I said to Rick as our new family happily polished off another pile of sandwiches, "it's beginning to cost a bomb in bread, butter, mayonnaise and roasted chickens from Petite Lucille!"

"Let me speak to Petite Lucille," replied Rick in his usual unfazed manner (Petite Lucille being the name we'd given to the giggling Amazon-like young woman in charge of a small store-cum-bar adjacent to the Casuarina Club). Petite Lucille who, like Delilah was head over flip flops-cum-paws in love with "Mr Rick", could not have been more helpful and made sure Delilah, Tom, Paul, Ringo, Kylie and Barry were served a daily helping of a rich, meaty stew and biscuits.

"Maybe in being kind we're also being bloody cruel for Christ only knows what will happen to the pooches when we leave," murmured Rick eyeing Delilah dozing by his feet, "despite Petite Lucille saying she'll keep up the good work."

"Added to which she certainly can't afford it," I said bluntly. "And even if I - we - were to leave a wad of cash with Lucille it wouldn't last for more than a week or two and a monthly cheque to a bank or even the Club to cover the costs is out of the question."

Rick and I didn't mention the obvious, namely what guarantee did we have that the animals would even see another meal once we had left. On the return flight to London Rick and I repeatedly berated ourselves for having lulled the poor animals into such a short-lived, comfortable lifestyle. On our last evening the Rick along with me and the six pooches sat on the moonlit staring at the gentle ways breaking lace-like on the silvery sand.

"Dear Robin, I can't begin to thank you enough," murmured Rick gently fondling Delilah's ears, "it's been a marvellous ten days, the greatest of fun in perhaps one of the most beautiful places on the planet." He gave me a soft, dimpled smile. "And if you feel I've let you down in any way . . ."

"You mean the bed thing?" I replied with a grin. "Rick, even if I *had* wanted a torrid tumble or two it would have been out of the question seeing we did have six others sharing the bed!"

Of all the paradisiacal tropical islands I have visited Mauritius remains unchallenged. With its miles of coral reef, turquoise and aquamarine coloured sea, golden beaches, languidly waving Casuarina trees, palm trees and mountainous interior the island is breathtakingly beautiful. And where else in the world would you find water lily pads two to three metres in diameter?

I did challenge Rick to a game of water lily hopscotch on a visit to Sir Seewoosagur Ramgoolah's famous Pamplemousse Botanical Gardens but was turned down. Maybe if the six pooches had been in tow Rick would have positively jumped at the challenge.

*

Back from Mauritius I found myself caught up in numerous spin-offs from The Albert Dock, including another block of apartments in Hyde Park Gate and two private houses in another marina-type development known as Chelsea Harbour. The new development boasted the elegant Belvedere Tower, an imposing eighteen storey block of flats overlooking The Thames, a yacht marina, the Chelsea Harbour Design Centre with its three majestic Regency glass domes housing over a hundred and twenty design showrooms, a five star hotel and a selection of luxury riverside houses.

Through Tracy Reed I was introduced to Sally Burton, widow of the actor Richard Burton, who - in the beginning hinted at a being that rarity, a dream client - a hint which soon became a nuance. Sally owned a large Georgian-style house in Bayswater's exclusive Porchester Terrace. My unusual suggestion of a pair of gilded Louis XV1 armchairs upholstered in a pistachio-coloured cowhide pattern printed on ivory silk moiré for her elegant but rather "safe" drawing room was greeted with positive glee and after this minor breakthrough there was no holding the adventurous Sally back.

Dubbed "Sally B" by the imitable JW as opposed to "that bitch Burton" by some of the lesser impressed workmen, Sally at first could do no wrong. However one soon learned her easy smile could quickly switch to a forbidding scowl (shades of Peter Sellers). Whereas JW soon learned to tread carefully (laugh when she laughed and remain silent when she was silent) one or two other trades didn't and the atmosphere was strained to say the least.

Encouraged by the success of the "Louis twins" and Sally's ongoing enthusiasm for "something a bit more adventurous" she ended up with a sumptuous dining room literally "wrapped" in a swirling burgundy and black lacquer plus a vanilla and lemon ice cream-coloured staircase described by Tracy as "positively mouth-watering"!

The pièce de résistance however had to be Sally's study. "Daringly" papered in a deep burgundy by the former designer (about the only colour of note she seemed to have introduced in the whole house) we took it from there.

First things first; the glaring white ceiling and impractical white carpet simply had to go. This resulted in JW repainting the ceiling in a burgundy swirl as so as to complement the wallpaper instead of alienating it: the walls decorated with a plethora of gold frames displaying Richard Burton's many tributes and diplomas. Sally's preference for a carpet was something traditional "but traditional with a difference". Enter Colleen Berry of Berry Designs whose exclusive hand-painted silks and hand painted canvas rugs were the talk among those designer's and decorators "in the know".

A few weeks later saw a team from Berry Designs fitting wall to wall sisal matting in the study followed by a group of artists who, armed with the appropriate working drawings done to scale, went on to painstakingly create a hand painted Aubusson style carpet on the sisal background. Delighted with the result I suggested to Sally the top flight of stairs leading to her office again be covered in sisal only this time "scattered" with hand painted cornflowers to match the fabric used for the curtains and covers in the airy, top floor room.

On thanking Colleen for the exemplary work carried out by her team of artists her response was not what I expected with Colleen saying I no uncertain terms, "No matter *what* Mrs Burton thinks I can assure you Robin my girls will *never* set foot in that woman's house again". After considerable probing I learned how one of the girl artists on politely asking "Mrs Burton" if she could "use the loo" had been told to walk across the road and use the facilities of a nearby hotel. Sally's behaviour must have been catching as a similar incident was to occur involving another carpet layer a few weeks later.

Sally eventually moved to Australia to be close to her brother and his family and though there was talk of Berry Designs creating another unique sisal "talking point" for her new haven "Down Under" I never broached the subject with Colleen and much to my relief I heard nothing more on the subject.

Years later I dedicated *Oysters Aweigh,* one of the books in my highly successful *La Di Da Di Bloody Da!* series to Sally who had the temerity to suggest a few changes to the proposed dedication!

In 2003 the BBC produced a brilliant drama titled *Burton & Taylor* starring as far as I am concerned two of England's most brilliant actors, Helena Bonham Carter and Dominic West. On seeing the film it again led to the inevitable recurring question, "Why Richard? Why?" In my mind's eye Elizabeth Taylor will always remain Burton's one and only Krupp Diamond and anything else a pale imitation. I only met Elizabeth Taylor once at a charity AIDS luncheon at the Mirabelle in London where I spent about ten minutes talking to this magical person who genuinely sparkled instead of appearing apathetic.

Meanwhile David and Lita Young purchased what I can only describe as "Hollywood's idea of a Spanish hacienda in the Sussex countryside" and I was more than delighted to add a touch of "*Olé*" to the sprawling property. The extensive verdant grounds included numerous outbuildings, a comfortable guest cottage, a swimming pool, a tennis court and a large pond eventually transformed into a placid, miniature lake by a local landscape artist. I enjoyed my "away days" to Sussex and would leave early for the drive to house situated a few miles from the small town of Petworth and the famous 17th-century Petworth House and after a worthwhile morning on site treat myself to a pub lunch at The Black Horse Inn in the town serving what I claim can only be the best Eggs Benedict in all of England. A Freudian slip perhaps?

Lita was (and still is) a positive dynamo and never stops with her charities and various projects. Therefore I was not at all surprised when she telephoned asking me to meet her and David in the Regent's Park apartment to discuss "enlarging the entrance hall and replacing the large screen in the drawing room with a handsome Adam fireplace".

I duly redecorated the enlarged entrance hall in tone of aubergine and ivory with a bordered carpet to match; turned the former maid's room into a small breakfast room and as Karen the eldest daughter was about to get married, changed her former en suite bedroom with its definite "teenager's look" into something more sophisticated. Judith, her younger sister, was also leaving the roost and moved to a fun flat in London's charming Little Venice which saw her former en suite bedroom turned into a stylish study for David.

At the start of the eighties David Young had become heavily involved in politics and was regarded by Prime Minister Margaret Thatcher as her "blue-eyed boy" and given a life peerage in 1984 making him Baron Young of Graffham.

It was during the refurbishment of the Regent's Park apartment the second "carpet" incident occurred when Ted one of the carpet layers from Harrow Carpets, a true salt of the earth type and a trouper, asked Lita if he could "please use the toilet" and was told without any due hesitation to make use of the "facilities" at the nearby Baker Street Station.

On being told of the slight fracas by an indignant Ted (he ended up using the "facilities in the bleedin' Porter's Lodge") I diplomatically replied, "C'mon Ted, you know how fussy women can be. You'd just put down brand new carpet in her Ladyship's loo for Christ's sake. And while we all aim to please she could have been seriously concerned about your personal aim!"

Oh, the trials and tribulations of being an interior designer!

To this day, some thirty five years on, Ted and Doug the factory manager still laughingly talk about the Ted being "truly pissed off in more ways than one".

On being told of "Ted's trauma" another client Joyce Freed and a great friend of Lita's was heard to say waspishly, "Unlike myself who was born a lady they had to make Lita one!"

Ouch!

I was duly invited to Karen's wedding to Bernard Rix where I was introduced by a smiling Lita to the guest of honour, the formidable Margaret Thatcher.

"Prime Minister, this is Mr Robin Anderson the interior designer who designed our apartment in York Terrace," gushed Lita.

Proffering her hand The Iron Lady eyed me steadily from beneath a pair of alarmingly hooded lids and said in a slow, low, elocuted voice, "You did a good job."

Looking at the Iron Lady's expressionless face I was tempted to give a questioning glance over my shoulder as if checking out "the good job" on the floor behind me!

*

To confirm and to illustrate the fact I was over the trials and tribulations caused by the dastardly Sheik of Araby for which I still held Richard Reynolds partly responsible, I hired the Marie Antoinette Suite at the Ritz for a glittering, midmorning champagne soiree. Among the many guests were my four firm favourites: Margaret, Duchess of Argyll, Ben Colman, Peter Coats and Lita Young. On receiving the final bill for my preening my immediate reaction was a gasped, "C'mon Beesle. Chop! Chop! Time to stop playing your harp and find your Robble a new client!"

A week later Lita and David introduced me to another David; David Li a business associate from Hong Kong and his svelte wife Penny who were in the process of purchasing a house off Belgrave Square. The couple had seen the Young's apartment in Regent's Park and fallen in love with the décor. After several consultations with the couple I was more or less left to my own devices. On showing Penny a stunning circular antique rosewood dining table and a set of chairs I considered and ideal match I was told to go ahead and buy the furniture and once I had done this would I have chairs and table sprayed ivory "to match the cornice and woodwork" in the new apricot and ivory dining room.

Giving my client a tight smile I muttered an almost inaudible "of course" while simultaneously thinking, *I'm sorry but no, a thousand times no, the client is* not *always right but thinking of all the feelthy lucre Beesle and Lita have sent my way, Penny can have the antiques with a fucking* polka dot *finish as long as she's happy!*

SAMBA, CARMEN MIRANDA & MACHU POPPINS

A well-deserved break following the warranted success of the massive Park West property redevelopment saw me - literally - triumphantly *Flying Down to Rio* courtesy of British Caledonian from Gatwick, London's second airport. Seated comfortably next to a chunky, dark haired, sombre-faced young Latino who sullenly introduced himself as "Walter" before turning his attention back to a well-thumbed paper back (his message coming across loud and clear) I gave a small inner sigh of relief. *Thank God for small mercies*, I thought, *No boring small talk and with luck, a few hours undisturbed kip*. Accompanied by a glass of white wine I turned *my* attention to *Lover and Gamblers*, the latest best-selling Jackie Collins which I reluctantly set aside while dinner was served. Half an hour later saw me back in the company of Miss Collins accompanied by a couple of VSOP brandies. Finally it was time for the brightly smiling and very camp air steward to distribute tartan-patterned blankets and bid us a cheery "good night".

Falling into a fitful VSOP doze I was literally *jerked* awake by a warm hand feverishly fumbling with the zip to my fly. Instinctively I placed my hand on Walter's hand only to find it clutched in a strong grasp and redirected to Walter's open fly on to what could only be described as Rio's answer to the Leaning Tower of Pisa without the leaning. Eyes tightly shut Walter proceeded to do what most schoolboys do and being an accommodating soul I followed suit.

Despite the subdued lighting in the cabin I was acutely conscious of our bobbing tartan-patterned blankets energetically doing their own very individual version of the Highland Fling. I am convinced all would have gone unnoticed had it not been for Walter the Wanker (how else could I refer to him?) suddenly becoming Walter the Wailing Wanker!

On disembarking at Rio's Galeão International Airport the following morning I deliberately ignored the smirking young steward's snide "Hope you enjoyed the flight sir; not *too* bumpy I trust?" as I made my way down the aircraft steps.

"Whereabouts are you staying in Rio?" hissed Walter as we stood by the carousel waiting for our respective luggage.

"The Sheraton," I hissed back furtively (Walter's cloak and dagger behaviour was catching), "and as we never er . . . never got round to properly introduced ourselves the name's Robin. Robin Anderson."

At the Sheraton I made myself known to Alan Bird, the Kuoni representative whose group I was joining on a trip titled *South American Panorama* and billed as "the trip of a lifetime".

"For what it's costing, it damn well should be," I growled at Alison on collecting my tickets and various brochures from Peter Lubbock Travel.

"You'll love it," smiled Alison, "you couldn't be in better hands."

How right she was with both Kuoni's and Walter's hands being as they say in the land of the Samba, *perfeito!*

Having been introduced by Alan to my fellow travellers I was also introduced to the irresistible Château Duvalier, a charming white wine and my constant companion for much of the trip.

Much to my surprise I received a call later from Walter the WW inviting me to lunch the next day.

"Sorry Walter," I said apologetically, "but I'm already tied up for most of the day with a morning visit to Corcovado to say hello to his nibs and then on to lunch somewhere along the Copacabana."

If Walter was puzzled by my reference to "his nibs" he didn't say so. "How about dinner then?" he softly replied.

Why not? I thought. *After all, if my VSOP befuddled brain serves me well Walter's answer to the Leaning Tower of Pisa was both spectacular and splatter-lar!*

"Sounds great Walter; I'd love to. Thank you and thanks again for your call."

I woke up to a Rio de Janeiro blanketed by grey, grey clouds and blustering rain, so much so the famous Sugar Loaf mountain could not be seen.

I stood surveying a towering "his nibs" as the rain continued to pour down relentlessly while his nibs - aka the 38 metre high statue of Christ, The Redeemer - standing with arms outstretched, remained impervious to the appalling weather. (Or maybe it was His way of snubbing Dad.)

Lunch at a restaurant on the famous Copacabana beach was a literal washout with the dispirited group "making do" with an adequate alternative selected by Alan. Compensation for the relentless rain was the utter enchantment of the mosaic pavement adjoining the beach. The undulating wave effect created by the Brazilian landscape architect Roberto Burle Marx proving to be not only stunning but - to me - quite remarkable.

Walter dully arrived almost an hour late to collect me for our presumed "hot date". To my surprise he was accompanied by a dazzlingly beautiful young woman.

"My cousin Rosa," he said on introducing us, "I have told her all about you!"

Ah, but did you tell her about Brazil's answer to the Highland Fling? In other words, my samba with your very large mamba?

We dined in a stylish restaurant - "Rosa's favourite" - and after a chaste kiss on the cheek from Walter and a giggling Rosa I was left standing on the steps of the Sheraton as the two zoomed off in Rosa's silver Mercedes-Benz 280SL.

"Ah well, some you lose," I muttered philosophically as I made my way to the bar for a late night rendezvous with my new friend Château Duvalier.

Despite having raised my glass in a definite *tchau* to Walter the WW (Portuguese for "goodbye") my gesture proved to be unfounded. Knowing my next stop would be Sao Paulo he was insistent I call a great friend of his who lived there. (I had learned during dinner the night before that Walter lived in Sao Paulo but would be staying with Rosa for a few days before venturing back home.)

Exit Walter the Wailing Wanker and enter Pedro the Pulsating Piston.

Two days later (still raining) we took a flight to Brasilia which, contrary to all its publicity, turned out to a major disappointment with its modernistic stained, grimy concrete buildings looking totally lost amidst the dilapidated roads and choking jungle. After a gloomy tour of this "fabled city of the future" it was a relief to return to Brasilia's alien looking airport for our flight to Sao Paulo.

"Fingers and legs crossed," I murmured as the plane prepared for take-off. "So far so not at all good.

To my increasing disappointment with the land of the Samba Sao Paulo proved itself an unattractive, claustrophobic city of seemingly endless skyscrapers and a permanent traffic jam. Whereas London is large and sprawling the endless, randomly scattered parks and squares take any feeling of being hemmed in while in New York all the tall buildings are contained on Manhattan alone, Sao Paulo is nothing but mile upon square mile of unattractive phallic-like skyscrapers. A gay fetishist's delight no doubt.

Thank goodness for my introduction to Walter the WW's Pedro and his amazing alternative to Sao Paulo's unattractive skyline. Towering yes, but not at all claustrophobic yet suitably jammed.

To the delight of all our next port of call acted as a giant eraser to the first few days of nonstop rain and general disillusionment with the weather, Brasilia and Sao Paulo. I stood staring entranced by the beauty of the cascading Iguaçu Falls. "Not as savage or as primitive as the Victoria Falls," I said to Alan, "much more civilised - if such a word can be used to describe a waterfall! - and er . . . comfortable; whatever that means!"

At Iguaçu we stayed at the enchanting Das Cataratas hotel. Built in Spanish Colonial style the magnificent rooms all boasted heavily polished wooden floors, dark wood curtains and, a first for me, hand painted rough linen curtains. From my bedroom balcony I had a stunning view of the Falls and the surrounding jungle. The Falls are situated on the borders of Brazil and Argentina and with its endless walkways and observation platforms I found myself overwhelmed by the beauty of it all. Adding to the magic of endless rambling walks were the myriads of colourful butterflies determined not to leave one alone. I was intrigued to note that once the sun had gone down the butterflies were happily replaced by hordes of velvet-winged bats.

On the first evening at Iguaçu I was wakened by a discreet knocking on my bedroom door and a hoarsely whispered, "Robin, are you awake?"

"Who's there?" I called.

"Batman, Robin!" came the somewhat slurred reply followed by a giggle and a hiccup.

"Batman?" I answered with a snicker as I made my way from the bed to the door. "Well good evening Mr Batman, this *is* a surprise," I added on opening the door to reveal a swaying Alan Bird.

"May Batman come in, Robin?" said Alan with a sloppy grin. "Er . . . I was rather hoping we could er . . . go for a ride in my Batmobile . . .?

"A ride in your Batmobile?" I quipped as I ushered him into the room. "Sounds fun and what better way to see Iguaçu from yet another vantage point."

"The Batmobile," announced Alan unzipping his fly and proudly dropping his trousers.

"Batmobile?" I said with a smirk. "That's no Batmobile, it's a bloody Megabat or Giant Flying Fox to give it a more appropriate name!"

*

From Iguaçu we flew to Asuncion the main city of Paraguay for a brief stopover before another two hours flight to La Paz, capital of Bolivia. The city of La Paz nestles in the crater of a former and reassuringly extinct volcano. The following day we visited the colourful local market where I was bedazzled by all the colours, especially the vibrant shocking pink which seemed to predominate. Another noticeable feature were the wonderfully coloured outfits worn by the women store holders comprised of wonderful quilted skirts and technicoloured shawls all topped - literally - with a black bowler or black Derby-style hat. All pure and utter magic.

After the delights of the market we were taken on a tour of the appropriately named Valley of the Moon which proved not to be insomuch a valley but a vast maze of canyons and giant spires comprised of clay and sandstone. Very Buzz Aldrin!

After an exhausting day in this enchanting city it was early to bed (*sans* Batman and his Batmobile) before an early morning start for the long drive in sight of the magnificent snow-capped Andes to Lake Titicaca. Lake

Titicaca (how we smutty school children used to snigger whenever the name "Titicaca" came up during a geography lesson), billed as the highest lake on the planet appeared ahead of us in the form of a vast sheet of blue glass reflecting the clear, azure blue sky. Leaving the bus at the small Hydrofoil station at Huatajata we boarded a hydrofoil for our journey across the lake to Puno and on to Juliaca. I was fascinated by the floating islands we travelled past. These islands made from bundles of reeds were home to endless Indians. As I said to Batman Bird, "Now that could certainly be a new look for RADC. Who needs a mundane houseboat when you could have your own floating island?" I was later informed by a waspish Alan in addition to "endless running water" most of the floating houses boasted a battery-operated TV set!

During the crossing we docked at a small island (not made of reeds) named Island of the Sun where after an exhausting climb up what appeared to be a series of never ending steps we reached the Fountain of Youth from which I drank from copiously. Forty plus years on perhaps the debilitating climb was worth it after all!

From Juliaca we took a train bound for Cuzco. While the majority of the group opted for the grandly named "Buffet Car", Batman Bird and I, along with a charming and very amiable American couple named Don and Cill opted for one of the local carriages and how right we were. Seated snugly on a pair of opposite-facing wooden benches Batman Bird, Don and I set about creating a Juliaca Punch; a lethal mixture of Fanta, Pisco, red wine and a dash of pineapple juice. (Whilst I quite expected to see the universal Cola Cola sign in the depths of Peru I never expected to find fizzy Fanta on sale as well!)

Equally as intoxicating was the continuous stream of vendors who boarded the train at each stop and rushed through the carriages selling such treats as grilled Alpaca, spicy stuffed green and red peppers, riper than ripe runny cheeses and more before jumping from the train at the sound of several short blasts from the train's whistle.

Obviously there had to be some sort of local cabaret and this was provided by the packs of wild dogs running alongside the train and happily scavenging for the left overs tossed from the carriage windows. Bertram Mills and The Moscow State circuses eat your hearts out for when it came to aerial acrobatics nothing could compete with those leaping, twisting, somersaulting, snapping, yowling, panting ferocious dogs as they valiantly kept pace with the chugging train.

When asked to describe my first impression of Cuzco I would have immediately said, "Florence magically transported to the Andes" but on closer examination, Florence wearing a very decorative mantilla. Our hotel named the Hotel Picoaga, comprised of three former 16ty-century grand Spanish townhouses knocked into one large unit. With its cobbled courtyards and large, airy rooms reminiscent of Das Cataratas at Iguaçu the hotel was rightly described by an enchanted Cill as "Pure unadulterated bliss!" It was here I was somewhat taken aback to see colour bands in either a single, double or triple format enhancing the majority of ceilings in the public areas. On asking if they were part of the original décor I was assured they were.

"So much for RA thinking his colour bands were a startlingly new happening in the world of twentieth century design," I muttered sourly to nobody in particular.

A visit to the immense cathedral which dominates the main square could easily turn out to be a shock for anyone with racist tendencies; the shock coming (ha!) from the first sighting of the gigantic statue of a black Christ figure as opposed to the pale, gaunt figure found in similar circumstances.

"Obviously *this* Jesus guy never heard of sunblock," quipped Don.

"Or if he had, he didn't apply it very thoroughly," giggled Cill not to be outdone by her wisecracking companion.

The following day saw a few of the group taking the small train bound for the Machu Picchu, the 15th-century Inca city believed to have been a former royal estate or a sacred religious site for the Inca leaders. The city was supposedly destroyed by the Spanish in the 16th-century and lay hidden among the Andes until rediscovered the American explorer, Higham Bingham in 1917.

The small train chugged into a tiny station situated on the bank of the Urubamba River. Leaving the train we clambered into a dilapidated bus which with a nonstop spewing of exhaust fumes and noisy gear changing slowly advanced up a rough, precipitous track to until it finally drew to a jarring halt outside a cluster of tin shanties; our hotel for the night.

The lost city of Machu Picchu and its breathtaking setting defies any description and the only way to appreciate this incredible place is by seeing it for oneself. I was so taken by the initial impact of the city's magnificent terraces and buildings I made a vow then and there I would return. Adding to the charm and experience of the visit was the dilapidated delight of our hotel made up of a series of ramshackle buildings. (On my return several years later I was horrified by the changes having taken place from a series of hotels complete with air-conditioning, gourmet restaurants, sauna and spas.)

What passed for a bar served a strange mixture of wines, the inevitable Pisco and much to the surprise of Don, Cill, Batman Bird and myself seemingly endless bottles of Amaretto. To this day I still have no idea as to how a dozen or so bottles of this native of *Bella Italia* found their way to a broken-down bar high up in the Andes.

The following morning - no thanks to our imported "friend" - saw the four of us decidedly the worse for wear, delicately climb to the top of the smaller of the two peaks overlooking the ruins.

"Fuck me," said Don giving an Amaretto-infused burp as we sat catching our breath at the top. "That sure is one damn drink I'll never be able to face again!"

"Hear! Hear!" murmured Batman Bird.

"I feel quite dreadful," whimpered Cill, "but come what may, this view was worth the torturous climb."

*

Several years later when I *did* return to Machu Picchu and climbed the peak for a second time I did the climb virtually solo. On this occasion I was accompanied by a bottle of champagne courtesy of our hotel in Lima. Clearheaded and therefore much more appreciative of my surroundings despite a light rain, I seated myself comfortably on a boulder before popping the champagne cork and taking a hearty swallow.

"Goodness," said a plummy English male voice. "I spy with my jaundiced eye a solitary figure atop Machu Picchu sipping champers from a bottle no less? He can only be English!"

"But what a *handsome* champers-swigging Englishman," chirruped his female companion, a robust-looking young woman. "Hello there," she

510

continued, "we saw you setting off ahead of us from the hotel." She gave a light laugh. "Goodness, you must have simply flown up here. Er . . . I'm Louisa and this is Tarquin. Er . . . and you are?"

"Machu Poppins," I replied deadpan, "*sans* umbrella despite the unexpected rain."

"I *thought* you looked familiar," quipped Louisa. She turned to Tarquin, "Didn't *you* think it was Machu Poppins, Tarquin? Despite him not holding his trademark brolly?"

"Care for a sip of Machu P's poison?" I said proffering the bottle, "seeing I really shouldn't drink and fly."

"I thought you'd never ask," laughed Louisa stepping forward.

"Nor I," added Tarquin, a blond, Desmond Cumberbatch lookalike, "and guess what? While it's not quite champers it comes highly recommended." The word's "highly recommended" accompanied by a deft sleight of hand as he suddenly produced a bottle of Château Duvalier from his backpack. "And before you ask, Señor Poppins, yes, it *is* chilled and yes, Señor Tarquin *did* bring along a corkscrew."

"Damn, but no glasses as we weren't expecting guests." giggled Louisa.

"Who needs glasses when a bottle has a neck?" replied Señor Tarquin with a grin.

After such an introduction it was no wonder the three of us were inseparable for the rest of the trip.

*

We travelled back from Machu Picchu to Cuzco where Don, Cill, Batman Bird and I bade farewell to   the rest of the group travelling on to Lima and then London while the four of us flew to Iquitos, a small town on the banks of the Amazon River. From Iquitos we travelled down the Amazon on a giant paddle steamer and after a few hours chugging along the vast expanse of khaki-coloured water we docked alongside a small, nondescript jetty nestling in a clearing cut into the dense foliage lining the river bank. During the journey I watched with fascination endless schools of freshwater dolphins leaping from the river as they escorted the paddle steamer on to its next port of call. When they tell you the Amazon is impressive they simply do not do it justice. At one stage we literally could not see the opposite banks and could have been somewhere in the middle of the ocean as opposed to being inland on a river.

Our refuge for the next few nights was a marvellous establishment named Explorama Lodge which for me was pure Hollywood. The Lodge, a collection of thatched cabins on stilts joined by rope walkways set amidst lush green foliage interspersed with a myriad of orchids would have been a challenge for any established set designer (or interior designer). As far as I was concerned the concept was faultless.

I have to admit the last thing to ever cross my mind was a brief romance in the middle of the Amazon jungle but the unusual *does* happen and for me the "happening" took place on the evening of our arrival. Freshly showered and suitably "Peed and Geed" (Pucci and Gucci . . . what else for an evening in the Amazon jungle?) I was sitting at the dinner table waiting for Don, Cill and Batman Bird and toying with a large glass of the inevitable Chateau Duvalier when out of the blue Tommy suddenly made himself known. From that moment there was no looking back.

I stared transfixed as the unexpected guest who without so much as a "do you mind?" proceeded to swallow the remaining wine in my glass.

"Oi!" I snapped. ""Don't be so bloody rude!"

"Oh sir," giggled the tiny Indian wine steward skipping nimbly across to the table, "Do forgive our Tommy! Please . . . allow me to refill your glass, sir."

"Refill my glass?" I echoed. "No way am I going to drink from the same glass as him."

Ignoring the giggles coming from the neighbouring table I fixed Tommy with a glare and said in a suitable scathing aside to the giggling waiter. "After all, who knows where your Tommy's beak may have been?"

"Of course, sir," replied the wine steward, "I won't be a moment sir . . ."

"And as for you my friend," I said in a reprimanding voice to the unfazed Toucan bird staring expectantly at the empty glass, "there's a saying 'manners maketh man' and I see no reason why that shouldn't apply to a toucan . . . despite him being be one of the most dashing toucans in the whole of Amazonia!"

"Hear! Hear!" cried a woman diner from the neighbouring table. "Tommy did the same to us last night but unlike you young man, we weren't brave enough to chastise him!"

"Your glass sir," interrupted the wine steward placing a clean glass on the pristine white table cloth and deftly filling it. I looked at Tommy who was now staring at me balefully. "Thank you," I said to the wine steward. I nodded towards Tommy's empty glass. "You'd better top up Tommy's glass as well as I certainly don't wish for a repeat performance of him dunking his beak in my wine!"

"Of course, sir. Thank you sir." Eyeing Tommy who once again had his beak deeply immersed in the wine glass, the little Indian added sternly, "Now Tommy, don't forget to say 'thank you' to the kind gentlemen before you get too drunk."

"Who's this dapper fellow?" asked Cill on joining me at the table.

"My hot date," I replied, "and before you say *anything* Cill, *he* picked me up; not the other way round! White wine okay?"

"Lovely."

"White wine for the lady, please," I said to the hovering steward, "and as you can see Tommy is once again in need of a refill."

"Tommy?" quizzed Cill.

"Oh, I'm sorry . . . of course, you haven't been introduced," I laughed. "Cill, meet Tommy and Tommy, if you care to drag your damn beak out of your glass for a second, say 'hello' to Cill."

At the arrival to Batman Bird and Don a decidedly wobbly Tommy fluttered down from the table and made his way unsteadily towards another table of unsuspecting diners.

"Is it something I said?" quipped Don as we watched Tommy's unsteady departure.

"Too much competition for my gracious affections," replied Cill with a chuckle. She reached across and gave Don's hand a squeeze. "I'm sorry to tell you Don dear but if you hadn't turned up when you did I would had no hesitation in tottering off into the jungle with torrid Tommy despite his initial interest being in our lovely Robin."

Next day Tony, one of the genial guides at the Lodge happily confirmed Tommy's penchant for white wine. "I don't know how he does it," he said, "but if *I* put away each night what Tommy does, I'd never be able to get up the next morning."

On our way back to Lima two days later Cill confided to us that she was sure Tommy was a *Transylvanian* toucan as he was never seen during the day; keeping his handsome appearance under "flaps" as it were until evening.

Part of our visit to the Lodge included a day's walk through the jungle which included a stopover at a remote village inhabited by the primitive Quechua Indian tribe. It was here I, much to the amusement of Don, Cill and Batman Bird and the gathered villagers I bargained brazenly for the chief's splendid phallic necklace which I swore was more of a burden for the poor man than a blessing.

"Okay below but not above," quipped Don.

"Hear! Hear!" said Batman Bird.

"Gentlemen!" exclaimed Cill, "There happens to be a lady present."

On our walk back from the village I confirmed an earlier observation to my companions. "Apart from the really heavy growth we say along the river bank and along the tributary leading to the Lodge, it doesn't really give the impression of a *proper* impregnable jungle, does it?."

"Not surprising when you take into account the height of the trees and the almost impenetrable canopy of leaves up above," explained Tony the guide pointing upwards to the umbrella of green shading us. "They call this primary jungle and as you can see the sunlight never really quite gets through the thick foliage hence the impression of wading through a thick bog of decomposing leaves or compost." He added with a chuckle. "If you wish to see what I consider really impenetrable jungle - or secondary jungle to give it its correct term, you should visit Malaysia or the Philippines."

Needless to say we never saw any giant anacondas, piranha fish or devious alligators but my visit to the Amazon, the land of the Samba, Carmen Miranda and Machu Poppins remains a highlight of my extensive travels. So much so I paid, as already mentioned, the Lost City of the Incas a second visit where, despite an increasing plague of insensitive tourists, the impact on viewing the spectacular ruins for a second time easily equalled the wonderment of my first sighting. Apart from my meeting with Tarquin and Louisa I soon made friends with a dashing young Englishman best described as a balding Douglas Fairbanks Junior (no headless man scenario here I hasten to add) with a definite eye for the local ladies. The lady of the moment being our guide, a nubile young lady named Jo.

Over drinks during our first evening in Lima before flying on to Cuzco I learned the Englishman's name was Timothy Foster, a lawyer and head of his own firm. It so happened Martyn Bayer had been causing some concern following hints he had plans for returning to South Africa. On my return to England I made a few enquiries concerning Tim's firm and arranged a meeting with the man himself. Foster, Harrington Associates have been my lawyers ever since.

*

Having thoroughly enjoyed my *Flying Down to Rio* interlude I returned to London to find a multitude of new clients waiting as a result of having purchased one (or several) of the standard flats in the Park West complex. Among the new owners was Harold Gootrad and his elegant French partner, Jacqueline, who commissioned me to design a distinctive modern interior for two flats which I knocked into one.

"Margaret and I would like you to take a look at our flat in Plane Tree House," announced JB a few days after my return. "The place really needs a spectacular 'doing over' and we both agree you're the right guy for the job!"

I agreed to meet Margaret and JB on site the following day and was most impressed by the spacious flat, part of a modern block set at the top end of Kensington's exclusive Phillimore Gardens and overlooking the leafy canopy of Holland Park.

"I lof the view," purred Margaret with a seductive pout.

"And so you should!" quipped JB, "seeing it's a million quid one: if not more!"

Staring out at the autumnal colouring of the turning leave (the flat was on the fifth floor) I suddenly came up with the preposterous idea of "bringing the woods into the flat". However I didn't elaborate any further on the idea to JB and Margaret until I'd discussed the formidable task with JW.

"I'd like you to finish the entrance hall in an antique gold and once this is dry individually stick a variety of dried leaves, oak or whatever, on top of the gold and coating the finished areas with a clear varnish." I announced giving the startled man a reassuring smile. "Don't worry John. All you have to do is *stick* the leaves as I'm sure Steve or Ray can find a Louisville minion to collect them for you. Making it even easier for you is the fact I will be personally selecting the requisite leaves. No pick, just stick. Easy!"

"Jesus Rob," muttered JW looking at me askance. "*Jesus!*"

"Perhaps it will soften the blow," I added laughingly, "if you imagine JB and Margaret as the two *Babes in the Wood*; albeit a rather corpulent babe and a worldly-wise one."

JW was saved the daunting task of "leaf sticking in a most unusual way" (apologies to Noël Coward) thanks to me making one of my many "what's new and exciting" forays to the Mount Street showrooms of Toynbee-Clarke Interiors, one of London's most innovative stockists of wallpapers and fabrics.

"I don't believe it!" I said to Daphne Toynbee-Clarke; wife of George T-C the affable owner.

"Just arrived from one of our supplies in the States," announced Daphne, a smiling Dawn French lookalike, "very different, wouldn't you agree?"

"Not only different Daphs, but *exactly* what I had in mind for a contract I'm currently working on," I said excitedly eyeing the wallpaper sample of laminated autumnal leaves on a translucent background.

Playing on the woodland effect I installed a full-scale tree covered in artificial cherry blossom in what I wittily described as "Madam Butterfly Margaret's bathroom" complete with a pair of mother-of-pearl basins and mother-of-pearl extra wide bath specially commissioned from Godfrey Bonsack Baths whose lavish showroom happened to be situated in Mount Street directly opposite Toynbee-Clarke Interiors. With its mother-of-pearl bath, elaborate gold fittings, pink mosaic walls and floor plus a blossoming cherry tree who could ask for anything more? Margaret I am pleased to say "loffed" it. Adding to all the kitsch the kitchen boasted a climbing vine complete with purple grapes and a stuffed rooster silently crowing on the terracotta-tile window sill.

JB and Margaret were so enamoured with their "Shangri-La" (JB's words) in Plane Tree House they invited me to St. Tropez to view an old farmhouse in the hills above the town they intended to buy.

"I suggest you have a look and then come up with whatever you consider necessary to make it another show stopper," said JB. "Obviously Margaret and I will leave it up to you but we'd still like to see samples and sketches. "He gave a Diddy-like cackle. "Plus I'll need estimates for the whole exercise." He continued happily, "We've rented a villa for the summer - Margaret flew out over the weekend and I plan to join her on Friday - which means you can stay in the villa and the boys - I assume you'll be taking Steve and co along to have a look at the property (a statement, not a question) so I'll get Margaret to make reservations at a nearby *pension* or hotel. Any idea who else you'll be taking?"

Without any hesitation I named JW as well as Steve and Ray.

"Ah yes, the Rod Stewart lookalike who drives that customised black Chevi Blazer 4 x 4," quipped JB. "Good; then Rod can drive back the Merc I left out there last year!" He gave a snicker. "Maybe I should check *his* quotes more thoroughly!"

Ignoring the snide dig I said in a business-like manner, "Between us we'll be able to have all the quotes ready for your return to London or else they can be sent to you in St. Trop. I'll obviously be taking window measurements etcetera plus I will have the relevant colour cards sketches and the soft furnishing quotes ready for you and Margaret to approve within a few days. These aren't as vital as the building quotes but, if the tension proves to be too much I can always hop on a plane!"

"No need for that RA," replied JB with a grin. "Best I see you all back in London in approximately ten days' time. I'll be popping back for a day or two as I don't like being away from the office for more than a week or ten days if I can help it."

Being summer and due to the heavy demand for flights to the South of France we were unable to book a direct flight to Nice resulting in the four of us having to fly to Brussels where after a brief stopover we would take a connecting flight to Nice.

Disaster struck when we missed our connection in Brussels as a result of not registering the final call for boarding. Needless to say Steve and Ray (Steve in particular) were already celebrating their proposed visit to St. Tropez or, as described by an already salivating Steve, "The town of Brigitte Bardot and *ooh la la!*" and due to the two's raucous laughter the announcement went unheeded.

After an argument with the woman at the check-in desk who sneeringly informed us the next flight was fully booked and she would *try* to get us on to a flight the next day, I demanded to see the "fully booked passenger list" which showed the flight in question to be practically empty: but not before she summoned security claiming I had threatened her. Fortunately for us the security guard had obviously experienced similar incidents before involving the belligerent woman and after a few rapids instructions from the man she sullenly handed us our boarding cards. Adding insult to injury on our arrival at Nice Airport I discovered the pre-arranged hire car (a comfortable Fiat 130 saloon) had been reallocated to an earlier passenger due to our no-show at the scheduled time.

"We'll take whatever you have available," I said in desperation to the rental man.

Ten minutes later saw the four of us crammed inside a claustrophobic Renault 4 and with JW at the wheel we set off on the long journey to St. Tropez. Before we left the airport I telephoned Margaret to explain our delay and was told "not to worry" as she had everything "under control".

We spent the next morning surveying the old farmhouse JB was planning to buy. While Steve and Ray took measurements and made notes JW and I discussed the interiors.

"While I don't mind the bare brick which is apparent throughout," I said to JW, "I don't think it will be a hit with JB so let's make the brickwork a work of art in itself by painting sections of the brickwork in a different colour; in other words a geometric Mondrian-type wall mural or two with areas of plain colour to house the odd painting here and there."

I had already suggested to the three they wear swimming costumes under their clothes and bring a holdall with a couple of towels. "I leave it up to you whether or not you'll want to replace your wet cozzies with a pair of underpants!" I cheerfully announced, "And once we've completed our initial survey of the property we'll drive on to Pampelonne Beach for lunch and a swim."

A laughing Margaret had insisted we ditch the Renault and use her bright red Jeep CJ Renegade instead while she used JB's Merc.

Steve and Ray could not believe their eyes on seeing "boobs, bare boobs and more bare boobs" (JW was a bit more blasé having previously visited Charo del Palo beach on Lanzarote). I eyed the wide-eyed, wolf-whistling and yodelling Steve with disbelief. *And this is the same guy who came to my office and told me he was gay and Bobby telling me the two of them were having an affair?* I thought as JW expertly parked the jeep. *Obviously when it comes to whipping it in and whipping it out our Steve isn't all that fussy!*

The day ended on an even more bizarre note when I took the three for dinner in the port itself. By this stage Steve was well and truly into his cups and becoming more and more out of control. Having finished dinner we had moved to an outdoor café where we seated ourselves at table close to the cobbled street facing the bay. Steve, Ray and JW cheerfully settled for coffee and a couple of brandies while I ordered a grappa as a token to DLL.

"Ooh la la!" Steve suddenly yodelled on spotting a white-clad figure sashaying by. "Oi! *Monsieur!*"

Oh no, I thought eyeing the willowy, waspish young queen pause in mid-stride and give Steve a disdainful look. *For fuck's sake Steve. Belt up!*

"*Oui . . . paysan?*" sneered the young man, his mascaraed eyes narrowing dangerously as they homed in on a red-faced, sweating Steve.

"Er . . . la club for la dancing and la Brigitte Bardot?" called out Steve with a leering grin. "Fun, naughty boobies . . . er . . . *comprendez?*"

"That's fucking *Spanish*, Steve," hissed Ray.

"La!" moued the young queen pointing to a nearby doorway and obviously the entrance to some sort of club. Blowing Steve a kiss he added shrilly followed by a fiendish cackle. "*Un club pour la danse!*"

"Let's go!" bellowed Steve clambering clumsily to his feet.

"Must we?" I muttered nervously.

"Not to worry Rob," said JW reassuringly, "I'll make sure Stevie Wonder is kept in order!"

"Shit," I murmured on entering the club (a wink from JW in his tank-top and snug-fitting khakis had ensured us immediate entry), "Trans-*very*-sylvania here we come!"

Within seconds of having sat down and been almost press-ganged into buying a bottle of exorbitantly priced champagne we were approached by a voluptuous blonde transvestite dressed in a red strapless, figure-hugging dress. Fluttering her false eyelashes at a gaping Steve she proffered a ham-like gloved hand and said in a husky voice, "*Aimerais-je danser avec moi?*" ("Would sir like to dance with me?")

Barely able to stifle my laughter I watched a leering Steve as he shuffled off hand-in-hand with his Amazon partner towards the crowded dance floor. On reaching the dance floor Steve immediately embraced his willing partner in a bear-like hug accompanied by a wild gyrating of his hips.

"I think this definitely calls for a top up," muttered JW reaching for the champagne, "and judging from Stevie Wonder's antics on the dance floor we'll probably need another bottle . . ." his words cut short by a wild-eyed, huffing Steve storming back to the table.

"Steve!" I exclaimed. "Something wrong?"

"It's that bloomin' bird back there," gasped Steve. "She's got a fuckin' hard-on!"

*

As arranged an excruciatingly hungover Steve, not-so-hungover Ray and a clear-headed JW and RA met JB the following afternoon after his arrival from London.

"The house could be great," I assured him and Margaret. "Plus I've already managed a quick few sketches of a few ideas I'd like you to mull over before I make a proper presentation. Meanwhile, I'll go over any suggested building and decorating specifications with the lads when we get back to London. All estimates should be ready by the end of next week."

"Well done everybody, well done," said JB jovially, his tousled head bobbing enthusiastically and making him look more Ken Dodd diddy-like than ever. "And now, how about a celebratory dinner somewhere fun? Le Byblos perhaps."

"As long as the birds are kosher," muttered Steve.

*

The next morning Steve and I bade a cheerful farewell to JB and Margaret as we left for Nice to catch the morning flight for London while JW and Ray would be leaving in JB's Mercedes for their long drive back.

Prior to leaving for St. Tropez Steve and JW had left their cars parked at Scarsdale Studios; the plan being Steve would collect his car on his return with me and likewise JW on his return accompanied by Ray. Arriving at Heathrow we quickly cleared customs and within a matter of minutes were in a taxi bound for the studio.

On arrival I suggested Steve come in for another "celebratory drink" before driving home. The "celebratory drink" turned into several and lo and behold (read "ooh la la!") I found myself succumbing to the charms of a very loveable and surprisingly gentle Mr Edwards.

"Now I can see why Bobby Miller was so pleased with himself?" I said to Steve as he was leaving, "for when it comes to sporting a 'hard hat' Mr Edwards would take some beating!"

However, unlike Bob, my "hard hatting" with Steve remained a "one off".

Claiming he was "over the moon" with the proposed designs and JW's and Louisville's quotes were "okay", JB went on to say he would be letting us have a starting date "in due course". For reasons known only to him the information was never forthcoming. However I am sure Steve, Ray and JW never forgot our brief exploratory to the land of Brigitte Bardot, St. Tropez and "Ooh la la!"

*

Hot on the heels of Park West I was asked to undertake a similar venture involving a large thirties-style block of flats named Chelsea Cloisters situated in Sloane Avenue, Chelsea, a few minutes' walk from the iconic Art Deco Michelin Building.

Nowadays Chelsea Cloisters is notorious for the specialist services offered by the many foreign ladies of the night (or any time to suit) who appear to have taken over the building. What amuses is me is the number of times my books have been described as pornographic but this can only be a first when it comes to my skills as an interior designer!

MAGIC CARPET RIDES

During the late '80s and early '90s I made sure whenever possible to take a weekend or a week or two's break - three would have been a luxury - before dealing with punters new. In the '80s Russia was still seen as a country of little appeal to the tourist but I decided on a long weekend in Moscow and it was easy to see why. I flew from Heathrow to Moscow's Sheremetyevo International Airport via Aeroflot and was intrigued by the dismal interior of the aircraft: drab, uncomfortable seats and tatty pull curtains on the windows and a cabin crew apparently chosen from the butchest diesel or bull-dykes available who cajoled or bullied one into a snack more cardboard than caviar.

Being early December the weather was freezing and forewarned I stepped from the plane wearing a handsome, full-length Raccoon coat on top of a blazer, red roll-neck sweater (very subtle), corduroy trousers and brogues with a Fendi briefcase. I had also been instructed in no uncertain terms by a previous visitor to "the land of the hammer and sickle" to make sure I packed a golf ball. Ignoring the curious glances of the other well-wrapped passengers I followed Rodzher our guide who was there to greet me and other nervous members of our group making up a grand total of six excluding the guide.

I thought Rodzher definitely un-Russian and on asking tongue-in-cheek "Did you say Igor or Radomir? I didn't quite hear . . .?"

I was answered by a scornful, "Roger as in James Bond Roger Moore."

"In England we give out friends nicknames," I continued unperturbed. "Maybe, as you're going to be our friend for the next four days you'd allow me to call you 007?"

"007 like 007 James Bond?" questioned Rodzher, his face splitting into a gold-toothed grin. "*Da*, 007 is good. Roger likes 007 very much." He gave me another golden grin. "Do you have a nickname er . . ." he glanced at his clipboard, "Mr Anderson?"

Sorely tempted to say "Pussy Galore" I held back and replying with a smile said instead, "Yes 007, I do. My colleagues and friends call me RA."

"Then I too will call you by this RA," said Rodzher with a further flash of gold.

The short drive into the city through the snow-covered landscape could be best described as travelling through a winter wonderland. I was particularly taken by the acres of leafless silver birches looking exactly like an army of Jack Frosts dressed in sparkling white with black accoutrements. We checked in to the massive Inturist Hotel (not a typo) set in the very centre of the city on Tverskaya and Mochovaya Streets. The hotel, a grim, rectangular block reminiscent of Oxford Street's "sore thumb" Centre Point, was made up of twenty floors of some four hundred and thirty six rooms. I was intrigued to find a grim-faced equivalent of Aeroflot's cabin crew allocated to each floor of the hotel. Sitting with arms folded as they stonily watched the toing and froing of the guests they were obviously there to make sure nobody was having too much fun!

"We're foul and we scowl" could easily have been the slogan for these Michelin-like ladies.

In my Spartan like room (a double bed, a wardrobe, small upright chair and a table) I soon discovered the value of my golf ball seeing neither the basin nor bath possessed a plug. On tentatively placing the gleaming golf ball onto of the outlet to the basin it proved to be a love made in heaven; in other words a perfect fit. Likewise the bath. While my fellow tourists moaned and cursed as they valiantly tried to block the plugholes with a wad of sandpaper-like toilet paper I was happily (and smugly) able to fill both units almost to the brim.

Red Square was vast, sombre and not at all "tourist friendly". I was genuinely shocked by how small St. Basil's Cathedral looked sitting in the middle of the massive Square. Rodzher proudly informed us the Cathedral was commissioned by Ivor the Terrible in 1552 and completed in 1560. Unlike its richly decorated exterior and domes today the building was finished in white with gold-coloured onion domes, similar to the white-stone Kremlin as seen today. Despite Lenin wanting to have St. Basil's demolished in order for Red Square free of any obstacles for his planned massed parades his plan was thwarted; thanks to a Russian architect named Pyotr Baranovsky who refused categorically to do Lenin's bidding. The Cathedral was saved but Baranovsky's conservation efforts earned him five years in prison.

The Kremlin itself is magnificent and there is no other way (for me, anyway) to describe it. To write about it could never do the complex justice. In order to judge the Kremlin (like the Taj Mahal) one can only do this by visiting the site itself.

As the Bolshoi Ballet was not performing at the time I "made do" by paying a visit to the Kremlin Theatre where I sat through a very poor performance of *Madam Butterfly*. In this case a very tatty and tacky Butterfly.

A sight never to be forgotten was the changing of the guard next to Lenin's Tomb where the high-stepping guardsmen in their full-length overcoats were both balletic and majestic as they marched in unison, their coattails swinging from left to right and left again in perfect rhythm.

For an aspiring window designer the shop windows at GUM, Moscow's answer to Harrods would not have been seen as particularly inspirational. With their display of basic utensils buckets (I noted a display of buckets a plough and even a forlorn-looking stuffed sheep) GUM was sorely lacking in the luxury goods stakes.

Rodzher continued to be as good as his golden teeth in making sure we missed out on nothing during out brief visit. He ensured we travelled on the Moscow Metro the city's underground, albeit only between two stops, in order to view the elaborate stations with their ornate, cavernous ceilings, endless crystal chandeliers, panelled walkways and marble floors. Other outings included the Yuri Gagarin Space Museum and a visit to the Moscow State Circus: the latter proving to be a huge disappointment. After what I had been led to expect I can honestly say the acts witnessed were nothing more than poor cousins to any of the acts seen in Boswell's Circus in South Africa. One could not help but be impressed by the Lomonosov Moscow State University with its massive main building of thirty six floors and fifty seven metres high spire built on a site overlooking the city. Rodzher also informed us the University was home to some seven thousand students and the library contained nigh on nine million books.

On reflection I can honestly say I never once saw any of the milling, muffled, drably dressed shuffling Muscovites actually smile. Sad and drab is the only way to describe them and sad and drab is how I will always remember Moscow.

A decade on I would visit St. Petersburg which proved to be such a contrast to gloomy Moscow. In fairness I had visited Moscow in winter and when access to Russia wasn't as easy as it is today but I couldn't quite believe the two cities were part of the same country. St. Petersburg is dazzling to behold with its marvellous buildings including the stunning Winter Palace and Kazan Cathedral, canals and parks.

A case of *"raznitsa mezhdu melom I syrom"* as they say in Russia or "the difference between chalk and cheese" as we say in England.

*

As a child the head hunters of Borneo not only fired up my imagination they made me determined to visit Borneo "when I grew up".

Could Injima's ancestors have been head hunters? I would ask myself as I spied on the benign man serenely clipping the lawn or deadheading the zinnias or Barberton daisies. (Injima you may remember as the gardener of errant lawn clipping fame back in distant Gwelo.) *Did his great grandfather have a collection of enemies shrunken heads among the trophies in his hut?* I later learned - much to my disappointment - the shrinking of heads was not practiced among the tribes of Africa but parts of Asia (namely Borneo) and South America. As a result poor Injima soon lost his glamour!

Many years later I would become the proud possessor of a supposed shrunken head whom I promptly christened Migraine. Migraine sits proudly on my desk alongside another carved import; a bat-eared (or Robert-eared) carved elephant's head named Barrack.

As I had already travelled to Migraine's homeland of the Amazon why not venture in the opposite direction and explore Borneo? I had already planned a visit to Myanmar (formerly Burma) and Sri Lanka (formerly Ceylon) but decided Borneo should take priority. I flew to Kuala Lumpur and after a few days in this exciting, modern city travelled on to Sabah one of Borneo's two capitals. From Sabah my next stop was the famous Orangutan sanctuary at Sepilok where you can literally mingle with these enchanting great apes. My impression on meeting my first Orangutan "face to face" was "Wow! You're completely orange! Even your eyes! Talk about a giant jar of marmalade!" The meeting taking place on one of the jungle walkways made of roughly-hewn planks wending its way through the dense foliage. (Most definitely Amazon Tony's secondary jungle here.)

It didn't take long to learn these enchanting apes possessed a wicked sense of humour when it came to dealing with the more naïve and flashy tourists. Having met Caesar (I instinctively dubbed my first Orangutan "Caesar" after the lead in *The Plant of the Apes*) who stood staring at me, his massive frame blocking the walkway, I murmured politely, "Please, after you" as I stepped aside into the dense bushes. Giving cursory nod Caesar moved silently past. *I'm sure you're a very nice guy, Caesar,* I thought as I watched the giant ape continue on his gentle amble, *but in no way was I going to see who gave way first; even though I* am *a guest in your country!*

The next Orangutan I almost bumped in to I treated with the same respect and, unlike Caesar my moving aside saw me receiving what I swear was a mischievous wink from the orange giant whom I mentally christened Zira after the lady (ape) doctor in the film. It soon became obvious both Caesar and Zira were heavily in cahoots (if not the leaders) of what I would call "the bling brigade" a fearsome group of orange-coloured robbers. Their victims? Forget the sensibly dressed men or women in T shirts, sweaters, comfortable trainers and sensible shoes but view instead the complete opposite dressed as if attending a social event wearing and flaunting their designer labels and expensive jewellery.

I had gone to join the other tourists who had gathered a viewing platform to watch the wardens giving the Orangutans their mid-morning snack and couldn't resist giving one particularly flashy member of the "bling brigade" a glare and a "do you mind?" as she pushed me aside with her expensive camera in order to take a photograph. "Bloody Germans," I muttered taking in her plump, sunburned arms, pendant earrings, endless gold bracelets and diamante watch. "Not satisfied with nabbing sunloungers they're now jostling for the bigger picture . . ." my words cut short by a loud shriek coming from the Brunhilde lookalike as Caesar, Zira and cohorts suddenly swung down on to the platform where we were standing. To my delight I saw Caesar grab hold of the shrieking woman's camera, jerk the necklace from her plump neck and deftly slip of a couple of bracelets from her trembling arms. While Caesar dealt with Brunhilde, Zira and the others were dealing with the other tourists festooned with cameras and wearing similar pieces of jewellery.

In the ensuing chaos the laughing game wardens made a half-hearted attempt to chase the Orangutans away before setting about organising the whole purpose of us being on the viewing platform; namely the Orangutans mid-morning snack. It took a good ten minutes or so for the chief warden to calm down the sobbing and hysterical women while assuring the outraged Brunhildes and their equally outraged Fritzes (husbands) who'd lost cameras and watches it was only a game. In between interruptions he cheerfully explained it was a trick the Orangutans played on some of the more "selective" tourists. They would pretend to rob them but everyone would be able to collect all their belongings later from another viewing platform close by.

"Well done Caesar, Zira et al," I whispered as I watched the apes innocently tucking in to a veritable banquet of mixed fruits. "And how lucky for you RA that you're visiting Borneo now as opposed to the sixties where you and all *your* bling would have been irresistible to Caesar and the lovely Zira!"

Naturally - or unnaturally - it was love at first sight on seeing Caesar, Zira and the rest of the Orangutans, young and old, and on being told I could sponsor an orangutan for life did just that. I ended up the proud foster parent of - you guessed - baby versions of Caesar and Zira. Unlike poor Delilah, Tom, Paul, Ringo, Kylie and Barry, lucky Caesar and Zira were guaranteed a regular donation towards their wellbeing: a donation still going strong. The average life span of an Orangutan is thirty five to forty five years and if Caesar and Zira are no longer still happily "terrifying" the "bling brigade" hopefully their offspring are carrying on with the good work aided and abetted by my annual donation.

Adding to the delights of Sepilok was a visit to Mount Kinabulu. While I was there the British press was filled with the story of a group of British squaddies who had "gone missing" during a military exercise on the mountain.

"Pathetic, bloody pathetic," I murmured on reading the reports. "How could they have gotten themselves lost, for God's sake? Not only did I *climb* Kinabalu I did so wearing a Gucci blazer, chinos and my much-loved Gucci loafers!" What I *didn't* mention was the fact I'd taken a tourist bus which stopped at the beginning of what was called the "trek and scramble ascent" and took about four hours there and back. While the rest "trekked and scrambled" I enjoyed the spectacular views and dipped into my paperback while enjoying several glasses of Tiger beer.

A few days after my return to London I was somewhat taken aback by a tit-bit in Nigel Dempster's always entertaining *Mail Diary*. Captioned *Hail the Gucci trail blazer* Nigel wrote how *"our friend - the Argyll and Sutherland Highlander interior designer Robin Anderson"* waltzed up *Kinabulu while the squaddies floundered!"* Someone must have has too much Tiger Beer!

The gossip columnist writing under the pseudonym of William Hickey had christened me "The Argyll and Sutherland Highlander" in a leading "splash" at least a decade before when I invited Margaret Argyll to the much talked about premiere of the X-rated film *Caligula*. Knowing I was a friend of Clare, Duchess of Sutherland (whom I met through DLL) wicked "William" gave me a full page "expose" in his much-read (and loved) *William Hickey* column in *The Daily Express*. The article published on October 15th 1980 was headed *A non-starter for the Duchess* a mischievous read to say the least.

A non-starter for the Duchess

Confirmed bachelor-designer **Robin Anderson** *is the man society has affectionately dubbed 'The Argyll and Sutherland Highlander.' This is because he tickles the fancy, at different times, of both* **Margaret, Duchess of Argyll** *and* **Clare, Duchess of Sutherland** *- combined ages 139 - by "Confirmed alternatively squiring them to assorted soirees.*

Anderson, 41, confides "They're very great friends: Clare is more cosy; Margaret more show-bizzy.

To prove the point he is taking Margaret to the film event of the year; the opening in London of 'Caligula' - politely described in the States by influential Newsweek magazine as a 'two-and-a-half hour cavalcade of depravity'."

For some unknown reason Margaret opted out at the last minute and I ended up inviting Lady Connie McIndoe, widow of Sir "Archie" McIndoe the world-renowned plastic surgeon instead. I am sure certain more acerbic friends had a hey-day on hearing my other choice.

Nigel and his colleague Ross Benson seemed to enjoy writing the most bizarre snippets about Margaret and myself. Needless to say we enjoyed many a chuckle over them. Another such "chuckler" to appear in *The Express* and captioned *£1 million hands* ludicrously informed readers of the latest RA and "Marg of Arg" happening.

£1 million hands

They say his hands, which have regularly steered two old duchesses around the smartest knees-up in London, are among the most beautiful in the capital!

*And now confirmed bachelor **Robin Anderson** has taken the point and insured them for £1 million*

He told me: "I have to run my hands over a cactus plant in a television commercial I've made for a spiky aftershave. I didn't want anything to happen to them, but I had a tremendous job insuring them!

"Twaddle!" said the Duchess and I had to agree.

In complete contrast an article in the *Evening Standard* dated November 18, 1975 led to a great deal of backstabbing and envy. Titled *The Price on your Head* the article showed photographs of seventy two people from all walks of life along with their annual incomes. I appeared with an annual income of £15,000 compared to the likes of the Rt. Hon. Harold Wilson PM (£20,000 p.a.); Kenneth Barraclough, Chief Magistrate (£13,000 p.a.); Antony Page, an Assistant Bank Manager (£6,847 p.a.); Charles Eldridge, a City postman (£2,444 p.a.); Daniel Breen, an ambulance driver (£2,184 p.a.) and Pamela Youngman, a student nurse (£1,080 p.a.).

Today my equivalent of my so-called salary would be an eye-watering £118,547.65.

I must have inadvertently well and truly "pissed off" a journalist who under the ridiculous pseudonym of *Jonny Soothsayer* and writing for a frightful rag named *Scallywag* really would have won the equivalent of a Pulitzer Prize for penned rubbish. In an eyebrow-raising article emblazoned with the heading LILLEY'S LOVER'S LOVER SWALLOWS INSTEAD OF SNIFFS the dastardly *Jonny* excelled in what I took to be his usual load of the proverbial by suggesting I was MP Peter Lilley's lover and another of my lovers, having gulped down a whole bottle of amyl nitrate as opposed to taking a few sniffs was rushed to the local A & E where he subsequently died. Seeing I had never met Peter Lilley nor had a lover foolish enough to even consider taking a swig as opposed to a sniff of amyl nitrate, I have to give *Jonny Soothsayer* a hundred out of ten for his bizarre and wild imaginings.

As if the Peter Lilley saga wasn't enough I was again telephoned by some reporter asking if it was true I'd been "a thrillo on Portillo's pillow at school"! I quickly put Mr Slime in his place by informing him Michael Portillo had been a boarder at Harrow School in Harrow, England whereas I had been a day pupil at Milton Boys High in Bulawayo, Southern Rhodesia which would have made any pillow talk or even a pillow fight fairly improbable.

Obviously my role as a "thrillo" was short lived as any further interest in my private life became a welcoming zilch.

An incident which did take place and could have made headlines occurred a few months later prior to an evening spent in the (then) smoky congenial atmosphere of Ronnie Scott's world-renowned jazz club. I had planned to meet Ben for "a few - eek! - jars before 'bars'" at the Golden Lion pub in Dean Street before strolling on to nearby Firth Street. Thanks to a tense taxi driver with aspirations of being a second Stirling Moss I arrived early and found myself standing solo at the bar minding my own business and nursing a glass of white wine.

"I haven't see you here before," said a soft voice with a faint Scottish burr.

Thinking *At least he didn't use the tired old chat-up line 'do you come here often?* I gave a sidelong glance at the dark-haired, decidedly unsavoury-looking young man staring at me intently through a pair of dark rimmed glasses.

"I'm meeting a friend," I replied curtly.

"Oh . . . well do you mind if I talk to you until your friend arrives?" said the young man proffering his hand. "I'm Dennis; Dennis Nilsen."

Er . . . Robin Anderson . . ."

The pushy young man went on to inform me he was a bookkeeper (*With those looks I'm not surprised*, I thought evilly) before asking, "And what do you do, Robin?"

"I do interior design work," I replied crisply while thinking, *Jesus Ben, where are you when you're needed most?*

"My flat could certainly do with an interior designer," laughed Nilsen. "Maybe you should come round and have a drink one evening and give me a few ideas?"

Piss off arsehole, I thought. *You don't look as if you could afford a pot to piss in never mind a pot of paint!*

"Ah," I added in a relieved voice, "I've just spotted my friend." Gulping down the remainder of my wine I said with a tight smile, "Sorry but I have to go. Good luck with the redecorating."

Marching over to where Ben stood with his usual impish grin I grabbed him by the arm and said with a hiss, "Let's go somewhere else otherwise Mr Magoo over there will want to join us." I gave a mock shiver. "And I can assure Ben the guy's a total creepola-cum-crapola-cum-bloody nightmare."

Two years later the "total creepola-cum-crapola-cum-bloody nightmare" hit the headlines when the former bookkeeper was arrested in connection with the murder of a final total of fifteen rent boys or vagabonds in his Hampstead flat. After killing his victims Nilsen then dissected them before boiling certain parts and putting these down the waste disposal or flushing bits and pieces down the toilet.

"Jesus Ben!" I exclaimed on seeing Nilsen's photograph staring out from all the newspapers, "That was the nerdy arsehole chatting me up in the Golden Lion the night we went to Ronnie Scott's a couple of years ago." I gave a sniff and added with feigned indignation. "It says his victims were either rent boys or vagabonds. Please tell me I do *not* resemble a rent boy or vagabond even in one's wildest imaginings?"

Eyeing my Savile Row suit, Turnbull & Asser shirt, Hermès tie and de rigueur Gucci loafers Ben replied with a mischievous chuckle. "Eek Mumsie! Don't you always?"

A few years later I spotted author Brian Masters' in-depth book on Nilsen, *Killing For Company* during a Saturday browse in John Sandoe, a Chelsea bookshop and promptly bought a copy. I have always been a great fan of this fine writer. I doubt if Brain would remember meeting me but I had a fun dinner with him and the ballerina Doreen Wells way back in the sixties!

*

One of the many spinoffs following the regeneration of The Albert Dock was a request to design the main dining room and a secondary dining room for the prestigious Army & Navy Club located in the heat of St. James on Pall Mall. Founded in 1837 the original building was eventually replaced by a bland, unattractive box-like edifice in the mid-fifties. I was introduced to Major David Taylor, a charming man and the Club Secretary and after several site visits I submitted my ideas which were received with enthusiasm.

My concept for both rooms was what I called "updated trad"; a blending of the old with the new. The vast ceiling area was painted by the always-reliable JW in tones of navy blue, gold, ivory and terracotta (described by me to the startled committee as "symbolic Sistine") with the walls following suit. For the carpet I used the same motif as inspired by Jesse Hartley for the communal areas at the Albert Dock. To add an extra touch of glamour to the room I had the complete party wall separating the dining room from the kitchens faced in sepia mirror decorated with an enlarged applique effect taken from the geometric pattern of the carpet. Full length curtains were made of ivory slub silk and bordered in a wide contrasting band of navy blue.

For the secondary dining room I concentrated on a blending of various greens, gold and ivory and again adapted the pattern from the curtain fabric for as an applique for the bar front of silver as opposed to sepia. On this occasion JW was instructed to paint a triple banding of green gold and sepia to the ivory-coloured ceiling. ("More Spanish Cuzco than Sistine Chapel this time John," I said chirpily.)

On completion of the contract Major Taylor kindly invited me for a mid-morning celebratory glass of champagne along with two members of the Committee who "wished to meet Anderson". After introductions had been made and the champagne served the excited Major could hardly wait to tell me how Queen Elizabeth The Queen Mother, a regular guest, had described the newly decorated smaller dining room as "simply lovely".

"Her comment accompanied by a regal wave I assume?" I quipped.

"Why would Her Majesty have waved?" snapped one of the Committee members, a short, tubby man bristling with self-importance combined with a severe case of a "Napoleonic complex" or "Short Man Syndrome".

"Don't all queens wave?" I answered spikily fixing him with a challenging stare and thinking, *And if you aren't one poisonous, vicious, vindictive horrible little closet queen then I'm Arnold Schwarzenegger!*

"The only queens I've had the privilege to meet are Her Majesty The Queen Mother and the former Queen Sālote of Tonga at our present Queen's coronation and they didn't wave . . . well, not in private, so why do you say *all* queens wave?" barked the other Committee member, a dead ringer for a puffed-up Colonel Blimp.

"To keeps their arms supple, perhaps?" I said with a feigned chuckle.

"Arms supple? Arms supple?" blustered the old boy. "What's supple got to do with it?"

"One of the features I do admire in the room is the bar Mr Anderson managed to create in that particularly difficult niche to the right of the window, Trevor," interrupted Major Taylor diplomatically.

"Trevor" aka Colonel Blimp harrumphed and said, "As long as it's not too bloody new-fangled!"

"I'm not sure if I approve of the pattern used for the wall panels," sniped his diminutive companion (the panels were covered in the same fabric as the curtains but paper-backed). "A bit too new-fangled for my more traditional tastes." He gave me a glare. "But then some you win and some you lose."

Whereas the Major described my designs as "a breath of fresh air" I am quite sure the majority of members and guests must have huffed and puffed over the Army & Navy Club's bold new look. A few days later I met up with JW for a mid-morning drink and to discuss my ideas concerning a new contract.

"Jesus John," I said reaching for my Bloody Mary, "talk about a fucking time warp. Half the members make Colonel Blimp look a positive toy boy to Britannia's 'old gel'. And as for Major or whatever his rank Tom Thumb. I would have thought the Old Quebec rather than the A & N Club more up his very obviously *un-used street*!"

"The Old Quebec?" questioned JW.

"Otherwise known as The Elephant's Graveyard. It's a gay pub near to Marble Arch where all old queens go for one last try and sigh before they die."

"Sounds as if you know it well," replied JW with a mischievous grin as the two of us burst out laughing.

Another West End "plum" were the elaborate specialised paint effects to the elegant restaurant and the redecoration of the showrooms for Thomas Goode & Co., the exclusive china shop in Mayfair's South Audley Street. The owner's request for the restaurant was simply, "a ceiling and paint effects to outdo those of the Ritz restaurant".

"The ceiling and paint effects of the restaurant at the Ritz?" I murmured to myself. "We'll go one better than that and paint a ceiling to outdo the Sistine Chapel!"

RA and the "Sistine Chapel inspired ceiling" appeared in the BBC2 documentary *Modern Times* shown in 1995. Pointing up at the spectacular ceiling with its swirling rainbow coloured clouds I said mischievously to the cameras, "My homage to Michelangelo. A formidable task as one literally had to lie spread-eagled on the scaffolding in order to paint the wretched thing. But, according to rumour, I'm best at doing it while lying on my back".

Another RA witticism was to completely cover one of the walls in the showrooms with dozens of different patterned plates and name it *The Great Wall of China*. Said totally tongue-in-cheek I was somewhat surprised on finding the owner had gone ahead with my somewhat sarcastic suggestion.

*

Buoyed with the successes of The Albert Dock, The Army & Navy Club and numerous new clients I began planning more magic carpet rides between commitments. By this stage I had also treated myself to several weeklong breaks on Key West, an alcoholic fleshpot which after two visits saw the appeal of the island dwindle and after a third visit most definitely disappear. I enjoyed staying at the Pier House and the colourful, chaotic "celebrating the sunset" evenings spent at Mallory Dock plus endless forays to Sloppy Joe's aka "Hemmingway's Hangout", but at the end of the day I decided Key West with its much publicised Duval Street (apart from the relentless sunshine) could easily have been a substitute for Soho's famous "gay alley" or Romilly Street.

I've never been a fan of seething masses of shrieking, screeching "we're here for fun, fun, fun!" over- the-top queens and would visibly shudder on hearing another shrilled or bellowed greeting in some harsh, brash, nasal accent. Gazing around one of the many dance clubs along Duval Street I decided Key West was not for me. "Give me the sophistication of England and Europe any time," I murmured to nobody in particular. One guest staying at The Pier did suggest I pay a visit to Jacksonville and "maybe drive down to New Orleans". With a few days to spare I took up the debonair Rhett Butler lookalike's offer which turned out to be more a case of hoodwinked Scarlet O'Horror meets Ridiculous Rhett. No lark with this Clark I'm afraid to emphatically say. I ended up checking myself into the Ritz-Carlton and spent a deliciously self-indulgent three days in this colourful city. I became hooked on beignets, brandy milk punches and the endless jazz seemingly played everywhere. Years later I sat entranced through the film, *Midnight in the Garden of Good and Evil* while thoroughly immersing myself in the Jim Williams role so brilliantly portrayed by Kevin Spacey. Who needs Clark or Scarlet when you have Jim and Lady Chablis?

Having returned to South America where I visited Argentina and made a second pilgrimage (I don't use the word lightly) to Machu Picchu I decided it was time to take a break from the Incas and pay homage to another ancient people and therefore a change of tune. Instead of *Flying Down to Rio* I would now be travelling *South of the Border, Down Mexico Way* in order to meet the Aztecs and should one bump into a Gene Autry lookalike as opposed to a second-rate Rhett, so much the better.

My first stopover was Mexico City and after a day's break in the vast metropolis I was relieved to board a flight for Merida on the Yucatan Peninsula; the main purpose for my visit. Two days later I was perched on top of a pyramid at Chichen Itza, the famous Mayan city built in about 600 AD and inhabited until 1200 AD. One of the most intriguing (and gory) facts about Chichen Itza were the rules and regulations regarding a popular ballgame but a ball game with a difference. If your team lost, you all - literally - lost your heads. In other words you were decapitated as part of some bizarre, primitive sacrifice.

As I sat pondering what the likes of Diego Maradona and Danny Dalglish would have been thinking at the start of a game if the rules applied today, a voice suddenly boomed out as if reading my very thoughts, "A prime example where one wouldn't wish to be seen as a bad sport or even worse, a loser! Ho! Ho!"

"Bloody hell!" I exclaimed, "I *know* that voice but from where?"

I stared across at the neighbouring pyramid, my eyes focussing on two hunched-up elderly male figures, each as decrepit looking as the other.

"I don't believe it," I muttered, "It *can't* be but then if not, *why* not? If *I* can be here then why shouldn't he?"

I clambered to my feet and climbed down from my particular pyramid and made my way over to where the two were sitting discussing loudly the pros and cons of human sacrifices. Staring up at the animated but gruesome twosome I said softly, "Fuck me if it *isn't* him after all. Okay, he'd make Methuselah look a teenybopper on a good day but it's definitely *him*! Er. . . excuse me gentlemen," I called breaking into their conversation, "but you Sir on the right, is your name by any chance Ewer, *Jakes* Ewer, a former Professor at Rhodes University in South Africa?"

"Unless I've changed since breakfast I most certainly am," guffawed the elderly man, "and who the hell then are you?"

"Anderson er . . . Jakes. Robert Anderson . . . a friend of Shirley Ritchie and Alan Dashwood . . ."

"Shirley Ritchie? Alan Dashwood? Robert Anderson?" exclaimed Jakes, "But of *course* I remember you! I'm not bloody senile despite my appearance!" He gave a ragged laugh as he rose creakily to his feet and offered a palsied hand. "Imagine seeing you here of all places? How long ago since we last saw each other? Twenty something years?"

Jakes and his companion (no, it wasn't Griff despite the cropped hair nor was the aged figure carrying a pipe!) agreed to meet up later at the hotel for a pre-dinner drink but ended up doing a "no show". When I made a cursory check with the girl at reception to see if there was a message for me from "Professor or Dr Ewer" I was informed the Doctor and his companion had checked out earlier prior to a visit to the pyramids and their return to Mexico City.

"Well they're the losers despite keeping their heads," I replied with a smile. "Now, is there somewhere you would recommend for dinner?"

Most people would say a visit to Mexico wouldn't be complete without a visit to Acapulco. True to form I journeyed on to city which back in the fifties and sixties was considered the jet set hub of the universe. I was enchanted by the Acapulco's sparkling blue semi-circular bay and surrounding mountains but not at all enchanted by the fact I was mugged on the beach in front of my hotel while taking an after dinner stroll. Adding fuel to my fury was my stupidity at ignoring the myriad of signs within the hotel asking visitors to make sure they placed any valuables in the safe in one's room or leave these with the management. As a result of my mugging I was stripped of my very expensive gold Corum watch, a pair of gold cufflinks and my signet ring.

"Fuck the Aztecs, fuck the Mayans, fuck Acapulco, fuck Mexico and fuck me for being such a bloody idiot!" I stormed at my angry reflection in the bathroom of my suite. "To hell with this godforsaken place of shit, salsa and sombreros, I'm taking the first possible flight out of here!"

Instead of returning I telephoned Bob who was still staying with Frank Messina in LA. I explained what had happened whereupon Bob terminated the conversation by saying drily, "At least if you're mugged in LA the perpetrator's more likely to be by a dishy, pot head of a beach bum than a fucking wetback!"

I spent three days with Bob and Frank which in retrospect was a waste of time and money and I could have kicked myself for not returning directly to London. Bob was decidedly drunk when he and Frank met me at LAX Airport and Frank did not seem too pleased with my impromptu visit.

"He's drinking almost non-stop these days," muttered Frank when Bob was out of earshot. "Plus he now seems to have taken up residence in a leather bar nearby." He gave a shake of his handsome head. "It's almost as if he's gone into a downhill spiral since John went back to London."

"But he knew John had to go back," I replied. "Christ, he's got a dental surgery to run." I gave a snicker. "A *leather* bar? I never thought leather as being Bob's scene?"

"No doubt you'll find out, sooner than later," grizzled Frank.

As Frank predicted a few hours after my arrival Bob announced he was headed for the Eagle and would l like to tag along.

"But I thought we'd agreed to have dinner with Belmont? Your suggestion seeing he's always asking after Robin," said Frank (Belmont being Belmont Spironi an artist friend I had met through Frank on a previous visit to LA).

"Did I? Did we?" replied Bob with a sloppy grin. "Well then, you two go along because *I* am off to the Eagle." He added spikily. "Maybe he'll even talk Robin into buying another painting."

Frank and I duly met up with Belmont and after a pleasant evening said out goodnights, Belmont returning to his studio and Frank and I back to Frank's house in West Hollywood.

"Shit! Bloody Miller!" exclaimed Frank thumping the steering wheel with his fist after parking outside. He gave me a sidelong glance. "Do you mind RA if we drop by the Eagle and bring him home otherwise Christ only knows where he'll end up?"

"Not at all Frank if it makes you feel happier," I replied. I stared at Frank. "You said earlier this has been going on for some time?"

"Ever since John left." He gave a sigh. "I have a feeling the parting wasn't all that amicable, the result leading to Bob going slightly off the rails."

"Maybe we can have a go at getting him to come back to London?" I suggested.

"We most certainly can but try," said Frank with a sigh, "but I wouldn't bet on it." He pulled into a vacant parking space. "We're here. I suggest you wait here while I go and grab him. "He gave a grimace. "I can assure you RA this his place isn't for the squeamish."

"Are you sure you don't want me to come I with you?"

"Come into *that* place looking like an ad from GQ? You must be joking!" grunted Frank opening the driver's door and hefting himself out. Five minutes later he was back holding on to a struggling, dishevelled and highly abusive Bob. "Shut *up* Bob," hissed Frank bundling him in to the back of the car. "Just shut the fuck up!"

Turning on the ignition an obviously seething Frank drove off with a screaming of tyres while Bob continued to rant and hurl abuse from the back seat.

"Jesus Frank," I muttered aghast. "What the hell happened in there?"

Staring stonily ahead Frank said with a growl. "Not much apart from the fact I found his madam back there being publicly fucked on one of the pool tables."

(Vivid details of Bob's hijinks and more in LA are luridly described in my novel *Bobette - The Ups & Downs of a Total (Male) Tart.*)

The following morning Bob seemed to have forgotten the happenings of the previous evening. However he declined my invitation to lunch with the other Bob, Bob Hanley, at The Polo Lounge (Frank having left earlier for his own workplace).

"Bob," I said, "what the fuck's going on? If you need to talk about what's bothering you please feel free . . ."

"I'm fine," murmured Bob followed by a waspish, "When did you say you were leaving?"

On my return from lunch I packed and left a note for Frank (Bob was out) saying I had had a change of mind and would be leaving for London that evening. It was only after the Seat Belt sign was turned off I felt able to relax.

Again somebody - maybe DLL - must have been looking after me for a few days after my return Mexico was hit by a severe earthquake. Whereas Acapulco was subjected to what was described as a minor tsunami, Mexico City was not so lucky. Horrifying figures showed at least 10,000 people killed with some 30,000 injured and endless buildings damaged.

On hearing about the disaster I couldn't help thinking, "Now if the bastard who mugged me had done so in Mexico City . . . who knows?"

*

Undeterred by my Mexican misadventure my next exploratory venture abroad saw me paying much looked forward visit to the Land of the Rising Sun. I had always been fascinated by the art and culture of this faraway, exotic land, my interest kindled by the lectures on Japanese art I had attended at University. Images of works by Hokusai, Utamaro, Sesshū Tōyō, Hassegawa Tōhaka and many more had made a lasting impression and I was determined to visit the land of their inspiration one day.

Until I travelled to Japan I could truly say one of the most breathtaking sights I had been privileged to witness was the magical, mystical Taj Mahal at Agra. I arrived at the Taj about half an hour before sunrise and before the fountains serving the long mirror-like ponds leading up to the ivory white mausoleum were turned on. This meant the luminous building was reflected several times in sheets of silver and a sight never to be forgotten or equalled: until Japan.

I sat on one of the benches facing the Taj watching the magnificent building slowly turning from a silvery sheen to a soft rose colour and literally beginning to sparkle and twinkle as the sun's rays began to catch the endless semiprecious stones decorating the façade. To my delight I was invited inside the actual building itself where I found myself gently scattered with rose petals. Unbelievable.

After the Taj Mahal I travelled on to Udaipur where I stayed at the Lake Palace Hotel, another reflected masterpiece but still a very poor second to the unique Taj Mahal: until Japan.

Sadly most visitors tend to overlook the Black Taj across the Yamuna River from the Taj Mahal. The Black Taj said to be the resting place for the Mughal emperor Shah Jahan who had built the Taj Mahal in memory of his third wife, Mumtaz Mahal.

I landed at Tokyo's bustling Narita International Airport where I was met by a travel representative and swept in to the city where I was briskly checked in to the new Imperial Hotel, the original of which was designed by Frank Lloyd-Wright whom I had admired since my Bulawayo days. On my first evening in Tokyo I stood gazing in wonderment from the balcony on the 14th floor at shadowy Hibiya Park and the dazzling city below.

From Tokyo I travelled on to Kyoto which was like walking into a Hokusai painting with one major exception. Having been told about the numerous small restaurants which are focussed around the mail railway station I decided "the proof of the purin was in eating" (purin being the Japanese for pudding and a type of crème caramel) and treated myself to a delicious lunch in one of the tiny eateries. I was about to clamber onto the UP escalator when to my delighted surprise I spotted a Geisha girl - chalk white face, black wig, kimono, platform shoes et al - carrying two large plastic carrier bags emblazoned with the name Yokado, one of the largest grocery chains in Japan - sailing serenely past on the DOWN escalator. Talk about the very old meets the very new!

In Kyoto I found myself among the audience at the famous Minami-za Kabuki Theatre where I sat bedazzled but confused through several acts of what appeared to be an ongoing bizarre and at the same time totally unique performance. Years later a kabuki theatre would take centre stage in my novel, *Wow! Pow! & Persuasions!* the fourth Miz M and Miz K adventure tale in my bestselling *La Di Da Di Blooody Da!* series.

Every moment spent in Japan was a moment of unfettered delight. I remember watching the immaculate landscape passing by as we sped along on the famous Bullet Train. *Why even the trees look as if they've just been washed and blow dried!* I kept thinking.

I visited Hiroshima and apart from the "preserved" ruins of the former Prefectural Industrial Promotional Hall now known as the A-bomb Dome or Hiroshima Peace Memorial, one could easily have been in Miami or San Diego thanks to the tree-lined boulevards and towering buildings.

Competing with the Taj Mahal in the sheer wonderment stakes the accolade must surely go to the Shinto shrine on the island of Itsukushima best known for its "floating" Torii gate. Here the giant vermillion gate reflected in the azure blue sea gives the impression of floating on the placid surface.

This is further highlighted by its inverted reflection of the shrine. As with my first impression of the Taj Mahal I must have stood for at least an hour gazing at the spellbinding sight.

While Japan proved to be a land of total enchantment so did the people. I found the Japanese to be charming, polite and, after the tackiness of the West, refreshingly civilised. Since my first visit to this wondrous place I have been fortunate enough to have revisited The Land of the Rising Sun twice and have never been disappointed. To me Japan is utter magic. On each subsequent visit I made sure I returned to Tokyo's Nezu Museum where I stood in humble and silent homage facing Ogata Korin's golden panels blossoming irises in what I can only describe as chimerical splendour. Like Japan the panels - to me - remain utterly breathtaking.

As for Mount Fujiama, how could Hokusai disappoint his worshipping fans by limiting himself to a mere thirty six woodcuts depicting the famous sleeping volcano? Āh sō Hokusai!

After the impact of Japan it would be unfair to try and find a Far East equivalent. I was impressed by the magnitude of the Great Wall of China (on which I danced a nifty Charleston in a tribute to Bobby Van Husenof Sandy Wilson's *The Boyfriend* fame: the character I played when at Rhodes University) and the sights of the Forbidden City, Beijing, the Terracotta

Army and dazzling Shanghai but flashbacks to Japan made me realise which place in the Far East I still considered *numero uno.*

I was appalled by the sheer dilapidation and general filth of Myanmar (Burma). Viewings of endless pagodas reminded of the mishmash that is Bangkok. I visited the notorious River Kwai and spent a sobering hour at the tranquil Taukkyan War Cemetery where 6.374 Allied soldiers are buried. Not the happiest of memories.

At the end of the day Lieutenant B.F. Pinkerton remains the undisputed winner!

*

Bob Miller finally returned to London and much to my surprise gave me a call. Having declined my luncheon invitations in LA he graciously accepted a last minute invitation to a "boyz only" lunch I was giving on the same for six other friends. I have to confess Bob's invitation was offered "on the spur of the moment" due to an apologetic, last minute cancellation by one of my guests. As predicted Bob arrived drunk (according to what he told me on the phone the following day he had stopped at several pubs for "a sip or two of Dutch courage") and took his place at the opposite end of the table where he sat slumped while regarding his fellow diners with a slack smile.

My guests included PR maestro John Addy otherwise known as "The Adder" due to his poisonous wit; a red-faced not always genial Charles Gray; the Marshallene; Ben; PR wunderkind Peter Stiles and Tony Hutt (of black cock fame!).

While the sweet course was being served I glanced to where Bob was sitting and, much to my relief, saw him chatting happily to Peter Stiles seated on his left. A few minutes later I homed in on Bob's empty chair.

Hmm, must have slipped out to the loo, I thought as I returned my attention back to Charles seated on my right. Seconds later there came an audible gasp from Peter followed by the beginning of a grin. As I was giving Peter a questioning look the remaining conversation was suddenly interrupted by Charles Gray uttering a loud "Harrumph" before starting to talk animatedly to a sniggering Peter Stiles.

What the fuck's going on? I thought before it struck me. Bob hadn't sneaked off to the loo but crawled under the table instead in order to begin what Peter described as "a potential blowjob marathon" instead. Alarmed John Addy could easily suffer a heart attack or a stroke should he find himself suddenly unzipped and voraciously gobbled up by "marathon Miller" I scrambled from my chair and fell to my knees before lifting the base of the tablecloth and bawling, "Cut it out Bob! *Now!*"

A chastened Bob meekly returned to his seat and proceeded to attack his waiting crème brûlée as if nothing untoward had happened.

I saw Bob a few times after his "tribute to Linda Lovelace performance" as Ben laughingly dubbed my last minute guest's surprise manoeuvre. By this stage Bob was no longer living in Ivor Court with John and after several moves ended up living alone in a gloomy council block in Camberwell. Remembering the fun times we'd spent together I duly invited Bob to lunch (strictly à deux) but having been stood up a third time I reluctantly gave up.

Accepting Bob had a drink problem and becoming more and more unpredictable in his behaviour and outrageous slurred aspersions against all and sundry ranging from the local postman to Luciano Pavarotti, I did my best to keep in touch through a series of dutiful (and concerned) phone calls but nine times out of ten his phone remained unanswered. When he did answer our conversations were one-sided with me attempting to make sense out of his incoherent gurgling. A sad and depressing final curtain to a colourful life.

When it came to his Pavarotti "claim to fame" Bob glibly described a luncheon at The Coral Sands Motel in LA where he and a few others were supposedly joined by the so-called singer who introduced himself as "Master of the High C" and was accompanied by "a sickly, frail-looking young male".

"Talk about Laurel and Hardy," said Bob with a giggle.

Having been told the names of the other guests attending the clandestine luncheon which included both his lover at the time and a former lover (busy Bob) I duly contacted both for verification. John Leach vaguely recalled the event but couldn't confirm "any names" while a former lover of Bob's named Michael Sullivan currently living in LA denied even being there.

Pavarotti was not the only one to suffer from such "Bobisms" or hallucinations. When a young man Bob apparently gave Richard Greene aka Robin Hood a blowjob "in Bricket Wood" (I could find no trace of the 1950s series being filmed in the area) and "slept with Frank Ifield" of *When I'm Calling You* fame. Say no more! At least Charles Clore and I escaped unscathed.

*

In 1978 Barry Manilow decided to enthral a world-wide audience with his rhythmic rendition of *Copacabana*. Like all his fans captured and enraptured by his singing and the song's exotic Cuban beat I had vivid mental images of Havana with its varied architecture ranging from Colonial baroque to Neo-classical, Art Nouveau and Art Deco all set in a fifties time warp. This "frozen in time" was further substantiated by mental pictures of vast, chrome-infested fin-tailed cars and the city's inhabitants, all of whom appeared to have stepped out of *Guys & Dolls*, the musical by Frank Loesser and Abe Burrows set in the much-glamorised 1930s New York underworld.

Fidel Castro's Cuba, I am happy to say, did not disappoint me one iota. I found the Cubans friendly and most welcoming despite the political problems fed to us on a daily basis by meddlesome news media. Obviously I saw what I was allowed to see. In Moscow one was greeted with what I call a typical Russian scowl whereas in Cuba on was greeted by a dazzling smile.

A highlight of my stay in Havana - apart from the endless mojitos! - was evening spent in the outdoor-but-not-quite Tropicana nightclub where I witnessed a stage show-cum-cabaret which today still remains unbeatable. Not even "za starr of the Lido" could have held a torch to any of the performers. I have seen shows of a similar vein all over the world but the evening spent at the Tropicana remains unique. I spent several days touring the island and once again was impressed by the civility of the Cuban people and their zest for living.

*

Having given up the Studio and having "made a killing" with the sale of the Park West apartment I took a leasehold on a bijou apartment a stone's throw away from the King's Road and a few minutes stagger home from Daphne's, Bibendum, The Brasserie and other such fine eateries. Naturally the new apartment was done up in typical RA style. I dubbed this

545

my "safari sanctuary" due to the golden tones of "the savannah" used throughout with the added impact of a leopard skin print. Instead of relying on the natural tawny colourings sported by a leopard I changed these to red, gold, black an ivory. Who said a leopard couldn't change its spots?

Further proof of a "spot changing leopard" were the antics of "Mr Ryott from Arsehole" himself (Petal's Caribbean name for DBR in case the reader is having a "craft moment") who took it upon himself to invite a limp, whickering-voiced, equally sanctimonious younger soul named David Johnston for a clandestine few days at the family villa near Faro in Portugal. No doubt a firm case of a braying DBR promising the equally neighing, youthful Johnston a weekend of wicked fun in the sun. Unfortunately something went horribly wrong with the two eager lovers destined never to meet due to DBR - in some strange never-to-be explained way - losing his leg. In other words, following a mysterious accident (read misadventure) en route to collect the irresistible David Johnston for their cloak-and-dagger few days of fun in the sun, DBR ended up with a broken leg. Following "complications" the aspiring lothario ended up having his right leg amputated instead.

Naturally "Robun" got the blame seeing "the young man" (or DBR's "Circe" as Ben referred to him) happened to know me and therefore I must have been responsible for the introduction. In retrospect the two could have met at one of my many "boyz only" cocktail parties.

On being told of "Circe's" misadventure Ben's comeback was typically "Ben". "Eek Mumsie! I've heard of people losing their *heads* over love but never a leg!"

"Another version of 'head over high heels in love' perhaps?" added a friend.

*

Suddenly it was 1990.

To celebrate the New Year I was invited to a lavish Sunday brunch given by Edith Foxwell now elevated from the former tongue-in-cheek "Lady Edith Fuckswell" to the "Disco Dowager" despite her affiliation with the Embassy Club being well and truly over. At the brunch Edith went out of her way to make sure I was introduced to two young men, Paul Giggle and Simon Leslie who had recently set up a glossy monthly magazine titled *Impression.*

"Edith's told us *all* about you," enthused Paul, a devastatingly good-looking twenty-something year old Tatum Channing lookalike (or Tab Hunter for the "golden oldies"). He gave a sidelong glance at Simon (definitely more John Candy than Tatum Channing). "Er . . . and we were wondering if you would be interested in writing one or two articles for our magazine."

"On what?" I replied only half paying attention to Paul's question, "seeing I'm quite sure I wouldn't be capable of contributing anything of interest for a gay magazine."

"It's not a *gay* magazine!" expostulated Simon. He looked at Paul. "We're not *gay*! *Impression* is a glossy monthly of general interest rather like *The London Magazine!*"

"Oops! My mistake," I replied cheerfully. "It's only because you know Edith . . ."

"*Everybody* knows Lady Edith but that doesn't necessarily mean they're gay!" snapped Simon.

"We were thinking of articles relating to interior design," intercepted Paul.

"As I said, my mistake," I murmured contritely. I gave the two a placatory smile. "Articles on interior design? Sounds interesting."

"Why not give us a call and, if possible, drop by and see us sometime next week if you think you *may* be interested," said Simon somewhat spikily as he handed me a business card. "Our offices are in King's Road; above Macdonald's." He added with a grin. "Hard to miss."

"Why not indeed?" I replied pocketing the card. "I live literally round the corner so any day or any time to suit as I appear to be in-between clients at the moment."

"We'll also pay you," said Simon sharply. "Unlike some of those other freebies floating around we wouldn't expect you to submit an article and not be paid!"

"Now I'll most definitely give you a call, "I replied cheerfully.

I started writing feature articled for *Impression* the following week and found myself thoroughly enjoying the challenge plus I was taken aback by the support and enthusiasm I received from the various suppliers and dealers I approached in connection with the article of the moment. It didn't take long before I said to myself, "Talk about déjà vu and fun days all those years ago on *The Bulawayo Chronicle* and wielding my poison pen on behalf of *Stekel* but why not take it one step further and write a novel? A rather bitchy tome based on an extremely bitchy interior designer? After all it's a world I most certainly know about!"

I began working on *Regina* but progress was deliciously interrupted (as opposed to rudely) by a new contract which saw my efforts as a budding author temporarily shelved. (*Regina* was eventually published in 1998. The book was among the many displayed at the annual Book Fair at Earl's Court followed by a book signing at Hatchards in Piccadilly.)

Closely following in the wake of Bob's stumbling footsteps Ben's copious drinking had also become a major problem. Despite our close friendship Ben had never been one to "open up" about his innermost concerns and feelings (when discussing this with DLL all those years back we had both decided it must have had something to do with the fact he was adopted) and it was not long before a worried David Harvey contacted me and ask if we could meet. Over lunch Harvey professed his concern regarding Ben's behaviour and his growing dependency on the two Cs; cocaine and cannabis.

Here again I remembered Pete the Wheel and his concern over Ben's "delving into drugs" when Ben had so kindly suggested Pete help me with setting up The Grove.

On my return to the flat I made myself a mug of coffee before settling down in front of my desk. "Christ," I muttered to the silent study, "First DLL and now - or so it seems - it won't be long before one says goodbye to Ben. As for Bob, like Tony before him, he's already a lost cause." I took a long look at myself in the mirror panel next to my desk. "Peggy, DLL and now Ben? Hold on in there DC (Donald Cameron); you never made Dosso but I'm going to make sure we spend a few weeks together either in the States or a place of your choice a.s.a.p. Damn sure!"

It soon reached the stage where Ben appeared to float in a permanent haze and daze of alcoholic fumes. Following a particularly slurred early morning call I warily agreed to meet him for lunch at Choy's, a popular Chinese restaurant in King's Road. Having agreed to meet at one o'clock Ben staggered in half an hour later. Anticipating his late arrival I had armed myself with a copy of Stephen King's *The Dark Half* and a mineral water.

Ben greeted me cheerily with a grinning "Eek Mumsie! You're looking well," before turning to the waiter and saying loudly, "a large vodka tonic please." He pointed to my glass. "Still on the wagon?"

"Yes and no," I muttered, "on and off . . ."

I sat half-listening to Ben as he burbled on about his latest find. "Take it from me Mumsie," he said in a stage whisper as he leant across the table, "forget about trying to find true love, it's a waste of time." Giving the impression of suddenly sobering up he added gently, "You and I both know there'll never be another David in your life; there couldn't be so please don't be offended by what I'm about to say. *Forget* the likes of your crooning Frenchman, Barry Justice, the Big T and that devious little Livingston and do what I now do. If it flies, floats of fuck . . . rent it!" Murmuring a "thank you" to the waiter Ben gave a chuckle. "Let me assure you Mumsie, whoever, wherever and *whatever* he's always there and quite willing to go gay for pay!" He gulped down half the contents of the glass and beckoned for a refill. "No financial burden, no thinking 'how the fuck can I get rid of him'. In other words a fun fuck and then forget it."

This would be the last time I saw Ben. When I think back to his newfound philosophy all I can say is "Ben, dear Ben, how right you were. If it flies, floats or fucks; rent it and if it's the latter you're after, find it, fuck it and forget it." Cynical but true. In other words "no names; no pack-drill" or "take no prisoners".

*

When I began writing in earnest in 2005 I made sure Bob received a complimentary copy of each publication and even dedicated my bestselling *Bobette - The Ups & Downs of a Total (male) Tart* to him. I was horrified when Bob told he was "riddled with cancer". By this stage I didn't quite know whether to take Bob seriously or not due to his very apparent Walter Mitty-like behaviour and was shocked when I heard several months later that he'd been found dead in his flat by a concerned neighbour.

Having seen the effects of too much alcohol on the likes of Ben, Barry and Bob I took a severe look at myself and decided it was time to call a halt. Having thoroughly enjoyed my "partaking of the evil grape" I literally downed my last alcoholic drink in January 2007 and haven't touched a drop since.

Today my "cocktails" involve a BVtini (Balsamic vinegar, iced water and a slice served in a wine glass) or a Tabascotini (Tabasco, sparkling mineral water, ice and a slice served in a martini glass).

*

Back to the nefarious 1990s.

While attending one of Liz's endless charity "dos" I was introduced to the legendary Ivana Trump and immediately drawn to this remarkable woman. Not only did I find Ivana to be even *more* glamorous than expected (my original expectations taking some beating) I found her to be warm, funny and thoroughly likeable.

To my unequivocal delight Ivana telephone a few days later to ask if I would be interested in helping her with the interior to an apartment she'd recently bought in exclusive Cadogan Square, Knightsbridge. Would I ever! I arranged to meet Ivana on site the following day to inspect the property and come up with some initial ideas.

"Honey, I leave it up to you," said Ivana in her charming Czech accent. "Liz and everyone says you're good, huh?"

Working with Ivana proved to be a positive joy. Once she had approved the various schemes we then spent several days exploring the lesser-known antique shops in the vicinity of Chelsea's Lots Road which, at the time, was still regarded as a bit of a backwater. Needless to say most of the dealers' jaws literally dropped when I walked into their premises accompanied by the instantly recognisable Ivana Trump.

Inside the Cadogan Square apartment I kept Ivana's well-known passion for animal prints to a minimum. Built in in the late 19th-century the high ceilinged rooms cry out for elaborate window treatments which saw the drawing room decorated in glowing red, pink and gold damasks and silks with the master bedroom decorated in different shades of ivory and gold. A neat staircase led to a mezzanine floor containing a guest room adjacent to a small balcony overlooking the drawing room. In the small guest room Ivana and I went wild with a leopard skin print!

Obviously delighted with the apartment Ivana then asked me if I would be interested in "working with her" on the interiors to her new yacht named, surprise, surprise, *IVANA*.

"I can't wait!" I replied, "And this time Ivana we can go overboard (no pun intended!) with your favourite animal prints!"

I telephoned and asked to be put through to Bernard Thorp himself.

"Good morning Bernardo," I said cheerfully, "I'll be bringing in a very special client tomorrow at around ten and expect 'champagne treatment' to say the least. Sorry Bernardo; no names. You'll simply have to wait and see but I promise you, you won't be let down!"

"Don't tell me you'll be bringing in Her Maj?" laughed Bernard.

"What? And usurp Queen Janet McCulloch?" I exclaimed. "I wouldn't dare!"

Bernard Thorp, always the showman, didn't let me down and on arrival Ivana was warmly greeted by the suave, smiling Edmund Purdom-lookalike and promptly offered a sparkling flute of Cristal champagne.

"Honey!" laughed Ivana taking a sip, "You vant Ivana to buy za whole showroom?"

Ivana was enchanted by the showroom. A tactful Bernard excused himself saying, "I'll leave you in the capable hands of RA, Mrs Trump. However, please feel free to call me should you have any further questions."

After an extremely cheerful chatty and absorbing two hours the two of us had schemed up the whole of *IVANA*.

Bearing in mind the yacht would be spending most of the time sailing around the sun-drenched Mediterranean we opted for what I described as "St Tropez" colours; namely a sparkling azure blue, aquamarine, shell pink, gold and dazzling white.

In the main salon plump scatter cushions of a pink, azure blue and aquamarine fan design on a white, moiré background nestled on white suede-covered sofas; the walls covered in a correlating suede embellished with a small coronet motif.

The master cabin was a riot of gold, aquamarine, azure and navy blue ropes and tassels swirling on the defining white moiré with walls covered in the background fabric. The same colours were used throughout the guest cabins with one "decked" out in a glowing leopard print.

Having schemed up *IVANA* I ordered various samples of the final colours chosen saying smoothly to Ivana, "For the record as it were Ivana and in case you want to match up a few extra bits and pieces back in the States", I asked Bernard to rejoin us and help finish off the remainder of the champagne. On hearing we would be catching a cab to take us to the Cipriani restaurant where we were lunching, a chivalrous Bernard offered to drive us there. Despite the slight frosting inside the car due to Ivana having insisted I sit in the back of the car with her while Bernard drove, we eventually reached our destination in Davies Street, Mayfair. Matters didn't improve on arrival when Ivana having said a "thank you" to Bernard turned to me and said with a mischievous smile, "Honey, you certainly have za cute chauffeur, huh?" With a loud revving of the engine a stony-faced Bernard zoomed off without so much as a backward glance.

I spent a frantic morning with Ivana within the hallowed precincts of Peter Jones (the store favoured by the Duchess of Cambridge and other yummy mummies) where with a suitably start struck, not-too-blessed with brains, swaggering young male sales assistant somehow managed to note down Ivana's rapid, gunfire-like decisions as we raced round the ground floor buying various household items.

Despite my offering the services of an established embroiderer ("I vant all za bedlinen and za towels to have za embroidery of za coronet") Ivana knew of "za perfect person" who would happily undertake the task as a favour. However she was not at all amused to discover "za perfect person" had ended up stitching all the pillow flaps together when embroirdering the monogram making them impossible to use. Having advised her to get "za perfect person" to cut round the monogram and reapply as a patch" I had to restrain myself from saying, "As the saying goes Ivana, if you pay with peanuts you get the monkeys!" for I am sure the lady in question - unlike me - would not have found my words of wisdom the least bit funny. I was later informed a second visit to Peter Jones saved the day and *IVANA* ended up with a double supply of pillowcases, albeit half of them somewhat scarred.

Having resolved this "Ivana drama" it was not long before I was faced with another setback when *IVANA* decided to go missing! I dread to think of the *oreccio* or ear bashing the poor captain must have received when docking at Livorno instead of La Spezia to take on the various items we had bought or prepared. Apart from this unfortunate hiccup the rest was er . . . plain sailing.

Inevitably a beaming Ivana and *IVANA* the yacht appeared in Hello Magazine and as already mentioned, Ivana's Knightsbridge apartment (and RA) featured in a BBC 2 documentary titled *The Fame Game.* The apartment also appeared In *Impression, Epicurean Life* plus Volume 1 of the Andrew Martin Interior Design Review (1997).

During the course of my many design discussions with Ivana I happened to mention Sally Burton's "sisal Aubusson".

"A fabulous idea for should you one day decide to buy a property on the harbour front in Saint Tropez," I suggested mischievously knowing Ivana to be a fan of the popular, hedonistic resort. "A carpet with a scattering of seashells perhaps?" I gave an inward snigger at the thought of Ivana in a pose reminiscent of Venus in Botticelli's painting *The Birth of Venus.*

"Painted sisal?" exclaimed Ivana. "Zis I have to see!"

I duly set up a mid-morning meeting at Porchester Terrace between the two ladies. With an extremely shaky hand upon my rapidly beating heart I can truthfully say Rudyard Kipling's famous mongoose Rikki-Tikki-Tavi and nasty Nagaina the cobra were nothing compared to these two tightly smiling ladies sitting opposite each other. Ivana a confident, preening bird-of-paradise in contrast to Sally Burton's drab peahen. Having finished our coffee Ivana crisply announced she had "seen enough, honey". Taking the hint I thanked Sally profusely her time and the "delicious coffee" (instant) and escorted Ivana out to the waiting car.

Ivana's reaction to the pained sisal was a smiling, "Very pretty but not very practical vhen you think of all za cigar ash and crumbs, huh? Tiles honey. Tiles."

Here endeth the lesson!

I am *not* a Rudyard Kipling type and therefore unable to cope with the likes of Rikki and Nagaina despite the potential profit following a meeting between sisal Sally and *The Birth of Venus.*

Despite all the publicity she generated I was still unaware of the full impact the name "Ivana" had on people until I was on a Christmas visit to Canada. One of the first ports of call before setting off on a train journey across the vast country to Vancouver was morning's sightseeing at Niagara Falls. Having done the "touristy bit" I was sitting enjoying a glass of wine in a nearby picturesque hotel-cum-Inn when I couldn't help overhearing an animated conversation between three portly (best described as "well-upholstered), somewhat formidable looking matronly ladies sitting at a nearby table.

"Oh my, I simply *love* your bracelet, Patsy!" carolled on viciously coiffed matron.

"Isn't it a *dream*?" crooned Patsy. "Just one of many delights from House of Ivana!"

"House of Ivana?" exclaimed Matron No. 3, "But so is this divine brooch I'm wearing!"

"Mine also!" yodelled Matron No. 2 determined not to be outdone.

"Excuse me ladies," I interrupted at my most charming, "but would you be referring to Ivana Trump by any chance?"

"Who else?" questioned Patsy somewhat snappishly, "After all there is only *one* Ivana!"

"It's simply because I happen to know the lady," I replied with a syrupy smile. "I had the privilege of designing her London apartment and her yacht named *IVANA.*" Giving an even more syrupy smile (if possible) I added teasingly, "What's more the aftershave I'm wearing is from Ivana's range of toiletries for men." (Now sadly discontinued.)

Forget an about-turn. From then on I could do no wrong as the three formidable matrons - shrieking with delight - insisted on me joining them for "another glass" accompanied by a Spanish Inquisition type interrogation on the subject of Ivana Trump.

As ca be expected I sang Ivana's praises; the three ladies sang Ivana's praises and I am sure this little scene would have led to the glamarous instigator herself being extremely happy.

*

A few days later another unexpected meeting took place in one of the bars at the ravishingly beautiful Château Lake Louise hotel overlooking the lake of the same name set in the province of Alberta.

Waiting to be served I heard a man say, "I'm sure it's him, Jenny. I'm sure it's Robin Anderson."

Turning in the direction of the familiar accented voice I spied a stocky, bearded middle-aged man and a petite, smiling woman whom I immediately took to be his wife.

"Good heavens!" I exclaimed, "Brian and Jenny Grainger. Imagine seeing you here?" I gave a light laugh. "You're not planning to tile the lake are you?"

(Brian and Jenny Grainger being the owners of Tiles of Newport based In Newport, Wales. I had been introduced to Brian in the late seventies and was delighted to find a homebased supplier of hand painted and handcrafted on a par with my favourite Italian supplier Franco Pecchioli.)

"Why? Are you planning to give us an order?" chuckled Brian, his fulsome beard jiggling like some cosy Father Christmas.

"Better late than never," I quipped seeing the last order I had placed with Brian must have been fifteen years earlier.

Jakes Ewer twenty years on in Mexico and now the Graingers fifteen years later in Canada, who's next? Brother dear and the dreaded Margaret in Outer Mongolia? I thought. *Best remove Mongolia from my "to do" list a.s.a.p.*

The next evening I joined Brian and Jenny on a torch-lit sleigh ride along the shores of the lake. Needless to say we made sure we were well-fortified with warming Whisky Macs for the ride.

I travelled by train from Toronto to Banff and from Banff journeyed on to Vancouver in the wake of the famous Canadian Pacific Railway known today as The Canadian. I sat dull-eyed watching the seemingly endless flat vistas of prairie and although impressed by the grandeur of the Rockies, having flown over the Andes, the Alps and viewed the Himalayas I didn't - unlike my fellow passengers - go overboard in my admiration. I enjoyed a visit to Vancouver Island but my overall impression of Canada was a shrugged "so what?" A vast amount of empty space occupied here and there by a small amount of rather bland albeit charming people.

*

An avid reader since my childhood I have always made sure a couple of paperbacks accompany me on my travels as well as be waiting for me at home. Nowadays with my travels somewhat curbed by my lack of mobility I spend a great deal of time when not writing on sitting in my favourite armchair and reading. A weekly "must" as previously mentioned is my visit to Waterstones bookshop in King's Road where the lively helpful staff always make sure at least three possible paperbacks are always set aside for me. I am a fast reader and three substantial paperbacks are very much part of my regular diet. The always cheerful Charlie is a hive of information when it comes to introducing a new author into the fold as well as recommending what he and his associate Maggie consider a "must read for RA".

A further divining-rod for a "must read" or the plural is my local library which again has an ever changing display of new reads.

I am a great fan of what I deem chiller and political thrillers and if they include a sense of humour -preferably dark and which I refer to as a sense of *tumour* - so much the better. A thin list of authors whose books never let me is like the proverbial piece of string: infinite. Firm favourites in the thriller category include Simon Kernick, Charles Cumming; Alan Furst; David Baldacci; Philip Kerr; Nelson DeMille; Peter May; Samuel Bjork; Henning Mankell; Lars Kepler: Jo Nesbø along with Bernard Minier. Nor should Tom Rob Smith and his *Child 44* trilogy be overlooked. When it comes to tongue-in-cheek humour-cum-tumour I rate - without a doubt - Carl Hiaasen as *numero uno*. For a definite "lump in the throat" I highly recommend *Christodora* by the brilliant Tim Murphy.

Prior to my teens I mentioned *The Swish of the Curtain* by Pamela Brown as my most memorable childhood read. As an adult, out of the *hundreds* of books I have read there is one I will go to my grave saying nothing can ever surpass. This is the *The Wild Highway* by Bill Drummond and Mark Manning. I must have read the book at least twenty times and each rereading still electrifies. To me the book is pure genius and far surpasses the much-lauded authors such as Updike, Roth and Vidal. If by some remote chance either Mr Drummond or Mr Manning should ever hear of or read my comments about *The Wild Highway* please note I really do take off my hat (or maybe you'd prefer my head?) to you both.

When it comes to the selling of my books I always remind people of a conversation which took place between myself and a determined-to-be taxi driver who kept giving me suspicious glances in the rear-view mirror.

After several minutes and several glances he said truculently, "It's quite legitimate ye know; guv. Me meter's totally *kosher* an' not all rigged if that's what yer thinkin'."

"Of that I am quite sure," I replied cheerfully. "However, I'm an author and knowing what I make per book I was simply calculating how many books this journey has cost me so far. So far we've reached the grand total of four and a half!"

On dropping me off at my destination the taxi driver asked sarcastically, "Can I ask 'ow many books then?"

"Eleven plus an extra one for the tip," I said dismissively.

"Yeah, well I didn't think I'd picked up bleedin' Mrs 'Arry Potter," he snorted before accelerating away.

"Ah, but you *did* happen to pick up Robin Anderson!" I called after the rapidly disappearing cab. "And until you've *read* a Robin Anderson you haven't even *begun* to exist!"

HALCYON DAZE

Having recently completed work on the refurbishment of a large, 16th-century manor house near to Reading in leafy Berkshire I finally had to admit - like so many fellow interior designers - I was another victim suffering from over-active POWFC or "Pissed Off With Fucking Clients" syndrome to give the crippling ailment its full name.

"After nearly fifty years of dealing with Mrs A's PMS or Mrs B's EHS (errant husband syndrome) enough is enough," I muttered to Abel Mabel, my skeleton companion and sounding board (read skull) to my endless opinions. "Obviously if this effing second Park West *had* raised its profitable head instead of causing me to end up in plaster I would have said an immediate 'yes' but as for the rest? Fucking forget it!" Staring thoughtfully at Abel Mabel who in turn sat "eyeing" me through her dark eye sockets I added contemplatively, "Writing for *Impression* etcetera has been both rewarding and even more important as far as I am concerned, the greatest of fun so why don't I sit down and write another *Regina*?"

Receiving not the slightest rattle in response from Abel Mabel I decided to ignore but continued with my ponderings, "Okay *Regina* wasn't exactly *Harry Potter* but it *did* cover a couple of trips abroad plus one or two spoilers. So think, Anderson: think. And as you've just been having a right old bitch about Berkshire's answer to Elizabeth Báthory (a 14th-century Hungarian serial killer) what would you wildest wishes be if you ever had the chance of true payback time in compensation for all her vileness? What would you do if you could take on the persona of Gilles de Rais (a 15th-century French serial killer) or Vlad the Impaler? (The 15th-century sadist said to have inspired the legend of Dracula.)

The answer came in a blinding flash; an interior designer who decides enough is enough and concludes revenge is a dish best *not* served cold but cold-blooded. However, the thought of gleefully eliminating one or two nightmares of his choice would be far too easy and much too mundane. In other words, what is the point of becoming a serial killer seeing once one's victim is dead he or she no longer suffer? In other words, end of story.

But if one decides to become a serial *mutilator* imagine the prolonged and delicious evilly reaped benefits with the victim having to live with the vengrful designer's ultimate "design" until the day he or she dies.

Within the next few minutes I allowed myself to be introduced to James Augustine-Jones the sinisterly charming, blood-stained hero of what would be the first of my "chiller thrillers" titled *Red Snapper*. As a result of the incredible self-discipline practiced during my years as a designer a new rigid, daily regime soon became standard. I have always been awake by five o'clock each morning and first on the agenda is a steaming mug of extra-strong black coffee (no sugar) accompanied by half an hour of hijinks as I run through my schedule for the day which nowadays covers whatever book, novella or play I happen to be working on.

Fate may have planned it as a bitter blow but after my decision to expose James Augustine-Jones - no holds whatsoever barred! - I was involved in an accident which saw me ending up with both legs and my left arm in plaster. I wittily announced to anyone who cared to listen I still had the use of my right hand and wasn't it obviously "a boon" seeing I really had no excuse for not "getting on" with the proposed *Red Snapper*.

The truth is (and nothing but the truth) I get such a kick, thrill or high - you name it - out of writing I find it a glorious self-indulgence as opposed to finding "something to do". *Red Snapper* - as with *Regna* and now all my books - was first written in longhand (I write as if I'm actually reading the "page turner" in front of me) before transferring the hieroglyphic-like scrawl on to the computer. This gives me the chance to add, subtract and look up any information or any details which may require expanding. Thus a single page in scrawled longhand easily extend to two printed pages on the computer or vice versa; the single paged reduced to a few, tightly edited lines.

Red Snapper was first published in 2007 and sold some fifty thousand copies with endless downloads on Kindle. In December of the same year I was a guest at Shirley Bassey's glittering 70th birthday celebration at Cliveden the country house made famous following the destructive

Profumo scandal in the sixties. Needless to say my birthday present for Shirley simply had to be a signed copy of *Red Snapper*.

Red Snapper was quickly followed by *Sebastian & Seline* (note the subtle difference in the spelling of *Sebastian*!) which remains my favourite RA. Hot on the steamy heels of *Sebastian & Seline* came *Versus*. I am convinced the incredible influence of Peggy Powell during my childhood was the catalyst behind the camp, glamorous, wise-cracking glamorous women who frequent my books: HM in *Ped Snapper*; Camilla Galsworthy in *Versus* and Clytemnestra in *Still Life - The Resurrection* to name but a few. I trust darling Peggy wouldn't be offended when I say a bit of her extravagant personality found its way into the characters of Miz Miranda Maracona and Miz Kookie Kombuis ("We are transvestites of taste; never tackiness") the over-top-heroines of the *La Di Da Di Bloody Da!* series who run a detective-cum-love company.

Miz M and Miz K as the two ladies call each other came into being while I was sitting in Balans in Old Compton Street, Soho prior to a meeting with one of the directors regarding the forthcoming book launch for *Red Snapper.* On hearing a loud, "Get you girl!" I glanced up from my copy of the *Daily Mail* and instantly homed in on two flamboyant transvestites - one black and one white - who not only looked much the worse for wear from the night before but went on to dissect their adventures, their sentences continually interrupted with shrieks of laughter. Cue for another "blinding flash".

It's so obvious, I thought with an inward chuckle, *I simply* have *to write a book involving two such over-the-top trannies for whom the world is not only their oyster but an endless string of pearls as well.* With my mind going firmly into overdrive I christened my two new heroines there and then. The white tranny would be called Miranda in honour of Carmen Miranda and Maracona; a play on the surname of Diego Maradona the full-bodied or bloodied football player. Something Miss M most definitely is not.

The newly christened Miranda Maracona's black companion proved to be more of a conundrum. *Hmm,* I thought, *not a Whoopi but equally - if not a tad more - as kooky . . . That's it! That's it! But on this special occasion a* Kookie *as opposed to kooky.* Another thought followed by, *And as for Kookie's surname . . . why not kombuis, the Afrikaans word for kitchen?* My two new creations allowing me to sit back with a self-satisfied expression on my face. *So all in all we now have Miss Kookie Kombuis and Miss Miranda*

Maracona. I gave the garrulous trannies a grateful smile (they were too engrossed in their conversation to notice) and jotted a few notes down on to a notepad. At that moment Charles Cotton one of the directors of the Balans Group appeared and suggested we go somewhere "more private to talk".

After our meeting I was disappointed to see my two heroines had disappeared but knowing they were well and truly ensconced in my mind as well as my notebook I wasn't too particularly put out. In the taxi back to Chelsea Miss Miranda and Miss Kookie were elevated to Miz M and Miz K. Added to which the two ladies instead of seeing themselves as merely "divine" decided they were utterly "*divoon*".

Gazing from the taxi as we shunted our way down Park Lane (a favourite London view which never fails to impress) I immediately knew the ladies first adventure tale could only be dedicated to the one and only Ivana Trump. "Right," I murmured, "I've got my two OTT heroines and I know who the book will be dedicated to so all I need is a rollicking, over-the-top plot and of course, a title. So think, Anderson. Think." For no apparent reason (unless it was sparked off by the statue of Nike, Winged Goddess of Victory atop the Wellington Arch at Hyde Park Corner) I suddenly remembered Dennis Paget's description of Bryan aka Lady Larkin. "Very la di da, isn't he?"

"La di da?" I pondered. "That's one thing Ivana can never be accused of as a more down-to-earth person would be difficult to find but somehow those three words are begging, simply *begging* . . . shit!" My mutterings severely interrupted by a screeching of brakes as the cab came to an abrupt halt. "Bloody hell!" I exclaimed, rocking in my seat.

"Sorry about that, guv'," said the cabdriver apologetically, "Bleedin' foreign drivers!"

"Not to worry, cabbie!" I replied with a grin. "Thanks to you braking like that you've just helped me solve a major problem!"

"I 'ave? I did?"

"You *have* indeed, cabbie. In fact you could say you've just helped sire and inspire *La Di Da Di Bloody Da!* which will be dedicated to the one and only Ivana Trump."

"'Elped sire an' inspire la di da di bloody da dedicated to the one and only Ivana Trump?" repeated the cabdriver eyeing me curiously in the rearview mirror. "Bloody 'ell."

*

La Di Da Di Bloody Da! was first published in 2009 and proved to be an immediate success receiving four star reviews in England and America. As a result of his subsequent glowing four and five star reviews on behalf of Amazon, Miz M and Miz K have christened Grady Harp, a top American reviewer, Grady *Golden* Harp. As the two ladies continually yodel and ululate, their *"divoon* Golden Grady" can do no wrong.

While Grady "Golden" Harp reigns supreme on America's West Coast Miz M and MIZ have an equally flattering admirer on America's East Coast in the form of Amos Lassen graciously dubbed AA or "Adorable Amos" by the two. With a Golden Grady and an Adorable Amos as staunch fans it appears neither of these two flamboyant ladies can put a stiletto wrong.

La Di Da Di Bloody Da! was quickly followed by *Trannies to Tiaras* and *Wow! Pow! & Persuasions!* with a further five in the series published to date. The two ladies are adamant "RA accompanies uz on at least two more journeys before he hangs up his Jimmy Choos". What does come as a surprise is the uncharacteristic modesty adopted by Miz M and Miz K whenever one mentions the worldly two have even been spotted on a bookshelf belonging to the Duchess of Cambridge.

Any mention of The Duchess of Cambridge takes me back to Booth Tarkington's 1918 best seller *The Magnificent Ambersons* which if written today would surely be named *The Magnificent Middletons* (the Middletons replacing the Morgan family in the original). I am a great fan of the Middleton clan including wayward Uncle Gary and in my cynical eyes Kate is a superstar who apart from epitomising elegance is without doubt the brightest star in the Royal firmament. I find Pippa a positive hoot as well as a real go-getter and mother, Carol, the type of determined woman as played by Virginia McKenna in her portrayal of Violette Szabo in the 1958 film *Carve Her Name with Pride* or Jean Paget in the earlier *A Town Like Alice* made in 1956. While son James remains a bit of an enigma I am sure I am not alone when I say debonair daddy George wins heads over when it comes to the terms "father complex" or sublime "sugar daddy".

*

Having started on the first draft of *Red Snapper* I received an out-of-the blue call from Rose Collis the author of several well-received biographies.

"I'm writing a book about the legendary Coral Browne," she informed me, "and Richard Compton-Miller whom I met a few days ago gave me your telephone number and suggested I get in touch as you were not only the interior of her sensational London flat but also a great friend."

"Good Heavens," I replied drily, "The Incompetent One becomes the Competent One! Why, thank you R.C.M."

I arranged to meet Rose for a coffee at Balans on Old Brompton Road and spent a delightful two hours with this very charming lady feeding her endless titbits about how it was to work with Coral and other fun anecdotes involving my friendship with her and subsequent friendship with husband Vincent Price. I was flattered by all Rose's references in her best-selling *This Effing Lady!* But not at all flattered by Jill Melford's venomous comments regarding the totally "new look" I created for Coral's Eaton Place apartment. "I walked in; it was stark and white - and I said, 'I get the feeling you're going to perform an appendectomy in here'." She went on to bemoan the fact all the pretty things and memorabilia "had gone".

My response on reading what Melford had to say regarding my design was a dismissive, "If she's such a bloody wonderful decorator or designer why didn't Coral commission *her* to redo the *effing* apartment! Apart from a fucking Ficus tree, a few green and white scatter cushions and a lot of theatrical jawing I wonder what else would she have done to bring out the best for Coral's prized collection of sphinxes?"

Through Rose I met Peter Burton the writer and stalwart campaigner for Gay Rights. Peter became a friend and reviewed several of my books. It was Peter who so wisely advised me to always "check, check, re-check and then check again" every manuscript and never, ever rely on any proof-readers ("wannabe authors") for a pristine copy.

At this stage I also met the glamorous and delightful Sally Farmiloe. Sally became a great RA supporter and always gave me laudatory reviews in *Hot Gossip* magazine. I dedicated my third chiller thriller *The Gallery* to this charming lady who sadly died in 2014 after a brave battle with cancer.

It was Sally (Farmiloe) who suggested I write a cookery book but a cookery book "with a difference" to which I dourly replied, "Seeing there are already enough such books out there to sink another Titanic what's the point? And while I consider myself a fairly competent cook if the truth be known I'm what I would call a con cook seeing I spend as little time possible with any preparation. Once the basics are done the dish is popped into the oven for an hour and that's it! Everything is served up with a dollop or two of crème fraiche and Bob, Rob or Robin's your uncle!"

To date I have a burgeoning file labelled *A Quickie In A Jiffie – or - How To Serve It Up In The Best Possible Haste*; the file containing "quickie recipes" from such luminaries as Ivana Trump, Shirley Bassey, Grady Harp, Julian Fellowes, Sally Farmiloe, Jess Conrad, Liz Brewer, Donatella Signorini and more. However the book will not be out "in a jiffie" but sometime in 2018.

Sally (Farmiloe) was also the catalyst behind my children's book *Four Zimbabwean Adventure Tales* which led to another unexpected snippet appearing in the *Daily Mail* in October, 2007.

"Once known as the Argyll and Sutherland Highlander because of the ladies he escorted - Margaret, Duchess of Sutherland and Clare, Duchess of Sutherland - bespoke interior designer Robin Anderson is about to burst into print.

At the age of sixty five, flamboyant Robin who decorated Ivana Trump's yacht with monogrammed moiré sheets, has discovered a talent for writing. 'I've just completed a series of children's stories set in Zimbabwe,' he tells me. They include Charlie The Cheetah and Bunti the Bushbaby.'

But the confirmed bachelor, who has sent Ivana a red rose to mark her formal engagement today has a wider repertoire. 'I have sveral other books due out. They are pornographic gay novels and include Red Snapper which is about a serial mutilator.

Let's hope they never get mixed up."

*

Young recipients of *Four Zimbabwean Adventure Tales* include Ivana Trump's first three grandchildren ("Honey! Knowing my family there'll be many more!"), Shirley Bassey's granddaughter along with The Duke and Duchess of Cambridge's children, Prince George and Princess Charlotte. A second children's book, *The Adventures of Tumble The Clumsy Tree* has been patiently waiting in the woods and should be stumbling into print sometime in 2019.

Despite the years rolling by I have never forgotten little Miffy, my first pet pooch who was so cruelly despatched by my mother, the vindictive, spiteful Cur; hence my devotion to DLL's Borgie and Dosso's Parigi. For many years I have been a strong supporter of London's world-renowned Battersea Dogs & Cats Home. Enter Miss Mollie and Miss Millie, two elderly Fox Terriers who are seen as the doyennes or figureheads for this amazing establishment. Another Fox Terrier of equal charms is Amos Lassen's Fox Terrier who I respectfully refer to as Miss Sophie and it was inevitable I would dedicate *Four Zimbabwean Adventure Tales* to these three gracious ladies.

A marvellous photograph showing Miss Sophie sitting comfortably on Amos's lap and reading *Four Zimbabwean Adventure Tales* appeared on Facebook.

Nor has the tremendous privilege and exhilaration of being part of Rupert Fothergill's Operation Noah involving the rescue of animals large and small from the growing waters of the Kariba Dam on the Mighty Zambezi ever been forgotten and I often think of the rescued animals' offspring and how they are coping with the daily problems of food, water and natural predators. *The Adventures of Lucy the Baboon and Charlie the Cheetah* vividly depict this amazing happening.

I am always baffled and immediately wary when I meet a person who doesn't appreciate animals and fascinated how an animal can also sense this. If it wasn't for the fact I live in an apartment in the centre of London I would be first in the queue at Battersea to give some poor unfortunate pooch a home. However I see owning a pooch as a commitment for life and unless you can offer any animal this promise then it is best to be a hundred percent honest and say a heart rendering "no".

*

Following the resounding success of *Red Snapper* I found myself inundated with invitations to give a talk about my life involving interior design, my writing for various magazines, the almost forgotten *Regina* and the sinister *Red Snapper*. Peter Burton helped considerably with the success of the latter by labelling the book "a feast of unsavoury delights".

Venues for my talks ranged from local libraries, several small theatres and last but not least, The Royal Festival Hall.

One display billed as "An Evening with Robin Anderson" complete with photographs of the author and the cover to *Red Snapper* appeared in one of the windows to the Kensington & Chelsea Library in Old Brompton Road. Accompanied by a banner displaying Peter Burton's promise for "an evening of unsavoury delights" I was amused to note the greater part of the audience comprised of demure or matronly grey-headed ladies with the occasional curious male and a sprinkling of queens; two of whom looked as if they had just stepped out of *La Cage Aux Folles*. Having delivered my talk and smilingly acknowledged the general applause hand I stood surveying the sea of faces and having said several "thank yous" added in my best *Golden Voice,* "Now, if there are any questions . . .?"

Immediately one buxom matron raised her hand and barked brusquely, "Mr Anderson, can you give me one good reason - and I am sure I am not alone in asking the question - why you had to be *quite* so graphic when describing the homosexual sex scenes in your book?"

Before I had a chance to ask what induced bothered to read *Red Snapper* in the first place she added with a derisive snort, "And before you ask me why I bought the book in the first it's because I was totally mislead by the comment, *A Feast of Unsavoury Delights*; A title which led me to think - as red snapper is a type of fish - your book would be a somewhat witty *cookery* book!"

Barely able to suppress my laughter I returned the matron's challenging gaze and said as if talking to a truculent child, "A cooking book is on the cards or, in chef speak, presently on the back burner but in answer to *your* question about the *homosexual* sex scenes *my* answer is quite straightforward. Like Gide, Isherwood and Gore Vidal the author of *Red Snapper* was once a practising homosexual but age has taken its wicked toll which means nowadays one has to sublimate instead of masturbate."

"I don't understand?" replied the woman in a puzzled voice. "Sublimate instead of masturbate?"

"What Mr Anderson *means* Madam is he's too old to cut the mustard or if *that's* also too difficult for you to understand, it's now a case of blowjobs instead of hand jobs," trilled one of the peroxided *La Cage Aux Folles* lookalikes. His strident interruption resulting in a stunned silence.

"Er . . . I take it there are no more questions," I murmured to the audience as they whispered and sniggered among themselves. "So thank you for coming along this evening. Refreshments are available downstairs." I gave a light laugh. "Plus, should you wish to buy a copy of my *novel* - remembering *Red Snapper* is a novel and *not* cookery book - copies are also available downstairs."

Much to my amusement I later saw the misled matron in animated conversation with Mademoiselle *La Cage Aux Folles* and his friend.

"Maybe the belligerent old bat's found her true *metier* at last and will soon be upstaging Monsieur Albin in St. Tropez!" commented Bob on hearing of my *grand success.*

"Or Robert Carrier in Camden Passage," I replied sourly. My reference being to the celebrity chef and cookery writer's popular sixties Islington restaurant.

I met Robert Carrier through Tony Galliers-Pratt. Ben and I spent many a fun evening at his Camden Passage restaurant and later at Hintlesham Hall, a lavish country restaurant near Ipswich in Suffolk. When Bob (as he was known to us) moved to Marrakech in the eighties Ben and I were frequent guests at his magical riad-cum-hotel-cum-restaurant Gastro MK.

To the acute dismay of its many loyal patrons La Popote closed down in 1998 and reinvented itself as Sacalini's which in turn became a frim favourite. Adding even more glamour to this gourmet area of Chelsea was the "new" Daphne's, purchased in 1993 by Mogens Tholstrup referred to as "a society Scandinavian" by top gossip columnist Nigel Dempster. I seemed to spend an enormous amount of time (and an extortionate amount of money) in these two establishments but can truly say the fun times there were worth every penny.

*

In the aftermath of my unfortunate but "spurring on" accident and my decreased mobility I found myself reverting to my Albion Gate penthouse days and starting to entertain at home as opposed to meeting one's guests in a restaurant. This also saw a more scrutinised type of guest and a reduction in numbers with me settling for four of us seated around the "coffin" table. Such intimate gatherings were further inspired by an overheard remark in Andreas, the greengrocer's shop on Chelsea Green. "I find one simply has no choice but to be much more frugal these days," announced a bejewelled matron beckoning her chauffeur to take the shopping bags from Nelson one of the sales assistants and a dead-ringer for Aiden Turner of *Poldark* fame. "Hence only *eight* punnets of strawberries today as opposed to my usual dozen seeing *darling* Andreas is charging a startling four pounds per punnet; but then he does assure me the strawberries are English born and bred. Or should that be home grown? Haw! Haw! Haw!"

Forgetting Andrea's price for a punnet (I am not a strawberry fan) I could not forget the woman's decision to be "more frugal" and therefore return to entertaining at home as opposed to eating out. I know from experience it costs a minimum of £200 plus for two if one visits a decent restaurant in Dicken's city where some of the streets appear to be literally paved with gold cards. Should one venture out to dinner then you may as well double the cost; and that's before you've even paid for the journeys there and back!

Despite it being an impossibility if I could have one final dinner party at a restaurant of my choice I would ask for it to be held at Dosso. My special guest would obviously be the one and only glorious David Lloyd-Lowles. Joining DLL and myself would be Ben Colman, Donald Cameron, Peter Coats, Coral Browne, Vincent Price, Lionel Bart, Margaret Argyll and Lesley (La) Lake. Sadly I have a strong suspicion my wonderful Peggy Powell would be out of her depth amidst all the camp banter.

Take my word for it, such a lunch could only be billed as *never* a "craft" moment!

And finally, the question to end all questions and one I am continually asked; of all my thirty something books which one is my favourite. In all honesty I would be hard pushed to name one whereas naming three would be easier. And while *Red Snapper* remains highly regarded my personal selection would be a gold medal for *The Gallery* followed by silver for *Sebastian & Seline* with *Still Life - The Resurrection* going for bronze.

THE END? SOMEHOW I DON'T THINK SO!

Robin Anderson. London. 2018.

BOOKS by ROBIN ANDERSON
www.robinandersonauthor-ott.com

NOVELS

Regina
Red Snapper
Sebastian & Seline
Versus
The Gallery
Divoon Daddy
Neos Helios
Amo, Amas, Amassive
Ceruse - A Cover-Up Extraordinaire
The Grin Reaper
The Go Blow Go Bar
Bobette - The Ups & Downs of a Total (Male) Tart!
Jan Unleashed!
Still Life - The Resurrection
Bruised Fruit
Defunct Gristle
Pau Dot Go
Crisp & Golden
Too Good to be Trué

La Di Da Di Bloody Da! Series

La Di Da Di Bloody Da!
Trannys to Tiaras!
Maharajas, Mystics & Masala!
Wow! Pow! & Persuasions!
Oysters Aweigh!
Triple Oh Heaven!
Rootin' Tootin' Khamun!
Aliens & Arabesques - Blast Off!

NOVELLAS

The Burning Bush
Bel Ragazzo Beautiful Boy - ? –
Swallow Dive

SHORT STORIES

6 + 6 + 6 - Eighteen Tales of Textual Titillation (Volume One)
6 + 6 + 6 - Eighteen Tales of Textual Titillation (Volume Two)
She Married a Zombie Truck Driver & Five other "Trucking" Tales

CHILDREN'S BOOKS

Four Zimbabwean Adventure Tales

PLAYS

The Burning Bush